Essentials of Management Information Systems

Eighth Edition

Kenneth C. Laudon
New York University

Jane P. Laudon
Azimuth Information Systems

PEARSON

Prentice Hall

Upper Saddle River, New Jersey 07458

Editor-in-Chief: David Parker
AVP/Executive Editor: Bob Horan
Product Development Manager: Ashley Santora
Assistant Editor: Kelly Loftus
Editorial Assistant: Christine Ietto
Media Project Manager: Denise Vaughn
Marketing Manager: Anne Howard
Marketing Assistant: Susan Osterlitz
Associate Managing Editor: Renata Butera
Project Manager, Production: Renata Butera, Carol Samet
Permissions Project Manager: Charles Morris
Senior Operations Supervisor: Arnold Vila
Operations Specialist: Michelle Klein
Art Director: Steven Frim
Interior Design: Ken Rosenblatt/Azimuth Interactive, Inc.
Cover Design: Steven Frim
Cover Illustration/Photo: Robert Harding/Digital Vision/Getty Images, Inc.
Illustration (Interior): Azimuth Interactive, Inc.
Director, Image Resource Center: Melinda Patelli
Manager, Rights and Permissions: Zina Arabia
Manager: Visual Research: Beth Brenzel
Manager, Cover Visual Research & Permissions: Karen Sanatar
Image Permission Coordinator: Angelique Sharps
Photo Researcher: Diane Austin
Composition: Azimuth Interactive, Inc.
Printer/Binder: Courier/Kendallville
Typeface: 10.5/12.5 Times LT Std

Credits and acknowledgments borrowed from other sources and reproduced, with permission, in this textbook appear on appropriate page within text (or on page P-1).

Microsoft® and Windows® are registered trademarks of the Microsoft Corporation in the U.S.A. and other countries. Screen shots and icons reprinted with permission from the Microsoft Corporation. This book is not sponsored or endorsed by or affiliated with the Microsoft Corporation.

If you purchased this book within the United States or Canada you should be aware that it has been wrongfully imported without the approval of the Publisher or the Author.

Pearson Education Ltd., London.
Pearson Education Singapore, Pte. Ltd
Pearson Education, Canada, Ltd
Pearson Education–Japan

Pearson Education Australia PTY, Limited
Pearson Education North Asia Ltd
Pearson Educación de Mexico, S.A. de C.V.
Pearson Education Malaysia, Pte. Ltd.
Pearson Education, Upper Saddle River, New Jersey

10 9 8 7 6 5 4 3 2 1
ISBN-13: 978-0-13-501353-3
ISBN-10: 0-13-501353-4

About the Authors

Kenneth C. Laudon is a Professor of Information Systems at New York University's Stern School of Business. He holds a B.A. in Economics from Stanford and a Ph.D. from Columbia University. He has authored twelve books dealing with electronic commerce, information systems, organizations, and society. Professor Laudon has also written over forty articles concerned with the social, organizational, and management impacts of information systems, privacy, ethics, and multimedia technology.

Professor Laudon's current research is on the planning and management of large-scale information systems and multimedia information technology. He has received grants from the National Science Foundation to study the evolution of national information systems at the Social Security Administration, the IRS, and the FBI. Ken's research focuses on enterprise system implementation, computer-related organizational and occupational changes in large organizations, changes in management ideology, changes in public policy, and understanding productivity change in the knowledge sector.

Ken Laudon has testified as an expert before the United States Congress. He has been a researcher and consultant to the Office of Technology Assessment (United States Congress), Department of Homeland Security, and to the Office of the President, several executive branch agencies, and Congressional Committees. Professor Laudon also acts as an in-house educator for several consulting firms and as a consultant on systems planning and strategy to several Fortune 500 firms.

At NYU's Stern School of Business, Ken Laudon teaches courses on Managing the Digital Firm, Information Technology and Corporate Strategy, Professional Responsibility (Ethics), and Electronic Commerce and Digital Markets. Ken Laudon's hobby is sailing.

Jane Price Laudon is a management consultant in the information systems area and the author of seven books. Her special interests include systems analysis, data management, MIS auditing, software evaluation, and teaching business professionals how to design and use information systems.

Jane received her Ph.D. from Columbia University, her M.A. from Harvard University, and her B.A. from Barnard College. She has taught at Columbia University and the New York University Stern School of Business. She maintains a lifelong interest in Oriental languages and civilizations.

The Laudons have two daughters, Erica and Elisabeth, to whom this book is dedicated.

Brief Contents

Complete Contents

II Information Technology Infrastructure 113

III Key System Applications for the Digital Age 265

Preface

We wrote this book for business school students who wanted an in-depth look at how business firms use information technologies and systems to achieve corporate objectives. Information systems are one of the major tools available to business managers for achieving operational excellence, developing new products and services, improving decision making, and achieving competitive advantage.

When interviewing potential employees, business firms often look for new hires who know how to use information systems and technologies for achieving bottom-line business results. Regardless of whether you are an accounting, finance, management, operations management, marketing, or information systems major, the knowledge and information you find in this book will be valuable throughout your business career.

It's a New World of Business

A continuing stream of information technology innovations from the Internet to wireless networks to digital phone and cable systems are continuing to transform the business world. These innovations are enabling entrepreneurs and innovative traditional firms to create new products and services, develop new business models, and transform the day-to-day conduct of business. In the process, some old businesses, even industries, are being destroyed while new businesses are springing up.

For instance, the emergence of online music stores—driven by millions of consumers who prefer iPods and MP3 players—has forever changed the older business model of distributing music on physical devices, such as records and CDs. Online video rentals are similarly transforming the old model of distributing films through theaters and then through DVD rentals at physical stores. New high-speed broadband connections to the home have supported these two business changes.

E-commerce is back, generating over $200 billion in revenues in 2007, and growing at 25 percent a year. It is forever changing how firms design, produce and deliver their products and services. E-commerce has reinvented itself again, disrupting the traditional marketing and advertising industry and putting major media and content firms in jeopardy. MySpace and Facebook, along with other social networking sites such as YouTube, Photobucket, and Second Life, exemplify the new face of e-commerce in the 21st Century. They sell services. When we think of e-commerce we tend to think of selling physical products. While this iconic vision of e-commerce is still very powerful and the fastest growing form of retail in the U.S., growing up alongside is a whole new value stream based on selling services, not goods. It's a services model of e-commerce. Information systems and technologies are the foundation of this new services-based e-commerce.

Likewise, the management of business firms has changed: With new mobile phones, high-speed wireless Wi-Fi networks, and wireless laptop computers, remote salespeople on the road are only seconds away from their managers' questions and oversight. The growth of enterprise-wide information systems with extraordinarily rich data means that managers no longer operate in a fog of confusion, but instead have online, nearly instant, access to the really important information they need for accurate and timely decisions. In addition to their public uses on the Web, wikis and blogs are becoming important corporate tools for communication, collaboration, and information sharing.

The Eighth Edition: The Complete Solution for the MIS Curriculum

Since its inception, this text has helped to define the MIS course around the globe. This edition continues to be authoritative, but is also more customizable, flexible, and geared to meeting the needs of different colleges, universities, and individual instructors. This book is now part of a complete learning package that includes the core text and an extensive Companion Web site.

The core text consists of 12 chapters with hands-on projects covering the most essential topics in MIS. The Companion Web site provides more in-depth coverage of chapter topics, video cases, career resources, additional case studies, supplementary chapter material, interactive quizzes, and data files for hands-on projects.

THE CORE TEXT

The core text provides an overview of fundamental MIS concepts using an integrated framework for describing and analyzing information systems. This framework shows information systems composed of people, organization, and technology elements and is reinforced in student projects and case studies.

A diagram accompanying each chapter-opening case graphically illustrates how people, organization, and technology elements work together to create an information system solution to the business challenges discussed in the case.

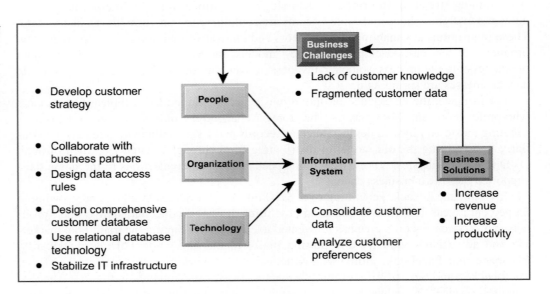

Chapter Organization

Each chapter contains the following elements:

- A chapter-opening case describing a real-world organization to establish the theme and importance of the chapter
- A diagram analyzing the opening case in terms of the people, organization, and technology model used throughout the text
- A series of Student Learning Objectives
- Two Interactive Sessions with Case Study Questions and MIS in Action projects
- A Hands-On MIS section featuring a Dirt Bikes USA running case project, a hands-on application software project, and a project to develop Internet skills
- A Learning Tracks section identifying supplementary material on the Companion Web site
- A chapter Review Summary keyed to the Student Learning Objectives

- A list of Key Terms that students can use to review concepts
- Review Questions for students to test their comprehension of chapter material
- Discussion Questions raised by the broader themes of the chapter
- A Video Case (available on the Companion Web site)
- A Teamwork project to develop teamwork and presentation skills
- A chapter-ending case study for students to apply chapter concepts

KEY FEATURES

We have enhanced the text to make it more interactive, leading-edge, and appealing to both students and instructors. The eighth edition includes the following features and learning tools:

Business-Driven with Real-World Examples

The text helps students see the direct connection between information systems and business performance. It describes the main business objectives driving the use of information systems and technologies in corporations all over the world: operational excellence; new products and services; customer and supplier intimacy; improved decision making; competitive advantage; and survival. In-text examples and case studies show students how specific companies use information systems to achieve these objectives.

Real-world examples from business and public organizations are used throughout the text to illustrate text concepts. All the case studies describe companies or organizations that are familiar to students, such as Google, MySpace, Photobucket, Wal-Mart, iTunes, NASCAR, Amazon, the NBA, and JetBlue.

Student Learning-Focused

Student Learning Objectives are organized around a set of study questions to focus student attention. Each chapter concludes with a Review Summary and Review Questions organized around these study questions.

Interactivity

There's no better way to learn about MIS than by doing MIS! We provide different kinds of hands-on projects where students can work with real-world business scenarios and data, and learn first hand what MIS is all about. These projects heighten student involvement in this exciting subject.

- **Hands-On MIS**. Each chapter concludes with a Hands-On MIS section containing three types of projects: a running case project, a hands-on application software exercise using Microsoft Excel, Access, or Web page development tools, and a project that develops Internet business skills.
- **Interactive Sessions**. Two short cases in each chapter have been redesigned as Interactive Sessions to be used in the classroom (or on Internet discussion boards) to stimulate student interest and active learning. Each case concludes with two types of activities: *Case Study Questions* and *MIS in Action*. The *Case Study Questions* provide topics for class discussion, Internet discussion, or written assignments. *MIS in Action* features hands-on Web activities for exploring issues discussed in the case more deeply.

Students practice using software in real-world settings for achieving operational excellence and enhancing decision making.

IMPROVING DECISION MAKING: USING DATABASES TO ANALYZE SALES TRENDS

Software skills: Database querying and reporting
Business skills: Sales trend analysis

You can find out how information systems improve management decision making in this exercise. Rather than guessing or relying on estimates and experience, managers today rely on information stored in databases. In this project, you will start out with raw transactional sales data and use Microsoft Access database software to develop queries and reports that help managers make better decisions about product pricing, sales promotions, and inventory replenishment. A part of the database is shown in the following figure.

On the Laudon Web site for Chapter 1, you can find a Store and Regional Sales Database developed in Microsoft Access. The database contains raw data on weekly store sales of computer equipment in various sales regions. You will use Access to manage the data and turn them into useful business information.

The database includes fields for store identification number, sales region number, item number, item description, unit price, units sold, and the weekly sales period when the sales were made.

Develop some reports and queries to make this information more useful for running the business. Sales and production managers want answers to the following questions:
- Which products should be restocked?
- Which stores and sales regions would benefit from a promotional campaign and additional marketing?
- When (what time of year) should products be offered at full price, and when should discounts be used?

You can easily modify the database table to find and report your answers. Print your reports and results of queries.

Store & Region Sales Database : Table

ID	Store No	Sales Region	Item No	Item Description	Unit Price	Units Sold	Week Ending
1	1	South	2005	17" Monitor	$229.00	28	10/27/2007
2	1	South	2005	17" Monitor	$229.00	30	11/24/2007
3	1	South	2005	17" Monitor	$229.00	9	12/29/2007
4	1	South	3006	101 Keyboard	$19.95	30	10/27/2007
5	1	South	3006	101 Keyboard	$19.95	35	11/24/2007
6	1	South	3006	101 Keyboard	$19.95	39	12/29/2007
7	1	South	6050	PC Mouse	$8.95	28	10/27/2007
8	1	South	6050	PC Mouse	$8.95	3	11/24/2007
9	1	South	6050	PC Mouse	$8.95	38	12/29/2007
10	1	South	8500	Desktop CPU	$849.95	25	10/27/2007

Record: 1 of 96

Each Dirt Bikes USA running case project requires students to use application software, Web tools, or analytical skills to solve a problem encountered by a simulated real-world company.

3.5 Hands-On MIS

The projects in this section give you hands-on experience analyzing a company's competitive strategy, using a database to improve decision making about business strategy, and using Web tools to configure and price an automobile.

IMPROVING DECISION MAKING: ANALYZING COMPETITIVE STRATEGY:

Software skills: Web browser software and presentation software
Business skills: Value chain and competitive forces analysis, business strategy formulation

This project provides an opportunity for you to develop the competitive strategy for a real-world business. You will use the Web to identify Dirt Bikes's competitors and the competitive forces in its industry. You'll use value chain analysis to determine what kinds of information systems will provide the company with a competitive advantage.

Dirt Bikes's management wants to be sure it is pursuing the right competitive strategy. You have been asked to perform a competitive analysis of the company using the Web to find the information you need. Prepare a report that analyzes Dirt Bikes using the value chain and competitive forces models. Your report should include the following:
- Which activities at Dirt Bikes create the most value?
- How does Dirt Bikes provide value to its customers?
- What other companies are Dirt Bikes's major competitors? How do their products compare in price to those of Dirt Bikes? What are some of the product features they emphasize?
- What are the competitive forces that can affect the industry?
- What competitive strategy should Dirt Bikes pursue?
- What information systems best support that strategy?
- (Optional) Use electronic presentation software to summarize your findings for management.

INTERACTIVE SESSION: TECHNOLOGY   The Databases Behind MySpace

MySpace.com, the popular social networking site, has experienced one of the greatest growth spurts in the history of the Internet. The site launched in November 2003 and by May 2007, it had 175 million member accounts. The challenge for MySpace has been to avoid technological letdowns that degrade Web site performance and frustrate its rapidly expanding network of users.

The technical requirements of a site like MySpace are vastly different from other heavily trafficked Web sites. Generally, a small number of people change the content on a news site a few times a day. The site may retrieve thousands of read-only requests from its underlying database without having to update the database. On MySpace, tens of millions of users are constantly updating their content, resulting in an elevated percentage of database interactions that require updates to the underlying database. Each time a user views a profile on MySpace, the resulting page is stitched together from database lookups that organize information from multiple tables stored in multiple databases residing on multiple servers.

In its initial phases, MySpace operated with two Web servers communicating with one database server and a Microsoft SQL Server database. Such a setup is ideal for small to medium-size sites because of its simplicity. At MySpace, the setup showed signs of stress as more users came aboard. At first, MySpace reduced the load by adding Web servers to handle the increased user requests. But when the number of accounts stretched to 500,000 in 2004, one database server was not sufficient. Deploying additional database servers is more complicated than adding Web servers because the data must be divided among multiple databases without any loss in accessibility or performance. MySpace deployed three SQL Server databases. One served as a master database, which received all new data and copied them to the other two databases. These databases focused on retrieving data for user page requests.

As MySpace approached 2 million accounts, the database servers approached their input/output capacity, which refers to the speed at which they could read and write data. This caused the site to lag behind in content updates. MySpace switched to a vertical partitioning model in which separate databases supported distinct functions of the Web site, such as the log-in screen, user profiles, and blogs.

However, the distinct functions also had occasion to share data, and this became problematic when the site reached 3 million accounts. Furthermore, some functions of the site grew too large to be served by only one database server. After considering a scale-up strategy of investing in more powerful and expensive servers, MySpace instead scaled out by adding many cheaper servers to share the database workload.

The more economical solution of a distributed architecture required a new design in which all of the servers combined to work as one logical computer. Under this design, the workload still needed to be spread out, which was accomplished by dividing the user accounts into groups of 1 million, and putting all the data related to those accounts in a separate instance of SQL Server.

Despite these gains in efficiency, the workload was not distributed evenly, which would sometimes cause an overload in the storage area for a particular database. MySpace tried to correct this issue manually, but the work was demanding and not an effective use of resources. So, MySpace switched to a virtualized storage architecture, which ended the practice of attaching disks dedicated to specific applications in favor of a single pool of storage space available to all applications. Under this arrangement, databases could write data to any available disk, thus eliminating the possibility of an application's dedicated disk becoming overloaded.

In 2005, MySpace also fortified its infrastructure by installing a layer of servers between the database servers and the Web servers to store and serve copies of frequently accessed data objects so that the site's Web servers wouldn't have to query the database servers with lookups as frequently.

Despite all these measures, MySpace still overloads more frequently than other major Web sites. Users have expressed frustration at not being able to log in or view certain pages. Log-in errors occur at a rate of 20 to 40 percent some days. Site activity continues to challenge the limitations of the technology. So far, the site's continued growth suggests that users are willing to put up with periodic "Unexpected Error" screens. MySpace developers continue to redesign the Web site's database, software, and storage systems to keep pace with its exploding growth, but their job is never done.

Sources: David F. Carr, "Inside MySpace.com," *Baseline Magazine*, January 16, 2007; Mark Brunelli, "Oracle Database 10g Powers Growing MySpace.com Competitor," SearchOracle.com, January 31, 2007; and Saul Hansell, "For MySpace, Making Friends Was Easy. Big Prophet Is Tougher," *The New York Times*, April 23, 2006.

CASE STUDY QUESTIONS

1. Describe how MySpace uses databases and database servers.

2. Why is database technology so important for a business such as MySpace?

3. How effectively does MySpace organize and store the data on its site?

4. What data management problems have arisen? How has MySpace solved, or attempted to solve, these problems?

MIS IN ACTION

Explore MySpace.com, examining the features and tools that are not restricted to registered members. Then answer the following questions:

1. Based on what you can view without registering, what are the entities in MySpace's database?

2. Which of these entities have some relationship to individual members?

3. Select one of these entities and describe the attributes for that entity.

Each chapter contains two Interactive Sessions on People, Organizations, or Technology using real-world companies to illustrate chapter concepts and issues.

MIS in Action projects encourage students to learn more about the companies and issues discussed in the case studies.

Assessment and AACSB Assessment Guidelines

The Association to Advance Collegiate Schools of Business (AACSB) is a not-for-profit corporation of educational institutions, corporations and other organizations that seeks to improve business education primarily by accrediting university business programs. As a part of its accreditation activities, the AACSB has developed an Assurance of Learning Program designed to ensure that schools do in fact teach students what they promise. Schools are required to state a clear mission, develop a coherent business program, identify student learning objectives, and then prove that students do in fact achieve the objectives.

We have attempted in this book to support AACSB efforts to encourage assessment-based education. The front end papers of this edition identify student learning objectives and anticipated outcomes for our Hands-on MIS projects. On the Laudon Web site is a more inclusive and detailed assessment matrix that identifies the learning objectives of each chapter and points to all the available assessment tools for ensuring students in fact do achieve the learning objectives. Because each school is different and may have different missions and learning objectives, no single document can satisfy all situations. The authors will provide custom advice on how to use this text in colleges with different missions and assessment needs. Please e-mail the authors or contact your local Prentice Hall representative for contact information.

For more information on the AACSB Assurance of Learning Program, and how this text supports assessment-based learning, please visit the Web site for this book.

Customization and Flexibility: New Learning Track Modules:

Our **Learning Tracks** feature gives instructors the flexibility to provide in-depth coverage of the topics they choose. A Learning Tracks section at the end of each chapter directs students to short essays or additional chapters on the Laudon Companion Web site. This supplementary content takes students deeper into MIS topics, concepts and debates; reviews basic technology concepts in hardware, software, database design, telecommunications, and other areas; and provide additional hands-on software instruction. The Eighth Edition includes new Learning Tracks on The Booming Job Market in IT Security, Hot New Careers in E-Commerce, Computer Forensics, Sarbanes-Oxley, Service Level Agreements, Building a Web Page, Excel Pivot Tables, and additional coverage of Computer Hardware and Software technology.

Author-Certified Test Bank and Supplements

- **Author-Certified Test Bank.** The authors have worked closely with skilled test item writers to ensure that higher level cognitive skills are tested. Test bank multiple choice questions include questions on content, but also include many questions that require analysis, synthesis, and evaluation skills.
- **Interactive PowerPoint Lecture Slides.** In addition to illuminating key concepts, class slides include four to five Interactive Sessions where students are encouraged to discuss in class the cases in the chapter or related issues in MIS, management, and business.

Globalization

This edition has even more global emphasis than previous editions. New material on globalization (Chapter 1), global workgroup collaboration (Chapter 2), software localization (Chapter 4), global security threats (Chapter 7), global supply chains (Chapter 8), global marketplaces (Chapter 9), managing global systems projects (Chapter 11), and offshore outsourcing (Chapter 11), accompanied by numerous examples of multinational and non-U.S. companies, show how to use IS in a global business environment.

Expanded Treatment of Project Management

A new chapter on *Building Information Systems and Managing Projects* (Chapter 11) teaches students how to implement MIS projects to obtain genuine business value.

New Leading-Edge Topics

The Laudons are always in the forefront in identifying what's new in MIS. This edition includes new coverage of the following leading-edge topics:

Globalization
Virtualization
Multicore processing
Cloud computing
Ajax
Web 2.0
Business uses of wikis and blogs
Social networking
Social shopping
Social bookmarking
Service level agreements
Offshore outsourcing

A Problem-Solving Perspective

Chapter 1 introduces a four-step problem-solving method that students can use throughout the course and for analyzing case studies. Students will learn how to identify a business problem, design alternative solutions, choose the correct solution, and implement the solution. We use the problem-solving perspective throughout the text to show how real-world companies identified and ultimately solved key business challenges using information systems and technologies.

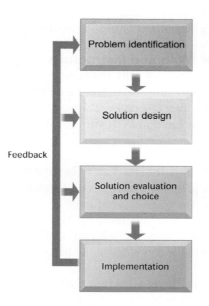

This four-step method helps students analyze information systems problems and develop solutions.

Career Resources

Career resources are integrated throughout the learning system. Each chapter shows why students need to know about the chapter and how this knowledge will help them in their future career. The Companion Web site offers extensive Career Resources, including job-hunting guides and instructions on how to build a Digital Portfolio demonstrating the business knowledge, application software proficiency, and Internet skills acquired from using the text. The portfolio can be included in a resume or job application or used as a learning assessment tool for instructors.

COMPANION WEB SITE

The Laudon/Laudon text is supported by an excellent Web site at **http://www.pren-hall.com/laudon** that reinforces and enhances text material with Learning Tracks supplements, the Dirt Bikes U.S.A. running case, video cases, data files for the Hands-on MIS projects, Career Resources and Digital Portfolio guide, an Interactive Study Guide, International Resources, additional case studies, and a special PowerPoint slide show on IT Careers custom-prepared by Ken Laudon. The Web site also features a secure password-protected faculty area from which instructors can obtain AACSB assessment tools and download the Instructor's Manual and suggested answers to the Hands-on MIS and other projects. The site has an improved online syllabus tool to help professors add their own personal syllabi to the site in minutes.

Instructional Support Materials

Instructor's Resource CD-ROM
Most of the support materials described in the following sections are conveniently available for adopters on the Instructor's Resource CD-ROM. The CD includes the Instructor's Manual, Lecture Notes, Test Item File, PowerPoint slides, and the helpful lecture tool "Image Library."

Image Library (on Web and Instructor's Resource CD-ROM)
The Image Library is an impressive resource to help instructors create vibrant lecture presentations. Almost every figure and photo in the text is provided and organized by chapter for convenience. These images and lecture notes can be imported easily into Microsoft PowerPoint to create new presentations or to add to existing ones.

Instructor's Manual (on Web and Instructor's Resource CD-ROM)
The Instructor's Manual features not only answers to review, discussion, case study, and group project questions but also an in-depth lecture outline, teaching objectives, key terms, teaching suggestions, and Internet resources. This supplement can be downloaded from the secure faculty section of the Laudon Web site and is also available on the Instructor's Resource CD-ROM.

Test Item File (on Web and Instructor's Resource CD-ROM)
The Test Item File is a comprehensive collection of true-false, multiple-choice, fill-in-the-blank, and essay questions. The questions are rated by difficulty level and the answers are referenced by section. An electronic version of the Test Item File is available in TestGen and TestGen conversions are available for BlackBoard or WebCT course management systems. All TestGen files are available for download at the Instructor Resource Center.

PowerPoint Slides (on Web and Instructor's Resource CD-ROM)
Electronic color slides created by Azimuth Interactive Corporation, Inc., are available in Microsoft PowerPoint. The slides illuminate and build on key concepts in the text. Faculty can download the PowerPoint slides from the Web site, and they are also provided on the Instructor's Resource CD-ROM.

Microsoft Office Tutorial Software
For instructors seeking application software training to use with this text, Prentice Hall is pleased to offer student training in Microsoft Office 2007. This item is not available as a stand-alone item but can be packaged with the Laudon/Laudon text at an additional charge. Contact your local Prentice Hall representative for more details.

Acknowledgments

The production of any book involves valued contributions from a number of persons. We would like to thank all of our editors for encouragement, insight, and strong support for many years. We thank Bob Horan for guiding the development of this edition and Kelly Loftus for her role in managing the project.

We praise Carol Samet for overseeing production for this project and thank Diane Austin for her fine photo research. Our special thanks go to our supplement authors for their work. We are indebted to Kenneth Rosenblatt for his assistance in the writing and production of the text and to Megan Miller for her help during production. We thank Diana R. Craig for her assistance with database topics.

Special thanks to colleagues at the Stern School of Business at New York University; to Professor Edward Stohr of Stevens Institute of Technology; to Professors Al Croker and Michael Palley of Baruch College and New York University; to Professor Lawrence Andrew of Western Illinois University; to Professors Walter Brenner and Lutz Kolbe of the University of St. Gallen; to Professor Donald Marchand of the International Institute for Management Development; and to Professor Daniel Botha of Stellenbosch University who provided additional suggestions for improvement. Thank you to Professor Ken Kraemer, University of California at Irvine, and Professor John King, University of Michigan, for more than a decade's long discussion of information systems and organizations. And a special remembrance and dedication to Professor Rob Kling, University of Indiana, for being my friend and colleague over so many years.

We also want to especially thank all our reviewers whose suggestions helped improve our texts. Reviewers for this edition include the following:

Joseph Blankenship, Youngstown State University
Nora Braun, Augsburg College
Rochelle Cadogan, Viterbo University
Wade Chumney, Belmont University
Angela Clark, University of South Alabama
Preston Clark, Cornell University
C. Lee Clarke, Augsburg College
Emilio Collar Jr., Western Connecticut State University
Jack Cook, Rochester Institute of Technology
Terry Freed, Penn State Harrisburg
Robert Fulkerth, Golden Gate University
Albert Hayashi, Loyola Marymount University
Patrick Jeffers, Iowa State University
Keith Jenkins, Judson College
Boyd Jones, The Catholic University of America
Larry Larson, University of Redlands
Farrokh Mamaghani, St. John Fisher College
Bernard Merkle, California Lutheran University
Fiona Fui-Hoon Nah, University of Nebraska-Lincoln
Laszlo Pook, Metropolitan State College of Denver
Michael Powers, Franklin University
David Rosi, Lower Columbia College
Werner Schenk, St. John Fisher College
Corinne Smolizza, St. Francis College
Timothy Stanton, Mount St. Mary's University
Claire Theriault-Perkins, University of Maine at Augusta
Bradley Watson, Franklin University
Marie Wright, Western Connecticut State University
James Yao, Montclair State University
Michael Yates, Robert Morris College

K.C.L.
J.P.L.

Information Systems in the Digital Age

P A R T I

1 **Business Information Systems in Your Career**

2 **E-Business: How Businesses Use Information Systems**

3 **Achieving Competitive Advantage with Information Systems**

Part I introduces the major themes and the problem-solving approaches that are used throughout the book. While surveying the role of information systems in today's businesses, this part raises several major questions: What is an information system? Why are information systems so essential in businesses today? How can information systems help businesses become more competitive? What do I need to know about information systems to succeed in my business career?

Business Information Systems in Your Career

CHAPTER 1

STUDENT LEARNING OBJECTIVES

After completing this chapter, you will be able to answer the following questions:

1. How are information systems transforming business and what is their relationship to globalization?

2. Why are information systems so essential for running and managing a business today?

3. What exactly is an information system? How does it work? What are its people, organization, and technology components?

4. How will a four-step method for business problem solving help you solve information system-related problems?

5. How will information systems affect business careers and what information systems skills and knowledge are essential?

CHAPTER OUTLINE

NBA TEAMS MAKE A SLAM DUNK WITH INFORMATION TECHNOLOGY

Basketball is a very fast-paced, high-energy sport but it's also big business. Professional teams that belong to the National Basketball Association (NBA) pay each of their players an average of $5 million each year. For that amount of money, member teams expect a great deal and are constantly on the watch for ways of improving their performance. During an 82-game season, every nuance a coach can pick up about a weakness in an opponent's offense or in the jump shot of one of his own players will translate into more points on the scoreboard, more wins, and ultimately more money for the team.

Traditional basketball game statistics failed to capture all of the details associated with every play and were not easily related to videotapes of games. As a result, decisions about changes in tactics or how to take advantage of opponents' weaknesses were based primarily on hunches and gut instincts. Coaches could not easily answer questions such as "Which types of plays are hurting us?" Now professional basketball coaches and managers are taking their cues from other businesses and learning how to make decisions based on hard data.

A company called Synergy Sports Technology has found a way to collect and organize fine-grained statistical data and relate the data to associated video clips. Synergy employs more than 30 people to match up videos of each play with statistical information on which players have the ball, what type of play is involved, and the result. Each game is dissected and tagged, play by play, using hundreds of descriptive categories and these data are linked to high-resolution video.

Coaches then use an index to locate the exact video clip in which they are interested and access the video at a protected Web site. Within seconds they are able to watch streaming video on the protected site or they can download it to laptops and even to Apple iPods. One NBA team puchased iPods for every player so they could review videos to help them prepare for their next game.

For example, if the Dallas Mavericks have just lost to the Phoenix Suns and gave up too many fast-break points, Mavericks coaches can use Synergy's service to see video clips of every Phoenix fast break in the game. They can also view every Dallas transitional situation for the entire season to see how that night's game compared with others. According to Dallas Mavericks owner Mark Cuban, "The system allows us to look at every play, in every way, and tie it back to stats. So we can watch how we played every pick and roll, track our success rate, and see how other teams are doing it."

The service helps coaches analyze the strengths and weaknesses of individual players. For example, Synergy's system has recorded every offensive step of the Mavericks' Dirk Nowitzki since he joined the NBA in 1998. The system can show how successfully he is driving right or left in either home or away games, with the ability to break games and player performance into increasingly finer-grained categories. If a user clicks on any statistic, that person will find video clips from the last three seasons of 20, 50, or even 2,000 plays that show Nowitzki making that particular move.

About 14 NBA teams have already signed up for Synergy's service and are using it to help them scout for promising high school and international players. Although nothing will ever replace the need to scout players in person, the service has reduced NBA teams' sky-rocketing travel costs.

Sources: Randall Stross, "Technology to Dissect Every Dunk and Drive," *The New York Times*, April 29, 2007; Bob Young, "Nothing but 'Net: NBA Stats Come to Life Online," *The Arizona Republic*, April 17, 2006; wkyc.com, accessed May 4, 2007; and www.nba.org, accessed May 4, 2007.

The challenges facing NBA teams show why information systems are so essential today. Like other businesses, professional basketball faces pressures from high costs, especially for team member salaries and travel to search for new talent. Teams are trying to increase revenue by improving employee performance, especially the performance of basketball team members.

The chapter-opening diagram calls attention to important points raised by this case and this chapter. To improve team performance, NBA coaches could have spent more time scrutinizing existing videos of their games, or management could have paid more money to recruit the most highly-ranked NBA players. They chose instead a new information system solution that provides them with better information to take advantage of their existing player resources.

The solution is based on an information system service provided by Synergy Sports Technology. Synergy staff members break down each game into a series of plays and then categorize each play by players, type of play, and the outcome. These data are tagged to the videos they describe to make the videos easy to search. NBA coaches and management can analyze the data to see which offensive and defensive moves are the most effective for each team player. Team members themselves can use iPods to download the videos to help them prepare for games. This innovative solution makes it possible for basketball management to use hard statistical data about players, plays, and outcomes to improve their decision making about what players should or shouldn't do to most effectively counter their opponents.

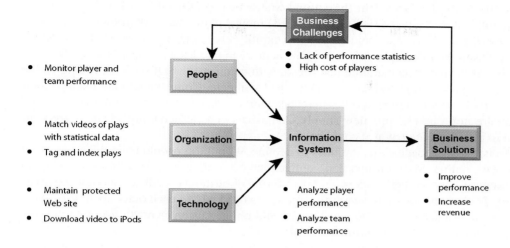

1.1 The Role of Information Systems in Business Today

It's not business as usual in America any more, or the rest of the global economy. In 2007, American businesses will invest nearly $1 trillion in information systems hardware, software, and telecommunications equipment—more than half of all capital investment in the United States. In addition, they will spend another $250 billion on business and management consulting and services—much of which involves redesigning firms' business operations to take advantage of these new technologies. More than half of all business investment in the United States each year involves information systems and technologies.

HOW INFORMATION SYSTEMS ARE TRANSFORMING BUSINESS

You can see the results of this massive spending around you every day by observing how people conduct business. More wireless cell phone accounts were opened in 2007 than telephone land lines installed. Cell phones, BlackBerrys, wireless handhelds, e-mail, and online conferencing over the Internet have all become essential tools of business. In 2007, more than 40 million businesses had dot-com Internet sites registered. Six million Americans purchase something every day on the Internet, 19 million research a product, and 38 million use a search engine. What this means is that if you and your business aren't connected to the Internet and wireless networks, chances are you are not being as effective as you could be (Pew Internet and American Life, 2007).

In 2006, FedEx moved in the United States nearly 200 million packages, mostly overnight, and the United Parcel Service (UPS) moved more than 570 million packages, as businesses sought to sense and respond to rapidly changing customer demand, reduce inventories to the lowest possible levels, and achieve higher levels of operational efficiency. Supply chains have become more fast paced, with companies of all sizes depending on the delivery of just-in-time inventory to help them compete. Companies today manage their inventories in near real time in order to reduce their overhead costs and get to market faster. If you are not a part of this new supply chain management economy, chances are your business is not as efficient as it could be.

As newspaper readership continues to decline, 94 million people read at least some of their news online. Sixty million bank online, and 55 million now read blogs, creating an explosion of new writers, readers, and new forms of customer feedback that did not exist before. This means your customers are empowered and talk to each other about your business products and services. Do you have a solid online customer relationship program in place? Is your marketing department listening?

E-commerce and Internet advertising are booming: Google's online ad revenues surpassed $10 billion in 2006. Internet advertising continues to grow at more than 15 percent a year, at the expense of traditional media, reaching more than $18 billion in revenues in 2007. Is your advertising department reaching this new Web-based customer base?

New federal security and accounting laws require many businesses to keep e-mail messages for five years. Coupled with existing occupational and health laws requiring firms to store employee chemical exposure data for up to 60 years, these laws are spurring the growth of digital information now estimated to be 5 exabytes, equivalent to 37,000 Libraries of Congress. Does your compliance department meet the minimal requirements for storing financial, health, and occupational information? If they don't, your entire business may be at risk.

Briefly, it's a new world of doing business, one that will greatly affect your future business career. Along with the changes in business come changes in jobs and careers. No matter whether you are a finance, accounting, management, marketing, operations management, or information systems major, how you work, where you work, and how well you are compensated will all be affected by business information systems. The purpose of this book is to help you understand and benefit from these new business realities.

GLOBALIZATION CHALLENGES AND OPPORTUNITIES: A FLATTENED WORLD

In 1492, Columbus reaffirmed what astronomers were long saying: the world was round and the seas could be safely sailed. As it turned out, the world was populated by peoples and languages living in near total isolation from one another, with great disparities in economic and scientific development. The world trade that ensued after Columbus's voyages has brought these peoples and cultures closer. The "industrial revolution" was really a world-wide phenomenon energized by expansion of trade among nations.

By 2005, journalist Thomas Friedman wrote an influential book declaring the world was now "flat," by which he meant that the Internet and global communications had greatly reduced the economic and cultural advantages of developed countries. U.S. and European countries were in a fight for their economic lives, competing for jobs, markets, resources, and even ideas with highly educated, motivated populations in low-wage areas in the less developed world (Friedman, 2005). This "globalization" presents you and your business with both challenges and opportunities.

A growing percentage of the economy of the United States and other advanced industrial countries in Europe and Asia depends on imports and exports. In 2007, more than 33 percent of the U.S. economy resulted from foreign trade, both imports and exports. In Europe and Asia, the number exceeds 50 percent. Many Fortune 500 U.S. firms derive half their revenues from foreign operations. For instance, more than half of Intel's revenues in 2006 came from overseas sales of its microprocessors. Toys for chips: 80 percent of the toys sold in the United States are manufactured in China, while about 90 percent of the PCs manufactured in China use American-made Intel or Advanced Micro Design (AMD) chips.

It's not just goods that move across borders. So too do jobs, some of them high-level jobs that pay well and require a college degree. In the past decade the U.S. lost several million manufacturing jobs to offshore, low-wage producers. But manufacturing is now a very small part of U.S. employment (less than 12 percent). In a normal year, about 300,000 service jobs move offshore to lower-wage countries, many of them in less-skilled information system occupations, but also including "tradable service" jobs in architecture, financial services, customer call centers, consulting, engineering, and even radiology.

On the plus side, the U.S. economy creates over 3.5 million new jobs a year, and employment in information systems, and the other service occupations listed previously, has expanded in sheer numbers, wages, productivity, and quality of work. Outsourcing has actually accelerated the development of new systems in the United States and worldwide. For the last several years there have been too few information systems majors to fill the demand of employers in the United States.

The challenge for you as a business student is to develop high-level skills through education and on-the-job experience that cannot be outsourced. The challenge for your business is to avoid markets for goods and services that can be produced offshore much less expensively. The opportunities are equally immense. You can learn how to profit from the lower costs available in world markets and the chance to serve a marketplace with billions of customers. You have the opportunity to develop higher-level and more profitable products and services. You will find throughout this book examples of companies and individuals who either failed or succeeded in using information systems to adapt to this new global environment.

What does globalization have to do with management information systems? That's simple: everything. The emergence of the Internet into a full-blown international communications system has drastically reduced the costs of operating and transacting on a global scale. Communication between a factory floor in Shanghai and a distribution center in Rapid Falls, South Dakota, is now instant and virtually free. Customers now can shop in a worldwide marketplace, obtaining price and quality information reliably 24 hours a day. Firms producing goods and services on a global scale achieve extraordinary cost reductions by finding low-cost suppliers and managing production facilities in other countries. Internet service firms, such as Google and eBay, are able to replicate their business models and services in multiple countries without having to redesign their expensive fixed-cost information systems infrastructure. Over half of eBay's revenues in 2007 originated outside the United States. Briefly, information systems enable globalization.

BUSINESS DRIVERS OF INFORMATION SYSTEMS

What makes information systems so essential today? Why are businesses investing so much in information systems and technologies? They do so to achieve six important business objectives: operational excellence; new products, services, and business models; customer and supplier intimacy; improved decision making; competitive advantage; and survival.

Operational Excellence
Businesses continuously seek to improve the efficiency of their operations in order to achieve higher profitability. Information systems and technologies are some of the most important tools available to managers for achieving higher levels of efficiency and productivity in business operations, especially when coupled with changes in business practices and management behavior.

Wal-Mart, the largest retailer on Earth, exemplifies the power of information systems coupled with brilliant business practices and supportive management to achieve world-class operational efficiency. In 2007, Wal-Mart achieved more than $348 billion in sales—nearly one-tenth of retail sales in the United States—in large part because of its Retail Link system, which digitally links its suppliers to every one of Wal-Mart's 5,289 stores worldwide. As soon as a customer purchases an item, the supplier monitoring the item knows to ship a replacement to the shelf. Wal-Mart is the most efficient retail store in the industry, achieving sales of more than $28 per square foot, compared to its closest competitor, Target, at $23 a square foot, with other retail firms producing less than $12 a square foot.

New Products, Services, and Business Models

Information systems and technologies are a major enabling tool for firms to create new products and services, as well as entirely new business models. A **business model** describes how a company produces, delivers, and sells a product or service to create wealth. Today's music industry is vastly different from the industry in 2000. Apple Inc. transformed an old business model of music distribution based on vinyl records, tapes, and CDs into an online, legal distribution model based on its own iPod technology platform. Apple has prospered from a continuing stream of innovations, including the original iPod, the iPod nano, the iTunes music service, the iPod video player, and the iPhone.

Customer and Supplier Intimacy

When a business really knows its customers and serves them well, the way they want to be served, the customers generally respond by returning and purchasing more. This raises revenues and profits. Likewise with suppliers: the more a business engages its suppliers, the better the suppliers can provide vital inputs. This lowers costs. How to really know your customers, or suppliers, is a central problem for businesses with millions of offline and online customers.

The Mandarin Oriental in Manhattan and other high-end hotels exemplify the use of information systems and technologies to achieve customer intimacy. These hotels use computers to keep track of guests' preferences, such as their preferred room temperature, check-in time, frequently dialed telephone numbers, and television programs, and store these data in a giant data repository. Individual rooms in the hotels are networked to a central network server computer so that they can be remotely monitored or controlled. When a customer arrives at one of these hotels, the system automatically changes the room conditions, such as dimming the lights, setting the room temperature, or selecting appropri-

With its stunning multi-touch display, full Internet browsing, digital camera, and portable music player, Apple's iPhone set a new standard for mobile phones. Other Apple products have transformed the music and entertainment industries.

ate music, based on the customer's digital profile. The hotels also analyze their customer data to identify their best customers and to develop individualized marketing campaigns based on customers' preferences.

JCPenney exemplifies the benefits of information systems-enabled supplier intimacy. Every time a dress shirt is bought at a JCPenney store in the United States, the record of the sale appears immediately on computers in Hong Kong at the TAL Apparel Ltd. supplier, a giant contract manufacturer that produces one in eight dress shirts sold in the United States. TAL runs the numbers through a computer model it developed and then decides how many replacement shirts to make, and in what styles, colors and sizes. TAL then sends the shirts to each JCPenney store, bypassing completely the retailer's warehouses. In other words, JCPenney's shirt inventory is near zero, as is the cost of storing it.

Improved Decision Making

Many business managers operate in an information fog bank, never really having the right information at the right time to make an informed decision. Instead, managers rely on forecasts, best guesses, and luck. The result is over- or underproduction of goods and services, misallocation of resources, and poor response times. These poor outcomes raise costs and lose customers. In the past 10 years, information systems and technologies have made it possible for managers to use real-time data from the marketplace when making decisions.

For instance, Verizon Corporation, one of the largest regional Bell operating companies in the United States, uses a Web-based digital dashboard to provide managers with precise real-time information on customer complaints, network performance for each locality served, and line outages or storm-damaged lines. Using this information, managers can immediately allocate repair resources to affected areas, inform consumers of repair efforts, and restore service fast.

Competitive Advantage

When firms achieve one or more of these business objectives—operational excellence; new products, services, and business models; customer/supplier intimacy; and improved decision making—chances are they have already achieved a competitive advantage. Doing things better than your competitors, charging less for superior products, and responding to customers and suppliers in real time all add up to higher sales and higher profits that your competitors cannot match.

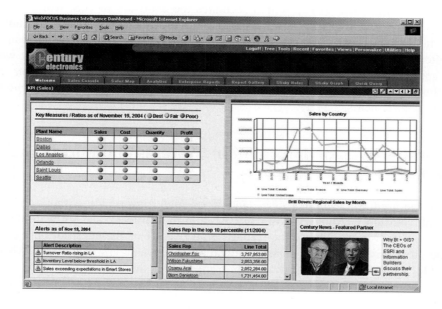

Information Builders' digital dashboard delivers comprehensive and accurate information for decision making. The graphical overview of key performance indicators helps managers quickly spot areas that need attention.

In a Toyota factory, the assembly line produces a superior product in less time, using less inventory, and having fewer defects than the competition. Toyota uses information systems to monitor inventory levels and manage production scheduling.

Perhaps no other company exemplifies all of these attributes leading to competitive advantage more than Toyota Motor Company, which we discuss in the following chapter. Toyota has become the world's largest auto maker because of its high level of efficiency and quality. Competitors struggle to keep up. Toyota's legendary Toyota Production System (TPS) focuses on organizing work to eliminate waste, making continuous improvements, and optimizing customer value. Information systems help Toyota implement the TPS and produce vehicles based on what customers have actually ordered.

Survival

Business firms also invest in information systems and technologies because they are necessities of doing business. Sometimes these necessities are driven by industry-level changes. For instance, after Citibank introduced the first automatic teller machines (ATMs) in the New York region in 1977 to attract customers through higher service levels, its competitors rushed to provide ATMs to their customers to keep up with Citibank. Today, virtually all banks in the United States have regional ATMs and link to national and international ATM networks, such as CIRRUS. Providing ATM services to retail banking customers is simply a requirement of being in and surviving in the retail banking business.

Many federal and state statutes and regulations create a legal duty for companies and their employees to retain records, including digital records. For instance, the Toxic Substances Control Act (1976), which regulates the exposure of U.S. workers to more than 75,000 toxic chemicals, requires firms to retain records on employee exposure for 30 years. The Sarbanes-Oxley Act (2002), which was intended to improve the accountability of public firms and their auditors, requires public companies to retain audit working papers and records, including all e-mails, for five years. Firms turn to information systems and technologies to provide the capability to respond to these information retention and reporting requirements.

1.2 Perspectives on Information Systems and Information Technology

So far we've used *information systems* and *technologies* informally without defining the terms. **Information technology (IT)** consists of all the hardware and software that a firm needs to use in order to achieve its business objectives. This includes not only computer machines, disk drives, handheld personal digital assistants, and, yes, even iPods (where they are used for a business purpose) but also software, such as the Windows or Linux operating systems, the Microsoft Office desktop productivity suite, and the many thousands of computer programs that can be found in a typical large firm. "Information systems" are more complex and can be best be understood by looking at them from both a technology and a business perspective.

WHAT IS AN INFORMATION SYSTEM?

An **information system (IS)** can be defined technically as a set of interrelated components that collect (or retrieve), process, store, and distribute information to support decision making and control in an organization. In addition to supporting decision making, coordination, and control, information systems may also help managers and workers analyze problems, visualize complex subjects, and create new products.

Information systems contain information about significant people, places, and things within the organization or in the environment surrounding it. By **information** we mean data that have been shaped into a form that is meaningful and useful to human beings. **Data**, in contrast, are streams of raw facts representing events occurring in organizations or the physical environment before they have been organized and arranged into a form that people can understand and use.

A brief example contrasting information and data may prove useful. Supermarket checkout counters scan millions of pieces of data, such as bar codes, that describe the product. Such pieces of data can be totaled and analyzed to provide meaningful information, such as the total number of bottles of dish detergent sold at a particular store, which brands of dish detergent were selling the most rapidly at that store or sales territory, or the total amount spent on that brand of dish detergent at that store or sales region (see Figure 1-1).

Three activities in an information system produce the information that organizations need to make decisions, control operations, analyze problems, and create new products or services. These activities are input, processing, and output (see Figure 1-2). **Input** captures or collects raw data from within the organization or from its external environment. **Processing** converts this raw input into a meaningful form. **Output** transfers the processed information to the people who will use it or to the activities for which it will be used.

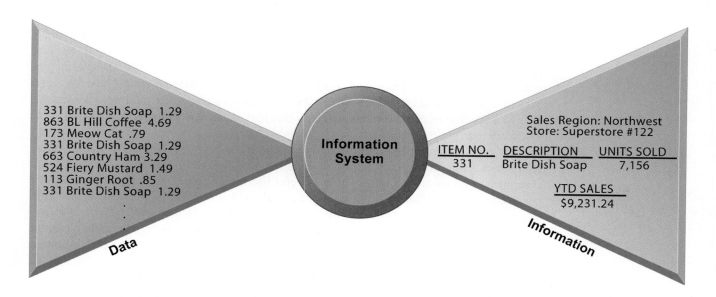

Figure 1-1
Data and Information
Raw data from a supermarket checkout counter can be processed and organized to produce meaningful information, such as the total unit sales of dish detergent or the total sales revenue from dish detergent for a specific store or sales territory.

Figure 1-2
Functions of an
Information System
*An information system
contains information
about an organization
and its surrounding
environment. Three basic
activities—input, pro-
cessing, and output—
produce the information
organizations need.
Feedback is output
returned to appropriate
people or activities in the
organization to evaluate
and refine the input.
Environmental actors,
such as customers,
suppliers, competitors,
stockholders, and regula-
tory agencies, interact
with the organization and
its information systems.*

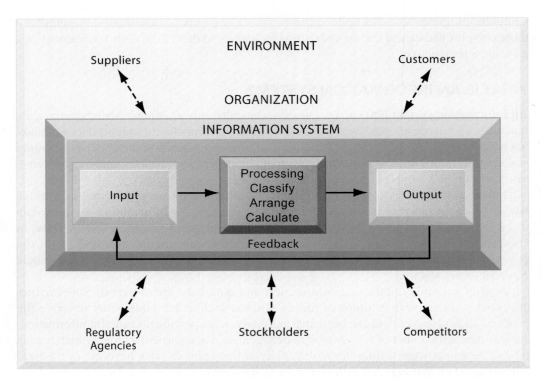

Information systems also require **feedback**, which is output that is returned to appropriate members of the organization to help them evaluate or correct the input stage.

In the NBA teams' system for analyzing basketball moves, there are actually two types of raw input. One consists of all the statistics about each play entered by Synergy Sports Technology's staff members—the player's name, team, date of game, game location, type of play, other players involved in the play, and the outcome. The other input consists of videos of the plays and games, which are captured as digital points of data for storage, retrieval, and manipulation by the computer.

Synergy Sports Technology server computers store these data and process them to relate data such as the player's name(s), type of play, and outcome to a specific video clip. The output consists of videos and statistics about specific players, teams, and plays. The system provides meaningful information, such as the number and type of defensive plays that were successful against a specific player, what types of offensive plays were the most successful against a specific team, or comparisons of individual player and team performance in home and away games.

Although computer-based information systems use computer technology to process raw data into meaningful information, there is a sharp distinction between a computer and a computer program and an information system. Electronic computers and related software programs are the technical foundation, the tools and materials, of modern information systems. Computers provide the equipment for storing and processing information. Computer programs, or software, are sets of operating instructions that direct and control computer processing. Knowing how computers and computer programs work is important in designing solutions to organizational problems, but computers are only part of an information system.

A house is an appropriate analogy. Houses are built with hammers, nails, and wood, but these do not make a house. The architecture, design, setting, landscaping, and all of the decisions that lead to the creation of these features are part of the house and are crucial for solving the problem of putting a roof over one's head. Computers and programs are the hammer, nails, and lumber of computer-based information systems, but alone they cannot produce the information a particular organization needs. To understand information systems, you must understand the problems they are designed to solve, their architectural and design elements, and the organizational processes that lead to these solutions.

IT ISN'T SIMPLY TECHNOLOGY: THE ROLE OF PEOPLE AND ORGANIZATIONS

To fully understand information systems, you will need to be aware of the broader organization, people, and information technology dimensions of systems (see Figure 1-3) and their power to provide solutions to challenges and problems in the business environment. We refer to this broader understanding of information systems, which encompasses an understanding of the people and organizational dimensions of systems as well as the technical dimensions of systems, as **information systems literacy**. Information systems literacy includes a behavioral as well as a technical approach to studying information systems. **Computer literacy**, in contrast, focuses primarily on knowledge of information technology.

The field of **management information systems (MIS)** tries to achieve this broader information systems literacy. MIS deals with behavioral issues as well as technical issues surrounding the development, use, and impact of information systems used by managers and employees in the firm.

DIMENSIONS OF INFORMATION SYSTEMS

Let's examine each of the dimensions of information systems—organizations, people, and information technology.

Organizations

Information systems are an integral part of organizations. And although we tend to think about information technology changing organizations and business firms, it is, in fact, a two-way street: The history and culture of business firms also affects how the technology is used and how it should be used. In order to understand how a specific business firm uses information systems, you need to know something about the structure, history, and culture of the company.

Organizations have a structure that is composed of different levels and specialties. Their structures reveal a clear-cut division of labor. A business firm is organized as a hierarchy, or a pyramid structure, of rising authority and responsibility. The upper levels of the hierarchy consist of managerial, professional, and technical employees, whereas the lower levels consist of operational personnel. Experts are employed and trained for different business functions, such as sales and marketing, manufacturing and production, finance and accounting,

**Figure 1-3
Information Systems Are More Than Computers**
Using information systems effectively requires an understanding of the organization, people, and information technology shaping the systems. An information system provides a solution to important business problems or challenges facing the firm.

and human resources. Information systems are built by the firm in order to serve these different specialties and different levels of the firm. Chapter 2 provides more detail on these business functions and organizational levels and the ways in which they are supported by information systems.

An organization accomplishes and coordinates work through this structured hierarchy and through its **business processes**, which are logically related tasks and behaviors for accomplishing work. Developing a new product, fulfilling an order, or hiring a new employee are examples of business processes.

Most organizations' business processes include formal rules that have been developed over a long time for accomplishing tasks. These rules guide employees in a variety of procedures, from writing an invoice to responding to customer complaints. Some of these business processes have been written down, but others are informal work practices, such as a requirement to return telephone calls from co-workers or customers, that are not formally documented. Information systems automate many business processes. For instance, how a customer receives credit or how a customer is billed is often determined by an information system that incorporates a set of formal business processes.

Each organization has a unique **culture**, or fundamental set of assumptions, values, and ways of doing things, that has been accepted by most of its members. Parts of an organization's culture can always be found embedded in its information systems. For instance, the United Parcel Service's concern with placing service to the customer first is an aspect of its organizational culture that can be found in the company's package tracking systems.

Different levels and specialties in an organization create different interests and points of view. These views often conflict. Conflict is the basis for organizational politics. Information systems come out of this cauldron of differing perspectives, conflicts, compromises, and agreements that are a natural part of all organizations.

People

A business is only as good as the people who work there and run it. Likewise with information systems—they are useless without skilled people to build and maintain them, and without people who can understand how to use the information in a system to achieve business objectives.

For instance, a call center that provides help to customers using an advanced customer relationship management system (described in later chapters) is useless if employees are not adequately trained to deal with customers, find solutions to their problems, and leave the customer feeling that the company cares for them. Likewise, employee attitudes about their jobs, employers, or technology can have a powerful effect on their abilities to use information systems productively.

Business firms require many different kinds of skills and people, including managers as well as rank-and-file employees. The job of managers is to make sense out of the many situations faced by organizations, make decisions, and formulate action plans to solve organizational problems. Managers perceive business challenges in the environment; they set the organizational strategy for responding to those challenges; and they allocate the human and financial resources to coordinate the work and achieve success. Throughout, they must exercise responsible leadership.

But managers must do more than manage what already exists. They must also create new products and services and even re-create the organization from time to time. A substantial part of management responsibility is creative work driven by new knowledge and information. Information technology can play a powerful role in helping managers develop novel solutions to a broad range of problems.

As you will learn throughout this text, technology is today relatively inexpensive, but people are very expensive. Because people are the only ones capable of business problem solving and converting information technology into useful business solutions, we spend considerable effort in this text looking at the people dimension of information systems.

Technology

Information technology is one of many tools managers use to cope with change. **Computer hardware** is the physical equipment used for input, processing, and output activities in an information system. It consists of the following: computers of various sizes and shapes; various input, output, and storage devices; and telecommunications devices that link computers together.

Computer software consists of the detailed, preprogrammed instructions that control and coordinate the computer hardware components in an information system. Chapter 4 describes the contemporary software and hardware platforms used by firms today in greater detail.

Data management technology consists of the software governing the organization of data on physical storage media. More detail on data organization and access methods can be found in Chapter 5.

Networking and telecommunications technology, consisting of both physical devices and software, links the various pieces of hardware and transfers data from one physical location to another. Computers and communications equipment can be connected in networks for sharing voice, data, images, sound, and video. A **network** links two or more computers to share data or resources, such as a printer.

The world's largest and most widely used network is the **Internet**. The Internet is a global "network of networks" that uses universal standards (described in Chapter 6) to connect millions of different networks in over 200 countries around the world.

The Internet has created a new "universal" technology platform on which to build new products, services, strategies, and business models. This same technology platform has internal uses, providing the connectivity to link different systems and networks within the firm. Internal corporate networks based on Internet technology are called **intranets**. Private intranets extended to authorized users outside the organization are called **extranets**, and firms use such networks to coordinate their activities with other firms for making purchases, collaborating on design, and performing other interorganizational work. For most business firms today, using Internet technology is a business necessity and a competitive advantage.

The **World Wide Web** is a service provided by the Internet that uses universally accepted standards for storing, retrieving, formatting, and displaying information in a page format on the Internet. Web pages contain text, graphics, animations, sound, and video and are linked to other Web pages. By clicking on highlighted words or buttons on a Web page, you can link to related pages to find additional information and links to other locations on the Web. The Web can serve as the foundation for new kinds of information systems such as UPS's Web-based package tracking system or Synergy Sports Technology's online service for delivering video linked to NBA team statistics.

All of these technologies, along with the people required to run and manage them, represent resources that can be shared throughout the organization and constitute the firm's **information technology (IT) infrastructure**. The IT infrastructure provides the foundation, or *platform*, on which the firm can build its specific information systems. Each organization must carefully design and manage its information technology infrastructure so that it has the set of technology services it needs for the work it wants to accomplish with information systems. Chapters 4 through 7 of this text examine each major technology component of information technology infrastructure and show how they all work together to create the technology platform for the organization.

The Interactive Session on Technology describes some of the typical technologies used in computer-based information systems today. UPS invests heavily in information systems technology to make its business more efficient and customer oriented. It uses an array of information technologies including bar code scanning systems, wireless networks, large mainframe computers, handheld computers, the Internet, and many different pieces of software for tracking packages, calculating fees, maintaining customer accounts, and managing logistics. As you read this case, try to identify the problem this company was facing, what alternative solutions were available to management, and how well the chosen solution worked.

United Parcel Service (UPS) started out in 1907 in a closet-sized basement office. Jim Casey and Claude Ryan—two teenagers from Seattle with two bicycles and one phone—promised the "best service and lowest rates." UPS has used this formula successfully for more than a century to become the world's largest ground and air package-distribution company. It is a global enterprise with more than 400,000 employees, 92,000 vehicles, and the world's eighth largest airline.

Today, UPS delivers more than 15 million parcels and documents each day in the United States and more than 200 other countries and territories. The firm has been able to maintain leadership in small-package delivery services despite stiff competition from FedEx and Airborne Express by investing heavily in advanced information technology. UPS spends more than $1 billion each year to maintain a high level of customer service while keeping costs low and streamlining its overall operations.

It all starts with the scannable bar-coded label attached to a package, which contains detailed information about the sender, the destination, and when the package should arrive. Customers can download and print their own labels using special software provided by UPS or by accessing the UPS Web site. Before the package is even picked up, information from the "smart" label is transmitted to one of UPS's computer centers in Mahwah, New Jersey, or Alpharetta, Georgia and sent to the distribution center nearest its final destination. Dispatchers at this center download the label data and use special software to create the most efficient delivery route for each driver that considers traffic, weather conditions, and the location of each stop. UPS estimates its delivery trucks saved 28 million miles and 3 million gallons of fuel in 2006 compared to the year before as a result of using this technology.

The first thing a UPS driver picks up each day is a handheld computer called a Delivery Information Acquisition Device (DIAD), which can access one of the wireless networks cell phones rely on. As soon as the driver logs on, his or her day's route is downloaded onto the handheld. The DIAD also automatically captures customers' signatures along with pickup and delivery information. Package tracking information is then transmitted to UPS's computer network for storage and processing. From there, the information can be accessed worldwide to provide proof of delivery to customers or to respond to customer

queries. It usually takes less than 60 seconds from the time a driver presses "complete" on the DIAD for the new information to be available on the Web.

Through its automated package tracking system, UPS can monitor and even re-route packages throughout the delivery process. At various points along the route from sender to receiver, bar code devices scan shipping information on the package label and feed data about the progress of the package into the central computer. Customer service representatives are able to check the status of any package from desktop computers linked to the central computers and respond immediately to inquiries from customers. UPS customers can also access this information from the company's Web site using their own computers or wireless devices.

Anyone with a package to ship can access the UPS Web site to track packages, check delivery routes, calculate shipping rates, determine time in transit, print labels, and schedule a pickup. The data collected at the UPS Web site are transmitted to the UPS central computer and then back to the customer after processing. UPS also provides tools that enable customers, such Cisco Systems, to embed UPS functions, such as tracking and cost calculations, into their own Web sites so that they can track shipments without visiting the UPS site.

UPS is now leveraging its decades of expertise managing its own global delivery network to manage logistics and supply-chain management for other companies. It created a UPS Supply Chain Solutions division that provides a complete bundle of standardized services to subscribing companies at a fraction of what it would cost to build their own systems and infrastructure. These services include supply-chain design and management, freight forwarding, customs brokerage, mail services, multimodal transportation, and financial services, in addition to logistics services.

Hired Hand Technologies, a Bremen, Alabama-based manufacturer of agricultural and horticultural equipment, uses UPS Freight services not only to track shipments but also to build its weekly manufacturing plans. UPS provides up-to-the-minute information about exactly when parts are arriving within 20 seconds.

Sources: Claudia Deutsch, "Still Brown, but Going High Tech," *The New York Times*, July 12, 2007; United Parcel Service, "LTL's High-Tech Infusion," *Compass*, Spring 2007; UPS Public Relations, "UPS Changes the Delivery Game with New Intercept Service," March 26, 2007; and www.ups.com, accessed May 11, 2007.

CASE STUDY QUESTIONS

1. What are the inputs, processing, and outputs of UPS's package tracking system?

2. What technologies are used by UPS? How are these technologies related to UPS's business model and business objectives?

3. What problems do UPS's information systems solve? What would happen if these systems were not available?

MIS IN ACTION

Explore the UPS Web site (www.ups.com) and answer the following questions:

1. What kind of information and services does the Web site provide for individuals, small businesses, and large businesses? List these services and write several paragraphs describing one of them, such as UPS Trade Direct or Automated Shipment Processing. Explain how you or your business would benefit from the service.

2. Explain how the Web site helps UPS achieve some or all of the strategic business objectives we described earlier in this chapter. What would be the impact on UPS's business if this Web site were not available?

Let's identify the organization, people, and technology elements in the UPS package tracking system we have just described. The organization element anchors the package tracking system in UPS's sales and production functions (the main product of UPS is a service—package delivery). It specifies the required procedures for identifying packages with both sender and recipient information, taking inventory, tracking the packages en route, and providing package status reports for UPS customers and customer service representatives.

The system must also provide information to satisfy the needs of managers and workers. UPS drivers need to be trained in both package pickup and delivery procedures and in how to use the package tracking system so that they can work efficiently and effectively.

Using a handheld computer called a Delivery Information Acquisition Device (DIAD), UPS drivers automatically capture customers' signatures along with pickup, delivery, and time card information. UPS information systems use these data to track packages while they are being transported.

UPS customers may need some training to use UPS in-house package tracking software or the UPS Web site.

UPS's management is responsible for monitoring service levels and costs and for promoting the company's strategy of combining low cost and superior service. Management decided to use automation to increase the ease of sending a package using UPS and of checking its delivery status, thereby reducing delivery costs and increasing sales revenues.

The technology supporting this system consists of handheld computers, bar code scanners, wired and wireless communications networks, desktop computers, UPS's central computer, storage technology for the package delivery data, UPS in-house package tracking software, and software to access the World Wide Web. The result is an information system solution to the business challenge of providing a high level of service with low prices in the face of mounting competition.

1.3 Understanding Information Systems: A Business Problem-Solving Approach

Our approach to understanding information systems is to consider information systems and technologies as solutions to a variety of business challenges and problems. We refer to this as a "problem-solving approach." Businesses face many challenges and problems, and information systems are one major way of solving these problems. All of the cases in this book illustrate how a company used information systems to solve a specific problem.

The problem-solving approach has direct relevance to your future career. Your future employers will hire you because you are able to solve business problems and achieve business objectives. Your knowledge of how information systems contribute to problem solving will be very helpful to both you and your employers.

THE PROBLEM-SOLVING APPROACH

At first glance, problem solving in daily life seems to be perfectly straightforward: A machine breaks down, parts and oil spill all over the floor, and, obviously, somebody has to do something about it. So, of course, you find a tool around the shop and start repairing the machine. After a cleanup and proper inspection of other parts, you start the machine, and production resumes.

No doubt some problems in business are this straightforward. But few problems are this simple in the real world of business. In real-world business firms, a number of major factors are simultaneously involved in problems. These major factors can usefully be grouped into three categories: *organization, technology,* and *people*. In other words, a whole set of problems is usually involved.

A MODEL OF THE PROBLEM-SOLVING PROCESS

There is a simple model of problem solving that you can use to help you understand and solve business problems using information systems. You can think of business problem-solving as a four-step process (see Figure 1-4). Most problem solvers work through this model on their way to finding a solution. Let's take a brief look at each step.

Problem Identification

The first step in the problem-solving process is to understand what kind of problem exists. Contrary to popular beliefs, problems are not like basketballs on a court simply waiting to be picked up by some "objective" problem solver. Before problems can be solved, there must be agreement in a business that a problem exists, about what the problem is, about what its causes are, and about what can be done about the problem given the limited resources of the organization. Problems have to be properly defined by people in an organization before they can be solved.

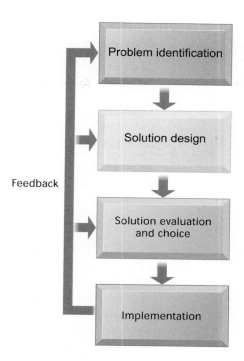

Figure 1-4
Problem Solving Is a Continuous Four-Step Process
During implementation and thereafter, the outcome must be continually measured and the information about how well the solution is working is fed back to the problem solvers. In this way, the identification of the problem can change over time, solutions can be changed, and new choices made, all based on experience.

For instance, what at first glance what might seem like a problem with employees not adequately responding to customers in a timely and accurate manner might in reality be a result of a older, out-of-date information system for keeping track of customers. Or it might be a combination of both poor employee incentives for treating customers well and an outdated system. Once you understand this critical fact, you can start to solve problems creatively. Finding answers to these questions will require fact gathering, interviews with people involved in the problem, and analysis of documents.

In this text, we emphasize three different and typical dimensions of business problems: organizations, technology, and people (see Table 1.1). Typical organizational problems include poor business processes (usually inherited from the past), unsupportive culture, political in-fighting, and changes in the organization's surrounding environment. Typical technology problems include insufficient or aging hardware, outdated software, inadequate database capacity, insufficient telecommunications capacity, and the incompatibility of old systems with new technology. Typical people problems include employee training, difficulties of evaluating performance, legal and regulatory compliance, ergonomics, poor or indecisive management, and employee support and participation. When you begin to analyze a business problem, you will find these dimensions are helpful guides to understanding the kind of problem with which you are working.

Solution Design

The second step is to design solutions to the problem(s) you have identified. As it turns out, there are usually a great many "solutions" to any given problem, and the choice of solution often reflects the differing perspectives of people in an organization. You should try to consider as many different solutions as possible so that you can understand the range of possible solutions. Some solutions emphasize technology; others focus on change in the organization and people aspects of the problem. As you will find throughout the text, most successful solutions result from an integrated approach in which new technologies are accompanied by changes in organization and people.

Choice

Choosing the "best" solution for your business firm is the next step in the process. Some of the factors to consider when trying to find the "best" single solution are the cost of the

TABLE 1.1

Dimensions of
Business Problems

Dimension	Description
Organizational dimensions	Outdated business processes
	Unsupportive culture and attitudes
	Political conflict
	Turbulent business environment, change
	Complexity of task
	Inadequate resources
Technology dimensions	Insufficient or aging hardware
	Outdated software
	Inadequate database capacity
	Insufficient telecommunications capacity
	Incompatibility of old systems with new technology
	Rapid technological change
People dimensions	Lack of employee training
	Difficulties of evaluating performance
	Legal and regulatory compliance
	Work environment
	Lack of employee support and participation
	Indecisive management
	Poor management

solution, the feasibility of the solution for your business given existing resources and skills, and the length of time required to build and implement the solution. Also very important at this point are the attitudes and support of your employees and managers. A solution that does not have the support of all the major interests in the business can quickly turn into a disaster.

Implementation

The best solution is one that can be implemented. Implementation of an information system solution involves building the solution and introducing it into the organization. This includes purchasing or building the software and hardware—the technology part of the equation. The software must be tested in a realistic business setting; then employees need to be trained, and documentation about how to use the new system needs to be written.

You will definitely need to think about change management. **Change management** refers to the many techniques used to bring about successful change in a business. Nearly all information systems require changes in the firm's business processes and, therefore, changes in what hundreds or even thousands of employees do every day. You will have to design new, more efficient business processes, and then figure out how to encourage employees to adapt to these new ways of doing business. This may require meeting sessions to introduce the change to groups of employees, new training modules to bring employees quickly up to speed on the new information systems and processes, and finally some kind of rewards or incentives to encourage people to enthusiastically support the changes.

Implementation also includes the measurement of outcomes. After a solution has been implemented, it must be evaluated to determine how well it is working and whether any additional changes are required to meet the original objectives. This information is fed back to the problem solvers. In this way, the identification of the problem can change over time, solutions can be changed, and new choices made, all based on experience.

Problem Solving: A Process, Not an Event

It is often assumed that once a problem is "solved," it goes away and can be forgotten about. And it is easy to fall into the trap of thinking about problem solving as an event that is "over" at some point, like a relay race or a baseball game. Often in the real world this does not happen. Sometimes the solution chosen does not work, and new solutions are required.

For instance, the U.S. National Aeronautics and Space Administration (NASA) spent more than $1 billion to fix a problem with shedding foam on the space shuttle. Experience proved the initial solution did not work. More often, the chosen solution partially works but needs a lot of continuous changes to truly "fit" the situation. Initial solutions are often rough approximations at first of what ultimately "works." Sometimes, the nature of the problem changes in a way that makes the initial solution ineffective. For instance, hackers create new variations on computer viruses that require continually evolving antivirus programs to hold in check. For all these reasons, problem solving is a continuous process rather than a single event.

THE ROLE OF CRITICAL THINKING IN PROBLEM SOLVING

It is amazingly easy to accept someone else's definition of a problem or to adopt the opinions of some authoritative group that has "objectively" analyzed the problem and offers quick solutions. You should try to resist this tendency to accept existing definitions of any problem. Through the natural flow of decision making, it is essential that you try to maintain some distance from any specific solution until you are sure you have properly identified the problem, developed understanding, and analyzed alternatives. Otherwise, you may leap off in the wrong direction, solve the wrong problem, and waste resources. You will have to engage in some critical-thinking exercises.

Critical thinking can be briefly defined as the sustained suspension of judgment with an awareness of multiple perspectives and alternatives. It involves at least four elements:
- Maintaining doubt and suspending judgment
- Being aware of different perspectives
- Testing alternatives and letting experience guide
- Being aware of organizational and personal limitations

Simply following a rote pattern of decision making, or a model, does not guarantee a correct solution. The best protection against incorrect results is to engage in critical thinking throughout the problem-solving process.

First, maintain doubt and suspend judgment. Perhaps the most frequent error in problem solving is to arrive prematurely at a judgment about the nature of the problem. By doubting all solutions at first and refusing to rush to a judgment, you create the necessary mental conditions to take a fresh, creative look at problems, and you keep open the chance to make a creative contribution.

Second, recognize that all interesting business problems have many dimensions and that the same problem can be viewed from different perspectives. In this text, we have emphasized the usefulness of three perspectives on business problems: technology, organizations, and people. Within each of these very broad perspectives are many subperspectives, or views. The *technology perspective*, for instance, includes a consideration of all the components in the firm's IT infrastructure and the way they work together. The *organization perspective* includes a consideration of a firm's business processes, structure, culture, and politics. The *people perspective* includes consideration of the firm's management, as well as employees as individuals and their interrelationships in workgroups.

You will have to decide for yourself which major perspectives are useful for viewing a given problem. The ultimate criterion here is usefulness: Does adopting a certain perspective tell you something more about the problem that is useful for solving the problem? If not, reject that perspective as being not meaningful in this situation and look for other perspectives.

The third element of critical thinking involves testing alternatives, or modeling solutions to problems, letting experience be the guide. Not all contingencies can be known in advance, and much can be learned through experience. Therefore, experiment, gather data, and reassess the problem periodically.

THE CONNECTION BETWEEN BUSINESS OBJECTIVES, PROBLEMS, AND SOLUTIONS

Now let's make the connection between business information systems and the problem-solving approach. At the beginning of this chapter we talked about the six reasons business firms invest in information systems and technologies. We identified six business objectives of information systems: operational excellence; new products, services, and business models; customer/supplier intimacy; improved decision making; strategic advantage; and survival. When firms cannot achieve these objectives, they become "challenges" or "problems" that receive attention. Managers and employees who are aware of these challenges often turn to information systems as one of the solutions, or the entire solution.

Review the diagram at the beginning of this chapter. The diagram shows how NBA teams' systems solved the business problem presented by intense competitive pressures of professional sports, the high cost of professional basketball players, and incomplete data on team and player performance. Its system provides a solution that takes advantage of computer capabilities for processing digital video data and linking them to team and player data. It helps NBA coaches and managers make better decisions about how to best use the talents of their players in both offensive and defensive maneuvers. The diagram also illustrates how people, technology, and organizational elements work together to create the systems.

Each chapter of this text begins with a diagram similar to this one to help you analyze the chapter-opening case. You can use this diagram as a starting point for analyzing any information system or information system problem you encounter.

Let's try to use what you have learned about problem-solving in the following Interactive Session. Saks Fifth Avenue, a leading U.S. luxury retail department store chain, was struggling to achieve profitability and hold on to market share. As you read this case ask yourself: Why was Saks experiencing this problem? What was the source of the problem? What caused the problem? What alternative solutions were available to management? What people, organization, and technology issues had to be addressed to solve the problem?

1.4 Information Systems and Your Career

Looking out to 2012, the U.S. economy will create 21.6 million new jobs, and 28.5 million existing jobs will open up as their occupants retire. More than 95 percent of the new jobs will be created in the service sector. Many of these new jobs and replacement jobs will require a college degree to perform (Statistical Abstract, 2006-2007; U.S. Bureau of Labor Statistics, 2006).

What this means is that U.S. business firms are looking for candidates who have a broad range of problem-solving skills—the ability to read, write, and present ideas—as well as the technical skills required for specific tasks. Regardless of your business school major, or your future occupation, information systems and technologies will play a major and expanding role in your day-to-day work and your career. Your career opportunities, and your compensation, will in part depend on your ability to help business firms use information systems to achieve their objectives.

HOW INFORMATION SYSTEMS WILL AFFECT BUSINESS CAREERS

In the following sections, we describe how specific occupations will be affected by information systems and what skills you should be building in order to function effectively in this new, emerging labor market. Let's look at the career opportunities for business school majors.

Accounting

There are about 1.1 million accountants in the U.S. labor force today, and the field is expected to expand by 20 percent to the year 2012, adding 200,000 new jobs, and a similar

INTERACTIVE SESSION: PEOPLE   How Can Saks Know Its Customers?

Since 1924, Saks Fifth Avenue has worked hard to lure shoppers into its stores. And for many years it did, delivering high-end, unique, and fashionable luxury merchandise. Most Saks stores are freestanding entities in high-profile shopping destinations or anchor stores in upscale malls. A shopper at Saks can expect to find an array of luxury apparel, shoes, accessories, jewelry, cosmetics, and gift items. Saks Fifth Avenue Enterprises conducts its merchandising, sales promotion, and store operating support functions for 54 locations around the United States from corporate offices in New York City.

But times have changed and luxury retailing has become a very crowded field. For the past decade the company has lost market share and sales to Neiman Marcus, Nordstrom, and other high-end retailers. Management tried to improve financial results by minimizing inventory. A walk through a typical Saks store in 2005 would have revealed holes in cosmetics cases where lipsticks were out of stock and basic men's dress shirts that were sold out. Even worse, what inventory stores carried turned off many shoppers because the focus was on young women with what one analyst called a "Hollywood bling-bling look."

What Saks lacked was an accurate picture of its customers. It hasn't fully figured out who are its core customers and how their buying preferences differ in Saks stores around the country. For example, the core shopper at Saks' New York store is in her mid-forties, preferring a largely "classic" style for work and slightly more modern looks for going out and for weekend wear. Saks' New York store is its flagship, generating approximately 20 percent of the company's annual revenue. But Saks' selection elsewhere was too New York-centric. In Birmingham, Alabama, customers were slightly younger and less conservative in taste, and traveled to Atlanta to buy designer clothing and handbags. The Saks Short Hills New Jersey store didn't carry enough high-end merchandise or clothing for men. Working women visit the Stamford store, but the nearby Greenwich location receives a greater number of women who do not work. Shoppers on the Saks Web site, which is the company's second largest source of revenue, are about seven years younger than the typical Saks customer and spend more per transaction.

In January 2006, Stephen Sadove was named Saks CEO and charged with turning the company around. Whereas some companies might choose to increase revenue by opening more stores, Saks focused on wringing more value from existing facilities. Sadove earmarked between $125 million and $150 million annually for store renovations. To help determine which merchandise to send to which stores, Sadove and his team developed a nine-box grid that cross-references the most popular styles at each store with the most common spending levels. The styles are categorized as Park Avenue for classic, uptown for modern, and Soho for trendy. Merchandise prices are categorized as good, better, and best, with very high-end items from designers such as Chanel, Gucci, Louis Vuitton, Oscar de la Renta, and Bill Blass filling in the "best" category. The grid will help Saks customize the inventory for each store and stock each with the optimum blend of goods. Saks watches the profitability and sales histories associated with its many vendors carefully.

The new strategy has already begun to bear fruit. Saks president and chief merchandising officer Ron Frasch says that the new approach to stocking has brought about "tremendous response." For example, the Saks Fifth Avenue flagship store in New York spent the first half of 2007 boosting the number of women's designer shoes it carries by almost 60 percent because shoes are one of the "hot areas in the store" right now. The most recent financial data for Saks Inc. show a net income of $54 million on revenues of $2.9 billion. Saks stores that were open for at least a year showed greater improvements in sales than the stores of chief rival Neiman Marcus.

The differences among the stores even permeate marketing strategy at Saks. National marketing campaigns have been complicated by the fact that fashion trends do not have equal appeal across the country. Saks is planning to place more emphasis on customized marketing for individual markets. The company is also experimenting with a computer system that helps the sales staff monitor the buying habits of customers so that the staff can be more productive. Management has declared that investments in technology are necessary for the success of the company's business and strategy, and therefore Saks will continue to upgrade its information systems with the goal of greater efficiency and productivity.

Sources: Vanessa O'Connell, "Park Avenue Classic or Soho Trendy?" *The Wall Street Journal*, April 20, 2007; "Saks Masters DC Flow-Through," *Packaging Digest*, July 2006; "Saks Incorporated Form 10-K for Fiscal Year Ended February 3, 2007," www.saks.com, April 3, 2007; Andrew Leckey, "High-end Strategy Has Saks Looking Better," *The Chicago Tribune*, April 15, 2007; Joseph Lazzaro, "Saks vs. Nordstrom: Battle of the Brands," www.bloggingstocks.com, April 12, 2007; and Chad Brand, "Saks: The Revival Is Worth Watching," *Seeking Alpha*, April 13, 2007.

CASE STUDY QUESTIONS

1. What is the problem affecting the performance of Saks?

2. What information does Saks need to solve this problem? What other pieces of data does Saks need in addition to those in its nine-box grid?

3. Where can Saks acquire this information?

4. What role should managers and employees have in designing the solution?

5. Design a report that represents the information Saks needs to implement its merchandising strategy.

6. How might a better understanding of customer preferences support Saks' strategy of improving existing facilities?

MIS IN ACTION

1. Explore the Saks Fifth Avenue Web site (www.saks.com). What are some of the features of the Web site that make it useful for selling luxury goods?

2. What information about customers can be collected at the Web site that would help Saks stock the items that customers want?

number of jobs to replace retirees. This above-average growth in accounting is in part driven by new accounting laws for public companies, greater scrutiny of public and private firms by government tax auditors, and a growing demand for management and operational advice.

Accountants can be broadly classified as public accountants, management accountants, government accountants, and internal auditors. Accountants provide a broad range of services to business firms including preparing, analyzing, and verifying financial documents; budget analysis; financial planning; information technology consulting; and limited legal services. A new specialty called "forensic accounting" investigates white-collar crimes, such as securities fraud and embezzlement, bankruptcies and contract disputes, and other possibly criminal financial transactions.

Accountants increasingly rely on information systems to summarize transactions, create financial records, organize data, and perform financial analysis. In fact, there is no way that firms today can perform even basic accounting functions without extensive investment in systems. As a result of new public laws, accountants are beginning to perform more technical duties, such as implementing, controlling, and auditing systems and networks, and developing technology plans and budgets.

What kinds of information system skills are really important for accounting majors given these changes in the accounting profession? Here is a short list:

- Knowledge of current and likely future changes in information technology, including hardware, software, and telecommunications, which will be used by public and private firms, government agencies, and financial advisors as they perform auditing and accounting functions. Also essential is an understanding of accounting and financial applications and design factors to ensure firms are able to maintain accounting records and perform auditing functions, and an understanding of system and network security issues, which are vital to protect the integrity of accounting systems.

- Understanding of enterprise systems capabilities for corporate-wide financial reporting on a global and national scale. Because so many transactions are occurring over the Internet, accountants need to understand online transaction and reporting systems, and how systems are used to achieve management accounting functions in an online, wireless, and mobile business environment.

Finance

Finance majors perform a wide variety of jobs in the U.S. economy. Financial managers develop financial reports, direct investment activities, and implement cash management strategies. There are about 600,000 financial managers in the U.S. labor force and this occupation is expected to grow by about 20 percent by 2012, adding about 120,000 new jobs and requiring the replacement of about 100,000 additional jobs.

Financial managers require strong system skills and play important roles in planning, organizing, and implementing information system strategies for their firms. Financial managers work directly with a firm's board of directors and senior management to ensure investments in information systems help achieve corporate goals and achieve high returns. The relationship between information systems and the practice of modern financial management and services is so strong that many advise finance majors to also co-major in information systems (and vice versa).

What kinds of information system skills should finance majors develop? Following is brief list:

- An understanding of likely future changes in information technology, including hardware, software, and telecommunications, that will be used by financial managers and financial service firms. This includes an understanding of financial applications and design factors to ensure firms are able to manage their investments, cash, and risks; new kinds of mobile and wireless applications to manage financial reporting; and development of online systems for financial transactions. As new trading systems emerge, financial service firms and managers will need to understand how these systems work and how they will change their firm's business.
- Knowledge of the new role played by enterprise-wide financial reporting systems on a global and national scale. As more and more transactions move online, finance majors need to understand online transaction reporting systems and management of online system investments.

Marketing

No field has undergone more technology-driven change in the past five years than marketing and advertising. The explosion in e-commerce activity described earlier in this chapter means that eyeballs are moving rapidly to the Internet. As a result, Internet advertising is the fastest-growing form of advertising, expanding at more than 30 percent annually and reaching $13 billion in 2006. (Other forms of marketing communications are growing at a much slower 5 percent rate.) All this means that branding products and communicating with customers are moving online at a fast pace.

Equities analysts depend heavily on information systems for organizing and analyzing vast quantities of financial data.

There are about 900,000 marketing, public relations, sales, and advertising managers in the U.S. labor force. This field is growing faster than average and is expected to add more than 200,000 jobs by 2012 and replace an additional 150,000 employees who are retiring. There is a much larger group of 2.6 million nonmanagerial employees in marketing-related occupations (art, design, entertainment, sports, and media) and more than 15.9 million employees in sales. These occupations together are expected to create an additional 1.8 million jobs by 2012.

Here are some of the general information systems skills on which marketing majors should focus:

- An ability to understand Internet and marketing database systems, and how they impact traditional marketing activities, such as brand development, production promotion, and sales. This would include an understanding of design factors to ensure firms are able to market their products, develop reports on product performance, retrieve feedback from customers, and manage product development.
- An understanding of how enterprise wide-systems for product management, sales force management, and customer relationship management are used to develop products that consumers want, to manage the customer relationship, and to manage an increasingly mobile sales force.

Operations Management in Services and Manufacturing

The growing size and complexity of modern industrial production and the emergence of huge global service companies have created a growing demand for employees who can coordinate and optimize the resources required to produce goods and services. Operations management as a discipline is directly relevant to three occupational categories: industrial production managers, administrative service managers, and operations analysts.

Production managers, administrative service managers and operations analysts will be employing information systems and technologies every day to accomplish their jobs, with extensive use of database and analytical software. Here are the general information systems skills on which operations management majors should focus:

- Knowledge of the changing hardware and software platforms that will be used in operations management. This would include an understanding of the role that databases, modeling tools, and business analytical software play in production and services management.
- An in-depth understanding of how enterprise-wide information systems for production management, supplier management, sales force management, and customer relationship management are used to achieve efficient operations and meet other firm objectives.

Management

Management is the largest single group in the U.S. business labor force with more than 14 million members, not including an additional 547,000 management consultants. Overall, the management corps in the United States is expected to expand faster than other occupational groups, adding about 3.8 million new jobs by 2012, with about 2 million replacement openings in this period as a result of retirements. There are more than 20 different types of managers tracked by the Bureau of Labor Statistics, all the way from chief executive officer, to human resource managers, production managers, project managers, lodging managers, medical managers, and community service managers.

The job of management has been transformed by information systems, and, arguably, it would be impossible to manage business firms today without the extensive use of information systems, even very small firms. Nearly all of the 14 million managers in the United States use information systems and technologies everyday to accomplish their jobs, from desktop productivity tools to applications coordinating the entire enterprise. Here are the general information systems skills on which management majors should focus:

- Knowledge of new hardware and software that can make management more efficient and effective, enhance leadership and coordination capabilities, and improve the achievement of corporate business objectives in the broadest sense. This would include an understanding of the role that databases play in managing information resources of the firm, and the role of new communication and collaboration technologies, such as wikis, blogs, and wireless and cellular computing.

- An in-depth understanding of how enterprise-wide information systems for production management, supplier management, sales force management, and customer relationship management are used to achieve efficient operations and help managers make better decisions for improving firm performance.

Information Systems

The information systems field is arguably one of the most fast changing and dynamic of all the business professions because information technologies are among the most important tools for achieving business firms' key objectives. The explosive growth of business information systems has generated a growing demand for information systems employees and managers who work with other business professionals to design and develop new hardware and software systems to serve the needs of business. Of the top 20 fastest-growing occupations through 2012, five are information systems occupations.

There are about 284,000 information system managers in the United States, with an estimated growth rate of 36 percent through 2012, expanding the number of new jobs by more than 100,000 new positions, with an additional 50,000 new hires required for replacements. As businesses and government agencies increasingly rely on the Internet for communication and computing resources, system and network security management positions are growing very rapidly.

Outsourcing and Offshoring The Internet has created new opportunities for outsourcing many information systems jobs, along with many other service sector and manufacturing jobs. Offshore outsourcing to low-wage countries has been controversial because U.S. workers fear it will reduce demand for U.S. information systems employment. However, this fear is overblown given the huge demand for new information system hires in the United States through 2012. In fact, reducing the cost of providing information technology services to U.S. corporations by offshoring labor-intensive and lower-level jobs may increase the demand for U.S.-based information system workers as firms find the price of investing in information technology falls relative to other investments while its power to increase revenues and profits grows.

There are two kinds of outsourcing: outsourcing to domestic U.S. firms and offshore outsourcing to low-wage countries, such as India and eastern European countries. Even this distinction becomes problematic as domestic service providers, such as IBM, develop global outsourcing centers in India.

The impact of *domestic* outsourcing on the overall demand for information technology employment through 2012 is most likely quite small. Service provider firms, such as Hewlett-Packard and Accenture, add domestic IT employees as they expand their domestic IT services, while domestic information systems departments lose some employees or do not hire new employees.

The impact of *offshore* outsourcing on U.S. domestic IT jobs is more problematic because, ostensibly, jobs that move offshore decrease demand for workers in the United States. The most common and successful offshore outsourcing projects involve production programming and system maintenance programming work, along with call center work related to customer relationship management systems. Hence, the largest impact of offshore outsourcing will mostly likely be on technical positions in information systems and less on managerial positions.

Inflation in Indian wages for technology work, coupled with the additional management costs incurred in outsourcing projects, is leading to a counter movement of jobs back to the United States. Moreover, while technical IS jobs can be outsourced easily, all those management and organizational tasks required in systems development—including business process design, customer interface, and supply chain management—often remain in the

United States. The net result is that offshore outsourcing will increase demand in the United States for managerial IS positions, while negatively impacting lower-level technical jobs (Tam and Range, 2007; Lohr, 2007).

Given all these factors in the IT labor market, on what kinds of skills should information system majors focus? Following is a list of general skills we believe will optimize employment opportunities:

- An in-depth knowledge of how new and emerging hardware and software can be used by business firms to make them more efficient and effective, enhance customer and supplier intimacy, improve decision making, achieve competitive advantage, and ensure firm survival. This includes an in-depth understanding of databases, database design, implementation, and management.

- An ability to take a leadership role in the design and implementation of new information systems, work with other business professionals to ensure systems meet business objectives, and work with software packages providing new system solutions.

INFORMATION SYSTEMS AND YOUR CAREER: WRAP-UP

Looking back at the information system skills required for specific majors, there are some common themes that affect all business majors. Following is a list of these common requirements for information system skills and knowledge:

- All business students, regardless of major, should understand how information systems and technologies can help firms achieve business objectives such as achieving operational efficiency, developing new products and services, and maintaining customer intimacy.
- Perhaps the most dominant theme that pervades this review of necessary job skills is the central role of databases in a modern firm. Each of the careers we have just described relies heavily in practice on databases.
- With the pervasive growth in databases comes inevitably an exponential growth in digital information and a resulting challenge to managers trying to understand all this information. Regardless of major, business students need to develop skills in analysis of information and helping firms understand and make sense out of their environments.
- All business majors need to be able to work with specialists and system designers who build and implement information systems. This is necessary to ensure that the systems that are built actually service business purposes and provide the information and understanding required by managers and employees.
- Each of the business majors will be impacted by changes in the ethical, social, and legal environment of business. Business school students need to understand how information systems can be used to meet business requirements for reporting to government regulators and the public and how information systems impact the ethical issues in their fields.

HOW THIS BOOK PREPARES YOU FOR THE FUTURE

This book is explicitly designed to prepare you for your future business career. It provides you with the necessary knowledge and foundation concepts for understanding the role of information systems in business organizations. You will be able to use this knowledge to identify opportunities for increasing the effectiveness of your business. You will learn how to use information systems to improve operations, create new products and services, improve decision making, increase customer intimacy, and promote competitive advantage.

Equally important, this book develops your ability to use information systems to solve problems that you will encounter on the job. You will learn how to analyze and define a business problem and how to design an appropriate information system solution. You will deepen your critical-thinking and problem-solving skills. The following features of the text and the accompanying learning package reinforce this problem-solving and career orientation.

A Framework for Describing and Analyzing Information Systems

The text provides you with a framework for analyzing and solving problems by examining the people, organizational, and technology components of information systems. This framework is used repeatedly throughout the text to help you understand information systems in business and analyze information systems problems.

A Four-Step Model for Problem Solving

The text provides you with a four-step method for solving business problems, which we introduced in this chapter. You will learn how to identify a business problem, design alternative solutions, choose the correct solution, and implement the solution. You will be asked to use this problem-solving method to solve the case studies in each chapter. Chapter 11 will show you how to use this approach to design and build new information systems.

Hands-on MIS Projects for Stimulating Critical Thinking and Problem Solving

Each chapter concludes with a series of hands-on MIS projects to sharpen your critical-thinking and problem-solving skills. These projects include the Dirt Bikes USA running case, hands-on application software problems, and projects for building Internet skills. For each of these projects, we identify both the business skills and the software skills required for the solution.

Career Resources

To make sure you know how the text is directly useful in your future business career, we've added a full set of Career Resources to help you with career development and job hunting.

Heads Up At the Beginning of each chapter is a Heads Up section showing exactly why you need to know about the contents of the chapter and how this knowledge will help you in your future career.

Digital Portfolio The companion Web site includes a template for preparing a structured digital portfolio to demonstrate the business knowledge, application software skills, Internet skills, and analytical skills you have acquired in this course. You can include this portfolio in your resume or job applications. Your professors can also use the portfolio to assess the skills you have learned.

Career Resources Web Site A Career Resources section on our companion Web site shows you how to integrate what you have learned in this course in your resume, cover letter, and job interview to improve your chances for success in the job market.

1.5 Hands-On MIS

The projects in this section give you hands-on experience in analyzing a real world company's information systems needs and requirements based on an understanding of its business, using a database to improve management decision making, and using Internet software for job hunting.

UNDERSTANDING INFORMATION SYSTEM REQUIREMENTS

Software skills: Presentation software
Business skills: Management analysis and information system recommendations

How do you know what information systems are really needed by a business and which are the most important? How should a company's structure or culture affect the building and use of information systems?

The Dirt Bikes case describes a real-world company that makes dirt bikes—a kind of motorcycle that is used off-road and often raced in competition. This case appears in every chapter with different assignments linked to the chapter contents. There is a complete description of the company, including its organizational structure, culture, management, and goals at the Laudon Web site for this text. The case contains spreadsheets and databases that complete the description of the company. The following is an illustration of the company's organization chart, showing how the company is organized.

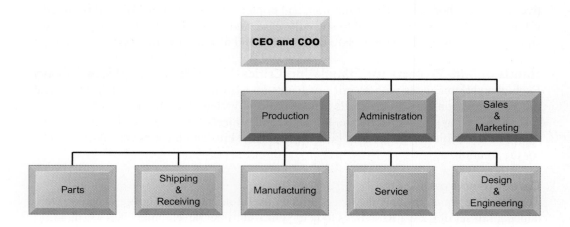

Dirt Bikes's management has asked you to prepare a management analysis of the company to help it assess the firm's current situation and future plans. Review Dirt Bikes's company history, organization chart, products and services, and sales and marketing in the Introduction to Dirt Bikes. Then prepare a report that addresses these questions:

- What are the company's goals and culture?
- What products and services does Dirt Bikes USA provide? How many types of products and services are available to customers? How does Dirt Bikes sell its products?
- How many employees are managers, production workers, or knowledge or information workers? Are there levels of management?
- What kinds of information systems and technologies would be the most important for a company such as Dirt Bikes?
- (Optional) Use electronic presentation software to summarize for management your analysis of Dirt Bikes.

IMPROVING DECISION MAKING: USING DATABASES TO ANALYZE SALES TRENDS

Software skills: Database querying and reporting
Business skills: Sales trend analysis

You can find out how information systems improve management decision making in this exercise. Rather than guessing or relying on estimates and experience, managers today rely on information stored in databases. In this project, you will start out with raw transactional sales data and use Microsoft Access database software to develop queries and reports that help managers make better decisions about product pricing, sales promotions, and inventory replenishment. A part of the database is shown in the following figure.

On the Laudon Web site for Chapter 1, you can find a Store and Regional Sales Database developed in Microsoft Access. The database contains raw data on weekly store sales of computer equipment in various sales regions. You will use Access to manage the data and turn them into useful business information.

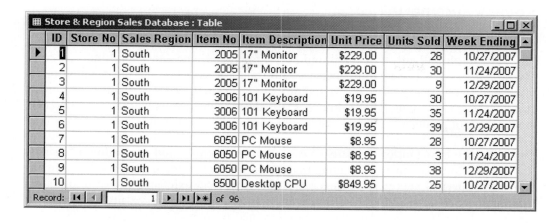

The database includes fields for store identification number, sales region number, item number, item description, unit price, units sold, and the weekly sales period when the sales were made.

Develop some reports and queries to make this information more useful for running the business. Sales and production managers want answers to the following questions:

- Which products should be restocked?
- Which stores and sales regions would benefit from a promotional campaign and additional marketing?
- When (what time of year) should products be offered at full price, and when should discounts be used?

You can easily modify the database table to find and report your answers. Print your reports and results of queries.

IMPROVING DECISION MAKING: USING THE INTERNET TO LOCATE JOBS REQUIRING INFORMATION SYSTEMS KNOWLEDGE

Software skills: Internet-based software
Business skills: Job searching

Visit job-posting Web sites such as Monster.com or hotjobs.com. Spend some time at the sites examining jobs for accounting, finance, sales, marketing, and human resources. Find two or three descriptions of jobs that require some information systems knowledge. What information systems knowledge do these jobs require? What do you need to do to prepare for these jobs? Write a one- to two-page report summarizing your findings.

LEARNING TRACKS

The following Learning Tracks provide content relevant to topics covered in this chapter:

1. How Much Does IT Matter?
2. Changing Business Environment for Information Technology
3. Business Information Value Chain

Review Summary

1 **How are information systems transforming business and what is their relationship to globalization?** E-mail, online conferencing, and cell phones have become essential tools for conducting business. Information systems are the foundation of fast-paced supply chains. The Internet allows businesses to buy, sell, advertise, and solicit customer feedback online. The Internet has stimulated globalization by dramatically reducing the costs of producing, buying, and selling goods on a global scale

2 **Why are information systems so essential for running and managing a business today?** Information systems are a foundation for conducting business today. In many industries, survival and even existence is difficult without extensive use of information technology. Businesses today use information systems to achieve six major objectives: operational excellence; new products, services, and business models; customer/supplier intimacy; improved decision making; competitive advantage; and day-to-day survival.

3 **What exactly is an information system? How does it work? What are its people, organization, and technology components?** From a technical perspective, an information system collects, stores, and disseminates information from an organization's environment and internal operations to support organizational functions and decision making, communication, coordination, control, analysis, and visualization. Information systems transform raw data into useful information through three basic activities: input, processing, and output. From a business perspective, an information system provides a solution to a problem or challenge facing a firm and represents a combination of people, organization, and technology elements.

The people dimension of information systems involves issues such as training, job attitudes, and management behavior. The technology dimension consists of computer hardware, software, data management technology, and networking/telecommunications technology, including the Internet. The organization dimension of information systems involves issues such as the organization's hierarchy, functional specialties, business processes, culture, and political interest groups.

4 **How will a four-step method for business problem solving help you solve information system-related problems?** Problem identification involves understanding what kind of problem is being presented and identifying people, organizational, and technology factors. Solution design involves designing several alternative solutions to the problem that has been identified. Choice entails selecting the best solution, taking into account its cost and the available resources and skills in the business. Implementation of an information system solution entails purchasing or building hardware and software, testing the software, providing employees with training and documentation, managing change as the system is introduced into the organization, and measuring the outcome. Problem solving requires critical thinking in which one suspends judgment to consider multiple perspectives and alternatives.

5 **How will information systems affect business careers and what information system skills and knowledge are essential?** Business careers in accounting, finance, marketing, operations management, management and human resources, and information systems all will need an understanding of how information systems help firms achieve major business objectives; an appreciation of the central role of databases; skills in information analysis and business intelligence; sensitivity to the ethical, social, and legal issues raised by systems; and the ability to work with technology specialists and other business professionals in designing and building systems.

Key Terms

Business model, 8	Extranets, 15	Internet, 15
Business processes, 14	Feedback, 12	Intranets, 15
Change management, 20	Information, 11	Management information
Computer hardware, 15	Information system, 11	systems (MIS), 13
Computer literacy, 13	Information systems	Network, 15
Computer software, 15	literacy, 13	Networking and telecommu-
Critical thinking, 21	Information technology	nications technology, 15
Culture, 14	(IT), 10	Output, 11
Data, 11	Information technology (IT)	Processing, 11
Data management	infrastructure, 15	World Wide Web, 15
technology, 15	Input, 11	

Review Questions

1. How are information systems transforming business and what is their relationship to globalization?
- Describe how information systems have changed the way businesses operate and their products and services.
- Describe the challenges and opportunities of globalization in a "flattened" world.

2. Why are information systems so essential for running and managing a business today?
- List and describe the six reasons why information systems are so important for business today.

3. What exactly is an information system? How does it work? What are its people, organization, and technology components?
- List and describe the organizational, people, and technology dimensions of information systems.
- Define an information system and describe the activities it performs.
- Distinguish between data and information and between information systems literacy and computer literacy.
- Explain how the Internet and the World Wide Web are related to the other technology components of information systems.

4. How will a four-step method for business problem solving help you solve information system-related problems?
- List and describe each of the four steps for solving business problems.
- Give some examples of people, organizational, and technology problems found in businesses.
- Describe the relationship of critical thinking to problem solving.
- Describe the role of information systems in business problem solving.

5. How will information systems affect business careers and what information system skills and knowledge are essential?
- Describe the role of information systems in careers in accounting, finance, marketing, management, and operations management and explain how careers in information systems have been affected by new technologies and outsourcing.
- List and describe the information system skills and knowledge that are essential for all business careers.

Discussion Questions

1. What are the implications of globalization when you have to look for a job? What can you do to prepare yourself for competing in a globalized business environment? How would knowledge of information systems help you compete?

2. If you were setting up the Web sites for NBA teams, what people, organization, and technology issues might you encounter?

Video Case

You will find a video case illustrating some of the concepts in this chapter on the Laudon Web site along with questions to help you analyze the case.

Teamwork

Analyzing a Business System

In a group with three or four classmates, find a description in a computer or business magazine of an information system used by an organization. Look for information about the company on the Web to gain further insight into the company, and prepare a brief description of the business. Describe the system you have selected in terms of its inputs, processes, and outputs and in terms of its organization, people, and technology features and the importance of the system to the company. If possible, use electronic presentation software to present your analysis to the class.

BUSINESS PROBLEM-SOLVING CASE

Is Second Life Ready for Business?

Second Life is a 3D virtual online world created by former RealNetworks CTO Philip Rosedale through Linden Lab, a company he founded in San Francisco in 1999. The world is built and owned by its users, who are called residents. Nearly 7 million people have signed up to be residents of Second Life's world, also known as the Grid. In May 2007, the usage stats on Second Life's Web site (www.secondlife.com) showed that just over 1.7 million residents had logged in over the previous 60 days. Second Life runs over the Internet using special software, called the Viewer, that users download to their desktops.

Second Life is not a game. Residents interact with each other in a 3-D social network. They can explore, socialize, collaborate, create, participate in activities, and purchase goods and services. The Second Life Web site says that its world is similar to a massively multiplayer online role playing game (MMORPG) but distinct in that

it allows nearly unlimited creativity and ownership over user-created content. When logged in, residents take on a digital persona, called an avatar. Each user may customize his or her own avatar, changing its appearance, its clothing, and even its form from human to humanoid or something altogether different.

Second Life has its own virtual economy and currency. The currency is the Linden Dollar, or Linden for short, and is expressed as L$. There is an open market for goods and services created on the Grid. Residents may acquire Lindens this way, or by using currency exchanges to trade real-world money for Lindens. The Linden has a real-world value, which is set by market pricing and tracked and traded on a proprietary market called the LindeX. A very modest percentage of residents earns a significant profit from dealing in the Second Life economy. One user, known on the Grid as Anshe Chung, has accumulated enough virtual real estate that she could sell it for an amount of Lindens equaling US$1 million. More common are the residents who gross enough to cover the expense of their participation in the world. According to statistics from Second Life, 304,499 residents spent money on the Grid during August 2007.

Basic membership in Second Life is free and includes most of the privileges of paid membership, except the right to own land. Residents with Premium memberships are eligible to own land on the Grid. The largest lots, or Entire Regions, measure 65,536 square meters (about 16 acres) and incur a monthly land use fee of US$195. Second Life also offers private islands, which are the same size as Entire Regions but require a one-time fee of US$1,675 plus monthly maintenance fees of US$295.

Residents create content for the Grid using tools provided by Second Life. For example, the software includes a 3-D modeling tool that enables users to construct buildings, landscapes, vehicles, furniture, and any other goods they can imagine. A standard library of animations and sounds enables residents to make gestures to one another. Basic communication is performed by typing in the manner of an instant message or chat session.

Users may also design and upload their own sounds, graphics, and animations to Second Life. Second Life has its own scripting language, Linden Scripting Language, which makes it possible for users to enhance objects in the virtual world with behaviors.

Although the concept of a 3-D virtual world is in its infancy, this has not stopped businesses, universities, and even governments from jumping into the fray to see what a virtual world has to offer them. The hope is that Second Life will be a birthing ground for new industries and transform business, commerce, marketing, and learning the same way that the Web did in the late twentieth and early twenty-first centuries.

The advertising and media industries have been early proponents of the technology, opening virtual offices to facilitate internal communications and to position themselves at the forefront of the digital landscape in order to recruit tech-savvy employees.

Crayon is a new-media marketing firm that has purchased an island on the Grid, named crayonville, to serve as its primary office. With employees scattered in real-world offices on both sides of the Atlantic, crayonville provides the firm with a new way to bring everyone together, even if the employees are represented by avatars. Crayon leaves its conference room open to the public unless matters of client confidentiality come into play. Employees communicate by text message and with Skype Internet telephony. The company is still evaluating the use of Second Life for client meetings.

A Second Life presence may convince potential clients that an advertising agency is on the cutting edge of

technology, and therefore able to market to consumers who are there as well. Leo Burnett, an ad agency with 2,400 employees, built an Ideas Hub on the Grid with the goal of bringing workers together to mingle and exchange ideas in a "creative lounge" environment. The company also plans to hold functions in its virtual space that were traditionally hosted in real-world spaces. Industry executives put the price tag of a Second Life business presence at $20,000.

Television and media companies are starting to use Second Life to attract viewers who have forsaken television for the Internet or to offer existing viewers a new medium for interacting with their brands. For example, visitors to the Second Life island for Major League Baseball (MLB) can mingle during the All-Star Game and watch the Home Run Derby. The average time they stayed was two hours, compared to 19 minutes at the MLB Web site.

What about Second Life would encourage companies like IBM to invest $10 million in exploring the possibilities of virtual business? For one, it can offer the following to support important business functions like customer service, product development, training, and marketing: a three-dimensional space in which a user can interact with visual and auditory content; custom content that can be altered and animated; a persistent presence that remains intact for future work even when users log off; and a community where like-minded people can gather to pursue activities of mutual interest.

IBM employees use their avatars to attend meetings in virtual meeting rooms where they can see PowerPoint slides while reading the text of a meeting or lecture or listen to it via a conference call. Virtual attendees can use instant messaging to send questions and receive answers from other avatars or the lecturer. Lynne Hamilton, who runs professional development classes for IBM's human resources (HR) department, uses Second Life for orienting new employees located in China and Brazil. An HR avatar will give a talk and then respond to text questions from the new employees.

Retailers such as Reebok, Adidas, American Apparel, and 1-800-Flowers.com have set up stores in Second Life, hoping that users will steer their avatars their way and buy goods to deliver to their real-world addresses. Some of these Second Life stores have links to the retailers' real-world Web sites where visitors can purchase actual physical goods. So far, these Second Life retailers' expectations are low, but they believe their virtual presence could enhance their brand image and provide new insights into how people might act in the online realm.

American Apparel initially set up its virtual store to test sales of virtual clothing to residents for their avatars. Feedback from consumers and observers quickly convinced American Apparel to link its virtual store with its real-world business. Customers who bought virtual clothing received discounts on American Apparel clothing purchases in the real world.

IBM researchers set up retail kiosks on the Grid that enable residents to shop for real-world Amazon.com products while the residents are in-world. Amazon cooperates by making the tools to develop in-world applications available.

Sears, Adidas, Dell, Circuit City, and Toyota have also developed Second Life identities. However, as of the writing of this case, their virtual stores are mostly empty. None of the major companies has bothered to provide "staff" for its virtual space. The social aspect of the shopping experience is not present. American Apparel recently closed its virtual clothing shop.

While it is too soon for companies to measure the return on their investment in Second Life, some have instantly recognized the value of user-created content, user investment, user input, and the cost-savings of leveraging all for new business opportunities. Prototyping in a virtual world is fast and cheap. Crescendo Design, a residential designer in Wisconsin, uses Second Life's 3-D modeling tools to give clients an inside view of their homes before they are constructed. Clients can suggest changes that would not be obvious from working from traditional blueprints, and the designer avoids mistakes that would be expensive to fix if made in the real world.

Institutions of higher education have purchased their own islands to create campuses where students and faculty can meet for real-time classwork or to hold informal discussions related to their classes. Second Life is a particular boon to distance learning. Insead, an international business school with real-world classes in France and Singapore, is building a virtual campus with rooms for virtual classroom lectures, research laboratories, and lounge areas for students to meet with professors, potential employers, and fellow classmates. Insead's Second Life presence will help it reduce travel and physical building expenses while bringing together students and professors from across the globe. Eventually students will be able to download documents, work in teams, and meet alumni online.

A number of companies, including Hewlett-Packard and global management consultancy Bain and Company, are experimenting with Second Life for screening prospective hires. Job seekers create an avatar representing themselves and communicate with executives of prospective employers by exchanging instant-message-like text messages. Some interviewees and employers report having trouble designing and controlling the movements of their avatars, and companies still need to interview their final selections face to face. But participating companies have found Second Life useful for narrowing the pool of candidates and trimming recruitment expenses.

From a popularity standpoint, Second Life is far behind social networks such as MySpace, which has 180 million users. MySpace and the soaring video-sharing site YouTube are both accessible through a familiar Web browser and do not require any additional software. A user who is willing to take the steps necessary to download and install the Second Life Viewer may find that his or her computer does not meet Second Life's minimum or recommended system requirements. This last factor is especially important for businesses who may need to reconfigure the systems of a large number of employees in order to get them on the Grid.

Still, support for Second Life continues to mount in many forms. Reuters, the global news service, has assigned a full-time reporter to the Grid. In-world, reporter Adam Pasick goes by the avatar Adam Reuters. He files real-world stories about virtual-world happenings. And eBay has decided to permit auctions of virtual goods from Second Life despite previously banning items from other virtual worlds and online games.

Sources: Alice LaPlante, "Second Life Opens for Business,"*Information Week*, February 26, 2007; Anjali Athavaley, "A Job Interview You Don't Have to Show Up For," *The Wall Street Journal*, June 20, 2007; Linda Zimmer, "How Viable is Virtual Commerce?" *Optimize Magazine*, January 2007; "Is Second Life a Pyramid Scheme?" News.com, accessed January 24, 2007; Dave Itzkoff, "A Brave New World for TV? Virtually?" *The New York Times*, June 24, 2007; David DeWitt, "Virtual-Reality Software Creates Parallel Campus, Enhances Education," *The Athens News*, January 29, 2007; Daniel Terdiman, "eBay to Exempt 'Second Life' Listings from Virtual Items Ban," News.com, January 29, 2007; and Mitch Wagner, "What Happens in Second Life, Stays in SL," *InformationWeek*, January 29, 2007.

Case Study Questions

1. What problems can Second Life help businesses solve?

2. Considering what you have learned about Second Life, how could you, as an individual, create a modest start-up business on the Grid? What goods would you sell? Why would this be a good choice of product? What, in simple terms, would your business plan be? Why would it work?

3. Visit eBay on the Web and see what Second Life items you can find listed for auction. How would you rate the activity surrounding these items? Are you surprised by what you see? Why or why not?

4. How important is interoperability between 3-D worlds such as Second Life and other Web sites such as Amazon, MySpace, and YouTube? Do you think that Second Life can survive and prosper on its own? What is the future of these entities? Separate or integrated?

5. What obstacles does Second Life have to overcome in order to become a mainstream business tool? Does it face fewer or more obstacles to become a mainstream educational tool? To what do you attribute the difference?

6. What kinds of businesses are most likely to benefit from a presence on Second Life? Why?

7. Would you like to interview for a job using Second Life? Why or why not?

8. Is Second Life a precursor of how business will be conducted in the future or a corporate experiment? Justify your answer.

E-Business: How Businesses Use Information Systems

CHAPTER 2

STUDENT LEARNING OBJECTIVES

After completing this chapter, you will be able to answer the following questions:

1. What are the major features of a business that are important for understanding the role of information systems?

2. How do information systems support the major business functions: sales and marketing, manufacturing and production, finance and accounting, and human resources?

3. How do systems serve the various levels of management in a business and how are these systems related?

4. How do enterprise applications, collaboration and communication systems, and intranets improve organizational performance?

5. What is the role of the information systems function in a business?

CHAPTER OUTLINE

INFORMATION SYSTEMS JOIN THE TUPPERWARE PARTY

Earl Tupper patented the airtight Tupper seal for food storage containers in 1947, but it wasn't catching on in retail stores. He turned to an engaging single mother, Brownie Wise, to help him sell his Tupperware through home demonstration parties. The strategy worked: Tupperware grew into a $1.7 billion company that sells through home parties in almost 100 countries using an independent sales force of 1.9 million members. A Tupperware party begins every two seconds somewhere in the world.

A few years ago, Tupperware faced another challenge. The company changed its U.S. operations from a distributorship model to a multilevel compensation structure. Tupperware's U.S. sales force mushroomed from three levels of compensation (sales consultant, manager, and distributor) to a dozen levels. Sales consultants are paid a commission for their own sales plus a smaller commission based on sales of consultants that they recruited to the business.

As a sales consultant became successful and recruited more people to the business, that person would be responsible for her paperwork plus paperwork from the people she had recruited on her downline sales team. These activities did not leave enough time for

the strategic tasks of selling and recruiting. Tupperware's order entry system was not able to handle peak demand during sales promotions and busy times of the year. To support growth and improve business processes for both the sales force and corporate staff, Tupperware needed a system that could handle an additional 5,000 users each month, send e-mail messages to 50,000 recipients at a time, and allow restricted access to documents based on an employee's job position in the company.

In 2004, Tupperware began implementing an integrated Web-based order management system called MyTupperware.com that relieves distributors from the task of entering the orders from everyone they recruited. Now each sales consultant enters her own orders.

The Web-based system serves as a portal that integrates with Tupperware's existing systems so that authorized users can access information from related systems with a single sign-on. Different groups in the company, such as sales promotion, training, and Web support, have tools to publish and retire Web content for specific audiences in the company on their own without requiring help from the company's information systems staff. The system also streamlines communications among corporate managers, support staff, and sales consultants, and provides better support to sales consultants in promoting product sales, recruiting new sales consultants, and managing downline sales teams.

The portal provides four levels of access. There is a home page accessible to consumers, which provides information on Tupperware products and increases brand awareness. A second level gives all sales consultants access to order entry, e-mail, a calendar, training materials, and list functions. A third level offers sales consultants who wish to pay a fee additional marketing and promotional features and tools to create their own e-commerce Web sites linked to My.Tupperware.com. The highest level lets users perform more promotional activities and links to higher compensation opportunities. Any sales consultant can choose any level of accessibility she wishes.

Tupperware chose Oracle Collaboration Suite and Oracle Portal software as the platform for the system because they enabled the company to integrate functions for data management, financial systems, calendar, and e-mail into a single secure environment that could scale up to meet future growth in Tupperware sales and sales consultants. The company had also been using other Oracle software for a decade, so it felt comfortable with Oracle products.

Tupperware finished rolling out My.Tupperware.com to 50,000 North American users in the final months of 2004. Reaction to the system has been very positive. The company is enhancing the system to provide online Web conferencing and voice and text messaging.

Sources: Molly Rose Teuke, "Sealing Success," *Profit Magazine*, February 2006; "Tupperware Brands Corporation Form 10-K," February 28, 2007; and www.tupperware.com, accessed June 3, 2007.

Tupperware's experience illustrates how much companies today rely on information systems to run their businesses and drive growth and profitability. Tupperware has a unique business model based on selling food storage and preparation products at home parties using a large independent sales force. In addition to introducing new products and entering new markets, Tupperware's continued growth depends on increasing the size of its sales force to expand its business. However, its information systems were inadequate for supporting its new multilevel compensation structure and continuing growth.

The chapter-opening diagram calls attention to important points raised by this case and this chapter. Tupperware management identified an opportunity to use information systems to improve business performance. To support increased sales activity, it could have tried to enhance its existing order entry system. But that would not have made much of a dent in sales reps' workload, and this solution would not have worked well with its new sales force organization. Tupperware management wisely opted for a new system that could not only support large numbers of users but could also automate more business processes performed by the sales reps.

The Oracle software made it possible to support additional levels of Tupperware consultants and gave individual consultants tools to process their own orders and set up personal e-commerce sites. To make the system effective, Tupperware had to revise its

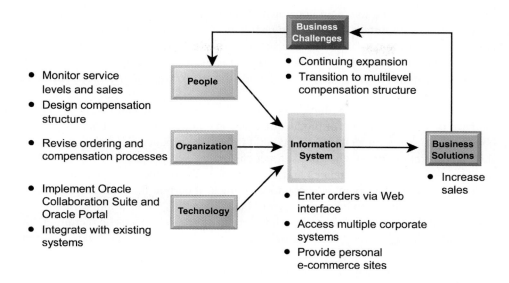

- Monitor service levels and sales
- Design compensation structure

- Revise ordering and compensation processes

- Implement Oracle Collaboration Suite and Oracle Portal
- Integrate with existing systems

Business Challenges
- Continuing expansion
- Transition to multilevel compensation structure

People

Organization

Technology

Information System
- Enter orders via Web interface
- Access multiple corporate systems
- Provide personal e-commerce sites

Business Solutions
- Increase sales

business processes for placing orders and compensating consultants. Tupperware's new ordering and compensation systems have reduced sales force workloads, increased productivity, and provided a new channel for reaching customers on the Web. The system has strategic implications: Tupperware has a high turnover rate among its sales force, and any change that enhances the recruitment, motivation, and retention of sales reps contributes to long-term growth and prosperity.

HEADS UP

This chapter provides you with an overview of how business firms use and organize information systems, and provides you with the basic vocabulary and concepts of business information systems that are used throughout the book. Many of the topics we cover here are covered in greater detail in later chapters, but this brief introduction to the entire field will help prepare you for later chapters and will quickly give you a better idea of the significant role that information systems play in a business.

2.1 Components of a Business

A **business** is a formal organization whose aim is to produce products or provide services for a profit—that is, to sell products at a price greater than the costs of production. Customers are willing to pay this price because they believe they receive a value greater than or equal to the sale price. Business firms purchase inputs and resources from the larger environment (suppliers who are often other firms). Employees of the firm transform these inputs by adding value to them in the production process. There are of course nonprofit firms and organizations, and government agencies that are complex formal organizations, that produce services and products but do not operate in order to produce a profit. Nevertheless, even these kinds of organizations consume resources from their environments, add value to these inputs, and deliver their outputs to constituents and customers. In general, the information systems found in nonprofit organizations are remarkably similar to those found in private industry.

ORGANIZING A BUSINESS: BASIC BUSINESS FUNCTIONS

Imagine that you wanted to set up your own business. Simply deciding to go into business would be the most important decision, but next would come the question of what product or what service you wanted to offer. The decision of what to produce is called a strategic choice because it determines who are your likely customers, the kinds of employees you will need, the production methods and facilities needed, the marketing themes, and many other choices.

Once you decide what to produce, what kind of organization would you need? First, you would have to design some sort of production division—an arrangement of people, machines, and business processes (procedures) that could produce the product. Second, you would need a sales and marketing group who could attract customers, sell the product, and keep track of after-sales issues, such as warranties and maintenance. Third, once you generate sales, you will need a finance and accounting group to keep track of current financial transactions, such as orders, invoices, disbursements, and payroll. In addition, this group would seek out sources of credit and finance. Finally, you would want a group of people to focus on recruiting, hiring, training, and retaining employees. Figure 2-1 summarizes the four basic functions found in every business.

If you were an entrepreneur or your business was very small with only a few employees, you would not need, and probably could not afford, all these separate groups of people. Instead, in small firms, you would be performing all these functions yourself or with a few others. No wonder small firms have a high mortality rate! In any event, even in small firms, the four basic functions of a firm are required. Larger firms often will have separate departments for each function: manufacturing and production, sales and marketing, finance and accounting, and human resources.

Figure 2-1 is also useful for thinking about the basic entities that make up a business. The five basic entities in a business with which it must deal are: suppliers, customers, employees, invoices/payments, and products and services. There are many other entities that a business must manage and monitor, but these are the basic ones at the foundation of any business.

BUSINESS PROCESSES

Once you identify the basic business functions and entities for your business, your next job will be to describe exactly how you want your employees to perform these functions.

Figure 2-1
The Four Major Functions of a Business
Every business, regardless of its size, must perform four functions to succeed. It must produce the product or service; market and sell the product; keep track of accounting and financial transactions; and perform basic human resources tasks, such as hiring and retaining employees.

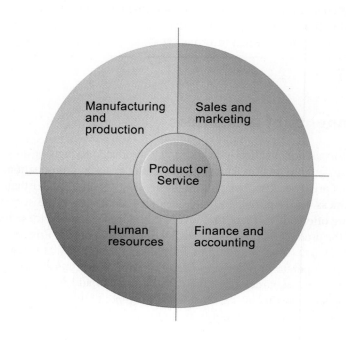

What specific tasks do you want your sales personnel to perform, in what order, and on what schedule? What steps do you want production employees to follow as they transform raw resources into finished products? How will customer orders be fulfilled? How will vendor bills be paid? The actual steps and tasks that describe how work is organized in a business are called **business processes**. A business process is a logically related set of activities that define how specific business tasks are performed.

Every business can be seen as a collection of business processes. Large businesses have thousands of business processes, some more important than others. To a large extent, the efficiency of a business firm depends on how well its business processes are designed and coordinated.

Many business processes are tied to a specific functional area. For example, the sales and marketing function would be responsible for identifying customers, and the human resources function would be responsible for hiring employees. Other business processes cross many different functional areas and require coordination across departments. For instance, consider the seemingly simply business process of fulfilling a customer order (see Figure 2-2). Initially, the sales department would receive a sales order. The order will pass first to accounting to ensure the customer can pay for the order either by a credit verification or request for immediate payment prior to shipping. Once the customer credit is established, the production department has to pull the product from inventory or produce the product. Then the product will need to be shipped (and this may require working with a logistics firm, such as UPS or FedEx). A bill or invoice will then have to be generated by the accounting department, and a notice will be sent to the customer indicating that the product has shipped. Sales will have to be notified of the shipment and prepare to support the customer by answering calls or fulfilling warranty claims.

What at first appears to be a simple process, fulfilling an order, turns out to be a very complicated series of business processes that require the close coordination of major functional groups in a firm. Second, to efficiently perform all the steps in the order fulfillment process requires a great deal of information and, in order to be efficient, the rapid flow of information both within the firm (with business partners, such as delivery firms) and with the customer.

The Interactive Session on Organizations provides more detail on the critical role played by business processes in firm productivity and competitive advantage. Toyota Motor Company has flourished in a highly competitive environment because it created a set of

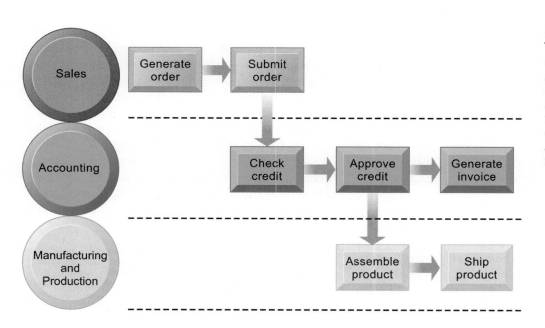

Figure 2-2
The Order Fulfillment Process
Fulfilling a customer order involves a complex set of steps that requires the close coordination of the sales, accounting, and manufacturing functions.

INTERACTIVE SESSION: ORGANIZATIONS Toyota As Number One

What company is the world's largest auto maker? For many years it was General Motors (GM), but in April 2007 that distinction passed to Toyota. Toyota sells over 9.5 million vehicles each year.

The company is also the world's most profitable automaker and the world's best automaker. The quality and reliability of Toyota vehicles are the gold standard of the industry, even among its lower-priced models. Customer loyalty is so high that Toyota can make sales without heavy discounting. And Toyota can produce a vehicle in significantly fewer hours than its competitors.

Key to the company's success in combining quality with efficiency is its vaunted Toyota Production System (TPS), which is based on lean manufacturing—eliminating waste while optimizing value. Toyota has based its business processes and information systems on the principles of just-in-time delivery, quality, and continuous improvement. By organizing its business processes and information systems around these principles, Toyota delivers value to the customer at a competitive price. Vehicle production is based on actual customer orders rather than best guesses of what to stock in dealer showrooms. The company only builds cars that customers want, when they want them, without additional delays or quality problems.

TPS is not an information system, but information technology has a critical role in supporting TPS so that it can drive Toyota's business processes. Toyota is likely to say that it does not have a technology strategy, but the role of the company's technology is to help its business strategy, which is to do away with waste, manufacture product without maintaining an inventory, and always improve production.

The key concepts of TPS are a just-in-time supply chain system and the ability to stop production to prevent defects (*Jidoka*). Jidoka is enhanced on the production floor by devices that enable line workers to stop the assembly line in order to correct mistakes or defects immediately. The devices range from a pull-rope or a button to monitoring software that provides real-time alerts of malfunctions in equipment or robots.

One of the best illustrations of Toyota's just-in-time supply chain system is the seat installation process. At the appropriate point in the assembly line, the system sends an electronic message to a Johnson Controls plant not far from the factory to place an order for the precise seat configuration needed for the specific car. Johnson Controls sends seats to the Toyota factory every four hours, in the exact sequence that they are needed on the assembly line. Such a precise system enables Toyota to operate without stored inventory, reduce errors, and satisfy customer demand for customized seat configurations quickly. Toyota developed its own software to manage this scheduling. The Assembly Line Control System (ALCS) is scalable for large and small plants, and runs on a combination of Hewlett-Packard and Windows 2000 host servers.

TPS also draws on other concepts. *Kaizen* is the component that seeks continuous improvement, often by eliminating waste from the system. A basic example of Kaizen is relocating a tool near the line so that a worker does not waste time going to get it when he or she needs it. A more advanced example is Toyota's Dealer Daily Internet portal, which, among other capabilities, enables car dealerships to make virtual swaps of the cars they are scheduled to receive so that they reduce the wait time for customers who have placed orders for specific cars.

Andons are visual controls that provide an up-to-the-minute look at how the production process is running. Electronic dashboards, overhead displays, and plasma screens all serve as Andons. They give supervisors an accurate report on what is happening on the assembly line. A green light signals that production is normal, a yellow light signals that a problem is under examination, and a red light means that the assembly line has stopped.

More advanced Andons are connected to the assembly line machinery and use plasma screens to report more detailed information, such as the type of equipment that failed, the operator's name, and the precise conditions under which the equipment malfunctioned. Toyota acquired the monitoring software, Activplant Performance Management Systems, from the Canadian company, Activplant.

Other auto companies have studied Toyota's methods but have had trouble imitating them. According to Jeffrey Liker, an expert on lean manufacturing, less than one percent of such organizations rate highly for their business processes. Liker attributes Toyota's success to the company's willingness "to commit to practicing the concepts behind TPS every day" despite the fact that it's difficult to do so.

Sources: Mel Duvall, "What's Driving Toyota?" *Baseline Magazine*, September 5, 2006; Dan Markovitz, "TPS—The Thinking Production System," themanufacturer.com, January 19, 2007; Ron Mott, "Toyota Culture Keeps Auto Giant in the Fast Lane," msnbc.com, January 18, 2007; "TPS (Toyota Production System)," Vorne.com, accessed January 26, 2007; and Sarah Perrin, "Corporate Profile: the Toyota Production System," AccountancyAge.com, December 4, 2006.

CASE STUDY QUESTIONS

1. What are the basic principles of Toyota's production system? To which areas of the organization do these principles apply?

2. How is TPS interconnected with the culture at Toyota? Are TPS and Toyota's culture interdependent? Could one exist without the other?

3. Describe how information systems support each of the business processes described in this case.

MIS IN ACTION

1. Select another industry, such as the airline industry or banking, and apply the principles of TPS to that industry. For instance, if you choose a bank, what are some examples of waste that you could try to eliminate? How would Jidoka be implemented? What are some examples of Andons that could be used? How would information systems support these practices? What obstacles might prevent Kaizen from being successful?

2. Some experts believe that lean manufacturing by itself is becoming less and less of a competitive advantage because there is a limit to how much waste you can remove from the production process. Go to www.industryweek.com (or use a search engine) and search for the article titled *Toyota's Real Secret: Hint, It's Not TPS* by John Teresko. Do you agree with the premise of the article? Why or why not? Based on the article and your reading of the case study, what strategies has Toyota implemented to counteract the notion that TPS and lean manufacturing do not offer unlimited opportunities for improvement?

finely tuned business processes and information systems that simultaneously promote agility, efficiency, and quality. It can respond instantly to customers and changes in the marketplace as events unfold, while working closely with suppliers and retailers. As you read this case, look for all the ways information systems support these business processes and the problems they solve.

MANAGING A BUSINESS AND FIRM HIERARCHIES

What is missing from Figures 2-1 and 2-2 is any notion of how to coordinate and control the four major functions, their departments, and their business processes. Each of these functional departments has its own goals and processes, and they obviously need to cooperate in order for the whole business to succeed. Business firms, like all organizations, achieve coordination by hiring managers whose responsibility is to ensure all the various parts of an organization work together. Firms coordinate the work of employees in various divisions by developing a hierarchy in which authority (responsibility and accountability) is concentrated at the top.

The hierarchy of management is composed of **senior management**, which makes long-range strategic decisions about products and services as well as ensures financial performance of the firm; **middle management**, which carries out the programs and plans of senior management; and **operational management**, which is responsible for monitoring the daily activities of the business. **Knowledge workers**, such as engineers, scientists, or architects, design products or services and create new knowledge for the firm, whereas **data workers**, such as secretaries or clerks, assist with paperwork at all levels of the firm. **Production or service workers** actually produce the product and deliver the service (see Figure 2-3).

Each of these groups has different needs for information given their different responsibilities, and each can be seen as major information constituents. Senior managers need sum-

Figure 2-3
Levels in a Firm
Business organizations are hierarchies consisting of three principal levels: senior management, middle management, and operational management. Information systems serve each of these levels. Scientists and knowledge workers often work with middle management.

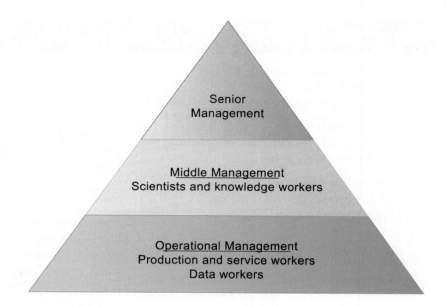

mary information that can quickly inform them about the overall performance of the firm, such as gross sales revenues, sales by product group and region, and overall profitability. Middle managers need more specific information on the results of specific functional areas and departments of the firm, such as sales contacts by the sales force, production statistics for specific factories or product lines, employment levels and costs, and sales revenues for each month or even each day. Operational managers need transaction-level information, such as the number of parts in inventory each day or the number of hours logged on Tuesday by each employee. Knowledge workers may need access to external scientific databases or internal databases with organizational knowledge. Finally, production or service workers need access to information from production machines, and service workers need access to customer records in order to take orders and answer questions from customers.

THE BUSINESS ENVIRONMENT

So far we have talked about business as if it operated in a vacuum. Nothing could be further from the truth. In fact, business firms depend heavily on their environments to supply capital, labor, customers, new technology, services and products, stable markets and legal systems, and general educational resources. Even a pizza parlor cannot survive long without a supportive environment that delivers the cheese, tomato sauce, and flour!

Figure 2-4 summarizes the key actors in the environment of every business. To stay in business, a firm must monitor changes in its environment and share information with the key entities in that environment. For instance, a firm must respond to political shifts, respond to changes in the overall economy (such as changes in labor rates and price inflation), keep track of new technologies, and respond to changes in the global business environment (such as foreign exchange rates). In its immediate environment, firms need to track and share information with suppliers, customers, stockholders, regulators, and logistic partners (such as shipping firms).

Business environments are constantly changing: new developments in technology, politics, customer preferences, and regulations happen all the time. In general, when businesses fail, it is often because they failed to respond adequately to changes in their environments.

For instance, changes in technology, such as the Internet, are forcing entire industries and leading firms to change their business models or suffer failure. The Chapter 3 opening case study describes how new technology—the Internet—is making the music industry's traditional business model based on distributing music on CDs obsolete. Another example is

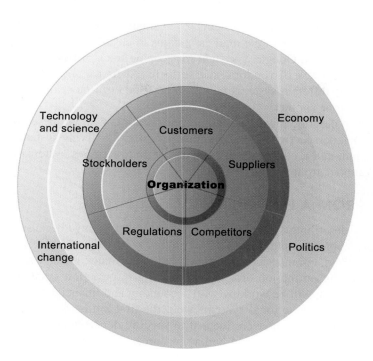

Figure 2-4
The Business Environment
To be successful, an organization must constantly monitor and respond to—or even anticipate—developments in its environment. A firm's environment includes specific groups with which the business must deal directly, such as customers, suppliers, and competitors as well as the broader general environment, including socioeconomic trends, political conditions, technological innovations, and global events.

the photography business. Digital photography has forced Eastman Kodak to downsize and move into digital cameras and Internet photography services because most of the consumer marketplace no longer wants to use traditional cameras with film.

THE ROLE OF INFORMATION SYSTEMS IN A BUSINESS

Until now we have not mentioned information systems. But from the brief review of business functions, entities, and environments, you can see the critical role that information plays in the life of a business. Up until the mid-1950s, firms managed all this information and information flow with paper records. During the past 50 years, more and more business information and the flow of information among key business actors in the environment has been computerized.

Businesses invest in information systems as a way to cope with and manage their internal production functions and to cope with the demands of key actors in their environments. Specifically, as we noted in Chapter 1, firms invest in information systems for the following business objectives:

- To achieve operational excellence (productivity, efficiency, agility)
- To develop new products and services
- To attain customer intimacy and service (continuous marketing, sales, and service; customization and personalization)
- To improve decision making (accuracy and speed)
- To achieve competitive advantage
- To ensure survival

2.2 Types of Business Information Systems

Now it is time to look more closely at how businesses use information systems to achieve these goals. Because there are different interests, specialties, and levels in an organization, there are different kinds of systems. No single system can provide all the information an organization needs. In fact large- and medium-size firms have thousands of computer programs and hundreds of different systems. Even small firms have a collection of different systems: a system for conducting e-mail campaigns to customers, a system for monitoring advertisements placed on Google, a system for keeping track of basic sales transactions, a system for keeping track of vendors, and so forth. At first glance it can be difficult to comprehend all the different systems in a business, and even more difficult to understand how they relate to one another.

We attempt to describe this complex situation by looking at all these different systems from two different perspectives: a functional perspective identifying systems by their major business function, and a constituency perspective that identifies systems in terms of the major organizational groups that they serve

SYSTEMS FROM A FUNCTIONAL PERSPECTIVE

We will start by describing systems using a functional perspective because this is the most straightforward approach, and, in fact, because this is how you will likely first encounter systems in a business. For instance, if you are a marketing major and take a job in marketing, you will be working on the job first with marketing information systems. If you are an accounting major, you will be working with accounting and financial systems first. From a historical perspective, functional systems were the first kinds of systems developed by business firms. These systems were located in specific departments, such as accounting, marketing and sales, production, and human resources. Let's take a close look at systems from this functional perspective.

Sales and Marketing Systems

The sales and marketing function is responsible for selling the organization's products or services. Marketing is concerned with identifying the customers for the firm's products or services, determining what customers need or want, planning and developing products and services to meet their needs, and advertising and promoting these products and services. Sales is concerned with contacting customers, selling the products and services, taking orders, and following up on sales. **Sales and marketing information systems** support these activities.

Table 2.1 shows that information systems are used in sales and marketing in a number of ways. Sales and marketing systems help senior management monitor trends affecting new products and sales opportunities, support planning for new products and services, and monitor the performance of competitors. Sales and marketing systems aid middle management by supporting market research and by analyzing advertising and promotional campaigns, pricing decisions, and sales performance. Sales and marketing systems assist operational management and employees in locating and contacting prospective customers, tracking sales, processing orders, and providing customer service support.

Figure 2-5 illustrates a sales information system used by retailers, such as The Gap or Target. Point-of-sale devices (usually handheld scanners at the checkout counter) capture data about each item sold, which update the sales system's figures about sales and send data about items sold to related systems dealing with items remaining in inventory and with production. These businesses use this information to track which items have been sold, to determine sales revenue, and to identify hot-selling items and other sales trends.

TABLE 2.1			
	System	**Description**	**Groups Served**
Examples of Sales and Marketing Information Systems	Order processing	Enter, process, and track orders	Operational management Employees
	Pricing analysis	Determine prices for products and services	Middle management
	Sales trend forecasting	Prepare five-year sales forecasts	Senior management

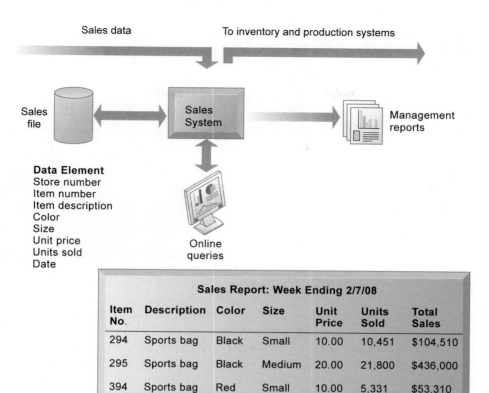

Sales data   To inventory and production systems

Sales file

Sales System

Management reports

Data Element
Store number
Item number
Item description
Color
Size
Unit price
Units sold
Date

Online queries

Sales Report: Week Ending 2/7/08						
Item No.	Description	Color	Size	Unit Price	Units Sold	Total Sales
294	Sports bag	Black	Small	10.00	10,451	$104,510
295	Sports bag	Black	Medium	20.00	21,800	$436,000
394	Sports bag	Red	Small	10.00	5,331	$53,310

Figure 2-5
Example of a Sales Information System
This system captures sales data at the moment the sale takes place to help the business monitor sales transactions and to provide information to help management analyze sales trends and the effectiveness of marketing campaigns.

Manufacturing and Production Systems

The manufacturing and production function is responsible for actually producing the firm's goods and services. Manufacturing and production systems deal with the planning, development, and maintenance of production facilities; the establishment of production goals; the acquisition, storage, and availability of production materials; and the scheduling of equipment, facilities, materials, and labor required to fashion finished products. **Manufacturing and production information systems** support these activities.

Table 2.2 shows some typical manufacturing and production information systems for each major organizational group. Senior management uses manufacturing and production systems that deal with the firm's long-term manufacturing goals, such as where to locate new plants or whether to invest in new manufacturing technology. Manufacturing and production systems for middle management analyze and monitor manufacturing and production costs and resources. Operational management uses manufacturing and production systems that deal with the status of production tasks.

Most manufacturing and production systems use some sort of inventory system, as illustrated in Figure 2-6. Data about each item in inventory, such as the number of units

System	Description	Groups Served
Machine control	Controls the actions of machines and equipment	Operational management
Production planning	Decides when and how many products should be produced	Middle management
Facilities location	Decides where to locate new production facilities	Senior management

TABLE 2.2

Examples of Manufacturing and Production Information Systems

Figure 2-6
Overview of an Inventory System
This system provides information about the number of items available in inventory to support manufacturing and production activities.

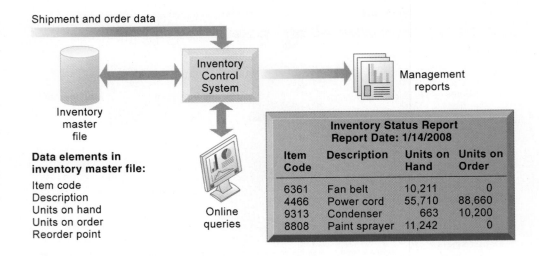

depleted because of a shipment or purchase or the number of units replenished by reordering or returns, are either scanned or keyed into the system. The inventory master file contains basic data about each item, including the unique identification code for each item, a description of the item, the number of units on hand, the number of units on order, and the reorder point (the number of units in inventory that triggers a decision to reorder to prevent a stockout). Companies can estimate the number of items to reorder, or they can use a formula for calculating the least expensive quantity to reorder called the *economic order quantity*. The system produces reports that give information about such things as the number of each item available in inventory, the number of units of each item to reorder, or items in inventory that must be replenished.

Finance and Accounting Systems

The finance function is responsible for managing the firm's financial assets, such as cash, stocks, bonds, and other investments, to maximize the return on these financial assets. The finance function is also in charge of managing the capitalization of the firm (finding new financial assets in stocks, bonds, or other forms of debt). To determine whether the firm is getting the best return on its investments, the finance function must obtain a considerable amount of information from sources external to the firm.

The accounting function is responsible for maintaining and managing the firm's financial records—receipts, disbursements, depreciation, payroll—to account for the flow of funds in a firm. Finance and accounting share related problems—how to keep track of a firm's financial assets and fund flows. They provide answers to questions such as these: What is the current inventory of financial assets? What records exist for disbursements, receipts, payroll, and other fund flows?

Table 2.3 shows some of the typical **finance and accounting information systems** found in large organizations. Senior management uses finance and accounting systems to establish long-term investment goals for the firm and to provide long-range forecasts of the firm's financial performance. Middle management uses systems to oversee and control the

TABLE 2.3

Examples of Finance and Accounting Information Systems

System	Description	Groups Served
Accounts receivable	Tracks money owed the firm	Operational management
Budgeting	Prepares short-term budgets	Middle management
Profit planning	Plans long-term profits	Senior management

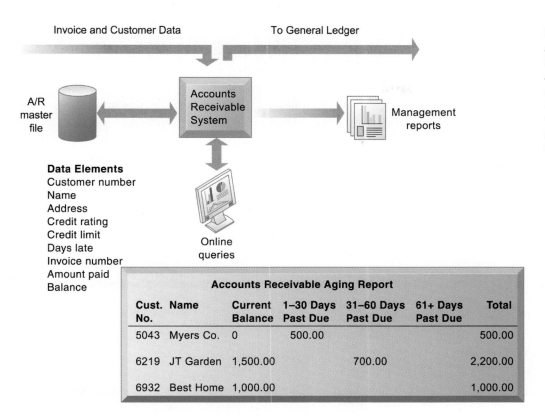

Figure 2-7
An Accounts Receivable System
An accounts receivable system tracks and stores important customer data, such as payment history, credit rating, and billing history.

firm's financial resources. Operational management uses finance and accounting systems to track the flow of funds in the firm through transactions, such as paychecks, payments to vendors, securities reports, and receipts.

Figure 2-7 illustrates an accounts receivable system, which keeps track of what customers who have made purchases on credit owe to a company. Every invoice generates an "account receivable"—that is, the customer owes the firm money. Some customers pay immediately in cash, but others are granted credit. The accounts receivable system records each invoice in a master file that also contains information on each customer, including that person's credit rating. The system also keeps track of all the bills outstanding and can produce a variety of output reports, both on paper and on the computer screen, to help the business collect bills. The system also answers queries about a customer's credit rating and payment history.

Human Resources Systems

The human resources function is responsible for attracting, developing, and maintaining the firm's workforce. **Human resources information systems** support activities such as identifying potential employees, maintaining complete records on existing employees, and creating programs to develop employees' talents and skills.

Human resources systems help senior management identify the manpower requirements (skills, educational level, types of positions, number of positions, and cost) for meeting the firm's long-term business plans. Middle management uses human resources systems to monitor and analyze the recruitment, allocation, and compensation of employees. Operational management uses human resources systems to track the recruitment and placement of the firm's employees (see Table 2.4).

Figure 2-8 illustrates a typical human resources system for employee record keeping. It maintains basic employee data, such as the employee's name, age, sex, marital status, address, educational background, salary, job title, date of hire, and date of termination. The system can produce a variety of reports, such as lists of newly hired employees, employees who are terminated or on leaves of absence, employees classified by job type or

TABLE 2.4

Examples of Human
Resources Information
Systems

System	Description	Groups Served
Training and development	Tracks employee training, skills, and performance appraisals	Operational management
Compensation analysis	Monitors the range and distribution of employee wages, salaries, and benefits	Middle management
Human resources planning	Plans the long-term labor force needs of the organization	Senior management

**Figure 2-8
An Employee
Record Keeping
System**
*This system maintains
data on the firm's
employees to support
the human resources
function.*

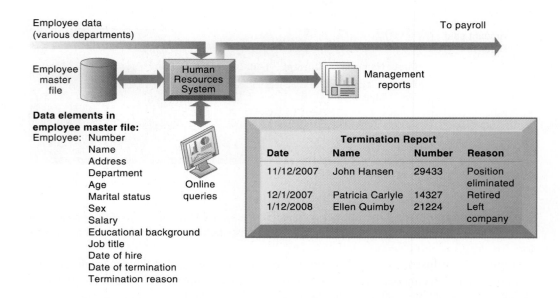

educational level, or employee job performance evaluations. Such systems are typically designed to provide data that can satisfy federal and state record keeping requirements for Equal Employment Opportunity (EEO) and other purposes.

The Interactive Session on People describes a human resources system with a strategic orientation. Google is one of the world's most leading-edge, rapidly growing companies. It is best known for its powerful Internet search engine, but it is also the source of numerous other technology-based products and services. Innovation and knowledge are key business drivers. Google obviously has very special human resources requirements and prizes highly intelligent employees who can work in teams yet think outside the box. As you read this case, try to identify the problem this company was facing; what alternative solutions were available to management; how well the chosen solution worked; and the people, organization, and technology issues that had to be addressed when developing the solution.

SYSTEMS FROM A CONSTITUENCY PERSPECTIVE

Although a functional perspective is very useful for understanding how business systems serve specific functions, this perspective does not tell us how systems help managers manage the firm. Here we need a perspective that examines systems in terms of the various levels of management and types of decisions that they support. Each of three main management

INTERACTIVE SESSION: PEOPLE   Google's New Search for the Best and the Brightest

What would it take to work for Google? Its employees are among the best and the brightest. The typical Google employee achieved perfect grades in school, on top of perfect SAT scores. If you were looking for an engineering position at Google, your grade point average had to be 3.7 or better. Experienced workers whose past grades and test scores did not reach Google's high standards were ruled out.

The few applicants who made the initial cutoff told tales of an exceptionally rigorous hiring process that in some cases included as many as a dozen on-site interviews. Google was also known to challenge prospective hires with complicated brainteasers. These practices helped the company build an organization where the sharpest minds could flourish amidst Google's freewheeling and competitive culture.

Google's work force has roughly doubled over the past few years, reaching more than 12,200 by the end of March 2007. Lazlo Bock, who was recruited from General Electric to be Google's vice president of people operations in March 2006, anticipated that the company would double in size once again in 2007 and require approximately 200 new hires per week. This rapid workforce expansion forced Google to re-examine its employee recruiting processes. Was there another way for Google to take the 100,000 job applications it receives monthly and recruit enough worthwhile candidates to satisfy its desperate need for engineers, sales representatives, and other positions?

Bock believes in research findings saying that grades and interviews are not totally reliable predictors of job performance. And indeed, Google has found that high academic performance is not always correlated with success on the job. So Google decided to gather quantitative information about people's backgrounds to pinpoint good candidates for employment.

In the summer of 2006, Google employees who had been on the job for at least five months filled out a 300-question survey designed by an organizational psychologist that covered a broad spectrum of questions. The survey included questions about skills (What programming languages are you familiar with?), behavior (Is your workspace messy or neat?), personality (Are you an extrovert or an introvert?), and non-traditional factors (What magazines do you subscribe to?).

Bock was willing to consider that a great variety of factors could be associated with personality traits that would be effective predictors of success. He pointed out that it is fairly common to find employees with their dogs in the Google offices. Therefore, it was worth asking whether pet ownership is related to a personality trait that makes for a successful Google employee. Google also asked questions such as, "Have you ever set a world record in anything?" "At what age did you first get excited about computers?" "Have you ever made a profit from a catering business or dog walking?" and "Have you ever established a nonprofit organization?" The questions were designed to create a profile of a worker that included his or her attitudes, behavior, personality, and life experiences.

Mathematicians at Google gathered the data from the current employee survey and lined them up against 25 different measures of job performance, including supervisor and peer reviews, compensation, and the ability to make the company a better place to work. The results of the data analysis populated a score matrix that rated potential employees on a scale of zero to 100 on how likely they were to thrive at Google. The initial survey showed that there was no single way to determine who would be the best candidates for every type of position that Google offers. However, the company created separate surveys to distill the best candidates in specific areas including engineering, sales, finance, and human resources.

Google's use of quantitative data is not unique. Other companies have used a wide range of tests to assess skills, intelligence, and personality, including biographical surveys similar to Google's.

Initially, only a small percentage of job applicants were evaluated with the survey approach, but it was slated for a full rollout in January 2007. It was still too early to tell whether Google's revamped recruiting and hiring techniques yielded the desired results. Michael Mumford, a University of Oklahoma psychology professor specializing in talent assessment, notes that this type of test can be effective, but that companies should not rely too heavily on oddball factors. The company also had to address resistance to the idea that a computer running an algorithm is better equipped to identify talent than a human.

In the meantime, Google has been exploring additional ways to condense the hiring process, including cutting the number of interviews for some positions down to two, and changing the format of interviewer feedback from free-form text and a single score to a multifaceted evaluation with four attributes and multiple scores. Bock believes that Google hiring practices are producing results: more people are being hired for what their experience indicated they would be able to accomplish.

Sources: Saul Hansell, "Google Answer to Filling Jobs Is an Algorithm," *The New York Times*, January 3, 2007; Miguel Helft, "In Fierce Competition, Google Finds Novel Ways to Feed Hiring Machine, " *The New York Times*, May 28, 2007; and Kevin J. Delaney, "Google Adjusts Hiring Process As Needs Grow," *The Wall Street Journal*, October 26, 2006.

CASE STUDY QUESTIONS

1. Did Google's traditional hiring practices create business problems? Explain your answer.

2. Is Google's quantitative approach to hiring a good solution to its employee recruiting problems? Why or why not?

3. What role does culture play in Google's hiring preferences?

4. What kind of system or systems described in this chapter are discussed in this case? What are the inputs, processes, and outputs?

5. Create a list of ten questions that you think might be appropriate for Google's job applicant survey. Justify each question with a short explanation of why the answer would be useful.

6. If you were applying for a job at Google, how would you want to be evaluated? Which evaluation techniques do you think favor your strengths? Which techniques might expose your weaknesses?

MIS IN ACTION

Explore the Google Jobs page at http://www.google.com/intl/en/jobs/index.html, and then answer the following questions:

1. What resources does Google provide for prospective employees on its Web site?

2. Find a Google job listing that interests you and determine whether you will have the necessary skills to interview for the job when you graduate. What skills are you lacking? How did the job posting make you feel about your chances of landing the job you want?

3. Imagine that you are preparing for a job interview at Google. Use the company's Web site to learn about the company and come up with three questions that you can ask your interviewer about the company. List your three questions along with links to the pages of the Web site that inspired your questions and descriptions of the content of those pages.

groups we described earlier uses a different type of system to deliver the information required to manage the company.

Transaction Processing Systems

Operational managers need systems that keep track of the elementary activities and transactions of the organization, such as sales, receipts, cash deposits, payroll, credit decisions, and the flow of materials in a factory. **Transaction processing systems (TPS)** provide this kind of information. A transaction processing system is a computerized system that performs and records the daily routine transactions necessary to conduct business, such as sales order entry, hotel reservations, payroll, employee record keeping, and shipping.

The principal purpose of systems at this level is to answer routine questions and to track the flow of transactions through the organization. How many parts are in inventory? What happened to Mr. Williams's payment? To answer these kinds of questions, information generally must be easily available, current, and accurate.

At the operational level, tasks, resources, and goals are predefined and highly structured. The decision to grant credit to a customer, for instance, is made by a lower-level supervisor according to predefined criteria. All that must be determined is whether the customer meets the criteria. The systems illustrated in Figures 2-7 and 2-8 are transaction processing systems.

Managers need TPS to monitor the status of internal operations and the firm's relations with the external environment. TPS are also major producers of information for the other types of systems. (For example, the accounts receivable system illustrated in Figure 2-7, along with other accounting TPS, supplies data to the company's general ledger system, which is responsible for maintaining records of the firm's income and expenses and for producing reports such as income statements and balance sheets.)

Transaction processing systems are often so central to a business that TPS failure for a few hours can lead to a firm's demise and perhaps that of other firms linked to it. Imagine what would happen to UPS if its package tracking system were not working! What would the airlines do without their computerized reservation systems?

Management Information Systems and Decision-Support Systems

Middle management needs systems to help with monitoring, controlling, decision-making, and administrative activities. The principal question addressed by such systems is this: Are things working well?

In Chapter 1, we defined management information systems as the study of information systems in business and management. The term **management information systems (MIS)** also designates a specific category of information systems serving middle management. MIS provide middle managers with reports on the organization's current performance. This information is used to monitor and control the business and predict future performance.

MIS summarize and report on the company's basic operations using data supplied by transaction processing systems. The basic transaction data from TPS are compressed and usually presented in reports that are produced on a regular schedule. Today, many of these reports are delivered online. Figure 2-9 shows how a typical MIS transforms transaction-level data from inventory, production, and accounting into MIS files that are used to provide managers with reports. Figure 2-10 shows a sample report from this system.

MIS serve managers primarily interested in weekly, monthly, and yearly results, although some MIS enable managers to drill down to see daily or hourly data if required. MIS generally provide answers to routine questions that have been specified in advance and have a predefined procedure for answering them. For instance, MIS reports might list the total pounds of lettuce used this quarter by a fast-food chain or, as illustrated in Figure 2-10, compare total annual sales figures for specific products to planned targets. These systems generally are not flexible and have little analytical capability. Most MIS use simple routines, such as summaries and comparisons, as opposed to sophisticated mathematical models or statistical techniques.

Decision-support systems (DSS) support nonroutine decision making for middle management. They focus on problems that are unique and rapidly changing, for which the procedure for arriving at a solution may not be fully predefined in advance. They try to

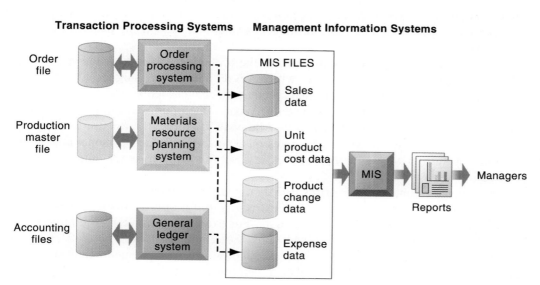

Figure 2-9
How Management Information Systems Obtain Their Data from the Organization's TPS
In the system illustrated by this diagram, three TPS supply summarized transaction data to the MIS reporting system at the end of the time period. Managers gain access to the organizational data through the MIS, which provides them with the appropriate reports.

Figure 2-10
Sample MIS Report
This report, showing summarized annual sales data, was produced by the MIS in Figure 2-9.

Consolidated Consumer Products Corporation Sales by Product and Sales Region: 2008

PRODUCT CODE	PRODUCT DESCRIPTION	SALES REGION	ACTUAL SALES	PLANNED	ACTUAL versus PLANNED
4469	Carpet Cleaner	Northeast	4,066,700	4,800,000	0.85
		South	3,778,112	3,750,000	1.01
		Midwest	4,867,001	4,600,000	1.06
		West	4,003,440	4,400,000	0.91
	TOTAL		16,715,253	17,550,000	0.95
5674	Room Freshener	Northeast	3,676,700	3,900,000	0.94
		South	5,608,112	4,700,000	1.19
		Midwest	4,711,001	4,200,000	1.12
		West	4,563,440	4,900,000	0.93
	TOTAL		18,559,253	17,700,000	1.05

answer questions such as these: What would be the impact on production schedules if we were to double sales in the month of December? What would happen to our return on investment if a factory schedule were delayed for six months?

Although DSS use internal information from TPS and MIS, they often bring in information from external sources, such as current stock prices or product prices of competitors. These systems use a variety of models to analyze data, or they condense large amounts of data into a form in which decision makers can analyze them. DSS are designed so that users can work with them directly; these systems explicitly include user-friendly software.

An interesting, small, but powerful DSS is the voyage-estimating system of a subsidiary of a large American metals company that exists primarily to carry bulk cargoes of coal, oil, ores, and finished products for its parent company. The firm owns some vessels, charters others, and bids for shipping contracts in the open market to carry general cargo. A voyage-estimating system calculates financial and technical voyage details. Financial calculations include ship/time costs (fuel, labor, capital), freight rates for various types of cargo, and port expenses. Technical details include a myriad of factors, such as ship cargo capacity, speed, port distances, fuel and water consumption, and loading patterns (location of cargo for different ports).

The system can answer questions such as the following: Given a customer delivery schedule and an offered freight rate, which vessel should be assigned at what rate to maximize profits? What is the optimal speed at which a particular vessel can optimize its profit and still meet its delivery schedule? What is the optimal loading pattern for a ship bound for the U.S. West Coast from Malaysia? Figure 2-11 illustrates the DSS built for this company. The system operates on a powerful desktop personal computer, providing a system of menus that makes it easy for users to enter data or obtain information.

This voyage-estimating DSS draws heavily on analytical models. Other types of DSS are less model driven, focusing instead on extracting useful information to support decision making from massive quantities of data. For example, Intrawest—the largest ski operator in North America—collects and stores vast amounts of customer data from its Web site, call center, lodging reservations, ski schools, and ski equipment rental stores. It uses special software to analyze these data to determine the value, revenue potential, and loyalty of each customer so managers can make better decisions on how to target their marketing programs. The system segments customers into seven categories based on

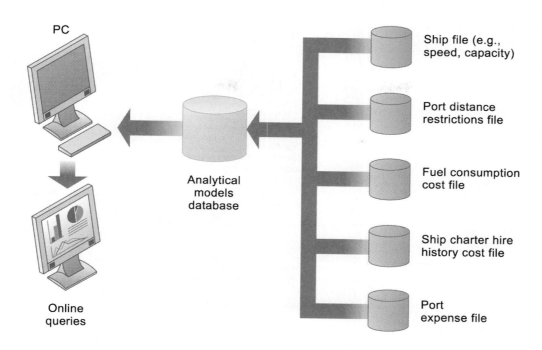

PC

Analytical models database

Online queries

Ship file (e.g., speed, capacity)

Port distance restrictions file

Fuel consumption cost file

Ship charter hire history cost file

Port expense file

Figure 2-11
Voyage-Estimating Decision-Support System
This DSS operates on a powerful PC. It is used daily by managers who must develop bids on shipping contracts.

needs, attitudes, and behaviors, ranging from "passionate experts" to "value-minded family vacationers." The company then e-mails video clips that would appeal to each segment to encourage more visits to its resorts.

Sometimes you'll hear DSS referred to as *business intelligence systems* because they focus on helping users make better business decisions. You'll learn more about them in Chapters 5 and 10.

Executive Support Systems

Senior managers need systems that address strategic issues and long-term trends, both in the firm and in the external environment. They are concerned with questions such as these: What will employment levels be in five years? What are the long-term industry cost trends, and where does our firm fit in? What products should we be making in five years? What new acquisitions would protect us from cyclical business swings?

Executive support systems (ESS) help senior management make these decisions. ESS address nonroutine decisions requiring judgment, evaluation, and insight because there is no agreed-on procedure for arriving at a solution. ESS provide a generalized computing and communications capacity that can be applied to a changing array of problems.

ESS are designed to incorporate data about external events, such as new tax laws or competitors, but they also draw summarized information from internal MIS and DSS. They filter, compress, and track critical data, displaying the data of greatest importance to senior managers. For example, the CEO of Leiner Health Products, the largest manufacturer of private-label vitamins and supplements in the United States, has an ESS that provides on his desktop a minute-to-minute view of the firm's financial performance as measured by working capital, accounts receivable, accounts payable, cash flow, and inventory.

ESS present graphs and data from many sources through an interface that is easy for senior managers to use. Often the information is delivered to senior executives through a **portal**, which uses a Web interface to present integrated personalized business content. You will learn more about other applications of portals in Chapters 9 and 10.

Figure 2-12 illustrates a model of an ESS. It consists of workstations with menus, interactive graphics, and communications capabilities that can be used to access historical

Figure 2-12
Model of an
Executive Support
System
This system pools data
from diverse internal and
external sources and
makes them available to
executives in an easy-to-
use form.

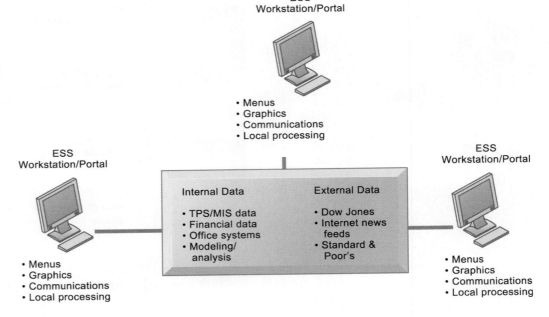

and competitive data from internal corporate systems and external databases such as Dow Jones News/Retrieval or the Gallup Poll. More details on leading-edge applications of DSS and ESS can be found in Chapter 10.

RELATIONSHIP OF SYSTEMS TO ONE ANOTHER

The systems we have just described are interrelated, as illustrated in Figure 2-13. TPS are typically a major source of data for other systems, whereas ESS are primarily a recipient of data from lower-level systems. The other types of systems may exchange data with each other as well. Data also may be exchanged among systems serving different functional areas. For example, an order captured by a sales system may be transmitted to a manufacturing system as a transaction for producing or delivering the product specified in the order or to an MIS for financial reporting. In most organizations, these systems have been loosely integrated.

2.3 Systems That Span the Enterprise

Reviewing all the different types of systems we have just described, you might wonder how a business can manage all the information in these different systems. You might also wonder how costly it is to maintain so many different systems. And you might wonder how these different systems can share information and how managers and employees can coordinate their work. In fact, these are all excellent questions and challenges for businesses today.

ENTERPRISE APPLICATIONS

Getting all the different kinds of systems in a company to work together is a major challenge. Typically, corporations are put together both through normal "organic" growth and through acquisition of smaller firms. Over a period of time, corporations end up with a collection of systems, most of them older, and face the challenge of getting them all to "talk" with one another and work together as one corporate system. There are several solutions to this problem.

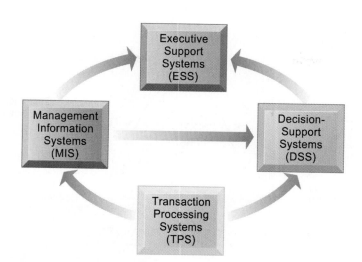

Figure 2-13
Interrelationships Among Systems
The various types of systems in the organization have interdependencies. TPS are major producers of information that is required by many other systems in the firm, which, in turn, produce information for other systems. These different types of systems have been loosely coupled in most organizations.

One solution is to implement **enterprise applications**, which are systems that span functional areas, focus on executing business processes across the business firm, and include all levels of management. Enterprise applications help businesses become more flexible and productive by coordinating their business processes more closely and integrating groups of processes so they focus on efficient management of resources and customer service.

There are four major enterprise applications: enterprise systems, supply chain management systems, customer relationship management systems, and knowledge management systems. Each of these enterprise applications integrates a related set of functions and business processes to enhance the performance of the organization as a whole. Figure 2-14 shows that the architecture for these enterprise applications encompasses processes spanning the entire organization and, in some cases, extending beyond the organization to customers, suppliers, and other key business partners.

Enterprise Systems

A large organization typically has many different kinds of information systems built around different functions, organizational levels, and business processes that cannot automatically exchange information. Managers might have a hard time assembling the data they need for a comprehensive, overall picture of the organization's operations. For instance, sales personnel might not be able to tell at the time they place an order whether the items that were ordered are in inventory, customers cannot track their orders, and manufacturing cannot communicate easily with finance to plan for new production. This fragmentation of data in hundreds of separate systems degrades organizational efficiency and business performance.

For example, Alcoa, the world's leading producer of aluminum and aluminum products with operations spanning 41 countries and 500 locations, had initially been organized around lines of business, each of which had its own set of information systems. Many of these systems were redundant and inefficient. Alcoa's costs for executing requisition-to-pay and financial processes were much higher and its cycle times were longer than those of other companies in its industry. (Cycle time refers to the total elapsed time from the beginning to the end of a process.) The company could not operate as a single worldwide entity (Oracle, 2005; Sullivan, 2005).

Enterprise systems, also known as *enterprise resource planning (ERP) systems*, solve this problem by collecting data from various key business processes in manufacturing and production, finance and accounting, sales and marketing, and human resources and storing the data in a single central data repository. This makes it possible for information that was previously fragmented in different systems to be shared across the firm and for different parts of the business to work more closely together (see Figure 2-15).

Figure 2-14
Enterprise Application Architecture
Enterprise applications automate processes that span multiple business functions and organizational levels and may extend outside the organization.

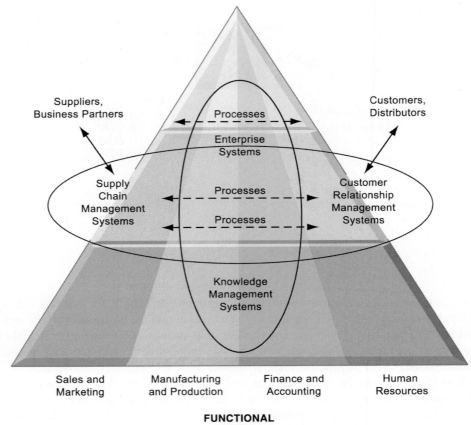

Enterprise systems speed communication of information throughout the company, making it easier for businesses to coordinate their daily operations. When a customer places an order, the data flow automatically to other parts of the company that are affected by them. The order transaction triggers the warehouse to pick the ordered products and schedule shipment. The warehouse informs the factory to replenish whatever has depleted.

Figure 2-15
Enterprise Systems
Enterprise systems integrate the key business processes of an entire firm into a single software system that enables information to flow seamlessly throughout the organization. These systems focus primarily on internal processes but may include transactions with customers and vendors.

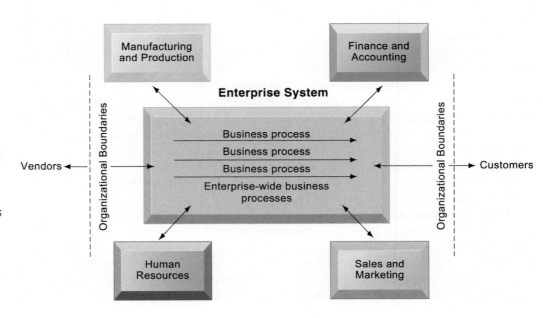

The accounting department is notified to send the customer an invoice. Customer service representatives track the progress of the order through every step to inform customers about the status of their orders.

Enterprise systems give companies the flexibility to respond rapidly to customer requests while producing and stocking inventory only with what is needed to fulfill existing orders. Their ability to increase accurate and on-time shipments, minimize costs, and increase customer satisfaction adds to firm profitability.

After implementing enterprise software from Oracle, Alcoa eliminated many redundant processes and systems. The enterprise system helped Alcoa reduce requisition-to-pay cycle time (the total elapsed time from the time a purchase requisition is generated to the time the payment for the purchase is made) by verifying receipt of goods and automatically generating receipts for payment. Alcoa's accounts payable transaction processing dropped 89 percent. Alcoa was able to centralize financial and procurement activities, which helped the company reduce nearly 20 percent of its worldwide costs. The company expects continued use of the enterprise system to reduce inventory by 25 percent, increase productivity by 15 percent, reduce materials costs by 5 percent, and improve customer service by 20 percent.

Enterprise systems provide much valuable information for improving management decision making. Corporate headquarters has access to up-to-the-minute data on sales, inventory, and production and uses this information to create more accurate sales and production forecasts. Enterprise systems provide company-wide information to help managers analyze overall product profitability or cost structures. For example, Alcoa's new enterprise system includes functionality for global human resources management that shows correlations between investment in employee training and quality; measures the company-wide costs of delivering services to employees; and measures the effectiveness of employee recruitment, compensation, and training.

Supply Chain Management Systems

Supply chain management (SCM) systems help businesses manage relationships with their suppliers. These systems provide information to help suppliers, purchasing firms, distributors, and logistics companies share information about orders, production, inventory levels, and delivery of products and services so that they can source, produce, and deliver goods and services efficiently. The ultimate objective is to get the right amount of their products from their source to their point of consumption with the least amount of time and with the lowest cost.

If a company and its supply network do not have accurate information, they will most likely be saddled by excessive inventories, inaccurate manufacturing plans, and missed production schedules. Inability to move products efficiently through the supply chain raises costs while degrading customer service.

For example, until it implemented a supply chain management system from SAP, Alcan Packaging had trouble fulfilling customer orders for its packaging materials for food, pharmaceuticals, and cosmetics. It did not have the information to make good decisions about how much to produce, how to allocate personnel, or how to meet the delivery dates requested by customers. It would go from working employees overtime one month to cutting back staff the next. It could not accurately project when it would meet shipment requirements (SAP, 2005).

Table 2.5 describes how firms can benefit from supply chain management systems. These systems increase firm profitability by lowering the costs of moving and making products and by enabling managers to make better decisions about how to organize and schedule sourcing, production, and distribution. Alcan expects its supply chain management system to reduce overtime by 25 percent, reduce setup costs by up to 7.5 percent, and reduce carrying inventory by up to 10 percent.

Supply chain management systems are one type of **interorganizational system** because they automate the flow of information across organizational boundaries. You will find examples of other types of interorganizational information systems throughout this text

TABLE 2.5

How Information
Systems Facilitate
Supply Chain
Management

Information from supply chain management systems helps firms
Decide when and what to produce, store, and move
Rapidly communicate orders
Track the status of orders
Check inventory availability and monitor inventory levels
Reduce inventory, transportation, and warehousing costs
Track shipments
Plan production based on actual customer demand
Rapidly communicate changes in product design

**Figure 2-16
Example of a Supply
Chain Management
System**
*Customer orders,
shipping notifications,
optimized shipping plans,
and other supply chain
information flow among
Haworth's Warehouse
Management System
(WMS), Transportation
Management System
(TMS), and its back-end
corporate systems.*

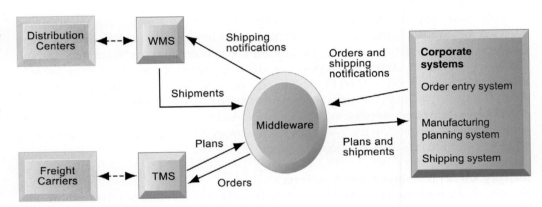

because such systems make it possible for firms to link electronically to customers and to outsource their work to other companies.

Figure 2-16 illustrates supply chain management systems used by Haworth Incorporated, a world-leading manufacturer and designer of office furniture. Haworth's 15 North American manufacturing facilities are located in North Carolina, Arkansas, Michigan, Mississippi, Texas, Ontario, Alberta, and Quebec. These facilities supply inventory to distribution centers in Michigan, Pennsylvania, Georgia, and Arkansas.

Haworth's Transportation Management System (TMS) examines customer orders, factory schedules, carrier rates and availability, and shipping costs to produce optimal lowest-cost delivery plans. These plans are generated daily and updated every 15 minutes. The TMS works with Haworth's Warehouse Management System (WMS), which tracks and controls the flow of finished goods from Haworth's distribution centers to its customers. Acting on shipping plans from TMS, WMS directs the movement of goods based on immediate conditions for space, equipment, inventory, and personnel. Haworth uses special "middleware" software to link its TMS and WMS to order entry, manufacturing planning, and shipping systems and to pass customer orders, shipping plans, and shipping notifications among the applications.

Customer Relationship Management Systems

Customer relationship management (CRM) systems help firms manage their relationships with their customers. CRM systems provide information to coordinate all of the business processes that deal with customers in sales, marketing, and service to optimize revenue, customer satisfaction, and customer retention. This information helps firms identify, attract, and retain the most profitable customers; provide better service to existing customers; and increase sales.

In the past, a firm's processes for sales, service, and marketing were highly compartmentalized, and these departments did not share much essential customer information. Some information on a specific customer might be stored and organized in terms of that person's account with the company. Other pieces of information about the same customer might be organized by products that were purchased. There was no way to consolidate all of this information to provide a unified view of a customer across the company.

For example, until recently, Saab U.S.A., which imports and distributes Saab vehicles to U.S. dealerships, had a splintered view of its customers. It had been engaging customers through three channels: its dealer network, a customer assistance center dealing with service inquiries, and a lead management center handling marketing and information requests from prospective customers. Each of these channels maintained customer data in its own systems. Fragmented customer data meant that a prospective customer might receive a direct mail offer from Saab one week and e-mail with an unrelated offer from a third-party marketing company the next week. The local dealer might not know about either of these offers, which prevented the dealer from delivering an effective pitch when the prospect visited the showroom. Lead quality was highly variable, so many dealers ignored the leads and the company had no way of tracking leads faxed to dealers.

CRM systems try to solve this problem by integrating the firm's customer-related processes and consolidating customer information from multiple communication channels—telephone, e-mail, wireless devices, retail outlets, or the Web. Detailed and accurate knowledge of customers and their preferences helps firms increase the effectiveness of their marketing campaigns and provide higher-quality customer service and support.

After Saab U.S.A. implemented three CRM applications for automotive dealers from Oracle-Siebel Systems, it was able to have a 360-degree view of each customer, including prior service-related questions and all the marketing communication the customer had ever received. Saab can track the status of referred leads by monitoring events, such as the salesperson's initial call to the customer and the scheduling and completion of a test drive.

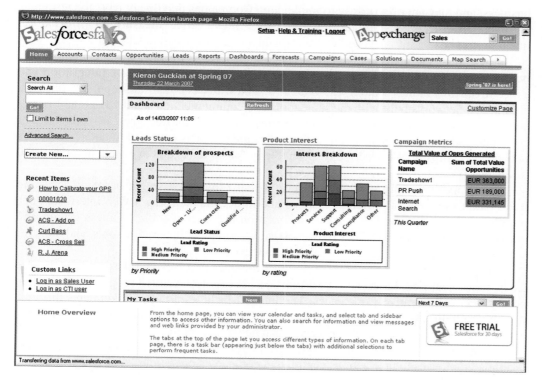

Illustrated here are some of the capabilities of Salesforce.com, a market-leading provider of on-demand customer relationship management (CRM) software. CRM systems integrate information from sales, marketing, and customer service.

The systems provide detailed information to measure the sales results of specific leads, and target leads are directed more precisely to the right salespeople at the right dealerships. Since the CRM applications were implemented, Saab's follow-up rate on sales leads has increased from 38 to 50 percent and customer satisfaction rose from 69 to 75 percent (Picarille, 2004; Siebel, 2005).

Knowledge Management Systems

The value of a firm's products and services is based not only on its physical resources but also on intangible knowledge assets. Some firms perform better than others because they have better knowledge about how to create, produce, and deliver products and services. This firm knowledge is difficult to imitate, unique, and can be leveraged into long-term strategic benefits. **Knowledge management systems (KMS)** enable organizations to better manage processes for capturing and applying knowledge and expertise. These systems collect all relevant knowledge and experience in the firm, and make it available wherever and whenever it is needed to improve business processes and management decisions. They also link the firm to external sources of knowledge.

KMS support processes for acquiring, storing, distributing, and applying knowledge, as well as processes for creating new knowledge and integrating it into the organization. They include enterprise-wide systems for managing and distributing documents, graphics, and other digital knowledge objects; systems for creating corporate knowledge directories of employees with special areas of expertise; office systems for distributing knowledge and information; and knowledge work systems to facilitate knowledge creation. Other knowledge management applications use intelligent techniques that codify knowledge for use by other members of the organization and tools for knowledge discovery that recognize patterns and important relationships in large pools of data.

We examine enterprise systems and systems for supply chain management and customer relationship management in greater detail in Chapter 8 and cover knowledge management applications in Chapter 10.

INTRANETS AND EXTRANETS

Enterprise applications create deep-seated changes in the way the firm conducts its business, and they are often costly to implement. Companies that do not have the resources to invest in enterprise applications can still achieve some measure of information integration by using intranets and extranets, which we introduced in Chapter 1.

Intranets and extranets are really more technology platforms than specific applications, but they deserve mention here as one of the tools firms use to increase integration and expedite the flow of information within the firm, and with customers and suppliers. Intranets are internal networks built with the same tools and communication standards as the Internet and are used for the internal distribution of information to employees, and as repositories of corporate policies, programs, and data. Extranets are intranets extended to authorized users outside the company. We describe the technology for intranets and extranets in more detail in Chapter 6.

An intranet typically centers on a portal that provides a single point of access to information from several different systems and to documents using a Web interface. Such portals can be customized to suit the information needs of specific business groups and individual users, if required. They may also feature e-mail, collaboration tools, and tools for searching internal corporate systems and documents.

For example, SwissAir's corporate intranet for sales provides its salespeople with sales leads, fares, statistics, libraries of best practices, access to incentive programs, discussion groups, and collaborative workspaces. The intranet includes a Sales Ticket capability that displays bulletins about unfilled airplane seats around the world to help the sales staff work with colleagues and with travel agents who can help them fill those seats.

Companies can connect their intranets to internal company transaction systems, enabling employees to take actions central to a company's operations, such as checking the status of an order or granting a customer credit. SwissAir's intranet connects to its reservation system. GUESS Jeans has an intranet called ApparelBuy.com that links to its core order processing systems.

Extranets expedite the flow of information between the firm and its suppliers and customers. SwissAir uses an extranet to provide travel agents with fare data from its intranet electronically. GUESS Jeans allows store buyers to order merchandise electronically from ApparelBuy.com. The buyers can use this extranet to track their orders through fulfillment or delivery.

COLLABORATION AND COMMUNICATION SYSTEMS: "INTERACTION" JOBS IN A GLOBAL ECONOMY

With all these systems and information, you might wonder how is it possible to make sense out of them? How do people working in firms pull it all together, work towards common goals, and coordinate plans and actions? Information systems can't make decisions, hire or fire people, sign contracts, agree on deals, or adjust the price of goods to the marketplace.

The number of people who perform these tasks in a firm is growing. A recent report from the consulting firm McKinsey and Company argued that 41 percent of the U.S. labor force is now composed of jobs where interaction (talking, e-mailing, presenting, and persuading) is the primary value-adding activity. Blue collar production jobs are now down to 15 percent of the labor force, and transactional jobs (filling out forms or reports or accepting payments) are now 25 percent of the labor force. Moreover, the "interaction" jobs are the fastest-growing: 70 percent of all new jobs created since 1998 are interaction jobs.

With globalization, firms have teams around the globe in different time zones working on the same problem, so the need for continuous interaction and communication around the clock has greatly expanded. Working 24/7 is not just a problem for call centers but involves a much larger group of managers and employees than in the past.

These interaction jobs involve knowledge and problem-solving experience that can't be put into an information system. Jobs such as sales representative, marketing manager, stock analyst, corporate lawyer, business strategist, or operations manager require sharing information and interacting with other people. Here are some business decisions that require knowledge based on collaboration and interaction:

- How much should we charge for this service?
- What kind of discount should we give this customer who is considering our competitor?
- Should we sign a three-year contract with a vendor, or would we be safer with a one-year contract?
- Should we make a special deal with our largest distributor, or work with all distributors on an equal basis?
- Should we put our price list on the Web site where our competitors can see it?
- Where should we be looking for new lines of business?

The answers to these questions generally cannot be found in structured information systems like those we have described earlier in this chapter. True, these systems help managers and employees by making essential information available. But what's needed to complete these decisions is face-to-face interaction with other employees, managers, vendors, and customers, along with systems that allow them to communicate, collaborate, and share ideas.

We now briefly introduce some of the enterprise-wide information system solutions used by business firms for this purpose. They include Internet-based collaboration environments, e-mail and instant messaging (IM), cell phones and wireless handhelds, social networking, wikis, and virtual worlds. Chapters 6, 9, and 10 describe these solutions in greater detail.

In the past, these collaboration and communication systems were not considered an essential part of the information systems field, or even an IT management concern. Today this has changed, and our view of information systems is extended to include these vital management tools.

Internet-Based Collaboration Environments

Teams of employees who work together from many different locations around the world need tools to support workgroup collaboration. These tools provide storage space for team documents, a space separate from corporate e-mail for team communications, group calendars, and an audio-visual environment where members can "meet" face to face in a live video conference. Groupware products such as IBM's Lotus Notes Collaboration Suite, Microsoft Office Groove, and the WebEx Internet conferencing system provide these capabilities.

E-mail and Instant Messaging (IM)

Worldwide, there are an estimated 120 billion legitimate e-mail messages sent each day with about 80 billion originating in the United States. One in six people in the world use e-mail. There are also about 12 billion instant messages sent every day, 8 billion of which originate in business networks. E-mail and instant messaging have been embraced by corporations as a major communication and collaboration tool supporting interaction jobs (Radicatti Group, 2007).

Cell Phones and Wireless Handhelds

Over 8 million people are BlackBerry subscribers in the United States, using wireless devices made by Research in Motion for e-mail, text messaging, instant messaging, phone, and wireless Internet connections. Of the 250 million cell phone subscribers in the United States, 90 million are business subscribers (eMarketer, 2007). Cell phones today are a basic part of a firm's telecommunications infrastructure for supporting professionals and other employees whose primary job is to talk with one another, with customers and vendors, and with their managers. Cell phones and BlackBerrys are digital devices, and the data generated by their communications may be stored in large corporate systems for later review and use in legal proceedings.

Social Networking

Most of us have visited social networking sites such as MySpace, Facebook, and Friendster, which feature tools to help people share their interests and interact. Social networking sites such as LinkedIn.com provide networking services to business professionals, while other niche sites have sprung up to serve lawyers, doctors, engineers, and even dentists. IBM is building a Community Tools component into its Lotus Notes collaboration software to add social networking features. Users will be able to submit questions to others in the company and receive answers via instant messaging. Social networking tools are quickly becoming a corporate tool for sharing ideas and collaborating among interaction-based jobs in the firm.

Wikis

Wikis are a type of Web site that makes it easy for users to contribute and edit text content and graphics without any knowledge of Web page development or programming techniques. The most well-known wiki is Wikipedia, one of the largest collaboratively edited reference projects in the world. It relies on volunteers, makes no money, accepts no advertising, and is used by 35 million people in the United States alone. It has become the world's most successful online encyclopedia, with over 20 percent of the online reference market.

Wikis are ideal tools for storing and sharing company knowledge and insights. Enterprise software vendor SAP AG has a wiki that acts as a base of information for people outside the company, such as customers and software developers who build programs that interact with SAP software. In the past, those people asked and sometimes answered questions in an informal way on SAP online forums, but that was an inefficient system, with people asking and answering the same questions over and over.

At Intel Corporation, employees built their own internal wiki in 2006, and it has been edited about 100,000 times and viewed more than 27 million times by Intel employees. The most common search is for the meaning of Intel acronyms, such as EASE for "employee access support environment" and POR for "plan of record." Other popular resources include a page about software-engineering processes at the company. Wikis are destined to become the major repository for unstructured corporate knowledge in the next five years in part because they are so much less costly than formal knowledge management systems and they can be much more dynamic and current.

Virtual Worlds

The case study concluding Chapter 1 features a detailed description of Second Life, an online 3-D virtual world where 7 million "residents" have established lives by building graphical representations of themselves known as avatars. Organizations such as IBM and Insead, an international business school with campuses in France and Singapore, are using this virtual world to house online meetings, training sessions, and "lounges." Real-world people represented by avatars meet, interact, and exchange ideas at these virtual locations. Communication takes place in the form of text messages similar to instant messages.

E-BUSINESS, E-COMMERCE, AND E-GOVERNMENT

The systems and technologies we have just described are transforming firms' relationships with customers, employees, suppliers, and logistic partners into digital relationships using networks and the Internet. So much business is now enabled by or based upon digital networks that we use the terms *electronic business* and *electronic commerce* frequently throughout this text. **Electronic business**, or **e-business**, refers to the use of digital technology and the Internet to execute the major business processes in the enterprise. E-business includes activities for the internal management of the firm and for coordination with suppliers and other business partners. It also includes **electronic commerce**, or **e-commerce**. E-commerce is the part of e-business that deals with the buying and selling of goods and services over the Internet. It also encompasses activities supporting those market transactions, such as advertising, marketing, customer support, security, delivery, and payment.

The technologies associated with e-business have also brought about similar changes in the public sector. Governments on all levels are using Internet technology to deliver information and services to citizens, employees, and businesses with which they work. **E-government** refers to the application of the Internet and networking technologies to digitally enable government and public sector agencies' relationships with citizens, businesses, and other arms of government. In addition to improving delivery of government services, e-government can make government operations more efficient and also empower citizens by giving them easier access to information and the ability to network electronically with other citizens. For example, citizens in some states can renew their driver's licenses or apply for unemployment benefits online, and the Internet has become a powerful tool for instantly mobilizing interest groups for political action and fund-raising.

2.4 The Information Systems Function in Business

We've seen that businesses need information systems to operate today and that they use many different kinds of systems. But who is responsible for running these systems? Who is responsible for making sure the hardware, software, and other technologies used by these systems are running properly and are up to date? End users manage their systems from a business standpoint, but managing the technology requires a special information systems function.

In all but the smallest of firms, the **information systems department** is the formal organizational unit responsible for information technology services. The information systems department is responsible for maintaining the hardware, software, data storage, and networks that comprise the firm's IT infrastructure. We describe IT infrastructure in detail in Chapter 4.

THE INFORMATION SYSTEMS DEPARTMENT

The information systems department consists of specialists, such as programmers, systems analysts, project leaders, and information systems managers. **Programmers** are highly trained technical specialists who write the software instructions for computers. **Systems analysts** constitute the principal liaisons between the information systems groups and the rest of the organization. It is the systems analyst's job to translate business problems and requirements into information requirements and systems. **Information systems managers** are leaders of teams of programmers and analysts, project managers, physical facility managers, telecommunications managers, or database specialists. They are also managers of computer operations and data entry staff. In addition, external specialists, such as hardware vendors and manufacturers, software firms, and consultants, frequently participate in the day-to-day operations and long-term planning of information systems.

In many companies, the information systems department is headed by a **chief information officer (CIO)**. The CIO is a senior manager who oversees the use of information technology in the firm. Today's CIOs are expected to have a strong business background as well as information systems expertise and to play a leadership role in integrating technology into the firm's business strategy. Large firms today also have positions for a chief security officer, chief knowledge officer, and chief privacy officer, all of whom work closely with the CIO.

The **chief security officer (CSO)** is in charge of information systems security for the firm and is responsible for enforcing the firm's information security policy (see Chapter 7). (Sometimes this position is called the *chief information security officer (CISO),* where information systems security is separated from physical security.) The CSO is responsible for educating and training users and information systems specialists about security, keeping management aware of security threats and breakdowns, and maintaining the tools and policies chosen to implement security.

Information systems security and the need to safeguard personal data have become so important that corporations collecting vast quantities of personal data have established positions for a **chief privacy officer (CPO)**. The CPO is responsible for ensuring that the company complies with existing data privacy laws.

The **chief knowledge officer (CKO)** is responsible for the firm's knowledge management program. The CKO helps design programs and systems to find new sources of knowledge or to make better use of existing knowledge in organizational and management processes.

End users are representatives of departments outside of the information systems group for whom applications are developed. These users are playing an increasingly large role in the design and development of information systems.

In the early years of computing, the information systems group was composed mostly of programmers who performed very highly specialized but limited technical functions. Today, a growing proportion of staff members are systems analysts and network specialists, with the information systems department acting as a powerful change agent in the organization. The information systems department suggests new business strategies and new information-based products and services, and coordinates both the development of the technology and the planned changes in the organization.

INFORMATION SYSTEMS SERVICES

Services provided by the information systems department include the following:
- Computing platforms provide computing services that connect employees, customers, and suppliers into a coherent digital environment, including large mainframes, desktop and laptop computers, servers, and wireless handheld devices.
- Telecommunications services provide data, voice, and video connectivity to employees, customers, and suppliers.

- Data management services store and manage corporate data, and provide capabilities for analyzing the data.
- Application software services provide development and support services for the firm's business systems, including enterprise-wide capabilities, such as enterprise resource planning, customer relationship management, supply chain management, and knowledge management systems, that are shared by all business units.
- Physical facilities management services develop and manage the physical installations required for computing, telecommunications, and data management services.
- IT management services plan and develop the infrastructure, coordinate with the business units for IT services, manage accounting for the IT expenditure, and provide project management services.
- IT standards services provide the firm and its business units with policies that determine which information technology will be used, when, and how.
- IT educational services provide training in system use to employees and offer managers training in how to plan for and manage IT investments.
- IT research and development services provide the firm with research on potential future information systems projects and investments that could help the firm differentiate itself in the marketplace.

In the past, firms generally built their own software and managed their own computing facilities. Today, many firms are turning to external vendors to provide these services (see Chapters 4 and 11) and are using their information systems departments to manage these service providers.

2.5 Hands-On MIS

The projects in this section give you hands-on experience analyzing a company's financial and sales data to assess business performance and profitability, using a spreadsheet to improve decision making about suppliers, and using Internet software to plan efficient transportation routes.

ANALYZING FINANCIAL PERFORMANCE

Software skills: Spreadsheet charts and formulas
Business skills: Financial statement analysis

As part of your analysis of the company for management, you have been asked to analyze data on Dirt Bikes's financial performance. Review Dirt Bikes's selected financial data in the Introduction to Dirt Bikes, which can be found at the Laudon Web site. There you will find Dirt Bikes's income statement and summary balance sheet data from 2005 to 2007, annual sales of Dirt Bikes models between 2003 and 2007, and total domestic versus international sales between 2003 and 2007.

			Sales by Model				
5							
6			Sales by Model				
7	Model	2003	2004	2005	2006	2007	
8	Enduro 250	1201	1663	2291	2312	2195	
9	Enduro 550	2832	3290	3759	4078	3647	
10	Moto 300	1755	1932	2454	2615	2627	
11	Moto 450	463	598	661	773	823	
12	TOTAL	6251	7483	9165	9778	9292	
13							

Use spreadsheet software to create graphs of Dirt Bikes's sales history from 2003 to 2007 and its domestic versus international sales from 2003 to 2007. Select the type of graph that is most appropriate for presenting the data you are analyzing.

Use the instructions at the Laudon Web site and your spreadsheet software to calculate the gross and net margins in Dirt Bikes's income statements from 2005 to 2007. You can also create graphs showing trends in selected pieces of Dirt Bikes's income statement and balance sheet data if you wish. (You may want to rearrange the historical ordering of the data if you decide to do this.)

Prepare an addition to your management report that answers these questions:

- What are Dirt Bikes's best- and worst-performing products? What is the proportion of domestic to international sales? Have international sales grown relative to domestic sales?
- Are sales (revenues) growing steadily, and, if so, at what rate? What is the cost of goods sold compared to revenues? Is it increasing or decreasing? Are the firm's gross and net margins increasing or decreasing? Are the firm's operating expenses increasing or decreasing? Is the firm heavily in debt? Does it have assets to pay for expenses and to finance the development of new products and information systems?
- (Optional) Use electronic presentation software to summarize your analysis of Dirt Bikes's performance for management.

IMPROVING DECISION MAKING: USE A SPREADSHEET TO SELECT SUPPLIERS

Software skills: Spreadsheet date functions, data filtering, DAVERAGE function
Business skills: Analyzing supplier performance and pricing

In this exercise, you will learn how to use spreadsheet software to improve management decisions about selecting suppliers. You will start with raw transactional data about suppliers organized as a large spreadsheet list. You will use the spreadsheet software to filter the data based on several different criteria to select the best suppliers for your company.

You run a company that manufactures aircraft components. You have many competitors who are trying to offer lower prices and better service to customers, and you are trying to determine whether you can benefit from better supply chain management. At the Laudon Web site for Chapter 2, you will find a spreadsheet file that contains a list of all of the items that your firm has ordered from its suppliers during the past three months. The fields in the spreadsheet file include vendor name, vendor identification number, purchaser's order number, item identification number and item description (for each item ordered from the vendor), cost per item, number of units of the item ordered (quantity), total cost of each order, vendor's accounts payable terms, order date, and actual arrival date for each order.

Prepare a recommendation of how you can use the data in this spreadsheet database to improve your decisions about selecting suppliers. Some criteria to consider for identifying

	A	B	C	D	E	F	G	H	I	J	K
2					Orders and Suppliers						
3											
4	Vendor Name	Vendor No.	Order No.	Item No.	Item Description	Item Cost	Quantity	Cost per order	A/P Terms	Order Date	Arrival Date
5	Spacetime Technologies	2	A0111	6489	O-Ring	$ 3.00	900	$ 2,700.00	25	10/10/07	10/18/07
6	Steelpin Inc.	6	A0115	5319	Shielded Cable/ft.	$ 1.10	17,500	$ 19,250.00	30	08/20/07	08/31/07
7	Steelpin Inc.	6	A0123	4312	Bolt-nut package	$ 3.75	4,250	$ 15,937.50	30	08/25/07	09/01/07
8	Steelpin Inc.	6	A0204	5319	Shielded Cable/ft.	$ 1.10	16,500	$ 18,150.00	30	09/15/07	10/05/07
9	Steelpin Inc.	6	A0205	5677	Side Panel	$ 195.00	120	$ 23,400.00	30	11/02/07	11/13/07
10	Steelpin Inc.	6	A0207	4312	Bolt-nut package	$ 3.75	4,200	$ 15,750.00	30	09/01/07	09/10/07
11	Alum Sheeting	5	A0223	4224	Bolt-nut package	$ 3.95	4,500	$ 17,775.00	30	10/15/07	10/20/07
12	Alum Sheeting	5	A0433	5417	Control Panel	$ 255.00	500	$ 127,500.00	30	10/20/07	10/27/07
13	Alum Sheeting	5	A0443	1243	Airframe fasteners	$ 4.25	10,000	$ 42,500.00	30	08/08/07	08/14/07
14	Alum Sheeting	5	A0446	5417	Control Panel	$ 255.00	406	$ 103,530.00	30	09/01/07	09/10/07
15	Spacetime Technologies	2	A0533	9752	Gasket	$ 4.05	1,500	$ 6,075.00	25	09/20/07	09/25/07
16	Spacetime Technologies	2	A0555	6489	O-Ring	$ 3.00	1,100	$ 3,300.00	25	10/05/07	10/10/07
17	Spacetime Technologies	2	A0622	9752	Gasket	$ 4.05	1,550	$ 6,277.50	25	09/25/07	10/05/07
18	Spacetime Technologies	2	A0666	5125	Shielded Cable/ft.	$ 1.15	15,000	$ 17,250.00	25	10/01/07	10/15/07
19	Spacetime Technologies	2	A0777	6489	O-Ring	$ 3.00	1,050	$ 3,150.00	25	10/29/07	11/10/07
20	Spacetime Technologies	2	A1222	4111	Bolt-nut package	$ 3.55	4,200	$ 14,910.00	25	09/15/07	10/15/07

preferred suppliers include the supplier's track record for on-time deliveries, suppliers offering the best accounts payable terms, and suppliers offering lower pricing when the same item can be provided by multiple suppliers. Use your spreadsheet software to prepare reports to support your recommendations.

ACHIEVING OPERATIONAL EXCELLENCE: USING INTERNET SOFTWARE TO PLAN EFFICIENT TRANSPORTATION ROUTES

In this exercise, you will use the same online software tool that businesses use to map out their transportation routes and select the most efficient route. The MapQuest (www.mapquest.com) Web site includes interactive capabilities for planning a trip. The software on this Web site can calculate the distance between two points and provide itemized driving directions to any location.

You have just started working as a dispatcher for Cross-Country Transport, a new trucking and delivery service based in Cleveland, Ohio. Your first assignment is to plan a delivery of office equipment and furniture from Elkhart, Indiana (at the corner of E. Indiana Ave. and Prairie Street) to Hagerstown, Maryland (corner of Eastern Blvd. N. and Potomac Ave.). To guide your trucker, you need to know the most efficient route between the two cities. Use MapQuest to find the route that is the shortest distance between the two cities. Use MapQuest again to find the route that takes the least time. Compare the results. Which route should Cross-Country use?

LEARNING TRACKS

The following Learning Tracks provide content relevant to topics covered in this chapter:

1. Challenges of Using Business Information Systems
2. Organizing the Information Systems Function

Review Summary

1 **What are the major features of a business that are important for understanding the role of information systems?** A business is a formal complex organization producing products or services for a profit. Businesses have specialized functions, such as finance and accounting, human resources, manufacturing and production, and sales and marketing. Business organizations are arranged hierarchically into levels of management. A business process is a logically related set of activities that defines how specific business tasks are performed. Business firms must monitor and respond to their surrounding environments.

2 **How do information systems support the major business functions: sales and marketing, manufacturing and production, finance and accounting, and human resources?** Sales and marketing systems help the firm identify customers for the firm's products or services, develop products and services to meet customers' needs, promote the products and services, sell the products and services, and provide ongoing customer support. Manufacturing and production systems deal with the planning, development, and production of products and services, and control the flow of production. Finance and accounting systems keep track of the firm's financial assets and fund flows. Human resources systems maintain employee records; track employee skills, job performance, and training; and support planning for employee compensation and career development.

3 **How do systems serve the various levels of management in a business and how are these systems related?** Systems serving operational management are transaction processing systems (TPS), such as payroll or order processing, that track the flow of the daily routine transactions necessary to conduct business. Management information systems (MIS) and decision-support systems (DSS) support middle management. Most MIS reports condense information from TPS and are not highly analytical. DSS support management decisions that are unique and rapidly changing, using advanced analytical models and data analysis capabilities. Executive support systems (ESS) support senior management by providing data that are often in the form of graphs and charts delivered via portals using many sources of internal and external information.

4 **How do enterprise applications, collaboration and communication systems, and intranets improve organizational performance?** Enterprise applications (enterprise systems, supply chain management systems, customer relationship management systems, and knowledge management systems) are designed to coordinate multiple functions and business processes. Enterprise systems integrate the key internal business processes of a firm into a single software system to improve coordination, efficiency, and decision making. Supply chain management systems help the firm manage its relationship with suppliers to optimize the planning, sourcing, manufacturing, and delivery of products and services. Customer relationship management uses information systems to coordinate all of the business processes surrounding the firm's interactions with its customers to optimize firm revenue and customer satisfaction. Knowledge management systems enable firms to optimize the creation, sharing, and distribution of knowledge. Jobs where interaction is the primary value-adding activity benefit from collaboration and communication systems. Intranets and extranets use Internet technology and standards to assemble information from disparate systems and present it to the user in a Web page format. Extranets make portions of private corporate intranets available to outsiders.

5 **What is the role of the information systems function in a business?** The information systems department is the formal organizational unit responsible for information technology services. It is responsible for maintaining the hardware, software, data storage, and networks that comprise the firm's IT infrastructure. The department consists of specialists, such as programmers, systems analysts, project leaders, and information systems managers, and is often headed by a CIO.

Key Terms

Business, 41
Business processes, 43
Chief information officer (CIO), 68
Chief knowledge officer (CKO), 68
Chief privacy officer (CPO), 68
Chief security officer (CSO), 68
Customer relationship management (CRM) systems, 62
Data workers, 45
Decision-support systems (DSS), 55
Electronic business (e-business), 67
Electronic commerce (e-commerce), 67

E-government, 67
End users, 68
Enterprise applications, 59
Enterprise systems, 59
Executive support systems (ESS), 57
Finance and accounting information systems, 50
Human resources information systems, 51
Information systems department, 67
Information systems managers, 68
Interorganizational system, 61
Knowledge management systems (KMS), 64
Knowledge workers, 45

Management information systems (MIS), 55
Manufacturing and production information systems, 49
Middle management, 45
Operational management, 45
Portal, 57
Production or service workers, 45
Programmers, 68
Sales and marketing information systems, 48
Senior management, 45
Supply chain management (SCM) systems, 61
Systems analysts, 68
Transaction processing systems (TPS), 54

Review Questions

1. What are the major features of a business that are important for understanding the role of information systems?
- Define a business and describe the major business functions.
- Define business processes and describe the role they play in organizations.
- Identify and describe the different levels in a business firm and their information needs.
- Explain why environments are important for understanding a business.

2. How do information systems support the major business functions: sales and marketing, manufacturing and production, finance and accounting, and human resources?
- List and describe the information systems serving each of the major functional areas of a business.

3. How do systems serve the various levels of management in a business and how are these systems related?
- Describe the characteristics of transaction processing systems (TPS) and role they play in a business.
- Describe the characteristics of MIS and explain how MIS differ from TPS and from DSS.
- Describe the characteristics of DSS and explain how DSS differ from ESS.
- Describe the relationship between TPS, MIS, DSS, and ESS.

4. How do enterprise applications, collaboration and communication systems, and intranets improve organizational performance?
- Explain how enterprise applications improve organizational performance.
- Define enterprise systems and describe how they change the way an organization works.
- Define supply chain management systems and describe how they benefit businesses.
- Define customer relationship management systems and describe how they benefit businesses.
- Describe the role of knowledge management systems in the enterprise.
- List and describe the various types of collaboration and communication systems.
- Explain how intranets and extranets help firms integrate information and business processes.

5. What is the role of the information systems function in a business?
- Describe how the information systems function supports a business.
- Compare the roles played by programmers, systems analysts, information systems managers, the chief information officer (CIO), chief security officer (CSO), and chief knowledge officer (CKO).

Discussion Questions

1. How could information systems be used to support the order fulfillment process illustrated in Figure 2-2? What are the most important pieces of information these systems should capture? Explain your answer.

2. Adopting an enterprise application is a key business decision as well as a technology decision. Do you agree? Why or why not? Who should make this decision?

Video Case

You will find a video case illustrating some of the concepts in this chapter on the Laudon Web site along with questions to help you analyze the case.

Teamwork

Describing Management Decisions and Systems

With a group of three or four other students, find a description of a manager in a corporation in *Business Week*, *Forbes*, *Fortune*, or another business magazine. Write a description of the kinds of decisions this manager has to make and the kind of information that manager would need for those decisions. Suggest how information systems could supply this information. If possible, use presentation software to present your findings to the class.

BUSINESS PROBLEM-SOLVING CASE

JetBlue Hits Turbulence

In February 2000, JetBlue started flying daily to Fort Lauderdale, Florida and Buffalo, New York, promising top-notch customer service at budget prices. The airline featured new Airbus A320 planes with leather seats, each equipped with a personal TV screen, and average one-way fares of only $99 per passenger.

JetBlue was able to provide this relatively luxurious flying experience by using information systems to automate key processes, such as ticket sales (online sales dominate) and baggage handling (electronic tags help track luggage). Jet Blue prided itself on its "paperless processes."

JetBlue's investment in information technology enabled the airline to turn a profit by running its business at 70 percent of the cost of larger competitors. At the same time, JetBlue filled a higher percentage of its seats, employed non-union workers, and established enough good will to score an impressive customer retention rate of 50 percent.

Initially, JetBlue flew only one type of plane from one vendor: the Airbus A320. This approach enabled the airline to standardize flight operations and maintenance procedures to a degree that resulted in considerable savings. CIO Jeff Cohen used the same simple-is-better strategy for JetBlue's information systems.

Cohen depended almost exclusively on Microsoft software products to design JetBlue's extensive network of information systems. (JetBlue's reservation system and systems for managing planes, crews, and scheduling are run by an outside contractor.) Using a single vendor provided a technology framework in which Cohen could keep a small staff and favor in-house development of systems over outsourcing and relying on consultants. The benefit was stable and focused technology spending. JetBlue spent only 1.5 percent of its revenue on information technology, as opposed to the 5 percent spent by competitors.

JetBlue's technology strategy helped create a pleasing flying experience for passengers. As president and chief operating officer Dave Barger put it, "Some people say airlines are powered by fuel, but this airline is powered by its IT infrastructure." JetBlue consistently found itself at the top of J.D. Power and Associates customer satisfaction surveys. JetBlue believed it had learned to work lean and smart.

The big question was whether JetBlue would be able to maintain its strategy and its success as the airline grew. By the end of 2006, the company was operating 500 flights daily in 50 cities and had $2.4 billion in annual revenue. Along the way, JetBlue committed to purchasing a new plane every five weeks through 2007, at a cost of $52 million each. Through all of this, JetBlue remained true to its formula for success and customers continued to return.

February 14, 2007, was a wake-up call. A fierce ice storm struck the New York City area that day and set in motion a string of events that threatened JetBlue's sterling reputation and its stellar customer relationships. JetBlue made a fateful decision to maintain its schedule in the belief that the horrible weather would break. JetBlue typically avoided pre-canceling flights because passengers usually preferred to have a delayed arrival than to camp out at a terminal or check into a hotel. If the airline had guessed correctly, it would have kept its revenue streams intact and made the customers who were scheduled to fly that day very happy. Most other airlines began canceling flights early in the day, believing it was the prudent decision even though passengers would be inconvenienced and money would be lost.

The other airlines were correct. Nine JetBlue planes left their gates at John F. Kennedy International Airport and were stranded on the tarmac for at least six hours. The planes were frozen in place or trapped by iced-over access roads, as was the equipment that would de-ice or move the aircraft. Passengers were confined inside the planes for up to ten and one-half hours. Supplies of food and water on the planes ran low and toilets in the restrooms began to back up. JetBlue found itself in the middle of a massive dual crisis of customer and public relations.

JetBlue waited too long to solicit help for the stranded passengers because the airline figured that the planes would be able to take off eventually. Meanwhile, the weather conditions and the delays or cancellations of other flights caused customers to flood JetBlue's reservations system, which could not handle the onslaught. At the same time, many of the airline's pilots and flight crews were also stranded and unable to get to locations where they could pick up the slack for crews that had just worked their maximum hours without rest, but did not actually go anywhere. Moreover, JetBlue did not have a system in place for the rested crews to call in and have their assignments rerouted.

The glut of planes and displaced or tired crews forced JetBlue to cancel more flights the next day, a Thursday. And the cancellations continued daily for nearly a week, with the Presidents' Day holiday week providing few opportunities for rebooking. On the sixth day, JetBlue cancelled 139 of 600 flights involving 11 other airports.

JetBlue's eventual recovery was of little solace to passengers who were stranded at the airport for days and missed reservations for family vacations. Overall, more than 1,100 flights were cancelled, and JetBlue lost $30 million. The airline industry is marked by low profit margins and high fixed costs, which means that even short revenue droughts, such as a four-day shutdown, can have devastating consequences for a carrier's financial stability.

Throughout the debacle, JetBlue's CEO David G. Neeleman was very visible and forthcoming with accountability and apologies. He was quoted many times, saying things such as, "We love our customers and we're horrified by this. There's going to be a lot of apologies."

Neeleman also admitted to the press that JetBlue's management was not strong enough and its communica-

tions system was inadequate. The department responsible for allocating pilots and crews to flights was too small. Some flight attendants were unable to get in touch with anyone who could tell them what to do for three days. With the breakdown in communications, thousands of pilots sand flight attendants were out of position, and the staff could neither find them nor tell them where to go.

JetBlue had grown too fast, and its low-cost IT infrastructure and systems could not keep up with the business. JetBlue was accustomed to saving money both from streamlined information systems and lean staffing. Under normal circumstances, the lean staff was sufficient to handle all operations, and the computer systems functioned well below their capacity. However, the ice storm exposed the fragility of the infrastructure as tasks such as rebooking passengers, handling baggage, and locating crew members became impossible.

Although Neeleman asserted in a conference call that JetBlue's computer systems were not to blame for its meltdown, critics of the company pointed out that JetBlue lacked systems to keep track of off-duty flight crews and lost baggage. Its reservation system could not expand enough to meet the high customer call volume. Navitaire, headquartered in Minneapolis, hosts the reservation system for JetBlue as well as for a dozen other discount airlines. The Navitaire system was configured to accomodate up to 650 agents at one time, which was more than sufficient under normal circumstances. During the Valentine's Day crisis, Navitaire was able to tweak the system to accomodate up to 950 agents simultaneously, but that was still not enough.

Moreover, JetBlue could not find enough qualified employees to staff its phones. The company employs about 1,500 reservation agents who work primarily from their homes, linking to its Navitaire Open Skies reservation system using an Internet-based voice communications system. Many ticketholders were unable to determine the status of their flights because the phone lines were jammed. Some callers received a recording that directed them to JetBlue's Web site. The Web site stopped responding because it could not handle the spike in visitors, leaving many passengers with no way of knowing whether they should make the trip to the airport.

JetBlue lacked a computerized system for recording and tracking lost bags. It did have a system for storing information such as the number of bags checked in by a passenger and bag tag identification numbers. But the system could not record which bags had not been picked up or their location. There was no way for a JetBlue agent to use a computer to see if a lost bag for a particular passenger was among the heap of unclaimed bags at airports where JetBlue was stranded. In the past,

JetBlue management did not feel there was a need for such a system because airport personnel were able to look up passenger records and figure out who owned leftover bags. When so many flights were canceled, the process became unmanageable.

JetBlue uses several applications provided by outsourcing vendor Sabre Airline Solutions of Southlake, Texas to manage, schedule, and track planes and crews and to develop actual flight plans. Sabre's FliteTrac application interfaces with the Navitaire reservation system to provide managers with information about flight status, fuel, passenger lists, and arrival times. Sabre's CrewTrac application tracks crew assignments and provides pilots and flight attendants access to their schedules via a secure Web portal. JetBlue uses a Navitaire application called SkySolver to determine how to redeploy planes and crews to emerge from flight disruptions. However, JetBlue found out during the Valentine's Day emergency that SkySolver was unable to transfer the information quickly to JetBlue's Sabre applications. And even if these systems had worked properly together, JetBlue would have probably been unable to locate all of its flight crews to redirect them. It did not have a system to keep track of off-duty crew members. Overtaxed phone lines prevented crew members from calling into headquarters to give their locations and availability for work.

JetBlue's response to its humiliating experience was multifaceted. On the technology front, the airline deployed new software that sends recorded messages to pilots and flight attendants to inquire about their availability. When the employees return the calls, the information they supply is entered into a system that stores the data for access and analysis. From a staffing standpoint, Neeleman promised to train 100 employees from the airline's corporate office to serve as backups for the departments that were stretched too thin by the effects of the storm.

JetBlue attempted to address its customer relations and image problems by creating a customer bill of rights to enforce standards for customer treatment and airline behavior. JetBlue would be penalized when it failed to provide proper service, and customers who were subjected to poor service would be rewarded. JetBlue set the maximum time for holding passengers on a delayed plane at five hours. The company changed its operational philosophy to make more accomodation for inclement weather.

An opportunity to test its changes arrived for JetBlue just one month after the incident that spurred the changes. Faced with another snow and ice storm in the northeast United States on March 16, 2007, JetBlue cancelled 215 flights, or about a third of its total daily slate. By canceling early, management hoped to ensure that its flight crews would be accessible and available when needed, and that airport gates would be kept clear in case flights that were already airborne had to return.

In the wake of its winter struggles, JetBlue was left to hope that its customers would be forgiving and that its losses could be offset. Neeleman pointed out that only about 10,000 of JetBlue's 30 million annual customers were inconvenienced by the airline's weather-related breakdowns. On May 10, 2007, JetBlue's Board of Directors removed Neeleman as CEO, placing him in the role of non-executive chairman. According to Liz Roche, managing partner at Customers Incorporated, a customer relationship management research and consulting firm, "JetBlue demonstrated that it's an adolescent in the airline industry and that it has a lot of learning and growing up to do."

Sources: Doug Bartholomew and Mel Duvall, "What Really Happened at JetBlue," *Baseline Magazine*, April 1, 2007; "JetBlue Cancels Hundreds of Flights," The Associated Press, accessed via www.nytimes.com, March 16, 2007; Susan Carey and Darren Everson, "Lessons on the Fly: JetBlue's New Tactics," *The Wall Street Journal*, February 27, 2007; Eric Chabrow, "JetBlue's Management Meltdown," *CIO Insight*, February 20, 2007; Jeff Bailey, "Chief 'Mortified' by JetBlue Crisis," *The New York Times*, February 19, 2007 and "Long Delays Hurt Image of JetBlue," *The New York Times*, February 17, 2007; Susan Carey and Paula Prada, "Course Change: Why JetBlue Shuffled Top Rank," *The Wall Street Journal*, May 11, 2007; Coreen Bailor, JetBlue's Service Flies South," *Customer Relationship Management*, May 2007; Thomas Hoffman, "Out-of-the-Box Airline Carries Over Offbeat Approach to IT," *Computerworld*, March 11, 2003; and Stephanie Overby, "JetBlue Skies Ahead," *CIO Magazine*, July 1, 2002.

Case Study Questions

1. What types of information systems and business functions are described in this case?

2. What is JetBlue's business model? How do its information systems support this business model?

3. What was the problem experienced by JetBlue in this case? What people, organization, and technology factors were responsible for the problem?

4. Evaluate JetBlue's response to the crisis. What solutions did the airline come up with? How were these solutions implemented? Do you think that JetBlue found the correct solutions and implemented them correctly? What other solutions can you think of that JetBlue hasn't tried?

5. How well is JetBlue prepared for the future? Are the problems described in this case likely to be repeated? Which of JetBlue's business processes are most vulnerable to breakdowns? How much will a customer bill of rights help?

Achieving Competitive Advantage with Information Systems

CHAPTER 3

STUDENT LEARNING OBJECTIVES

After completing this chapter, you will be able to answer the following questions:

1. How does Porter's competitive forces model help companies develop competitive strategies using information systems?

2. How do the value chain and value web models help businesses identify opportunities for strategic information system applications?

3. How do information systems help businesses use synergies, core competencies, and network-based strategies to achieve competitive advantage?

4. How do competing on a global scale and promoting quality enhance competitive advantage?

5. What is the role of business process reengineering (BPR) in enhancing competitiveness?

Chapter Outline

APPLE'S ITUNES: MUSIC'S NEW GATEKEEPER

Where do you buy most of the music you listen to? Up until 2003, you would have purchased CDs from a retail store, such as Tower Records or Wal-Mart, and you would have listened to the music on a boom box or portable CD player. Today, you're probably downloading the music from the Internet and playing it on a portable music player. That portable music player is most likely to be an Apple iPod storing songs from Apple's online iTunes Store.

The iPod was launched in 2001 and the iTunes Store in 2003 as the company changed its business strategy to include digital entertainment and consumer devices as well as computers. iTunes was an instant hit, selling 1.4 million songs in its first week. iTunes and iPod became a major revenue stream for the company.

Apple's online music delivery system helped revolutionize the way music is sold and played. CD sales have been declining for the past seven years, but digital music sales are climbing. Over 100 million iPods have been sold worldwide, and iTunes is now one of the largest sellers of music in the United States. It sold 1.2 billion songs in 2006 alone.

Apple nearly monopolizes digital music sales, which are climbing as CD sales continue to fall and is the third-largest music retailer in the United States.

Apple's iTunes and iPod have also emerged as key forces in how hit tunes and hit albums are created. In the past, radio deejays wielded the power to make or break hit songs and hit albums by selecting what played on the air. More recently, it has been MTV. Now iTunes and Apple have supplanted these music gatekeepers.

The iTunes Store home page displays several dozen albums, TV shows, and movie downloads for sale from among the 6 million such goods the Apple site offers. The promotional impact of appearing on the iTunes Store home page viewed by roughly 1 million people each day is equivalent to a CD being displayed at the checkout stands of all 940 Best Buy stores or featured on the front page of Wal-Mart's ad circular.

In other words, the artists and music groups who are chosen to populate the iTunes Store home page get a tremendous boost. Placement on the iTunes Store home page has put an unknown band on the map, generating millions of dollars in sales. Other groups who are not displayed so prominently may remain forever in obscurity.

In exchange for placement on the iTunes Store home page, a music group may be required to give iTunes exclusive access to new songs, special discount pricing, or interviews with band members. Most other retailers seek exclusive offerings, but Apple wields enormous clout, especially with slightly out-of-mainstream music. Although some artists have complained that iTunes "bullies" them into supplying exclusive content, most recording labels are eager to cooperate because of iTunes's ability to drive sales. Dozens of iTunes editors and label-relations staff collaborate each week to determine what selections will populate the iTunes Store home page when it is refreshed every Tuesday.

During the week when an album is featured on the iTunes Store home page, it often sells about five times more copies on average at that Web site than it does in the following three to five weeks when the album is no longer featured. For example, when Warner Music Group's Rhino Entertainment was trying to promote a few older Prince titles, it negotiated with Apple to give four albums, including "Purple Rain," prominent placements in the iTunes Store. These albums were priced at $7.99 each, two dollars less than Apple's standard album price. As a result of the prime display, digital sales of "Purple Rain" rose fivefold and sales of "The Very Best of Prince" more than doubled.

Sources: Nick Wingfield and Ethan Smith, "Music's New Gatekeeper," *The Wall Street Journal*, March 9, 2007 and Greg Sandoval, "Apple's iTunes Overtakes Amazon in Overall Music Sales," CNET News.com, June 22, 2007.

The story of Apple and iTunes illustrates some of the ways that information systems help businesses compete—and also the challenges of sustaining a competitive advantage. Apple was noted for innovative, user-friendly computers and software, but it was always overshadowed by PCs running Microsoft Windows and software products. As long as Apple was an underdog in the PC industry, it could not keep growing. Founder and CEO Steve Jobs recognized that the Internet was a new channel for selling music and entertainment and started developing products and services to tap the emerging digital entertainment market.

The chapter-opening diagram calls attention to important points raised by this case and this chapter. Apple's management saw there was an opportunity to use information technology to expand its product line and sources of revenue. It developed series of new products (the iPod, iPod nano, and iPod video) and software for online music delivery (iTunes) to tap into the growing trend for downloading music from the Internet rather than buying CDs in a physical store. Apple's digital music and video products and services helped the company change its strategic direction so that it derives more of its revenue from digital entertainment. The iPod and iTunes are information system-based products that provide a strategic advantage.

These products have had a much wider impact than just changing Apple's business model—they have helped transform the entire music industry. Nearly 20 percent of all music sold in the United States is downloaded from the Internet, with digital music sales growing at

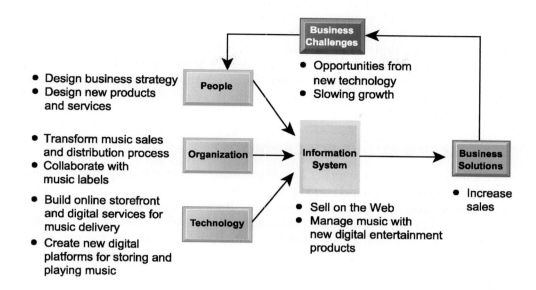

a rate of 50 percent each year. Apple's iTunes Store has become a major force in determining hit songs, albums, and artists. This has created some problems and tension for the traditional music recording industry, but it has also opened up new promotional opportunities, especially for lesser-known independent labels.

HEADS UP

In the past decade, firms using the Internet and the Web, and other kinds of information systems, have created entirely new products and services, and entire new industries and businesses. Other firms have achieved operational excellence and much closer relationships with customers and suppliers. In so doing, these firms often have achieved competitive advantages over others. Every business student and future manager should know about the strategic uses of information technology.

3.1 Using Information Systems to Achieve Competitive Advantage

In almost every industry you examine, you will find that some firms do better than most others. There's almost always a stand-out firm. In the automotive industry, Toyota is considered a superior performer. In pure online retail, Amazon is the leader; in off-line retail, Wal-Mart, the largest retailer on earth, is the leader. In online music, Apple's iTunes is considered the leader with more than 75 percent of the downloaded music market, and in the related industry of digital music players, the iPod is the leader. In Web search, Google is considered the leader.

Firms that "do better" than others are said to have a competitive advantage over others: They either have access to special resources that others do not, or they are able to use commonly available resources more efficiently—usually because of superior knowledge and information assets. In any event, they do better in terms of revenue growth, profitability, or productivity growth (efficiency), all of which ultimately in the long run translate into higher stock market valuations than their competitors.

But why do some firms do better than others and how do they achieve competitive advantage? How can you analyze a business and identify its strategic advantages? How can you develop a strategic advantage for your own business? And how do information systems contribute to strategic advantages? One answer to these questions is Michael Porter's competitive forces model.

PORTER'S COMPETITIVE FORCES MODEL

Arguably, the most widely used model for understanding competitive advantage is Michael Porter's **competitive forces model** (see Figure 3-1). This model provides a general view of the firm, its competitors, and the firm's environment. Recall in Chapter 2 we described the importance of a firm's environment and the dependence of firms on environments. Porter's model is all about the firm's general business environment. In this model, five competitive forces shape the fate of the firm.

Traditional Competitors
All firms share market space with other competitors who are continuously devising new, more efficient ways to produce by introducing new products and services, and attempting to attract customers by developing their brands and imposing switching costs on their customers.

New Market Entrants
In a free economy with mobile labor and financial resources, new companies are always entering the marketplace. In some industries, there are very low barriers to entry, whereas in other industries, entry is very difficult. For instance, it is fairly easy to start a pizza business or just about any small retail business, but it is much more expensive and difficult to enter the computer chip business, which has very high capital costs and requires significant expertise and knowledge that is hard to obtain. New companies have several possible advantages: They are not locked into old plants and equipment, they often hire younger workers who are less expensive and perhaps more innovative, they are not encumbered by old worn-out brand names, and they are "more hungry" (more highly motivated) than traditional occupants of an industry. These advantages are also their

Figure 3-1
Porter's Competitive Forces Model
In Porter's competitive forces model, the strategic position of the firm and its strategies are determined not only by competition with its traditional direct competitors but also by four forces in the industry's environment: new market entrants, substitute products, customers, and suppliers.

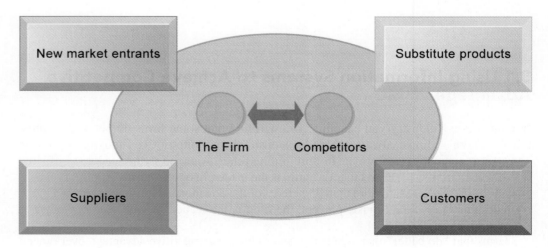

weakness: They depend on outside financing for new plants and equipment, which can be expensive; they have a less-experienced workforce; and they have little brand recognition.

Substitute Products and Services

In just about every industry, there are substitutes that your customers might use if your prices become too high. New technologies create new substitutes all the time. Even oil has substitutes: Ethanol can substitute for gasoline in cars; vegetable oil for diesel fuel in trucks; and wind, solar, coal, and hydro power for industrial electricity generation. Likewise, Internet telephone service can substitute for traditional telephone service, and fiber-optic telephone lines to the home can substitute for cable TV lines. And, of course, an Internet music service that allows you to download music tracks to an iPod is a substitute for CD-based music stores. The more substitute products and services in your industry, the less you can control pricing and the lower your profit margins.

Customers

A profitable company depends in large measure on its ability to attract and retain customers (while denying them to competitors), and charge high prices. The power of customers grows if they can easily switch to a competitor's products and services, or if they can force a business and its competitors to compete on price alone in a transparent marketplace where there is little product differentiation, and all prices are known instantly (such as on the Internet). For instance, in the used college textbook market on the Internet, students (customers) can find multiple suppliers of just about any current college textbook. In this case, online customers have extraordinary power over used-book firms.

Suppliers

The market power of suppliers can have a significant impact on firm profits, especially when the firm cannot raise prices as fast as suppliers can. The more different suppliers a firm has, the greater control it can exercise over suppliers in terms of price, quality, and delivery schedules. For instance, manufacturers of laptop PCs almost always have multiple competing suppliers of key components, such as keyboards, hard drives, and display screens.

INFORMATION SYSTEM STRATEGIES FOR DEALING WITH COMPETITIVE FORCES

So what is a firm to do when it is faced with all these competitive forces? And how can the firm use information systems to counteract some of these forces? How do you prevent substitutes and inhibit new market entrants? How do you become the most successful firm in an industry in terms of profit and share price (two measures of success)?

Basic Strategy 101: Align the IT with the Business Objectives

The basic principle of IT strategy for a business is to ensure the technology serves the business, and not the other way around. The research on IT and business performance has found that (a) the more successfully a firm can align its IT with its business goals, the more profitable it will be, and (b) only about one-quarter of firms achieve alignment of IT with business. About half of a business firm's profits can be explained by alignment of IT with business (Luftman, 2003; Henderson, et al., 1996).

Most businesses get it wrong: IT takes on a life of its own and does not serve management and shareholder interests very well. Instead of business people taking an active role in shaping IT to the enterprise, they ignore it, claim to not understand IT, and tolerate failure in the IT area as just a nuisance to work around. Such firms pay a hefty price in poor performance. Successful firms and managers understand what IT can do and how it works, take an active role in shaping its use, and measure its impact on revenues and profits.

So how do you as a manager achieve this alignment of IT with business? In the following sections, we discuss some basic ways to do this, but here's a summary:
- Identify your business strategy and goals.
- Break these strategic goals down into concrete activities and processes.
- Identify how you will measure progress towards the business goals (e.g. metrics).
- Ask yourself "How can information technology help me achieve progress towards our business goals and how it will improve our business processes and activities?"
- Measure actual performance. Let the numbers speak.

Let's see how this works out in practice. There are four generic strategies, each of which often is enabled by using information technology and systems: low-cost leadership, product differentiation, focus on market niche, and strengthening customer and supplier intimacy.

Low-Cost Leadership

Use information systems to achieve the lowest operational costs and the lowest prices. The classic example is Wal-Mart. By keeping prices low and shelves well stocked using a legendary inventory replenishment system, Wal-Mart became the leading retail business in the United States. Wal-Mart's continuous replenishment system sends orders for new merchandise directly to suppliers as soon as consumers pay for their purchases at the cash register. Point-of-sale terminals record the bar code of each item passing the checkout counter and send a purchase transaction directly to a central computer at Wal-Mart headquarters. The computer collects the orders from all Wal-Mart stores and transmits them to suppliers. Suppliers can also access Wal-Mart's sales and inventory data using Web technology.

Because the system replenishes inventory with lightning speed, Wal-Mart does not need to spend much money on maintaining large inventories of goods in its own warehouses. The system also enables Wal-Mart to adjust purchases of store items to meet customer demands. Competitors, such as Sears, have been spending 24.9 percent of sales on overhead. But by using systems to keep operating costs low, Wal-Mart pays only 16.6 percent of sales revenue for overhead. (Operating costs average 20.7 percent of sales in the retail industry.)

Wal-Mart's continuous inventory replenishment system uses sales data captured at the checkout counter to transmit orders to restock merchandise directly to its suppliers. The system enables Wal-Mart to keep costs low while fine-tuning its merchandise to meet customer demands.

Wal-Mart's continuous replenishment system is also an example of an **efficient customer response system**. An efficient customer response system directly links consumer behavior to distribution and production and supply chains. Wal-Mart's continuous replenishment system provides such an efficient customer response. Dell Inc.'s assemble-to-order system, described in the following discussion, is another example of an efficient customer response system.

Product Differentiation

Use information systems to enable new products and services, or greatly change the customer convenience in using your existing products and services. For instance, Google continuously introduces new and unique search services on its Web site, such as Google Maps. By purchasing PayPal, an electronic payment system, in 2003, eBay made it much easier for customers to pay sellers and expanded use of its auction marketplace. Apple created iPod, a unique portable digital music player, plus a unique online Web music service where songs can be purchased for 99 cents. Continuing to innovate, Apple recently introduced a portable iPod video player and music-playing cell phone.

Manufacturers and retailers are starting to use information systems to create products and services that are customized and personalized to fit the precise specifications of individual customers. Dell Inc. sells directly to customers using assemble-to-order manufacturing. Individuals, businesses, and government agencies can buy computers directly from Dell, customized with the exact features and components they need. They can place their orders directly using a toll-free telephone number or by accessing Dell's Web site. Once Dell's production control receives an order, it directs an assembly plant to assemble the computer using components from an on-site warehouse based on the configuration specified by the customer.

Lands' End customers can use its Web site to order jeans, dress pants, chino pants, and shirts custom-tailored to their own specifications. Customers enter their measurements into a form on the Web site, which then transmits each customer's specifications over a network to a computer that develops an electronic made-to-measure pattern for that customer. The individual patterns are used to drive fabric-cutting equipment at a manufacturing plant. Lands' End has almost no extra production costs because the process does not require

On the Dell Inc. Web site, customers can select the options they want and order their computer custom built to these specifications. Dell's assemble-to-order system is a major source of competitive advantage.

additional warehousing, production overruns, and inventories, and the cost to the customer is only slightly higher than that of a mass-produced garment. This ability to offer individually tailored products or services using the same production resources as mass production is called **mass customization**.

Table 3.1 lists a number of companies that have developed IS-based products and services that other firms have found difficult to copy.

Focus on Market Niche

Use information systems to enable a specific market focus, and serve this narrow target market better than competitors. Information systems support this strategy by producing and analyzing data for finely tuned sales and marketing techniques. Information systems enable companies to analyze customer buying patterns, tastes, and preferences closely so that they efficiently pitch advertising and marketing campaigns to smaller and smaller target markets.

The data come from a range of sources—credit card transactions, demographic data, purchase data from checkout counter scanners at supermarkets and retail stores, and data collected when people access and interact with Web sites. Sophisticated software tools find patterns in these large pools of data and infer rules from them that can be used to guide decision making. Analysis of such data drives one-to-one marketing where personal messages can be created based on individualized preferences. For example, Hilton Hotels' OnQ system analyzes detailed data collected on active guests in all of its properties to determine the preferences of each guest and each guest's profitability. Hilton uses this information to give its most profitable customers additional privileges, such as late check-outs. Contemporary customer relationship management (CRM) systems feature analytical capabilities for this type of intensive data analysis (see Chapters 2 and 8).

The Interactive Session on Organizations describes how AutoNation is mining customer data to determine which models and options they are most likely to buy and then using that information to make better decisions about stocking inventory. But it is having trouble getting car manufacturers to use their findings from the data to drive production. As you read this case, try to identify the problem this company is facing; what alternative solutions are available to management; and the people, organization, and technology issues that have to be addressed when developing the solution.

Strengthen Customer and Supplier Intimacy

Use information systems to tighten linkages with suppliers and develop intimacy with customers. Chrysler Corporation uses information systems to facilitate direct access from suppliers to production schedules, and even permits suppliers to decide how and when to ship suppliers to Chrysler factories. This allows suppliers more lead time in producing goods. On the customer side, Amazon keeps track of user preferences for book and CD purchases, and can recommend titles purchased by others to its customers. Strong linkages to customers and suppliers increase switching costs, and loyalty to your firm.

TABLE 3.1 IS-Enabled New Products and Services Providing Competitive Advantage		
Amazon: One-click shopping	Amazon holds a patent on one-click shopping that it licenses to other online retailers
Online music: Apple iPod and iTunes	An integrated handheld player backed up with an online library of 6 million songs
Golf club customization: Ping	Customers can select from more than 1 million different golf club options; a build-to-order system ships their customized clubs within 48 hours
Online person-to-person payment: PayPal.com	Enables transfer of money between individual bank accounts and between bank accounts and credit card accounts

INTERACTIVE SESSION: ORGANIZATIONS   Can Detroit Make the Cars Customers Want?

Burger King lets you "have it your way." Your local car dealer is usually not quite so customer friendly. A typical ready-to-buy car shopper may walk into the dealership with an idea of how much he or she wants to spend and which features the car should include for that price.

Many dealers will order a customized vehicle for a customer, but such an order usually adds six to eight weeks to the transaction. The customer who wants to buy on the spot must choose from cars on the lot that the manufacturer has already configured, priced, and shipped. Despite manufacturer incentives and rebates to entice customers to purchase, dealers often have a glut of new cars sitting in their lots for months at a time that no one wants to buy. The swollen inventory and slow turnaround hurt dealers because they must borrow money to pay for the cars the manufacturers ship.

AutoNation, the largest chain of car dealers in the United States, is no exception. With over $19 billion in annual revenue, AutoNation is the leading seller of automobiles in the country. The company has 257 dealerships in 16 states and sells four percent of all new cars sold in the United States. But it, too, has excessive inventory that it can't easily sell.

Why don't auto manufacturers try harder to produce the car models and options customers actually want? One reason is that their manufacturing processes are not set up to do so and have been geared toward optimizing the efficiency of the production plant. It has become imperative for the manufacturers to keep their plants running regardless of demand to pay for the rising costs of employee healthcare and pensions. Furthermore, auto workers must be paid most of their salaries regardless of whether they are working, so the manufacturers want them working all the time. Pushing out factory-friendly vehicles keeps revenue streams flowing because the automakers are paid as soon as the cars ship to the dealers.

These days, with so many options available for cars, this manufacturing strategy makes less sense. For example, a dealer in Florida may get stuck with four-wheel drive SUVs that, while in demand in climates that see regular snowfall, have little appeal to drivers in the Sunshine State. Similarly, a mid-priced car that is so loaded with options that it reaches luxury prices will be passed over in favor of the better car.

Historically, dealers have been independent or small chains selling a single brand of car and having little bargaining power. They had to accept whatever the auto manufacturers shipped them even if it was bad for business. With the growth of chains like AutoNation, the dealers have gained more power in the relationship.

AutoNation's CEO Michael J. Jackson is pressuring the Big Three to cut back on production and focus on building cars that customers actually want. Jackson's intent is not simply to tell automakers what to do. He wants to show them the way. AutoNation already has experience working with data on the habits of car buyers and the most popular configurations of all makes of vehicles. The work started when the company put forth a major effort to consolidate the customer lists from its hundreds of dealerships.

AutoNation used proprietary analytic software as well as assistance from DME, a marketing firm with expertise in creating customized direct mail campaigns. AutoNation no longer sends out the same mailing to every customer who has opted to be on the mailing list. The chain has divided customers into 62 groups that receive mailings that have been customized for each group with relevant sales pitches and service specials. Service revenues in particular have received a boost from this sort of targeted marketing. AutoNation's goal for its data is to offer products and services that its customers want rather than sifting through its data to find customers that might want the products it already has.

AutoNation is now applying these principles of market intelligence to auto manufacturing. By mining consumer data, Jackson wants to pinpoint the few configurations of each vehicle among thousands of possible variations that are most popular with buyers. That way, the manufacturers can focus on building these vehicles in the numbers that the data dictate.

Ford, GM, and Chrysler have all expressed their support for Jackson's attempts to integrate customer data with auto manufacturing processes. Mark LaNeve, head of North American sales and marketing for GM, suggested that his company might collaborate with Jackson on the creation of a predictive modeling system to bring production in line with consumer demand. At the same time, LaNeve is not overly concerned about inventory levels and does not think that the industry is in crisis. Jackson may still have a lot of campaigning to do before market intelligence and auto manufacturing truly co-exist.

Sources: Neal E. Boudette, "Big Dealer to Detroit: Fix How You Make Cars," *The Wall Street Journal*, February 9, 2007; Rob Preston, "Down to Business: Engage with Customers, Don't Just Humor Them," *InformationWeek*, February 24, 2007; John Gaffney, "AutoNation Solves Customer Information Gridlock," CRM News, October 21, 2004; Sharon Silke Carty, "Chrysler Wrestles with High Levels of Inventory as Unsold Vehicles Sit on Lots," *USA Today*, November 2, 2006; "Chrysler's Inventory Casts Long Shadow on Detroit," Reuters, November 5, 2006.

CASE STUDY QUESTIONS

1. Why is AutoNation having a problem with its inventory? Why is this also a problem for auto manufacturers such as GM, Ford, and Chrysler? How is this problem impacting the business performance of AutoNation and of the auto manufacturers?

2. What pieces of data does AutoNation need to determine which cars to stock in each of its dealerships? How can it obtain these data?

3. What is AutoNation's solution to its problem? What obstacles must AutoNation overcome to implement its solution? How effective will the solution be?

MIS IN ACTION

Explore AutoNation.com, examining all of its features and capabilities. Then answer the following questions.

1. How does this Web site help AutoNation forge closer ties with customers and potential customers?

2. What information could AutoNation collect from its Web site that would help it determine which makes and models of cars are of most interest to potential buyers?

Table 3.2 summarizes the competitive strategies we have just described. Some companies focus on one of these strategies, but you will often see companies pursuing several of them simultaneously. For example, Dell Inc. has tried to emphasize low cost as well as the ability to customize its personal computers. Parker Hannifin, described in the Interactive Session on People, competes by offering products with unique features, but it also must compete on the basis of cost for products that can be obtained from many other sources. Parker Hannifin's management uses information systems to help it implement this strategy, but it initially had trouble working this strategy out. As you read this case, try to identify the problem this company is facing; what alternative solutions are available to management; and the people, organization, and technology issues that have to be addressed when developing the solution.

Implementing any of these strategies is no simple matter. But it is possible, as evidenced by the many firms that obviously dominate their markets and that have used information systems to enable their strategies. As shown by the Parker Hannifin case and other cases

TABLE 3.2 Four Basic Competitive Strategies	**Strategy**	**Description**	**Example**
	Low-cost leadership	Use information systems to produce products and services at a lower price than competitors while enhancing quality and level of service	Wal-Mart
	Product differentiation	Use information systems to differentiate products, and enable new services and products	Google, eBay, Apple, Lands' End
	Focus on market niche	Use information systems to enable a focused strategy on a single market niche; specialize	AutoNation Harrah's
	Customer and supplier intimacy	Use information systems to develop strong ties and loyalty with customers and suppliers	Chrysler Corporation Amazon.com

INTERACTIVE SESSION: PEOPLE   Parker Hannifin Finds the Right Price

Parker Hannifin Corporation, headquartered in Cleveland, Ohio, is a $9.4 billion business that manufacturers and sells industrial parts for motion control systems such as fluid power systems and electromechanical controls. Parker Hannifin also produces components and systems for fluid purification, fuel control, air conditioning, refrigeration, and thermal management.

Overall, Parker Hannifin's 57,000 employees manufacture 800,000 parts in 292 plants covering 35 states in the United States and 46 foreign countries. The company has 417,000 customers in nearly every manufacturing, processing, and transportation industry. Parker Hannifin produces tens of thousands of different products, which are often custom-engineered.

When Donald Washkewicz took over as CEO in 2000, he found Parker Hannifin in a profit margin slump. As Washkewicz saw it, the company was holding itself back by using a pricing strategy that severely limited profit margin growth. Management determined the prices of all products by adding a flat percentage to the cost of production and delivery. Generally, the markup for any product was 35 percent. This scheme was popular among managers because of its simplicity.

Under this pricing model, it did not matter how good a product was in comparison to previous versions of the same product or to similar products offered by competitors. Even if the market allowed for an increase in profit margin, Parker Hannifin was not taking advantage of the opportunity. Additionally, if the company refined a production process to manufacture a product for less money, the selling price of the product dropped with the cost.

Washkewicz decided that his company required a strategic pricing system where prices are determined by what the market will bear based on demand or the value as perceived by the customer. Parker Hannifin was selling itself short by not exploring how much customers were willing to pay for specific products. Some industries charge premium prices based on factors such as the calendar or special circumstances. For example, airline tickets to Europe cost more in the summer than they do in the winter because they are in greater demand.

Washkewicz had to approach a change in pricing strategy carefully. With greater competition from a global economy and many customers in heavy cost-cutting modes, manufacturers had to think twice about raising prices. For Parker Hannifin, the pricing issue was complicated by the fact that approximately half of its products were custom-designed for a single customer.

To help tackle the transition to a strategic pricing plan, Washkewicz enlisted consultants and created the position of vice president of corporate strategic pricing. Together, they had to convince the company's managers that making such a significant change at a company known for its conservative culture was the right move. Washkewicz backed up his position with the observations he made on a tour of Parker Hannifin's facilities around the world in 2000. He saw positive signs in many aspects of the business: rising productivity, new accounts, and advantageous acquisitions. Yet, the company consistently came up short in its return on invested capital, as measured against similar manufacturers.

The company's pricing methods were based on an old system adopted in the 1990s that used "a cookbook approach" for calculating prices. Managers input the costs of producing each item into a computer, which then generated a suggested base price. That approach ignored instances in which Parker Hannifin had a unique or superior product for which the company could demand a higher price. But to identify these opportunities, the company needed much more sophisticated software that could analyze many other factors besides costs, with numerous combinations of products, customers, and terms of sale.

The consultants Washkewicz hired conducted a survey of Parker Hannifin's entire catalog of products and assigned each product to a category labeled A, B, C, or D. The A category represented products that the company produced in high volume and that were subject to outside competition. Due to these factors, such products were poor candidates for flexible pricing. Moving down the line of categories toward D, the products became increasingly specialized due to their rarity, their lack of competition, their niche, their quality, or the speed with which Parker Hannifin delivered them. It was with these products that the company could achieve higher returns.

The survey showed that approximately one-third of Parker Hannifin's products were priced too low. The company raised these prices by an average of 5 percent, with some going up by as much as 60 percent. In some cases, the data dictated that products receive reduced prices. Of course, distributors and customers quickly expressed their displeasure with the elevated prices. Parker Hannifin educated the distributors about the advantages of its products, enabling the distributors to convince customers that the products were worth the new prices. Eventually, most customers understood the logic behind the pricing strategy and found Parker Hannifin still to be their best source for purchasing.

The company installed new software from Vanguard's Graphical Performance Series (GPS). The software combines data from multiple sources and uses the rules established by Parker Hannifin's new pricing methodology, taking into account factors such as pricing averages, product volume, and customer type. Initially the company's strategic pricing process used report writer and spreadsheet software but had to be completed manually. Using GPS, the entire process is automated, and the information is distributed automatically to users at all levels of the organization. Parker Hannifin's product management group uses this information in its product development process to determine which products will be the most profitable.

Washkewicz assigned a pricing guru to implement strategic pricing in every one of the company's 115 divisions. Since then, Parker Hannifin's return on investment has increased steadily, up to 21 percent in 2006 from 7 percent in 2002. In that same period, the company's net income jumped from $130 million to $673 million. Pricing guru Sheila Konopka summarized Washkewicz's willingness to ask the difficult question and change a culture thusly: "If we could make 35% margin for a big order—that was great. Nobody asked: 'Why not 45%?'"

Sources: Timothy Aeppel, "Seeking Perfect Prices, CEO Tears Up the Rules," *The Wall Street Journal*, March 27, 2007; "Parker-Hannifin Corporation Form 10-K," For the fiscal year ended June 30, 2006, accessed via www.parker.com, April 16, 2007; Carl Howe, "Parker-Hannifin Does Pricing the Right Way," SeekingAlpha.com, March 29, 2007; Joseph Ogando, "Parker's Innovation Strategy," www.designnews.com, March 26, 2007; and Joseph Ogando, "Parker Develops Smarter Seal," www.designnews.com, March 26, 2007.

CASE STUDY QUESTIONS

1. What is strategic pricing? How does it work? What data are required?

2. What role do information systems play in strategic pricing? What role do people play in getting a strategic pricing system to work?

3. What kind of impact does strategic pricing have on a business such as Parker Hannifin?

4. What other kinds of businesses could benefit from strategic pricing?

5. How are value chain and competitive forces analysis related to Parker Hannifin's strategic pricing?

MIS IN ACTION

Briefly explore Parker Hannifin's Web site. Click on the Markets section and select one of its markets to examine in greater detail. Click on Products for the market you have selected and answer the following questions:

1. What products does Parker Hannifin produce for the market you selected?

2. Which of these products are likely to be Category A products? Which are likely to be Category D products? To answer this question, review the product description and also search the Web to see if you can find competing products.

throughout this book, successfully using information systems to achieve a competitive advantage requires a precise coordination of technology, organizations, and people. Indeed, as many have noted with regard to Wal-Mart, Dell, and Amazon, the ability to successfully implement information systems is not equally distributed, and some firms are much better at it than others. It is not simply a matter of purchasing computers and plugging them into the wall socket. We discuss these topics throughout the book.

THE INTERNET'S IMPACT ON COMPETITIVE ADVANTAGE

The Internet has nearly destroyed some industries and has severely threatened more. The Internet has also created entirely new markets and formed the basis for thousands of new businesses. The first wave of e-commerce transformed the business world of books, music, and air travel. In the second wave, eight new industries are facing a similar transformation scenario: telephone services, movies, television, jewelry, real estate, hotels, bill payments, and software. The breadth of e-commerce offerings grows, especially in travel, information clearinghouses, entertainment, retail apparel, appliances, and home furnishings.

For instance, the printed encyclopedia industry and the travel agency industry have been nearly decimated by the availability of substitutes over the Internet. Likewise, the Internet has had a significant impact on the retail, music, book, brokerage, and newspaper industries. At the same time, the Internet has enabled new products and services, new business models, and new industries to spring up every day from eBay and Amazon, to iTunes and Google. In this sense, the Internet is "transforming" entire industries, forcing firms to change how they do business.

Because of the Internet, the traditional competitive forces are still at work, but competitive rivalry has become much more intense (Porter, 2001). Internet technology is based on universal standards that any company can use, making it easy for rivals to compete on price alone and for new competitors to enter the market. Because information is available to everyone, the Internet raises the bargaining power of customers, who can quickly find the lowest-cost provider on the Web. Profits have been dampened. Some industries, such as the travel industry and the financial services industry, have been more impacted than others. Table 3.3 summarizes some of the potentially negative impacts of the Internet on business firms identified by Porter.

However, contrary to Porter's somewhat negative assessment, the Internet also creates new opportunities for building brands and building very large and loyal customer bases that are willing to pay a premium for the brand, for example, Yahoo!, eBay, BlueNile, RedEnvelope, Amazon, and many others. In addition, as with all IT-enabled business initiatives, some firms are far better at using the Internet than other firms are, which creates new strategic opportunities for the successful firms.

THE BUSINESS VALUE CHAIN MODEL

Although the Porter model is very helpful for identifying competitive forces and suggesting generic strategies, it is not very specific about what exactly to do, and it does not provide a methodology to follow for achieving competitive advantages. If your goal is to achieve operational excellence, where do you start? Here's where the business value chain model is helpful.

The **value chain model** highlights specific activities in the business where competitive strategies can best be applied (Porter, 1985) and where information systems are most likely to have a strategic impact. This model identifies specific, critical leverage points where a

Competitive Force	Impact of the Internet
Substitute products or services	Enables new substitutes to emerge with new approaches to meeting needs and performing functions
Customers' bargaining power	Availability of global price and product information shifts bargaining power to customers
Suppliers' bargaining power	Procurement over the Internet tends to raise bargaining power over suppliers; suppliers can also benefit from reduced barriers to entry and from the elimination of distributors and other intermediaries standing between them and their users
Threat of new entrants	The Internet reduces barriers to entry, such as the need for a sales force, access to channels, and physical assets; it provides a technology for driving business processes that makes other things easier to do
Positioning and rivalry among existing competitors	Widens the geographic market, increasing the number of competitors and reducing differences among competitors; makes it more difficult to sustain operational advantages; puts pressure to compete on price

TABLE 3.3

Impact of the Internet on Competitive Forces and Industry Structure

firm can use information technology most effectively to enhance its competitive position. The value chain model views the firm as a series or chain of basic activities that add a margin of value to a firm's products or services. These activities can be categorized as either primary activities or support activities (see Figure 3-2).

Primary activities are most directly related to the production and distribution of the firm's products and services, which create value for the customer. Primary activities include inbound logistics, operations, outbound logistics, sales and marketing, and service. Inbound logistics includes receiving and storing materials for distribution to production. Operations transforms inputs into finished products. Outbound logistics entails storing and distributing finished products. Sales and marketing includes promoting and selling the firm's products. The service activity includes maintenance and repair of the firm's goods and services.

Support activities make the delivery of the primary activities possible and consist of organization infrastructure (administration and management), human resources (employee recruiting, hiring, and training), technology (improving products and the production process), and procurement (purchasing input).

Now you can ask at each stage of the value chain, "How can we use information systems to improve operational efficiency and improve customer and supplier intimacy?" This will force you to critically examine how you perform value-adding activities at each stage and how the business processes might be improved. For example, value chain analysis would indicate that Parker Hannifin should improve its processes for product pricing and product development. You can also begin to ask how information systems can be used to improve the relationship with customers and with suppliers who lie outside the firm value chain but belong to the firm's extended value chain where they are absolutely critical to your success. Here, supply chain management systems that coordinate the flow of resources into your firm, and customer relationship management systems that coordinate your sales and support employees with customers are two of the most common system applications that result from a business value chain analysis. We discuss these enterprise applications in detail later in Chapter 8.

Figure 3-2
The Value Chain Model

This figure provides examples of systems for both primary and support activities of a firm and of its value partners that would add a margin of value to a firm's products or services.

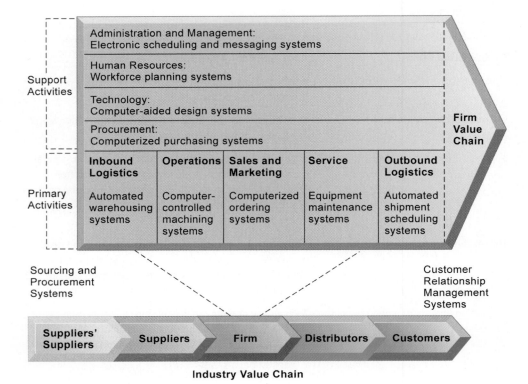

Industry Value Chain

Using the business value chain model will also cause you to consider benchmarking your business processes against your competitors or others in related industries, and identifying industry best practices. **Benchmarking** involves comparing the efficiency and effectiveness of your business processes against strict standards and then measuring performance against those standards. Industry **best practices** are usually identified by consulting companies, research organizations, government agencies, and industry associations as the most successful solutions or problem-solving methods for consistently and effectively achieving a business objective.

Once you have analyzed the various stages in the value chain at your business, you can come up with candidate applications of information systems. Then, once you have a list of candidate applications, you can decide which to develop first. By making improvements in your own business value chain that your competitors might miss, you can achieve competitive advantage by attaining operational excellence, lowering costs, improving profit margins, and forging a closer relationship with customers and suppliers. If your competitors are making similar improvements, then at least you will not be at a competitive disadvantage—the worst of all cases!

Extending the Value Chain: The Value Web

Figure 3-2 shows that a firm's value chain is linked to the value chains of its suppliers, distributors, and customers. After all, the performance of most firms depends not only on what goes inside a firm but also on how well the firm coordinates with direct and indirect suppliers, delivery firms (logistics partners, such as FedEx or UPS), and, of course, customers.

How can information systems be used to achieve strategic advantage at the industry level? By working with other firms, industry participants can use information technology to develop industry-wide standards for exchanging information or business transactions electronically, which force all market participants to subscribe to similar standards. Such efforts increase efficiency, making product substitution less likely and perhaps raising entry costs—thus discouraging new entrants. Also, industry members can build industry-wide, IT-supported consortia, symposia, and communications networks to coordinate activities concerning government agencies, foreign competition, and competing industries.

Looking at the industry value chain encourages you to think about how to use information systems to link up more efficiently with your suppliers, strategic partners, and customers. Strategic advantage derives from your ability to relate your value chain to the value chains of other partners in the process. For instance, if you are Amazon.com, you would want to build systems that

- Make it easy for suppliers to display goods and open stores on the Amazon site
- Make it easy for customers to pay for goods
- Develop systems that coordinate the shipment of goods to customers
- Develop shipment tracking systems for customers

In fact, this is exactly what Amazon has done to make it one of the Web's most satisfying online retail shopping sites.

Internet technology has made it possible to create highly synchronized industry value chains called value webs. A **value web** is a collection of independent firms that use information technology to coordinate their value chains to produce a product or service for a market collectively. It is more customer driven and operates in a less linear fashion than the traditional value chain.

Figure 3-3 shows that this value web synchronizes the business processes of customers, suppliers, and trading partners among different companies in an industry or in related industries. These value webs are flexible and adaptive to changes in supply and demand. Relationships can be bundled or unbundled in response to changing market conditions. Firms will accelerate time to market and to customers by optimizing their value web relationships to make quick decisions on who can deliver the required products or services at the right price and location.

Figure 3-3
The Value Web
The value web is a networked system that can synchronize the value chains of business partners within an industry to respond rapidly to changes in supply and demand.

SYNERGIES, CORE COMPETENCIES, AND NETWORK-BASED STRATEGIES

A large corporation is typically a collection of businesses. Often, the firm is organized financially as a collection of strategic business units, and the returns to the firm are directly tied to the performance of all the strategic business units. For instance, General Electric—one of the largest industrial firms in the world—is a collection of aerospace, heavy manufacturing, electrical appliance, medical imaging, electronics, and financial services firms called business units. Information systems can improve the overall performance of these business units by promoting communication, synergies, and core competencies among the units.

Synergies

The idea of synergies is that when the output of some units can be used as inputs to other units, or two organizations can pool markets and expertise, these relationships lower costs and generate profits. Recent bank and financial firm mergers, such as the merger of JPMorgan Chase and Bank One Corporation and Bank of America and FleetBoston Financial Corporation, occurred precisely for this purpose.

One use of information technology in these synergy situations is to tie together the operations of disparate business units so they can act as a whole. For example, merging with Bank One provided JPMorgan Chase with a massive network of retail branches in the Midwest and Southwest. Information systems would help the merged banks lower retailing costs and increase cross-marketing of financial products.

Enhancing Core Competencies

Yet another way to use information systems for competitive advantage is to think about ways that systems can enhance core competencies. The argument is that the performance of all business units can increase insofar as these business units develop, or create, a central core of competencies. A **core competency** is an activity for which a firm is a world-class leader. Core competencies may involve being the world's best miniature parts designer, the best package delivery service, or the best thin-film manufacturer. In general, a core competency relies on knowledge that is gained over many years of experience and a first-class research organization, or simply key people who follow the literature and stay abreast of new external knowledge.

Any information system that encourages the sharing of knowledge across business units enhances competency. Such systems might encourage or enhance existing competencies and help employees become aware of new external knowledge; such systems might also help a business leverage existing competencies to related markets.

For example, Procter & Gamble (P&G), a world leader in brand management and consumer product innovation, uses a series of systems to enhance its core competencies. P&G uses an intranet called InnovationNet to help people working on similar problems share ideas and expertise. The system connects those working in research and development (R&D), engineering, purchasing, marketing, legal affairs, and business information systems around the world, using a portal to provide browser-based access to documents, reports, charts, videos, and other data from various sources. In 2001, InnovationNet added a directory of subject matter experts who can be tapped to give advice or collaborate on problem solving and product development, and created links to outside research scientists and 150 entrepreneurs who are searching for new, innovative products worldwide.

Network-Based Strategies

Internet and networking technology have spawned strategies that take advantage of firms' abilities to create networks or network with each other. Network-based strategies include the use of network economics and a virtual company model.

Business models based on a network may help firms strategically by taking advantage of **network economics**. In traditional economics—the economics of factories and agriculture—production experiences diminishing returns. The more any given resource is applied to production, the lower the marginal gain in output, until a point is reached where the additional inputs produce no additional outputs. This is the law of diminishing returns, and it is the foundation for most of modern economics.

In some situations, the law of diminishing returns does not work. For instance, in a network, the marginal costs of adding another participant are about zero, whereas the marginal gain is much larger. The larger the number of subscribers in a telephone system or the Internet, the greater the value to all participants because each user can interact with more people. It is no more expensive to operate a television station with 1,000 subscribers than with 10 million subscribers. The value of a community of people grows with size, whereas the cost of adding new members is inconsequential.

From this network economics perspective, information technology can be strategically useful. Internet sites can be used by firms to build *communities of users*—like-minded customers who want to share their experiences. This can build customer loyalty and enjoyment, and build unique ties to customers. eBay, the giant online auction site, and iVillage, an online community for women, are examples. Both businesses are based on networks of millions of users, and both companies have used the Web and Internet communication tools to build communities. The more people offering products on eBay, the more valuable the eBay site is to everyone because more products are listed, and more competition among suppliers lowers prices. Network economics also provide strategic benefits to commercial software vendors. The value of their software and complementary software products increases as more people use them, and there is a larger installed base to justify continued use of the product and vendor support.

Another network-based strategy uses the model of a virtual company to create a competitive business. A **virtual company**, also known as a *virtual organization*, uses networks to link people, assets, and ideas, enabling it to ally with other companies to create and distribute products and services without being limited by traditional organizational boundaries or physical locations. One company can use the capabilities of another company without being physically tied to that company. The virtual company model is useful when a company finds it cheaper to acquire products, services, or capabilities from an external vendor or when it needs to move quickly to exploit new market opportunities and lacks the time and resources to respond on its own.

Fashion companies, such as GUESS, Ann Taylor, Levi Strauss, and Reebok, enlist Hong Kong-based Li & Fung to manage production and shipment of their garments. Li & Fung handles product development, raw material sourcing, production planning, quality assurance, and shipping. Li & Fung does not own any fabric, factories, or machines, outsourcing all of its work to a network of more than 7,500 suppliers in 37 countries all over the world. Customers place orders to Li & Fung over its private extranet. Li & Fung then sends instructions to appropriate raw material suppliers and factories where the clothing is produced. The Li & Fung extranet tracks the entire production process for each order. Working as a virtual company keeps Li & Fung flexible and adaptable so that it can design and produce the products ordered by its clients in short order to keep pace with rapidly changing fashion trends.

DISRUPTIVE TECHNOLOGIES: RIDING THE WAVE

Sometimes a new technology comes along like a tsunami and destroys everything in its path. Some firms are able to create these tsunamis and ride the wave to profits; others learn quickly and are able to swim with the current; still others are obliterated because their products, services, and business models are obsolete. They may be very efficient at doing what no longer needs to be done! There are also cases where no firms benefit, and all the gains go to consumers (firms fail to capture any profits). Business history is filled with examples of **disruptive technologies**. Table 3.4 describes just a few disruptive technologies from the past and some from the likely near-term future.

Disruptive technologies are tricky. Firms that invent disruptive technologies as "first movers" do not always benefit if they lack the resources to really exploit the technology or fail to see the opportunity. The MITS Altair 8800 is widely considered the first PC, but its inventors did not take advantage of their first-mover status. Second movers, so-called

TABLE 3.4 Disruptive Technologies: Winners and Losers	Technology	Description	Winners and Losers
	Transistor (1947)	Low power, compact, semiconductor switch that destroyed the vacuum tube industry	Transistor manufacturing firms win (Texas Instruments), while vacuum tube manufacturers decline (RCA, Sylvania)
	Microprocessor chips (1971)	Thousands and eventually millions of transistors on a silicon chip	Microprocessor firms win (Intel, Texas Instruments), while transistor firms (GE) decline
	Personal computers (1975)	Small, inexpensive, but fully functional desktop computers	PC manufacturers (HP, Apple, IBM) and chip manufacturers (Intel) prosper, while mainframe (IBM) and minicomputer (DEC) firms lose
	PC word processing software (1979)	Inexpensive, limited but functional text editing and formatting for personal computers	PC and software manufacturers (Microsoft, HP, Apple) prosper, while the typewriter industry disappears
	World Wide Web (1989)	A global database of digital files and "pages" instantly available	Owners of online content and news benefit, while traditional publishers (newspapers, magazines, and broadcast television) lose

TABLE 3.4

Continued...

Internet music (1998) services	Repositories of downloadable music on the Web with acceptable fidelity	Owners of online music collections (MP3.com, iTunes), telecommunications providers who own Internet backbone (ATT, Verizon), and local Internet service providers win, while record label firms and music retailers lose (Tower Records)
PageRank algorithm	A method for ranking Web pages in terms of their popularity to supplement Web search by key terms	Google wins (it owns the patent), while traditional key word search engines (Alta Vista) lose
Online video search algorithms	Using a family of techniques from speech recognition to text classification in order to make large video collections easily searchable	Online video search companies (Blinkx) win, while traditional search engines at Yahoo!, Amazon, and even Google are challenged
Software as Web service	Using the Internet to provide remote access to online software	Online software services companies (Salesforce.com) win, while traditional "boxed" software companies (Microsoft, SAP, Oracle) lose
Online print services	Using the Internet to provide remote access to digital printers and online designers	Online print process firms gain (digitalpressonline.com), while traditional printers lose (RR Donnelly)

"fast followers" such as IBM and Microsoft, reaped the rewards. ATMs revolutionized retail banking, but the inventor, Citibank, was copied by other banks, and ultimately all banks used ATMs with the benefits going mostly to the consumers. Google was not a first mover in search but an innovative follower that was able to patent a powerful new search algorithm called PageRank. So far it has been able to hold onto its lead while most other search engines have faded down to small market shares.

3.2 Competing on a Global Scale

Look closely at your jeans or sneakers. Even if they have a U.S. label, they were probably designed in California and stitched together in Hong Kong or Guatemala using materials from China or India. Call up Microsoft Help, or Verizon Help, and chances are good you will be speaking to a customer service representative located in India.

Consider the path to market for a Hewlett-Packard (HP) laptop computer, which is illustrated in Figure 3-4. The idea for the product and initial design came from HP's Laptop Design Team in the United States. HP headquarters in Houston approved the concept. Graphics processors were designed in Canada and manufactured in Taiwan. Taiwan and South Korea provided the liquid-crystal display screens and many of the memory chips. The laptop's hard disk drive came from Japan. Sources in China, Japan, Singapore, South Korea, and the United States supplied other components. Laptop assembly took place in China. Contractors in Taiwan did the machine's engineering design and collaborated with the Chinese manufacturers.

Figure 3-4
An HP Laptop's Path to Market
Hewlett-Packard and other electronics companies assign distribution and production of their products to a number of different countries.

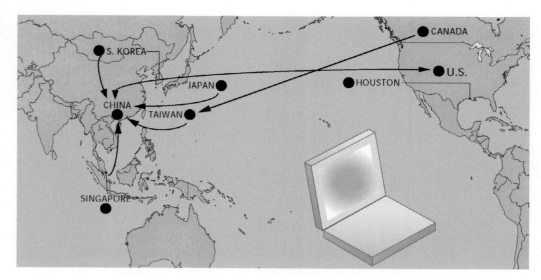

Firms pursuing a global strategy benefit from economies of scale and resource cost reduction (usually wage cost reduction). HP spread design, sourcing, and production for its laptops over multiple countries overseas to reduce logistics, tariffs, and labor costs. Digital content firms that produce Hollywood movies are able to sell millions more copies of DVDs of popular films by using foreign markets.

THE INTERNET AND GLOBALIZATION

Up until the mid-1990s, competing on a global scale was dominated by huge multinational firms, such as General Electric, General Motors, Toyota, and IBM. These large firms could afford huge investments in factories, warehouses, and distribution centers in foreign countries and proprietary networks and systems that could operate on a global scale. The emergence of the Internet into a full-blown international communications system has drastically reduced the costs of operating on a global scale, deepening the possibilities for large companies but simultaneously creating many opportunities for small and medium-sized firms.

The global Internet, along with internal information systems, puts manufacturing firms in nearly instant contact with their suppliers; Internet telephony permits millions of service calls to U.S. companies to be answered in India and Jamaica, just as easily and cheaply as if the help desk were in New Jersey or California. Likewise, the Internet makes it possible to move very large computer files with hundreds of graphics, or complex industrial designs, across the globe in seconds.

Small and medium-sized firms have created an entirely new class of "micromultinational firms." For instance, CEO Brad Oberwager runs Sundia, a company which sells watermelon juice and fruit in the United States and Europe, out of his San Francisco home. Oberwager has employees in other parts of the United States as well as in India and the Philippines, and they use Web-based information systems to manage and coordinate. A Sundia employee in the Philippines is able to take orders from a Boston grocery store for watermelon juice made from Mexican fruit. The juice is squeezed in Washington State and payment goes to Oberwager in California (Copeland, 2006).

GLOBAL BUSINESS AND SYSTEM STRATEGIES

There are four main ways of organizing businesses internationally: domestic exporter, multinational, franchiser, and transnational, each with different patterns of organizational structure or governance. In each type of global business organization, business functions may be centralized (in the home country), decentralized (to local foreign units), and coordinated (all units participate as equals).

The **domestic exporter** strategy is characterized by heavy centralization of corporate activities in the home country of origin. Production, finance/accounting, sales/marketing, human resources, and strategic management are set up to optimize resources in the home country. International sales are sometimes dispersed using agency agreements or subsidiaries, but foreign marketing is still totally reliant on the domestic home base for marketing themes and strategies. Caterpillar Corporation and other heavy capital-equipment manufacturers fall into this category of firm.

A **multinational** strategy concentrates financial management and control out of a central home base while decentralizing production, sales, and marketing operations to units in other countries. The products and services on sale in different countries are adapted to suit local market conditions. The organization becomes a far-flung confederation of production and marketing facilities in different countries. Many financial service firms, along with a host of manufacturers, such as General Motors, Chrysler, and Intel, fit this pattern.

Franchisers have the product created, designed, financed, and initially produced in the home country but rely heavily on foreign personnel for further production, marketing, and human resources. Food franchisers, such as McDonald's and Starbucks, fit this pattern. McDonald's created a new form of fast-food chain in the United States and continues to rely largely on the United States for inspiration of new products, strategic management, and financing. Nevertheless, local production of some items, local marketing, and local recruitment of personnel are required.

Transnational firms have no single national headquarters but instead have many regional headquarters and perhaps a world headquarters. In a **transnational** strategy, nearly all the value-adding activities are managed from a global perspective without reference to national borders, optimizing sources of supply and demand wherever they appear and taking advantage of any local competitive advantages. There is a strong central management core of decision making but considerable dispersal of power and financial muscle throughout the global divisions. Few companies have actually attained transnational status, but Citigroup, Sony, and Nestlé are attempting this transition.

Nestlé, the largest food and beverage company in the world, is one of the world's most globalized companies, with nearly 250,000 employees at 500 facilities in 200 countries. Nestlé launched a $2.4 billion initiative to adopt a single set of business processes and systems for procurement, distribution, and sales management using mySAP enterprise software. All of Nestlé's worldwide business units use the same processes and systems for making sales commitments, establishing factory production schedules, billing customers, compiling management reports, and reporting financial results. Nestlé has learned how to operate as a single unit on a global scale.

GLOBAL SYSTEM CONFIGURATION

Figure 3-5 depicts four types of systems configuration for global business organizations. *Centralized systems* are those in which systems development and operation occur totally at the domestic home base. *Duplicated systems* are those in which development occurs at the home base but operations are handed over to autonomous units in foreign locations. *Decentralized systems* are those in which each foreign unit designs its own unique solutions and systems. *Networked systems* are those in which systems development and operations occur in an integrated and coordinated fashion across all units.

As can be seen in Figure 3-5, domestic exporters tend to have highly centralized systems in which a single domestic systems development staff develops worldwide applications. Multinationals allow foreign units to devise their own systems solutions based on local needs with few, if any, applications in common with headquarters (the exceptions being financial reporting and some telecommunications applications). Franchisers typically develop a single system, usually at the home base, and then replicate it around the world. Each unit, no matter where it is located, has identical applications. Firms such as Nestlé

Figure 3-5
Global Business
Organization and
Systems
Configurations
*The large Xs show the
dominant patterns, and
the small Xs show the
emerging patterns.
For instance, domestic
exporters rely
predominantly on
centralized systems,
but there is continual
pressure and some
development of decen-
tralized systems in local
marketing regions.*

SYSTEM CONFIGURATION	Strategy			
	Domestic Exporter	Multinational	Franchiser	Transnational
Centralized	X			
Duplicated			X	
Decentralized	x	X	x	
Networked		x		X

organized along transnational lines use networked systems that span multiple countries using powerful telecommunications networks and a shared management culture that crosses cultural barriers.

3.3 Competing on Quality and Design

Quality has developed from a business buzzword into a very serious goal for many companies. Quality is a form of differentiation. Companies with reputations for high quality, such as Lexus or Nordstrom, are able to charge premium prices for their products and services. Information systems have a major contribution to make in this drive for quality. In the services industries in particular, quality strategies are generally enabled by superior information systems and services.

WHAT IS QUALITY?

Quality can be defined from both producer and customer perspectives. From the perspective of the producer, quality signifies conformance to specifications or the absence of variation from those specifications. The specifications for a telephone might include one that states the strength of the phone should be such that it will not be dented or otherwise damaged by a drop from a four-foot height onto a wooden floor. A simple test will allow this specification to be measured.

A customer definition of quality is much broader. First, customers are concerned with the quality of the physical product—its durability, safety, ease of use, and installation. Second, customers are concerned with the quality of service, by which they mean the accuracy and truthfulness of advertising, responsiveness to warranties, and ongoing product support. Finally, customer concepts of quality include psychological aspects: the company's knowledge of its products, the courtesy and sensitivity of sales and support staff, and the reputation of the product.

Today, as the quality movement in business progresses, the definition of quality is increasingly from the perspective of the customer. Customers are concerned with getting value for their dollar and product fitness, performance, durability, and support.

Many companies have embraced the concept of **total quality management (TQM)**. Total quality management makes quality the responsibility of all people and functions within an organization. TQM holds that the achievement of quality control is an end in itself. Everyone is expected to contribute to the overall improvement of quality—the engineer who avoids design errors, the production worker who spots defects, the sales representative who presents the product properly to potential customers, and even the secretary who avoids typing mistakes. TQM derives from quality management concepts developed by American quality experts, such as W. Edwards Deming and Joseph Juran, but the Japanese popularized it.

Another quality concept that is being widely implemented today is six sigma, which Amazon.com used to reduce errors in order fulfillment. **Six sigma** is a specific measure of quality, representing 3.4 defects per million opportunities. Most companies cannot achieve this level of quality but use six sigma as a goal to implement a set of methodologies and techniques for improving quality and reducing costs. Studies have repeatedly shown that the earlier in the business cycle a problem is eliminated, the less it costs the company. Thus, quality improvements not only raise the level of product and service quality but they can also lower costs.

HOW INFORMATION SYSTEMS IMPROVE QUALITY

Let's examine some of the ways companies face the challenge of improving quality to see how information systems can be part of the process.

Reduce Cycle Time and Simplify the Production Process

Studies have shown that probably the best single way to reduce quality problems is to reduce **cycle time**, which refers to the total elapsed time from the beginning of a process to its end. Shorter cycle times mean that problems are caught earlier in the process, often before the production of a defective product is completed, saving some of the hidden costs of producing it. Finally, finding ways to reduce cycle time often means finding ways to simplify production steps. The fewer steps in a process, the less time and opportunity for an error to occur. Information systems help eliminate steps in a process and critical time delays.

800-Flowers, a multimillion-dollar company selling flowers by telephone or over the Web, used to be a much smaller company that had difficulty retaining its customers. It had poor service, inconsistent quality, and a cumbersome manual order-taking process. Telephone representatives had to write each order, obtain credit card approval, determine which participating florist was closest to the delivery location, select a floral arrangement, and forward the order to the florist. Each step in the manual process increased the chance of human error, and the whole process took at least a half hour. Owners Jim and Chris McCann installed a new information system that downloads orders taken in telecenters or over the Web to a central computer and electronically transmits them to local florists. Orders are more accurate and arrive at the florist within two minutes.

Benchmark

Companies achieve quality by using benchmarking to set strict standards for products, services, and other activities, and then measuring performance against those standards. Companies may use external industry standards, standards set by other companies; internally developed high standards; or some combination of the three. L.L.Bean, the Freeport, Maine, outdoor clothing company, used benchmarking to achieve an order-shipping accuracy of 99.9 percent. Its old batch order fulfillment system could not handle the surging volume and variety of items to be shipped. After studying German and Scandinavian companies with leading-edge order fulfillment operations, L.L.Bean carefully redesigned its order fulfillment process and information systems so that orders could be processed as soon as they were received and shipped within 24 hours.

Use Customer Demands to Improve Products and Services

Improving customer service, making customer service the number one priority, will improve the quality of the product itself. Delta Airlines decided to focus on its customers, installing a customer care system at its airport gates. For each flight, the airplane seating chart, reservations, check-in information, and boarding data are linked in a central database. Airline personnel can track which passengers are on board regardless of where they checked in and use this information to help passengers reach their destination quickly, even if delays cause them to miss connecting flights.

Improve Design Quality and Precision

Computer-aided design (CAD) software has made a major contribution to quality improvements in many companies, from producers of automobiles to producers of razor blades.

A **computer-aided design (CAD) system** automates the creation and revision of designs, using computers and sophisticated graphics software. The software enables users to create a digital model of a part, a product, or a structure and make changes to the design on the computer without having to build physical prototypes.

Clarion Malaysia, a manufacturer of sound and car audio electronics, used a CAD system to reduce the amount of time to design its products while creating new designs and improving their quality. Clarion implemented Catia V5 CAD software from Dassault Systems and IBM. Before implementing this software, Clarion Malaysia's designers needed 14 months to complete a new design model for a product. The software enables the company's design teams to complete a model in less than nine months. The time savings allow the company to be more competitive and to make more design revisions, which has improved product quality. Catia V5 has three-dimensional modeling capabilities that helped Clarion users grasp the nuances of design and see errors that would have been expensive if not detected until production.

Improve Production Precision and Tighten Production Tolerances

For many products, quality can be enhanced by making the production process more precise, thereby decreasing the amount of variation from one part to another. CAD software often produces design specifications for tooling and manufacturing processes, saving additional time and money while producing a manufacturing process with far fewer problems. The user of this software is able to design a more precise production system, a system with tighter tolerances, than could ever be done manually. Clarion Malaysia's Catia software provided product data to tooling suppliers, which enabled them to cut tooling preparation time by 60 percent

3.4 Competing on Business Processes

Technology alone is often not enough to make organizations more competitive, efficient, or quality-oriented. The organization itself may need to be changed to take advantage of the

Computer-aided design (CAD) systems improve the quality and precision of product design by performing much of the design and testing work on the computer.

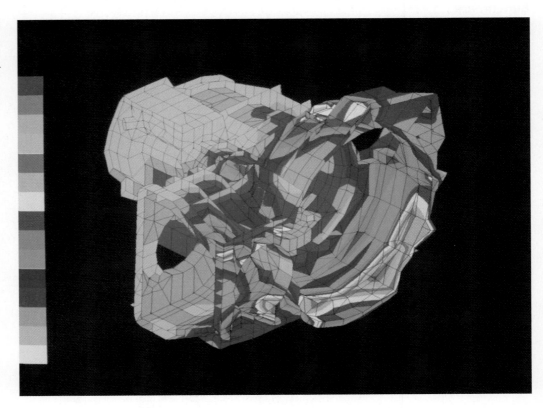

power of information technology. Sometimes these changes require minor adjustments in work activities, but, often, entire business processes may need to be redesigned. This radical rethinking and redesign of business processes to take advantage of information systems is called **business process reengineering (BPR)**.

BUSINESS PROCESS REENGINEERING

In business process reengineering, the steps required to accomplish a particular task are combined and streamlined to eliminate repetitive and redundant work. To reengineer successfully, the business must ask some basic questions: Why do we do what we do? Why do we do it the way we do? If we could start from scratch, what would we do now and how would we do it? Then the business needs to reinvent these processes anew, without regard to traditional responsibilities of workgroups, departments, or divisions.

Here's how reengineering worked for banks engaged in mortgage processing: The application process for a home mortgage used to take about six to eight weeks and cost about $3,000. The goal of mortgage banks, such as Wells Fargo, Washington Mutual, and JPMorgan Chase, has been to reduce that cost to $1,000 and the time to obtain a mortgage to about one week (see Figure 3-6).

In the past, a mortgage applicant filled out a paper loan application. The bank entered the application into its computer system. Specialists, such as credit analysts and underwriters from perhaps eight different departments, accessed and evaluated the application individually. If the loan application was approved, the closing was scheduled. After the closing, bank specialists dealing with insurance or funds in escrow serviced the loan. This "desk-to-desk" assembly-line approach might take up to 17 days.

The banks replaced the sequential desk-to-desk approach with a speedier "work cell" or team approach. Now, loan originators in the field enter the mortgage application directly into laptop computers. Software checks the application transaction to make sure that all of the information is correct and complete. The loan originators transmit the loan applications over a network to regional production centers. Instead of working on the application individually, the credit analysts, loan underwriters, and other specialists convene electronically, working as a team to approve the mortgage.

After closing, another team of specialists sets up the loan for servicing. The entire loan application process can take as little as two days. Loan information is easier to access than before, when the loan application could be in eight or nine different departments. Loan originators also can dial into the bank's network to obtain information on mortgage loan costs or to check the status of a loan for the customer.

By radically rethinking their approaches to mortgage processing, mortgage banks have achieved remarkable efficiencies. They have not focused on redesigning a single business process but instead they have reexamined the entire set of logically connected processes required to obtain a mortgage.

To support the new mortgage application process, the banks have implemented workflow and document management software. **Workflow management** is the process of streamlining business procedures so that documents can be moved easily and efficiently. Workflow and document management software automates processes, such as routing documents to different locations, securing approvals, scheduling, and generating reports. Two or more people can work simultaneously on the same document, allowing much quicker completion time. Work need not be delayed because a file is out or a document is in transit. And with a properly designed indexing system, users will be able to retrieve files in many different ways, based on the content of the document.

STEPS IN EFFECTIVE REENGINEERING

One of the most important strategic decisions that a firm can make is not deciding how to use computers to improve business processes but rather understanding what business processes need improvement. When systems are used to strengthen the wrong business

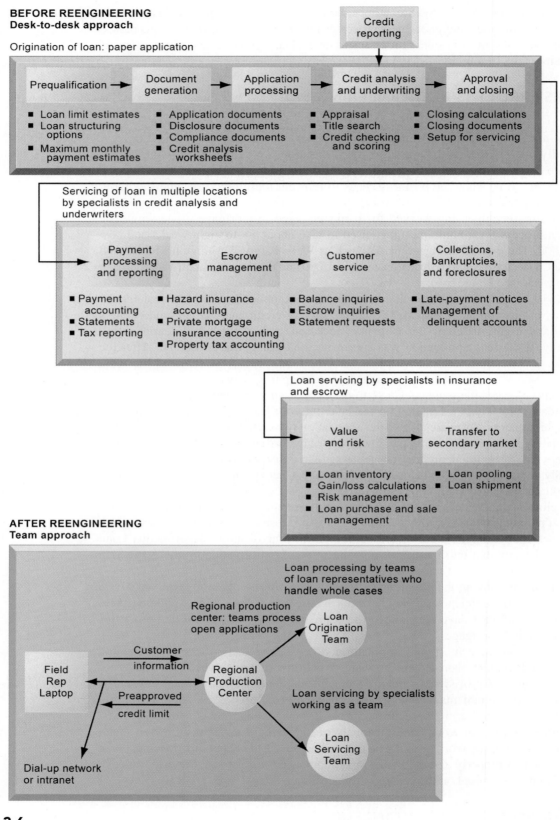

Figure 3-6
Redesigning Mortgage Processing in the United States
By redesigning their mortgage processing systems and the mortgage application process, mortgage banks are able to reduce the costs of processing the average mortgage from $3,000 to $1,000 and reduce the time of approval from six weeks to one week or less. Some banks are even preapproving mortgages and locking interest rates on the same day the customer applies.

model or business processes, the business can become more efficient at doing what it should not do. As a result, the firm becomes vulnerable to competitors who may have discovered the right business model. Considerable time and cost may also be spent improving business processes that have little impact on overall firm performance and revenue. Managers need to determine what business processes are the most important to focus on when applying new information technology and how improving these processes will help the firm execute its strategy.

Management must also understand and measure the performance of existing processes as baselines. If, for example, the objective of reengineering is to reduce time and cost in developing a new product or filling an order, the business needs to measure the time and cost consumed by the unchanged process. For instance, before reengineering, Cemex, the international provider of cement and ready-mix concrete, required an average time of three hours to make a delivery. After Cemex's processes were reengineered, average delivery time dropped to 20 minutes.

Following these steps does not automatically guarantee that reengineering will always be successful. Many reengineering projects do not achieve breakthrough gains in business performance because the organizational changes are often very difficult to manage. Managing change is neither simple nor intuitive, and companies committed to reengineering need a good change-management strategy (see Chapter 11).

3.5 Hands-On MIS

The projects in this section give you hands-on experience analyzing a company's competitive strategy, using a database to improve decision making about business strategy, and using Web tools to configure and price an automobile.

IMPROVING DECISION MAKING: ANALYZING COMPETITIVE STRATEGY

Software skills: Web browser software and presentation software
Business skills: Value chain and competitive forces analysis, business strategy
           formulation

This project provides an opportunity for you to develop the competitive strategy for a real-world business. You will use the Web to identify Dirt Bikes's competitors and the competitive forces in its industry. You'll use value chain analysis to determine what kinds of information systems will provide the company with a competitive advantage.

Dirt Bikes's management wants to be sure it is pursuing the right competitive strategy. You have been asked to perform a competitive analysis of the company using the Web to find the information you need. Prepare a report that analyzes Dirt Bikes using the value chain and competitive forces models. Your report should include the following:

- Which activities at Dirt Bikes create the most value?
- How does Dirt Bikes provide value to its customers?
- What other companies are Dirt Bikes's major competitors? How do their products compare in price to those of Dirt Bikes? What are some of the product features they emphasize?
- What are the competitive forces that can affect the industry?
- What competitive strategy should Dirt Bikes pursue?
- What information systems best support that strategy?
- (Optional) Use electronic presentation software to summarize your findings for management.

IMPROVING DECISION MAKING: USING A DATABASE TO CLARIFY BUSINESS STRATEGY

Software skills: Database querying and reporting; database design
Business skills: Reservation systems; customer analysis

In this exercise, you'll use database software to analyze the reservation transactions for a hotel and use that information to fine-tune the hotel's business strategy and marketing activities.

The Presidents' Inn is a small three-story hotel on the Atlantic Ocean in Cape May, New Jersey, a popular northeastern U.S. resort. Ten rooms overlook side streets, 10 rooms have bay windows that offer limited views of the ocean, and the remaining 10 rooms in the front of the hotel face the ocean. Room rates are based on room choice, length of stay, and number of guests per room. Room rates are the same for one to four guests. Fifth and sixth guests must pay an additional $20 charge each per day. Guests staying for seven days or more receive a 10 percent discount on their daily room rates.

Business has grown steadily during the past 10 years. Now totally renovated, the inn uses a romantic weekend package to attract couples, a vacation package to attract young families, and a weekday discount package to attract business travelers. The owners currently use a manual reservation and bookkeeping system, which has caused many problems. Sometimes two families have been booked in the same room at the same time. Management does not have immediate data about the hotel's daily operations and income.

ID	Guest First Name	Guest Last Name	Room	Room Type	Arrival Date	Departure Date	No of Guests	Daily Rate
1	Barry	Lloyd	Hayes	Bay-window	12/1/2007	12/4/2007	2	$150.00
2	Michael	Lunsford	Cleveland	Ocean	12/1/2007	12/9/2007	3	$112.50
3	Kim	Kyuong	Coolidge	Bay-window	12/4/2007	12/7/2007	1	$150.00
4	Edward	Holt	Washington	Ocean	12/1/2007	12/3/2007	4	$325.00
5	Thomas	Collins	Lincoln	Ocean	12/9/2007	12/13/2007	2	$300.00
6	Paul	Bodkin	Coolidge	Bay-window	12/1/2007	12/3/2007	2	$150.00
7	Randall	Battenburg	Washington	Ocean	12/4/2007	12/12/2007	2	$292.50
8	Calvin	Nowotney	Lincoln	Ocean	12/2/2007	12/4/2007	1	$300.00
9	Homer	Gonzalez	Lincoln	Ocean	12/5/2007	12/7/2007	5	$320.00
10	David	Sanchez	Jefferson	Bay-window	12/5/2007	12/7/2007	2	$175.00

At the Laudon Web site for Chapter 3, you will find a database for hotel reservation transactions developed in Microsoft Access. Illustrated below are some sample records from that database.

Develop some reports that provide information to help management make the business more competitive and profitable. Your reports should answer the following questions:
- What is the average length of stay per room type?
- What is the average number of visitors per room type?
- What is the base income per room (i.e., length of visit multiplied by the daily rate) during a specified period of time?
- What is the strongest customer base?

After answering these questions, write a brief report describing what the database information reveals about the current business situation. Which specific business strategies might be pursued to increase room occupancy and revenue? How could the database be improved to provide better information for strategic decisions?

IMPROVING DECISION MAKING: USING WEB TOOLS TO CONFIGURE AND PRICE AN AUTOMOBILE

Software skills: Internet-based software
Business skills: Researching product information and pricing

In this exercise, you will use software at Web sites for selling cars to find product information about a car of your choice and use that information to make an important purchase decision. You will also evaluate two of these sites as selling tools.

You are interested in purchasing a new Ford Escape (if you are personally interested in another car, domestic or foreign, investigate that one instead). Go to the Web site of CarsDirect (www.carsdirect.com) and begin your investigation. Locate the Ford Escape. Research the various specific automobiles available in that model and determine which you prefer. Explore the full details about the specific car, including pricing, standard features, and options. Locate and read at least two reviews if possible. Investigate the safety of that model based on the U.S. government crash tests performed by the National Highway Traffic Safety Administration if those test results are available. Explore the features for locating a vehicle in inventory and purchasing directly. Finally, explore the other capabilities of the CarsDirect site for financing.

Having recorded or printed the information you need from CarsDirect for your purchase decision, surf the Web site of the manufacturer, in this case Ford (www.ford.com). Compare the information available on Ford's Web site with that of CarsDirect for the Ford Escape. Be sure to check the price and any incentives being offered (which may not agree with what you found at CarsDirect). Next, find a dealer on the Ford site so that you can view the car before making your purchase decision. Explore the other features of Ford's Web site.

LEARNING TRACKS

The following Learning Tracks provide content relevant to topics covered in this chapter:

1. Challenges of Information Systems for Competitive Advantage

---

Try to locate the lowest price for the car you want in a local dealer's inventory. Which site would you use to purchase your car? Why? Suggest improvements for the sites of CarsDirect and Ford.

Review Summary

1 **How does Porter's competitive forces model help companies develop competitive strategies using information systems?** In Porter's competitive forces model, the strategic position of the firm, and its strategies, are determined by competition with its traditional direct competitors but also they are greatly affected by new market entrants, substitute products and services, suppliers, and customers. Information systems help companies compete by maintaining low costs, differentiating products or services, focusing on market niche, strengthening ties with customer and suppliers, and increasing barriers to market entry with high levels of operational excellence. Information systems are most successful when the technology is aligned with business objectives.

2 **How do the value chain and value web models help businesses identify opportunities for strategic information system applications?** The value chain model highlights specific activities in the business where competitive strategies and information systems will have the greatest impact. The model views the firm as a series of primary and support activities that add value to a firm's products or services. Primary activities are directly related

to production and distribution, whereas support activities make the delivery of primary activities possible. A firm's value chain can be linked to the value chains of its suppliers, distributors, and customers. A value web consists of information systems that enhance competitiveness at the industry level by promoting the use of standards and industry-wide consortia, and by enabling businesses to work more efficiently with their value partners.

3 **How do information systems help businesses use synergies, core competences, and network-based strategies to achieve competitive advantage?** Because firms consist of multiple business units, information systems achieve additional efficiencies or enhanced services by tying together the operations of disparate business units. Information systems help businesses leverage their core competencies by promoting the sharing of knowledge across business units. Information systems facilitate business models based on large networks of users or subscribers that take advantage of network economics. A virtual company strategy uses networks to link to other firms so that a company can use the capabilities of other companies to build, market, and distribute products and services. Disruptive technologies provide strategic opportunities, although "first movers" do not necessarily obtain long-term benefit.

4 **How do competing on a global scale and promoting quality enhance competitive advantage?** Information systems and the Internet can help companies operate internationally by facilitating coordination of geographically dispersed units of the company and communication with faraway customers and suppliers. Information systems can enhance quality by simplifying a product or service, facilitating benchmarking, reducing product development cycle time, and improving quality and precision in design and production.

5 **What is the role of business process reengineering (BPR) in enhancing competitiveness?** Organizations often have to change their business processes in order

Key Terms

Benchmarking, 93
Best practices, 93
Business process reengineering (BPR), 103
Competitive forces model, 82
Computer-aided design (CAD) system, 102
Core competency, 94
Cycle time, 101
Disruptive technologies, 96

Domestic exporter, 99
Efficient customer response system, 85
Franchiser, 99
Mass customization, 86
Multinational, 99
Network economics, 95
Primary activities, 92
Quality, 100
Six sigma, 101

Strategic transitions, 00
Support activities, 92
Total quality management (TQM), 100
Transnational, 99
Value chain model, 91
Value web, 93
Virtual company, 95
Workflow management, 103

Review Questions

1. How does Porter's competitive forces model help companies develop competitive strategies using information systems?
- Define Porter's competitive forces model and explain how it works.
- List and describe four competitive strategies enabled by information systems that firms can pursue.

- Describe how information systems can support each of these competitive strategies and give examples.
- Explain why aligning IT with business objectives is essential for strategic use of systems.

2. How do the value chain and value web models help businesses identify opportunities for strategic information system applications?
- Define and describe the value chain model.
- Explain how the value chain model can be used to identify opportunities for information systems.
- Define the value web and show how it is related to the value chain.
- Explain how the value web helps businesses identify opportunities for strategic information systems.
- Describe how the Internet has changed competitive forces and competitive advantage.

3. How do information systems help businesses use synergies, core competencies, and network-based strategies to achieve competitive advantage?
- Explain how information systems promote synergies and core competencies.
- Describe how promoting synergies and core competencies enhances competitive advantage.
- Explain how businesses benefit by using network economics.
- Define and describe a virtual company and the benefits of pursuing a virtual company strategy.
- Explain how disruptive technologies create strategic opportunities.

4. How do competing on a global scale and promoting quality enhance competitive advantage?
- Describe how globalization has increased opportunities for businesses.
- List and describe the four main ways of organizing a business internationally and the types of systems configuration for global business organizations.
- Define quality and compare the producer and consumer definitions of quality.
- Describe the various ways in which information systems can improve quality.

5. What is the role of business process reengineering (BPR) in enhancing competitiveness?
- Define business process reengineering (BPR) and explain how it helps firms become more competitive.
- Define workflow management and explain how it is related to BPR.
- List and describe the steps companies should take to make sure BPR is successful.

Discussion Questions

1. It has been said that there is no such thing as a sustainable competitive advantage. Do you agree? Why or why not?

2. What are some of the issues to consider in determining whether the Internet would provide your business with a competitive advantage?

Video Case

You will find a video case illustrating some of the concepts in this chapter on the Laudon Web site along with questions to help you analyze the case.

Teamwork

Identifying Opportunities for Strategic Information Systems

With a group of three or four students, select a company described in *The Wall Street Journal, Fortune, Forbes*, or another business publication. Visit the company's Web site to find additional information about that company and to see how the firm is using the Web. On the basis of this information, identify important business processes and the firm's business strategy. Suggest information systems that might give that particular business a competitive advantage, including those based on Internet technology, if appropriate. If possible, use electronic presentation software to present your findings to the class.

BUSINESS PROBLEM-SOLVING CASE

YouTube, the Internet, and the Future of Movies

The Internet has transformed the music industry. Sales of CDs in retail music stores have been declining while sales of songs downloaded through the Internet to iPods and other portable music players are skyrocketing. And the music industry is still contending with millions of people illegally downloading songs for free. Will the motion picture industry have a similar fate?

Increased levels of high-speed Internet access, powerful PCs with DVD readers and writers, portable video devices, and leading-edge file sharing services have made downloading of video content faster and easier than ever. Free and often illegal video downloads are currently outpacing paid video downloads by four to one. But the Internet is also providing new ways for movie and television studios to distribute and sell their content, and they are trying to take advantage of that opportunity.

In April 2006, six movie studios, including Warner Brothers, Sony Pictures, Universal, MGM, and Paramount, reached an agreement with Web site Movielink to sell movies online via download. Until that time, Movielink had offered movie downloads as rentals, which, like the video-on-demand model, the customer could watch for only 24 hours. Sony, MGM, and Lions Gate also reached agreements with a Movielink competitor, CinemaNow, which is partially owned by Lions Gate. Warner Brothers also expanded its presence by entering into relationships with video downloading services Guba.com and BitTorrent. The studios moved to build on the momentum created by the success of the iTunes music store, which demonstrated that consumers were very willing to pay for legal digital downloads of copyrighted material. At the same time, they hoped that entering the download sales market would enable them to confront the piracy issue in their industry earlier in its development than the music industry was able to do.

What remained a question was whether the studios could replicate the success of iTunes. The initial pricing schemes certainly did not offer the same appeal as Apple's $0.99 per song or $9.99 per CD. Movielink set the price for new movies at $20 to $30. Older movies were discounted to $10. Movielink was counting on the fact that customers would pay more for the immediacy of downloading a movie in their homes, as opposed to visiting a bricks-and-mortar store such as Circuit City or an online store such as Amazon.com, both of which sell new DVDs for less than $15.

However, even if customers were willing to pay a little extra, they were getting less for their money. Most movie downloads did not come with the extra features that are common with DVD releases. Moreover, the downloaded movies were programmed for convenient viewing on computer screens, but transporting them from the computer to the TV screen involved a more complicated process than most consumers were willing to tackle. Neither Movielink nor CinemaNow offered a movie format that could be burned to a DVD and played on a regular DVD player. In fact, CinemaNow downloads were limited to use on a single computer. To watch these movies on a television screen, users would need to have Windows Media Center, which is designed to connect to a TV, or special jacks and cables.

An additional obstacle for both the technology and the consumer to overcome was data transmission speeds over the Internet. Even using a high-speed Internet connection, high-quality movie files, which generally surpassed 1 gigabyte in file size, required in the neighborhood of 90 minutes to download completely.

Right around the time that the studios were making their foray into Web distribution, a new challenge emerged. YouTube, which started up in February 2005, quickly became the most popular video-sharing Web site in the world. Even though YouTube's original mission was to provide an outlet for amateur filmmakers, digital rights management issues immediately emerged.

Sure enough, video clips of copyrighted Hollywood movies and television shows soon proliferated on YouTube right alongside the video diaries created by teenagers with webcams and the amateur films created by film students. YouTube measures to discourage its users from posting illegal clips included limiting the length of videos to 10 minutes and removing videos at the request of the copyright owner. It was, however, a losing battle. Clips from popular movies and shows were often posted by multiple users, and they could be reposted as quickly as they were removed. And watching a two-hour movie in twelve 10-minute pieces proved to be a small price to pay to view the movie for free.

No one knows how much Hollywood-derived content is submitted to YouTube without the studios' permission. Academics and media executives estimate it ranges from 30 to 70 percent.

When Google purchased YouTube in 2006 for $1.65 billion, the site gained considerable clout in the media world. With YouTube reporting 100 million video views per day and becoming one of the most visited Web sites on the entire Web, the major production studios were not going to stand idly by while someone else profited off of movies that cost them an average of $95 million to make. NBC Universal, for example, assigned three employees to search YouTube every day for property that had been posted without permission. NBC Universal makes over 1,000 requests per month to remove its material from YouTube.

Of course, in the end, the chase probably is not worthwhile. Rick Cotton, NBC Universal's general counsel, admitted, "There is only so much we can do." Rather than pursue an unachievable goal, some of the major studios, including NBC Universal, Time Warner's Warner Brothers Entertainment, and News Corporation's Twentieth Century Fox, sought more constructive solutions. They entered into negotiations with YouTube to establish licensing agreements that would make copyrighted content available legally. The licensing model was already in place between YouTube and several major music companies. Furthermore, YouTube had already engineered successful arrangements with major studios to market movies on the site.

The studios clearly recognize the value of getting exposure for their movies on such a heavily trafficked Web site. Marc Shmuger, chairman of Universal Pictures, noted that his company's marketing team distributed promotional video clips of all its new films to

Web sites such as YouTube. Of course, the studios could not expect users to voluntarily ignore illegal clips in favor of the approved ones, or even discern the difference between them. So, it made sense for the movie industry to follow the lead of the music industry, where the focus shifted from killing off illegal uploads to taking advantage of digital music as a new source of revenue.

What happens when the two sides can't agree on terms? In some cases, the studios have to tread lightly because of their diverse interests in the media. For example, News Corporation also owns MySpace, which itself houses untold numbers of unauthorized music and video clips that are posted by users. The delicate balance between vigilance and public relations surfaced in January 2007 when News Corporation filed a subpoena in a U.S. District Court to compel Google to turn over the identity of a user who uploaded episodes of the Fox Television programs *24* and *The Simpsons* to YouTube. Fox was simply looking to protect its copyrights, but the network risked angering fans of the shows, as well as fans of YouTube, if it pursued the individual too aggressively. Moreover, News Corporation could come across as hypocritical for seeking to punish a YouTube user while so many of users of MySpace were permitted to engage in the same behavior.

In early 2007, YouTube revealed its intention to explore a revenue-sharing model. By sharing revenue with content creators, YouTube might be able to return the focus of the site to its original purpose, and steer users away from the practice of uploading their favorite copyrighted material. Metacafe and Revver, two other video-sharing sites, already had such models in place. Metacafe's producer rewards program pays users $5 for every 1,000 views once their original creations surpass a threshold of 20,000 views. Revver attaches pay-per-click advertisements to the end of videos and then splits evenly the revenue generated by ad clicks with the video creator.

Sharing revenue would improve YouTube's image in the eyes of both advertisers and users. Advertisers would know that they weren't sponsoring stolen material and tacitly approving of YouTube's profiting from content it had no right to possess. Users would be more motivated to produce and upload high-quality original videos knowing that YouTube wasn't getting all of the financial reward. One possible danger is the temptation for users to steal high-quality content and pass it off as their own in order to reap the rewards. Therefore, it is critical for YouTube to continue developing the filtering and digital fingerprinting technology that it has promised.

Whatever the motion picture studios' relationship to YouTube, it remains to be seen whether streaming video can actually be profitable. Screen Digest, a London research firm, forecasts that 55 percent of the video content watched in the United States in 2010 will be in the form of video streams—44 billion of them. However, that 55 percent of the video content will only account for 15 percent of the revenues produced by video content. A large part of the problem is that the videos that are most popular online are the least attractive to advertisers due to inappropriate or objectionable material, or because they are simply dull.

For all of the players in the movie game—studios, video-sharing sites, rental companies—partnerships and revenue sharing seem the best choice for maximizing the revenue streams made possible by new technology. However, that hasn't stopped the various players from continuing to seek the next competitive edge in order to get a bigger piece of the pie. Netflix introduced a streaming video service that enables subscribers to watch movies on their PCs instantaneously with no fees beyond what a subscriber is already paying for a membership. The membership level determines how many hours of streaming video the subscriber receives per month. Blockbuster launched its Total Access program to give online movie renters additional convenience. In addition to returning their movies through the mail, subscribers may return them to a Blockbuster store and receive a free movie or game rental.

The studios continue to seek out more partners for movie downloads. The six major studios reached an agreement with Wal-Mart to allow the discount-shopping giant to sell movie downloads from its Web site. Wal-Mart joined iTunes, CinemaNow, Amazon, and others who already had such deals. All will now compete on pricing and ease-of-use of their Web sites. Two things are certain: technology will continue to advance—Apple, AOL, and others planned devices to broadcast video from computers directly to televisions; and lawyers will continue to argue concepts such as liability and fair use.

Sources: Laura M. Holson, "Hollywood Asks YouTube: Friend or Foe?" *The New York Times*, January 15, 2007; Catherine Holahan, "Google and YouTube: A Catch-22," *BusinessWeek*, January 26, 2007 and "Upload Video, Download Cash on YouTube?" *BusinessWeek*, January 30, 2007; eMarketer, "Illegal Video Downloads Outpace Legal Downloads Four to One," January 16, 2007; "User-Generated Web Sites in Clicks-to-Cash Dilemma," Reuters, accessed via Yahoo! News, January 15, 2007; "The Odd Couple," The Associated Press, accessed via TheAge.com.au, February 1, 2007; Eric Benderoff, "Web Sites Begin to Pay for Content," *The Baltimore Sun*, January 31, 2007; Adrian McCoy, "Netflix, Blockbuster Launch New Services," *Pittsburgh Post-Gazette*, January 31, 2007; Dan Blacharski, "Blog Insights: YouTube and the Copyright Dilemma," *ITWorld*, February 5, 2007; Greg Sandoval, "Does YouTube Have a Control Problem?" *CNET News*, February 5, 2007; and Jennifer LeClaire, "YouTube.com Stirs Napster Memories in Digital Movie Era," *TechNewsWorld*, February 5, 2007.

Case Study Questions

1. What competitive forces have challenged the movie industry? What problems have these forces created? What changes have these problems caused the movie and televisions studios to make?

2. Describe the impact of disruptive technology on the motion picture industry.

3. How have the movie studios responded to YouTube? What is the goal of the response? What can the movie studios learn from the music industry's dealings with online digital music and copyright infringement?

4. Should motion picture companies continue to use YouTube to promote their new films? Why or why not?

5. Go to YouTube.com and search for videos from your favorite movie or television show. What do you find on the site? To whom do you assign more responsibility for unauthorized copyrighted material appearing on the site, the users who uploaded it or YouTube? If you wrote or produced a television show or movie, what would be a fair arrangement for your work to appear on YouTube? Would you allow your work to circulate freely on the Internet? If not, how should you be compensated? What measures would you be willing to take to enforce your copyright?

Information Technology Infrastructure

P A R T

II

Part II provides the technical foundation for understanding information systems by examining hardware, software, databases, networking technologies, and tools and techniques for security and control. This part answers questions such as these: What technologies and tools do businesses today need to accomplish their work? What do I need to know about these technologies to make sure they enhance the performance of my firm? How are these technologies likely to change in the future?

IT Infrastructure: Hardware and Software

CHAPTER 4

STUDENT LEARNING OBJECTIVES

After completing this chapter, you will be able to answer the following questions:

1. What are the components of IT infrastructure?

2. What are the major computer hardware, data storage, input, and output technologies used in business?

3. What are the major types of computer software used in business?

4. What are the most important contemporary hardware and software trends?

5. What are the principal issues in managing hardware and software technology?

CHAPTER OUTLINE

UNIVERSITY OF PITTSBURGH MEDICAL CENTER'S TECHNOLOGY CURE

The University of Pittsburgh Medical Center (UPMC) is a $6 billion integrated health care enterprise and a widely recognized leader in using information technology for health care. UPMC puts great demands on its information systems to operate 19 hospitals, a network of other care sites, and international and commercial ventures. With 43,000 employees, it is the largest employer in western Pennsylvania. It is a national leader in implementing electronic medical records.

UPMC was such a heavy user of information technology that demand for additional servers and storage technology was growing by 20 percent each year. Integrating the systems of a new hospital it acquired or adding new information systems increased the complexity of its infrastructure, making it increasingly difficult to manage. UPMC was setting up a separate server for every application, and its servers and other computers were running a number of different operating systems, including several versions of UNIX and Windows. UPMC had to manage technologies from many different vendors, including Hewlett-Packard (HP), Sun Microsystems, Microsoft, and IBM.

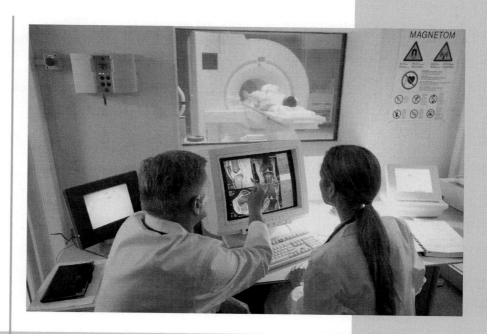

To reduce costs and simplify its IT infrastructure, UPMC turned to IBM. In 2005, UPMC selected IBM as its primary server and storage technology provider with the goal of reducing UPMC's IT infrastructure spending by 20 percent. IBM would also provide help in managing the people, process, and technology issues surrounding the overhaul of UPMC's IT infrastructure. Both organizations agreed to work together on developing applications to jointly market to other hospitals and health care firms.

IBM recommended that UPMC use virtualization to reduce the number of servers it needed to run its applications. Virtualization makes it possible to put many applications on a single physical server but give each its own instance of the operating system, so what appear to be many separate applications and operating systems are running on a single machine. It standardized UNIX applications on IBM's AIX version of the UNIX operating system running on IBM System p5 595 servers and used VMware technology to consolidate more than 1,000 physical servers on just 20 IBM System x servers. As a result, server utilization rates have increased from 3 percent per server to nearly 80 percent, the same staff are able to support 150 percent more server capacity, and the space required for servers has been reduced by 40 percent.

UPMC also used IBM technology to consolidate its storage infrastructure to three enterprise-wide storage pools, enhancing utilization, flexibility, and management. International Data Corporation's Health Industry Insights service estimated that UPMC's server virtualization project alone will save $18 million to $22 million over the next three years by reducing costs for new hardware, floor space, and staffing.

Sources: David F. Carr, "Major Surgery," *Baseline Magazine*, July 2007 and IBM, "University of Pittsburgh Medical Center Boosts Efficiency and Cost Savings with IBM Virtualization Technology," April 9, 2007.

The University of Pittsburgh Medical Center is highly dependent on information technology for its daily operations and patient care. But UPMC is a large organization with many local branches, new units to integrate, and a massive amount of data to store and process. Its IT infrastructure used technology from many different vendors. It was so complex and massive that it had become difficult to manage, and its server and storage needs were growing at 20 percent each year.

UPMC could have kept adding more hardware each year, but this would have made its infrastructure even more complex and added to IT costs. But this is an organization with a very large amount of information to manage that would benefit from an enterprise-wide approach to managing computers, storage, and networks. UPMC chose instead to standardize its technology as much as possible on IBM platforms and to use virtualization technology to reduce the number of servers required to run its applications. This solution lowered costs, increased resource utilization rates, and made UPMC's IT infrastructure easier to maintain and manage.

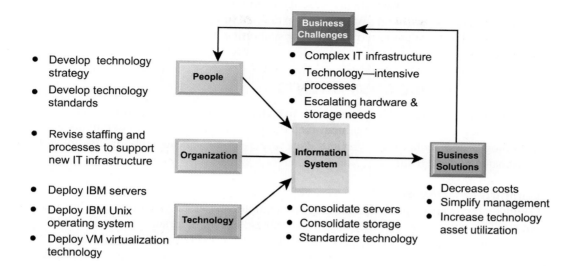

- Develop technology strategy
- Develop technology standards

- Revise staffing and processes to support new IT infrastructure

- Deploy IBM servers
- Deploy IBM Unix operating system
- Deploy VM virtualization technology

Business Challenges
- Complex IT infrastructure
- Technology—intensive processes
- Escalating hardware & storage needs

People

Organization

Technology

Information System

- Consolidate servers
- Consolidate storage
- Standardize technology

Business Solutions
- Decrease costs
- Simplify management
- Increase technology asset utilization

HEADS UP

This chapter describes the kind of software and hardware you will need to operate a business. In your business career, you will inevitably be making decisions about what information technology to buy, from whom to buy it, and how much to spend for it. You will need to know how to select technology that enhances the performance of your business, is cost effective, and is appropriate for the kind of work you will be doing.

4.1 IT Infrastructure: Computer Hardware

If you want to know why American businesses spend about $2 trillion every year on computing and information systems, just consider what it would take for you personally to set up a business or manage a business today. Businesses today require a wide variety of computing equipment, software, and communications capabilities simply to operate and solve basic business problems. Obviously, you need computers, and, as it turns out, a wide variety of computers are available, including desktops, laptops, and handhelds.

Do your employees travel or do some work from home? You will want to equip them with laptop computers (over half the computers sold in the U.S. are laptops). If you are employed by a medium to large business, you will also need larger server computers, perhaps an entire data center or server farm with hundreds or even thousands of servers. Google, for instance, is able to answer 80 million queries a day in the United States, most within one second, by using a massive network of 450,000 PC servers linked together to spread the workload.

You will also need plenty of software. Each computer will require an operating system and a wide range of application software capable of dealing with spreadsheets, documents, and data files. Unless you are a single-person business, you will most likely want to have a network to link all the people in your business together and perhaps your customers and suppliers. As a matter of fact, you will probably want several networks: a local area network connecting employees in your office and remote access capabilities so employees can share e-mail and computer files while they are out of the office. You will also want all your employees to have access to land and cell phone networks and the Internet. Finally, to make all this equipment and software work harmoniously, you will also need the services of trained people to help you run and manage this technology.

All of these elements we have just described combine to make up the firm's *information technology (IT) infrastructure*, which we first defined in Chapter 1. A firm's IT infrastructure provides the foundation, or platform, for supporting all the information systems in the business.

INFRASTRUCTURE COMPONENTS

IT infrastructure today is composed of five major components: computer hardware, computer software, data management technology, networking and telecommunications technology, and technology services (see Figure 4-1). These components must be coordinated with each other.

Computer Hardware

Computer hardware consists of technology for computer processing, data storage, input, and output. This component includes large mainframes, servers, midrange computers, desktop and laptop computers, handheld personal digital assistants (PDAs), and mobile devices for accessing corporate data and the Internet. It also includes equipment for gathering and inputting data, physical media for storing the data, and devices for delivering the processed information as output.

Computer Software

Computer software includes both system software and application software. **System software** manages the resources and activities of the computer. **Application software** applies the computer to a specific task for an end user, such as processing an order or generating a mailing list. Today, most system and application software is no longer custom programmed but rather is purchased from outside vendors. We describe these types of software in detail in Section 4.2.

Data Management Technology

In addition to physical media for storing the firm's data, businesses need specialized software to organize the data and make them available to business users. **Data management software** organizes, manages, and processes business data concerned with inventory, customers, and vendors. Chapter 5 describes data management software in detail.

Figure 4-1
IT Infrastructure
Components
A firm's IT infrastructure is composed of hardware, software, data management technology, networking technology, and technology services.

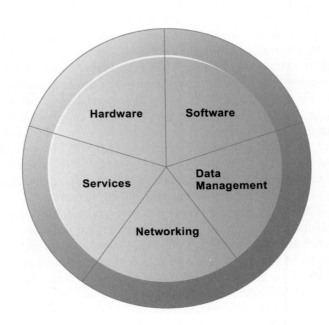

Networking and Telecommunications Technology

Networking and telecommunications technology provides data, voice, and video connectivity to employees, customers, and suppliers. It includes technology for running a company's internal networks, services from telecommunications/telephone services companies, and technology for running Web sites and linking to other computer systems through the Internet. Chapter 6 provides an in-depth description of these technologies.

Technology Services

Businesses need people to run and manage the other infrastructure components we have just described and to train employees in how to use these technologies for their work. Chapter 2 described the role of the information systems department, which is the firm's internal business unit set up for this purpose. Today, many businesses supplement their in-house information systems staff with external technology consultants. Even large firms do not have the staff, the skills, the budget, or the necessary experience to implement and run the wide array of technologies that would be required. When businesses need to make major system changes or implement an entirely new IT infrastructure, they typically turn to external consultants to help them with systems integration.

Systems integration means ensuring that the new infrastructure works with the firm's older, so-called legacy systems and that the new elements of the infrastructure work with one another. **Legacy systems** are generally older transaction processing systems created for mainframe computers that continue to be used to avoid the high cost of replacing or redesigning them.

There are many thousands of technology vendors supplying IT infrastructure components and services and an equally large number of ways of putting them together. This chapter is about the hardware and software components of infrastructure you will need to run a business. Chapter 5 describes the data management component, and Chapter 6 is devoted to the networking and telecommunications technology component. Chapter 7 deals with hardware and software for ensuring that information systems are reliable and secure, and Chapter 8 discusses software for enterprise applications.

TYPES OF COMPUTERS

Business firms face many different challenges and problems that can be solved by computers and information systems. In order to be efficient, firms need to match the right computer hardware to the nature of the business challenge, neither overspending nor underspending for the technology.

Computers come in an array of sizes with differing capabilities for processing information, from the smallest handheld devices to the largest mainframes and supercomputers. Table 4.1 illustrates the different broad categories of computers and their relative performance.

Although there are many factors that enter into a computer system's performance, one way to think about the performance of computers is to measure how long it takes them to perform a FLOPS (FLoating point Operations Per Second). A floating point operation is essentially long division. The faster a computer system can calculate long division problems, the higher its overall performance. Computers range in power from about 500 FLOPS (a handheld) to more than a trillion FLOPS for supercomputers.

If you're working alone or with a few other people in a small business, you'll probably be using a desktop or laptop **personal computer (PC)**. You might carry around a mobile device with some computing capability, such as a BlackBerry, iPhone or Palm handheld, or other high-end cell phone. If you're doing advanced design or engineering work requiring powerful graphics or computational capabilities, you might use a **workstation**, which fits on a desktop but has more powerful mathematical and graphics-processing capabilities than a PC.

If your business has a number of computers networked together or maintains a Web site, it will need a **server**. Server computers are specifically optimized to support a computer

TABLE 4.1

Computer Performance

Computer	Processor/Speed	Performance	Comment
Personal digital assistant (PDA) Palm handheld	Intel™ XScale/ 312 MHz	~500 FLOPS	PDAs are generally asked to perform one task at a time by the operator. Most of the processing power is used to draw the screen and handle voice messages.
Personal computer Dell XPS 720 H2C	Intel Core 2 Extreme (quad-core) processor/3.67 GHz,	4 Giga FLOPS	High-end game machine. Most PCs used in business are 1–3 GHz, with 2 GFLOPS performance, plenty for word processing, Web surfing, and spreadsheets.
Server computer (midrange computer) SUN Sun Fire E6900 Server	UltraSPARC IV+/1.8 GHz	~48 Giga FLOPS	Up to 24 processors can be used with this powerful server.
Mainframe computer IBM System z9 Enterprise Class	System z9 Integrated Information Processor/Equal to 100 or more distributed processors	~1 Tera FLOPS	Up to 60 logical partitions, each with 64-bit central memory addressability.
SuperComputer IBM Blue Gene/P	4 PowerPC 450 processors per chip/850 MHz	~1 Peta FLOPS	Configured with 294,912 PowerPC processors on 72 racks. A chip of 4 processors capable of 13.6 billion operations per second.
Distributed Computing Grid Folding@home	Various PC processors, whatever is available on the Internet.	~125 Peta FLOPS	A volunteer program with approximately 250,000 CPUs online; the largest and fastest online distributed computing project devoted to study protein folding.

network, enabling users to share files, software, peripheral devices (such as printers), or other network resources. Servers are classified as **midrange computers**.

Servers have become important components of firms' IT infrastructures because they provide the hardware platform for electronic commerce. By adding special software, they can be customized to deliver Web pages, process purchase and sale transactions, or exchange data with systems inside the company. You will sometimes find many servers linked together to provide all the processing needs for large companies. If your company has to process millions of financial transactions or customer records, you will need several midrange computers or a single large mainframe to solve these challenges.

Mainframe computers first appeared in the mid-1960s, and are still used by large banks, insurance companies, stock brokerages, airline reservation systems, and government agencies to keep track of hundreds of thousands, or even millions, of records and transactions. A **mainframe** is a large-capacity, high-performance computer that can process large amounts of data very rapidly. Airlines, for instance, use mainframes to process upwards of 3,000 reservation transactions per second.

IBM, the leading mainframe vendor, has repurposed its mainframe systems so they can be used as giant servers for large-scale enterprise networks and corporate Web sites. A single IBM mainframe can run enough instances of Linux or Windows server software to replace thousands of smaller Windows-based servers.

A **supercomputer** is a specially designed and more sophisticated computer that is used for tasks requiring extremely rapid and complex calculations with thousands of variables, millions of measurements, and thousands of equations. Supercomputers traditionally have been used in engineering analysis of structures, scientific exploration and simulations, and military work, such as classified weapons research and weather forecasting. A few private business firms use supercomputers. For instance, Volvo and most other automobile manufacturers use supercomputers to simulate vehicle crash tests.

If you are a long-term weather forecaster, such as the National Oceanic and Atmospheric Administration (NOAA), or the National Hurricane Center, and your challenge is to predict the movement of weather systems based on hundreds of thousands of measurements, and thousands of equations, you would want access to a supercomputer or a distributed network of computers called a grid.

Grid computing involves connecting geographically remote computers into a single network to create a "virtual supercomputer" by combining the computational power of all computers on the grid. Grid computing takes advantage of the fact that most computers in the United States use their central processing units on average only 25 percent of the time, leaving 75 percent of their capacity available for other tasks. By using the combined power of thousands of PCs and other computers networked together, the grid is able to solve complicated problems at supercomputer speeds at far lower cost.

Private firms are beginning to use computing grids because of their greater reliability than supercomputers, higher capacity, and lower cost. For example, Citigroup is implementing grid computing for analyzing complex financial products, harnessing 7,000 processors in Texas and London (Crosman, 2007).

Computer Networks and Client/Server Computing

Unless you are in a small business with a stand-alone computer, you'll be using networked computers for most processing tasks. The use of multiple computers linked by a communications network for processing is called **distributed processing**. **Centralized processing**, in which all processing is accomplished by one large central computer, is much less common.

One widely used form of distributed processing is **client/server computing**. Client/server computing splits processing between "clients" and "servers." Both are on the network, but each machine is assigned functions it is best suited to perform. The **client** is the user point of entry for the required function and is normally a desktop or laptop computer. The user generally interacts directly only with the client portion of the application. The server provides the client with services. Servers store and process shared data and also perform functions such as managing printers, backup storage, and network activities such as security, remote access, and user authentication. Figure 4-2 illustrates the client/server computing concept. Computing on the Internet uses the client/server model (see Chapter 6).

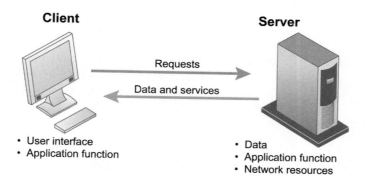

Client

Server

Requests

Data and services

- User interface
- Application function

- Data
- Application function
- Network resources

Figure 4-2
Client/Server Computing

In client/server computing, computer processing is split between client machines and server machines linked by a network. Users interface with the client machines.

Figure 4-2 illustrates the simplest client/server network, consisting of a client computer networked to a server computer, with processing split between the two types of machines. This is called a *two-tiered client/server architecture*. Whereas simple client/server networks can be found in small businesses, most corporations have more complex, multitiered (often called **N-tier**) **client/server architectures**, in which the work of the entire network is balanced over several different levels of servers, depending on the kind of service being requested (see Figure 4-3).

For instance, at the first level a **Web server** will serve a Web page to a client in response to a request for service. Web server software is responsible for locating and managing stored Web pages. If the client requests access to a corporate system (a product list or price information, for instance), the request is passed along to an **application server**. Application server software handles all application operations between a user and an organization's back-end business systems. The application server may reside on the same computer as the Web server or on its own dedicated computer. Chapters 5 and 6 provide more detail on other pieces of software that are used in multitiered client/server architectures for e-commerce and e-business.

STORAGE, INPUT, AND OUTPUT TECHNOLOGY

In addition to hardware for processing data, you will need technologies for data storage, and input and output. Storage and input and output devices are called *peripheral devices* because they are outside the main computer system unit.

Secondary Storage Technology
Electronic commerce and electronic business, and regulations such as Sarbanes-Oxley, have made storage a strategic technology. The amount of data that companies now need to store is doubling every 12 to 18 months. The primary storage technologies are magnetic disks, optical disc, magnetic tape, and storage networks.

Magnetic Disks The most widely used secondary storage medium today is the **magnetic disk**. PCs have *hard drives*, and large mainframe or midrange computer systems have multiple hard disk drives because they require immense disk storage capacity in the gigabyte and terabyte range. Some PCs use floppy disks, but they have been largely supplanted by *USB flash drives*, also known as USB drives. A USB flash drive provides portable flash memory storage by plugging into a computer's USB port. It can provide up to 64 gigabytes of portable storage capacity and is small enough to fit into a pocket.

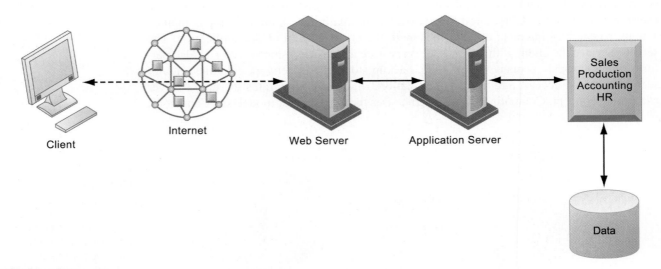

Figure 4-3
A Multitiered Client/Server Network (N-Tier)
In a multitiered client/server network, client requests for service are handled by different levels of servers.

Large computers with massive storage requirements use a disk technology called *RAID* (*Redundant Array of Inexpensive Disks*). RAID devices package more than 100 disk drives, a controller chip, and specialized software into a single, large unit delivering data over multiple paths simultaneously.

Optical Discs Optical discs use laser technology to store massive quantities of data in a highly compact form. They are available for both PCs and large computers. The most common optical disc system used with PCs is called **CD-ROM (compact disc read-only memory)**. A 4.75-inch compact disc for PCs can store up to 660 megabytes. Optical discs are most appropriate for applications where enormous quantities of unchanging data must be stored compactly for easy retrieval or for applications combining text, sound, and images.

CD-ROM is read-only storage. No new data can be written to it; it can only be read. *CD-RW (CD-ReWritable)* technology has been developed to allow users to create rewritable optical discs for applications requiring large volumes of storage where the information is only occasionally updated.

Digital video discs (DVDs) are optical discs the same size as CD-ROMs but of even higher capacity. They can hold a minimum of 4.7 gigabytes of data, enough to store a full-length, high-quality motion picture. DVDs are being used to store video and digitized text, graphics, and audio data. Rewritable DVD drives and media are now available.

Magnetic Tape Magnetic tape is an older storage technology that still is employed for secondary storage of large quantities of data that are needed rapidly but not instantly. It stores data sequentially and is relatively slow compared to the speed of other secondary storage media. In order to find an individual record stored on magnetic tape, such as an employment record, the tape must be read from the beginning up to the location of the desired record.

Storage Networking Large firms are turning to network-based storage technologies to deal with the complexity and cost of mushrooming storage requirements. **Storage area networks (SANs)** connect multiple storage devices on a separate high-speed network dedicated to storage. The SAN creates a large central pool of storage that can be rapidly accessed and shared by multiple servers (see Figure 4-4).

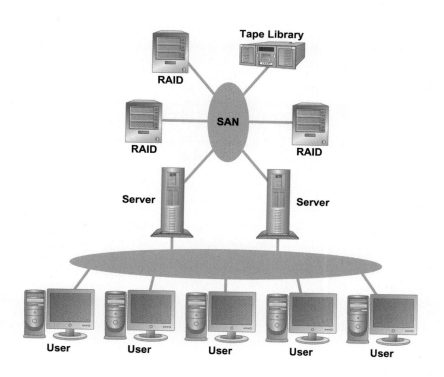

Figure 4-4
A Storage Area Network (SAN)
A typical SAN consists of a server, storage devices, and networking devices, and is used strictly for storage. The SAN stores data on many different types of storage devices, providing data to the enterprise. The SAN supports communication between any server and the storage unit as well as between different storage devices in the network.

Input and Output Devices

Human beings interact with computer systems largely through input and output devices. **Input devices** gather data and convert them into electronic form for use by the computer, whereas **output devices** display data after they have been processed. Table 4.2 describes the principal input and output devices.

TABLE 4.2

Input and Output Devices

Input Device	Description
Keyboard	Principal method of data entry for text and numerical data.
Computer mouse	Handheld device with point-and-click capabilities that is usually connected to the computer by a cable. The computer user can move the mouse around on a desktop to control the cursor's position on a computer display screen, pushing a button to select a command. Trackballs and touch pads often are used in place of the mouse as pointing devices on laptop PCs.
Touch screen	Device that allows users to enter limited amounts of data by touching the surface of a sensitized video display monitor with a finger or a pointer. Often found in information kiosks in retail stores, restaurants, and shopping malls.
Optical character recognition	Device that can translate specially designed marks, characters, and codes into digital form. The most widely used optical code is the bar code, which is used in point-of-sale systems in supermarkets and retail stores. The codes can include time, date, and location data in addition to identification data.
Magnetic ink character recognition (MICR)	Technology used primarily in check processing for the banking industry. Characters on the bottom of a check identify the bank, checking account, and check number and are preprinted using special magnetic ink. A MICR reader translates these characters into digital form for the computer.
Pen-based input	Handwriting-recognition devices, such as pen-based tablets, notebooks, and notepads, that convert the motion made by an electronic stylus pressing on a touch-sensitive tablet screen into digital form.
Digital scanner	Device that translates images, such as pictures or documents, into digital form; essential component of image-processing systems.
Audio input	Voice input devices that convert spoken words into digital form for processing by the computer. Microphones and tape cassette players can serve as input devices for music and other sounds.
Sensors	Devices that collect data directly from the environment for input into a computer system. For instance, today's farmers can use sensors to monitor the moisture of the soil in their fields to help them with irrigation.

Output Device	Description
Cathode ray tube (CRT)	Electronic gun that shoots a beam of electrons illuminating pixels on a display screen. Laptop computers use flat-panel displays, which are less bulky than CRT monitors.
Printers	Devices that produce a printed hard copy of information output. They include impact printers (such as dot matrix printers) and nonimpact printers (such as laser, inkjet, and thermal transfer printers).
Audio output	Voice output devices that convert digital output data back into intelligible speech. Other audio output, such as music, can be delivered by speakers connected to the computer.

Batch and Online Input and Processing

Information systems collect and process information in one of two ways: through batch or through online processing. In **batch processing**, transactions, such as orders or payroll time cards, are accumulated and stored in a group or batch until the time when, because of some reporting cycle, it is efficient or necessary to process them. Batch processing is found primarily in older systems where users need only occasional reports. In **online processing**, the user enters transactions into a device (such as a data entry keyboard or bar code reader) that is directly connected to the computer system. The transactions usually are processed immediately. Most processing today is online processing. Batch systems often use tape as a storage medium, whereas online processing systems use disk storage, which permits immediate access to specific items.

CONTEMPORARY HARDWARE TRENDS

The exploding power of computer hardware and networking technology has dramatically changed how businesses organize their computing power, putting more of this power on networks. We look at six trends: technology convergence, nanotechnology, edge computing, autonomic computing, virtualization, and multicore processors.

The Integration of Computing and Telecommunications Platforms

Arguably the most dominant theme in hardware platforms today is the convergence of telecommunications and computing platforms to the point where, increasingly, computing takes place over the network. You can see this convergence at several levels.

Communication devices, such as cell phones, are taking on functions of handheld computers or morphing into wireless handhelds. For instance, the Apple iPhone integrates a phone, digital camera, digital music player, and handheld computer capable of surfing the Web in a single device. Television, radio, and video are moving toward all-digital production and distribution.

The growing success of Internet telephone systems (now the fastest-growing type of telephone service) demonstrates how historically separate telecommunications and computing platforms are converging toward a single network—the Internet. Chapter 6 describes the convergence of computing and telecommunications in greater depth.

Nanotechnology

Over the years, microprocessor manufacturers have been able to exponentially increase processing power while shrinking chip size by finding ways to pack more transistors into less space. They are now turning to nanotechnology to shrink the size of transistors down to the width of several atoms. **Nanotechnology** uses individual atoms and molecules to create computer chips and other devices that are thousands of times smaller than current technologies permit. IBM and other research labs have created transistors from nanotubes and other electrical devices and have developed a manufacturing process for producing nanotube processors economically (Figure 4-5).

Edge Computing

Edge computing is a multitier, load-balancing scheme for Web-based applications in which significant parts of Web site content, logic, and processing are performed by smaller, less expensive servers located nearby the user in order to increase response time and resilience while lowering technology costs. In this sense, edge computing is another technique like grid computing and on-demand computing for using the Internet to share the workload experienced by a firm across many computers located remotely on the network.

Figure 4-6 illustrates the components of edge computing. There are three tiers in edge computing: the local client; the nearby edge computing platform, which consists of servers positioned at any of the 5,000-plus Internet service providers in the United States; and enterprise computers located at the firm's main data center. The edge computing platform is owned by a service firm, such as Akamai, which employs about 15,000 edge servers around the United States.

Figure 4-5
Examples of
Nanotubes
Nanotubes are tiny tubes about 10,000 times thinner than a human hair. They consist of rolled up sheets of carbon hexagons, have potential uses as minuscule wires or in ultra-small electronic devices, and are very powerful conductors of electrical current.

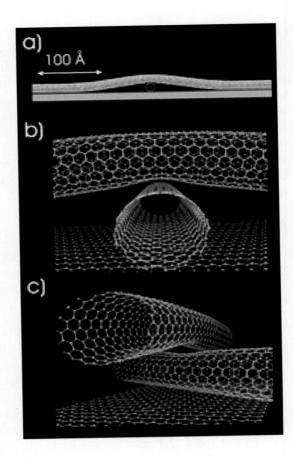

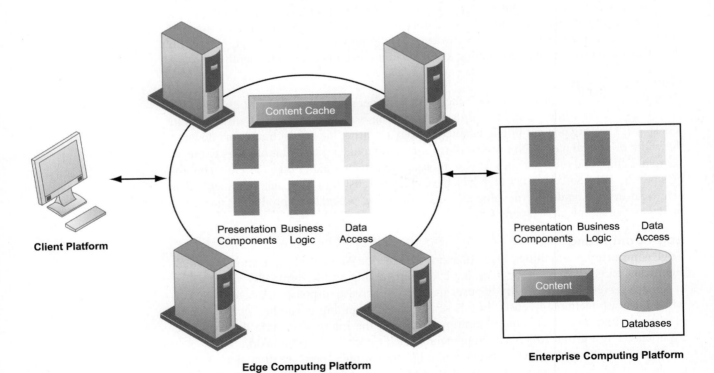

Figure 4-6
Edge Computing Platform
Edge computing involves the use of the Internet to balance the processing load of enterprise platforms across the client and edge computing platform.

In an edge platform application, the edge servers initially process requests from the user client computer. Presentation components, such as static Web page content, reusable code fragments, and interactive elements gathered on forms, are delivered by the edge server to the client. Database and business logic elements are delivered by the enterprise computing platform.

Autonomic Computing

With large systems encompassing many thousands of networked devices, computer systems have become so complex today that some experts believe they may not be manageable in the future. One approach to dealing with this problem from a computer hardware perspective is to employ autonomic computing. **Autonomic computing** is an industry-wide effort to develop systems that can configure themselves, optimize and tune themselves, heal themselves when broken, and protect themselves from outside intruders and self-destruction. Imagine, for instance, a desktop PC that could know it was invaded by a computer virus. Instead of blindly allowing the virus to invade, the PC would identify and eradicate the virus or, alternatively, turn its workload over to another processor and shut itself down before the virus destroyed any files.

You can glimpse some of these capabilities in your desktop system. For instance, virus and firewall protection software can detect viruses on PCs, automatically defeat the viruses, and alert operators. These programs can be updated automatically as the need arises by connecting to an online virus protection service such as McAfee. You can see autonomic computing occur nearly every day on your computer as Microsoft, Apple, and Sun automatically update their users' computers when they are connected to the Internet.

Virtualization and Multicore Processors

As companies deploy hundreds or thousands of servers, many have discovered that they are spending almost as much on electricity to power and cool their systems as they did on purchasing the hardware. Energy consumed by data centers doubled between 2000 and 2005. Cutting power consumption in data centers is now a major business challenge. The Interactive Session on Technology examines this problem. As you read this case, try to identify the alternative solutions for this problem and the advantages and disadvantages of each.

This Interactive Session and the chapter-opening case describe organizations curbing hardware proliferation and power consumption by using virtualization to reduce the number of computers required for processing. **Virtualization** is the process of presenting a set of computing resources (such as computing power or data storage) so that they can all be accessed in ways that are not restricted by physical configuration or geographic location. Server virtualization enables companies to run more than one operating system at the same time on a single machine. Most servers run at just 10 to 15 percent of capacity, and virtualization can boost server utilization rates to 70 percent or higher. Higher utilization rates translate into fewer computers required to process the same amount of work.

For example, the Denver Health and Hospital Authority servers mushroomed from 10 in 1996 to 220 in 2005, with server utilization rates averaging below 20 percent and 90 percent of the servers running a single application. The health care organization used virtualization to consolidate the work of 15 physical servers onto two machines running 15 virtual servers.

Server virtualization software runs between the operating system and the hardware, masking server resources, including the number and identity of physical servers, processors, and operating systems, from server users. VMware is the leading server virtualization software vendor for Windows and Linux systems. Microsoft offers its own Virtual Server product and has built virtualization capabilities into the newest version of Windows Server.

In addition to reducing hardware and power expenditures, virtualization allows businesses to run their legacy applications on older versions of an operating system on the same server as newer applications. Virtualization also facilitates centralization of hardware administration.

INTERACTIVE SESSION: TECHNOLOGY   Computing Goes Green

Computer rooms are becoming too hot to handle. Data-hungry tasks such as video on demand, music downloads, exchanging photos, and maintaining Web sites require more and more power-hungry machines. Between 2000 and 2007, the number of servers in corporate data center servers increased from 5.6 million to an estimated 12 million in the United States, and 29 million worldwide. During the same period, the total annual cost of electricity for data center servers jumped from $1.3 billion to $2.7 billion in the United States and from $3.2 billion to $7.2 billion across the world.

What's more, the heat generated from all of these severs is causing equipment to fail. Firms are forced to spend even more on cooling their data centers or to find other solutions. Some organizations spend more money to keep their data centers cool than they spend to lease the property itself. Cooling costs have helped raise the average annual utility bill of a 100,000-square-foot data center to $5.9 million. It is a vicious cycle, as companies must pay to power their servers, and then pay again to keep them cool and operational. Cooling a server requires roughly the same number of kilowatts of energy as running one. All this additional power consumption has a negative impact on the environment and as well as corporate operating costs.

At Pomona Valley Hospital Medical Center in Pomona, California, a 6,000-square-foot data center housed so many servers that the room temperature skyrocketed to nearly 100 degrees. IT managers aim to keep such rooms in the 60s. The elevated temperature caused server malfunctions and one case of outright failure. The hospital resolved the issue by investing $500,000 in a network of overhead air conditioners. Temperatures now hover at 64 degrees.

Emerson Network Power of St. Louis offers a cooling solution called Liebert XD that sits directly on top of server racks and conditions the air with pipes containing waterless refrigerant. US Internet Corp., a regional ISP in Minneapolis, installed the Liebert XD product to combat the 90-degree temperatures in one of its data centers. Without the system, US Internet was suffering from daily breakdowns of servers and storage drives.

Another cooling solution comes from Degree Controls Inc., based in Milford, New Hampshire. Degree Controls installs floor tiles equipped with powerful fans that blow cool air directly onto servers. The tiles cost $1,800 each. HP now offers an energy management system named Dynamic Smart Cooling that directs cool air to the hot spots in a data center.

Some of the world's most prominent firms are tackling their power consumption issues with one eye toward saving the environment and the other toward saving dollars. Google, Microsoft, and HSBC are all building data centers that will take advantage of hydroelectric power. Salesforce.com plans to offset its carbon footprint by investing in renewable energy projects and alternative energy sources. Sun Microsystems permits over 14,000 employees to telecommute at least twice a week. None of these companies claim that their efforts will save the world, but they do demonstrate recognition of a growing problem and the commencement of the green computing era.

IT managers also have hardware and software options that conserve power. Some organizations are choosing to use thin client computers, which are very basic terminal machines that connect directly to servers and consume significantly less power than normal desktop clients. A call center operated by Verizon Wireless in Chandler, Arizona, replaced 1,700 PCs with thin clients from Sun Microsystems and saw its power consumption go down by one-third. Sun states that, on average, its thin clients use less than half of the electricity that PCs require.

Two years ago, City University of New York adopted software called Surveyor made by Verdiem Corp. for its 20,000 PCs. The software enables IT managers to have the computers turn themselves off when they are inactive at night. Surveyor has trimmed 10 percent from CUNY's power bills, creating an annual savings of around $320,000. Quad Graphics Inc., of Sussex, Wisconsin, also deployed Surveyor after tests indicated savings on power of 35 to 50 percent, or up to $70,000 annually, were possible.

Microsoft's latest desktop PC operating system, Windows Vista, has enhanced sleep features that reduce power consumption by much greater margins than the standby modes in previous versions of Windows. In sleep mode, computers may draw as little as 3 to 4 watts of power versus 100 watts for an idle computer that is not asleep.

HP launched a three-year initiative to reduce its power costs by 20 to 25 percent through a consolidation of servers and data centers. The company uses the program as a selling point when it pitches its services to clients. Businesses also have the options of using more efficient chips in their servers. In 2006, Intel introduced new Dual-Core Intel Xeon 7100 microprocessors that achieve "nearly three times better performance per watt" than their predecessors.

Virtualization is a highly effective tool for more cost-effective greener computing because it reduces the number of servers required to run a firm's applications. The University of Pittsburgh Medical Center, described in the chapter-opening case, and Swinerton Construction in San Francisco are among many firms that have benefited from this technology. Swinerton saved $140,000 in one year alone by using virtualization, which included a $50,000 savings in power and cooling costs as well as reductions in its server purchases.

Sources: Jim Carlton, "IT Managers Make a Power Play," *The Wall Street Journal*, March 27, 2007, and "IT Managers Find Novel Ways to Cool Powerful Servers," *The Wall Street Journal*, April 10, 2007; and Marianne Kolbasuk McGee, "Data Center Electricity Bills Double," *Information Week*, February 17, 2007, and "What Every Tech Pro Should Know About 'Green Computing,'" *Information Week*, March 10, 2007.

CASE STUDY QUESTIONS

1. What business and social problems does data center power consumption cause?

2. What solutions are available for these problems? Which are the most environment-friendly?

3. What are the business benefits and costs of these solutions?

4. Should all firms move toward green computing? Why or why not?

MIS IN ACTION

Perform an Internet search on the phrase "green computing" and then answer the following questions:

1. How would you define green computing?

2. Who are some of the leaders of the green computing movement? Which corporations are leading the way? Which environmental organizations are playing an important role?

3. What are the latest trends in green computing? What kind of impact are they having?

4. What can individuals do to contribute to the green computing movement? Is the movement worthwhile?

Multicore Processors Another way to reduce power requirements and hardware sprawl is to use multicore processors. A **multicore processor** is an integrated circuit to which two or more processors have been attached for enhanced performance, reduced power consumption and more efficient simultaneous processing of multiple tasks. This technology enables two processing engines with reduced power requirements and heat dissipation to perform tasks faster than a resource-hungry chip with a single processing core. Today you will find dual-core processors in PCs and quad-core processors in servers. Sun Microsystems's UltraSparc TI chip for managing Web applications has 8 processors, and Intel is working on an 80-processor chip.

4.2 IT Infrastructure: Computer Software

In order to use computer hardware, you will need software, which provides the detailed instructions that direct the computer's work. System software and application software are interrelated and can be thought of as a set of nested boxes, each of which must interact closely with the other boxes surrounding it. Figure 4-7 illustrates this relationship. The system software surrounds and controls access to the hardware. Application software must work through the system software in order to operate. End users work primarily with application software. Each type of software must be specially designed for a specific machine to ensure its compatibility.

OPERATING SYSTEM SOFTWARE

The system software that manages and controls the computer's activities is called the **operating system**. Other system software consists of computer language translation

Figure 4-7
The Major Types of Software
The relationship between the system software, application software, and users can be illustrated by a series of nested boxes. System software—consisting of operating systems, language translators, and utility programs—controls access to the hardware. Application software, including programming languages and "fourth-generation" languages, must work through the system software to operate. The user interacts primarily with the application software.

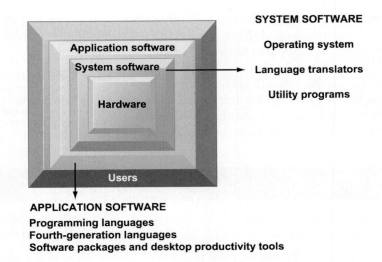

SYSTEM SOFTWARE

Operating system

Language translators

Utility programs

APPLICATION SOFTWARE
Programming languages
Fourth-generation languages
Software packages and desktop productivity tools

programs that convert programming languages into machine language that can be understood by the computer and utility programs that perform common processing tasks, such as copying, sorting, or computing a square root.

The operating system is the computer system's chief manager, enabling the system to handle many different tasks and users at the same time. The operating system allocates and assigns system resources, schedules the use of computer resources and computer jobs, and monitors computer system activities. The operating system provides locations in primary memory for data and programs, and controls the input and output devices, such as printers, terminals, and telecommunication links. The operating system also coordinates the scheduling of work in various areas of the computer so that different parts of different jobs can be worked on at the same time. Finally, the operating system keeps track of each computer job and may also keep track of who is using the system, of what programs have been run, and of any unauthorized attempts to access the system.

PC and Server Operating Systems

Like any other software, the software you use on your PC or corporate server is based on specific operating systems and computer hardware. Software written for one operating system generally cannot run on another. Table 4.3 compares leading PC and server operating systems. These include the Windows family of operating systems (Windows Vista, Windows XP, Windows Server 2003), UNIX, Linux, and the Macintosh operating system.

The operating system controls the way users interact with the computer. Contemporary PC operating systems and many types of contemporary application software use a **graphical user interface**, often called a **GUI**, which makes extensive use of icons, buttons, bars, and boxes to perform tasks.

Microsoft's Windows family of operating systems has both client and server versions and a streamlined GUI. Windows systems can perform multiple programming tasks simultaneously and have powerful networking capabilities, including the ability to access information from the Internet. **Windows Vista** features improved security, diagnostics, and networking; desktop searching; and support for multimedia. It has versions for home, small business, and enterprise users.

Windows operating systems for network servers provide network management functions, including tools for creating and operating Web sites and other Internet services. They include Windows Server 2003, which has multiple versions for small, medium, and large businesses, and businesses that have massive computer centers and processing requirements.

UNIX is an interactive, multiuser, multitasking operating system developed by Bell Laboratories in 1969 to connect various machines together and is highly supportive of

TABLE 4.3

Leading PC and Server Operating Systems

Operating System	Features
Windows Vista	Most recent Windows operating system. Includes improved security; desktop searching; and synchronization with mobile devices, cameras, and Internet services, as well as better support for video and TV.
Windows XP	Reliable, robust operating system for powerful PCs with versions for both home and corporate users. Features support of Internet access; multimedia; and group collaboration; along with powerful networking, security, and corporate management capabilities.
Windows Server 2003	Most recent Windows operating system for servers.
UNIX	Used for powerful PCs, workstations, and network servers. Supports multitasking, multiuser processing, and networking. Is portable to different models of computer hardware.
Linux	Open source, reliable alternative to UNIX and Windows operating systems that runs on many different types of computer hardware and can be modified by software developers.
Mac OS X	Operating system for the Macintosh computer. Is stable and reliable, with powerful search capabilities, support for video and image processing, and an elegant user interface. Most recent version is Leopard.

communications and networking. UNIX is often used on workstations and servers, and provides the reliability and scalability for running large systems on high-end servers. UNIX can run on many different kinds of computers and can be easily customized. Application programs that run under UNIX can be ported from one computer to run on a different computer with little modification. Graphical user interfaces have been developed for UNIX. UNIX poses some security problems because multiple jobs and users can access the same files simultaneously. Vendors have developed different versions of UNIX that are incompatible, thereby limiting software portability.

Linux is a UNIX-like operating system that can be downloaded from the Internet free of charge or purchased for a small fee from companies that provide additional tools for the software. It is free, reliable, compactly designed, and capable of running on many different hardware platforms, including servers, handheld computers, and consumer electronics.

Linux has become popular as a robust low-cost alternative to UNIX and the Windows operating systems. For example, E-Trade Financial saves $13 million annually with improved computer performance by running Linux on a series of small inexpensive IBM servers instead of large expensive Sun Microsystems servers running Sun's proprietary version of UNIX.

Linux plays a major role in the back office, running Web servers and local area networks in about 25 percent of the U.S. server market. Its use in desktop computers is growing steadily. IBM, HP, Intel, Dell, and Sun have made Linux a central part of their offerings to corporations, and major software vendors are starting to provide versions of their products that can run on Linux. Both IBM and Sun offer Linux-based office tools for free or a minimal charge of $50.

Linux is an example of **open source software**, which provides all computer users with free access to its program code, so they can modify the code to fix errors or to make improvements. Open source software, such as Linux, is not owned by any company or individual. A global network of programmers and users manages and modifies the software, usually without being paid to do so. Open source software is by definition not restricted to any specific operating system or hardware technology, although most open source software is currently based on a Linux or UNIX.

APPLICATION SOFTWARE AND DESKTOP PRODUCTIVITY TOOLS

Today, businesses have access to an array of tools for developing their application software. These include traditional programming languages, fourth-generation languages, application software packages and desktop productivity tools, software for developing Internet applications, and software for enterprise integration. It is important to know which software tools and programming languages are appropriate for the work your business wants to accomplish.

Application Programming Languages for Business

For business applications, the most important programming languages have been COBOL, C, C++, and Visual Basic. **COBOL (Common Business Oriented Language)** was developed in the early 1960s for processing large data files with alphanumeric characters (mixed alphabetic and numeric data) and for business reporting. C is a powerful and efficient language developed in the early 1970s that combines machine portability with tight control and efficient use of computer resources. C is used primarily by professional programmers to create operating systems and application software, especially for PCs. C++ is a newer version of C that has all the capabilities of C plus additional features for working with software objects. Unlike traditional programs, which separate data from the actions to be taken on the data, a software **object** combines data and procedures. Chapter 11 describes object-oriented software development in detail. Visual Basic is a widely used visual programming tool and environment for creating applications that run on Microsoft Windows operating systems. A **visual programming language** allows users to manipulate graphic or iconic elements to create programs.

Fourth-Generation Languages

Fourth-generation languages consist of a variety of software tools that enable end users to develop software applications with minimal or no technical assistance or that enhance professional programmers' productivity. Fourth-generation languages tend to be nonprocedural, or less procedural, than conventional programming languages. Procedural languages require specification of the sequence of steps, or procedures, that tell the computer what to do and how to do it. Nonprocedural languages need only specify what has to be accomplished rather than provide details about how to carry out the task. Some of these nonprocedural languages are *natural languages* that enable users to communicate with the computer using conversational commands resembling human speech.

Table 4.4 shows that there are seven categories of fourth-generation languages: PC software tools, query languages, report generators, graphics languages, application generators, application software packages, and very high-level programming languages. The table lists the tools in order of ease of use by nonprogramming end users. End users are most likely to work with PC software tools and query languages. **Query languages** are software tools that provide immediate online answers to requests for information that are not predefined, such as "Who are the highest-performing sales representatives?" Query languages are often tied to data management software (described later in this section) and to database management systems (see Chapter 5).

Table 4.4

Categories of Fourth-Generation Languages

Fourth-Generation Tool	Description	Example	
PC software tools	General-purpose application software packages for PCs.	WordPerfect Microsoft Access	Oriented toward end users
Query language	Languages for retrieving data stored in databases or files. Capable of supporting requests for information that are not predefined.	SQL	↑
Report generator	Extract data from files or databases to create customized reports in a wide range of formats not routinely produced by an information system. Generally provide more control over the way data are formatted, organized, and displayed than query languages.	Crystal Reports	
Graphics language	Retrieve data from files or databases and display them in graphic format. Some graphics software can perform arithmetic or logical operations on data as well.	SAS Graph Systat	
Application generator	Contain preprogrammed modules that can generate entire applications, including Web sites, greatly speeding development. A user can specify what needs to be done, and the application generator will create the appropriate program code for input, validation, update, processing, and reporting.	FOCUS Microsoft FrontPage	
Application software package	Software programs sold or leased by commercial vendors that eliminate the need for custom-written, in-house software.	Oracle PeopleSoft HCM mySAP ERP	↓
Very high-level programming language	Generate program code with fewer instructions than conventional languages, such as COBOL or FORTRAN. Designed primarily as productivity tools for professional programmers.	APL Nomad2	Oriented toward IS professionals

Software Packages and Desktop Productivity Tools

Much of the software used in businesses today is not custom programmed but consists of application software packages and desktop productivity tools. A **software package** is a prewritten, precoded, commercially available set of programs that eliminates the need for individuals or organizations to write their own software programs for certain functions. There are software packages for system software, but most package software is application software.

Software packages that run on mainframes and larger computers usually require professional programmers for their installation and support. Desktop productivity software packages for word processing, spreadsheets, data management, presentation graphics, and Web browsers are the most widely used software tools among business and consumer users.

Word Processing Software If you work in an office or attend school, you probably use word processing software every day. **Word processing software** stores text data electronically as a computer file rather than on paper. The word processing software allows the user to make changes in the document electronically, with formatting options to make changes in line spacing, margins, character size, and column width. Microsoft Word and WordPerfect are popular word processing packages.

Most word processing software has advanced features that automate other writing tasks: spelling checkers; style checkers (to analyze grammar and punctuation); thesaurus programs; mail merge programs, which link letters or other text documents with names and addresses in a mailing list; and capabilities for creating and accessing Web pages.

Businesses that need to create highly professional looking brochures, manuals, or books will likely use desktop publishing software for this purpose. Desktop publishing software provides more control over the placement of text, graphics, and photos in the layout of a page than does word processing software. Adobe PageMaker and QuarkXpress are two popular desktop publishing packages.

Spreadsheet Software Spreadsheets are valuable for applications in which numerous calculations with pieces of data must be related to each other. It organizes data into a grid of columns and rows. When you change a value or values, all other related values on the spreadsheet will be automatically recomputed.

You will often see spreadsheets in applications that require modeling and "what-if" analysis. After the user has constructed a set of mathematical relationships, the spreadsheet can be recalculated instantaneously using a different set of assumptions. Spreadsheet packages include graphics functions to present data in the form of line graphs, bar graphs, or pie charts, and the ability to read and create Web files. The most popular spreadsheet package is Microsoft Excel. Figure 4-8 illustrates the output from a spreadsheet for a break-even analysis and its accompanying graph.

Data Management Software Although spreadsheet programs are powerful tools for manipulating quantitative data, data management software, which we defined earlier in this chapter, is more suitable for creating and manipulating lists and for combining information from different files. PC database management packages have programming features and easy-to-learn menus that enable nonspecialists to build small information systems.

**Figure 4-8
Spreadsheet
Software**

Spreadsheet software organizes data into columns and rows for analysis and manipulation. Contemporary spreadsheet software provides graphing abilities for a clear, visual representation of the data in the spreadsheets. This sample break-even analysis is represented as numbers in a spreadsheet as well as a line graph for easy interpretation.

Total fixed cost	19,000.00
Variable cost per unit	3.00
Average sales price	17.00
Contribution margin	14.00
Break-even point	1,357

Custom Neckties Pro Forma Income Statement

Units sold	0.00	679	1,357	2,036	2,714
Revenue	0	11,536	23,071	34,607	46,143
Fixed cost	19,000	19,000	19,000	19,000	19,000
Variable cost	0	2,036	4,071	6,107	8,143
Total cost	19,000	21,036	23,071	25,107	27,143
Profit/Loss	(19,000)	(9,500)	0	9,500	19,000

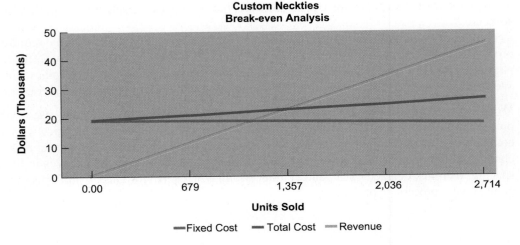

Custom Neckties
Break-even Analysis

Data management software typically has facilities for creating files and databases and for storing, modifying, and manipulating data for reports and queries. Popular database management software for the personal computer includes Microsoft Access, which has been enhanced to publish data on the Web. We discuss data management software in greater detail in Chapter 5.

Presentation Graphics Presentation graphics software allows users to create professional-quality graphics presentations. This software can convert numeric data into charts and other types of graphics and can include multimedia displays of sound, animation, photos, and video clips. The leading presentation graphics packages include capabilities for computer-generated slide shows and translating content for the Web. Microsoft PowerPoint and Lotus Freelance Graphics are popular presentation graphics packages.

Software Suites You will often see the major desktop productivity tools bundled together as a software suite. Microsoft Office is an example. There are a number of different versions of Office for home and business users, but the core desktop tools include Word word processing software; Excel spreadsheet software; Access database software; PowerPoint presentation graphics software; and Outlook, a set of tools for e-mail, scheduling, and contact management. Microsoft **Office 2007** features a new icon-driven Ribbon interface and enhanced capabilities to support collaborative work on the Web, publish Web documents, and update documents with information from the Web.

Low-cost alternatives to Microsoft Office are Sun Microsystems's *StarOffice* and *OpenOffice* (which can be downloaded over the Internet). Google recently launched a suite of Web-based desktop productivity tools that run over the Internet called Google Apps. The Interactive Session on Organizations discusses the capabilities of Google's tools in greater detail and whether they pose a challenge to Microsoft Office. As you read this case, try to determine what problems Google Apps are designed to solve and whether this online software suite is a viable alternative to productivity software on the desktop.

Web Browsers Web browsers are easy-to-use software tools for displaying Web pages and for accessing the Web and other Internet resources. Web browser software features a point-and-click GUI that can be employed throughout the Internet to access and display information stored on computers at other Internet sites. Browsers can display or present graphics, audio, and video information, as well as traditional text, and they allow you to click on-screen buttons or highlighted words to link to related Web sites. Web browsers have become the primary interface for accessing the Internet or for using networked systems based on Internet technology. The leading Web browsers today are Microsoft's Internet Explorer, Mozilla Firefox, and Netscape Navigator.

SOFTWARE FOR THE WEB: JAVA, AJAX, AND HTML

Special software tools help businesses build Web sites and applications that run on the Web. Java and Ajax are used for building applications that run on the Web and HTML is used for creating Web pages.

Java

Java is an operating system-independent, processor-independent, object-oriented programming language that has become a leading interactive programming environment for the Web. Java enables users to work with data on networked systems using Web browsers, reducing the need to write specialized software. At the enterprise level, Java is used for more complex e-commerce and e-business applications that require communication with an organization's back-end transaction processing systems.

Nearly all Web browser software has a Java platform built in. The Java platform has migrated into cell phones, automobiles, music players, game machines, and, finally, into set-top cable television systems serving interactive content.

INTERACTIVE SESSION: ORGANIZATIONS Will Google Take Over the Desktop?

The competition between Google and Microsoft is heating up another notch. Google has dominated Web search and ad placement technologies, while Microsoft has a near-monopoly on desktop office productivity and operating system software. Now Google is challenging Microsoft on the desktop as well.

In August 2006, Google launched Google Apps for Your Domain, a suite of Web-based applications targeted at small and midsize businesses. Google Apps bundled the company's e-mail, calendar, instant messaging, and Web site creation applications. The package was made available free of charge. Google designed the suite to be hosted in its own data center, but enabled customers to brand the components using their own domain names. The package also included management tools for those companies that had experienced IT professionals.

In February 2007, Google released Google Apps Premier Edition, which added its Docs word processing and Spreadsheets applications with the other tools in Google Apps for Your Domain. The Premier Edition also included APIs (application programming interfaces) to facilitate integration with a company's existing applications and the ability to build a customized home page with a single sign-on for all of a company's applications. An Apps user can save his or her files on Google's servers and access them anywhere that connects to the Internet using a standard Web browser. Multiple users are able to share files and work on them simultaneously online.

The charge for all of this: only $50 per year per employee—one-tenth the cost of Microsoft Office Professional Edition, which runs $499 for a single copy. The $50 license came with 10 gigabytes of storage for Gmail (e-mail) with no ads, a guaranteed performance level of 99.9-percent uptime, and tech support by phone 24 hours a day, seven days a week. Companies using the Web-based Google Apps save support costs because they do not have to hire their own IT workers to maintain the software.

Google Apps provides only basic functionality in its word processing and spreadsheet programs and lacks database and electronic presentation software to compete with Microsoft Access and PowerPoint. Microsoft's spreadsheet and word processing programs are far more powerful and rich in features than those offered by Google. However most Office users don't even use half of these features, so Google's value proposition is compelling.

Google positioned its productivity applications as "collaboration components" to Microsoft Office, especially in the context of larger businesses. Google did hope that its Gmail users who typically attached Office documents to their e-mail messages would instead move them to Google Apps for editing and sharing. Part of the company's overall business strategy was to encourage users to store both personal and business data on Google's servers where Google could appropriately match up documents with targeted ads.

Microsoft tried to counter Google by enhancing its Office 2007 suite with more capabilities for integrating with common business applications and additional collaboration tools. It introduced a new Office Live suite comprising Web design tools, a Web hosting service, and e-mail, calendar, contact manager, and online collaboration tools. At $39.95 per month, Office Live could not compete with Google Apps Premier Edition on price, and was not as integrated with the other productivity tools as Google Apps.

Google does, however, have major obstacles to overcome. Users must be connected to the Internet to use Google Apps. Microsoft Office users can work offline, which is a big advantage to mobile workers. Office, particularly Excel, is also entrenched in the business world. Although Google's document and spreadsheet files are interoperable with Microsoft's, companies may be hesitant to switch to Google's products, regardless of the savings.

Google must also face security issues. SF Bay Pediatrics, a medical clinic in San Francisco, implemented Google Apps in December 2006. The doctors at the clinic are enthusiastically collaborating on treatments and techniques using Google Docs. However, the clinic cannot use the services for sensitive information, such as patient records, because the hosted setup does not comply with HIPAA regulations for safeguarding privacy and security of medical records. According to Forrester Research, some large companies are wary of Google Apps because the data are not encrypted in Google's systems. Rajen Sheth, project manager for enterprise at Google, responds, "We put the security around [the data]. We provide a variety of security mechanisms to prevent penetration into the data center [with] strong perimeter security." Google practices what it preaches by storing its own data and intellectual property on the same system.

Google is probably more capable of backing up and protecting data than most small companies. However, Google's terms of service do contain language about the company not being responsible for lost data.

Small companies appear to be highly enthusiastic about the Google tools. According to Jason Winship, managing principal at Sea Change Management, "They are simple to use, they enable previously known levels of realtime collaboration." General Electric and Procter & Gamble are testing the tools, but only a few large organizations have been known to adopt Google Apps so far.

One of the largest Google Apps adopters to date is Arizona State University, where 40,000 students and faculty members are already using Google Gmail. ASU is using the free version of Apps, and will continue to reap the benefits of a no-cost solution as the university expands from 65,000 students to 90,000 over the next four years. ASU technology officer Adrian Sannier is also looking forward to the school's e-mail system and other applications being upgraded with the speed and innovation of Google's development team, rather than at the pace of a university IT department.

Sources: Paul McDougall, "Google Business Apps Shows the Changing Battle for Workers' Desktops," *InformationWeek*, February 24, 2007; Richard Martin, "Computer Science 101: A Case Study in Google Applications," *InformationWeek*, March 24, 2007; Harry McCracken, "PC World's Techlog: Google Apps vs. Microsoft Office," www.pcworld.com, February 22, 2007; and Chloe Albanesius, "Google Slyly Pushing Google Apps into Businesses," *PC Magazine*, accessed via Yahoo! News, April 26, 2007.

CASE STUDY QUESTIONS

1. What are the benefits of using Google Apps? What kinds of businesses are most likely to benefit? What kinds are least likely to benefit?

2. What reasons might a business have to continue using Microsoft Office for desktop productivity?

3. Search the Web for an article titled *Microsoft Office Live Vs. Google Apps For Your Domain* by Preston Gralla from September 2006. Do you agree with the author's conclusion?

MIS IN ACTION

Explore the Google Apps Web site. View the quick tour and comprehensive overview of the product, noting all the features and capabilities. Then answer the following question:

1. How could Google Apps be used by a small but growing events planning business to run the company? The business consists of an owner and three employees, who work with both individuals and companies to plan parties and large meetings. Two live in New York City, ones lives in Washington, D.C., and one lives in Boston. They all have laptops connected to the Internet. Their work involves soliciting clients; communicating with clients and vendors such as photographers, printers, musicians, caterers, and florists; and preparing budgets and bills for services.

Java software is designed to run on any computer or computing device, regardless of the specific microprocessor or operating system the device uses. Java achieves this neat trick by using a Java virtual machine built for each type of computer and operating system. The virtual machine enables it to run Java applications. A Macintosh PC, an IBM PC running Windows, a Sun server running UNIX, and even a smart cell phone or PDA can share the same Java application, reducing the costs of software development and creating the same user experience regardless of what kind of computer the user is working with.

In network environments, such as the Internet, Java is used to create miniature programs called *applets* that are designed to reside on centralized network servers. The network delivers to client computers only the applets required for a specific function. With Java applets residing on a network, a user can download only the software functions and data that he or she needs to perform a particular task, such as analyzing the revenue from one sales territory. The user does not need to maintain large software programs or data files on his or her desktop machine.

	Plain English	HTML
TABLE 4.5 Examples of HTML	Subcompact	<TITLE>Automobile</TITLE>
	4 passenger	<LI>4 passenger
	$16,800	<LI>$16,800

Ajax

Have you ever filled out a Web order form, made a mistake, and then had to start all over gain after a long wait for a new order form page to appear on your computer screen? Or visited a map site, clicked the North arrow once, and waited some time for an entire new page to load? **Ajax** (Asynchronous JavaScript and XML) is another Web development technique for creating interactive Web applications that prevents all of this inconvenience.

Ajax allows a client and server to exchange small pieces of data behind the scene so that an entire Web page does not have to be reloaded each time the user requests a change. So if you click North on a map site, such as Google Maps, the server downloads just that part of the application that changes with no wait for an entirely new map. You can also grab maps in map applications and move the map in any direction without forcing a reload of the entire page. Ajax uses JavaScript programs downloaded to your client to maintain a near-continuous conversation with the server you are using, making the user experience more seamless.

Hypertext Markup Language (HTML)

Hypertext markup language (HTML) is a page description language for specifying how text, graphics, video, and sound are placed on a Web page and for creating dynamic links to other Web pages and objects. Using these links, a user need only point at a highlighted keyword or graphic, click on it, and immediately be transported to another document. Table 4.5 illustrates some sample HTML statements.

HTML programs can be custom written, but they also can be created using the HTML authoring capabilities of Web browsers or of popular word processing, spreadsheet, data management, and presentation graphics software packages. HTML editors, such as Microsoft FrontPage and Adobe GoLive, are more powerful HTML authoring tool programs for creating Web pages.

WEB SERVICES

Web services refer to a set of loosely coupled software components that exchange information with each other using universal Web communication standards and languages. They can exchange information between two different systems regardless of the operating systems or programming languages on which the systems are based. They can be used to build open-standard, Web-based applications linking systems of two different organizations, and they can also be used to create applications that link disparate systems within a single company. Web services are not tied to any one operating system or programming language, and different applications can use them to communicate with each other in a standard way without time-consuming custom coding.

The foundation technology for Web services is **XML**, which stands for **extensible markup language**. This language was developed in 1996 by the World Wide Web Consortium (W3C, the international body that oversees the development of the Web) as a more powerful and flexible markup language than HTML for Web pages. Whereas HTML is limited to describing how data should be presented in the form of Web pages, XML can perform presentation, communication, and storage of data. In XML, a number is not simply a number; the XML tag specifies whether the number represents a price, a date, or a ZIP code. Table 4.6 illustrates some sample XML statements.

Plain English	XML
Subcompact	<AUTOMOBILETYPE="Subcompact">
4 passenger	<PASSENGERUNIT="PASS">4</PASSENGER>
$16,800	<PRICE CURRENCY="USD">$16,800</PRICE>

TABLE 4.6

Examples of XML

By tagging selected elements of the content of documents for their meanings, XML makes it possible for computers to manipulate and interpret their data automatically and perform operations on the data without human intervention. Web browsers and computer programs, such as order processing or enterprise resource planning (ERP) software, can follow programmed rules for applying and displaying the data. XML provides a standard format for data exchange, enabling Web services to pass data from one process to another.

Web services communicate through XML messages over standard Web protocols. *SOAP*, which stands for *Simple Object Access Protocol*, is a set of rules for structuring messages that enables applications to pass data and instructions to one another. *WSDL* stands for *Web services description language*; it is a common framework for describing the tasks performed by a Web service and the commands and data it will accept so that it can be used by other applications. *UDDI*, which stands for *Universal Description, Discovery, and Integration*, enables a Web service to be listed in a directory of Web services so that it can be easily located. Companies discover and locate Web services through this directory much as they would locate services in the Yellow Pages of a telephone book. Using these protocols, a software application can connect freely to other applications without custom programming for each different application with which it wants to communicate. Everyone shares the same standards.

The collection of Web services that are used to build a firm's software systems constitutes what is known as a service-oriented architecture. A **service-oriented architecture (SOA)** is set of self-contained services that communicate with each other to create a working software application. Business tasks are accomplished by executing a series of these services. Software developers reuse these services in other combinations to assemble other applications as needed.

Virtually all major software vendors, such as IBM, Microsoft, Sun, and HP, provide tools and entire platforms for building and integrating software applications using Web services. IBM includes Web service tools in its WebSphere e-business software platform, and Microsoft has incorporated Web services tools in its Microsoft .NET platform.

Dollar Rent-A-Car's systems use Web services to link its online booking system with Southwest Airlines's Web site. Although both companies' systems are based on different technology platforms, a person booking a flight on Southwest.com can reserve a car from Dollar without leaving the airline's Web site. Instead of struggling to get Dollar's reservation system to share data with Southwest's information systems, Dollar used Microsoft .NET Web services technology as an intermediary. Reservations from Southwest are translated into Web services protocols, which are then translated into formats that can be understood by Dollar's computers.

Other car rental companies have linked their information systems to airline companies' Web sites before. But without Web services, these connections had to be built one at a time. Web services provide a standard way for Dollar's computers to "talk" to other companies' information systems without having to build special links to each one. Dollar is now expanding its use of Web services to link directly to the systems of a small tour operator and a large travel reservation system as well as a wireless Web site for mobile phones and PDAs. It does not have to write new software code for each new partner's information systems or each new wireless device (see Figure 4-9).

Figure 4-9
How Dollar Rent-A-Car Uses Web Services
Dollar Rent-A-Car uses Web services to provide a standard intermediate layer of software to "talk" to other companies' information systems. Dollar Rent-A-Car can use this set of Web services to link to other companies' information systems without having to build a separate link to each firm's systems.

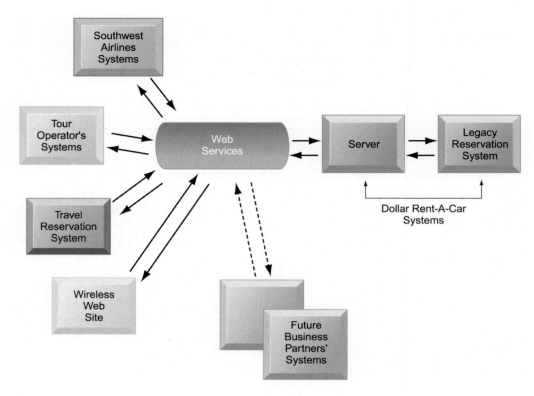

SOFTWARE TRENDS

Today there are many more sources for obtaining software and many more capabilities for users to create their own customized software applications. Expanding use of open source software, cloud computing, mashups, and widgets exemplify this trend.

Open Source Software

Arguably the most influential software trend is the movement towards open source software. As noted earlier, open source software is developed by a community of programmers around the world, who make their programs available to users under one of several different licensing schemes. Essentially, users of the software can use the software as is, modify it at will, and even include it in for-profit software applications.

The open source movement started out small in 1983 (when it was called "hippie software"), but it has since grown to be a major part of corporate computing infrastructure, as the foundation for programs such as Linux, and Apache, the most widely used Web server software. Today you can find thousands of open source computer programs to accomplish everything from e-commerce shopping carts and funds clearance to salesforce management.

Ubuntu is becoming increasingly popular as a low-cost open source alternative to Microsoft desktop products. It features a Linux-based operating system that is community-developed, updated regularly for free, and designed to be user-friendly. The software comes bundled with open source tools for desktop productivity (OpenOffice), Web browsing (Firefox), instant messaging, and graphics editing.

Cloud Computing, Mashups, and Widgets

In the past, software such as Microsoft Word or Adobe Illustrator came in a box and was designed to operate on a single machine. Today, you are more likely to download the software from the vendor's Web site to your machine or, increasingly, to use the software as a service delivered over the Internet. The term **cloud computing** is becoming popular for describing Web-based applications that are stored and accessed via the "cloud" of the

Internet. The software and the data they use are hosted on powerful servers in massive data centers, and can be accessed by anyone with an Internet connection and standard Web browser.

Google has teamed up with IBM to promote cloud computing, and it offers numerous Web-based applications, including the Google Apps desktop productivity tools described in this chapter's Interactive Session on Organizations. Microsoft is also starting to offer more software as services delivered on the Internet, including its Windows Live and Office Live suites. Windows Live includes updated e-mail and messaging programs, a photo-sharing application, and a writing tool for blogs. Office Live includes tools for building and hosting a Web site, e-mail support, and sharing projects, all of which are stored on Microsoft servers and accessed over the Internet.

The software you use for both personal and business tasks may consist of large, self-contained programs, or it may be composed of interchangeable components that integrate freely with other applications on the Internet. Individual users and entire companies mix and match these software components to create their own customized applications and to share information with others and the resulting software applications are called **mashups**.

The idea is to take different sources and produce a new work that is "greater than" the sum of its parts. Part of the movement called Web 2.0, and in the spirit of musical mashups, Web mashups combine the capabilities of two or more online applications to create a kind of hybrid that provides more customer value than the original sources alone. One area of great innovation is the mashup of mapping and satellite image software with local content. For instance, ChicagoCrime.org combines Google Maps with crime data for the city of Chicago. Users can search by location, police beat, or type of crime, and the results are displayed as color-coded map points on a Google Maps map. Google, Yahoo!, and Microsoft now offer tools to allow other applications to pull in information from their map and satellite images with relatively little programming.

You have performed a mashup if you have ever personalized your Facebook profile or your blog with a capability to display videos or slide shows. The small pieces of software code which enable users to embed content from one site into a Web page or another Web site are called widgets. **Widgets** are small software programs that can be added to Web pages or placed on the desktop to provide additional functionality. For example, the Flixter widget on Facebook profiles transports users to a place where they can list the films they have seen along with their ratings and reviews, view their friends' ratings and reviews, and find out what's playing in theaters.

Web widgets run inside a Web page or blog. Desktop widgets integrate content from an external source into the user's desktop to provide services such as a calculator, dictionary, or display of current weather conditions. The Apple Dashboard, Microsoft Windows Sidebar (in Vista), and Google Desktop Gadgets provide desktop widgets.

Widgets can also provide storefront windows for advertising and selling products and services. Random House Inc. has a widget that enables visitors to its Web site to click through to purchase new book releases from its online store. Amazon.com and Wal-Mart have toolbar widgets that enable surfers to search their Web stores while staying on their social network or another personal page. Widgets have become so powerful and useful that Facebook and Google launched programs to attract developers of widgets for their Web sites.

4.3 Managing Hardware and Software Technology

Selection and use of computer hardware and software technology has a profound impact on business performance. We now describe the most important issues you will face when managing hardware and software technology: capacity planning and scalability; determining the total cost of technology assets; determining whether to own and maintain your own hardware, software and other infrastructure components or lease them from an external technology service provider; and managing software localization.

CAPACITY PLANNING AND SCALABILITY

E-commerce and e-business are placing heavy new demands on hardware technology. Much larger processing and storage resources are required to process and store the surging digital transactions flowing between different parts of the firm, and between the firm and its customers and suppliers. Many people using a Web site simultaneously place great strains on a computer system, as does hosting large numbers of interactive Web pages with data-intensive graphics or video.

Managers and information systems specialists now need to pay more attention to hardware capacity planning and scalability than before. **Capacity planning** is the process of predicting when a computer hardware system becomes saturated. It considers factors such as the maximum number of users that the system can accommodate at one time; the impact of existing and future software applications; and performance measures, such as minimum response time for processing business transactions. Capacity planning ensures that the firm has enough computing power for its current and future needs. For example, the Nasdaq Stock Market performs ongoing capacity planning to identify peaks in the volume of stock trading transactions and to ensure it has enough computing capacity to handle large surges in volume when trading is very heavy.

Although information systems specialists perform capacity planning, input from business managers is essential. Business managers need to determine acceptable levels of computer response time and availability for the firm's mission-critical systems to maintain the level of business performance they expect. New applications, mergers and acquisitions, and changes in business volume all impact computer workload and must be considered when planning hardware capacity.

Scalability refers the ability of a computer, product, or system to expand to serve a large number of users without breaking down. Electronic commerce and electronic business both call for scalable IT infrastructures that have the capacity to grow with the business as the size of a Web site and number of visitors increase. Organizations must make sure they have sufficient computer processing, storage, and network resources to handle surging volumes of digital transactions and to make such data immediately available online.

TOTAL COST OF OWNERSHIP (TCO) OF TECHNOLOGY ASSETS

When you calculate how much your hardware and software cost, their purchase price is only the beginning. You must also consider ongoing administration costs for hardware and software upgrades, maintenance, technical support, training, and even utility and real estate costs for running and housing the technology. The **total cost of ownership (TCO)** model can be used to analyze these direct and indirect costs to help determine the actual cost of owning a specific technology. Table 4.7 describes the most important TCO components to consider in a TCO analysis.

When all these cost components are considered, the TCO for a PC might run up to three times the original purchase price of the equipment. "Hidden costs" for support staff, downtime, and additional network management can make distributed client/server architectures—especially those incorporating handheld computers and wireless devices—more expensive than centralized mainframe architectures.

Many large firms are saddled with redundant, incompatible hardware and software because their departments and divisions have been allowed to make their own technology purchases. These firms could reduce their TCO through greater centralization and standardization of their hardware and software resources. Companies could reduce the size of the information systems staff required to support their infrastructure if the firm minimized the number of different computer models and pieces of software that employees are allowed to use.

USING TECHNOLOGY SERVICE PROVIDERS

Some of the most important questions facing managers are "How should we acquire and maintain our technology assets? Should we build software applications ourselves or

Hardware acquisition	Purchase price of computer hardware equipment, including computers, terminals, storage, and printers
Software acquisition	Purchase or license of software for each user
Installation	Cost to install computers and software
Training	Cost to provide training to information systems specialists and end users
Support	Cost to provide ongoing technical support, help desks, and so forth
Maintenance	Cost to upgrade the hardware and software
Infrastructure	Cost to acquire, maintain, and support related infrastructure, such as networks and specialized equipment (including storage backup units)
Downtime	Lost productivity if hardware or software failures cause the system to be unavailable for processing and user tasks
Space and energy	Real estate and utility costs for housing and providing power for the technology

TABLE 4.7

Total Cost of Ownership (TCO) Cost Components

outsource them to an external contractor? Should we purchase and run them ourselves or rent them from external service providers?" In the past, most companies ran their own computer facilities and developed their own software. Today, more and more companies are obtaining their hardware and software technology from external service vendors.

Outsourcing

A number of firms are **outsourcing** the maintenance of their IT infrastructures and the development of new systems to external vendors. They may contract with an external service provider to run their computer center and networks, to develop new software, or to manage all of the components of their IT infrastructures, as did Procter & Gamble (P&G). P&G agreed to pay HP $3 billion to manage its IT infrastructure, computer center operations, desktop and end-user support, network management, and applications development and maintenance for global operations in 160 countries.

Specialized Web hosting services are available for companies that lack the financial or technical resources to operate their own Web sites. A **Web hosting service** maintains a large Web server, or a series of servers, and provides fee-paying subscribers with space to maintain their Web sites. The subscribing companies may create their own Web pages or have the hosting service, or a Web design firm, create them. Some services offer *co-location*, in which the firm actually purchases and owns the server computer housing its Web site but locates the server in the physical facility of the hosting service.

Firms often retain control over their hardware resources but outsource custom software development or maintenance to outside firms, frequently firms that operate offshore in low-wage areas of the world. When firms outsource software work outside their national borders, the practice is called **offshore software outsourcing**. Offshore firms provided about $10 billion in software services to the United States in 2006, which is about 2 percent of the combined U.S. software plus software services budget (about $500 billion). Until recently, this type of software development involved lower-level maintenance, data entry, and call center operations, but with the growing sophistication and experience of offshore firms, particularly in India, more and more new program development is taking place offshore. Chapter 11 discusses offshore software outsourcing in greater detail.

In order to manage their relationship with an outsourcer or technology service provider, firms will need a contract that includes a **service level agreement (SLA)**. The SLA is a formal contract between customers and their service providers that defines the specific responsibilities of the service provider and the level of service expected by the customer.

SLAs typically specify the nature and level of services provided, criteria for performance measurement, support options, provisions for security and disaster recovery, hardware and software ownership and upgrades, customer support, billing, and conditions for terminating the agreement.

On-Demand Computing

Even if firms continue to run their own IT infrastructures, they now have the option to rent additional infrastructure capacity on an as-needed basis. **On-demand computing** refers to firms off-loading peak demand for computing power to remote, large-scale data processing centers. In this manner, firms can reduce their technology expenditures by investing just enough to handle average processing loads and paying for only as much additional computing power as the market demands. Another term for on-demand computing is *utility computing*, which suggests that firms purchase computing power from central computing utilities and pay only for the amount of computing power they use, much as they would pay for electricity. Amazon.com, described in the chapter-ending case study, is expanding its business to offer on-demand computing services. IBM, HP, and Sun Microsystems also offer on-demand services.

In addition to lowering the cost of owning hardware resources, on-demand computing gives firms greater agility to use technology. On-demand computing shifts firms from having a fixed infrastructure capacity toward a highly flexible infrastructure, some of it owned by the firm, and some of it rented from giant computer centers run by technology specialists. This arrangement frees firms to launch entirely new business processes that they would never attempt with a fixed infrastructure.

Software as a Service (SaaS)

It is clear that software will be increasingly be delivered and used over networks as a service. Earlier in this chapter, we described cloud computing, in which software is delivered as a service over the Internet. In addition to free or low-cost tools for individuals and small businesses provided by Google or Yahoo!, enterprise software and other complex business functions are available as services from the major commercial software vendors. Instead of buying and installing software programs, subscribing companies rent the same functions from these services, with users paying either on a subscription or per-transaction basis. Services for delivering and providing access to software remotely as a Web-based service are now referred to as **Software as a Service (SaaS)**.

A leading example is Salesforce.com, which provides on-demand software services for customer relationship management, including salesforce automation, partner relationship management, marketing, and customer service. It includes tools for customization, integrating its software with other corporate applications, and creating new applications.

If you are running a business, especially a small business, you might find it much easier to "rent" software from another firm and avoid the expense and difficulty of installing, operating, and maintaining the hardware and software on your own. Such reasons convinced the Patriots Trail Girl Scouts, described in Chapter 11, to use a service providing QuickBase software to run their order management system.

Companies considering the SaaS model need to carefully assess the costs and benefits of the service, weighing all people, organizational, and technology issues, including the ability to integrate with existing systems and deliver a level of service and performance that is acceptable for the business. In some cases, the cost of renting software can add up to more than purchasing and maintaining the application in-house. Yet there may be benefits to paying more for software as a service if this decision allows the company to focus on core business issues instead of technology challenges.

MANAGING SOFTWARE LOCALIZATION FOR GLOBAL BUSINESS

If you are operating a global company, all of the management issues we have just described will be affected by the need to create systems that can be realistically used by multiple business units in different countries. Although English has become a kind of standard business language, this is truer at higher levels of companies and not throughout the middle and lower ranks. Software may have to be built with local language interfaces before a new information system can be successfully implemented worldwide.

These interfaces can be costly and messy to build. Menu bars, commands, error messages, reports, queries, online data entry forms, and system documentation may need to be translated into all the languages of the countries where the system will be used. To be truly useful for enhancing productivity of a global workforce, the software interfaces must be easily understood and mastered quickly. The entire process of converting software to operate in a second language is called *software localization*.

Global systems must also consider differences in local cultures and business processes. Cross-functional systems such as enterprise and supply chain management systems are not always compatible with differences in languages, cultural heritages, and business processes in other countries.

In a global systems environment, all of these factors add to the TCO and will influence decisions about whether to outsource or use technology service providers.

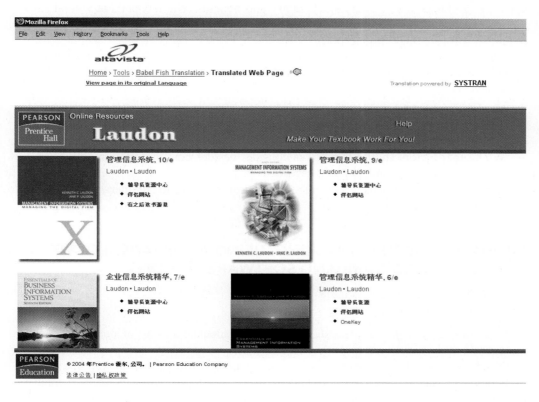

This page from the Pearson Prentice Hall Web site for Laudon text books was translated into Chinese using AltaVista Babel Fish translation tools. Web sites and software interfaces for global systems may have to be translated into multiple languages to accomodate users in other parts of the world.

4.4 Hands-On MIS

The projects in this section give you hands-on experience in using spreadsheet software to help a real-world company make a rent versus buy decision about new manufacturing software, using spreadsheet software to evaluate alternative desktop systems, and using Web research to budget for a sales conference.

IMPROVING DECISION MAKING: MAKING THE RENT VERSUS BUY DECISION FOR HARDWARE AND SOFTWARE

Software skills: Spreadsheet formulas, electronic presentation software (optional)
Business skills: Technology rent vs. buy decision, TCO analysis

This project provides an opportunity for you help a real-world company make a decision about whether to rent or buy new technology. You will use spreadsheet software to compare the total three-year cost of licensing and maintaining new manufacturing software or renting the software from a SaaS provider.

Dirt Bikes would like to implement new production planning, quality control, and scheduling software for use by 25 members of its manufacturing staff. Management is trying to determine whether to purchase the software from a commercial vendor along with any hardware required to run the software or to use a hosted software solution from a SaaS provider. (The hosted software runs on the service provider's computer.) You have been asked to help management with this rent versus buy decision by calculating the total cost of each option over a three-year period.

The costs of purchasing the software (actually for purchasing a license from the vendor to use its software package) include the initial purchase price of the software (licensing fee of $100,000 paid in the first year), the cost of implementing and customizing the software in the first year ($20,000), one new server to run the software (a first-year purchase of $4,000), one information systems specialist devoting half of his or her time to supporting the software ($55,000 in full-time annual salary and benefits with a 3-percent annual salary increase each year after the first year), user training in the first year ($10,000), and the cost of annual software upgrades ($5,000).

The costs of renting hosted software are the rental fees ($2,500 annually per user), implementation and customization costs ($12,000 in the first year), and training ($10,000 in the first year).

- Use your spreadsheet software to calculate the total cost of renting or purchasing this software over a three-year period. Identify the lowest-price alternative that meets Dirt Bikes's requirements.
- What other factors should Dirt Bikes consider besides cost in determining whether to rent or buy the hardware and software?
- (Optional) If possible, use electronic presentation software to summarize your findings for management.

IMPROVING DECISION MAKING: USING A SPREADSHEET TO EVALUATE HARDWARE AND SOFTWARE OPTIONS

Software skills: Spreadsheet formulas
Business skills: Technology pricing

In this exercise, you will use spreadsheet software to calculate the cost of alternative desktop systems.

You have been asked to obtain pricing information on hardware and software for an office of 30 people. Using the Internet, get pricing for 30 PC desktop systems (monitors, computers, and keyboards) manufactured by Lenovo, Dell, and HP/Compaq as listed at their respective corporate Web sites. (For the purposes of this exercise, ignore the fact that desktop systems usually come with preloaded software packages.) Also obtain pricing on 15 monochrome desktop printers manufactured by HP and by Xerox. Each desktop system must satisfy the minimum specifications shown in the following table:

Minimum Desktop Specifications	
Processor speed	3 GHz
Hard drive	250 GB
RAM	1 GB
CD-RW/DVD-ROM speed	48 speed
Monitor (diagonal measurement)	17 inches

Each desktop printer must satisfy the minimum specifications shown in the following table:

Minimum Monochrome Printer Specifications	
Print speed	12 pages per minute
Print resolution	600 × 600
Network ready?	Yes
Maximum price/unit	$1,000

After pricing the desktop systems and printers, obtain pricing on 30 copies of the most recent versions of Microsoft Office and Sun StarOffice desktop productivity packages, and on 30 copies of Microsoft Windows Vista Business. The application software suite packages come in various versions, so be sure that each package contains programs for word processing, spreadsheet analysis, database analysis, graphics preparation, and e-mail.

Prepare a spreadsheet showing your research results for the desktop systems, for the printers, and for the software. Use your spreadsheet software to determine the desktop system, printer, and software combination that will offer both the best performance and pricing per worker. Because every two workers will share one printer (15 printers/30 systems), assume only half a printer cost per worker in the spreadsheet. Assume that your company will take the standard warranty and service contract offered by each product's manufacturer.

IMPROVING DECISION MAKING: USING WEB RESEARCH TO BUDGET FOR A SALES CONFERENCE

In this exercise, you will use software at various online travel sites to arrange transportation and lodging for a large sales force to attend a sales conference at two alternative locations. You will use that information to calculate total travel and lodging costs and decide where to hold the conference.

Software skills: Internet-based software
Business skills: Researching transportation and lodging costs

The Foremost Composite Materials Company is planning a two-day sales conference for October 19–20, starting with a reception on the evening of October 18. The conference consists of all-day meetings that the entire sales force, numbering 125 sales representatives and their 16 managers, must attend. Each sales representative requires his or her own room, and the company needs two common meeting rooms, one large enough to hold the entire sales force plus a few visitors (200) and the other able to hold half the force. Management has set a budget of $95,000 for the representatives' room rentals. The hotel must also have such services as overhead and computer projectors, as well as a business center and banquet facilities. It also should have facilities for the company reps to be able to work in their rooms and to enjoy themselves in a swimming pool or gym facility. The company would like to hold the conference in either Miami or Marco Island, Florida.

Foremost usually likes to hold such meetings in Hilton- or Marriott-owned hotels. Use the Hilton and Marriott Web sites to select a hotel in whichever of these cities that would enable the company to hold its sales conference within its budget.

Link to the two sites' home pages, and search them to find a hotel that meets Foremost's sales conference requirements. Once you have selected the hotel, locate flights arriving the afternoon prior to the conference because the attendees will need to check in the day before and attend your reception the evening prior to the conference. Your attendees will be coming from Los Angeles (54), San Francisco (32), Seattle (22), Chicago (19), and Pittsburgh (14). Determine costs of each airline ticket from these cities. When you are finished, create a budget for the conference. The budget will include the cost of each airline ticket, the room cost, and $60 per attendee per day for food.

- What was your final budget?
- Which did you select as the best hotel for the sales conference and why?

LEARNING TRACKS

The following Learning Tracks provide content relevant to topics covered in this chapter:

1. How Computer Hardware and Software Work
2. Evolution of IT Infrastructure
3. Technology Drivers of IT Infrastructure Evolution
4. IT Infrastructure: Management Opportunities, Challenges, and Solutions
5. Service Level Agreements

Review Summary

1 **What are the components of IT infrastructure?** IT infrastructure consists of the shared technology resources that provide the platform for the firm's specific information system applications. Major IT infrastructure components include computer hardware, software, data management technology, networking and telecommunications technology, and technology services.

2 **What are the major computer hardware, data storage, input, and output technologies used in business?** Computers are categorized as mainframes, midrange computers, PCs, workstations, or supercomputers. Mainframes are the largest computers; midrange computers can be servers; PCs are desktop or laptop machines; workstations are desktop machines with powerful mathematical and graphic capabilities; and supercomputers are sophisticated, powerful computers that can perform massive and complex computations rapidly. Computing power can be further increased by creating a computational grid that combines the computing power of all the computers on a network. In the client/server model of computing, computer processing is split between "clients" and "servers" connected via a network. The exact division of tasks between client and server depends on the application.

The principal secondary storage technologies are magnetic disk, optical disc, and magnetic tape. Optical CD-ROM and DVD discs can store vast amounts of data compactly and some types are rewritable. Storage area networks (SANs) connect multiple storage devices on a separate high-speed network dedicated to storage. The principal input devices are keyboards, computer mice, touch screens, magnetic ink and optical character recognition devices, pen-based instruments, digital scanners, sensors, audio input devices, and radio-frequency identification devices. The principal output devices are cathode ray tube terminals, printers, and audio output devices.

3 **What are the major types of computer software used in business?** The two major types of software are system software and application software. System software coordinates the various parts of the computer system and mediates between application software and computer hardware. Application software is used to develop specific business applications.

The system software that manages and controls the activities of the computer is called the operating system. Leading PC and server operating systems include Windows Vista, Windows XP, Windows Server 2003, UNIX, Linux, and the Macintosh operating system. Linux is a powerful, resilient open source operating system that can run on multiple hardware platforms and is used widely to run Web servers.

The principal programming languages used in business application software include COBOL, C, C++, and Visual Basic. Fourth-generation languages are less procedural than conventional programming languages and enable end users to perform many software tasks that previously required technical specialists. They include popular PC desktop productivity tools, such as word processing, spreadsheet, data management, presentation graphics, and Web browser software. Java is an operating-system- and hardware-independent programming language that is the leading interactive programming environment for the Web. HTML is a page description language for creating Web pages.

Web services are loosely coupled software components based on XML and open Web standards that can work with any application software and operating system. They can be used as components of Web-based applications linking the systems of two different organizations or to link disparate systems of a single company.

4 **What are the most important contemporary hardware and software trends?** Increasingly, computing is taking place over a network with computing and telecommunications platforms increasingly integrated. Edge computing balances the processing load for Web-based applications by distributing parts of the Web content, logic, and processing among multiple servers. In autonomic computing, computer systems have capabilities for automatically configuring and repairing themselves. Open source software is proliferating because it allows users to modify the software at will and use it as a platform for new derivative applications. Mashups and widgets are the building blocks of new software applications and services using the cloud computing model.

5 **What are the principal issues in managing hardware and software technology?** Managers and information systems specialists need to pay special attention to hardware capacity planning and scalability to ensure that the firm has enough computing power for its current and future needs. Businesses also need to balance the costs and benefits of building and maintaining their own hardware and software versus outsourcing or using an on-demand computing model. The total cost of ownership (TCO) of the organization's technology assets includes not only the original cost of computer hardware and software but also costs for hardware and software upgrades, maintenance, technical support, and training. Companies with global operations need to manage software localization.

Key Terms

Ajax, 138
Application server, 122
Application software, 118
Autonomic computing, 127
Batch processing, 125
C, 132
Capacity planning, 142
CD-ROM (compact disc read-only memory), 123
Centralized processing, 121
Client, 121
Client/server computing, 121
Cloud computing, 140
COBOL (COmmon Business Oriented Language), 132
Data management software, 118
Digital video disc (DVD), 123
Distributed processing, 121
Edge computing, 125
Extensible markup language (XML), 138
Fourth-generation languages, 132
Graphical user interface (GUI), 130
Grid computing, 121

Hypertext markup language (HTML), 138
Input devices, 124
Java, 135
Legacy systems, 119
Linux, 00
Magnetic disk, 122
Magnetic tape, 123
Mainframe, 120
Mashups, 141
Midrange computers, 120
Multicore processor, 129
Nanotechnology, 125
N-tier client/server architectures, 122
Object, 132
Office 2007, 135
Offshore software outsourcing, 143
On-demand computing, 144
Online processing, 125
Open-source software, 132
Operating system, 129
Output devices, 124
Outsourcing, 143
Personal computer (PC), 119
Presentation graphics, 135
Query languages, 132

SaaS (Software as a Service), 144
Scalability, 142
Server, 119
Service level agreement (SLA), 143
Service-oriented architecture (SOA), 139
Software package, 133
Spreadsheet, 134
Storage area networks (SANs), 123
Supercomputer, 121
System software, 118
Total cost of ownership (TCO), 142
UNIX, 130
Virtualization, 127
Visual programming language, 132
Web browsers, 135
Web hosting service, 143
Web server, 122
Web services, 138
Widget, 141
Windows Vista, 130
Word processing software, 133
Workstation, 119

Review Questions

1. What are the components of IT infrastructure?
- Define information technology (IT) infrastructure and describe each of its components.

2. What are the major computer hardware, data storage, input, and output technologies used in business?
- List and describes the various type of computers available to businesses today.
- Define the client/server model of computing and describe the difference between a two-tiered and n-tier client/server architecture.
- List the most important secondary storage media and the strengths and limitations of each.
- List and describe the major computer input and output devices.
- Distinguish between batch and online processing.

3. What are the major types of computer software used in business?
- Distinguish between application software and system software and explain the role played by the operating system of a computer.
- List and describe the major PC and server operating systems.

- Name and describe each category of fourth-generation software tool and explain how fourth-generation languages differ from conventional programming languages.
- Name and describe the major desktop productivity software tools.
- Explain how Java and HTML are used in building applications for the Web.
- Define Web services, describe the technologies they use, and explain how Web services benefit businesses.

4. What are the most important contemporary hardware and software trends?
- Define and describe grid computing, edge computing, autonomic computing, virtualization, and multicore processing.
- Explain why open source software is so important today and its benefits for business.
- Define cloud computing, mashups, and widgets and explain how they benefit individuals and businesses.

5. What are the principal issues in managing hardware and software technology?
- Explain why managers need to pay attention to capacity planning and scalability of technology resources.
- List and describe the cost components used to calculate the TCO of technology assets.
- Describe the benefits of outsourcing, on-demand computing, and SaaS for businesses.
- Explain why software localization has become an important management issue for global companies.

Discussion Questions

1. Why is selecting computer hardware and software for the organization an important business decision? What people, organization, and technology issues should be considered when selecting computer hardware and software?

2. Should organizations use software service providers for all their software needs? Why or why not? What people, organization, and technology factors should be considered when making this decision?

Video Case

You will find a video case illustrating some of the concepts in this chapter on the Laudon Web site along with questions to help you analyze the case.

Teamwork

Evaluating Server Operating Systems

Form a group with three or four of your classmates. One group should research and compare the capabilities and costs of Linux versus the most recent version of the Windows operating system for servers. Another group should research and compare the capabilities and costs of Linux versus UNIX. Each group should present its findings to the class, using electronic presentation software, if possible.

BUSINESS PROBLEM-SOLVING CASE

Amazon's New Store: Utility Computing

Looking for a good deal on that DVD box set of "The West Wing" or the last Harry Potter book? Since opening as an online bookstore in 1995, Amazon.com has morphed into a virtual superstore with product offerings to 36 categories, including furniture, jewelry, clothing, and groceries. But what if what you really need is a place to store several terabytes of data? Or the computing power of 100 Linux servers? Now you can get those from Amazon too.

Over its first 12 years, Amazon.com committed $2 billion to refine the information technology infrastructure that was largely responsible for making it the top online retailer in the world. Following the burst of the dot com bubble in 2001, Amazon focused heavily on modernizing its data centers and software so that it could add new features to its product pages such as discussion forums and software for audio and video.

In March 2006, Amazon introduced the first of several new services that founder Jeff Bezos hoped would transform its future business. With Simple Storage Service (S3) and, later, Elastic Compute Cloud (EC2), Amazon entered the utility computing market. The company had realized that the benefits of its $2 billion investment in technology could also be valuable to other companies.

Amazon had tremendous computing capacity, but like most companies, only used a small portion of it at any one time. Moreover, the Amazon infrastructure was considered by many to be among the most robust in the world. So, the one-time bookseller exposed the guts of its entire system over the Internet to any developer who could make use of them. Amazon began to sell its computing power on a per-usage basis, just like a power company sells electricity.

S3 is a data storage service that is designed to make Web-scale computing easier and more affordable for developers. Customers pay 15 cents per gigabyte of data stored per month on Amazon's network of disk drives. There is also a charge of 20 cents per gigabyte of data transferred. The service has neither a minimum fee nor a start-up charge. Customers pay for exactly what they use and no more. Data may be stored as objects ranging in size from 1 byte to 5 gigabytes, with an unlimited number of objects permitted. Using S3 does not require any client software, nor does it require the user to set up any hardware. Amazon designed S3 to provide a fast, simple, and inexpensive method for businesses to store data on a system that is scalable and reliable. S3 promises 99.99-percent availability through a mechanism of fault tolerance that fixes failures without any downtime.

Working in conjunction with S3, EC2 enables businesses to utilize Amazon's servers for computing tasks, such as testing software. Using EC2 incurs charges of 10 cents per instance-hour consumed. An instance supplies the user with the equivalent of a 1.7 GHz x86 processor with 1.75 GB of RAM, a 160 GB hard drive, and 250 Mbps of bandwidth on the network. The service also includes 20 cents per GB of data traffic inbound and outbound per month, as well as the standard S3 pricing for storing an Amazon Machine Image (AMI), which contains the applications, libraries, data, and configuration settings that a business uses to run its processes.

What does Amazon specifically bring to utility computing? Business writer Nicholas Carr states "Amazon is coming to it fresh, without any baggage. As a result, it's been able to target the current sweet spot for utility computing—startups and smaller companies that have Web-based businesses and need highly scalable systems." Amazon distinguishes itself from traditional utility computing vendors in that it views its Web services as a standalone business, as opposed to as an appendage to a large corporation.

According to Adam Selipsky, vice president of product management and developer relations for Amazon Web Services (AWS), Amazon is really a technology company that can bring a wealth of engineering prowess and experience to independent developers and corporations by allowing them to run their processes on Amazon's computer systems. Selipsky also emphasizes that AWS is not simply about providing great amounts of storage capacity and server time. AWS creates the opportunity for others to work at Web scale without making the mistakes that Amazon has already made and learned from. Simplicity and ease-of-use are not generally terms that go along with building a Web-scale application, but they are major selling points for AWS. Users build on the services through APIs made available by Amazon.

From the very beginning, customers have responded strongly to S3 and EC2. Competition to secure test slots for EC2 was intense, and the slots were all taken within five hours of the program's launch. Bezos targeted micro-sized businesses and Web startups as customers for AWS, but the services have also attracted some midsize businesses and potential big players in e-business.

Webmail.us provides e-mail management services for thousands of companies around the world from its Blacksburg, Virginia, headquarters. When the company needed to increase its short-term storage capacity and the redundancy of its primary data backups, it selected S3 as its storage provider. Webmail.us sends more than a terabyte of data to Amazon to store with S3 every week. Bill Boebel, cofounder and chief technology officer of Webmail.us, was very pleased that his company was able to create a simple interface with which Amazon can accept the abundant small files that his company manages. Other backup systems have had difficulty handling the typical Webmail.us backup load, and most hosting companies would require a custom application to handle such data. Webmail.us even used EC2 to develop its storage interface. According to CEO Pat Matthews, Amazon immediately reduced his company's data backup costs by 75 percent.

Powerset is an up-and-coming search engine company based in San Francisco that wants to focus its time, and the $12.5 million it has raised, on its core business, natural language search technology. By using S3 and EC2, Powerset saves upfront cash expenditure, and eliminates the risk that building an infrastructure will take longer than expected. Many of the traditional utility computing suppliers charge around one dollar per CPU hour, or 10 times what Amazon charges.

Powerset's CEO Barney Pell says that the pay-as-you go model is very important because his company does not know how fast it will grow. What he does know is that the demand for Powerset's service will come in bursts, and trying to predict hardware needs is a dangerous game. If Powerset overestimates its peak usage capacity, the company will waste money on unnecessary hardware. If the company underestimates peak usage, it could fail to meet its users' expectations and damage its business. With AWS in place, Powerset never has to worry about being unable to add computing power when a spike in usage occurs.

As Powerset prepares to launch its search engine to the public in 2007, it is using EC2 for the rigorous and crucial background work of reading and indexing Web pages. The company is looking into whether EC2 will meet the needs of the run-time application that processes the search queries users will submit when the search engine goes live.

SmugMug Inc., an online photo-sharing startup, was immediately drawn to the ease with which it could back up photos on Amazon's S3. Storing its users' photos on Amazon's devices prevents SmugMug from having to purchase its own additional storage and saves the company $500,000 per year. CEO Don MacAskill anticipates that future annual savings could reach $1 million.

As with any large business initiative, there are issues for Amazon to confront before anyone can declare AWS to be a successful venture. Larger businesses may be more inclined to use a more established com-

pany, especially one with more experience hosting core applications and data. Currently, Amazon's flexible, pay-as-you-go model gives the company a competitive advantage over companies that require service contracts.

However, according to Daniel Golding, vice president of Tier 1 Research, the established companies, such as IBM, HP, and Sun Microsystems, may follow Amazon's lead and offer utility computing without service-level agreements (SLAs). Complicating the matter is that some companies are wary of using a supplier that does not offer SLAs, which guarantee the availability of services in terms of time. Golding suggests that Amazon may have launched a major shift in the industry, but others will reap the rewards while Amazon may suffer for it.

One more challenge for Amazon is the viability of AWS itself. Will the services actually function as planned? The company's track record with new technology projects is mixed. Amazon launched its A9.com search site with much fanfare, but the site never really caught on with users. Moreover, the growth of AWS could be harmful to Amazon's Web services line as well as to its retail line if Amazon does not position itself to handle a dramatic increase in demand on its infrastructure. AWS customers could drop the service, and Amazon.com could falter. January 2007 saw the first significant outage of S3 servers. Customers voiced their frustrations of receiving slow service and error messages. Faulty hardware installed during an upgrade caused the problem, which was resolved quickly. However, a quick explanation and resolution did not stop some users from questioning whether Amazon is capable of being their solution for hosted storage going forward.

AWS has charmed some high-profile clients. Microsoft uses S3 to increase software download speeds for its users. Linden Lab, creator of the online virtual world Second Life, uses the service to alleviate the pounding its servers take when the company releases its frequent software upgrades.

For now, the potential of AWS is being converted into performance mostly by tech savvy developers with financial backing. As more developers contribute and the services evolve, Amazon hopes one day to make it possible for anyone with an idea and an Internet connection to begin to put together the next Amazon.com.

Sources: Edward Cone, "Amazon at Your Service," *CIO Insight*, January 7, 2007; Robert D. Hof, "So You Wanna Be a Web Tycoon? Amazon Can Help," www.webworkerdaily.com, January 24, 2007; "Amazon's Hosted Storage Hits Bump," ZDNet.com, January 8, 2007; Thomas Claburn, "Open Source Developers Build on Amazon Web Services," TechWeb.com, January 12, 2007; "Useful Technology™ Leverages Amazon Web Services," Business Wire, accessed via Forbes.com, January 25, 2007; and Mamoon Yunus, Rizwan Mallal, and Dave Shaffer, "Amazon EC2 and Oracle SOA Suite a Strong Combo," *Dr. Dobb's Journal*, January 14, 2007.

Case Study Questions

1. What technology services does Amazon provide? What are the business advantages to Amazon and to subscribers of these services? What are the disadvantages to each? What kinds of businesses are likely to benefit from these services?

2. How do the concepts of capacity planning, scalability, and TCO apply to this case? Apply these concepts both to Amazon and to subscribers of its services.

3. Search the Internet for companies that supply utility computing. Select two or three such companies and compare them to Amazon. What services do these companies provide? What promises do they make about availability? What is their payment model? Who is their target client? If you were launching a Web startup business, would you choose one of these companies over Amazon for technology services? Why or why not? Would your answer change if you were working for a larger company and had to make a recommendation to the CIO?

4. Name three examples each of IT infrastructure hardware components and software components that are relevant to this case. Describe how these components fit into or are used by Amazon's Web services and/or the customers that subscribe to these services.

5. Think of an idea for a Web-based startup business. Explain how this business could utilize Amazon's S3 and EC2 services.

Foundations of Business Intelligence: Databases and Information Management

CHAPTER 5

STUDENT LEARNING OBJECTIVES

After completing this chapter, you will be able to answer the following questions:

1. How does a relational database organize data and how does it differ from an object-oriented database?

2. What are the principles of a database management system?

3. What are the principal tools and technologies for accessing information from databases to improve business performance and decision making?

4. What is the role of information policy and data administration in the management of organizational data resources?

5. Why is data quality assurance so important for a business?

CHAPTER OUTLINE

NASCAR RACES TO MANAGE ITS DATA

The National Association for Stock Car Auto Racing, better known as NASCAR, is on its way to becoming America's most popular spectator sport. In 2005, 75 million people attended NASCAR races, the highest number of attendees of any sport in the United States. NASCAR racing is second only to the National Football League (NFL) in television ratings. From 1995 to 2004, NASCAR's fan base ballooned from 63 million to 75 million, and retail sales of NASCAR-licensed merchandise jumped more than 250 percent, from approximately $600 million to $2.1 billion.

What's wrong with this picture? Not much, except NASCAR management thinks the company can still do better. It thinks it can grow NASCAR's fan base even more, especially in areas outside the South where NASCAR has traditionally been most popular. But NASCAR needs the right data to identify who its fans are, and it is having trouble putting all those data together.

Until about five years ago, NASCAR considered information systems a back-office function. Its entire race process—obtaining credentials for sponsors, running races, managing relationships with sponsors, and paying drivers and their

teams—was heavily manual and paper-oriented. Race tracks did not have technology to transmit race data effectively.

The picture changed after NASCAR started recruiting top-notch executives from Fortune 500, sports, and media companies who appreciated what IT could do for a business. Roger Lovell, NASCAR's Managing Director of IT, was empowered to launch an IT-enabled business transformation.

Lovell and his team of information systems specialists developed a scalable, stable IT infrastructure, standardized NASCAR's desktop computing technology, and implemented a plan to beef up systems security. They began gathering more data electronically about driver performance during a race and analyzing the data so fans could follow drivers' performance similar to the way baseball uses batting averages. In 2006, NASCAR implemented a state-of-the-art Mobile Technology Center to collect and process timing and scoring data as races take place.

Now Lovell and Roger VanDerSnick, NASCAR's vice president of marketing, are working on building a single comprehensive database of racing car fans that could be shared with business partners and used for marketing to those fans. Such a database provides a better understanding of NASCAR fans' demographic profiles, behaviors, and preferences for targeting offers such as NASCAR-branded merchandise, opportunities to meet drivers at races, or products and services from sponsors. In addition to generating revenue, these initiatives would increase fan loyalty, help NASCAR attract new sponsors, and convince existing sponsors to increase their spending.

Creating a consolidated fan database is challenging because the data are housed in many disparate databases. NASCAR.com has its own database as does the NASCAR members club and each driver's fan club. It is likely that these databases do not store fan data in a consistent manner, so the data will need to be "cleansed" for discrepancies, inconsistencies, and errors, and restructured to fit a single standard format. NASCAR and its partners will have to establish rules for using a consolidated fan database so that NASCAR fans are not bombarded with excessive marketing appeals and the privacy agreements that racing teams, drivers, and sponsors have established with their own fans are respected. Stoneacre Partners, who built a relational database for the Official NASCAR Membership Club, is in charge of the project.

Sources: Meridith Levinson, "IT Supercharges NASCAR," *CIO Magazine*, February 1, 2006; K.C. Jones, "NASCAR Revs Up Data Center on Wheels," *InformationWeek*, May 19, 2006; www.onmc.com, accessed June 16, 2007; and www.nascar.com, accessed June 16, 2007.

NASCAR's experience illustrates the importance of data management and database systems for business. NASCAR has experienced phenomenal growth. But its future growth and business performance depend on what it can or can't do with its customer data. How businesses store, organize, and manage their data has a tremendous impact on organizational effectiveness.

The chapter-opening diagram calls attention to important points raised by this case and this chapter. Management decided that NASCAR's business strategy needed to focus on creating customer intimacy. Data about NASCAR fans and potential customers had been stored in a number of different databases where they could not be easily retrieved and analyzed. NASCAR did not have all the information it needed for identifying all of its existing and potential fans to market its products and services.

In the past, NASCAR had used heavily manual paper processes to manage its information. This solution was no longer viable as the organization grew larger. A more appropriate solution was to integrate NASCAR customer data from all of its disparate sources into a single comprehensive fan database. In addition to using appropriate technology, NASCAR had to correct and reorganize the data into a standard format and establish rules with its business partners for accessing information in the new database.

A comprehensive fan database helps NASCAR and its partners boost profitability by making it easier to target potential customers for their products and services. The database

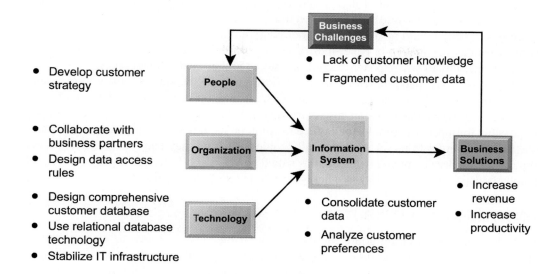

- Develop customer strategy
- Collaborate with business partners
- Design data access rules
- Design comprehensive customer database
- Use relational database technology
- Stabilize IT infrastructure

Business Challenges
- Lack of customer knowledge
- Fragmented customer data

People

Organization

Technology

Information System
- Consolidate customer data
- Analyze customer preferences

Business Solutions
- Increase revenue
- Increase productivity

improves operational efficiency and decision making by having more complete customer data available and making it easier to access the data. By helping NASCAR understand its own customers better, the database increases the opportunities for selling to these customers and the chances that new products and services will be successful.

HEADS UP

This chapter focuses on databases and how businesses use databases to achieve their objectives. Small and large companies alike use databases to record business transactions, control inventories, manage employees, and achieve customer and supplier intimacy. Once these data are properly organized in database management systems, the data can be analyzed, and the resulting information can be used to develop new businesses, achieve operational excellence, inform management decision making, and help the firm fulfill its reporting requirements to higher authorities. Entire businesses, such as UPS, credit card companies, and Google, are based on databases. It would not be an overstatement to say that databases are the foundation of business today and that most businesses would fail should their databases cease to exist.

5.1 The Database Approach to Data Management

A **database** is a collection of related files containing records on people, places, or things. One of the most successful databases in modern history is the telephone book. The telephone book is a collection of records on people and businesses who use telephones. The telephone book lists four pieces of information for each phone user: last name, first name, address, and phone number. It also contains information on businesses and business categories, such as auto dealers or plumbing suppliers. The telephone book draws its information from a database with files for customers, business classifications, and area codes and geographic regions.

Prior to the development of digital databases, a business would use large filing cabinets filled with paper files to store information on transactions, customers, suppliers, inventory, and employees. They would also use lists, laboriously collated and typed by hand, to quickly summarize the information in paper files. You can still find paper-based manual databases in most doctors' offices where patient records are stored in thousands of paper files.

Needless to say, paper-based databases are extremely inefficient and costly to maintain, often contain inaccurate data, are slow, and make it difficult to access the data in a timely fashion. Paper-based databases are also extremely inflexible. For instance, it would be nearly impossible for a paper-based doctor's office to combine its files on prescriptions with its files on patients in order to produce a list of all people for whom they had prescribed a specific drug. For a modern computer database, this would be very easy. In fact, a powerful feature of computer databases is the ability to quickly relate one set of files to another.

ENTITIES AND ATTRIBUTES

How do you start thinking about the data for your business and how to manage them? If you are starting up or running a business, you will have to identify the data you will need to run your business. Typically, you will be using data on categories of information, such as customers, suppliers, employees, orders, products, shippers, and perhaps parts. Each of these generalized categories representing a person, place, or thing on which we store and maintain information is called an **entity**. Each entity has specific characteristics, called **attributes**. For example, the entity SUPPLIER has specific attributes, such as the supplier's name and address, which would most likely include street, city, state, and ZIP code. The entity PART typically has attributes such as part description, price of each part (unit price), and supplier who produced the part.

ORGANIZING DATA IN A RELATIONAL DATABASE

If you stored this information in paper files, you would probably have a file on each entity and its attributes. In an information system, a database organizes the data much the same way, grouping related pieces of data together. The **relational database** is the most common type of database today. Relational databases organize data into two-dimensional tables (called relations) with columns and rows. Each table contains data on an entity and its attributes. For the most part, there is one table for each business entity. So, at the most basic level, you will have one table for customers, and a table each for suppliers, parts in inventory, employees, and sales transactions.

Let's look at how a relational database would organize data about suppliers and parts. Take the SUPPLIER table, which is illustrated in Figure 5-1. It consists of a grid of columns and rows of data. Each individual element of data about a supplier, such as the supplier name,

Figure 5-1
A Relational Database Table
A relational database organizes data in the form of two-dimensional tables. Illustrated here is a table for the entity SUPPLIER showing how it represents the entity and its attributes. Supplier_Number is the key field.

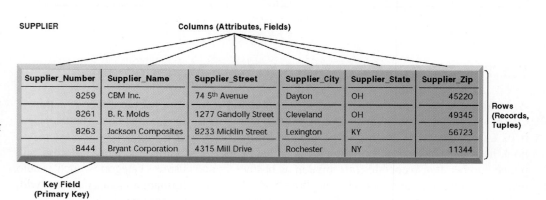

street, city, state, and ZIP code, is stored as a separate **field** within the SUPPLIER table. Each field represents an attribute for the entity SUPPLIER. Fields in a relational database are also called columns.

The actual information about a *single supplier* that resides in a table is called a row. Rows are commonly referred to as **records**, or, in very technical terms, as **tuples**.

Note that there is a field for Supplier_Number in this table. This field uniquely identifies each record so that the record can be retrieved, updated, or sorted, and it is called a **key field**. Each table in a relational database has one field that is designated as its **primary key**. This key field is the unique identifier for all the information in any row of the table, and this primary key cannot be duplicated.

We could use the supplier's name as a key field. However, if two different suppliers had the same name (which does happen from time to time), supplier name would not uniquely identify each, so it is necessary to assign a special identifier field for this purpose. For example, if you had two suppliers, both named "CBM," but one was based in Dayton and another in St. Louis, it would be easy to confuse them. However, if each has a unique Supplier_Number, such confusion is prevented.

We also see that the address information has been separated into four separate fields: Supplier_Street, Supplier_City, Supplier_State, and Supplier_Zip. Data are separated into the smallest elements that one would want to access separately to make it easy to select only the rows in the table that match the contents of one field, such as all the suppliers in Ohio (OH). The rows of data can also be sorted by the contents of the Supplier_State field to get a list of suppliers by state regardless of their cities.

So far, the SUPPLIER table does not have any information about the parts that a particular supplier provides for your company. PART is a separate entity from SUPPLIER, and fields with information about parts should be stored in a separate PART table (see Figure 5-2).

Why not keep information on parts in the same table as suppliers? If we did that, each row of the table would contain the attributes of both PART and SUPPLIER. Because one supplier could supply more than one part, the table would need many extra rows for a single supplier to show all the parts that supplier provided. We would be maintaining a great deal of redundant data about suppliers, and it would be difficult to search for the information on any individual part because you would not know whether this part is the first or fiftieth part in this supplier's record. A separate table, PART, should be created to store these three fields and solve this problem.

The PART table would also have to contain another field, Supplier_Number, so that you would know the supplier for each part. It would not be necessary to keep repeating all the

PART

Part_Number	Part_Name	Unit_Price	Supplier_Number
137	Door latch	22.00	8259
145	Side mirror	12.00	8444
150	Door molding	6.00	8263
152	Door lock	31.00	8259
155	Compressor	54.00	8261
178	Door handle	10.00	8259

Primary Key   **Foreign Key**

Figure 5-2
The PART Table
Data for the entity PART have their own separate table. Part_Number is the primary key and Supplier_Number is the foreign key, enabling users to find related information from the SUPPLIER table about the supplier for each part.

information about a supplier in each PART record because having a Supplier_ Number field in the PART table allows you to "look up" the data in the fields of the SUPPLIER table.

Notice that Supplier_Number appears in both the SUPPLIER and PART tables. In the SUPPLIER table, Supplier_Number is the primary key. When the field Supplier_Number appears in the PART table it is called a **foreign key** and is essentially a look-up field to look up data about the supplier of a specific part. Note that the PART table would itself have its own primary key field, Part_Number, to uniquely identify each part. This key is not used to link PART with SUPPLIER but might be used to link PART with a different entity.

As we organize data into tables, it is important to make sure that all the attributes for a particular entity apply only to that entity. If you were to keep the supplier's address with the PART record, that information would not really relate only to PART; it would relate to both PART and SUPPLIER. If the supplier's address were to change, it would be necessary to alter the data in every PART record rather than only once in the SUPPLIER record.

ESTABLISHING RELATIONSHIPS

Now that we've broken down our data into a SUPPLIER table and a PART table, we must make sure we understand the relationship between them. A schematic called an **entity-relationship diagram** is used to clarify table relationships in a relational database. The most important piece of information provided by an entity-relationship diagram is the manner in which two tables are related to each other. Tables in a relational database may have one-to-one, one-to-many, and many-to-many relationships.

An example of a one-to-one relationship might be a situation where a human resources system must store confidential data about employees. It might store data, such as the employee name, date of birth, address, and job position in one table, and confidential data about that employee, such as salary or pension benefits, in another table. These two tables pertaining to a single employee would have a one-to-one relationship because each record in the EMPLOYEE table with basic employee data has only one related record in the table storing confidential data.

The relationship between the SUPPLIER and PART entities in our database is a one-to-many relationship: Each supplier can supply more that one part, but each part has only one supplier. For every record in the SUPPLIER table, there may be many related records in the PART table.

Figure 5-3 illustrates how an entity-relationship diagram would depict this one-to-many relationship. The boxes represent entities. The lines connecting the boxes represent relationships. A line connecting two entities that ends in two short marks designates a one-to-one relationship. A line connecting two entities that ends with a crow's foot topped by a short mark indicates a one-to-many relationship. Figure 5-3 shows that each PART has only one SUPPLIER, but many PARTs can be provided by the same SUPPLIER.

We would also see a one-to-many relationship if we wanted to add a table about orders to our database because one supplier services many orders. The ORDER table would only contain the Order_Number and Order_Date. Figure 5-4 illustrates a report showing an order of parts from a supplier. If you look at the report, you can see that the information on the top-right portion of the report comes from the ORDER table. The actual line items ordered are listed in the lower portion of the report.

Figure 5-3
A Simple Entity-Relationship Diagram
This diagram shows the relationship between the entities SUPPLIER and PART.

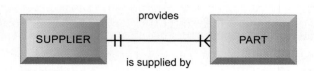

Order Number: 3502
Order Date: 1/15/2008

Supplier Number: 8259
Supplier Name: CBM Inc.
Supplier Address: 74 5th Avenue, Dayton, OH 45220

Order_Number	Part_Number	Part_Quantity	Part_Name	Unit_Price	Extended Price
3502	137	10	Door latch	22.00	$220.00
3502	152	20	Door lock	31.00	620.00
3502	178	5	Door handle	10.00	50.00
			Order Total:		$890.00

Figure 5-4
Sample Order Report
The shaded areas show which data came from the SUPPLIER, LINE_ITEM, and ORDER tables. The database does not maintain data on Extended Price or Order Total because they can be derived from other data in the tables.

Because one order can be for many parts from a supplier and a single part can be ordered many times on different orders, this creates a many-to-many relationship between the PART and ORDER tables. Whenever a many-to-many relationship exists between two tables, it is necessary to link these two tables in a table that joins this information. Creating a separate table for a line item in the order would serve this purpose. This table is often called a *join table* or an *intersection relation*. This join table contains only three fields: Order_Number and Part_Number, which are used only to link the ORDER and PART tables, and Part_Quantity. If you look at the bottom-left part of the report, this is the information coming from the LINE_ITEM table.

We would thus wind up with a total of four tables in our database. Figure 5-5 illustrates the final set of tables, and Figure 5-6 shows what the entity-relationship diagram for this set of tables would look like. Note that the ORDER table does not contain data on the extended price because that value could be calculated by multiplying Unit_Price by Part_Quantity. This data element can be derived when needed using information that already exists in the PART and LINE_ITEM tables. Order Total is another derived field calculated by totaling the extended prices for items ordered.

The process of streamlining complex groups of data to minimize redundant data elements and awkward many-to-many relationships, and increase stability and flexibility is called **normalization.** A database that has been properly designed and normalized will be easy to maintain, and will minimize duplicate data. The Learning Tracks at the end of this chapter direct you to more detailed discussions of normalization, entity-relationship diagramming, and database design on the Laudon Web site.

Relational database systems try to enforce **referential integrity** rules to ensure that relationships between coupled tables remain consistent. When one table has a foreign key that points to another table, you may not add a record to the table with the foreign key unless there is a corresponding record in the linked table. In the database we have just created, the foreign key Supplier_Number links the PART table to the SUPPLIER table. We may not add a new record to the PART table for a part with supplier number 8266 unless there is a corresponding record in the SUPPLIER table for supplier number 8266. We must also delete the corresponding record in the PART table if we delete the record in the SUPPLIER table for supplier number 8266. In other words, we shouldn't have parts from nonexistent suppliers!

The example provided here for parts, orders, and suppliers is a simple one. Even in a very small business, you will have tables for other important entities, such as customers, shippers, and employees. A very large corporation might have databases with thousands of entities (tables) to maintain. What is important for any business, large or small, is to have a good data model that includes all of its entities and the relationships among them, one that is organized to minimize redundancy, maximize accuracy, and make data easily accessible for reporting and analysis.

PART

Part_Number	Part_Name	Unit_Price	Supplier_Number
137	Door latch	22.00	8259
145	Side mirror	12.00	8444
150	Door molding	6.00	8263
152	Door lock	31.00	8259
155	Compressor	54.00	8261
178	Door handle	10.00	8259

LINE_ITEM

Order_Number	Part_Number	Part_Quantity
3502	137	10
3502	152	20
3502	178	5

ORDER

Order_Number	Order_Date
3502	1/15/2008
3503	1/16/2008
3504	1/17/2008

SUPPLIER

Supplier_Number	Supplier_Name	Supplier_Street	Supplier_City	Supplier_State	Supplier_Zip
8259	CBM Inc.	74 5th Avenue	Dayton	OH	45220
8261	B. R. Molds	1277 Gandolly Street	Cleveland	OH	49345
8263	Jackson Components	8233 Micklin Street	Lexington	KY	56723
8444	Bryant Corporation	4315 Mill Drive	Rochester	NY	11344

Figure 5-5
The Final Database Design with Sample Records
The final design of the database for suppliers, parts, and orders has four tables. The LINE_ITEM table is a join table that eliminates the many-to-many relationship between ORDER and PART.

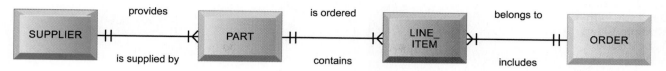

Figure 5-6
Entity-Relationship Diagram for the Database with Four Tables
This diagram shows the relationship between the entities SUPPLIER, PART, LINE_ITEM, and ORDER.

It cannot be emphasized enough: If the business does not get its data model right, the system will not be able to serve the business right. The company's systems will not be as effective as they could be because they will have to work with data that may be inaccurate, incomplete, or difficult to retrieve. Understanding the organization's data and how they should be represented in a database is perhaps the most important lesson you can learn from this course.

For example, Famous Footwear, a shoe store chain with more than 800 locations in 49 states, could not achieve its goal of having "the right style of shoe in the right store for sale at the right price" because its database was not properly designed for rapidly adjusting store inventory. The company had an Oracle relational database running on an IBM AS/400 midrange computer, but the database was designed primarily for producing standard reports for management rather than for reacting to marketplace changes. Management could not obtain precise data on specific items in inventory in each of its stores. The company had to work around this problem by building a new database where the sales and inventory data could be better organized for analysis and inventory management.

5.2 Database Management Systems

Now that you have started creating the files and identifying the data required by your business, you will need a database management system to help you manage and use the data. A **database management system (DBMS)** is a specific type of software for creating, storing, organizing, and accessing data from a database. Microsoft Access is a DBMS for desktop systems, whereas DB2, Oracle Database, and Microsoft SQL Server are DBMS for large mainframes and midrange computers. MySQL is a popular open-source DBMS, and Oracle Database Lite is a DBMS for small handheld computing devices. All of these products are relational DBMS that support a relational database.

The DBMS relieves the end user or programmer from the task of understanding where and how the data are actually stored by separating the logical and physical views of the data. The *logical view* presents data as end users or business specialists would perceive them, whereas the *physical view* shows how data are actually organized and structured on physical storage media, such as a hard disk.

The database management software makes the physical database available for different logical views required by users. For example, for the human resources database illustrated in Figure 5-7, a benefits specialist might require a view consisting of the employee's name, social security number, and health insurance coverage. A payroll department member might need data such as the employee's name, social security number, gross pay, and net pay. The data for all of these views is stored in a single database, where it can be more easily managed by the organization.

Figure 5-7
Human Resources Database with Multiple Views
A single human resources database provides many different views of data, depending on the information requirements of the user. Illustrated here are two possible views, one of interest to a benefits specialist and one of interest to a member of the company's payroll department.

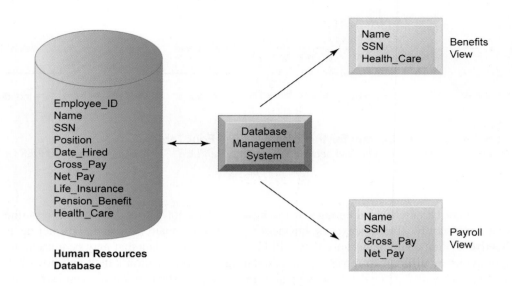

OPERATIONS OF A RELATIONAL DBMS

In a relational database, tables can be easily combined to deliver data required by users, provided that any two tables share a common data element. Let's return to the database we set up earlier with PART and SUPPLIER tables illustrated in Figures 5-1 and 5-2.

Suppose we wanted to find in this database the names of suppliers who could provide us with part number 137 or part number 150. We would need information from two tables: the SUPPLIER table and the PART table. Note that these two tables have a shared data element: Supplier_Number.

In a relational database, three basic operations, as shown in Figure 5-8, are used to develop useful sets of data: select, project, and join. The *select* operation creates a subset consisting of all records in the file that meet stated criteria. Select creates, in other words, a subset of rows that meet certain criteria. In our example, we want to select records (rows) from the PART table where the Part_Number equals 137 or 150. The *join* operation combines relational tables to provide the user with more information than is available in individual tables. In our example, we want to join the now-shortened PART table (only parts 137 or 150 will be presented) and the SUPPLIER table into a single new table.

The *project* operation creates a subset consisting of columns in a table, permitting the user to create new tables that contain only the information required. In our example, we want to extract from the new table only the following columns: Part_Number, Part_Name, Supplier_Number, and Supplier_Name (see Figure 5-8).

CAPABILITIES OF DATABASE MANAGEMENT SYSTEMS

A DBMS includes capabilities and tools for organizing, managing, and accessing the data in the database. The most important are its data definition capability, data dictionary, and data manipulation language.

DBMS have a **data definition** capability to specify the structure of the content of the database. It would be used to create database tables and to define the characteristics of the fields in each table. This information about the database would be documented in a **data dictionary**. A data dictionary is an automated or manual file that stores definitions of data elements and their characteristics. Microsoft Access has a rudimentary data dictionary capability that displays information about the name, description, size, type, format, and other properties of each field in a table (see Figure 5-9). Data dictionaries for large corporate databases may capture additional information, such as usage; ownership (who in the

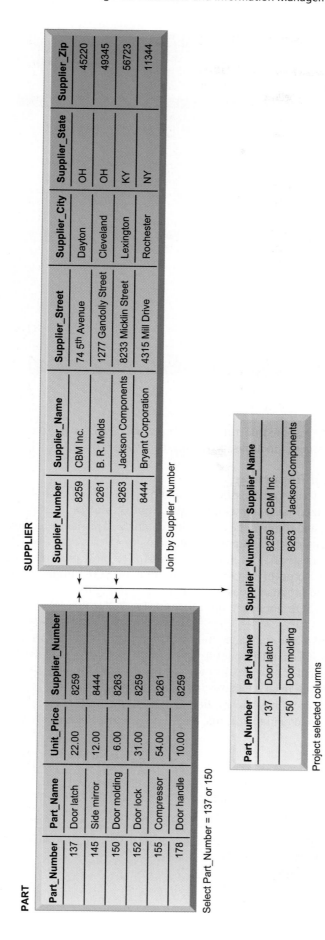

SUPPLIER

Supplier_Number	Supplier_Name	Supplier_Street	Supplier_City	Supplier_State	Supplier_Zip
8259	CBM Inc.	74 5th Avenue	Dayton	OH	45220
8261	B. R. Molds	1277 Gandolly Street	Cleveland	OH	49345
8263	Jackson Components	8233 Micklin Street	Lexington	KY	56723
8444	Bryant Corporation	4315 Mill Drive	Rochester	NY	11344

Join by Supplier_Number

PART

Part_Number	Part_Name	Unit_Price	Supplier_Number
137	Door latch	22.00	8259
145	Side mirror	12.00	8444
150	Door molding	6.00	8263
152	Door lock	31.00	8259
155	Compressor	54.00	8261
178	Door handle	10.00	8259

Select Part_Number = 137 or 150

Part_Number	Part_Name	Supplier_Number	Supplier_Name
137	Door latch	8259	CBM Inc.
150	Door molding	8263	Jackson Components

Project selected columns

Figure 5-8
The Three Basic Operations of a Relational DBMS
The select, project, and join operations enable data from two different tables to be combined and only selected attributes to be displayed.

Figure 5-9
Access Data
Dictionary Features
*Microsoft Access has a
rudimentary data dictio-
nary capability that dis-
plays information about
the size, format, and
other characteristics of
each field in a database.
Displayed here is the
information maintained in
the SUPPLIER table. The
small key icon to the left
of Supplier_Number indi-
cates that it is a key
field.*

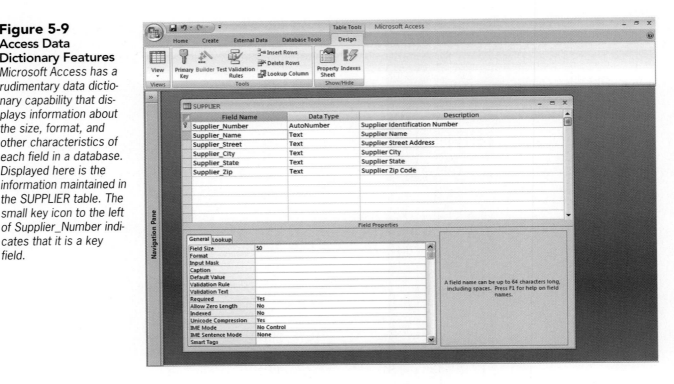

organization is responsible for maintaining the data); authorization; security; and the
individuals, business functions, programs, and reports that use each data element.

Querying and Reporting

DBMS include tools for accessing and manipulating information in databases. Most DBMS
have a specialized language called a **data manipulation language** that is used to add,
change, delete, and retrieve the data in the database. This language contains commands that
permit end users and programming specialists to extract data from the database to satisfy
information requests and develop applications. The most prominent data manipulation language today is **Structured Query Language**, or **SQL**. Figure 5-10 illustrates the SQL
query that would produce the new resultant table in Figure 5-8. You can find out more about
how to perform SQL queries in our Learning Tracks for this chapter, which can be found on
the Laudon Web site.

Users of DBMS for large and midrange computers, such as DB2, Oracle, or SQL Server,
would employ SQL to retrieve information they needed from the database. Microsoft Access
also uses SQL, but it provides its own set of user-friendly tools for querying databases and
for organizing data from databases into more polished reports.

Microsoft Access has capabilities to help users create queries by identifying the tables
and fields they want and the results, and then selecting the rows from the database that meet

Figure 5-10
**Example of an SQL
Query**
*Illustrated here are the
SQL statements for a
query to select suppliers
for parts 137 or 150.
They produce a list with
the same results as
Figure 5-8.*

SELECT PART.Part_Number, PART.Part_Name, SUPPLIER.Supplier_Number,
SUPPLIER.Supplier_Name
FROM PART, SUPPLIER
WHERE PART.Supplier_Number = SUPPLIER.Supplier_Number AND
Part_Number = 137 OR Part_Number = 150;

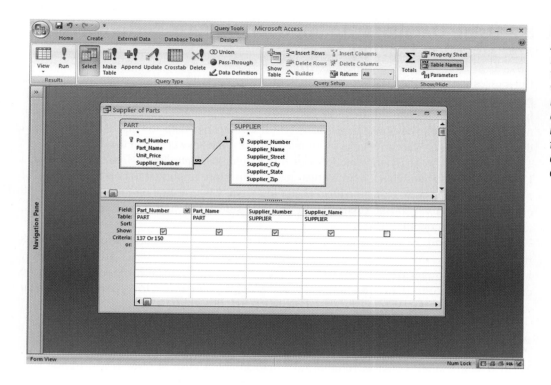

Figure 5-11
An Access Query
Illustrated here is how the query in Figure 5–10 would be constructed using Microsoft Access query-building tools. It shows the tables, fields, and selection criteria used for the query.

particular criteria. These actions in turn are translated into SQL commands. Figure 5-11 illustrates how the same query as the SQL query to select parts and suppliers in Figure 5-10 would be constructed using Microsoft Access.

DBMS typically include capabilities for report generation so that the data of interest can be displayed in a more structured and polished format than would be possible just by querying. Crystal Reports is a popular report generator for large corporate DBMS, although it can also be used with Microsoft Access.

Microsoft Access also has capabilities for developing desktop system applications. These include tools for creating data entry screens, reports, and developing the logic for processing transactions. These capabilities are primarily used by information systems specialists.

OBJECT-ORIENTED DATABASES

Many applications today and in the future require databases that can store and retrieve not only structured numbers and characters but also drawings, images, photographs, voice, and full-motion video. DBMS designed for organizing structured data into rows and columns are not well suited to handling graphics-based or multimedia applications. Object-oriented databases are better suited for this purpose.

An **object-oriented DBMS** stores the data and procedures that act on those data as objects that can be automatically retrieved and shared. Object-oriented database management systems (OODBMS) are becoming popular because they can be used to manage the various multimedia components or Java applets used in Web applications, which typically integrate pieces of information from a variety of sources.

Although object-oriented databases can store more complex types of information than relational DBMS, they are relatively slow compared with relational DBMS for processing large numbers of transactions. Hybrid **object-relational DBMS** systems are now available to provide capabilities of both object-oriented and relational DBMS.

5.3 Using Databases to Improve Business Performance and Decision Making

Businesses use their databases to keep track of basic transactions, such as paying suppliers, processing orders, serving customers, and paying employees. But they also need databases to provide information that will help the company run the business more efficiently, and help managers and employees make better decisions. If a company wants to know which product is the most popular or who is its most profitable customer, the answer lies in the data.

For example, by analyzing data from customer credit card purchases, Louise's Trattoria, a Los Angeles restaurant chain, learned that quality was more important than price for most of its customers, who were college-educated and liked fine wine. Acting on this information, the chain introduced vegetarian dishes, more seafood selections, and more expensive wines, raising sales by more than 10 percent.

In a large company, with large databases or large systems for separate functions, such as manufacturing, sales, and accounting, special capabilities and tools are required for analyzing vast quantities of data and for accessing data from multiple systems. These capabilities include data warehousing, data mining, and tools for accessing internal databases through the Web.

DATA WAREHOUSES

What if you wanted concise, reliable information about current operations, trends, and changes across the entire company? If you worked in a large company, this might be difficult because data are often maintained in separate systems, such as sales, manufacturing, or accounting. Some of the data you needed might be found in the sales system, and other pieces in the manufacturing system. Many of these systems are older legacy systems that use outdated data management technologies or file systems where information is difficult for users to access.

You might have to spend an inordinate amount of time locating and gathering the data you needed, or you would be forced to make your decision based on incomplete knowledge. If you wanted information about trends, you might also have trouble finding data about past events because most firms only make their current data immediately available. Data warehousing addresses these problems.

WHAT IS A DATA WAREHOUSE?

A **data warehouse** is a database that stores current and historical data of potential interest to decision makers throughout the company. The data originate in many core operational transaction systems, such as systems for sales, customer accounts, and manufacturing, and may include data from Web site transactions. The data warehouse consolidates and standardizes information from different operational databases so that the information can be used across the enterprise for management analysis and decision making.

Figure 5-12 illustrates how a data warehouse works. The data warehouse makes the data available for anyone to access as needed, but it cannot be altered. A data warehouse system also provides a range of ad hoc and standardized query tools, analytical tools, and graphical reporting facilities. Many firms use intranet portals to make the data warehouse information widely available throughout the firm.

DATA MARTS

Companies often build enterprise-wide data warehouses, where a central data warehouse serves the entire organization, or they create smaller, decentralized warehouses called data marts. A **data mart** is a subset of a data warehouse in which a summarized or highly focused portion of the organization's data is placed in a separate database for a specific population of users. For example, a company might develop marketing and sales data marts to

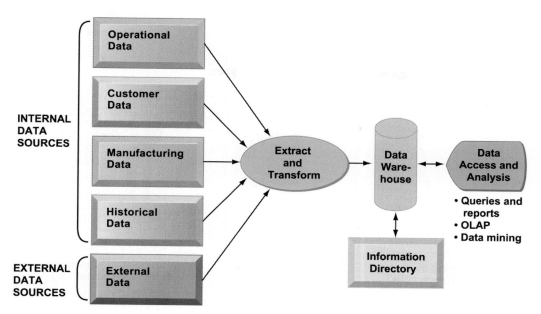

Figure 5-12
Components of a Data Warehouse
The data warehouse extracts current and historical data from multiple operational systems inside the organization. These data are combined with data from external sources and reorganized into a central database designed for management reporting and analysis. The information directory provides users with information about the data available in the warehouse.

deal with customer information. A data mart typically focuses on a single subject area or line of business, so it usually can be constructed more rapidly and at lower cost than an enterprise-wide data warehouse.

BUSINESS INTELLIGENCE, MULTIDIMENSIONAL DATA ANALYSIS, AND DATA MINING

Once data have been captured and organized in data warehouses and data marts, they are available for further analysis. A series of tools enables users to analyze these data to see new patterns, relationships, and insights that are useful for guiding decision making. These tools for consolidating, analyzing, and providing access to vast amounts of data to help users make better business decisions are often referred to **business intelligence (BI)**. Principal tools for business intelligence include software for database querying and reporting, tools for multidimensional data analysis (online analytical processing), and data mining tools.

When we think of *intelligence* as applied to humans, we typically think of people's ability to combine learned knowledge with new information and change behaviors in such a way that they succeed at their task or adapt to a new situation. Likewise, business intelligence provides firms with the capability to amass information; develop knowledge about customers, competitors, and internal operations; and change decision-making behavior to achieve higher profitability and other business goals.

For instance, Harrah's Entertainment, the second-largest gambling company in its industry, continually analyzes data about its customers gathered when people play its slot machines or use Harrah's casinos and hotels. Harrah's marketing department uses this information to build a detailed gambling profile, based on a particular customer's ongoing value to the company. For instance, business intelligence lets Harrah's know the favorite gaming experience of a regular customer at one of its Midwest riverboat casinos, along with that person's preferences for room accomodations, restaurants, and entertainment. This information guides management decisions about how to cultivate the most profitable customers, encourage those customers to spend more, and attract more customers with high revenue-generating potential. Business intelligence has improved Harrah's profits so much that it has become the centerpiece of the firm's business strategy.

Figure 5-13
Business Intelligence
A series of analytical tools works with data stored in databases to find patterns and insights for helping managers and employees make better decisions to improve organizational performance.

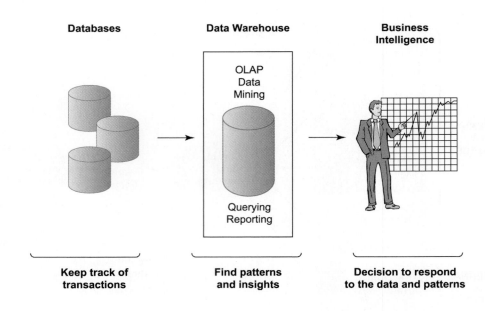

Figure 5-13 illustrates how business intelligence works. The firm's operational databases keep track of the transactions generated by running the business. These databases feed data to the data warehouse. Managers use business intelligence tools to find patterns and meanings in the data. Managers then act on what they have learned from analyzing the data by making more informed and intelligent business decisions.

This section will introduce you to the most important business intelligence technologies and tools. We will provide more detail about business intelligence applications in the Chapter 10 discussion of decision making.

Online Analytical Processing (OLAP)

Suppose your company sells four different products—nuts, bolts, washers, and screws—in the East, West, and Central regions. If you wanted to ask a fairly straightforward question, such as how many washers sold during the past quarter, you could easily find the answer by querying your sales database. But what if you wanted to know how many washers sold in each of your sales regions and compare actual results with projected sales?

To obtain the answer, you would need **online analytical processing (OLAP)**. OLAP supports multidimensional data analysis, enabling users to view the same data in different ways using multiple dimensions. Each aspect of information—product, pricing, cost, region, or time period—represents a different dimension. So, a product manager could use a multidimensional data analysis tool to learn how many washers were sold in the East in June, how that compares with the previous month and the previous June, and how it compares with the sales forecast. OLAP enables users to obtain online answers to ad hoc questions such as these in a fairly rapid amount of time, even when the data are stored in very large databases, such as sales figures for multiple years.

Figure 5-14 shows a multidimensional model that could be created to represent products, regions, actual sales, and projected sales. A matrix of actual sales can be stacked on top of a matrix of projected sales to form a cube with six faces. If you rotate the cube 90 degrees one way, the face showing will be product versus actual and projected sales. If you rotate the cube 90 degrees again, you will see region versus actual and projected sales. If you rotate 180 degrees from the original view, you will see projected sales and product versus region. Cubes can be nested within cubes to build complex views of data. A company would use either a specialized multidimensional database or a tool that creates multidimensional views of data in relational databases.

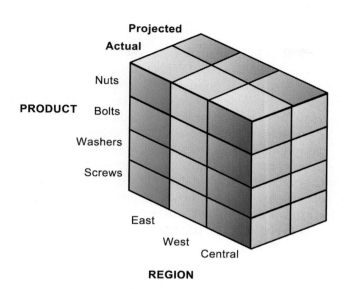

Figure 5-14
Multidimensional Data Model
The view that is showing is product versus region. If you rotate the cube 90 degrees, the face that will show is product versus actual and projected sales. If you rotate the cube 90 degrees again, you will see region versus actual and projected sales. Other views are possible.

DATA MINING

Traditional database queries answer such questions as, "How many units of product number 403 were shipped in February 2008?" OLAP, or multidimensional analysis, supports much more complex requests for information, such as, "Compare sales of product 403 relative to plan by quarter and sales region for the past two years." With OLAP and query-oriented data analysis, users need to have a good idea about the information for which they are looking.

Data mining is more discovery driven. Data mining provides insights into corporate data that cannot be obtained with OLAP by finding hidden patterns and relationships in large databases and inferring rules from them to predict future behavior. The patterns and rules are used to guide decision making and forecast the effect of those decisions. The types of information obtainable from data mining include associations, sequences, classifications, clusters, and forecasts.

* *Associations* are occurrences linked to a single event. For instance, a study of supermarket purchasing patterns might reveal that, when corn chips are purchased, a cola drink is purchased 65 percent of the time, but when there is a promotion, cola is purchased 85 percent of the time. This information helps managers make better decisions because they have learned the profitability of a promotion.

* In *sequences*, events are linked over time. We might find, for example, that if a house is purchased, a new refrigerator will be purchased within two weeks 65 percent of the time, and an oven will be bought within one month of the home purchase 45 percent of the time.

* *Classification* recognizes patterns that describe the group to which an item belongs by examining existing items that have been classified and by inferring a set of rules. For example, businesses such as credit card or telephone companies worry about the loss of steady customers. Classification helps discover the characteristics of customers who are likely to leave and can provide a model to help managers predict who those customers are so that the managers can devise special campaigns to retain such customers.

* *Clustering* works in a manner similar to classification when no groups have yet been defined. A data mining tool can discover different groupings within data, such as finding affinity groups for bank cards or partitioning a database into groups of customers based on demographics and types of personal investments.

* Although these applications involve predictions, *forecasting* uses predictions in a different way. It uses a series of existing values to forecast what other values will be.

For example, forecasting might find patterns in data to help managers estimate the future value of continuous variables, such as sales figures.

These systems perform high-level analyses of patterns or trends, but they can also drill down to provide more detail when needed. There are data mining applications for all the functional areas of business, and for government and scientific work. One popular use for data mining is to provide detailed analyses of patterns in customer data for one-to-one marketing campaigns or for identifying profitable customers.

For example, Virgin Mobile Australia uses a data warehouse and data mining to increase customer loyalty and roll out new services. The company created a data warehouse that consolidated data from its enterprise system, customer relationship management system, and customer billing systems in a massive database. Data mining has enabled management to determine the demographic profile of new customers and relate it to the handsets they purchased as well as to the performance of each store and point-of-sale campaign, consumer reactions to new products and services, customer attrition rates, and the revenue generated by each customer.

Predictive analysis uses data mining techniques, historical data, and assumptions about future conditions to predict outcomes of events, such as the probability a customer will respond to an offer or purchase a specific product. For example, the U.S. division of The Body Shop International plc used predictive analysis with its database of catalog, Web, and retail store customers to identify customers who were more likely to make catalog purchases. That information helped the company build a more precise and targeted mailing list for its catalogs, improving the response rate for catalog mailings and catalog revenues.

Data mining is both a powerful and profitable tool, but it poses challenges to the protection of individual privacy. Data mining technology can combine information from many diverse sources to create a detailed "data image" about each of us—our income, our driving habits, our hobbies, our families, and our political interests. The question of whether companies should be allowed to collect such detailed information about individuals is discussed in Chapter 12. The Interactive Session on Management explores the debate about whether large databases housing DNA profiles used in crime-fighting pose a threat to privacy and social well-being.

DATABASES AND THE WEB

Many companies are using the Web to make some of the information in their internal databases available to customers and business partners. Prospective customers might use a company's Web site to view the company's product catalog or to place an order. The company in turn might use the Web to check inventory availability for that product from its supplier. That supplier in turn may have to check with its own suppliers as well as delivery firms needed to ship the products on time.

These actions involve accessing and (in the case of ordering) updating corporate databases through the Web. Suppose, for example, a customer with a Web browser wants to search an online retailer's database for pricing information. Figure 5-15 illustrates how that customer might access the retailer's internal database over the Web. The user would access

Figure 5-15
Linking Internal Databases to the Web

Users access an organization's internal database through the Web using their desktop PCs and Web browser software.

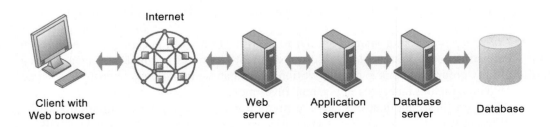

Client with
Web browser

Internet

Web
server

Application
server

Database
server

Database

INTERACTIVE SESSION: MANAGEMENT   DNA Databases: Crime Fighting Weapon or Threat to Privacy?

On December 2, 1996, Cherie Morrisette, age 11, left her apartment on the south side of Jacksonville, Florida after arguing with her sister about washing the dishes. Six days later, her body was found 13 miles away in the St. Johns River. Detectives classified the case as a homicide, but could not locate a suspect for 10 years. Then on March 16, 2006, detectives in Colchester, Connecticut announced that Robert Shelton Mitchell, age 43, of New Britain, Connecticut would be charged with the murder.

A DNA profile of bodily fluid left by the murderer at the crime scene had been developed by the Biology Laboratory of the Florida Department of Law Enforcement and sent to the nationwide DNA bank. There it matched a DNA sample provided by Mr. Mitchell to the Connecticut sex offenders' registry in 2003 while he was in prison on another charge.

DNA evidence has become a potent crime-fighting tool, allowing a criminal to be identified by his or her own genes. Computer analysis can discover the identity of a criminal by matching DNA from blood, hair, saliva, or other bodily fluids left at a crime scene with a DNA profile in a database. A laboratory creates a profile of specific agreed-upon genetic segments of the DNA molecule for a specific individual and stores that information in a database. To identify a particular individual, the laboratory compares the profile produced from a sample of unknown DNA with the profile produced from a sample belonging to an identified individual to see if there is a match.

Law enforcement agencies around the world are increasingly relying on DNA evidence. U.S. law enforcement agencies use databases of DNA profiles created by the states and linked through the FBI's Combined DNA Index System (CODIS). The CODIS system, authorized by Congress in 1994, allows law enforcement officials to exchange and compare DNA profiles at the local, state, and national levels. As of April 2007, CODIS had data on more than 4.6 million profiles. The samples on which the DNA profiles are based, primarily blood or saliva, are kept at forensic laboratories around the country. All 50 states, the FBI, and the U.S. Army work with this system.

The CODIS system has helped law enforcement officials identify suspects in more than 11,000 cases. It helped solve two "cold" murders in Kansas, identify two-decade-old remains of a missing California child, and capture a predator terrorizing young boys in Houston.

DNA identification is also helpful in proving innocence. Lawyer Barry Scheck's Innocence Project at the Cardozo School of Law in Yeshiva University has used DNA identification to free more than 200 people who had been wrongly convicted. Law schools at the University of Wisconsin, the University of Washington, and Santa Clara University have similar innocence projects.

According to Joseph M. Polisar, president of the International Association of Chiefs of Police, DNA testing "is the fingerprint technology of this century... The potential for us in the criminal justice field to solve crimes with this technology is boundless."

Despite all their benefits, DNA databases remain controversial. Privacy advocates and defense lawyers believe genetic databases pose risks to the innocent if they contain data on people who are not convicted criminals. In some instances, DNA has been collected from witnesses or others to eliminate them from police inquiries. DNA has also been collected from families of suspects to determine whether suspects should continue to be pursued. The Justice Department is completing rules to allow the collection of DNA from anyone arrested or detained by federal authorities, including illegal immigrants detained by federal agents. Some state legislators have also advocated expanding the FBI national DNA database to include juveniles.

Most people aren't violent criminals, including those who commit misdemeanors, and their inclusion in a national DNA database exposes them to risks they would not otherwise face. People who collect and analyze DNA can make mistakes. (Sloppy DNA collection and laboratory procedures resulted in at least one wrongful conviction in Houston and may have affected the outcome of the O.J. Simpson trial.) There may be valid reasons for an innocent person's DNA to be at a crime scene that police might choose to disregard. Innocent people may be caught up in a criminal investigation when their DNA from a single hair or spot of saliva on a drinking glass appears in a public or private place where they had every right to be.

Critics have also pointed out that expanding the FBI's DNA database would create large backlogs in the FBI's laboratory that logs, analyzes, and stores federal DNA samples. The lab might have to process an additional 250,000 to 1 million samples per year. There has already been an enormous increase in DNA samples to be processed but no new resources for the FBI's laboratory.

Sources: Julia Preston, "U.S. Set to Begin a Vast Expansion of DNA Sampling," *The Wall Street Journal*, February 5, 2007; Patrick McGeehan, "New York Plan for DNA Data in Most Crimes," *The New York Times*, May 14, 2007; Stacey Stowe, "10 Years after Girl's Murder, DNA Link Results in Arrest" and Harlan Levy, "Caught Up in DNA's Growing Web," *The New York Times*, March 17, 2006; and "Genetic Privacy," www.epic.org, accessed August 3, 2007.

1. What are the benefits of DNA databases?

2. What problems do DNA databases pose?

3. Who should be included in a national DNA database? Should it be limited to convicted felons? Explain your answer.

4. Who should be able to use DNA databases?

Explore the Web site for the Combined DNA Index System (CODIS) and answer the following questions:

1. How does CODIS work? How is it designed?

2. What information does CODIS maintain?

3. Who is allowed to use CODIS?

4. How does CODIS aid criminal investigations?

the retailer's Web site over the Internet using Web browser software on his or her client PC. The user's Web browser software would request data from the organization's database, using HTML commands to communicate with the Web server.

Because many "back-end" databases cannot interpret commands written in HTML, the Web server would pass these requests for data to software that translates HTML commands into SQL so that they can be processed by the DBMS working with the database. In a client/server environment, the DBMS resides on a dedicated computer called a **database server**. The DBMS receives the SQL requests and provides the required data. The information is transferred from the organization's internal database back to the Web server for delivery in the form of a Web page to the user.

Figure 5-15 shows that the software working between the Web server and the DBMS could be an application server running on its own dedicated computer (see Chapter 4). The application server software handles all application operations, including transaction processing and data access, between browser-based computers and a company's back-end business applications or databases. The application server takes requests from the Web server, runs the business logic to process transactions based on those requests, and provides connectivity to the organization's back-end systems or databases. Alternatively, the software for handling these operations could be a custom program or a CGI script. A CGI script is a compact program using the *Common Gateway Interface (CGI)* specification for processing data on a Web server.

There are a number of advantages to using the Web to access an organization's internal databases. First, everyone knows how to use Web browser software, and employees require much less training than if they used proprietary query tools. Second, the Web interface requires few or no changes to the internal database. Companies leverage their investments in older systems because it costs much less to add a Web interface in front of a legacy system than to redesign and rebuild the system to improve user access. For this reason, most large Fortune 500 firms all have back-end legacy databases running on mainframe computers that are linked to "front-end" software that makes the information available in the form of a Web page to users on request.

Accessing corporate databases through the Web is creating new efficiencies and opportunities, and, in some cases, it is even changing the way business is being done. ThomasNet.com provides an up-to-date directory of information from more than 700,000 suppliers of industrial products, such as chemicals, metals, plastics, rubber, and automotive equipment. Formerly called Thomas Register, the company used to send out huge paper catalogs with this information. Now, it provides this information to users online via its Web site and has become a smaller, leaner company.

INTERACTIVE SESSION: TECHNOLOGY — The Databases Behind MySpace

MySpace.com, the popular social networking site, has experienced one of the greatest growth spurts in the history of the Internet. The site launched in November 2003 and by May 2007, it had 175 million member accounts. The challenge for MySpace has been to avoid technological letdowns that degrade Web site performance and frustrate its rapidly expanding network of users.

The technical requirements of a site like MySpace are vastly different from other heavily trafficked Web sites. Generally, a small number of people change the content on a news site a few times a day. The site may retrieve thousands of read-only requests from its underlying database without having to update the database. On MySpace, tens of millions of users are constantly updating their content, resulting in an elevated percentage of database interactions that require updates to the underlying database. Each time a user views a profile on MySpace, the resulting page is stitched together from database lookups that organize information from multiple tables stored in multiple databases residing on multiple servers.

In its initial phases, MySpace operated with two Web servers communicating with one database server and a Microsoft SQL Server database. Such a setup is ideal for small to medium-size sites because of its simplicity. At MySpace, the setup showed signs of stress as more users came aboard. At first, MySpace reduced the load by adding Web servers to handle the increased user requests. But when the number of accounts stretched to 500,000 in 2004, one database server was not sufficient. Deploying additional database servers is more complicated than adding Web servers because the data must be divided among multiple databases without any loss in accessibility or performance. MySpace deployed three SQL Server databases. One served as a master database, which received all new data and copied them to the other two databases. These databases focused on retrieving data for user page requests.

As MySpace approached 2 million accounts, the database servers approached their input/output capacity, which refers to the speed at which they could read and write data. This caused the site to lag behind in content updates. MySpace switched to a vertical partitioning model in which separate databases supported distinct functions of the Web site, such as the log-in screen, user profiles, and blogs.

However, the distinct functions also had occasion to share data, and this became problematic when the site reached 3 million accounts. Furthermore, some functions of the site grew too large to be served by only one database server. After considering a scale-up strategy of investing in more powerful and expensive servers, MySpace instead scaled out by adding many cheaper servers to share the database workload.

The more economical solution of a distributed architecture required a new design in which all of the servers combined to work as one logical computer. Under this design, the workload still needed to be spread out, which was accomplished by dividing the user accounts into groups of 1 million, and putting all the data related to those accounts in a separate instance of SQL Server.

Despite these gains in efficiency, the workload was not distributed evenly, which would sometimes cause an overload in the storage area for a particular database. MySpace tried to correct this issue manually, but the work was demanding and not an effective use of resources. So, MySpace switched to a virtualized storage architecture, which ended the practice of attaching disks dedicated to specific applications in favor of a single pool of storage space available to all applications. Under this arrangement, databases could write data to any available disk, thus eliminating the possibility of an application's dedicated disk becoming overloaded.

In 2005, MySpace also fortified its infrastructure by installing a layer of servers between the database servers and the Web servers to store and serve copies of frequently accessed data objects so that the site's Web servers wouldn't have to query the database servers with lookups as frequently.

Despite all these measures, MySpace still overloads more frequently than other major Web sites. Users have expressed frustration at not being able to log in or view certain pages. Log-in errors occur at a rate of 20 to 40 percent some days. Site activity continues to challenge the limitations of the technology. So far, the site's continued growth suggests that users are willing to put up with periodic "Unexpected Error" screens. MySpace developers continue to redesign the Web site's database, software, and storage systems to keep pace with its exploding growth, but their job is never done.

Sources: David F. Carr, "Inside MySpace.com," *Baseline Magazine*, January 16, 2007; Mark Brunelli, "Oracle Database 10g Powers Growing MySpace.com Competitor," SearchOracle.com, January 31, 2007; and Saul Hansell, "For MySpace, Making Friends Was Easy. Big Prophet Is Tougher," *The New York Times*, April 23, 2006.

CASE STUDY QUESTIONS

1. Describe how MySpace uses databases and database servers.

2. Why is database technology so important for a business such as MySpace?

3. How effectively does MySpace organize and store the data on its site?

4. What data management problems have arisen? How has MySpace solved, or attempted to solve, these problems?

MIS IN ACTION

Explore MySpace.com, examining the features and tools that are not restricted to registered members. Then answer the following questions:

1. Based on what you can view without registering, what are the entities in MySpace's database?

2. Which of these entities have some relationship to individual members?

3. Select one of these entities and describe the attributes for that entity.

Other companies have created entirely new businesses based on access to large databases through the Web. One is the social networking site MySpace, which helps users stay connected with each other or meet new people. MySpace features music, comedy, videos, and "profiles" with information supplied by 175 million users about their age, hometown, dating preferences, marital status, and interests. It maintains a massive database to house and manage all of this content. Because the site grew so rapidly, it had to make a series of changes to its underlying database technology. The Interactive Session on Technology explores this topic. As you read this case, try to identify the problem MySpace is facing; what alternative solutions are available to management; and the people, organization, and technology issues that have to be addressed when developing the solution.

5.4 Managing Data Resources

Setting up a database is only a start. In order to make sure that the data for your business remain accurate, reliable, and readily available to those who need it, your business will need special policies and procedures for data management.

ESTABLISHING AN INFORMATION POLICY

Every business, large and small, needs an information policy. Your firm's data are an important resource, and you don't want people doing whatever they want with them. You need to have rules on how the data are to be organized and maintained, and who is allowed to view the data or change them.

An **information policy** specifies the organization's rules for sharing, disseminating, acquiring, standardizing, classifying, and inventorying information. Information policies lay out specific procedures and accountabilities, identifying which users and organizational units can share information, where information can be distributed, and who is responsible for updating and maintaining the information. For example, a typical information policy would specify that only selected members of the payroll and human resources department would have the right to change and view sensitive employee data, such as an employee's salary or social security number, and that these departments are responsible for making sure that such employee data are accurate.

If you are in a small business, the information policy would be established and implemented by the owners or managers. In a large organization, managing and planning for information as a corporate resource often requires a formal data administration function. **Data administration** is responsible for the specific policies and procedures through which data can be managed as an organizational resource. These responsibilities include developing information policy, planning for data, overseeing logical database design and data dictionary development, and monitoring how information systems specialists and end-user groups use data.

A large organization will also have a database design and management group within the corporate information systems division that is responsible for defining and organizing the structure and content of the database, and maintaining the database. In close cooperation with users, the design group establishes the physical database, the logical relations among elements, and the access rules and security procedures. The functions it performs are called **database administration**.

ENSURING DATA QUALITY

A well-designed database and information policy will go a long way toward ensuring that the business has the information it needs. However, additional steps must be taken to ensure that the data in organizational databases are accurate and remain reliable.

What would happen if a customer's telephone number or account balance were incorrect? What would be the impact if the database had the wrong price for the product you sold? Data that are inaccurate, untimely, or inconsistent with other sources of information create serious operational and financial problems for businesses. When faulty data go unnoticed, they often lead to incorrect decisions, product recalls, and even financial losses.

According to Forrester Research, 20 percent of U.S. mail and commercial package deliveries were returned because of incorrect names or addresses. The Gartner Group consultants reported that more than 25 percent of the critical data in large Fortune 1000 companies' databases is inaccurate or incomplete, including bad product codes and product descriptions, faulty inventory descriptions, erroneous financial data, incorrect supplier information, and incorrect employee data. Gartner believes that customer data degrades at a rate of 2 percent per month, making poor data quality a major obstacle to successful customer relationship management (Gage and McCormick, 2005).

Some of these data quality problems are caused by redundant and inconsistent data produced by multiple systems feeding a data warehouse. For example, the sales ordering system and the inventory management system might both maintain data on the organization's products. However, the sales ordering system might use the term *Item Number* and the inventory system might call the same attribute *Product Number*. The sales, inventory, or manufacturing systems of a clothing retailer might use different codes to represent values for an attribute. One system might represent clothing size as "extra large," whereas the other system might use the code "XL" for the same purpose. During the design process for the warehouse database, data describing entities, such as a customer, product, or order, should be named and defined consistently for all business areas using the database.

If a database is properly designed and enterprise-wide data standards established, duplicate or inconsistent data elements should be minimal. Most data quality problems, however, such as misspelled names, transposed numbers, or incorrect or missing codes, stem from errors during data input. The incidence of such errors is rising as companies move their businesses to the Web and allow customers and suppliers to enter data into their Web sites that directly update internal systems.

Think of all the times you have received several pieces of the same direct mail advertising on the same day. This is very likely the result of having your name maintained multiple times in a database. Your name may have been misspelled or you used your middle initial on one occasion and not on another or the information was initially entered onto a paper form and not scanned properly into the system. Because of these inconsistencies, the database would treat you as different people! We often receive redundant mail addressed to Laudon, Lavdon, Lauden, or Landon.

Before a new database is in place, organizations need to identify and correct their faulty data and establish better routines for editing data once their database is in operation. Analysis of data quality often begins with a **data quality audit**, which is a structured survey of the accuracy and level of completeness of the data in an information system. Data quality audits can be performed by surveying entire data files, surveying samples from data files, or surveying end users for their perceptions of data quality.

Data cleansing, also known as *data scrubbing*, consists of activities for detecting and correcting data in a database that are incorrect, incomplete, improperly formatted, or redundant. Data cleansing not only corrects data but also enforces consistency among different sets of data that originated in separate information systems. Specialized data-cleansing software is available to automatically survey data files, correct errors in the data, and integrate the data in a consistent company-wide format.

5.5 Hands-On MIS

The projects in this section give you hands-on experience in redesigning a customer database for targeted marketing, creating a database for inventory management, and using the Web to search online databases for overseas business resources.

IMPROVING DECISION MAKING: REDESIGNING THE CUSTOMER DATABASE

Software skills: Database design, querying, and reporting
Business skills: Customer profiling

Dirt Bikes USA sells primarily through its distributors. It maintains a small customer database with the following data: customer name, address (street, city, state, ZIP code), telephone number, model purchased, date of purchase, and distributor. The database is illustrated below and you can find it on the Laudon Web site for Chapter 5. These data are collected by its distributors when they make a sale and are then forwarded to Dirt Bikes. Dirt Bikes would like to be able to market more aggressively to its customers.

CustomerID	Last Name	First Name	Street	City	State	Zip	Phone	Model	Date	Distributor
1	Mann	Dwight	23 Colby Lane	Tacoma	WA	98109	(253) 123-4333	Enduro 250	2/12/2008	J&J Cycle
2	Porter	William	3 Pinehill Rd.	Logan	UT	84321	(435) 797-3322	Enduro 250	3/27/2008	WX Cycle
3	Higgins	Daniel	38 Ryder Rd.	Lincoln	NE	68526	(402) 471-6950	Moto 450	7/11/2007	All-Terrain Cycle
4	Langan	Howard	8 Belle Ave.	Flagstaff	AZ	86002	(928) 382-5877	Moto 450	1/12/2008	Cycle World
5	Delgado	Luis	66 Skyview Terr	Las Cruces	NM	88003	(505) 582-4301	Moto 300	10/5/2007	Ben's Cycles
6	Stratman	Philip	722 Donald Dr.	Hayward	CA	94541	(714) 278-5564	Moto 450	3/21/2007	Don's Off Road
7	Yates	Gerry	11 Buena Vista	Ventura	CA	93012	(805) 413-7922	Enduro 250	5/16/2008	Lightning Cycles
8	Mickel	Paul	523 Grant St.	Norman	OK	73072	(405) 325-1971	Moto 300	4/17/2008	WX Cycle
9	Podell	James	68 Clinton St.	Pocatello	ID	83202	(208) 251-4967	Enduro 550	5/18/2007	Performance Cycles
10	Lowe	Mark	95 Canyon Dr.	Pomona	CA	91767	(909) 869-3955	Moto 300	12/5/2007	KB Racing

The marketing department would like to be able to send customers e-mail notices of special racing events and of sales on parts. It would also like to learn more about customers' interests and tastes: their ages, years of schooling, another sport in which they are interested, and whether they attend dirt bike racing events. Additionally, Dirt Bikes would like to know whether customers own more than one motorcycle. (Some Dirt Bikes customers own two or three motorcycles purchased from Dirt Bikes USA or other manufacturers.) If a motorcycle was purchased from Dirt Bikes, the company would like to know the date of purchase, model purchased, and distributor. If the customer owns a non-Dirt Bikes motorcycle, the company would like to know the manufacturer and model of the other motorcycle (or motorcycles) and the distributor from whom the customer purchased that motorcycle.

- Redesign Dirt Bikes's customer database so that it can store and provide the information needed for marketing. You will need to develop a design for the new customer database and then implement that design using database software. Consider using multiple tables in your new design. Populate each new table with 10 records.
- Develop several reports that would be of great interest to Dirt Bikes's marketing and sales department (for example, lists of repeat Dirt Bikes customers, Dirt Bikes customers who attend racing events, or the average ages and years of schooling of Dirt Bikes customers) and print them.

ACHIEVING OPERATIONAL EXCELLENCE: BUILDING A RELATIONAL DATABASE FOR INVENTORY MANAGEMENT

Software skills: Database design, querying, and reporting
Business skills: Inventory management

In this exercise, you will use database software to design a database for managing inventory for a small business. Sylvester's Bike Shop, located in San Francisco, California, sells road, mountain, hybrid, leisure, and children's bicycles. Currently, Sylvester's purchases bikes from three suppliers, but plans to add new suppliers in the near future. This rapidly growing business needs a database system to manage this information.

Initially, the database should house information about suppliers and products. The database will contain two tables: a supplier table and a product table. The reorder level refers to the number of items in inventory that triggers a decision to order more items to prevent a stockout. (In other words, if the number of units of a particular item in inventory falls below the reorder level, the item should be reordered.) The user should be able to perform several queries and produce several managerial reports based on the data contained in the two tables.

Using the information found in the tables on the Laudon Web site for Chapter 5, build a simple relational database for Sylvester's. Once you have built the database, perform the following activities.

- Prepare a report that identifies the five most expensive bicycles. The report should list the bicycles in descending order from most expensive to least expensive, the quantity on hand for each, and the markup percentage for each.
- Prepare a report that lists each supplier, its products, the quantities on hand, and associated reorder levels. The report should be sorted alphabetically by supplier. Within each supplier category, the products should be sorted alphabetically.
- Prepare a report listing only the bicycles that are low in stock and need to be reordered. The report should provide supplier information for the items identified.
- Write a brief description of how the database could be enhanced to further improve management of the business. What tables or fields should be added? What additional reports would be useful?

IMPROVING DECISION MAKING: SEARCHING ONLINE DATABASES FOR OVERSEAS BUSINESS RESOURCES

Software skills: Online databases
Business skills: Researching services for overseas operations

Internet users have access to many thousands of Web-enabled databases with information on services and products in faraway locations. This project develops skills in searching these online databases.

Your company is located in Greensboro, North Carolina, and manufactures office furniture of various types. You have recently acquired several new customers in Australia, and a study you commissioned indicates that, with a presence there, you could greatly increase your sales. Moreover, your study indicates that you could do even better if you actually manufactured many of your products locally (in Australia). First, you need to set up an office in Melbourne to establish a presence, and then you need to begin importing from the United States. You then can plan to start producing locally.

You will soon be traveling to the area to make plans to actually set up an office, and you want to meet with organizations that can help you with your operation. You will need to engage people or organizations that offer many services necessary for you to open your office, including lawyers, accountants, import-export experts, telecommunications equipment and support, and even trainers who can help you to prepare your future employees to work for you. Start by searching for U.S. Department of Commerce advice on doing business in Australia. Then try the following online databases to locate companies that you would like to meet with during your upcoming trip: Australian Business Register (abr.gov.au), Australia Trade Now (australiatradenow.com), and the Nationwide Business Directory of Australia (www.nationwide.com.au). If necessary, you could also try search engines such as Yahoo! and Google.

- List the companies you would contact to interview on your trip to determine whether they can help you with these and any other functions you think vital to establishing your office.
- Rate the databases you used for accuracy of name, completeness, ease of use, and general helpfulness.
- What does this exercise tell you about the design of databases?

LEARNING TRACKS

The following Learning Tracks provide content relevant to topics covered in this chapter:

1. Database Design, Normalization, and Entity-Relationship Diagramming
2. Introduction to SQL

Review Summary

1 How does a relational database organize data and how does it differ from an object-oriented database? The relational database is the primary method for organizing and maintaining data today in information system. It organizes data in two-dimensional tables with rows and columns called relations. Each table contains data about an entity and its attributes. Each row represents a record and each column represents an attribute or field. Each table also contains a key field to uniquely identify each record for retrieval or manipulation. An entity-relationship diagram graphically depicts the relationship between entities (tables) in a relational database. The process of breaking down complex groupings of data and streamlining them to minimize redundancy and awkward many-to-many relationships is called normalization. An object-oriented DBMS stores data and procedures that act on the data as objects, and it can handle multimedia as well as characters and numbers.

2 What are the principles of a database management system? A database management system (DBMS) consists of software that permits centralization of data and data management so that businesses have a single consistent source for all their data needs. A single database services multiple applications. The DBMS separates the logical and physical views of data so that the user does not have to be concerned with its physical location. The principal capabilities of a DBMS includes a data definition capability, a data dictionary capability, and a data manipulation language.

3 **What are the principal tools and technologies for accessing information from databases to improve business performance and decision making?** A data warehouse consolidates current and historical data from many different operational systems in a central database designed for reporting and analysis. Data warehouses support multidimensional data analysis, also known as online analytical processing (OLAP). OLAP represents relationships among data as a multidimensional structure, which can be visualized as cubes of data and cubes within cubes of data. Data mining analyzes large pools of data, including the contents of data warehouses, to find patterns and rules that can be used to predict future behavior and guide decision making. Conventional databases can be linked to the Web or a Web interface to facilitate user access to an organization's internal data.

4 **What is the role of information policy and data administration in the management of organizational data resources?** Developing a database environment requires policies and procedures for managing organizational data as well as a good data model and database technology. A formal information policy governs the maintenance, distribution, and use of information in the organization. In large corporations, a formal data administration function is responsible for information policy, as well as for data planning, data dictionary development, and monitoring data usage in the firm.

5 **Why is data quality assurance so important for a business?** Data that are inaccurate, incomplete, or inconsistent create serious operational and financial problems for businesses if they lead to inaccurate decisions about the actions that should be taken by the firm. Assuring data quality involves using enterprise-wide data standards, databases designed to minimize inconsistent and redundant data, data quality audits, and data cleansing software.

Key Terms

Attributes, 160	Database, 159	Object-oriented DBMS, 169
Business intelligence (BI), 171	Database administration, 179	Object-relational DBMS, 169
Data administration, 179	Database management system (DBMS), 165	Online analytical processing (OLAP), 172
Data cleansing, 180	Database server, 176	Predictive analysis, 174
Data definition language, 166	Entity, 160	Primary key, 161
Data dictionary, 166	Entity-relationship diagram, 162	Records, 161
Data manipulation language, 168	Field, 161	Referential integrity, 163
Data mart, 170	Foreign key, 162	Relational database, 160
Data mining, 173	Information policy, 178	Structured Query Language (SQL), 168
Data quality audit, 180	Key field, 161	Tuples, 161
Data warehouse, 170	Normalization, 163	

Review Questions

1. How does a relational database organize data and how does it differ from an object-oriented database?
- Define and explain the significance of entities, attributes, and key fields.
- Define a relational database and explain how it organizes and stores information.
- Explain the role of entity-relationship diagrams and normalization in database design.
- Define an object-oriented database and explain how it differs from a relational database.

2. What are the principles of a database management system?
- Define a database management system (DBMS) and describe how it works and its benefits to organizations.
- Define and compare the logical and a physical view of data.
- Define and describe the three operations of a relational database management system.
- Name and describe the three major capabilities of a DBMS.

3. What are the principal tools and technologies for accessing information from databases to improve business performance and decision making?
- Define a data warehouse and describe how it works.
- Define business intelligence and explain how it is related to database technology.
- Describe the capabilities of online analytical processing (OLAP).
- Define data mining, describe what types of information can be obtained from it, and explain how does it differs from OLAP.
- Explain how users can access information from a company's internal databases through the Web.

4. What is the role of information policy and data administration in the management of organizational data resources?
- Define information policy and data administration and explain how they help organizations manage their data.

5. Why is data quality assurance so important for a business?
- List and describe the most common data quality problems.
- List and describe the most important tools and techniques for assuring data quality.

Discussion Questions

1. It has been said that you do not need database management software to create a database environment. Discuss.

2. To what extent should end users be involved in the selection of a database management system and database design?

Video Case

You will find a video case illustrating some of the concepts in this chapter on the Laudon Web site along with questions to help you analyze the case.

Teamwork

Identifying Entities and Attributes in an Online Database

With a group of two or three of your fellow students, select an online database to explore, such as AOL Music or the Internet Movie Database. Explore these Web sites to see what information they provide. Then list the entities and attributes that they must keep track of in their databases. If possible, diagram the relationship between the entities you have identified. If possible, use electronic presentation software to present your findings to the class.

BUSINESS PROBLEM-SOLVING CASE

Can HP Mine Success from an Enterprise Data Warehouse?

Hewlett-Packard, the $98.5 billion manufacturer of personal computers, server computers, printers, and provider of consulting services, is in the middle of a business transformation. The company is trying to reduce yearly spending by its information technology department by 30 percent over five years. HP expects information technology expenditures to drop from just over $3 billion in 2003 to $2.1 billion in 2008. HP is reducing its information system applications from 5,000 to 1,500 and consolidating 85 computer centers to six. HP's current IT infrastructure employs between 19,000 and 22,000 servers. The consolidation will decrease the total by 8,000 to 9,000.

The success of HP's business transformation may hinge on one particular project. HP is building a 400-terabyte data warehouse to serve the entire enterprise. If successful, the data warehouse will dispose of 17 different database technologies and unite 14,000 databases currently in use. If the initiative fails, HP would join a long list of organizations that have been confounded by the complexity of implementing enterprise-wide databases.

From an internal perspective, HP's data warehouse aims to give its workforce access to data in real time with no departmental or geographic boundaries. HP's numerous systems and applications had serious data management problems. CEO Mark Hurd had difficulty collecting and analyzing "consistent, timely data spanning different parts of the business." Some systems tracked sales and pricing by product, while others tracked sales information geographically. Commonly used financial information, such as gross margins to measure profitability, were calculated differently from business unit to business unit. The company was obtaining information from more than 750 data marts.

Lack of data consistency dragged down sales and profits. Compiling information about the business from various systems could take up to a week, so managers had to make decisions based on relatively stale data. Seemingly simple questions, such as how much the company was spending on marketing across its different businesses, were difficult to answer. Without a consistent view of the enterprise, senior executives struggled with decisions on matters such as the size of sales and service teams assigned to particular systems.

HP CIO Randy Mott began consolidating the data marts in November 2005 into a single data warehouse serving the entire enterprise. He created a team composed of 300 people who were running the data

marts and charged them with modeling the enterprise-wide database that would be the foundation of the data warehouse. They had to make sure that the data would always be up to date, consistent for the entire enterprise, and complete.

The company launched its enterprise data warehouse in May 2006 to coincide with its consolidation of applications and data centers. To date, HP has consolidated hundreds of data marts into just over 200. The data warehouse contains 180 terabytes of raw data and 75 terabytes of functional data. At some point in 2008, the size should double and the data warehouse will be complete. Fifty thousand HP workers will utilize the data warehouse. All HP financial data will be able to be accessed via the data warehouse.

HP believes so strongly in its development of the system that the company is trying to sell its expertise to other companies that are seeking data warehouse technology. HP is marketing a product called Neoview, which has been developed from the proprietary work that the company has done in creating its own data warehouse.

More than 100 database specialists and software developers at HP are perfecting the system's dexterity with table joins and giving it the ability to perform analysis functions at the same time that it is managing new incoming data. HP is also enhancing Neoview's management and monitoring tools.

The servers employed by the Neoview system utilize Itanium processors from Intel, so they meet industry standards and are far more versatile than servers with proprietary technology. The system is also highly scalable and promises availability 99.999 percent of the time.

HP's first customer for the Neoview database system was Bon-Ton Stores, which operates 272 department stores and 7 furniture stores in 23 states. Bon-Ton purchased a 7-terabyte Neoview system for a data warehouse that includes merchandise, customer, and supplier data for merchandise analysis and marketing. One of the database tables for the warehouse has more than 4 billion rows. Bon-Ton's CIO James Lance reported that the Neoview system exceeded expectations.

Wal-Mart signed up for Neoview to work with its strategic Retail Link system, which allows its 20,000 suppliers to access data about the movement and sales of their products in its stores. For over a decade Wal-Mart has operated one of the largest commercial data warehouses in the world with more than 1,000 Terabytes of sales information on every item sold in its stores.

Wal-Mart uses the data warehouse to analyze in-store sales, but it would like to do more with the data to determine the ideal mix of items for each store's customers and to place these items in stores where they are most likely to be purchased.

HP has been able to sell the Neoview technology by differentiating it from typical data warehouses, which are costly, use proprietary technology, and tend to focus on one area of a business rather than an entire enterprise. For example, airlines have data warehouses for yield management and telecommunications carriers have data warehouses to minimize customer attrition. A true enterprise data warehouse would have all these entities plus data on employees, customer service, marketing campaigns, and financial reporting—in other words, all of the data used by the company.

Wal-Mart had been using Teradata's data warehousing platform to support Retail Link. It will continue using Teradata, but will allow Neoview to shoulder some of the workload. Wal-Mart's chief technology officer (CTO) Nancy Stewart reported that selection of Neoview was a "price-performance decision." After several months of testing production loads and accuracy of query results, Stewart reported that "Neoview fits right into that environment of extreme high availability and high performance." Wal-Mart put Neoview into production in early June 2007.

Very few companies have built an all-inclusive data warehouse serving the entire enterprise. They require enormous work to organize and integrate all the data as well as knowledge of database technology and design principles. Businesses are changing constantly due to corporate mergers and global expansion, making today's data warehouse out of date tomorrow. There are also political turf issues. Not all departments want to depend on a central data warehouse supported by a centralized information systems staff for their data-analysis needs. All of HP's departmental users initially resisted the idea of a central data warehouse.

HP will emphasize cost and flexibility. Neoview's hardware can be used to run other applications aside from those connected to the data warehouse. The company does not see a current product that serves as the comprehensive enterprise data warehouse that it intends Neoview to be. Other data warehouses in use do not come close to incorporating 100 percent of a company's data, which is HP's goal for its own data warehouse and Neoview.

HP anticipates luring companies to Neoview that have not been previously interested in such technology by beating the competition on price and simplicity. Using industry-standard hardware should complement this strategy. Most information technology managers should be able to work with the familiar components of Neoview, whereas the pool of people with the knowledge to run most data warehouses is quite shallow. According to database expert Jim Gray, "Right now, it takes far too much expertise to install and use the systems for data mining."

One way in which HP intends to address the issue of complexity is to preconfigure Neoview installations for a particular industry and the workload and applications that the industry requires. Neoview will be a complete solution in a box with on-site management and remote support from HP. Mott hopes to convince potential customers that the cost of running multiple data marts is equal to or greater than the cost of a data warehouse, which will ultimately be a better solution for a business.

Sources: Christopher Lawton, "Data, Data Everywhere," *The Wall Street Journal*, September 24, 2007; Mary Hayes Weier, "HP Data Warehouse Lands in Wal-Mart's Shopping Cart," *InformationWeek*, August 6, 2007; John Foley, "Inside Hewlett-Packard's Data Warehouse Gamble," *InformationWeek*, January 6, 2007; and Paul A. Strassmann, "7 Places to Clean the Clutter in I.T.," *Baseline Magazine*, January 31, 2007.

Case Study Questions

1. Identify the problem described in this case. What people, organization, and technology factors were responsible for creating this problem?

2. What solution has HP chosen to fix this problem? Did management select the best solution alternative?

3. How much will HP's database experience and technology help HP and its clients build all-inclusive data warehouses?

4. How much will Neoview help HP and its clients create enterprise-wide data warehouses? Explain your answer.

5. If you were in charge of developing an enterprise-wide data warehouse for your company, describe the steps you would have to take to complete this project. List and describe all people, organization, and technology issues that must be addressed to build an enterprise-wide data warehouse successfully.

Telecommunications, the Internet, and Wireless Technology

CHAPTER **6**

STUDENT LEARNING OBJECTIVES

After completing this chapter, you will be able to answer the following questions:

1. What are the principal components of telecommunications networks and key networking technologies?

2. What are the main telecommunications transmission media and types of networks?

3. How do the Internet and Internet technology work and how do they support communication and e-business?

4. What are the principal technologies and standards for wireless networking, communication, and Internet access?

5. Why are radio frequency identification (RFID) and wireless sensor networks valuable for business?

Chapter Outline

HYATT REGENCY OSAKA USES WIRELESS NETWORKING FOR HIGH-TOUCH SERVICE

Hyatt Hotels are known for the "Hyatt Touch," and the Hyatt Regency Osaka (HRO) is no exception. This urban resort hotel in the Hyatt International hotel chain is located in the new Cosmo Square business district some distance from central Osaka. It features approximately 500 guest rooms and 19 rooms for conferences and other functions spread over 28 floors. With the hotel industry increasingly competitive, HRO searched for ways of providing a superior environment for guests and encouraging repeat visits despite its less convenient location. The hotel turned to technology for a solution.

Working with Nomura research and Intel Corporation, HRO implemented a mobile wireless local area network (LAN) using Internet standards to provide integrated voice and data coverage across the entire hotel. The hotel initially deployed 25 wireless-enabled notebook computers using Intel Centrino mobile technology and 60 handheld mobile devices based on Intel XScale technology. Both types of devices can handle voice phone calls as well as data communication and their quality of service is comparable to HRO's wired voice system. The wireless infrastructure also provides guests with high-speed Internet access.

Before this system was installed, HRO staff members were only able to communicate using fixed-line telephones and pagers. The new wireless network enables these employees to communicate via wireless handhelds or notebook PCs wherever they are working. HRO estimates this technology has saved 60 hours per year per staff member or a total of 4800 hours annually. This time savings from increased employee productivity can be spent on more personal attention to guests and face-to-face customer service.

The ability to access information online from anywhere in the hotel allows every employee to "act as a concierge," responding accurately and immediately to guest inquiries. If, for example, a guest asks a bell captain a question, the bell caption can access the information from HRO's intranet from his wireless PDA and reply to the guest on the spot. The ability to share and access information also makes it easier to provide customized services to guests. For example, if a guest reports she prefers a different kind of pillow than the one in her room, the staff can immediately check online the information maintained about that guest from past visits and provide exactly what she wants on the spot. That sort of memorable service makes guests want to visit again.

The wireless LAN has been a big hit with guests who use it to access the Internet from the hotel lobbies, conference center, meeting rooms, and guest rooms. Increasingly, the availability of high-speed Internet access in conference facilities has become an essential requirement for corporate conventions and seminars. Providing wireless Internet service for conferences could potentially generate several million yen in additional revenues for the hotel.

Sources: Intel Corporation, "VoIP Enables VIP Service at Hyatt Regency Osaka," 2006; Intel Corporation, "Pilot Project Using Mobile IP-Centrex to Build an Integrated Voice and Data Environment," www. intel.com, accessed August 14, 2006; and www.osaka.regency.hyatt.com, accessed July 2, 2007.

Hyatt Regency Osaka (HRO) illustrates some of the powerful new capabilities—and opportunities—provided by contemporary networking technology. HRO used Internet and wireless networking technology to provide staff and guests with voice and data communication capabilities, as well as wireless Internet access, anywhere in the hotel. The technology enabled HRO to provide superior customer service and made it a hotel of choice.

The chapter-opening diagram calls attention to important points raised by this case and this chapter. The hotel industry is exceptionally competitive. HRO's location is not optimal. HRO management could have lowered rates to attract customers. However, operating costs are high, and the hotel has a luxury image. Instead, HRO's management chose a strategy of focusing on a superior customer experience to distinguish it from competitors.

HRO's outdated networking and voice technology made it difficult to provide this experience. The hotel switched to networks based on the Internet protocol and wireless technology. These improvements saved staff time and enabled more employees to serve customers. HRO's wireless technology is also providing new guest services, which increase revenue and customer satisfaction. HRO had to redesign its processes for serving guests and redesign employee jobs to take advantage of the new technology.

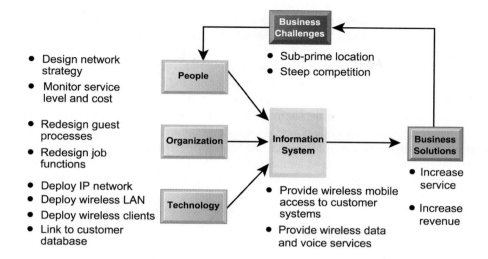

6.1 Telecommunications and Networking in Today's Business World

If you run or work in a business, you cannot do without networks. You need to communicate rapidly with your customers, suppliers, and employees. Until about 1990, you would have used the postal system or telephone system with voice or fax for business communication. Today, however, you and your employees use computers and e-mail, the Internet, cell phones, and mobile computers connected to wireless networks for this purpose. Networking and the Internet are now nearly synonymous with doing business.

NETWORKING AND COMMUNICATION TRENDS

Firms in the past used two fundamentally different types of networks: telephone networks and computer networks. Telephone networks historically handled voice communication, and computer networks handled data traffic. Telephone networks were built by telephone companies throughout the twentieth century using voice transmission technologies (hardware and software), and these companies almost always operated as regulated monopolies throughout the world. Computer networks were originally built by computer companies seeking to transmit data between computers in different locations.

Thanks to continuing telecommunications deregulation and information technology innovation, telephone and computer networks are slowly converging into a single digital network using shared Internet-based standards and equipment. Telecommunications providers, such as AT&T and Verizon, today offer data transmission, Internet access, wireless telephone service, and television programming as well as voice service. Cable companies, such as Cablevision and Comcast, now offer voice service and Internet access. Computer networks have expanded to include Internet telephone and limited video services. Increasingly, all of these voice, video, and data communications are based on Internet technology.

Both voice and data communication networks have also become more powerful (faster), more portable (smaller and mobile), and less expensive. For instance, the typical Internet connection speed in 2000 was 56 kilobits per second, but today more than 60 percent of U.S. Internet users have high-speed **broadband** connections provided by telephone and cable TV companies running at one million bits per second. The cost for this service has fallen exponentially, from 25 cents in 2000, to less than 1 cent today.

Increasingly, voice and data communication as well as Internet access are taking place over broadband wireless platforms, such as cell phones, handheld digital devices, and PCs in wireless networks. In fact, mobile wireless broadband Internet access (2.5G and 3G cellular, which we describe in section 6.4) is the fastest-growing form of Internet access in 2008, growing at a 96 percent compound annual growth rate. Fixed wireless broadband (Wi-Fi) is growing at a 28 percent compound annual growth rate, the second fastest growing form of Internet access.

WHAT IS A COMPUTER NETWORK?

If you had to connect the computers for two or more employees together in the same office, you would need a computer network. Exactly what is a network? In its simplest form, a network consists of two or more connected computers. Figure 6-1 illustrates the major hardware, software, and transmission components used in a simple network: a client computer and a dedicated server computer, network interfaces, a connection medium, network operating system software, and either a hub or a switch.

Each computer on the network contains a network interface device called a **network interface card (NIC)**. Most personal computers today have this card built into the motherboard. The connection medium for linking network components can be a telephone wire, coaxial cable, or radio signal in the case of cell phone and wireless local-area networks (Wi-Fi networks).

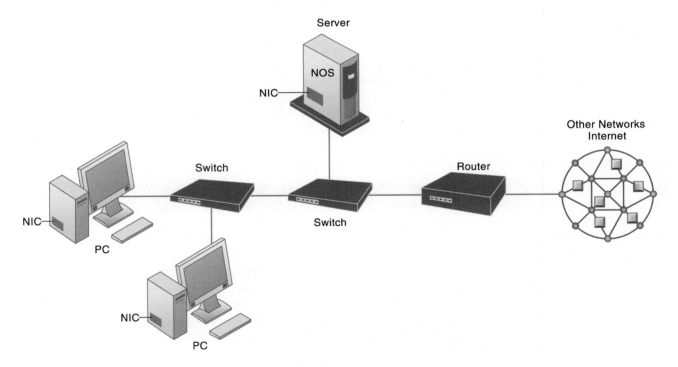

Figure 6-1
Components of a Simple Computer Network
Illustrated here is a very simple computer network, consisting of computers, a network operating system residing on a dedicated server computer, cable (wiring) connecting the devices, network interface cards (NIC), switches, and a router.

The **network operating system (NOS)** routes and manages communications on the network and coordinates network resources. It can reside on every computer in the network, or it can reside primarily on a dedicated server computer for all the applications on the network. A network server computer is a computer on a network that performs important network functions for client computers, such as serving up Web pages, storing data, and storing the network operating system (and hence controlling the network). Server software, such as Microsoft Windows Server, Linux, and Novell NetWare, are the most widely used network operating systems.

Most networks also contain a switch or a hub acting as a connection point between the computers. **Hubs** are very simple devices that connect network components, sending a packet of data to all other connected devices. A **switch** has more intelligence than a hub and can filter and forward data to a specified destination on the network.

What if you want to communicate with another network, such as the Internet? You would need a router. A **router** is a special communications processor used to route packets of data through different networks, ensuring that the data sent gets to the correct address.

Networks in Large Companies

The network we have just described might be suitable for a small business. But what about large companies with many different locations and thousands of employees? As a firm grows, and collects hundreds of small local area networks (LANs), these networks can be tied together into a corporate-wide networking infrastructure. The network infrastructure for a large corporation consists of a large number of these small local area networks linked to other local area networks and to firmwide corporate networks. A number of powerful servers support a corporate Web site, a corporate intranet, and perhaps an extranet. Some of these servers link to other large computers supporting backend systems.

Figure 6-2 provides an illustration of these more complex, larger scale corporate-wide networks. Here you can see that the corporate network infrastructure supports a mobile sales

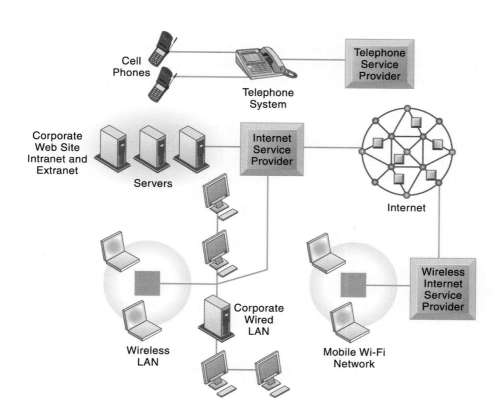

**Figure 6-2
Corporate Network Infrastructure**
Today's corporate network infrastructure is a collection of many different networks from the public switched telephone network, to the Internet, to corporate local area networks linking workgroups, departments, or office floors.

force using cell phones; mobile employees linking to the company Web site or internal company networks using mobile wireless local area networks (Wi-Fi networks); and a videoconferencing system to support managers across the world. In addition to these computer networks, the firm's infrastructure usually includes a separate telephone network that handles most voice data. Many firms are dispensing with their traditional telephone networks and using Internet telephones that run on their existing data networks (described later).

As you can see from this figure, a large corporate network infrastructure uses a wide variety of technologies—everything from ordinary telephone service and corporate data networks to Internet service, wireless Internet, and wireless cell phones. One of the major problems facing corporations today is how to integrate all the different communication networks and channels into a coherent system that enables information to flow from one part of the corporation to another, from one system to another. As more and more communication networks become digital, and based on Internet technologies, it will become easier to integrate them.

KEY DIGITAL NETWORKING TECHNOLOGIES

Contemporary digital networks and the Internet are based on three key technologies: client/server computing, the use of packet switching, and the development of widely used communications standards (the most important of which is Transmission Control Protocol/Internet Protocol, or TCP/IP) for linking disparate networks and computers.

Client/Server Computing

We introduced client/server computing in Chapter 4. Client/server computing is a distributed computing model in which some of the processing power is located within small, inexpensive client computers, and resides literally on desktops, laptops, or in handheld devices. These powerful clients are linked to one another through a network that is controlled by a network server computer. The server sets the rules of communication for the network and provides every client with an address so others can find it on the network.

Client/server computing has largely replaced centralized mainframe computing in which nearly all of the processing takes place on a central large mainframe computer. Client/server computing has extended computing to departments, workgroups, factory floors, and other parts of the business that could not be served by a centralized architecture. The Internet is the largest implementation of client/server computing.

Packet Switching

Packet switching is a method of slicing digital messages into parcels called packets, sending the packets along different communication paths as they become available, and then reassembling the packets once they arrive at their destinations (see Figure 6-3). Prior to the development of packet switching, computer networks used leased, dedicated telephone circuits to communicate with other computers in remote locations. In circuit-switched networks, such as the telephone system, a complete point-to-point circuit is assembled, and then communication can proceed. These dedicated circuit-switching techniques were expensive and wasted available communications capacity—the circuit was maintained regardless of whether any data were being sent.

Packet switching makes much more efficient use of the communications capacity of a network. In packet-switched networks, messages are first broken down into small fixed bundles of data called packets. The packets include information for directing the packet to the right address and for checking transmission errors along with the data. The packets are transmitted over various communications channels using routers, each packet traveling independently. Packets of data originating at one source will be routed through many different paths and networks before being reassembled into the original message when they reach their destinations.

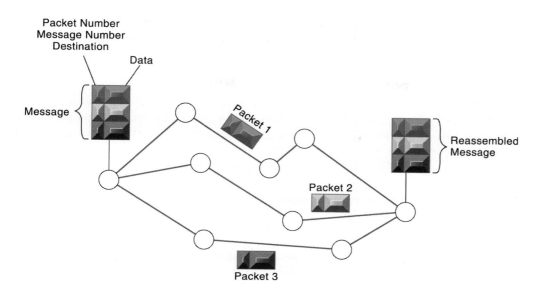

Figure 6-3
Packed-Switched Networks and Packet Communications
Data are grouped into small packets, which are transmitted independently over various communications channels and reassembled at their final destination.

TCP/IP and Connectivity

In a typical telecommunications network, diverse hardware and software components need to work together to transmit information. Different components in a network communicate with each other only by adhering to a common set of rules called protocols. A **protocol** is a set of rules and procedures governing transmission of information between two points in a network.

In the past, many diverse proprietary and incompatible protocols often forced business firms to purchase computing and communications equipment from a single vendor. But today corporate networks are increasingly using a single, common, worldwide standard called **Transmission Control Protocol/Internet Protocol (TCP/IP)**. TCP/IP was developed during the early 1970s to support U.S. Department of Defense Advanced Research Projects Agency (DARPA) efforts to help scientists transmit data among different types of computers over long distances.

TCP/IP uses a suite of protocols, the main ones being TCP and IP. TCP refers to the Transmission Control Protocol (TCP), which handles the movement of data between computers. TCP establishes a connection between the computers, sequences the transfer of packets, and acknowledges the packets sent. IP refers to the Internet Protocol (IP), which is responsible for the delivery of packets and includes the disassembling and reassembling of packets during transmission. Figure 6-4 illustrates the four-layered Department of Defense reference model for TCP/IP.

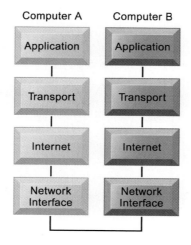

Figure 6-4
The Transmission Control Protocol/Internet Protocol (TCP/IP) Reference Model
This figure illustrates the four layers of the TCP/IP reference model for communications.

1. *Application layer.* The application layer enables client application programs to access the other layers and defines the protocols that applications use to exchange data. One of these application protocols is the Hypertext Transfer Protocol (HTTP), which is used to transfer Web page files.
2. *Transport layer.* The transport layer is responsible for providing the application layer with communication and packet services. This layer includes TCP and other protocols.
3. *Internet layer.* The Internet layer is responsible for addressing, routing, and packaging data packets called IP datagrams. The Internet Protocol is one of the protocols used in this layer.
4. *Network interface layer.* At the bottom of the reference model, the network interface layer is responsible for placing packets on and receiving them from the network medium, which could be any networking technology.

Two computers using TCP/IP are able to communicate even if they are based on different hardware and software platforms. Data sent from one computer to the other passes downward through all four layers, starting with the sending computer's application layer and passing through the network interface layer. After the data reach the recipient host computer, they travel up the layers and are reassembled into a format the receiving computer can use. If the receiving computer finds a damaged packet, it asks the sending computer to retransmit it. This process is reversed when the receiving computer responds.

6.2 Communications Networks

Let's look more closely at alternative networking technologies available to businesses.

Signals: Digital vs. Analog

There are two ways to communicate a message in a network: either an analog signal or a digital signal. An *analog signal* is represented by a continuous waveform that passes through a communications medium and has been used for voice communication. The most common analog devices are the telephone handset, the speaker on your computer, or your iPod earphone, all of which create analog wave forms that your ear can hear.

A *digital signal* is a discrete, binary waveform, rather than a continuous waveform. Digital signals communicate information as strings of two discrete states: one bit and zero bits, which are represented as on-off electrical pulses. Computers use digital signals, so if you want to use the analog telephone system to send digital data, you'll need a device called a **modem** to translate digital signals into analog form (see Figure 6-5). *Modem* stands for modulation/demodulation.

There are many different kinds of networks and ways of classifying them. One way of looking at networks is in terms of their geographic scope (see Table 6.1).

**Figure 6-5
Functions of the Modem**
A modem is a device that translates digital signals from a computer into analog form so that they can be transmitted over analog telephone lines. The modem also translates analog signals back into digital form for the receiving computer.

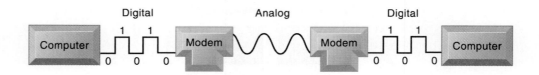

Type	Area
Local area network (LAN)	Up to 500 meters (half a mile); an office or floor of a building
Campus area network (CAN)	Up to 1,000 meters (a mile); a college campus or corporate facility
Metropolitan area network (MAN)	A city or metropolitan area
Wide area network (WAN)	A transcontinental or global area

TABLE 6.1

Types of Networks

Local Area Networks

If you work in a business that uses networking, you are probably connecting to other employees and groups via a local area network. A **local area network (LAN)** is designed to connect personal computers and other digital devices within a half-mile or 500-meter radius. LANs typically connect a few computers in a small office, all the computers in one building, or all the computers in several buildings in close proximity. LANs can link to long-distance wide area networks (WANs, described later in this section) and other networks around the world using the Internet.

Review Figure 6-1, which could serve as a model for a small LAN that might be used in an office. One computer is a dedicated network file server, providing users with access to shared computing resources in the network, including software programs and data files. The server determines who gets access to what and in which sequence. The router connects the LAN to other networks, which could be the Internet or another corporate network, so that the LAN can exchange information with networks external to it. The most common LAN operating systems are Windows, Linux, and Novell. Each of these network operating systems supports TCP/IP as their default networking protocol.

Ethernet is the dominant LAN standard at the physical network level, specifying the physical medium to carry signals between computers, access control rules, and a standardized set of bits used to carry data over the system. Originally, Ethernet supported a data transfer rate of 10 megabits per second (Mbps). Newer versions, such as Fast Ethernet and Gigabit Ethernet, support data transfer rates of 100 Mbps and 1 Gbps, respectively, and are used in network backbones.

The LAN illustrated in Figure 6-1 uses a client/server architecture where the network operating system resides primarily on a single file server, and the server provides much of the control and resources for the network. Alternatively, LANs may use a **peer-to-peer** architecture. A peer-to-peer network treats all processors equally and is used primarily in small networks with 10 or fewer users. The various computers on the network can exchange data by direct access and can share peripheral devices without going through a separate server.

In LANs using the Windows Server family of operating systems, the peer-to-peer architecture is called the *workgroup network model* in which a small group of computers can share resources, such as files, folders, and printers, over the network without a dedicated server. The Windows *domain network model*, in contrast, uses a dedicated server to manage the computers in the network.

Larger LANs have many clients and multiple servers, with separate servers for specific services, such as storing and managing files and databases (file servers or database servers), managing printers (print servers), storing and managing e-mail (mail servers), or storing and managing Web pages (Web servers).

Sometimes LANs are described in terms of the way their components are connected together, or their **topology**. There are three major LAN topologies: star, bus, and ring (see Figure 6-6).

Figure 6-6
Network Topologies
The three basic network topologies are the bus, star, and ring.

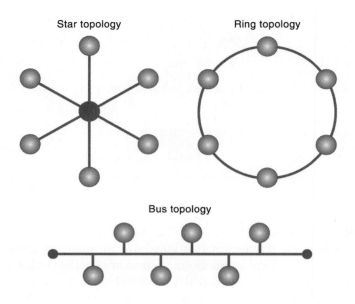

In a star topology, all devices on the network connect to a single hub. Figure 6-6 illustrates a simple **star topology** in which all network components connect to a single hub. All network traffic flows through the hub. In an *extended star network*, multiple layers or hubs are organized into a hierarchy.

In a bus topology, one station transmits signals, which travel in both directions along a single transmission segment. All of the signals are broadcast in both directions to the entire network. All machines on the network receive the same signals, and software installed on the clients enables each client to listen for messages addressed specifically to it. The **bus topology** is the most common Ethernet topology.

A **ring topology** connects network components in a closed loop. Messages pass from computer to computer in only one direction around the loop, and only one station at a time may transmit. The ring topology is primarily found in older LANs using Token Ring networking software.

Metropolitan and Wide Area Networks

Wide area networks (WANs) span broad geographical distances—entire regions, states, continents, or the entire globe. The most universal and powerful WAN is the Internet. Computers connect to a WAN through public networks, such as the telephone system or private cable systems, or through leased lines or satellites. A **metropolitan area network (MAN)** is a network that spans a metropolitan area, usually a city and its major suburbs. Its geographic scope falls between a WAN and a LAN.

PHYSICAL TRANSMISSION MEDIA

Networks use different kinds of physical transmission media, including twisted wire, coaxial cable, fiber optics, and media for wireless transmission. Each has advantages and limitations. A wide range of speeds is possible for any given medium depending on the software and hardware configuration.

Twisted Wire

Twisted wire consists of strands of copper wire twisted in pairs and is an older type of transmission medium. Many of the telephone systems in buildings had twisted wires installed for analog communication, but they can be used for digital communication as well. Although an older physical transmission medium, the twisted wires used in today's LANs, such as CAT5, can obtain speeds up to 1 Gbps. Twisted-pair cabling is limited to a maximum recommended run of 100 meters (328 feet).

Coaxial Cable

Coaxial cable, similar to that used for cable television, consists of thickly insulated copper wire, which can transmit a larger volume of data than twisted wire. Cable was used in early local area networks and is still used today for longer (more than 100 meters) runs in large buildings. Coaxial has speeds up to 1 Gbps.

Fiber Optics and Optical Networks

Fiber-optic cable consists of bound strands of clear glass fiber, each the thickness of a human hair. Data are transformed into pulses of light, which are sent through the fiber-optic cable by a laser device at rates varying from 500 kilobits to several trillion bits per second in experimental settings. Fiber-optic cable is considerably faster, lighter, and more durable than wire media, and is well suited to systems requiring transfers of large volumes of data. However, fiber-optic cable is more expensive than other physical transmission media and harder to install.

Until recently, fiber-optic cable had been used primarily for the high-speed network backbone, which handles the major traffic. Now telecommunications companies are starting to bring fiber lines into the home for new types of services, such as ultra high-speed Internet access and on-demand video.

Wireless Transmission Media

Wireless transmission is based on radio signals of various frequencies. **Microwave systems**, both terrestrial and celestial, transmit high-frequency radio signals through the atmosphere and are widely used for high-volume, long-distance, point-to-point communication. Microwave signals follow a straight line and do not bend with the curvature of the earth. Therefore, long-distance terrestrial transmission systems require that transmission stations be positioned about 37 miles apart. Long-distance transmission is also possible by using communication satellites as relay stations for microwave signals transmitted from terrestrial stations.

Communication satellites are typically used for transmission in large, geographically dispersed organizations that would be difficult to network using cabling media or terrestrial microwave. For instance, BP Amoco uses satellites for real-time data transfer of oil field exploration data gathered from searches of the ocean floor. Using geosynchronous satellites, exploration ships transfer these data to central computing centers in the United States for use by researchers in Houston, Tulsa, and suburban Chicago. Figure 6-7 illustrates how this system works.

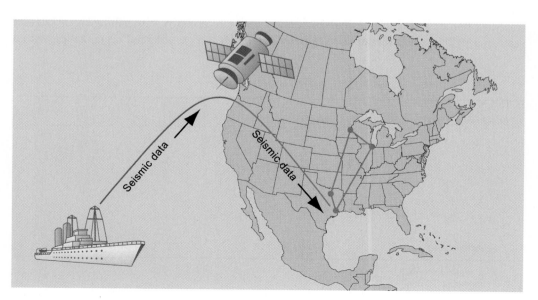

Figure 6-7
BP Amoco's Satellite Transmission System
Communication satellites help BP Amoco transfer seismic data between oil exploration ships and research centers in the United States.

Cellular systems use radio waves to communicate with radio antennas (towers) placed within adjacent geographic areas called cells. Communications transmitted from a **cell phone** to a local cell pass from antenna to antenna—cell to cell—until they reach their final destination.

Wireless networks are supplanting traditional wired networks for many applications and creating new applications, services, and business models. In Section 6.4 we provide a detailed description of the applications and technology standards driving the "wireless revolution."

Transmission Speed

The total amount of digital information that can be transmitted through any telecommunications medium is measured in bits per second (bps). One signal change, or cycle, is required to transmit one or several bits; therefore, the transmission capacity of each type of telecommunications medium is a function of its frequency. The number of cycles per second that can be sent through that medium is measured in **hertz**—one hertz is equal to one cycle of the medium.

The range of frequencies that can be accommodated on a particular telecommunications channel is called its **bandwidth**. The bandwidth is the difference between the highest and lowest frequencies that can be accommodated on a single channel. The greater the range of frequencies, the greater the bandwidth and the greater the channel's transmission capacity. Table 6.2 compares the transmission speeds of the major types of media.

6.3 The Global Internet

We all use the Internet, and many of us cannot do without it. It has become an indispensable personal and business tool. But what exactly is the Internet? How does it work, and what does Internet technology have to offer for business? Let's look at the most important Internet features.

WHAT IS THE INTERNET?

The Internet has become the world's most extensive public communication system and now rivals the global telephone system in reach and range. It is also the world's largest implementation of client/server computing and internetworking, linking millions of individual networks all over the world. This gigantic network of networks began in the early 1970s as a U.S. Department of Defense network to link scientists and university professors around the world.

Most homes and small businesses connect to the Internet by subscribing to an Internet service provider. An **Internet service provider (ISP)** is a commercial organization with a

TABLE 6.2	
Typical Speeds and Costs of Telecommunications Transmission Media	

Medium	Speed
Twisted wire	Up to 1 Gbps
Microwave	Up to 600+ Mbps
Satellite	Up to 600+ Mbps
Coaxial cable	Up to 1 Gbps
Fiber-optic cable	Up to 6+ Tbps

Mbps = megabits per second
Gbps = gigabits per second
Tbps = terabits per second

permanent connection to the Internet that sells temporary connections to retail subscribers. EarthLink, NetZero, AT&T Yahoo!, and Microsoft Network (MSN) are ISPs. Individuals also connect to the Internet through their business firms, universities, or research centers that have designated Internet domains.

There are a variety of services for ISP Internet connections. Connecting via a traditional telephone line and modem (at a speed of 56.6 Kbps) used to be the most common form of connection worldwide, but it is quickly being replaced by broadband connections. Digital Subscriber Line (DSL), cable and satellite Internet connections, and T lines provide these broadband services.

Digital subscriber line (DSL) technologies operate over existing telephone lines to carry voice, data, and video at transmission rates ranging from 385 Kbps all the way up to 9 Mbps. **Cable Internet connections** provided by cable television vendors use digital cable coaxial lines to deliver high-speed Internet access to homes and businesses. They can provide high-speed access to the Internet of up to 10 Mbps. In areas where DSL and cable services are unavailable, it is possible to access the Internet via satellite, although some satellite Internet connections have slower upload speeds than these other broadband services.

T1 and T3 are international telephone standards for digital communication. They are leased, dedicated lines suitable for businesses or government agencies requiring high-speed guaranteed service levels. **T1 lines** offer guaranteed delivery at 1.54 Mbps, and **T3 lines** offer delivery at 45 Mbps.

INTERNET ADDRESSING AND ARCHITECTURE

The Internet is based on the TCP/IP networking protocol suite described earlier in this chapter. Every computer on the Internet is assigned a unique **Internet Protocol (IP) address**, which currently is a 32-bit number represented by four strings of numbers ranging from 0 to 255 separated by periods. For instance, the IP address of www.microsoft.com is 207.46.250.119.

When a user sends a message to another user on the Internet, the message is first decomposed into packets using the TCP protocol. Each packet contains its destination address. The packets are then sent from the client to the network server and from there on to as many other servers as necessary to arrive at a specific computer with a known address. At the destination address, the packets are reassembled into the original message.

The Domain Name System

Because it would be incredibly difficult for Internet users to remember strings of 12 numbers, a **Domain Name System (DNS)** converts IP addresses to domain names. The **domain name** is the English-like name that corresponds to the unique 32-bit numeric IP address for each computer connected to the Internet. DNS servers maintain a database containing IP addresses mapped to their corresponding domain names. To access a computer on the Internet, users need only specify its domain name.

DNS has a hierarchical structure (see Figure 6-8). At the top of the DNS hierarchy is the root domain. The child domain of the root is called a top-level domain, and the child domain of a top-level domain is called is a second-level domain. Top-level domains are two-and three-character names you are familiar with from surfing the Web, for example, .com, .edu, .gov, and the various country codes such as .ca for Canada or .it for Italy. Second-level domains have two parts, designating a top-level name and a second-level name—such as buy.com, nyu.edu, or amazon.ca. A host name at the bottom of the hierarchy designates a specific computer on either the Internet or a private network.

The most common domain extensions currently available and officially approved are shown in the following list. Countries also have domain names such as .uk, .au, and .fr (United Kingdom, Australia, and France, respectively). In the future, this list will expand to include many more types of organizations and industries.

Figure 6-8
The Domain Name System
The Domain Name System is a hierarchical system with a root domain, top-level domains, second-level domains, and host computers at the third level.

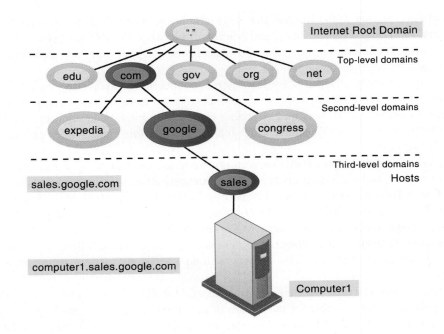

.com	Commercial organizations/businesses
.edu	Educational institutions
.gov	U.S. government agencies
.mil	U.S. military
.net	Network computers
.org	Nonprofit organizations and foundations
.biz	Business firms
.info	Information providers

Internet Architecture and Governance

Internet data traffic is carried over transcontinental high-speed backbone networks that generally operate today in the range of 45 Mbps to 2.5 Gbps (see Figure 6-9). These trunk lines are typically owned by long-distance telephone companies (called network service providers) or by national governments. Local connection lines are owned by regional telephone and cable television companies in the United States that connect retail users in homes and businesses to the Internet. The regional networks lease access to ISPs, private companies, and government institutions.

No one "owns" the Internet, and it has no formal management. However, worldwide Internet policies are established by a number of professional organizations and government bodies, including the Internet Architecture Board (IAB), which helps define the overall structure of the Internet; The Internet Corporation for Assigned Names and Numbers (ICANN), which assigns IP addresses; and The World Wide Web Consortium (W3C), which sets hypertext markup language (HTML) and other programming standards for the Web.

These organizations influence government agencies, network owners, ISPs and software developers with the goal of keeping the Internet operating as efficiently as possible. The Internet must also conform to the laws of the sovereign nation-states in which it operates, as well as the technical infrastructures that exist within the nation-states. Although in the early years of the Internet and the Web there was very little legislative or executive interference, this situation is changing as the Internet plays a growing role in the distribution of information and knowledge, including content that some find objectionable.

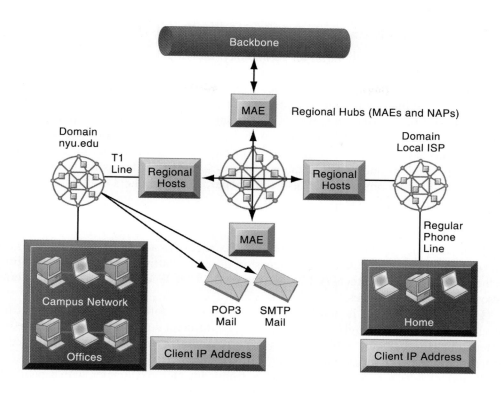

Figure 6-9
Internet Network Architecture
The Internet backbone connects to regional networks, which in turn provide access to Internet service providers, large firms, and government institutions. Network access points (NAPs) and metropolitan area exchanges (MAEs) are hubs where the backbone intersects regional and local networks and where backbone owners connect with one another.

The Internet is not "free," even though some college students believe they do not pay for their access. In fact, everyone who uses the Internet pays some fee—hidden or otherwise—to maintain the network. Each organization pays for its own networks and its own local Internet connection services, a part of which is paid to the long-distance trunk line owners. The costs of e-mail and other Internet connections tend to be far lower than equivalent voice, postal, or overnight delivery costs, making the Internet a very inexpensive communications medium. It is also a very fast method of communication, with messages arriving anywhere in the world in a matter of seconds, or a minute or two at most.

The Future Internet: IPv6 and Internet2

The Internet was not originally designed to handle the transmission of massive quantities of data and billions of users. Because many corporations and governments have been given large blocks of millions of IP addresses to accommodate current and future workforces, and because of sheer Internet population growth, the world will run out of available IP addresses using the existing addressing convention by 2012 or 2013. Under development is a new version of the IP addressing schema called *Internet Protocol version 6 (IPv6)*, which uses 128-bit addresses (2 to the power of 128), or more than a quadrillion possible unique addresses.

Internet2 and Next-Generation Internet (NGI) are consortia representing 200 universities, private businesses, and government agencies in the United States that are working on a new, robust, high-bandwidth version of the Internet. They have established several new high-performance backbone networks with bandwidths ranging from 2.5 Gbps to 9.6 Gbps. Internet2 research groups are developing and implementing new technologies for more effective routing practices; different levels of service, depending on the type and importance of the data being transmitted; and advanced applications for distributed computation, virtual laboratories, digital libraries, distributed learning, and tele-immersion. These networks do not replace the public Internet, but they do provide test beds for leading-edge technology that may eventually migrate to the public Internet.

INTERNET SERVICES AND COMMUNICATION TOOLS

The Internet is based on client/server technology. Individuals using the Internet control what they do through client applications on their computers, such as Web browser software. The data, including e-mail messages and Web pages, are stored on servers. A client uses the Internet to request information from a particular Web server on a distant computer, and the server sends the requested information back to the client over the Internet. Chapters 4 and 5 describe how Web servers work with application servers and database servers to access information from an organization's internal information systems applications and their associated databases. Client platforms today include not only PCs and other computers but also cell phones, small handheld digital devices, and other information appliances.

Internet Services

A client computer connecting to the Internet has access to a variety of services. These services include e-mail, electronic discussion groups, chatting and instant messaging, Telnet, **File Transfer Protocol** (**FTP**), and the World Wide Web. Table 6.3 provides a brief description of these services.

Each Internet service is implemented by one or more software programs. All of the services may run on a single server computer, or different services may be allocated to different machines. Figure 6-10 illustrates one way that these services might be arranged in a multitiered client/server architecture.

E-mail enables messages to be exchanged from computer to computer, with capabilities for routing messages to multiple recipients, forwarding messages, and attaching text documents or multimedia files to messages. Although some organizations operate their own internal electronic mail systems, most e-mail today is sent through the Internet.

Nearly 90 percent of U.S. workplaces have employees communicating interactively using **chat** or instant messaging tools. Chatting enables two or more people who are simultaneously connected to the Internet to hold live, interactive conversations. Chat systems now support voice and video chat as well as written conversations. Many online retail businesses offer chat services on their Web sites to attract visitors, to encourage repeat purchases, and to improve customer service.

Instant messaging is a type of chat service that enables participants to create their own private chat channels. The instant messaging system alerts the user whenever someone on his or her private list is online so that the user can initiate a chat session with other individuals. Instant messaging systems for consumers include Yahoo! Messenger and AOL Instant Messenger. Companies concerned with security use proprietary instant messaging systems such as Lotus Sametime.

TABLE 6.3

Major Internet
Services

Capability	Functions Supported
E-mail	Person-to-person messaging; document sharing
Chatting and instant messaging	Interactive conversations
Newsgroups	Discussion groups on electronic bulletin boards
Telnet	Logging on to one computer system and doing work on another
File Transfer Protocol (FTP)	Transferring files from computer to computer
World Wide Web	Retrieving, formatting, and displaying information (including text, audio, graphics, and video) using hypertext links

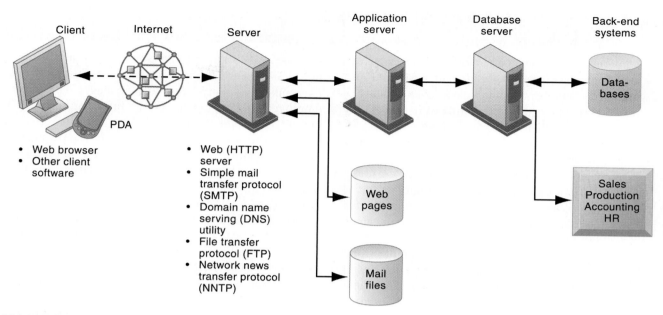

Figure 6-10
Client/Server Computing on the Internet
Client computers running Web browser and other software can access an array of services on servers over the Internet. These services may all run on a single server or on multiple specialized servers.

Newsgroups are worldwide discussion groups posted on Internet electronic bulletin boards on which people share information and ideas on a defined topic, such as radiology or rock bands. Anyone can post messages on these bulletin boards for others to read. Many thousands of groups exist that discuss almost all conceivable topics.

Employee use of e-mail, instant messaging, and the Internet is supposed to increase worker productivity, but the accompanying Interactive Session on People shows that this may not always be the case. Many company managers now believe they need to monitor their employees' online activity. But is this ethical? Although there are some strong business reasons why companies may need to monitor their employees' e-mail and Web activities, what does this mean for employee privacy?

Voice over IP

The Internet has also become a popular platform for voice transmission and corporate networking. **Voice over IP (VoIP)** technology delivers voice information in digital form using packet switching, avoiding the tolls charged by local and long-distance telephone networks (see Figure 6-11). Calls that would ordinarily be transmitted over public telephone networks would travel over the corporate network based on the Internet Protocol, or the public Internet. Voice calls can be made and received with a desktop computer equipped with a microphone and speakers or with a VoIP-enabled telephone.

Telecommunications service providers (such as Verizon) and cable firms (such as Time Warner and Cablevision) provide VoIP services. Skype, acquired by eBay, offers free VoIP worldwide using a peer-to-peer network, and Google has its own free VoIP service.

Although there are up-front investments required for an IP phone system, VoIP can reduce communication and network management costs by 20 to 30 percent. For example, VoIP saves Virgin Entertainment Group $700,000 per year in long-distance bills (Hoover, 2006). In addition to lowering long-distance costs and eliminating monthly fees for private lines, an IP network provides a single voice-data infrastructure for both telecommunications and computing services. Companies no longer have to maintain separate networks or provide support services and personnel for each different type of network.

INTERACTIVE SESSION: PEOPLE   Monitoring Employees on Networks: Unethical or Good Business?

As Internet use has exploded worldwide, so have the use of e-mail and the Web for personal business at the workplace. A number of studies have concluded that at least 25 percent of employee online time is spent on non-work-related Web surfing, and perhaps as many as 90 percent of employees receive or send personal e-mail at work.

Many companies have begun monitoring their employee use of e-mail, blogs, and the Internet, often without employee knowledge. A study by Forrester Consulting found that 37.8 percent of U.S. companies with 1,000 or more workers employ people to read through employees' outbound e-mail. A similar study by the American Management Association concluded that 55 percent of U.S. companies retain and review employee e-mail messages and that 76 percent monitor their Web connections. Although U.S. companies have the legal right to monitor employee Internet and e-mail activity while they are at work, is such monitoring unethical, or is it simply good business?

Managers worry about the loss of time and employee productivity when employees are focusing on personal rather than company business. Too much time on personal business, on the Internet or not, can mean lost revenue or overbilled clients. Some employees may be charging time they spend trading their personal stocks online or pursuing other personal business to clients, thus overcharging the clients.

If personal traffic on company networks is too high, it can also clog the company's network so that legitimate business work cannot be performed. Potomac Hospital in Woodridge, Virginia found its computing resources were limited by a lack of bandwidth caused by employees using the hospital's Internet connections to access radio stations and download music and video files.

When employees use e-mail or the Web at employer facilities or with employer equipment, anything they do, including anything illegal, carries the company's name. Therefore, the employer can be traced and held liable. Management in many firms fear that racist, sexually explicit, or other potentially offensive material accessed or traded by their employees could result in adverse publicity and even lawsuits for the firm. Even if the company is found not to be liable, responding to lawsuits could cost the company tens of thousands of dollars.

Companies also fear leakage of confidential information and trade secrets through e-mail or blogs. Ajax Boiler, based in Santa Ana, California, learned that one of its senior managers was able to access the network of a former employer and read the e-mail of that company's human resources manager. The Ajax employee was trying to gather information for a lawsuit against the former employer.

Companies that allow employees to use personal e-mail accounts at work face legal and regulatory trouble if they do not retain those messages. E-mail today is an important source of evidence for lawsuits, and companies are now required to retain all of their e-mail messages for longer periods than in the past. Courts do not discriminate about whether e-mails involved in lawsuits were sent via personal or business e-mail accounts. Not producing those e-mails could result in a five-to six-figure fine.

U.S. companies have the legal right to monitor what employees are doing with company equipment during business hours. The question is whether electronic surveillance is an appropriate tool for maintaining an efficient and positive workplace. Some companies try to ban all personal activities on corporate networks—zero tolerance. Others block employee access to specific Web sites or limit personal time on the Web using software that enables IT departments to track the Web sites employees visit, the amount of time employees spend at these sites, and the files they download. Ajax uses software from SpectorSoft Corporation that records all the Web sites employees visit, time spent at each site, and all e-mails sent.

Some firms have fired employees who have stepped out of bounds. Nearly one-third of the companies surveyed in the Forrester Consulting study had fired at least one employee within the last year for breaking company e-mail rules.

No solution is problem free, but many consultants believe companies should write corporate policies on employee e-mail and Internet use. The policies should include explicit ground rules that state, by position or level, under what circumstances employees can use company facilities for e-mail, blogging, or Web surfing. The policies should also inform employees whether these activities are monitored and explain why.

The rules should be tailored to specific business needs and organizational cultures. For example, although some companies may exclude all employees from visiting sites that have explicit sexual material, law firm or hospital employees may require access to these sites. Investment firms will need to allow many of their employees access to other investment sites.

A company dependent on widespread information sharing, innovation, and independence could very well find that monitoring creates more problems than it solves.

Sources: Katherine Wegert, "Workers Can Breach Security Knowingly Or Not," Dow Jones News Service, June 24, 2007; Andrew Blackman, "Foul Sents," *The Wall Street Journal*, March 26, 2007; Alex Mindlin, "You've Got Someone Reading Your E-Mail," *The New York Times*, June 12, 2006; and Darrell Dunn, "Who's Watching Now?" *InformationWeek*, February 27, 2006.

CASE STUDY QUESTIONS

1. Should managers monitor employee e-mail and Internet usage? Why or why not?

2. Describe an effective e-mail and Web use policy for a company.

MIS IN ACTION

Explore the Web site of online employee monitoring software such as SpectorSoft, NetVizor, SpyTech, or Activity Monitor and answer the following questions:

1. What employee activities does this software track? What can an employer learn about an employee by using this software?

2. How can businesses benefit from using this software?

3. How would you feel if your employer used this software where you work to monitor what you are doing on the job? Explain your response.

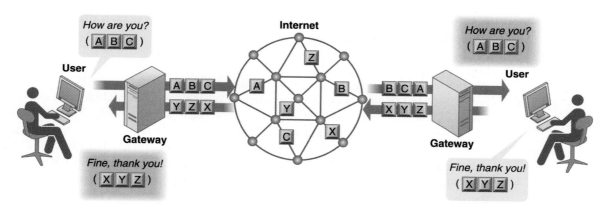

Figure 6-11
How Voice over IP Works
An VoIP phone call digitizes and breaks up a voice message into data packets that may travel along different routes before being reassembled at the final destination. A processor nearest the call's destination, called a gateway, arranges the packets in the proper order and directs them to the telephone number of the receiver or the IP address of the receiving computer.

Another advantage of VoIP is its flexibility. Unlike the traditional telephone network, phones can be added or moved to different offices without rewiring or reconfiguring the network. With VoIP, a conference call is arranged by a simple click-and-drag operation on the computer screen to select the names of the conferees. Voice mail and e-mail can be combined into a single directory.

Virtual Private Networks

What if you had a marketing group charged with developing new products and services for your firm with members spread across the United States. You would want to be able to e-mail each other and communicate with the home office without any chance that outsiders could intercept the communications. In the past, one answer to this problem was to work with large private networking firms who offered secure, private, dedicated networks to customers. But this was an expensive solution. A much less expensive solution is to create a virtual private network within the public Internet.

A **virtual private network** (**VPN**) is a secure, encrypted, private network that has been configured within a public network to take advantage of the economies of scale and management facilities of large networks, such as the Internet (see Figure 6-12). A VPN provides your firm with secure, encrypted communications at a much lower cost than the same capabilities offered by traditional non-Internet providers who use their private networks to secure communications. VPNs also provide a network infrastructure for combining voice and data networks.

Several competing protocols are used to protect data transmitted over the public Internet, including Point-to-Point Tunneling Protocol (PPTP). In a process called *tunneling*, packets of data are encrypted and wrapped inside IP packets. By adding this wrapper around a network message to hide its content, business firms create a private connection that travels through the public Internet.

THE WORLD WIDE WEB

You have probably used the World Wide Web to download music, to find information for a term paper, or to obtain news and weather reports. The Web is the most popular Internet service. It's a system with universally accepted standards for storing, retrieving, formatting, and displaying information using a client/server architecture. Web pages are formatted using hypertext with embedded links that connect documents to one another and that also link pages to other objects, such as sound, video, or animation files. When you click a graphic and a video clip plays, you have clicked a hyperlink. A typical **Web site** is a collection of Web pages linked to a home page.

Hypertext

Web pages are based on a standard hypertext markup language (HTML), which formats documents and incorporates dynamic links to other documents and pictures stored in the same or remote computers (see Chapter 4). Web pages are accessible through the Internet because Web browser software operating your computer can request Web pages stored on an Internet host server using the **Hypertext Transfer Protocol** (**HTTP**). HTTP is the communications standard used to transfer pages on the Web. For example, when you type a Web address in your browser, such as www.sec.gov, your browser sends an HTTP request to the sec.gov server requesting the home page of sec.gov.

HTTP is the first set of letters at the start of every Web address, followed by the domain name, which specifies the organization's server computer that is storing the document. Most

Figure 6-12
A Virtual Private Network Using the Internet
This VPN is a private network of computers linked using a secure "tunnel" connection over the Internet. It protects data transmitted over the public Internet by encoding the data and "wrapping" them within the Internet Protocol (IP). By adding a wrapper around a network message to hide its content, organizations can create a private connection that travels through the public Internet.

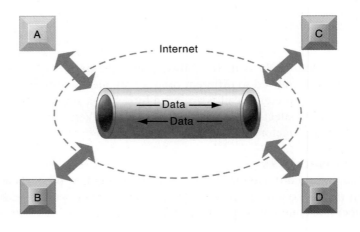

companies have a domain name that is the same as or closely related to their official corporate name. The directory path and document name are two more pieces of information within the Web address that help the browser track down the requested page. Together, the address is called a **uniform resource locator (URL)**. When typed into a browser, a URL tells the browser software exactly where to look for the information. For example, in the following URL

http://www.megacorp.com/content/features/082602.html

http names the protocol used to display Web pages, *www.megacorp.com* is the domain name, *content/features* is the directory path that identifies where on the domain Web server the page is stored, and *082602.html* is the document name and the name of the format it is in (it is an HTML page).

Web Servers

A Web server is software for locating and managing stored Web pages. It locates the Web pages requested by a user on the computer where they are stored and delivers the Web pages to the user's computer. Server applications usually run on dedicated computers, although they can all reside on a single computer in small organizations.

The most common Web server in use today is Apache HTTP Server, which controls 70 percent of the market. Apache is an open source product that is free of charge and can be downloaded from the Web. Microsoft's Internet Information Services is the second most commonly used Web server, with a 21-percent market share.

Searching for Information on the Web

No one knows for sure how many Web pages really exist. The surface Web is the part of the Web that search engines visit and about which information is recorded. For instance, Google visited about 50 billion pages in 2007, although publicly it acknowledges indexing more than 25 billion. But there is a "deep Web" that contains an estimated 800 billion additional pages, many of them proprietary (such as the pages of *The Wall Street Journal* Online, which cannot be visited without an access code) or that are stored in protected corporate databases.

Search Engines Obviously, with so many Web pages, finding specific Web pages that can help you or your business, nearly instantly, is an important problem. The question is, How can you find the one or two pages you really want and need out of billions of indexed Web pages? **Search engines** attempt to solve the problem of finding useful information on the Web nearly instantly, and, arguably, they are the "killer app" of the Internet era. Today's search engines can sift through HTML files, files of Microsoft Office applications, and .PDF files, with developing capabilities for searching audio, video, and image files. There are hundreds of different search engines in the world, but the vast majority of search results are supplied by three top providers: Google, Yahoo!, and Microsoft.

Web search engines started out in the early 1990s as relatively simple software programs that roamed the nascent Web, visiting pages, and gathering information about the content of each page. The first search engines were simple keyword indexes of all the pages they visited, leaving the user with lists of pages that may not have been truly relevant to their search.

In 1994, Stanford University computer science students David Filo and Jerry Yang created a hand-selected list of their favorite Web pages and called it "Yet Another Hierarchical Officious Oracle," or Yahoo!. Yahoo! was not initially a search engine but rather an edited selection of Web sites organized by categories the editors found useful, but it has since developed its own search engine capabilities.

In 1998, Larry Page and Sergey Brin, two other Stanford computer science students, released their first version of Google. This search engine was different: Not only did it index each Web page's words but it also ranked search results based on the relevance of each page. Page patented the idea of a page ranking system (PageRank System), which essentially measures the popularity of a Web page by calculating the number of sites that link to that page. Brin contributed a unique Web crawler program that indexed not only keywords on a page but also combinations of words (such as authors and the titles of their articles). These two ideas became the foundation for the Google search engine. Figure 6-13 illustrates how Google works.

Web sites for locating information such as Yahoo!, Google, and MSN have become so popular and easy to use that they also serve as major portals for the Internet. (see Chapter 9). Their search engines have become major shopping tools by offering what is now called **search engine marketing**. When users enter a search term at Google, MSN, Yahoo!, or any of the other sites serviced by these search engines, they receive two types of listings: sponsored links, for which advertisers have paid to be listed (usually at the top of the search results page) and unsponsored "organic" search results. In addition, advertisers can purchase tiny text boxes on the side of the Google and MSN search results page. The paid, sponsored advertisements are the fastest-growing form of Internet advertising and are powerful new marketing tools that precisely match consumer interests with advertising messages at the right moment (see the chapter-ending case study). Search engine marketing monetizes the value of the search process.

In 2007, 58 million people a day used a search engine, producing about 8 billion searches a month. There are hundreds of search engines but the top three (Google, Yahoo!, and MSN) account for 86 percent of all searches (see Figure 6-14).

Although search engines were originally built to search text documents, the explosion in online video and images has created a demand for search engines that can quickly find specific videos. In October 2007, YouTube (owned by Google) stored about 64 million videos, 3 billion minutes worth, growing at 20 percent a month, and having over 130 mil-

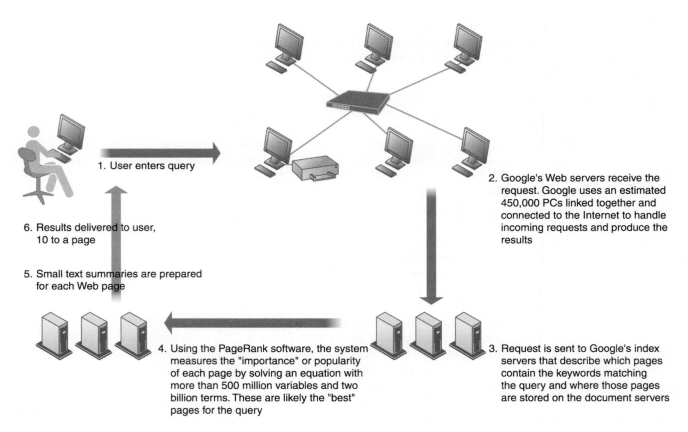

Figure 6-13
How Google Works
The Google search engine is continuously crawling the Web, indexing the content of each page, calculating its popularity, and storing the pages so that it can respond quickly to user requests to see a page. The entire process takes about one-half second.

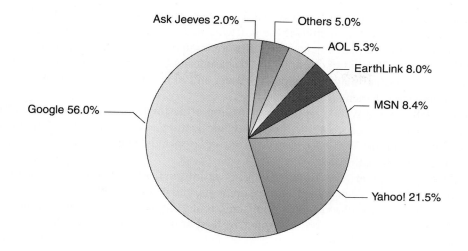

Figure 6-14
Major Web Search Engines
Google is the most popular search engine on the Web, handling 56 percent of all Web searches. Sources: Based on data from ClickZ.com, 2007; Nielsen/Net Ratings, 2007; and Searchenginewatch.com, 2007.

lion unique visitors in a month (Hof, 2007). The words "dance," "love," "music" and "girl" are all exceedingly popular in titles of YouTube videos, and searching on these keywords produces a flood of responses even though the actual contents of the video may have nothing to do with the search term. Searching videos is challenging because computers are not very good or quick at recognizing digital images. Some search engines have started indexing movies scripts so it will be possible to search on dialogue to find a movie. One of the most popular video search engines is Blinkx.com which stores 18 million hours of video and employs a large group of human classifiers who check the contents of uploaded videos against their titles.

Intelligent Agent Shopping Bots Chapter 10 describes the capabilities of software agents with built-in intelligence that can gather or filter information and perform other tasks to assist users. **Shopping bots** use intelligent agent software for searching the Internet for shopping information. Shopping bots such as MySimon or Google Product Search can help people interested in making a purchase filter and retrieve information about products of interest, evaluate competing products according to criteria the users have established, and negotiate with vendors for price and delivery terms. Many of these shopping agents search the Web for pricing and availability of products specified by the user and return a list of sites that sell the item along with pricing information and a purchase link.

The Semantic Web Most of the Web's content today is designed for humans to read and for computers to display, not for computer programs to analyze and manipulate. Search engines can discover when a particular term or keyword appears in a Web document, but they do not really understand its meaning or how it relates to other information on the Web. The **Semantic Web** is a collaborative effort led by the World Wide Web Consortium to make Web searching more efficient by reducing the amount of human involvement in searching for and processing Web information.

The Semantic Web is still in its infancy. Further development requires extensive work to establish specific meanings for data on the Web, categories for classifying the data, and relationships between classification categories. Once some of this work takes place, computers will be able to make more sense of the Web, intelligent agents will be capable of performing sophisticated search tasks, and data in Web pages will be able to be processed automatically.

Web 2.0

If you have shared photos over the Internet at Flickr or another photo site, blogged, looked up a word on Wikipedia or contributed information yourself, you have used services that are part of **Web 2.0**. Today's Web sites don't just contain static content—they enable people to collaborate, share information, and create new services online. Web 2.0 refers to these second-generation interactive Internet-based services.

The innovations that distinguish Web 2.0 are mashups, blogs, RSS, and wikis. Mashups, which we introduced in Chapter 4, are software services that enable users and system developers to mix and match content or software components to create something entirely new. For example, Yahoo's photo storage and sharing site Flickr combines photos with other information about the images provided by users and tools to make it usable within other programming environments.

With Web 2.0, the Web is not just a collection of destination sites but a source of data and services that can be combined to create applications users need. Web 2.0 software applications run on the Web itself instead of the desktop and bring the vision of Web-based computing closer to realization.

A **blog**, the popular term for a Weblog, is an informal yet structured Web site where subscribing individuals can publish stories, opinions, and links to other Web sites of interest. Blogs have become popular personal publishing tools, but they are also have business uses (see Chapters 9 and 10). For example, Wells Fargo uses blogs to help executives communicate with employees and customers. One of these blogs is dedicated to student loans.

If you are an avid blog reader, you might use RSS to keep up with your favorite blogs without constantly checking them for updates. **RSS**, which stands for Rich Site Summary or Really Simple Syndication, syndicates Web site content so that it can be used in another setting. RSS technology pulls specified content from Web sites and feeds it automatically to users' computers, where it can be stored for later viewing.

To receive an RSS information feed, you need to install aggregator or news reader software that can be downloaded from the Web. (Microsoft Internet Explorer has added RSS reading capabilities.) Alternatively, you can establish an account with an aggregator Web site. You tell the aggregator to collect all updates from a given Web page, or list of pages, or gather information on a given subject by conducting Web searches at regular intervals. Once subscribed, you automatically receive new content as it is posted to the specified Web site. A number of businesses use RSS internally to distribute updated corporate information. Wells Fargo uses RSS to deliver news feeds that employees can customize to see the business news of greatest relevance to their jobs.

Blogs allow visitors to add comments to the original content, but they do not allow visitors to change the original posted material. **Wikis**, in contrast, are collaborative Web sites where visitors can add, delete, or modify content on the site, including the work of previous authors. Wiki comes from the Hawaiian word for "quick." Probably the best-known wiki site is Wikipedia, the massive online open-source encyclopedia to which anyone can contribute. But wikis are also used for business. For example, Motorola sales representatives use wikis for sharing sales information. Instead of developing a different pitch for every client, reps reuse the information posted on the wiki.

INTRANETS AND EXTRANETS

Organizations use Internet networking standards and Web technology to create private networks called *intranets*. We introduced intranets in Chapter 1, explaining that an intranet is an internal organizational network that provides access to data across the enterprise. It uses the existing company network infrastructure along with Internet connectivity standards and software developed for the World Wide Web. Intranets create networked applications that can run on many different kinds of computers throughout the organization, including mobile handheld computers and wireless remote access devices. Hyatt Regency Osaka's intranet described in the chapter-opening case is an example.

Whereas the Web is available to anyone, an intranet is private and is protected from public visits by **firewalls**—security systems with specialized software to prevent outsiders from entering private networks (see Chapter 7). Intranet software technology is the same as that of the World Wide Web. A simple intranet can be created by linking a client computer with a Web browser to a computer with Web server software using a TCP/IP network with software to keep unwanted visitors out.

Extranets

A firm creates an extranet to allow authorized vendors and customers to have limited access to its internal intranet. For example, authorized buyers could link to a portion of a company's intranet from the public Internet to obtain information about the costs and features of the company's products. The company uses firewalls to ensure that access to its internal data is limited and remains secure; firewalls also authenticate users, making sure that only authorized users access the site.

Both intranets and extranets reduce operational costs by providing the connectivity to coordinate disparate business processes within the firm and to link electronically to customers and suppliers. Extranets often are employed for collaborating with other companies for supply chain management, product design and development, and training efforts.

6.4 The Wireless Revolution

If you have a cell phone, do you use it for taking and sending photos, sending text messages, or downloading music clips? Do you take your laptop to class or to the library to link up to the Internet? If so, you are part of the wireless revolution! Cell phones, laptops, and small handheld devices have morphed into portable computing platforms that let you perform some of the computing tasks you used to do at your desk.

Wireless communication helps businesses more easily stay in touch with customers, suppliers, and employees and provides more flexible arrangements for organizing work. Wireless technology has also created new products, services, and sales channels, which we discuss in Chapter 9.

If you require mobile communication and computing power or remote access to corporate systems, you can work with an array of wireless devices: cell phones, personal digital assistants (PDAs), and smart phones. Personal computers are also starting to be used in wireless transmission.

Personal digital assistants (PDAs) are small, handheld computers featuring applications such as electronic schedulers, address books, memo pads, and expense trackers. Models with digital cell phone capabilities such as e-mail messaging, wireless access to the Internet, voice communication, and digital cameras are called **smartphones**.

CELLULAR SYSTEMS

Cell phones and smartphones have become all-purpose devices for digital data transmission, with storage and processing power equivalent to a PC six or seven years ago. In addition to voice communication, mobile phones are now used for transmitting text and e-mail messages, instant messaging, digital photos, and short video clips; for playing music and games; for surfing the Web; and even for transmitting corporate data.

For example, employees at Pitney Bowes, a Stamford, Connecticut mail-management company, use BlackBerry smartphones to report on which parts they use on repair jobs while they are in the field. Instant availability of this information helped the company lower inventory levels by 15 percent and emergency part orders by 90 percent (Vascellaro, 2007).

Cellular Network Standards and Generations

Digital cellular service uses several competing standards. In Europe and much of the rest of the world outside the United Sates, the standard is Global System for Mobile Communication (GSM). GSM's strength is its international roaming capability. There are GSM cell phone systems in the United States, including T-Mobile and Cingular.

The major standard in the United States is Code Division Multiple Access (CDMA), which is the system used by Verizon and Sprint. CDMA was developed by the military during World War II. It transmits over several frequencies, occupies the entire spectrum, and randomly assigns users to a range of frequencies over time. In general, CDMA is cheaper to implement, is more efficient in its use of spectrum, and provides higher quality throughput of voice and data than GSM.

Most digital cellular systems still have data transmission speeds that are too slow for comfortable Internet access. They have become very popular, however, for sending and receiving short text messages.

Wireless carriers are rolling out more powerful cellular networks called **third-generation (3G) networks**, with transmission speeds ranging from 384 Kbps for mobile users in, say, a car, to more than 2 Mbps for stationary users. This is sufficient transmission capacity for video, graphics, and other rich media, in addition to voice, making 3G networks suitable for wireless broadband Internet access and always-on data transmission. 3G networks are widely used in Japan, South Korea, Taiwan, Hong Kong, Singapore, and parts of northern Europe.

However, 3G services are still not available in most U.S. locations, so U.S. cellular carriers have upgraded their networks to support higher-speed transmission. These interim 2.5G networks provide data transmission rates ranging from 30 to 384 Kbps, enabling cell phones to be used for Web access, music downloads, and other broadband services.

WIRELESS COMPUTER NETWORKS AND INTERNET ACCESS

If you have a laptop computer, you might be able to use it to access the Internet as you move from room to room in your dorm, or table to table in your university library. An array of technologies provide high-speed wireless access to the Internet for PCs and other wireless handheld devices as well as for cell phones. These new high-speed services have extended Internet access to numerous locations that could not be covered by traditional wired Internet services.

Bluetooth

Bluetooth is the popular name for the 802.15 wireless networking standard, which is useful for creating small **personal area networks (PANs)**. It links up to eight devices within a 10-meter area using low-power, radio-based communication and can transmit up to 722 Kbps in the 2.4 GHz band.

Wireless phones, pagers, computers, printers, and computing devices can use Bluetooth to communicate with each other and even operate each other without direct user intervention (see Figure 6-15). For example, a person could direct a notebook computer to send a

Figure 6-15
A Bluetooth Network (PAN)
Bluetooth enables a variety of devices, including cell phones, PDAs, wireless keyboards and mice, PCs, and printers, to interact wirelessly with each other within a small 30-foot (10-meter) area. In addition to the links shown, Bluetooth can be used to network similar devices to send data from one PC to another, for example.

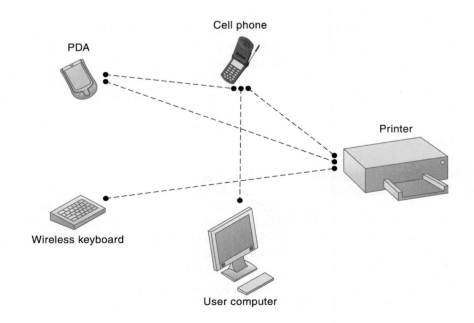

document file wirelessly to a printer. Bluetooth connects wireless keyboards and mice to PCs or cell phones to earpieces without wires. Bluetooth has low power requirements, making it appropriate for battery-powered handheld computers, cell phones, or PDAs.

Although Bluetooth lends itself to personal networking, it has uses in large corporations. For example, Federal Express drivers use Bluetooth to transmit the delivery data captured by their handheld PowerPad computers to cellular transmitters, which forward the data to corporate computers. Drivers no longer need to spend time docking their handheld units physically in the transmitters, and Bluetooth has saved FedEx $20 million per year.

Wi-Fi

The 802.11 set of standards for wireless LANs is also known as **Wi-Fi** (for wireless fidelity). There are three standards in this family: 802.11a, 802.11b, and 802.11g. 802.11n is an emerging standard for increasing the speed and capacity of wireless networking.

The 802.11a standard can transmit up to 54 Mbps in the unlicensed 5 GHz frequency range and has an effective distance of 10 to 30 meters. The 802.11b standard can transmit up to 11 Mbps in the unlicensed 2.4 GHz band and has an effective distance of 30 to 50 meters, although this range can be extended outdoors by using tower-mounted antennas. The 802.11g standard can transmit up to 54 Mbps in the 2.4 GHz range. 802.11n will transmit at more than 200 Mbps.

802.11b was the first wireless standard to be widely adopted for wireless LANs and wireless Internet access. 802.11g is increasingly used for this purpose, and dual-band systems capable of handling 802.11b and 802.11g are available.

In most Wi-Fi communication, wireless devices communicate with a wired LAN using access points. An access point is a box consisting of a radio receiver/transmitter and antennas that links to a wired network, router, or hub.

Figure 6-16 illustrates an 802.11 wireless LAN that connects a small number of mobile devices to a larger wired LAN. Most wireless devices are client machines. The servers that the mobile client stations need to use are on the wired LAN. The access point controls the wireless stations and acts as a bridge between the main wired LAN and the wireless LAN. (A bridge connects two LANs based on different technologies.) The access point also controls the wireless stations.

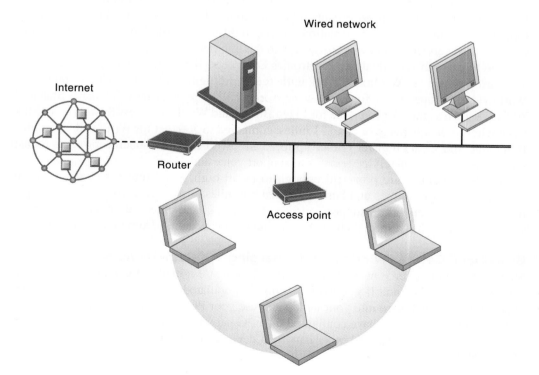

Figure 6-16
An 802.11 Wireless LAN
Mobile laptop computers equipped with wireless network interface cards link to the wired LAN by communicating with the access point. The access point uses radio waves to transmit network signals from the wired network to the client adapters, which convert them into data that the mobile device can understand. The client adapter then transmits the data from the mobile device back to the access point, which forwards the data to the wired network.

Laptop PCs now come equipped with chips to receive Wi-Fi signals. Older models may need an add-in wireless network interface card.

Wi-Fi and Wireless Internet Access

The 802.11 standard also provides wireless access to the Internet using a broadband connection. In this instance, an access point plugs into an Internet connection, which could come from a cable TV line or DSL telephone service. Computers within range of the access point use it to link wirelessly to the Internet.

Businesses of all sizes are using Wi-Fi networks to provide low-cost wireless LANs and Internet access. Wi-Fi hotspots are springing up in hotels, airport lounges, libraries, cafes, and college campuses to provide mobile access to the Internet. Dartmouth College is one of many campuses where students now use Wi-Fi for research, course work, and entertainment.

Hotspots typically consist of one or more access points positioned on a ceiling, wall, or other strategic spot in a public place to provide maximum wireless coverage for a specific area. Users in range of a hotspot are able to access the Internet from their laptops. Some hotspots are free or do not require any additional software to use; others may require activation and the establishment of a user account by providing a credit card number over the Web.

Wi-Fi technology, however, poses several challenges. Right now, users cannot freely roam from hotspot to hotspot if these hotspots use different Wi-Fi network services. Unless the service is free, users would need to log on to separate accounts for each service, each with its own fees.

One major drawback of Wi-Fi is its weak security features, which make these wireless networks vulnerable to intruders. We provide more detail about Wi-Fi security issues in Chapter 7.

Another drawback of Wi-Fi networks is susceptibility to interference from nearby systems operating in the same spectrum, such as wireless phones, microwave ovens, or other wireless LANs. Wireless networks based on the 802.11n specification will solve this problem by using multiple wireless antennas in tandem to transmit and receive data and technology called *MIMO* (multiple input multiple output) to coordinate multiple simultaneous radio signals.

WiMax

A surprisingly large number of areas in the United States and throughout the world do not have access to Wi-Fi or fixed broadband connectivity. The range of Wi-Fi systems is no more than 300 feet from the base station, making it difficult for rural groups that don't have cable or DSL service to find wireless access to the Internet.

The Institute of Electrical and Electronics Engineers (IEEE) developed a new family of standards known as WiMax to deal with these problems. **WiMax**, which stands for Worldwide Interoperability for Microwave Access, is the popular term for IEEE Standard 802.16, known as the "Air Interface for Fixed Broadband Wireless Access Systems." WiMax has a wireless access range of up to 31 miles, compared to 300 feet for Wi-Fi and 30 feet for Bluetooth, and a data transfer rate of up to 75 Mbps. The 802.16 specification has robust security and quality-of-service features to support voice and video.

WiMax antennas are powerful enough to beam high-speed Internet connections to rooftop antennas of homes and businesses that are miles away. Sprint Nextel is building a national WiMax network to support video, video calling, and other data-intensive wireless services and Intel has a special chips that facilitate WiMax access from mobile computers.

Broadband Cellular Wireless and Emerging Wireless Services

Suppose your sales force needs to access the Web or use e-mail but cannot always find a convenient Wi-Fi hotspot. If you work in a highly-populated area with 3G cellular service, you can plug a small card into your laptop and use your PC on the cellular network. Major cellular telephone carriers have configured their 3G networks to provide anytime, anywhere broadband access for PCs and other handheld devices at transmission rates ranging from 300 to 500 Kbps.

What if you want to use your cell phone for extensive Web surfing? One option is to use a 3G network for high-speed broadband access. (About 15 percent of wireless handsets in the United States are capable of handling 3G services.) Another is to use a cell phone that is Wi-Fi enabled. Over 80 different cell phone handsets, including the Apple iPhone, now have Wi-Fi capabilities or the ability to roam from Wi-Fi to cellular networks when Wi-Fi is not available. A few models support voice service over Wi-Fi networks.

RFID AND WIRELESS SENSOR NETWORKS

Mobile technologies are creating new efficiencies and ways of working throughout the enterprise. In addition to the wireless systems we have just described, radio frequency identification (RFID) systems and wireless sensor networks are having a major impact.

Radio Frequency Identification (RFID)

Radio frequency identification (RFID) systems provide a powerful technology for tracking the movement of goods throughout the supply chain. RFID systems use tiny tags with embedded microchips containing data about an item and its location to transmit radio signals over a short distance to special RFID readers. The RFID readers then pass the data over a network to a computer for processing. Unlike bar codes, RFID tags do not need line-of-sight contact to be read.

The RFID tag is electronically programmed with information that can uniquely identify an item plus other information about the item, such as its location, where and when it was made, or its status during production. Embedded in the tag is a microchip for storing the data. The rest of the tag is an antenna that transmits data to the reader.

The reader unit consists of an antenna and radio transmitter with a decoding capability attached to a stationary or handheld device. The reader emits radio waves in ranges anywhere from 1 inch to 100 feet, depending on its power output, the radio frequency employed, and surrounding environmental conditions. When an RFID tag comes within the range of the reader, the tag is activated and starts sending data. The reader captures these data, decodes them, and sends them back over a wired or wireless network to a host computer for further processing (see Figure 6-17). Both RFID tags and antennas come in a variety of shapes and sizes.

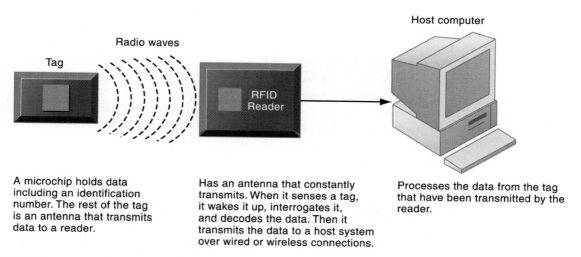

Figure 6-17
How RFID Works
RFID uses low-powered radio transmitters to read data stored in a tag at distances ranging from 1 inch to 100 feet. The reader captures the data from the tag and sends them over a network to a host computer for processing.

Active RFID tags are powered by an internal battery and typically enable data to be rewritten and modified. Active tags can transmit for hundreds of feet but cost $5 and upward per tag. Automated toll-collection systems such as New York's EZ Pass use active RFID tags.

Passive RFID tags do not have their own power source and obtain their operating power from the radio frequency energy transmitted by the RFID reader. They are smaller, lighter, and less expensive than active tags, but only have a range of several feet.

In inventory control and supply chain management, RFID systems capture and manage more detailed information about items in warehouses or in production than bar coding systems. If a large number of items are shipped together, RFID systems track each pallet, lot, or even unit item in the shipment. This technology may help companies improve receiving and storage operations by enhancing their ability to "see" exactly what stock is stored in warehouses or on retail store shelves.

The cost of RFID tags used to be too high for widespread use, but now it is approaching 10 cents per passive tag in the United States. As the price decreases, RFID is starting to become cost-effective for some applications.

In addition to installing RFID readers and tagging systems, companies may need to upgrade their hardware and software to process the massive amounts of data produced by RFID systems—transactions that could add up to tens or hundreds of terabytes.

Special software is required to filter, aggregate, and prevent RFID data from overloading business networks and system applications. Applications will need to be redesigned to accept massive volumes of RFID-generated data frequently and to share those data with other applications. Major enterprise software vendors, including SAP and Oracle-PeopleSoft, now offer RFID-ready versions of their supply chain management applications.

The Interactive Session on Organizations deals with these issues. Wal-Mart has required its top suppliers to use passive RFID tags on cases and pallets shipped to its stores to help it track and record inventory flow. Both Wal-Mart and its suppliers have been proceeding slowly because of difficulties in RFID implementation.

Wireless Sensor Networks

If your company wanted state-of-the art technology to monitor building security or detect hazardous substances in the air, it might deploy a wireless sensor network. **Wireless sensor networks (WSNs)** are networks of interconnected wireless devices that are embedded into the physical environment to provide measurements of many points over large spaces. These devices have built-in processing, storage, and radio frequency sensors and antennas. They are linked into an interconnected network that routes the data they capture to a computer for analysis.

These networks range from hundreds to thousands of nodes. Because wireless sensor devices are placed in the field for years at a time without any maintenance or human intervention, they must have very low power requirements and batteries capable of lasting for years.

Figure 6-18 illustrates one type of wireless sensor network, with data from individual nodes flowing across the network to a server with greater processing power. The server acts as a gateway to a network based on Internet technology.

Wireless sensor networks are valuable in areas such as monitoring environmental changes; monitoring traffic or military activity; protecting property; efficiently operating and managing machinery and vehicles; establishing security perimeters; monitoring supply chain management; or detecting chemical, biological, or radiological material.

6.5 Hands-On MIS

The projects in this section give you hands-on experience designing Internet applications to increase employee efficiency, using spreadsheet software to improve selection of telecommunications services, and using Web search engines for business research.

INTERACTIVE SESSION: ORGANIZATIONS Wal-Mart Grapples with RFID

Wal-Mart was always known for its ultra-efficient distribution systems that kept operating costs much lower than its rivals. But now its costs are climbing faster than those of competitors such as Costco and Target, and this retail giant is looking for a new breakthrough to maintain its price advantage. It appears to be pinning its hopes on RFID. Wal-Mart management believes that implementing this technology will help the company wring new efficiencies out of its retail stores, warehouses, and suppliers.

Wal-Mart has been RFID-enabling its retail stores and distribution centers, while ordering its top suppliers to use RFID tags on all products they ship. The objective is to reduce out-of-stock items by tracking item locations more precisely as items move from the receiving dock to store shelves. Wal-Mart is selling RFID as a technology that will eventually save everyone money.

Wal-Mart wants RFID readers installed at store receiving docks to record the arrival of pallets and cases of goods shipped with RFID tags. The RFID reader reads the tags a second time just as the cases are brought onto the sales floor from back-room storage areas. Software uses sales data from Wal-Mart's point-of-sale systems and the RFID data about the number of cases brought out the sales floor to figure out which items will soon be depleted and automatically generates a list of items to pick in the warehouse to replenish store shelves before they run out. This information helps Wal-Mart reduce out-of-stock items, increase sales, and further shrink its costs.

Wal-Mart is sharing all its RFID data with suppliers through its Retail Link extranet. The RFID data improve inventory management because suppliers know exactly where their goods are located within 30 minutes of the goods' movement from one part of a Wal-Mart store to another. Sales improve because the system allows Wal-Mart to always have products in stock.

Despite these benefits, the RFID implementations have not progressed exactly as planned. Wal-Mart initially hoped to have up to 12 of its 130 distribution centers using RFID by January 2006. As of October 2007, only five have implemented the technology, along with 600 of Wal-Mart's 60,000 suppliers and 600 Wal-Mart retail stores.

Costs of RFID tags, readers, and supporting systems are a barrier. In addition to buying large quantities of RFID tags, the suppliers have to purchase additional hardware—RFID readers, transponders, antennas, and software to track and analyze the data.

Suppliers also have to pay for new software programs to integrate the RFID software with their inventory and manufacturing systems and to change some of their business processes. Meeting Wal-Mart's RFID requirements might run over $20 million for a large supplier.

RFID tags still cost 10 to 15 cents apiece and must be attached by hand at the warehouse. These tags, particularly the least expensive types, may not perform properly when they are near certain liquids, metals, or porous objects. To ensure accuracy and proper performance, suppliers may have to use more expensive tags. RFID-tagging a case of goods might easily cost a supplier an additional 40 to 50 cents per case. A large supplier that shipped 15 million cases and pallets to Wal-Mart each year would be spending an extra $6 million in tag costs.

Some Wal-Mart suppliers report benefits from RFID. Pacific Coast Producers, which sells Wal-Mart $400 million worth of packaged and canned fruit each year, started RFID-tagging a handful of products to meet Wal-Mart's requirements in 2005. It integrated the RFID data with other corporate systems. The company reports it is able to see from the RFID-generated data which stores are not doing a good job of keeping its products on shelves so that it can work with Wal-Mart to improve those stores' performance. Pacific Coast plans to RFID-tag more items for Wal-Mart within the next few years.

Other suppliers off the record say they do not expect any return from their RFID investments for years, if at all. They have refrained from publicly criticizing Wal-Mart, which buys $260 billion products annually. For some Wal-Mart suppliers, achieving a return on their RFID investment is less important than keeping the giant retailer happy. As Howard Stockdale, chief information officer of Beaver Street Fisheries put it, "Do you want to risk the business by not being in the game?"

Wal-Mart CIO Rollin Ford insists that RFID technology is producing solid results in the company's supply chain operations, including a 30 percent improvement in out-of-stock rates in stores where RFID has been deployed. The company expects to RFID-enable 400 more retail stores in 2007.

Sources: Mel Duvall, "Radio Interference," *Baseline*, October 2007; Mary Hayes Weier, "Supplier Likes What It's Getting from Wal-Mart's RFID Push," *InformationWeek*, September 17, 2007; Laurie Sullivan, Gary McWilliams, "Wal-Mart's Radio-Tracked Inventory Hits Static," *The Wall Street Journal*, February 15, 2007; Sunil Chopra and Manmohan S. Sodhi, "In Search of RFID's Sweet Spot," *The Wall Street Journal*, March 3, 2007.

CASE STUDY QUESTIONS

1. How is RFID technology related to Wal-Mart's business model? How does it benefit suppliers?

2. What people, organization, and technology factors explain why Wal-Mart suppliers have had trouble implementing RFID systems?

3. What conditions would make adopting RFID more favorable for suppliers?

4. Should Wal-Mart require all its suppliers to use RFID? Why or why not? Explain your answer.

MIS IN ACTION

Explore the RFID Privacy Page at the Electronic Privacy Information Center (EPIC) www.epic.org/privacy/rfid) and answer the following questions:

1. Describe some RFID applications that might pose a threat to privacy. What information does RFID enable them to track?

2. How do these applications threaten personal privacy? How serious is this threat?

3. Should these RFID applications be deployed? Why or why not? Justify your answer.

Figure 6-18
A Wireless Sensor Network
The small circles represent lower-level nodes and the larger circles represent high-end nodes. Lower-level nodes forward data to each other or to higher-level nodes, which transmit data more rapidly and speed up network performance.

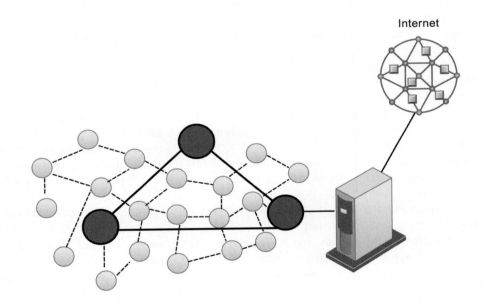

ACHIEVING OPERATIONAL EXCELLENCE: USING INTERNET TOOLS TO INCREASE EFFICIENCY AND PRODUCTIVITY

Software skills: Web browser software and presentation software
Business skills: Employee productivity analysis

In this project, you will suggest applications of Internet technology to help a employees at real-world company work more efficiently.

Dirt Bikes's management is concerned about how much money is being spent communicating with people inside and outside the company and on obtaining information about developments in the motorcycle industry and the global economy. You have been asked to investigate how Internet tools and technology could be used to help Dirt Bikes employees communicate and obtain information more efficiently. Dirt Bikes provides Internet access to all its employees who use desktop computers.

- How could the various Internet tools help employees at Dirt Bikes? Create a matrix showing what types of employees and business functions would benefit from using each type of tool and why.
- How could Dirt Bikes benefit from intranets for its sales and marketing, human resources, and manufacturing and production departments? Select one of these departments and describe the kind of information that could be provided by an intranet for that department. How could this intranet increase efficiency and productivity for that department?
- (Optional) If possible, use electronic presentation software to summarize your findings for management.

IMPROVING DECISION MAKING: USING SPREADSHEET SOFTWARE TO EVALUATE WIRELESS SERVICES

Software skills: Spreadsheet formulas, formatting
Business skills: Analyzing telecommunications services and costs

In this project, you will use the Web to research alternative wireless services and use spreadsheet software to calculate wireless service costs for a sales force.

You would like to equip your sales force of 35 based in Cincinnati, Ohio, with mobile phones that have capabilities for voice transmission, text messaging, and taking and sending photos. Use the Web to select a wireless service provider that provides nationwide service as well as good service in your home area. Examine the features of the mobile handsets offered by each of these vendors. Assume that each of the 35 salespeople will need to spend three hours per day during business hours (8 A.M. to 6 P.M.) on mobile voice communication, send 30 text messages per day, and five photos per week. Use your spreadsheet software to determine the wireless service and handset that will offer the best pricing per user over a two-year period. For the purposes of this exercise, you do not need to consider corporate discounts.

ACHIEVING OPERATIONAL EXCELLENCE: USING WEB SEARCH ENGINES FOR BUSINESS RESEARCH

Software skills: Web search tools
Business skills: Researching new technologies

This project will help develop your Internet skills in using Web search engines for business research.

You have heard that ethanol is a promising alternative fuel for motor vehicles, and you would like to learn more about how it is made and where it is used. Use the following search engines to obtain that information: Yahoo!, Google, and MSN. If you wish, try some other search engines as well. Compare the volume and quality of information you find with each search tool. Which tool is the easiest to use? Which produced the best results for your research? Why?

LEARNING TRACKS

The following Learning Tracks provide content relevant to topics covered in this chapter:

1. Computing and Communications Services Provided by Commercial Communications Vendors
2. Broadband Network Services and Technologies
3. Cellular System Generations
4. Wireless Applications for Customer Relationship Management, Supply Chain Management, and Healthcare

Review Summary

1 **What are the principal components of telecommunications networks and key networking technologies?** A simple network consists of two or more connected computers. Basic network components include computers, network interfaces, a connection medium, network operating system software, and either a hub or a switch. The networking infrastructure for a large company includes the traditional telephone system, mobile cellular communication, wireless local area networks, videoconferencing systems, a corporate Web site, intranets, extranets, and an array of local and wide area networks, including the Internet.

Contemporary networks have been shaped by the rise of client/server computing, the use of packet switching, and the adoption of Transmission Control Protocol/Internet Protocol (TCP/IP) as a universal communications standard for linking disparate networks and computers, including the Internet. Protocols provide a common set of rules that enable communication among diverse components in a telecommunications network.

2 **What are the main telecommunications transmission media and types of networks?** The principal physical transmission media are twisted copper telephone wire, coaxial copper cable, fiber-optic cable, and wireless transmission. Twisted wire enables companies to use existing wiring for telephone systems for digital communication, although it is relatively slow. Fiber-optic and coaxial cable are used for high-volume transmission but are expensive to install. Microwave and communications satellites are used for wireless communication over long distances.

Local area networks (LANs) connect PCs and other digital devices together within a 500-meter radius and are used today for many corporate computing tasks. Network components may be connected together using a star, bus, or ring topology. Wide area networks (WANs) span broad geographical distances, ranging from several miles to continents, and are private networks that are independently managed. Metropolitan area networks (MANs) span a single urban area.

Digital subscriber line (DSL) technologies, cable Internet connections, and T1 lines are often used for high-capacity Internet connections. Cable Internet connections provide high-speed access to the Web or corporate intranets at speeds of up to 10 Mbps. A T1 line supports a data transmission rate of 1.544 Mbps.

3 **How do the Internet and Internet technology work and how do they support communication and e-business?** The Internet is a worldwide network of networks that uses the client/server model of computing and the TCP/IP network reference model. Every computer on the Internet is assigned a unique numeric IP address. The Domain Name System (DNS) converts IP addresses to more user-friendly domain names. Worldwide Internet policies are established by organizations and government bodies, such as the Internet Architecture Board and the World Wide Web Consortium.

Major Internet services include e-mail, newgroups, chatting, instant messaging, Telnet, FTP, and the World Wide Web. Web pages are based on hypertext markup language (HTML) and can display text, graphics, video, and audio. Web site directories, search engines, and RSS technology help users locate the information they need on the Web. RSS, blogs, and wikis are features of Web 2.0. Web technology and Internet networking standards provide the connectivity and interfaces for internal private intranets and private extranets that can be accessed by many different kinds of computers inside and outside the organization.

Firms are also starting to realize economies by using Internet VoIP technology for voice transmission and by using virtual private networks (VPNs) as low-cost alternatives to private WANs.

4 **What are the principal technologies and standards for wireless networking, communication and Internet access?** Cellular networks are evolving toward high-speed, high-bandwidth, digital packet-switched, third-generation (3G) networks with speeds ranging from 384 Kbps to more than 2 Mbps for data transmission. However, most cellular communication today uses second-generation (2G) cellular networks or 2.5G networks that can support services such as Internet access, music downloading, and e-mail.

Major cellular standards include Code Division Multiple Access (CDMA), which is used primarily in the United States, and Global System for Mobile Communication (GSM), which is the standard in Europe and much of the rest of the world.

Standards for wireless computer networks include Bluetooth (802.15) for small personal area networks (PANs), Wi-Fi (802.11) for local area networks (LANs), and WiMax (802.16) for metropolitan area networks (MANs). 802.11b can transmit up to 11 Mbps in the unlicensed 2.4 GHz band and has an effective distance of 30 to 50 meters. It is the most widely used standard for creating wireless LANs and providing broadband wireless Internet access.

PC and high-end cell phone models can use either 3G networks or Wi-Fi for wireless broadband Internet access.

5 **Why are radio frequency identification (RFID) and wireless sensor networks valuable for business?** Radio frequency identification (RFID) systems provide a powerful technology for tracking the movement of goods by using tiny tags with embedded data about an item and its location. RFID readers read the radio signals transmitted by these tags and pass the data over a network to a computer for processing. Wireless sensor networks (WSNs) are networks of interconnected wireless sensing and transmitting devices that are embedded into the physical environment to provide measurements of many points over large spaces.

Key Terms

Bandwidth, 200
Blog, 212
Bluetooth, 214
Broadband, 192
Bus topology, 198
Cable Internet
   connections, 201
Cell phone, 200
Chat, 204
Coaxial cable, 199
Digital subscriber line
   (DSL), 201
Domain Name System
   (DNS), 201
Domain name, 201
E-mail, 204
Fiber-optic cable, 199
File Transfer Protocol
   (FTP), 204
Firewalls, 212
Hertz, 200
Hotspots, 216
Hubs, 193
Hypertext Transfer Protocol
   (HTTP), 208

Instant messaging, 204
Internet Protocol (IP)
   address, 201
Internet service provider
   (ISP), 200
Internet2, 203
Local area network
   (LAN), 197
Metropolitan area network
   (MAN), 198
Microwave systems, 199
Modem, 196
Network interface card
   (NIC), 192
Network operating system
   (NOS), 193
Packet switching, 194
Peer-to-peer, 197
Personal area networks
   (PANs), 214
Personal digital assistants
   (PDAs), 213
Protocol, 195
Radio frequency identifica-
   tion (RFID), 217

Ring topology, 198
Router, 193
RSS, 212
Search engines, 209
Search engine marketing, 210
Semantic Web, 211
Shopping bots, 211
Smartphones, 213
Star topology, 198
Switch, 193
T1 lines, 201
T3 lines, 201
Third-generation (3G)
   networks, 214
Topology, 197
Transmission Control
   Protocol/Internet Protocol
   (TCP/IP), 195
Twisted wire, 198
Uniform resource locator
   (URL), 209
Virtual private network
   (VPN), 208
Voice over IP (VoIP), 205
Web 2.0, 211

Review Questions

1. What are the principal components of telecommunications networks and key networking technologies?
- Describe the features of a simple network and the network infrastructure for a large company.
- Name and describe the principal technologies and trends that have shaped contemporary telecommunications systems.

2. What are the main telecommunications transmission media and types of networks?
- Name the different types of physical transmission media and compare them in terms of speed and cost.
- Define a local area network (LAN), describe its components and the functions of each component
- Name and describe the principal network topologies.

3. How do the Internet and Internet technology work and how do they support communication and e-business?
- Define the Internet, describe how it works and explain how it provides business value.
- Explain how the domain name and IP addressing system work.
- List and describe the principal Internet services.
- Define and describe VoIP and virtual private networks and explain how they provide value to businesses.
- List and describe alternative ways of locating information on the Web.
- Define and explain the difference between intranets and extranets. Explain how they provide value to businesses.

4. What are the principal technologies and standards for wireless networking, communication and Internet access?
- Define Bluetooth, Wi-Fi, WiMax, and 3G networks.
- Describe the capabilities of each and for which types of applications is each best suited.

5. Why are radio frequency identification (RFID) and wireless sensor networks valuable for business?
- Define radio frequency identification (RFID), explain how it works and how it provides value to businesses.
- Define wireless sensor networks, explain how they work and describe the kinds of applications that use them.

Discussion Questions

1. Network design is a key business decision as well as a technology decision. Why?

2. Should all major retailing and manufacturing companies switch to RFID? Why or why not?

Video Case

You will find a video case illustrating some of the concepts in this chapter on the Laudon Web site along with questions to help you analyze the case.

Teamwork

Evaluating Smartphones

Form a group with three or four of your classmates. Compare the capabilities of Apple's iPhone with a handset from another vendor with similar features. Your analysis should consider the purchase cost of each device, the wireless networks where each device can operate, plan and handset costs, and the services are available for each device. You should also consider other capabilities of each device, including the ability to integrate with existing corporate or PC applications. Which device would you select? What criteria would you use to guide your selection? If possible, use electronic presentation software to present your findings to the class.

BUSINESS PROBLEM-SOLVING CASE

Is Google Becoming Too Powerful?

The rise of Google has been fast and fierce since founders Sergey Brin and Larry Page began collaborating on a search engine in 1995 at Stanford University. Because Google was so effective, it quickly became the search engine of choice for Web users. Today, Google handles 56 percent of Web searches.

In addition to searching for Web pages, Google users can search for PDF, PostScript, text, Microsoft Office, Lotus, PowerPoint, image, and video files. Google claims to be one of the five most popular sites on the Internet with nearly 400 million unique users per month and more than 50 percent of its traffic coming from outside the United States.

Google's IT infrastructure is a closely-guarded secret because it is part of its competitive advantage. The best guess is that Google has up to 450,000 servers spread over at least 25 locations around the world. These servers use inexpensive off-the-shelf hardware to run a customized version of the Linux operating system and other critical pieces of custom software. These include MapReduce, a programming tool to simplify processing and create large data sets; Google WorkQueue, a system that groups queries and schedules them for distributed processing, and the Google File System, which keeps copies of data in several places so that the data will always be available even if a server fails.

According to a widely-cited estimate, Google only needs to spend $1 for every $3 its competitors spend to deliver a comparable amount of computing power. This inexpensive, flexible infrastructure explains the speed of Google Web searches and its ability to provide its users with such a vast array of Web-based services and software tools.

Most of Google's revenue comes from online advertising ($10.6 billion in 2006) and online search services. Google Search Services enable organizations to include the Google search engine on their own Web pages. This is a straightforward technology licensing arrangement—not groundbreaking, but profitable.

The side of Google that has driven its phenomenal growth and profits is its advertising program. In a fraction of a second, Google's technology can evaluate millions of variables about its users and advertisers, correlate them with millions of potential ads, and deliver the message to which each user is most likely to respond. Because this technology makes ads more relevant, users click on ads 50 to 100 percent more often on Google than on Yahoo!, creating a better return for advertisers. According to eMarketer, Google grabbed about 70 percent of all paid search advertising.

In 2000, Google launched AdWords, a self-service advertising program in which vendors bid to have their ads placed alongside the search results for specific search terms. In 2002, AdWords Select introduced cost-per-click (CPC) pricing so that advertisers only pay for their ads when users actually click on them. Google determines the placement of ads through a combination of the CPC and click-through (total number of clicks) rates so that the most relevant ads for a keyword string appear in the most prominent positions. The keyword-targeted ads appear throughout the Google Network, which includes America Online, Shopping.com, Ask.com, *The New York Times* on the Web, and many other high-profile Web sites.

AdWords has come under some fire for being vulnerable to a practice known as click-fraud, which we discuss in detail in Chapter 7. A business whose ad receives thousands of clicks from sources that have no intention of making a purchase may run through its marketing budget quickly. Unscrupulous businesses have tried to use click fraud to drive up the cost of competitors' ads and put them at a competitive disadvantage.

Google and its competitor Yahoo!, have been criticized for their vague response to the problem. Google credits customers for invalid clicks. It also has a system in place to detect click-fraud before customers are charged, but does not disclose details about its antifraud methods.

Google must also be concerned with legitimate offensives from its rivals. Yahoo has been sponsoring prominent academic economists and other researchers to find new ways of using its data about online consumer behavior to increase market share for its services and the revenue generated by its searches.

Microsoft has a history of diminishing or destroying its competitors by exploiting the fact that its Microsoft Windows operating system can be found on 95 percent of the world's personal computers. Netscape Navigator, Lotus 1-2-3, and WordPerfect have all been defeated in this manner.

Microsoft launched competing search service MSN Search in November 2004, followed by Windows Live Search two years later. Microsoft hoped that integrating search technology into Windows Vista and Office would boost its share of the search market, but so far that strategy has not panned out. Now Microsoft is trying to court businesses with a frequent-flier style rewards program. The company will pay large businesses in credits redeemable for Microsoft products and services based on the number of searches that employees perform with Windows Live Search. The challenge for IT departments will be convincing or forcing employees, who receive no personal reward, to change their search habits.

To Microsoft, Google has ceased being a search technology company and is now a software company, capable of infringing on the markets that Microsoft dominates. In the past, Microsoft has thwarted competition through strategic pricing and feature enhancements, as well as by tying its products together so that they are the most convenient to use. Microsoft may not find it so easy to thwart Google. Other software manufacturers had to rely on Windows as a platform on which to run their products. Since Google's applications are Web-based, and not tied to the Windows operating system, Microsoft cannot use its operating system monopoly to limit access to Google.

The Chapter 4 Interactive Session on Organizations discusses Google's online desktop productivity tools (Google Apps for Your Domain and Google Apps Premier Edition) as free or low-cost alternatives to Microsoft Office. How far Google can eat into Microsoft's software franchise is uncertain. But Microsoft fears Google's Web-based computing model could make it possible for computer users to bypass its products entirely.

Google is constantly looking for new ways to grow. Its AdSense program scans Web pages for target words and displays appropriate advertisements, enabling Web site operators to generate revenue from their sites. As with AdWords, Google only charges advertisers when their ads are clicked, so the advertisers spend far less than they would for ads in traditional media while reaching a global audience.

As a result of AdSense, Google quickly became an industry leader in targeted advertising. The company leveraged its strength in this area to expand ad sales to newspapers, magazines, radio, and television. Traditional advertising agencies fear that large corporations will soon give all of their advertising business to Google.

In April 2007 Google, in its largest acquisition deal ever, agreed to purchase the online advertising company DoubleClick for $3.1 billion. DoubleClick specializes in software for the placement of display ads and is the top ad server on the Web. Up until then, Google had earned most of its ad revenue from text ads generated by Web searches. DoubleClick added strength in banner and video ads as well as strong relationships with Web publishers, advertisers, and ad agencies. The acquisition cemented Google as a major advertising force. In May 2007, Microsoft, having lost out on DoubleClick, announced that it would purchase the online advertising firm aQuantive for $6 billion.

Google's moves into media and digital content have resulted in lawsuits. Google had already dealt with questions of copyright infringement in relation to its Google Library and Google News services. But when You Tube became the property of Google in 2006, for the price of $1 billion, most of the world's largest media conglomerates began jockeying for control of digital content on the Web. Viacom filed a suit against Google for damages along with an injunction to halt the activities of YouTube that represent copyright infringements. (See the Chapter 3 ending case study.) At issue are the innumerable video clips that users upload to YouTube featuring content from popular television shows, movies, and music videos that YouTube has not licensed.

NBC Universal and News Corporation have teamed up to launch their own video Web site, which will run television show clips and full-length movies on Yahoo, AOL, MSN, MySpace, and other partner sites.

Part of Google's success in launching new products is the frequency with which it does so. Marissa Mayer, the company's vice president of search products and user experience, confirms that Google expects to discard many of the products it develops. She says, "We should be able to put products out there and, without a lot of promotion, a good product will grow." The strategy suggests that as long as Google unleashes enough products, enough products will be successful.

However, not all of Google's ventures have been successful. Google's initiatives in print and radio ads have not had much impact. But to justify its high stock price, Google must continue to grow by expanding into other markets when online advertising matures.

Google has been pleased with the growth of its Gmail e-mail service, but raised the ire of privacy advocates because it uses the same technology as AdSense to place advertisements alongside messages. The selection of ads is based on the actual text of the messages, meaning that every Gmail message is read by an automated scanner.

Google is at a crossroads. Once the quirky startup that represented the public's hopes and dreams for the Internet, some now view the company as an arrogant, power-hungry behemoth. Google faces the same criticism of trying to stifle the competition that Microsoft faced at the zenith of its success. Google attributes its success to the fact that users simply like its products and services, and to say that the company is too powerful suggests that these users are making their choices incorrectly.

And Google continues to innovate. Its latest ventures include a telephone voice search, Google Voice Local Search, which enables users to dial an 800 number using speech recognition technology to answer queries about local businesses. Google also launched its Universal Search service, which combines the results from its Web, news, video, image, and other search services on one results page, with links to the separate services available at the top of every page.

Sources: Rob Hof, "Is Google Too Powerful?" *Business Week*, April 9, 2007; Kevin J. Delaney and Matthew Karnitschnig, "Viacom v. Google Could Shape Digital Future," *The Wall Street Journal*, March 14, 2007; Richard Siklos, "Push Comes to Shove for Control of Web Video," *The New York Times*, April 1, 2007; Randall Stross, "If at First You Don't Succeed, Write a Check," *The New York Times*, April 1, 2007; Louise Story and Miguel Helft, "Google Buys an Online Ad Firm for $3.1 Billion," *The New York Times*, April 14, 2007; "Inside Google's New-Product Process," *Business Week*, June 30, 2006; "Google Unifies Search Results," CNN.com, May 17, 2007; Ben Worthen, "The Enterprise Gets Googled," *CIO Magazine*, May 1, 2006; Steve Lohr and Saul Hansell, "Microsoft and Google Set to Wage Arms Race," *The New York Times*, May 2, 2006; David F. Carr, "How Google Works," *Baseline*, July, 2006; and Kevin J. Delaney, Hoping to Overtake Its Rivals, Yahoo Stocks Up on Academics" *The Wall Street Journa*l, August 25, 2006.

Case Study Questions

1. Evaluate Google using the competitive forces and value chain models. What are Google's sources of competitive advantage? How does Google provide value to the average user?

2. What problems and challenges does Google face in this case? What people, organization, and technology factors are responsible for these problems and challenges? Does Google's business strategy effectively address these challenges? Explain your answer.

3. How might a business owner benefit from the services offered by Google? Which Google services and products would be attractive to you if you owned a business? Why would you choose to use these particular products or services?

4. How can Google incorporate wireless technology into its business? Which wireless technologies in particular might lend themselves to extending Google's success? Visit Google's Web site and write a summary of the wireless/mobile services that Google currently offers. What other applications of mobile technology can you envision for the company?

5. What are the pros and cons of a company like Google extending its reach into new industries? How does Google's growth affect consumers? How does it impact the business world?

6. How successful do you think Google will be in the future?

Securing Information Systems

CHAPTER 7

STUDENT LEARNING OBJECTIVES

After completing this chapter, you will be able to answer the following questions:

1. Why are information systems vulnerable to destruction, error, and abuse?

2. What is the business value of security and control?

3. What are the components of an organizational framework for security and control?

4. What are the most important tools and technologies for safeguarding information resources?

CHAPTER OUTLINE

ONLINE GAMES NEED SECURITY, TOO

Have you ever played War Rock, Knight Online, or Sword of the New World? They are all massively multiplayer online games from K2 Network, which is based in Irvine, California. K2 currently has about 16 million registered users around the world. Its motto is "Gamers First," and it is known for its compelling titles, creative pricing, quality customer service, and frequent updates based on user requests.

If you have played any of these games, you have some idea of how much K2 puts into "Gamers First"—fantastic clothing and armor sets, fast-paced action, and the ability to control multiple characters at the same time, each with multiple stances and skills. Players are allowed to enter a game for free, but must buy digital "assets" from K2, such as swords to fight dragons, if they want to be deeply involved. The games can accomodate millions of players at once and are played simultaneously by people all over the world. What you may not see is how much K2 puts into protecting its Web sites from hacker attacks.

K2 would lose a great deal of money if its game sites were not working, as well as damage its brand reputation. It does not want hackers attacking its Web sites to extort money from players, to steal their gaming assets, or to steal customer information.

When K2 launched its first game in North America in 2003, it was using Secure Sockets Layer (SSL) certificates to encrypt communications with players buying its gaming assets. This did not offer enough protection against hackers who knew how to exploit flaws in Web applications, such as being able to enter commands into a Web browser that fools a database into revealing its contents. So K2 turned to two other security products—NetContinuum's NC-2000 AG firewall and Cenzic's ClickToSecure managed service. Using these tools in concert, K2 is able to detect flaws in its software, make sure those flaws are not reintroduced when new software is being developed, and protect its software against attacks. Cenzic's service remotely probes K2's applications as a hacker would and reports any vulnerabilities it finds, along with suggestions for eliminating them. Cenzic continually monitors hacker activity and upgrades its products to deal with new vulnerabilities and hacker techniques. NetContinuum's firewall is a box that sits in front of a Web server to examine network traffic and block suspicious traffic.

K2 spent nearly $250,000 on security in 2006 and expects to spend a similar amount in 2007. Management believes the money is well spent. K2's Web sites have never been breached.

Sources: Deborah Gage, "Stop Playing with Hackers," *Baseline*, February 2007 and www.k2network.com, accessed July 17, 2007.

The problems created by hackers for K2 Network and online game players illustrate some of the reasons why businesses need to pay special attention to information system security. Web sites such as those of K2 Network are vulnerable to malicious attacks designed to disable them and prevent their businesses from operating. If K2's game sites were not operational for even a day, the company would lose many millions of dollars, and possibly the loyalty of its subscribers.

The chapter-opening diagram calls attention to important points raised by this case and this chapter. K2's sites attract millions of people, making them attractive targets for hackers. The open nature of Internet connections makes Web applications vulnerable. Web software developers charged with getting new products to market quickly may not have detected all the vulnerabilities and errors.

K2 could have continued to rely on Secure Sockets Layer (SSL) encryption to secure communication with its players. But management realized this was not enough, and that the stakes were too high to allow hackers to exploit flaws in its Web applications. The company decided to make heavy investments in security technology to provide added layers of protection. It installed a firewall to filter out suspicious network traffic, and it subscribed to a service that monitors hacker activity, continually probes K2's software applications to detect vulnerabilities, and provides recommendations for eliminating them. The chosen solution has kept K2's game sites secure.

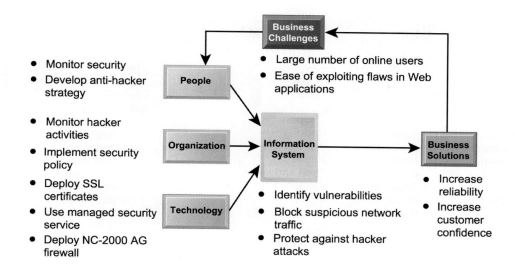

- Monitor security
- Develop anti-hacker strategy

- Monitor hacker activities
- Implement security policy
- Deploy SSL certificates
- Use managed security service
- Deploy NC-2000 AG firewall

People

Organization

Technology

Business Challenges

- Large number of online users
- Ease of exploiting flaws in Web applications

Information System

- Identify vulnerabilities
- Block suspicious network traffic
- Protect against hacker attacks

Business Solutions

- Increase reliability
- Increase customer confidence

HEADS UP

This chapter focuses on how to secure your information systems and the information inside them. As e-commerce and e-business have grown to encompass so much of our lives, we have all become much more aware of the need to secure digital information. Your customers expect you to keep their digital private information secure and confidential. As your business increasingly relies on the Internet, you will become vulnerable to a variety of attacks against your systems that could, if successful, put you out of business in a very short time. To protect your business, you will need to pay more attention to security and control than ever before.

7.1 System Vulnerability and Abuse

Can you imagine what would happen if you tried to link to the Internet without a firewall or antivirus software? Your computer would be disabled in a few seconds, and it might take you many days to recover. If you used the computer to run your business, you might not be able to sell to your customers or place orders with your suppliers while it was down. And you might find that your computer system had been penetrated by outsiders, who perhaps stole or destroyed valuable data, including confidential payment data from your customers. If too much data were destroyed or divulged, your business might never be able to operate!

In short, if you operate a business today, you need to make security and control a top priority. **Security** refers to the policies, procedures, and technical measures used to prevent unauthorized access, alteration, theft, or physical damage to information systems. **Controls** are methods, policies, and organizational procedures that ensure the safety of the organization's assets, the accuracy and reliability of its records, and operational adherence to management standards.

WHY SYSTEMS ARE VULNERABLE

When large amounts of data are stored in electronic form, they are vulnerable to many more kinds of threats than when they existed in manual form. Through communications networks,

Figure 7-1
Contemporary Security Challenges and Vulnerabilities
The architecture of a Web-based application typically includes a Web client, a server, and corporate information systems linked to databases. Each of these components presents security challenges and vulnerabilities. Floods, fires, power failures, and other electrical problems can cause disruptions at any point in the network.

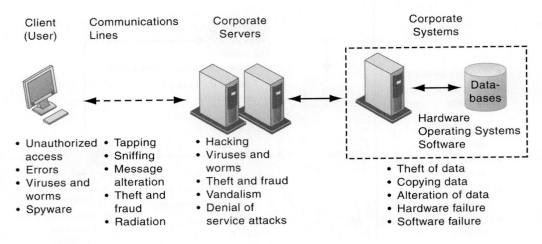

information systems in different locations are interconnected. The potential for unauthorized access, abuse, or fraud is not limited to a single location but can occur at any access point in the network.

Figure 7-1 illustrates the most common threats against contemporary information systems. They can stem from technical, organizational, and environmental factors compounded by poor management decisions. In the multi-tier client/server computing environment illustrated here, vulnerabilities exist at each layer and in the communications between the layers. Users at the client layer can cause harm by introducing errors or by accessing systems without authorization. It is possible to access data flowing over networks, steal valuable data during transmission, or alter messages without authorization. Radiation may disrupt a network at various points as well. Intruders can launch denial-of-service attacks or malicious software to disrupt the operation of Web sites. Those capable of penetrating corporate systems can destroy or alter corporate data stored in databases or files.

Systems malfunction if computer hardware breaks down, is not configured properly, or is damaged by improper use or criminal acts. Errors in programming, improper installation, or unauthorized changes cause computer software to fail. Power failures, floods, fires, or other natural disasters can also disrupt computer systems.

Domestic or offshore partnering with another company adds to system vulnerability if valuable information resides on networks and computers outside the organization's control. Without strong safeguards, valuable data could be lost, destroyed, or could fall into the wrong hands, revealing important trade secrets or information that violates personal privacy.

Internet Vulnerabilities

Large public networks, such as the Internet, are more vulnerable than internal networks because they are virtually open to anyone. The Internet is so huge that when abuses do occur, they can have an enormously widespread impact. When the Internet becomes part of the corporate network, the organization's information systems are even more vulnerable to actions from outsiders.

Computers that are constantly connected to the Internet, such as those that connect by cable modems or digital subscriber line (DSL) modems, are more open to penetration by outsiders because they use fixed Internet addresses for long periods, so they can be easily identified. (With dial-up service, a temporary Internet address is assigned for each session.) A fixed Internet address creates a fixed target for hackers.

Telephone service based on Internet technology (see Chapter 6) is more vulnerable than the switched voice network if it does not run over a secure private network. Most Voice over IP (VoIP) traffic over the public Internet is not encrypted, so anyone with a network can listen in on conversations. Hackers can intercept conversations or shut down voice service by flooding servers supporting VoIP with bogus traffic.

Vulnerability has also increased from widespread use of e-mail and instant messaging (IM). E-mail may contain attachments that serve as springboards for malicious software or unauthorized access to internal corporate systems. Employees may use e-mail messages to transmit valuable trade secrets, financial data, or confidential customer information to unauthorized recipients. Popular IM applications for consumers do not use a secure layer for text messages, so they can be intercepted and read by outsiders during transmission over the public Internet. Instant messaging activity over the Internet can in some cases be used as a back door to an otherwise secure network.

Wireless Security Challenges

Is it safe to log onto a wireless network at an airport, library, or other public location? It depends on how vigilant you are. Even the wireless network in your home is vulnerable because radio frequency bands are easy to scan. Both Bluetooth and Wi-Fi networks are susceptible to hacking by eavesdroppers.

Although the range of wireless fidelity (Wi-Fi) networks is only several hundred feet, it can be extended up to one-fourth of a mile using external antennae. Local area networks (LANs) using the 802.11 standard can be easily penetrated by outsiders armed with laptops, wireless cards, external antennae, and hacking software. Hackers use these tools to detect unprotected networks, monitor network traffic, and, in some cases, gain access to the Internet or to corporate networks. The chapter-ending case describes how poor wireless security may have enabled hackers to break into TJX Companies' corporate systems and steal credit card and personal data on nearly 46 million people.

Wi-Fi transmission technology was designed to make it easy for stations to find and hear one another. The *service set identifiers (SSIDs)* identifying the access points in a Wi-Fi network are broadcast multiple times and can be picked up fairly easily by intruders' sniffer programs (see Figure 7-2). Wireless networks in many locations do not have basic protections against **war driving**, in which eavesdroppers drive by buildings or park outside and try to intercept wireless network traffic.

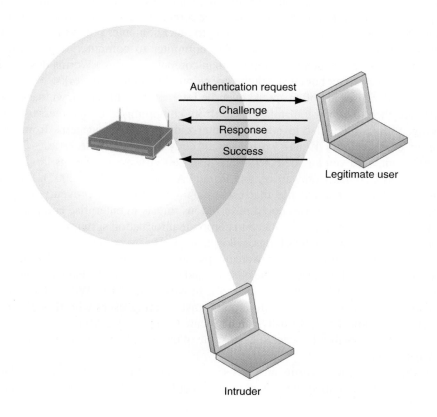

Figure 7-2
Wi-Fi Security Challenges
Many Wi-Fi networks can be penetrated easily by intruders using sniffer programs to obtain an address to access the resources of a network without authorization.

A hacker can employ an 802.11 analysis tool to identify the SSID. (Windows XP has capabilities for detecting the SSID used in a network and automatically configuring the radio NIC within the user's device.) An intruder that has associated with an access point by using the correct SSID is capable of accessing other resources on the network, using the Windows operating system to determine which other users are connected to the network, access their computer hard drives, and open or copy their files.

Intruders also use the information they have gleaned to set up rogue access points on a different radio channel in physical locations close to users to force a user's radio NIC to associate with the rogue access point. Once this association occurs, hackers using the rogue access point can capture the names and passwords of unsuspecting users.

The initial security standard developed for Wi-Fi, called Wired Equivalent Privacy (WEP), is not very effective. WEP is built into all standard 802.11 products, but its use is optional. Many users neglect to use WEP security features, leaving them unprotected. The basic WEP specification calls for an access point and all of its users to share the same 40-bit encrypted password, which can be easily decrypted by hackers from a small amount of traffic. Stronger encryption and authentication systems are now available, but users must be willing to install them.

MALICIOUS SOFTWARE: VIRUSES, WORMS, TROJAN HORSES, AND SPYWARE

Malicious software programs are referred to as **malware** and include a variety of threats, such as computer viruses, worms, and Trojan horses. A **computer virus** is a rogue software program that attaches itself to other software programs or data files in order to be executed, usually without user knowledge or permission. Most computer viruses deliver a "payload." The payload may be relatively benign, such as the instructions to display a message or image, or it may be highly destructive—destroying programs or data, clogging computer memory, reformatting a computer's hard drive, or causing programs to run improperly. Viruses typically spread from computer to computer when humans take an action, such as sending an e-mail attachment or copying an infected file.

Most recent attacks have come from **worms**, which are independent computer programs that copy themselves from one computer to other computers over a network. (Unlike viruses, they can operate on their own without attaching to other computer program files and rely less on human behavior in order to spread from computer to computer. This explains why computer worms spread much more rapidly than computer viruses.) Worms destroy data and programs as well as disrupt or even halt the operation of computer networks.

Worms and viruses are often spread over the Internet from files of downloaded software, from files attached to e-mail transmissions, or from compromised e-mail messages or instant messaging. Viruses have also invaded computerized information systems from "infected" disks or infected machines. E-mail worms are currently the most problematic.

In 2006, antivirus vendors detected more than 200 viruses and worms targeting mobile phones, such as CABIR, Comwarrior, and Frontal A (Gaur and Kiep, 2007). Frontal A, for example, installs a corrupted file that causes phone failure and prevents the user from rebooting. Mobile device viruses could pose serious threats to enterprise computing because so many wireless devices are now linked to corporate information systems.

Web 2.0 applications, such as blogs, wikis, and social networking sites such as MySpace, have emerged as new conduits for malware or spyware. These applications allow users to post software code as part of the permissible content, and such code can be launched automatically as soon as a Web page is viewed. For example, in November 2006, Wikipedia was compromised and used to distribute malware among unsuspecting users who thought they were obtaining information about a security patch (Secure Computing, 2007).

Table 7.1 describes the characteristics of some of the most harmful worms and viruses that have appeared to date.

Over the past decade, worms and viruses have cause billions of dollars of damage to corporate networks, e-mail systems, and data. According to Consumer Reports' State of the

TABLE 7.1

Examples of Malicious Code

Name	Type	Description
Netsky.P	Worm/ Trojan horse	First appeared in early 2003 and was still one of the most common computer worms in 2007. Spreads by gathering target e-mail addresses from the computers it infects, and sending e-mail to all recipients from the infected computer. Commonly used by bot networks to launch spam and denial-of-service attacks.
Sasser.ftp	Worm	First appeared in May 2004. Spread over the Internet by attacking random IP addresses. Causes computers to continually crash and reboot, and infected computers to search for more victims. Affected millions of computers worldwide, disrupting British Airways flight check-ins, operations of British coast guard stations, Hong Kong hospitals, Taiwan post office branches, and Australia's Westpac Bank. Sasser and its variants caused an estimated $14.8 billion to $18.6 billion in damages worldwide.
MyDoom.A	Worm	First appeared January 26, 2004. Spreads as an e-mail attachment. Sends e-mail to addresses harvested from infected machines, forging the sender's address. At its peak, this worm lowered global Internet performance by 10 percent and Web page loading times by as much as 50 percent. Was programmed to stop spreading after February 12, 2004.
Bagle	Worm	First appeared January 18, 2004. Infected PCs via an e-mail attachment, then used the PC e-mail addresses for replicating itself. Infected PCs and their data could be accessed by remote users and applications. Bagle.B stopped spreading after January 28, 2004, but other variants are still active. Has caused tens of millions of dollars in damage already.
Sobig.F	Worm	First detected on August 19, 2003. Spreads via e-mail attachments and sends massive amounts of mail with forged sender information. Deactivated itself on September 10, 2003, after infecting more than 1 million PCs and doing $5 to $10 billion in damage.
ILoveYou	Virus	First detected on May 3, 2000. Script virus written in Visual Basic script and transmitted as an attachment to e-mail with the subject line ILOVEYOU. Overwrites music, image, and other files with a copy of itself and did an estimated $10 billion to $15 billion in damage.
Melissa	Macro virus/worm	First appeared in March 1999. Word macro script mailing infected Word file to first 50 entries in user's Microsoft Outlook address book. Infected 15 to 29 percent of all business PCs, causing $300 million to $600 million in damage.

Internet survey, U.S. consumers lost $7.9 billion because of malware and online scams, and the majority of these losses came from malware (Software World, 2006).

A **Trojan horse** is a software program that appears to be benign but then does something other than expected. The Trojan horse is not itself a virus because it does not replicate but is often a way for viruses or other malicious code to be introduced into a computer system. The term *Trojan horse* is based on the huge wooden horse used by the Greeks to trick the Trojans into opening the gates to their fortified city during the Trojan War. Once inside the city walls, Greek soldiers hidden in the horse revealed themselves and captured the city.

An example of a modern-day Trojan horse is BotVoice.A, detected in July 2007. Once this Trojan horse is installed, it deletes everything from the victim's computer hard drive while repeating an audible message, "You have been infected." BotVoice.A infects computers running Windows operating systems and spreads via peer-to-peer file-sharing networks, CD-ROMs, or USB flash memory drives.

Some types of **spyware** also act as malicious software. These small programs install themselves surreptitiously on computers to monitor user Web surfing activity and serve up advertising. Thousands of forms of spyware have been documented. Harris Interactive found that 92 percent of the companies surveyed in its Web@Work study reported detecting spyware on their networks (Mitchell, 2006).

Many users find such spyware annoying and some critics worry about its infringement on computer users' privacy. Some forms of spyware are especially nefarious. **Key loggers** record every keystroke made on a computer to steal serial numbers for software, launch Internet attacks, gain access to e-mail accounts, obtain passwords to protected computer systems, or pick up personal information such as credit card numbers. Other spyware programs reset Web browser home pages, redirect search requests, or slow computer performance by taking up too much memory.

HACKERS AND COMPUTER CRIME

A **hacker** is an individual who intends to gain unauthorized access to a computer system. Within the hacking community, the term *cracker* is typically used to denote a hacker with criminal intent, although in the public press, the terms hacker and cracker are used interchangeably. Hackers and crackers gain unauthorized access by finding weaknesses in the security protections employed by Web sites and computer systems, often taking advantage of various features of the Internet that make it an open system that is easy to use.

Hacker activities have broadened beyond mere system intrusion to include theft of goods and information, as well as system damage and **cybervandalism**, the intentional disruption, defacement, or even destruction of a Web site or corporate information system. For example, on August 20, 2006, Pakistani hackers broke into the computer hosting the Web site of Kevin Mitnick, an ex-hacker turned security consultant, and replaced the home page with one displaying a vulgar message (Evers, 2006).

Spoofing and Sniffing

Hackers attempting to hide their true identities often spoof, or misrepresent, themselves by using fake e-mail addresses or masquerading as someone else. **Spoofing** also may involve redirecting a Web link to an address different from the intended one, with the site masquerading as the intended destination. For example, if hackers redirect customers to a fake Web site that looks almost exactly like the true site, they can then collect and process orders, effectively stealing business as well as sensitive customer information from the true site. We provide more detail on other forms of spoofing in our discussion of computer crime.

A **sniffer** is a type of eavesdropping program that monitors information traveling over a network. When used legitimately, sniffers help identify potential network trouble spots or criminal activity on networks, but when used for criminal purposes, they can be damaging and very difficult to detect. Sniffers enable hackers to steal proprietary information from anywhere on a network, including e-mail messages, company files, and confidential reports.

Denial-of-Service Attacks

In a **denial-of-service (DoS) attack**, hackers flood a network server or Web server with many thousands of false communications or requests for services to crash the network. The network receives so many queries that it cannot keep up with them and is thus unavailable to service legitimate requests. A **distributed denial-of-service (DDoS)** attack uses numerous computers to inundate and overwhelm the network from numerous launch points. For example, Bill O'Reilly's official Web site was bombarded by data that overloaded the system's firewalls for two days in early March 2007, forcing the site to be taken down to protect it (Schmidt, 2007).

Although DoS attacks do not destroy information or access restricted areas of a company's information systems, they often cause a Web site to shut down, making it impossible for legitimate users to access the site. For busy e-commerce sites, these attacks are costly; while the site is shut down, customers cannot make purchases. Especially vulnerable are small and midsize businesses whose networks tend to be less protected than those of large corporations.

Perpetrators of DoS attacks often use thousands of "zombie" PCs infected with malicious software without their owners' knowledge and organized into a **botnet**. Hackers create these botnets by infecting other people's computers with bot malware that opens a back door through which an attacker can give instructions. The infected computer then becomes a slave, or zombie, serving a master computer belonging to someone else. Once a hacker infects enough computers, her or she can use the amassed resources of the botnet to launch distributed denial-of-service attacks, phishing campaigns, or unsolicited "spam" e-mail.

In the first six months of 2007, security product provider Symantec observed over 5 million distinct bot-infected computers. Arguably, bots and bot networks are currently the single most important threat to the Internet and e-commerce because they can be used to launch very large scale attacks using many different techniques (Symantec, 2007). For example, the Storm worm, which was responsible for one of the largest e-mail attacks in the past few years, was propagated via a massive botnet of nearly 2 million computers (Gaudin, 2007). The Interactive Session on Technology provides more detail on the scope and severity of bot attacks.

Computer Crime

Most hacker activities are criminal offenses, and the vulnerabilities of systems we have just described make them targets for other types of computer crime as well. For example, Yung-Sun Lin was charged in January 2007 with installing a "logic bomb" program on the computers of his employer, Medco Health Solutions of Franklin Lakes, New Jersey. Lin's program could have erased critical prescription information for 60 million Americans (Gaudin, 2007). **Computer crime** is defined by the U.S. Department of Justice as "any violations of criminal law that involve a knowledge of computer technology for their perpetration, investigation, or prosecution." Table 7.2 provides examples of the computer as a target of crime and as an instrument of crime.

No one knows the magnitude of the computer crime problem—how many systems are invaded, how many people engage in the practice, or the total economic damage. According to one study by the Computer Crime Research Center, U.S. companies lose approximately $14 billion annually to cybercrimes. Many companies are reluctant to report computer crimes because the crimes may involve employees or the company fears that publicizing its vulnerability will hurt its reputation. The most economically damaging kinds of computer crime are DoS attacks, introducing viruses, theft of services, and disruption of computer systems.

Identity Theft

With the growth of the Internet and electronic commerce, identity theft has become especially troubling. **Identity theft** is a crime in which an imposter obtains key pieces of personal information, such as social security identification numbers, driver's license numbers, or credit card numbers, to impersonate someone else. The information may be used to obtain credit, merchandise, or services in the name of the victim or to provide the thief with false credentials. According to Javelin Strategy & Research, 8.4 million Americans were victims of identity theft in 2006, and they suffered losses totaling $49.3 billion (Stempel, 2007).

INTERACTIVE SESSION: TECHNOLOGY   Bot Armies Launch a Digital Data Siege

In Estonia, the Internet is almost as vital as running water. People use it routinely to vote, to file their taxes, and to shop or pay for parking with their cell phones. When the Estonian government began removing a bronze Soviet-era war memorial statue from a Tallinn park in April 2007, the move incited rioting by ethnic Russians. But the most violent protests took place over the Internet.

Major Estonian Web sites were subject to a massive and sustained distributed-denial-of-service attack that crippled the Web sites of Estonia's president, prime minister, Parliament, government agencies, national bank, and several daily newspapers. The attackers used a giant network of bots—as many as 1 million computers in Russia, Estonia, and other countries, including the United States, Canada, Brazil and Vietnam. They even rented time on other botnets. The attacks started around April 26 and lasted for nearly a month. The 10 largest assaults blasted streams of 90 megabits of data per second at Estonia's networks, lasting up to 10 hours each. This data load is equivalent to downloading the entire Windows XP operating system every six seconds for 10 hours.

Estonia's Computer Emergency Response team gathered security experts from Estonian Internet service providers, banks, government agencies, and authorities in other countries to help track down and block traffic from suspicious Internet addresses. Estonia had to close off large parts of its network to people outside the country and focused on trying to protect the most essential sites, including online banking. On May 10, the attackers' time on rented servers expired, and the botnet attacks fell off abruptly. The last major wave of attacks occurred on May 18.

Because it is so easy for attackers to conceal their Internet addresses and harness other computers to do their work, experts believe that the attackers would probably never be caught. They also believe that attacks such as these will become even more severe in the coming years, as bots are harnessed for more acts of cyberwarfare and other illicit activities.

Building and selling bots for malicious purposes has become a serious money-making enterprise. James Ancheta, a self-taught computer expert, pleaded guilty on January 23, 2006, in the U.S. District Court in Los Angeles to building and selling bots and using his network of thousands of bots to commit crimes. His botnet infected at least 400,000 computers, including machines at two U.S. Department of Defense facilities, and had installed unauthorized adware that earned him more than $60,000.

Ancheta also rented or sold bots to people interested in using them to send spam or launch DoS attacks to disable specific Web sites. Ancheta's botz4sale Web site offered access to up to 10,000 compromised PCs at one time for as little as 4 cents each.

To outwit law enforcement, Ancheta continually changed e-mail addresses, ISPs, domain names, and instant messaging handles. Eventually his luck ran out. The FBI arrested him on November 3, 2005, and shut down his operations. Ancheta was sentenced to 57 months in federal prison.

Could bot attacks like these be prevented? It's getting increasingly difficult. According to Michael Lines, chief security officer at credit reporting firm TransUnion, "There is no single technology or strategy to [solve] the problem." Even if people use antivirus and antispyware software and patch software vulnerabilities, new bots appear that target different vulnerabilities.

Hackers don't even have to write their own bot programs. They can download bot toolkits for free on the Internet. Ancheta modified Rxbot, a bot strain available for download at several Web sites, and had his bots report to an Internet Relay Chat (IRC) channel that he controlled. And as the Ancheta case revealed, people can even buy access to bots.

How do you know if your computers are being used in botnets? Warning signs include systems that seem to be running too slowly, have unusual spikes in network traffic, or get too many pop-up ads.

What can you do about it? At the very least, regularly patch software and keep firewalls and antivirus software up to date, including antivirus and filtering software for instant messaging. Companies should also use tools to monitor not only inbound network traffic for malware and suspicious behavior but also outbound traffic leaving the network, in the event this traffic contains malware from an infected computer that could be used to recruit additional bots.

The most common approach today when your network is being attacked by a botnet is to cut off all traffic to any servers that are being targeted, as the Estonian government did. This, however, isn't a way to solve the problem as much as it is a way to address immediate concerns. What is more effective, and more difficult, is to have cooperation among botnet victims, ISPs, and law enforcement worldwide. Trend Micro, a leading provide of antivirus software and online security tools, offers a free anti-botnet service that will notify users if their machine has been hijacked by a botnet or if information from their machine is being stolen and transmitted to the bot master.

Sources: Mark Landler and John Markoff, "War Fears Turn Digital After Data Siege in Estonia," *The New York Times*, May 29, 2007; Joaquim P. Menezs, "The Botnet Menace-and What You Can Do About It, "IT World Canada, June 4, 2007; Deborah Gage, "Security Case: How to Survive a Bot Attack," *Baseline*, February 6, 2007; Deborah Gage and Kim S. Nash, "When Bots Attack," *Baseline*, April 2006; and Robert Lemos, "Major Prison Time for Bot Master," *Security Focus*, May 9, 2006.

CASE STUDY QUESTIONS

1. What is the business impact of botnets?

2. What people, organization, and technology factors should be addressed in a plan to prevent botnet attacks?

3. How easy would it be for a small business to combat botnet attacks? A large business?

4. How would you know if your computer was part of a botnet? Explain your answer.

MIS IN ACTION

Read the article on "Robot Wars-How Botnets Work" by Massimiliano Romano, Simone Rosignoli, and Ennio Giannini at WindowsSecurity.com. Prepare an electronic presentation that summarizes your answers to the following questions:

1. What are botnets and how do they work?

2. What features do the most popular botnets offer?

3. How does a bot infect and control a host computer?

4. How can a bot attack be prevented?

COMPUTERS AS TARGETS OF CRIME

Breaching the confidentiality of protected computerized data

Accessing a computer system without authority

Knowingly accessing a protected computer to commit fraud

Intentionally accessing a protected computer and causing damage, negligently or deliberately

Knowingly transmitting a program, program code, or command that intentionally causes damage to a protected computer

Threatening to cause damage to a protected computer

COMPUTERS AS INSTRUMENTS OF CRIME

Theft of trade secrets

Unauthorized copying of software or copyrighted intellectual property, such as articles, books, music, and video

Schemes to defraud

Using e-mail for threats or harassment

Intentionally attempting to intercept electronic communication

Illegally accessing stored electronic communications, including e-mail and voice mail

Transmitting or possessing child pornography using a computer

TABLE 7.2

Examples of Computer Crime

Identify theft has flourished on the Internet, with credit card files a major target of Web site hackers. Moreover, e-commerce sites are wonderful sources of customer personal information—name, address, and phone number. Armed with this information, criminals are able to assume new identities and establish new credit for their own purposes.

One increasingly popular tactic is a form of spoofing called **phishing**. Phishing involves setting up fake Web sites or sending e-mail messages that look like those of legitimate businesses to ask users for confidential personal data. The e-mail message instructs recipients to update or confirm records by providing social security numbers, bank and credit card information, and other confidential data either by responding to the e-mail message, by entering the information at a bogus Web site, or by calling a telephone number. In October 2007, the OpenDNS PhishTank Annual Report found that the top two spoofed brands were eBay and PayPal, with a variety of banks, the IRS, and several large retailers (Amazon and Wal-Mart) rounding out the top 10 (OpenDNS, 2007).

New phishing techniques called evil twins and pharming are harder to detect. **Evil twins** are wireless networks that pretend to offer trustworthy Wi-Fi connections to the Internet, such as those in airport lounges, hotels, or coffee shops. The bogus network looks identical to a legitimate public network. Fraudsters try to capture passwords or credit card numbers of unwitting users who log on to the network.

Pharming redirects users to a bogus Web page, even when the individual types the correct Web page address into his or her browser. This is possible if pharming perpetrators gain access to the Internet address information stored by Internet service providers to speed up Web browsing and the ISP companies have flawed software on their servers that allows the fraudsters to hack in and change those addresses.

The U.S. Congress addressed the threat of computer crime in 1986 with the Computer Fraud and Abuse Act. This act makes it illegal to access a computer system without authorization. Most states have similar laws, and nations in Europe have comparable legislation. Congress also passed the National Information Infrastructure Protection Act in 1996 to make virus distribution and hacker attacks to disable Web sites federal crimes. U.S. legislation, such as the Wiretap Act, Wire Fraud Act, Economic Espionage Act, Electronic Communications Privacy Act, E-Mail Threats and Harassment Act, and Child Pornography Act, covers computer crimes involving intercepting electronic communication, using electronic communication to defraud, stealing trade secrets, illegally accessing stored electronic communications, using e-mail for threats or harassment, and transmitting or possessing child pornography.

Click Fraud

When you click on an ad displayed by a search engine, the advertiser typically pays a fee for each click, which is supposed to direct potential buyers to its products. **Click fraud** occurs when an individual or computer program fraudulently clicks on an online ad without any intention of learning more about the advertiser or making a purchase. Click fraud has become a serious problem at Google and other Web sites that feature pay-per-click online advertising (see the case study concluding Chapter 6.)

Some companies hire third parties (typically from low-wage countries) to fraudulently click on a competitor's ads to weaken them by driving up their marketing costs. Click fraud can also be perpetrated with software programs doing the clicking, and bot networks are often used for this purpose (review the Interactive Session on Technology). Search engines such as Google attempt to monitor click fraud but have been reluctant to publicize their efforts to deal with the problem.

Global Threats: Cyberterrorism and Cyberwarfare

The cybercriminal activities we have described—launching malware, bot networks, DoS attacks, and phishing probes—are borderless. Computer security firm Sophos reported that 34.2 percent of the malware it identified in 2006 originated in the United States, while 31

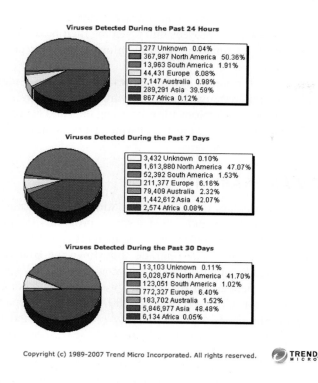

Viruses Detected During the Past 24 Hours

☐	277 Unknown	0.04%
■	367,987 North America	50.36%
■	13,963 South America	1.91%
☐	44,431 Europe	6.08%
☐	7,147 Australia	0.98%
■	289,291 Asia	39.59%
■	867 Africa	0.12%

Viruses Detected During the Past 7 Days

☐	3,432 Unknown	0.10%
■	1,613,880 North America	47.07%
■	52,392 South America	1.53%
☐	211,377 Europe	6.16%
☐	79,409 Australia	2.32%
■	1,442,612 Asia	42.07%
■	2,574 Africa	0.08%

Viruses Detected During the Past 30 Days

☐	13,103 Unknown	0.11%
■	5,028,975 North America	41.70%
■	123,051 South America	1.02%
☐	772,327 Europe	6.40%
■	183,702 Australia	1.52%
■	5,846,977 Asia	48.48%
■	6,134 Africa	0.05%

Malware is active throughout the globe. These three charts show the regional distribution of worms and computer viruses worldwide reported by Trend Micro over periods of 24 hours, 7 days, and 30 days. The virus count represents the number of infected files and the percentage shows the relative prevalence in each region compared to worldwide statistics for each measuring period.

percent came from China, and 9.5 percent from Russia (Australian IT News, 2007). The global nature of the Internet makes it possible for cybercriminals to operate—and to do harm—anywhere in the world.

Concern is mounting that the vulnerabilities of the Internet or other networks make digital networks targets for digital attacks by terrorists, foreign intelligence services, or other groups seeking to create widespread disruption and harm. Such cyberattacks might target the software that runs electrical power grids, air traffic control systems, or networks of major banks and financial institutions. At least 20 countries, including China, are believed to be developing offensive and defensive cyberwarfare capabilities. U.S. military networks and U.S. government agencies suffer hundreds of hacker attacks each year.

To deal with this threat, the U.S. Department of Homeland Security (DHS) has been charged with orchestrating activities to support critical information systems that safeguard critical infrastructures in the United States. Its responsibilities include promoting public and private information sharing about cyberattacks, threats, and vulnerabilities; developing national cyberanalysis and warning capabilities; incorporating cybersecurity into a comprehensive national plan for critical infrastructure protection; and coordinating with government and private sector groups to respond to cyberevents. The U.S. Department of Defense has joint task forces for computer network defense and for managing computer network attacks.

INTERNAL THREATS: EMPLOYEES

We tend to think the security threats to a business originate outside the organization. In fact, company insiders pose serious security problems. Employees have access to privileged information, and in the presence of sloppy internal security procedures, they are often able to roam throughout an organization's systems without leaving a trace.

Studies have found that user lack of knowledge is the single greatest cause of network security breaches. Many employees forget their passwords to access computer systems or allow co-workers to use them, which compromises the system. Malicious intruders seeking system access sometimes trick employees into revealing their passwords by pretending to be legitimate members of the company in need of information. This practice is called **social engineering**.

Both end users and information systems specialists are also a major source of errors introduced into information systems. End users introduce errors by entering faulty data or by not following the proper instructions for processing data and using computer equipment. Information systems specialists may create software errors as they design and develop new software or maintain existing programs.

SOFTWARE VULNERABILITY

Software errors pose a constant threat to information systems, causing untold losses in productivity. Growing complexity and size of software programs, coupled with demands for timely delivery to markets, have contributed to an increase in software flaws or vulnerabilities. For example, a flawed software upgrade shut down the BlackBerry e-mail service throughout North America for about 12 hours between April 17 and April 18, 2007. Millions of business users who depended on BlackBerry were unable to work, and BlackBerry's reputation for reliability was tarnished (Martin, 2007). The U.S. Department of Commerce National Institute of Standards and Technology (NIST) reported that software flaws (including vulnerabilities to hackers and malware) cost the U.S. economy $59.6 billion each year (NIST, 2005).

A major problem with software is the presence of hidden **bugs** or program code defects. Studies have shown that it is virtually impossible to eliminate all bugs from large programs. The main source of bugs is the complexity of decision-making code. A relatively small program of several hundred lines will contain tens of decisions leading to hundreds or even thousands of different paths. Important programs within most corporations are usually much larger, containing tens of thousands or even millions of lines of code, each with many times the choices and paths of the smaller programs.

Zero defects cannot be achieved in larger programs. Complete testing simply is not possible. Fully testing programs that contain thousands of choices and millions of paths would require thousands of years. Even with rigorous testing, you would not know for sure that a piece of software was dependable until the product proved itself after much operational use.

Flaws in commercial software not only impede performance but also create security vulnerabilities that open networks to intruders. Each year, security firms identify about 5,000 software vulnerabilities in Internet and PC software. For instance, in 2007, Symantec identified 39 vulnerabilities in Microsoft Internet Explorer, 34 in Mozilla browsers, 25 in Apple Safari, and 7 in Opera. Some of these vulnerabilities are critical (Symantec, 2007).

To correct software flaws once they are identified, the software vendor creates small pieces of software called **patches** to repair the flaws without disturbing the proper operation of the software. An example is Microsoft's XP Service Pack 2 (SP2) introduced in 2004, which features added firewall protection against viruses and intruders, capabilities for automatic security updates, and an easy-to-use interface for managing the security applications on the user's computer. It is up to users of the software to track these vulnerabilities, test, and apply all patches. This process is called patch management.

Because a company's IT infrastructure is typically laden with multiple business applications, operating system installations, and other system services, maintaining patches on all devices and services used by a company is often time-consuming and costly. Malware is being created so rapidly that companies have very little time to respond between the time a vulnerability and a patch are announced and the time malicious software appears to exploit the vulnerability.

7.2 Business Value of Security and Control

Many firms are reluctant to spend heavily on security because it is not directly related to sales revenue. However, protecting information systems is so critical to the operation of the business that it deserves a second look.

Companies have very valuable information assets to protect. Systems often house confidential information about individuals' taxes, financial assets, medical records, and job performance reviews. They also can contain information on corporate operations, including trade secrets, new product development plans, and marketing strategies. Government systems may store information on weapons systems, intelligence operations, and military targets. These information assets have tremendous value, and the repercussions can be devastating if they are lost, destroyed, or placed in the wrong hands. One study estimated that when the security of a large firm is compromised, the company loses approximately 2.1 percent of its market value within two days of the security breach, which translates into an average loss of $1.65 billion in stock market value per incident (Cavusoglu, Mishra, and Raghunathan, 2004).

Inadequate security and control may result in serious legal liability. Businesses must protect not only their own information assets but also those of customers, employees, and business partners. Failure to do so may open the firm to costly litigation for data exposure or theft. An organization can be held liable for needless risk and harm created if the organization fails to take appropriate protective action to prevent loss of confidential information, data corruption, or breach of privacy (see the chapter-ending case study). For example, B.J.'s Wholesale Club was sued by the U.S. Federal Trade Commission for allowing hackers to access its systems and steal credit and debit card data for fraudulent purchases. Banks that issued the cards with the stolen data sought $13 million from B.J.'s to compensate them for reimbursing card holders for the fraudulent purchases (McDougall, 2006). A sound security and control framework that protects business information assets can thus produce a high return on investment.

Strong security and control also increase employee productivity and lower operational costs. For example, Axia NextMedia Corp., a Calgary, Alberta firm that builds and manages open-access broadband networks, saw employee productivity go up and costs go down after it installed an information systems configuration and control system in 2004. Before then, Axia had lost valuable employee work time because of security or other network incidents that caused system outages. Between 2004 and 2007, the new configuration and control system saved the company $590,000 by minimizing system outages (Bartholomew, 2007).

LEGAL AND REGULATORY REQUIREMENTS FOR ELECTRONIC RECORDS MANAGEMENT

Recent U.S. government regulations are forcing companies to take security and control more seriously by mandating the protection of data from abuse, exposure, and unauthorized access. Firms face new legal obligations for the retention and storage of electronic records as well as for privacy protection.

If you work in the healthcare industry, your firm will need to comply with the Health Insurance Portability and Accountability Act (HIPAA) of 1996. **HIPAA** outlines medical security and privacy rules and procedures for simplifying the administration of healthcare billing and automating the transfer of healthcare data between healthcare providers, payers, and plans. It requires members of the healthcare industry to retain patient information for six years and ensure the confidentiality of those records. It specifies privacy, security, and electronic transaction standards for healthcare providers handling patient information, providing penalties for breaches of medical privacy, disclosure of patient records by e-mail, or unauthorized network access.

If you work in a firm providing financial services, your firm will need to comply with the **Gramm-Leach-Bliley Act**. The Financial Services Modernization Act of 1999, better known as the Gramm-Leach-Bliley Act after its congressional sponsors, requires financial institutions to ensure the security and confidentiality of customer data. Data must be stored on a secure medium. Special security measures must be enforced to protect such data on storage media and during transmittal.

If you work in a publicly traded company, your company will need to comply with the **Sarbanes-Oxley Act**. The Public Company Accounting Reform and Investor Protection Act of 2002, better known as Sarbanes-Oxley after its sponsors Senator Paul Sarbanes of Maryland and Representative Michael Oxley of Ohio, was designed to protect investors after the financial scandals at Enron, WorldCom, and other public companies. It imposes responsibility on companies and their management to safeguard the accuracy and integrity of financial information that is used internally and released externally. One of the Learning Tracks for this chapter discusses Sarbanes-Oxley in detail.

Sarbanes-Oxley is fundamentally about ensuring that internal controls are in place to govern the creation and documentation of information in financial statements. Because information systems are used to generate, store, and transport such data, the legislation requires firms to consider information systems security and other controls required to ensure the integrity, confidentiality, and accuracy of their data. Each system application that deals with critical financial reporting data requires controls to make sure the data are accurate. Controls to secure the corporate network, prevent unauthorized access to systems and data, and ensure data integrity and availability in the event of disaster or other disruption of service are essential as well.

ELECTRONIC EVIDENCE AND COMPUTER FORENSICS

Security, control, and electronic records management have become essential for responding to legal actions. Much of the evidence today for stock fraud, embezzlement, theft of company trade secrets, computer crime, and many civil cases is in digital form. In addition to information from printed or typewritten pages, legal cases today increasingly rely on evidence represented as digital data stored on portable floppy disks, CDs, and computer hard disk drives, as well as in e-mail, instant messages, and e-commerce transactions over the Internet. E-mail is currently the most common type of electronic evidence.

In a legal action, a firm is obligated to respond to a discovery request for access to information that may be used as evidence, and the company is required by law to produce those data. The cost of responding to a discovery request can be enormous if the company has trouble assembling the required data or the data have been corrupted or destroyed. Courts now impose severe financial and even criminal penalties for improper destruction of electronic documents.

An effective electronic document retention policy ensures that electronic documents, e-mail, and other records are well organized and accessible, and neither retained too long nor discarded too soon. It also reflects an awareness of how to preserve potential evidence for computer forensics. **Computer forensics** is the scientific collection, examination, authentication, preservation, and analysis of data held on or retrieved from computer storage media in such a way that the information can be used as evidence in a court of law. It deals with the following problems:

- Recovering data from computers while preserving evidential integrity
- Securely storing and handling recovered electronic data
- Finding significant information in a large volume of electronic data
- Presenting the information to a court of law

Electronic evidence may reside on computer storage media in the form of computer files and as *ambient data*, which are not visible to the average user. An example might be a file that has been deleted on a PC hard drive. Data that a computer user may have deleted on computer storage media can be recovered through various techniques. Computer forensics experts try to recover such hidden data for presentation as evidence.

An awareness of computer forensics should be incorporated into a firm's contingency planning process. The CIO, security specialists, information systems staff, and corporate legal counsel should all work together to have a plan in place that can be executed if a legal need arises. You can find out more about computer forensics in a Learning Track for this chapter.

7.3 Establishing a Framework for Security and Control

Even with the best security tools, your information systems won't be reliable and secure unless you know how and where to deploy them. You will need to know where your company is at risk and what controls you must have in place to protect your information systems. You will also need to develop a security policy and plans for keeping your business running if your information systems aren't operational.

INFORMATION SYSTEMS CONTROLS

Information systems controls are both manual and automated and consist of both general controls and application controls. **General controls** govern the design, security, and use of computer programs and the security of data files in general throughout the organization's information technology infrastructure. On the whole, general controls apply to all computerized applications and consist of a combination of hardware, software, and manual procedures that create an overall control environment.

General controls include software controls, physical hardware controls, computer operations controls, data security controls, controls over the systems implementation process, and administrative controls. Table 7.3 describes the functions of each of these controls.

Type of General Control	Description
Software controls	Monitor the use of system software and prevent unauthorized access of software programs, system software, and computer programs.
Hardware controls	Ensure that computer hardware is physically secure, and check for equipment malfunction. Organizations that are critically dependent on their computers also must make provisions for backup or continued operation to maintain constant service.
Computer operations controls	Oversee the work of the computer department to ensure that programmed procedures are consistently and correctly applied to the storage and processing of data. They include controls over the setup of computer processing jobs and backup and recovery procedures for processing that ends abnormally.
Data security controls	Ensure that valuable business data files on either disk or tape are not subject to unauthorized access, change, or destruction while they are in use or in storage.
Implementation controls	Audit the systems development process at various points to ensure that the process is properly controlled and managed.
Administrative controls	Formalized standards, rules, procedures, and control disciplines to ensure that the organization's general and application controls are properly executed and enforced.

TABLE 7.3

General Controls

Application controls are specific controls unique to each computerized application, such as payroll or order processing. They include both automated and manual procedures that ensure that only authorized data are completely and accurately processed by that application. Application controls can be classified as (1) input controls, (2) processing controls, and (3) output controls.

Input controls check data for accuracy and completeness when they enter the system. There are specific input controls for input authorization, data conversion, data editing, and error handling. Processing controls establish that data are complete and accurate during updating. Output controls ensure that the results of computer processing are accurate, complete, and properly distributed. You can find more detail about application and general controls in our Learning Tracks.

RISK ASSESSMENT

Before your company commits resources to security and information systems controls, it must know which assets require protection and the extent to which these assets are vulnerable. A risk assessment helps answer these questions and determine the most cost-effective set of controls for protecting assets.

A **risk assessment** determines the level of risk to the firm if a specific activity or process is not properly controlled. Business managers working with information systems specialists can determine the value of information assets, points of vulnerability, the likely frequency of a problem, and the potential for damage. For example, if an event is likely to occur no more than once a year, with a maximum $1,000 loss to the organization, it is not feasible to spend $20,000 on the design and maintenance of a control to protect against that event. However, if that same event could occur at least once a day, with a potential loss of more than $300,000 a year, $100,000 spent on a control might be entirely appropriate.

Table 7.4 illustrates sample results of a risk assessment for an online order processing system that processes 30,000 orders per day. The likelihood of each exposure occurring over a one-year period is expressed as a percentage. The next column shows the highest and lowest possible loss that could be expected each time the exposure occurred and an average loss calculated by adding the highest and lowest figures together and dividing by two. The expected annual loss for each exposure can be determined by multiplying the average loss by its probability of occurrence.

This risk assessment shows that the probability of a power failure occurring in a one-year period is 30 percent. Loss of order transactions while power is down could range from $5,000 to $200,000 (averaging $102,500) for each occurrence, depending on how long processing is halted. The probability of embezzlement occurring over a yearly period is about 5 percent, with potential losses ranging from $1,000 to $50,000 (and averaging $25,500) for each occurrence. User errors have a 98-percent chance of occurring over a yearly period, with losses ranging from $200 to $40,000 (and averaging $20,100) for each occurrence.

Once the risks have been assessed, system builders will concentrate on the control points with the greatest vulnerability and potential for loss. In this case, controls should focus on ways to minimize the risk of power failures and user errors because anticipated annual losses are highest for these areas.

TABLE 7.4 Online Order Processing Risk Assessment	Exposure	Probability of Occurrence (%)	Loss Range/ Average ($)	Expected Annual Loss ($)
	Power failure	30%	$5,000–$200,000 ($102,500)	$30,750
	Embezzlement	5%	$1,000–$50,000 ($25,500)	$1,275
	User error	98%	$200–$40,000 ($20,100)	$19,698

SECURITY POLICY

Once you have identified the main risks to your systems, your company will need to develop a security policy for protecting the company's assets. A **security policy** consists of statements ranking information risks, identifying acceptable security goals, and identifying the mechanisms for achieving these goals. What are the firm's most important information assets? Who generates and controls this information in the firm? What existing security policies are in place to protect the information? What level of risk is management willing to accept for each of these assets? Is it willing, for instance, to lose customer credit data once every 10 years? Or will it build a security system for credit card data that can withstand the once-in-a-100-year disaster? Management must estimate how much it will cost to achieve this level of acceptable risk.

The security policy drives policies determining acceptable use of the firm's information resources and which members of the company have access to its information assets. An **acceptable use policy (AUP)** defines acceptable uses of the firm's information resources and computing equipment, including desktop and laptop computers, wireless devices, telephones, and the Internet. The policy should clarify company policy regarding privacy, user responsibility, and personal use of company equipment and networks. A good AUP defines unacceptable and acceptable actions for every user and specifies consequences for noncompliance. For example, security policy at Unilever, the giant multinational consumer goods company, requires every employee equipped with a laptop or mobile handheld device to use a company-specified device and employ a password or other method of identification when logging onto the corporate network.

Authorization policies determine differing levels of access to information assets for different levels of users. **Authorization management systems** establish where and when a user is permitted to access certain parts of a Web site or a corporate database. Such systems allow each user access only to those portions of a system that person is permitted to enter, based on information established by a set of access rules.

The authorization management system knows exactly what information each user is permitted to access, as shown in Figure 7-3. This figure illustrates the security allowed for two sets of users of an online personnel database containing sensitive information, such as employees' salaries, benefits, and medical histories. One set of users consists of all employees who perform clerical functions, such as inputting employee data into the system. All individuals with this type of profile can update the system but can neither read nor update sensitive fields, such as salary, medical history, or earnings data. Another profile applies to a divisional manager, who cannot update the system but who can read all employee data fields for his or her division, including medical history and salary. These profiles are based on access rules supplied by business groups. The system illustrated in Figure 7-3 provides very fine-grained security restrictions, such as allowing authorized personnel users to inquire about all employee information except that in confidential fields, such as salary or medical history.

DISASTER RECOVERY PLANNING AND BUSINESS CONTINUITY PLANNING

If you run a business, you need to plan for events, such as power outages, floods, earthquakes, or terrorist attacks that will prevent your information systems and your business from operating. **Disaster recovery planning** devises plans for the restoration of computing and communications services after they have been disrupted. Disaster recovery plans focus primarily on the technical issues involved in keeping systems up and running, such as which files to back up and the maintenance of backup computer systems or disaster recovery services.

For example, MasterCard maintains a duplicate computer center in Kansas City, Missouri, to serve as an emergency backup to its primary computer center in St. Louis. Rather than build their own backup facilities, many firms contract with disaster recovery firms, such as Comdisco Disaster Recovery Services in Rosemont, Illinois, and SunGard

Figure 7-3
Security Profiles for a Personnel System
These two examples represent two security profiles or data security patterns that might be found in a personnel system. Depending on the security profile, a user would have certain restrictions on access to various systems, locations, or data in an organization.

SECURITY PROFILE 1

User: Personnel Dept. Clerk

Location: Division 1

Employee Identification
Codes with This Profile: 00753, 27834, 37665, 44116

Data Field Restrictions	Type of Access
All employee data for Division 1 only	Read and Update
• Medical history data	None
• Salary	None
• Pensionable earnings	None

SECURITY PROFILE 2

User: Divisional Personnel Manager

Location: Division 1

Employee Identification
Codes with This Profile: 27321

Data Field Restrictions	Type of Access
All employee data for Division 1 only	Read Only

Availability Services, headquartered in Wayne, Pennsylvania. These disaster recovery firms provide hot sites housing spare computers at locations around the country where subscribing firms can run their critical applications in an emergency. For example, Champion Technologies, which supplies chemicals used in oil and gas operations, is able to switch its enterprise systems from Houston to a SunGard hot site in Scottsdale, Arizona in two hours (Duvall, 2007).

Business continuity planning focuses on how the company can restore business operations after a disaster strikes. The business continuity plan identifies critical business processes and determines action plans for handling mission-critical functions if systems go down. For example, Deutsche Bank, which provides investment banking and asset management services in 74 different countries, has a well-developed business continuity plan that it continually updates and refines. It maintains full-time teams in Singapore, Hong Kong, Japan, India, and Australia to coordinate plans addressing loss of facilities, personnel, or critical systems so that the company can continue to operate when a catastrophic event occurs. Deutsche Bank's plan distinguishes between processes critical for business survival and those critical to crisis support and is coordinated with the company's disaster recovery planning for its computer centers.

Business managers and information technology specialists need to work together on both types of plans to determine which systems and business processes are most critical to the company. They must conduct a business impact analysis to identify the firm's most critical systems and the impact a systems outage would have on the business. Management must determine the maximum amount of time the business can survive with its systems down and which parts of the business must be restored first.

THE ROLE OF AUDITING

How does management know that information systems security and controls are effective? To answer this question, organizations must conduct comprehensive and systematic audits. An **MIS audit** examines the firm's overall security environment as well as controls governing individual information systems. The auditor should trace the flow of sample transactions through the system and perform tests, using, if appropriate,

Function: Loans Location: Peoria, IL	Prepared by: J. Ericson Date: June 16, 2008		Received by: T. Benson Review date: June 28, 2008	
Nature of Weakness and Impact	Chance for Error/Abuse		Notification to Management	
	Yes/No	Justification	Report date	Management response
User accounts with missing passwords	Yes	Leaves system open to unauthorized outsiders or attackers	5/10/08	Eliminate accounts without passwords
Network configured to allow some sharing of system files	Yes	Exposes critical system files to hostile parties connected to the network	5/10/08	Ensure only required directories are shared and that they are protected with strong passwords
Software patches can update production programs without final approval from Standards and Controls group	No	All production programs require management approval; Standards and Controls group assigns such cases to a temporary production status		

Figure 7-4
Sample Auditor's List of Control Weaknesses
This chart is a sample page from a list of control weaknesses that an auditor might find in a loan system in a local commercial bank.
This form helps auditors record and evaluate control weaknesses and shows the results of discussing those weaknesses with management, as well as any corrective actions taken by management.

automated audit software. The MIS audit may also examine data quality, as described in Chapter 5.

Security audits review technologies, procedures, documentation, training, and personnel. A thorough audit will even simulate an attack or disaster to test the response of the technology, information systems staff, and business employees.

The audit lists and ranks all control weaknesses and estimates the probability of their occurrence. It then assesses the financial and organizational impact of each threat. Figure 7-4 is a sample auditor's listing of control weaknesses for a loan system. It includes a section for notifying management of such weaknesses and for management's response. Management is expected to devise a plan for countering significant weaknesses in controls.

7.4 Technologies and Tools for Protecting Information Resources

Businesses have an array of tools and technologies for protecting their information resources. They include tools and technologies for securing systems and data, ensuring system availability, and ensuring software quality.

ACCESS CONTROL

Access control consists of all the policies and procedures a company uses to prevent improper access to systems by unauthorized insiders and outsiders. To gain access a user must be authorized and authenticated. **Authentication** refers to the ability to know that a person is who he or she claims to be. Access control software is designed to allow only authorized users to use systems or to access data using some method for authentication.

Authentication is often established by using passwords known only to authorized users. An end user uses a password to log on to a computer system and may also use passwords for accessing specific systems and files. However, users often forget passwords, share them, or choose poor passwords that are easy to guess, which compromises security. Password systems that are too rigorous hinder employee productivity. When employees must change complex passwords frequently, they often take shortcuts, such as choosing passwords that are easy to guess or writing down their passwords at their workstations in plain view. Passwords can also be "sniffed" if transmitted over a network or stolen through social engineering.

New authentication technologies, such as tokens, smart cards, and biometric authentication, overcome some of these problems. A **token** is a physical device, similar to an identification card, that is designed to prove the identity of a single user. Tokens are small gadgets that typically fit on key rings and display passcodes that change frequently. A **smart card** is a device about the size of a credit card that contains a chip formatted with access permission and other data. (Smart cards are also used in electronic payment systems.) A reader device interprets the data on the smart card and allows or denies access.

Biometric authentication uses systems that read and interpret individual human traits, such as fingerprints, irises, and voices, in order to grant or deny access. Biometric authentication is based on the measurement of a physical or behavioral trait that makes each individual unique. It compares a person's unique characteristics, such as the fingerprints, face, or retinal image, against a stored set profile of these characteristics to determine whether there are any differences between these characteristics and the stored profile. If the two profiles match, access is granted. Fingerprint and facial recognition technologies are just beginning to be used for security applications. About 10 percent of all new laptops sold in the United States come equipped with fingerprint identification devices.

FIREWALLS, INTRUSION DETECTION SYSTEMS, AND ANTIVIRUS SOFTWARE

Without protection against malware and intruders, connecting to the Internet would be very dangerous. Firewalls, intrusion detection systems, and antivirus software have become essential business tools.

Firewalls

Chapter 6 describes the use of *firewalls* to prevent unauthorized users from accessing private networks. A firewall is a combination of hardware and software that controls the flow of incoming and outgoing network traffic. It is generally placed between the organization's private internal networks and distrusted external networks, such as the Internet, although firewalls can also be used to protect one part of a company's network from the rest of the network (see Figure 7-5).

This NEC PC has a biometric fingerprint reader for fast yet secure access to files and networks. New models of PCs are starting to use biometric identification to authenticate users.

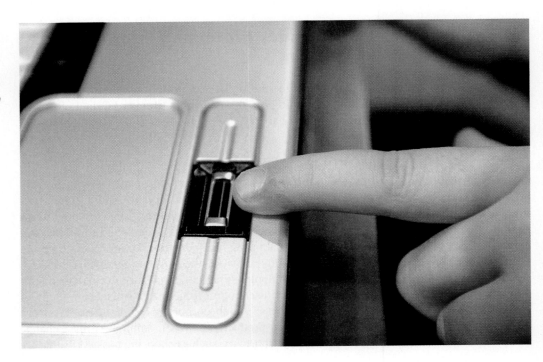

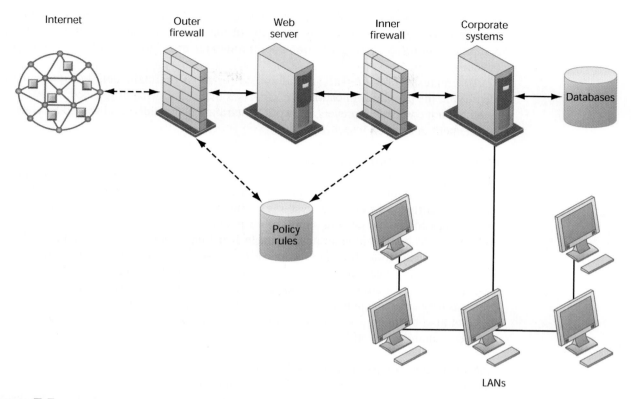

Figure 7-5
A Corporate Firewall
The firewall is placed between the firm's private network and the public Internet or another distrusted network to protect against unauthorized traffic.

The firewall acts like a gatekeeper who examines each user's credentials before access is granted to a network. The firewall identifies names, IP addresses, applications, and other characteristics of incoming traffic. It checks this information against the access rules that have been programmed into the system by the network administrator. The firewall prevents unauthorized communication into and out of the network.

In large organizations, the firewall often resides on a specially designated computer separate from the rest of the network, so no incoming request directly accesses private network resources. There are a number of firewall screening technologies, including static packet filtering, stateful inspection, Network Address Translation, and application proxy filtering. They are frequently used in combination to provide firewall protection.

Packet filtering examines selected fields in the headers of data packets flowing back and forth between the trusted network and the Internet, examining individual packets in isolation. This filtering technology can miss many types of attacks. *Stateful inspection* provides additional security by determining whether packets are part of an ongoing dialogue between a sender and a receiver. It sets up state tables to track information over multiple packets. Packets are accepted or rejected based on whether they are part of an approved conversation or whether they are attempting to establish a legitimate connection.

Network Address Translation (NAT) can provide another layer of protection when static packet filtering and stateful inspection are employed. NAT conceals the IP addresses of the organization's internal host computer(s) to prevent sniffer programs outside the firewall from ascertaining them and using that information to penetrate internal systems.

Application proxy filtering examines the application content of packets. A proxy server stops data packets originating outside the organization, inspects them, and passes a proxy to the other side of the firewall. If a user outside the company wants to communicate with a user inside the organization, the outside user first "talks" to the proxy application and the proxy application communicates with the firm's internal computer. Likewise, a computer user inside the organization goes through the proxy to talk with computers on the outside.

To create a good firewall, an administrator must maintain detailed internal rules identifying the people, applications, or addresses that are allowed or rejected. Firewalls can deter, but not completely prevent, network penetration by outsiders and should be viewed as one element in an overall security plan.

Intrusion Detection Systems

In addition to firewalls, commercial security vendors now provide intrusion detection tools and services to protect against suspicious network traffic and attempts to access files and databases. **Intrusion detection systems** feature full-time monitoring tools placed at the most vulnerable points or "hot spots" of corporate networks to detect and deter intruders continually. The system generates an alarm if it finds a suspicious or anomalous event. Scanning software looks for patterns indicative of known methods of computer attacks, such as bad passwords, checks to see if important files have been removed or modified, and sends warnings of vandalism or system administration errors. Monitoring software examines events as they are happening to discover security attacks in progress. The intrusion detection tool can also be customized to shut down a particularly sensitive part of a network if it receives unauthorized traffic.

Antivirus and Antispyware Software

Defensive technology plans for both individuals and businesses must include antivirus protection for every computer. **Antivirus software** is designed to check computer systems and drives for the presence of computer viruses and worms. Often the software eliminates the virus from the infected area. However, most antivirus software is effective only against malware already known when the software was written. To remain effective, the antivirus software must be continually updated. Antivirus products are available for mobile and hand-held devices.

Leading antivirus software vendors, such as McAfee, Symantec and Trend Micro, have enhanced their products to include protection against spyware. Anti-spyware software tools such as Ad-Aware, Spybot, and Spyware Doctor are also very helpful.

SECURING WIRELESS NETWORKS

Despite its flaws, WEP provides some margin of security if Wi-Fi users remember to activate it. A simple first step to thwart hackers is to assign a unique name to your network's SSID and instruct your router not to broadcast it. Corporations can further improve Wi-Fi security by using it in conjunction with virtual private network (VPN) technology when accessing internal corporate data.

In June 2004, the Wi-Fi Alliance industry trade group finalized the 802.11i specification (also referred to as Wi-Fi Protected Access 2 or WAP2) that replaces WEP with stronger security standards. Instead of the static encryption keys used in WEP, the new standard uses much longer keys that continually change, making them harder to crack. It also employs an encrypted authentication system with a central authentication server to ensure that only authorized users access the network.

ENCRYPTION AND PUBLIC KEY INFRASTRUCTURE

Many businesses use encryption to protect digital information that they store, physically transfer, or send over the Internet. **Encryption** is the process of transforming plain text or data into cipher text that cannot be read by anyone other than the sender and the intended receiver. Data are encrypted by using a secret numerical code, called an encryption key, that transforms plain data into cipher text. The message must be decrypted by the receiver.

Two methods for encrypting network traffic on the Web are SSL and S-HTTP. **Secure Sockets Layer (SSL)** and its successor Transport Layer Security (TLS) enable client and server computers to manage encryption and decryption activities as they communicate with each other during a secure Web session. **Secure Hypertext Transfer Protocol (S-HTTP)** is another protocol used for encrypting data flowing over the Internet, but it is limited to individual messages, whereas SSL and TLS are designed to establish a secure connection between two computers.

The capability to generate secure sessions is built into Internet client browser software and servers. The client and the server negotiate what key and what level of security to use. Once a secure session is established between the client and the server, all messages in that session are encrypted.

There are two alternative methods of encryption: symmetric key encryption and public key encryption. In symmetric key encryption, the sender and receiver establish a secure Internet session by creating a single encryption key and sending it to the receiver so both the sender and receiver share the same key. The strength of the encryption key is measured by its bit length. Today, a typical key will be 128 bits long (a string of 128 binary digits).

The problem with all symmetric encryption schemes is that the key itself must be shared somehow among the senders and receivers, which exposes the key to outsiders who might be able to intercept and decrypt the key. A more secure form of encryption called **public key encryption** uses two keys: one shared (or public) and one totally private as shown in Figure 7-6. The keys are mathematically related so that data encrypted with one key can be decrypted using only the other key. To send and receive messages, communicators first create separate pairs of private and public keys. The public key is kept in a directory and the private key must be kept secret. The sender encrypts a message with the recipient's public key. On receiving the message, the recipient uses his or her private key to decrypt it.

Digital certificates are data files used to establish the identity of users and electronic assets for protection of online transactions (see Figure 7-7). A digital certificate system uses a trusted third party, known as a certification authority (CA), to validate a user's identity. There are many CAs in the United States and around the world, including VeriSign, IdenTrust, and Australia's KeyPost. The CA verifies a digital certificate user's identity offline. This information is put into a CA server, which generates an encrypted digital certificate containing owner identification information and a copy of the owner's public key. The certificate authenticates that the public key belongs to the designated owner. The CA makes its own public key available publicly either in print or perhaps on the Internet. The recipient of an encrypted message uses the CA's public key to decode the digital certificate attached to the message, verifies it was issued by the CA, and then obtains the sender's public key and identification information contained in the certificate. Using this information, the recipient can send an encrypted reply. The digital certificate system would enable, for exam-

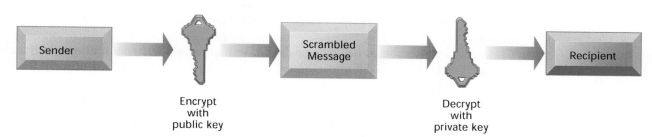

Figure 7-6
Public Key Encryption
A public key encryption system can be viewed as a series of public and private keys that lock data when they are transmitted and unlock the data when they are received. The sender locates the recipient's public key in a directory and uses it to encrypt a message. The message is sent in encrypted form over the Internet or a private network. When the encrypted message arrives, the recipient uses his or her private key to decrypt the data and read the message.

Figure 7-7
Digital Certificates
Digital certificates help establish the identity of people or electronic assets. They protect online transactions by providing secure, encrypted, online communication.

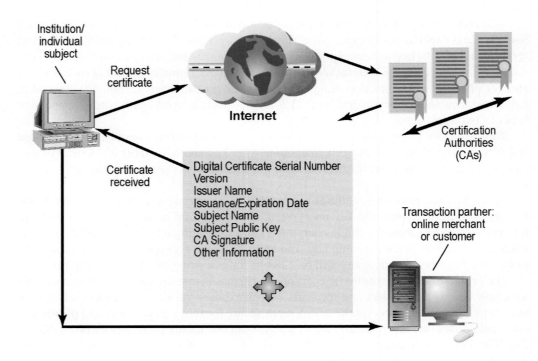

ple, a credit card user and a merchant to validate that their digital certificates were issued by an authorized and trusted third party before they exchange data. **Public key infrastructure (PKI)**, the use of public key cryptography working with a certificate authority, is now widely used in e-commerce.

ENSURING SYSTEM AVAILABILITY

As companies increasingly rely on digital networks for revenue and operations, they need to take additional steps to ensure that their systems and applications are always available. Firms such as those in the airline and financial services industries with critical applications requiring online transaction processing have traditionally used fault-tolerant computer systems for many years to ensure 100-percent availability. In **online transaction processing**, transactions entered online are immediately processed by the computer. Multitudinous changes to databases, reporting, and requests for information occur each instant.

Fault-tolerant computer systems contain redundant hardware, software, and power supply components that create an environment that provides continuous, uninterrupted service. Fault-tolerant computers use special software routines or self-checking logic built into their circuitry to detect hardware failures and automatically switch to a backup device. Parts from these computers can be removed and repaired without disruption to the computer system.

Fault tolerance should be distinguished from **high-availability computing**. Both fault tolerance and high-availability computing try to minimize downtime. **Downtime** refers to periods of time in which a system is not operational. However, high-availability computing helps firms recover quickly from a system crash, whereas fault tolerance promises continuous availability and the elimination of recovery time altogether.

High-availability computing environments are a minimum requirement for firms with heavy electronic commerce processing or for firms that depend on digital networks for their internal operations. High-availability computing requires backup servers, distribution of processing across multiple servers, high-capacity storage, and good disaster recovery and business continuity plans. The firm's computing platform must be extremely robust with scalable processing power, storage, and bandwidth.

Researchers are exploring ways to make computing systems recover even more rapidly when mishaps occur, an approach called **recovery-oriented computing**. This work includes designing systems that recover quickly, and implementing capabilities and tools to help operators pinpoint the sources of faults in multi-component systems and easily correct their mistakes.

The Interactive Session on Organizations describes the efforts of Salesforce.com to make sure its systems are always available to subscribers. Salesforce.com is a Web-based on-demand customer relationship management (CRM) and business services provider. Companies subscribing to its service use Salesforce.com's software programs running on Salesforce's servers. If Salesforce.com's services fail, they can't run their CRM applications. That's exactly what happened when Salesforce.com was hit by a series of service outages in late 2005 and 2006. As you read this case, try to identify the problem Salesforce.com encountered; what alternative solutions were available to management; and the people, organization, and technology issues that had to be addressed when developing the solution.

Controlling Network Traffic: Deep Packet Inspection

Have you ever tried to use your campus network and found it was very slow? It may be because your fellow students are using the network to download music or watch YouTube. Bandwith-consuming applications such as file-sharing programs, Internet phone service, and online video, are able to clog and slow down corporate networks, degrading performance. For example, Ball Sate University in Muncie, Indiana found its network had slowed because a small minority of students were using peer-to-peer file sharing programs to download movies and music.

A technology called **deep packet inspection (DPI)** helps solve this problem. DPI examines data files and sorts out low-priority online material while assigning higher priority to business-critical files. Based on the priorities established by a network's operators, it decides whether a specific data packet can continue to its destination or should be blocked or delayed while more important traffic proceeds. Using a DPI system from Allot Communications, Ball State was able to cap the amount of file-sharing traffic and assign it a much lower priority. Ball State's preferred network traffic speeded up (White, 2007).

Security Outsourcing

Many companies, especially small businesses, lack the resources or expertise to provide a secure high-availability computing environment on their own. They can outsource many security functions to **managed security service providers (MSSPs)** that monitor network activity and perform vulnerability testing and intrusion detection. Guardent, Counterpane, VeriSign, and Symantec are leading providers of MSSP services.

ENSURING SOFTWARE QUALITY

In addition to implementing effective security and controls, organizations can improve system quality and reliability by employing software metrics and rigorous software testing. Software metrics are objective assessments of the system in the form of quantified measurements. Ongoing use of metrics allows the information systems department and end users to jointly measure the performance of the system and identify problems as they occur. Examples of software metrics include the number of transactions that can be processed in a specified unit of time, online response time, the number of payroll checks printed per hour, and the number of known bugs per hundred lines of program code. For metrics to be successful, they must be carefully designed, formal, objective, and used consistently.

Early, regular, and thorough testing will contribute significantly to system quality. Many view testing as a way to prove the correctness of work they have done. In fact, we know that all sizable software is riddled with errors, and we must test to uncover these errors.

INTERACTIVE SESSION: ORGANIZATIONS   Can Salesforce.com On-Demand Remain in Demand?

Salesforce.com, headquartered in San Francisco, California, is the worldwide leader in on-demand customer relationship management (CRM) services. It offers hosted applications that manage customer information for sales, marketing, and customer support. Companies used Salesforce.com's applications for generating sales leads, maintaining customer records, and tracking customer interactions. As of January 31, 2007, Salesforce.com had about 29,800 customers and 646,000 paying subscriptions worldwide. More companies trust their vital customer and sales data to Salesforce.com than to any other on-demand CRM company in the world.

Imagine then, the impact if Salesforce.com's services are not available. That's exactly what happened during a six-week period in late 2005 and early 2006. Starting on December 20, 2005, Salesforce.com clients could not access the company's servers and obtain their customer records for more than three hours. A rare database software bug was the source of the problem. Oracle Database 10g and Oracle Grid Computing are key technologies for Salesforce.com's service and internal operations, and these tools are considered among the best in the business. Salesforce.com was careful not to blame Oracle for the outage, and instead focused on working with Oracle to eradicate the bug. It has not resurfaced since the initial occurrence. But with no access to customers' records, some businesses came to a standstill for the duration of the outage.

Salesforce.com experienced two more outages in January and several in early February attributed to "system performance issues." A January 30 performance problem was traced to a shortcoming in the company's database cluster, or collection of databases. Salesforce.com had to restart each database instance in the cluster, interrupting service to do so. Its service was down for about four hours. Even when the service was brought back up, its application programming interface was disabled for a few more hours.

On February 9, 2006, a primary hardware server failed and one of the company's four North American servers did not automatically recover. Salesforce.com had to restart the database running on this server manually. The outage lasted slightly more than one hour.

These service outages could not have occurred at a worse time. Salesforce.com was growing rapidly and seeking to attract more large customers with new software and services in addition to CRM. In January 2006, it launched AppExchange, an online marketplace for applications and Web services from other

vendors and developers that can be customized and integrated with Salesforce.com's CRM service. Salesforce.com would not be able to convince enterprise customers to let it run their applications if it could not guarantee that that its services were 100-percent reliable.

The outages caused some clients and analysts to ask whether Salesforce.com had run into capacity or scalability problems. At the time of the first incident, analysts agreed that a one-time outage would not cause a crisis of confidence on the part of clients. Many clients admitted that Salesforce.com had a better record of maintaining uptime than the clients' own companies did. What was of more concern to some clients was the failure of Salesforce.com to communicate adequately with its clients about the outage. They were left in the dark as to what exactly was happening with the on-demand service. At least one client (Mission Research, a Lancaster, Pennsylvania developer of fund-raising software) dropped Salesforce.com in favor of an internal system immediately on December 20, 2005.

In the weeks that followed that outage, it became apparent that the problems at Salesforce.com were not limited to a software bug. The recurring outages raised doubts about the fidelity of the service's infrastructure as a whole. These outages coincided with the end of the month and, for some companies, the end of the fiscal year. It was an extraordinarily inconvenient time to lose access to customer data.

The complaints from clients grew louder. They focused not only on the failure of the on-demand service but on poor customer service and a tepid response from Salesforce.com management. One particularly outraged client created a blog at gripeforce.blogspot.com to express his dissatisfaction with the service. The blogger, CRMGuy, described salespeople at Salesforce.com as arrogant and customer service representatives as interested only in selling more user licenses. Salesforce.com's CEO, Mark Benioff, was roundly criticized for downplaying the interruptions as minor. "Having the company's CEO minimize an outage that brings customer businesses to a halt as a 'minor issue' is not acceptable." Of course, there were plenty of clients who found the increasing downtime unacceptable as well.

Salesforce.com moved quickly to improve its client communication. The company used direct communications and customer support outlets to update clients on efforts to resolve service problems. By the end of February 2006, Salesforce.com had launched Trust.Salesforce.com, a Web site that displayed both real-time and historical data related to the performance of all key system components for its services. The site provided a measure of transparency into the level of database and service performance that clients were receiving, which they valued. Trust.Salesforce.com logs specific metrics, such as API transactions and page views. The site also gives general conditions using a color scheme to indicate service status for network nodes: green for OK, yellow for a performance issue, and red for an outage.

Even prior to the outages, Salesforce.com had been building up and redesigning its infrastructure to ensure better service. The company invested $50 million in Mirrorforce technology, a mirroring system that creates a duplicate database in a separate location and synchronizes the data instantaneously. If one database is disabled, the other takes over. Salesforce.com added two data centers on the East and West coasts in addition to its Silicon Valley facility and built an additional West Coast facility to support new product development. The company distributed processing for its larger customers among these centers to balance its

database load. The investment in Mirrorforce necessitated a complete overhaul of Salesforce.com's hardware and software.

Salesforce.com's accelerated growth and switch to the new data centers had contributed to the outages. But by March 2006, Salesforce.com had strengthened its IT infrastructure to the point where outages were no longer occurring. Salesforce.com stated that it already met availability standards of 99-percent uptime in 2005 and 2006, but it was still striving to achieve 99.999-percent availability. On the public relations front, spokesman Bruce Francis offered an apology and recognition of clients' frustrations. Francis said, "There's no such thing as a minor outage because we know that even one moment of degraded availability is a moment our customers can't do what they need to do."

Sources: Laton McCartney, "Salesforce.com: When On-Demand Goes Off," *Baseline Magazine*, January 7, 2007; John Pallatto, "Rare Database Bug Causes Salesforce.com Outage," eWeek.com, December 22, 2005 and "Salesforce.com Confirms 'Minor' CRM Outage," eWeek.com, January 6, 2006; Alorie Gilbert, "Salesforce.com Users Lament Ongoing Outages," cnet News.com, February 1, 2006; and Bill Snyder, "Salesforce.com Outage Strikes Again," TheStreet.com, January 6, 2006.

CASE STUDY QUESTIONS

1. How did the problems experienced by Salesforce.com impact its business?

2. How did the problems impact its customers?

3. What steps did Salesforce.com take to solve the problems? Were these steps sufficient?

4. List and describe other vulnerabilities discussed in this chapter that might create outages at Salesforce.com and measures to safeguard against them.

MIS IN ACTION

Go to www.salesforce.com, reviewing the sections on Security, Availability, Performance, and Scalability. Then answer the following questions:

1. How does Saleforce.com deliver world-class security at the application, facilities, and network level?

2. What provisions does Salesforce.com have in place for disaster recovery and availability?

3. Click on trust.salesforce.com. What kinds of performance metrics does it display?

4. If you ran a business, would you feel confident about using Salesforce.com's on-demand service? Why or why not?

Good testing begins before a software program is even written by using a *walkthrough*—a review of a specification or design document by a small group of people carefully selected based on the skills needed for the particular objectives being tested. Once developers start writing software programs, coding walkthroughs also can be used to review program code. However, code must be tested by computer runs. When errors are discovered, the source is found and eliminated through a process called *debugging*. You can find out more about the various stages of testing required to put an information system into operation in Chapter 11. Our Learning Tracks also contain descriptions of methodologies for developing software programs that also contribute to software quality.

7.5 Hands-On MIS

The projects in this section give you hands-on experience developing a disaster recovery plan, using spreadsheet software for risk analysis, and using Web tools to research security outsourcing services.

ACHIEVING OPERATIONAL EXCELLENCE: DEVELOPING A DISASTER RECOVERY PLAN

Software skills: Web browser and presentation software
Business skills: Disaster recovery planning

Management is concerned that Dirt Bikes's computer systems could be vulnerable to power outages, vandalism, computer viruses, natural disasters, or telecommunications disruptions. You have been asked to perform an analysis of system vulnerabilities and disaster recovery planning for the company. Your report should answer the following questions:

- What are the most likely threats to the continued operation of Dirt Bikes's systems?
- What would you identify as Dirt Bikes's most critical systems? What is the impact on the company if these systems cannot operate? How long could the company survive if these systems were down? Which systems are the most important to back up and restore in the event of a disaster?
- Use the Web to locate two disaster recovery services that could be used by a small business such as Dirt Bikes. Compare them in terms of the services they offer. Which should Dirt Bikes use? Exactly how could these services help Dirt Bikes recover from a disaster?
- (Optional) If possible use electronic presentation software to summarize your findings for management.

IMPROVING DECISION MAKING: USING SPREADSHEET SOFTWARE TO PERFORM A SECURITY RISK ASSESSMENT

Software skills: Spreadsheet formulas and charts
Business skills: Risk assessment

This project uses spreadsheet software to calculate anticipated annual losses from various security threats identified for a small company.

Mercer Paints is a small but highly regarded paint manufacturing company located in Alabama. The company has a network in place linking many of its business operations. Although the firm believes that its security is adequate, the recent addition of a Web site has become an open invitation to hackers. Management requested a risk assessment. The risk assessment identified a number of potential exposures. These exposures, their associated probabilities, and average losses are summarized in the following table.

Mercer Paints Risk Assessment		
Exposure	**Probability of Occurrence (%)**	**Average Loss ($)**
Malware attack	60%	$75,000
Data loss	12%	$70,000
Embezzlement	3%	$30,000
User errors	95%	$25,000
Threats from hackers	95%	$90,000
Improper use by employees	5%	$5,000
Power failure	15%	$300,000

- In addition to the potential exposures listed, you should identify at least three other potential threats to Mercer Paints, assign probabilities, and estimate a loss range.
- Use spreadsheet software and the risk assessment data to calculate the expected annual loss for each exposure.
- Present your findings in the form of a chart. Which control points have the greatest vulnerability? What recommendations would you make to Mercer Paints? Prepare a written report that summarizes your findings and recommendations.

IMPROVING DECISION MAKING: EVALUATING SECURITY OUTSOURCING SERVICES

Software skills: Web browser and presentation software
Business skills: Evaluating business outsourcing services

Businesses today have a choice of whether to outsource the security function or maintain their own internal staff for this purpose. This project will help develop your Internet skills in using the Web to research and evaluate security outsourcing services.

As an information systems expert in your firm, you have been asked to help management decide whether to outsource security or keep the security function within the firm. Search the Web to find information to help you decide whether to outsource security and to locate security outsourcing services.

- Present a brief summary of the arguments for and against outsourcing computer security for your company.
- Select two firms that offer computer security outsourcing services, and compare them and their services.
- Prepare an electronic presentation for management summarizing your findings. Your presentation should make the case as to whether or not your company should outsource computer security. If you believe your company should outsource, the presentation should identify which security outsourcing service should be selected and justify your selection.

LEARNING TRACKS

The following Learning Tracks provide content relevant to topics covered in this chapter:

1. The Booming Job Market in IT Security
2. The Sarbanes-Oxley Act
3. Computer Forensics
4. General and Application Controls for Information Systems
5. Management Challenges of Security and Control

Review Summary

1 **Why are information systems vulnerable to destruction, error, and abuse?** Digital data are vulnerable to destruction, misuse, error, fraud, and hardware or software failures. The Internet is designed to be an open system and makes internal corporate systems more vulnerable to actions from outsiders. Hackers can unleash denial-of-service (DoS) attacks or penetrate corporate networks, causing serious system disruptions. Wi-Fi networks can be easily penetrated by intruders using sniffer programs to obtain an address to access the resources of the network. Computer viruses and worms can disable systems and Web sites. Software presents problems because software bugs may be impossible to eliminate and because software vulnerabilities can be exploited by hackers and malicious software. End users often introduce errors.

2 **What is the business value of security and control?** Lack of sound security and control can cause firms relying on computer systems for their core business functions to lose sales and productivity. Information assets, such as confidential employee records, trade secrets, or business plans, lose much of their value if they are revealed to outsiders or if they expose the firm to legal liability. New laws, such as HIPAA, the Sarbanes-Oxley Act, and the Gramm-Leach-Bliley Act, require companies to practice stringent electronic records management and adhere to strict standards for security, privacy, and control. Legal actions requiring electronic evidence and computer forensics also require firms to pay more attention to security and electronic records management.

3 **What are the components of an organizational framework for security and control?** Firms need to establish a good set of both general and application controls for their information systems. A risk assessment evaluates information assets, identifies control points and control weaknesses, and determines the most cost-effective set of controls. Firms must also develop a coherent corporate security policy and plans for continuing business operations in the event of disaster or disruption. The security policy includes policies for acceptable use and authorization. Comprehensive and systematic MIS auditing helps organizations determine the effectiveness of security and controls for their information systems.

4 **What are the most important tools and technologies for safeguarding information resources?** Firewalls prevent unauthorized users from accessing a private network when it is linked to the Internet. Intrusion detection systems monitor private networks from suspicious network traffic and attempts to access corporate systems. Passwords, tokens, smart cards, and biometric authentication are used to authenticate system users. Antivirus software checks computer systems for infections by viruses and worms and often eliminates the malicious software, while antispyware software combats intrusive and harmful spyware programs. Encryption, the coding and scrambling of messages, is a widely used technology for securing electronic transmissions over unprotected networks. Digital certificates combined with public key encryption provide further protection of electronic transactions by authenticating a user's identity. Companies can use fault-tolerant computer systems or create high-availability computing environments to make sure that their information systems are always available. Use of software metrics and rigorous software testing help improve software quality and reliability.

Key Terms

Acceptable use policy (AUP), 247
Access control, 249
Antivirus software, 252
Application controls, 246
Authentication, 249
Authorization management systems, 247
Authorization policies, 247
Biometric authentication, 250
Botnet, 237
Bugs, 242
Business continuity planning, 248
Click fraud, 240
Computer crime, 237
Computer forensics, 244

Computer virus, 234
Controls, 231
Cybervandalism, 236
Deep packet inspection (DPI), 255
Denial-of-service (DoS) attack, 237
Digital certificates, 253
Disaster recovery planning, 247
Distributed denial-of-service (DDoS) attack, 237
Downtime, 254
Encryption, 252
Evil twins, 240
Fault-tolerant computer systems, 254

General controls, 245
Gramm-Leach-Bliley Act, 243
Hacker, 236
High-availability computing, 254
HIPAA, 243
Identity theft, 237
Intrusion detection systems, 252
Key loggers, 236
Malware, 234
Managed security service providers (MSSPs), 255
MIS audit, 248
Online transaction processing, 254
Patches, 242

Review Questions

1. Why are information systems vulnerable to destruction, error, and abuse?
- List and describe the most common threats against contemporary information systems.
- Define malware and distinguish among a virus, a worm, and a Trojan horse.
- Define a hacker and explain how hackers create security problems and damage systems.
- Define computer crime. Provide two examples of crime in which computers are targets and two examples in which computers are used as instruments of crime.
- Define identity theft and phishing and explain why identity theft is such a big problem today.
- Describe the security and system reliability problems created by employees.
- Explain how software defects affect system reliability and security.

2. What is the business value of security and control?
- Explain how security and control provide value for businesses.
- Describe the relationship between security and control and recent U.S. government regulatory requirements and computer forensics.

3. What are the components of an organizational framework for security and control?
- Define general controls and describe each type of general control.
- Define application controls and describe each type of application control.
- Describe the function of risk assessment and explain how it is conducted for information systems.
- Define and describe the following: security policy, acceptable use policy, authorization policy.
- Explain how MIS auditing promotes security and control.

4. What are the most important tools and technologies for safeguarding information resources?
- Name and describe three authentication methods.
- Describe the roles of firewalls, intrusion detection systems, and antivirus software in promoting security.
- Explain how encryption protects information.
- Describe the role of encryption and digital certificates in a public key infrastructure.
- Distinguish between fault-tolerant and high-availability computing, and between disaster recovery planning and business continuity planning.
- Describe measures for improving software quality and reliability.

Discussion Questions

1. Security isn't simply a technology issue, it's a business issue. Discuss.

2. If you were developing a business continuity plan for your company, where would you start? What aspects of the business would the plan address?

Video Case

You will find a video case illustrating some of the concepts in this chapter on the Laudon Web site along with questions to help you analyze the case.

Teamwork

Evaluating Security Software Tools

With a group of three or four students, use the Web to research and evaluate security products from two competing vendors, such as antivirus software, firewalls, or antispyware software. For each product, describe its capabilities, for what types of businesses it is best suited, and its cost to purchase and install. Which is the best product? Why? If possible, use electronic presentation software to present your findings to the class.

BUSINESS PROBLEM-SOLVING CASE

TXJ Companies' Credit Card Data Theft: The Worst Data Theft Ever?

Headquartered in Framingham, Massachusetts, TJX Companies is a $17 billion retailer with a global presence. The company's properties include 826 T.J. Maxx, 751 Marshalls, and 271 HomeGoods stores in the United States alone. On December 18, 2006, TJX management learned that its computer systems had been infiltrated by suspicious software, and intruders had stolen records with at least 45.7 million credit and debit card numbers. This is now the biggest known theft of credit card numbers in history. The TJX hackers also obtained personal information which could be used for identity theft, including driver license numbers, social security numbers, and military identification of 451,000 customers. The data theft took place over an eighteen-month period without anyone's knowledge.

How could this have happened? The thieves may have used several vulnerable entry points to TJX corporate systems. One was poorly secured computer kiosks located in many of TJX's retail stores, which let people apply for jobs electronically. These same kiosks also provide direct access to the company's internal corporate network. Hackers could have opened up the back of those terminals and inserted USB drives to install utility software that enabled them to turn the kiosks into remote terminals linked to TJX's networks. (The USB drives in the kiosks are normally used for plugging in mice or printers.) The TJX firewalls weren't set up to block malicious traffic coming from the kiosks.

Another entry point was wireless. The hackers may have used mobile data acess technology to penetrate the

wireless network at a Marshalls discount clothing store in St. Paul, Minnesota. They were able to decode data transmitted wirelessly between handheld price-checking devices, cash registers, and the store's computers, and the captured data helped them hack into the central TJX database, which stored customer transactions for T.J. Maxx, Marshalls, HomeGoods, and A.J. Wright stores in the United States and Puerto Rico, and for Winners and HomeSense stores in Canada.

TJX was still using the old Wired Equivalent Privacy (WEP) encryption system, which is relatively easy for hackers to crack. Other companies had switched to the more secure Wi-Fi Protected Access (WPA) standard with more complex encryption, but TJX did not make the change. An auditor later found that TJX had also neglected to install firewalls and data encryption on many of the computers using the wireless network, and didn't properly install another layer of security software it had purchased.

After the hackers tapped into the data transmitted by handheld equipment for communicating price markdowns and checking inventory, they used the data to crack encryption codes so they could digitally eavesdrop on employees logging into TJX's central database in Framingham. They stole one or more user names and passwords and used that information to set up their own accounts in the TJX system, amassing transaction data, including credit card numbers, into about 100 large files. They were able to access the TJX system from any computer connected to the Internet. Company investigators believe the hackers may have even stolen bank debit card information as customers making purchases waited for their transactions to be approved. TJX acknowledged in a Securities and Exchange Commission filing that it transmitted such data to banks without encryption, violating credit card company guidelines.

A little over a week after discovering the data breach, TJX began to notify the credit card, debit card, and check-processing companies it used that the intrusion had taken place. TJX finally reported the breach to the public in mid-January 2007.

The hackers sold the purloined data on the Internet on password-protected sites used by gangs who run up charges using fake credit cards printed with stolen numbers. Incidents of credit card fraud tied to TJX stores surfaced in the United States and abroad. Customers at Fidelity Homestead, the Louisiana savings bank, began seeing strange transactions on their credit card bills in November 2005—unauthorized purchases in Wal-Mart stores in Mexico and in supermarkets and other stores in southern California.

In March 2007, the Gainesville Police Department and the Florida Department of Law Enforcement arrested six people using fake credit cards with the stolen TJX data. They had purchased $8 million in gift cards from Wal-Mart and Sam's Club stores in 50 Florida counties, and used them to buy flat-screen TVs, computers, and other electronics.

The following July, the U.S. Secret Service arrested four more people in south Florida who had been using the stolen TJX customer data. The suspects were charged with belonging to an organized fraud ring that engaged in identity theft and counterfeit credit card trafficking. The arrests recovered about 200,000 stolen credit card numbers used in fraud losses calculated to be more than $75 million. The fraudsters had purchased the stolen credit card account numbers from known cybercriminals in Eastern Europe.

The revelation quickly directed attention to the way in which the company handled its customers' financial data. In question was whether TJX was adhering to the security rules established by Visa and MasterCard for storing such data, known as the Payment Card Industry (PCI) Data Security Standard. According to these rules, merchants are not supposed to maintain certain types of cardholder data in their systems because the data facilitate the creation of fraudulent card accounts. Communications between Visa and card-issuing financial institutions revealed that TJX did violate this principle by holding onto data for years, rather than for the short amount of time they are actually needed.

Avivah Litan, research director for the Gartner consulting firm, suggested that TJX did not store the data intentionally. Instead, legacy systems that were implemented before hackers were a serious threat accounted for the security catastrophe. Complying with the PCI regulations and fortifying security do not provide a clear return on investment.

TJX was guilty of storing data from Track 2 of the magnetic strip on Visa cards. This area of the strip houses the account number, expiration date, and security code. It does not include names and addresses, which are stored on Track 1. Even though the thieves could not use the data for identity theft, the Track 2 data are sufficient for fabricating false credit cards.

Although the PCI standards are rigorous, merchants who fail to abide by them remain eligible to process electronic payments. The merchant banks who provide the financial network and card readers that let stores accept credit and debit card purchases are subject to fines from Visa of up to $500,000 for accepting transactions from merchants who do not follow PCI rules. In addition to the requirements for storing sensitive data, PCI mandates secure networks with firewalls; systems passwords that are different than the vendor defaults; encryption of sensitive data that crosses public networks, such as the Internet; and up-to-date antivirus software.

TJX responded to the intrusion by launching an investigation with the assistance of a computer security firm. The company advised customers to monitor their accounts for fraudulent activities and established help centers available by a toll-free number and online. The FBI and local authorities, including the Massachusetts Attorney General, also began investigations. In addition to capturing data from the TJX systems, the hacker had covered his tracks by deleting and altering log files, changing clock settings, and relocating data. This made it more difficult to determine which records were accessed and when. In fact, in its 10-K filing to the SEC, TJX admitted that it might never identify much of the stolen data.

Banks that issue credit and debit cards have so far borne the brunt of the TJX losses from fraudulent credit card charges rather than the retailers who accepted the fraudulent cards, the credit card networks such as MasterCard and Visa, or TJX itself. They may have to spend $300 million just to replace the stolen cards, in addition to covering fraudulent purchases. However, lobbyists for banking associations are pushing for laws to place full financial responsibility for any credit card fraud-related losses on the company that allowed its security system to be breached.

Consumer groups and banks have filed lawsuits against TJX and its merchant banks for failing to protect account data. Lawsuits were also filed in six Canadian provinces seeking compensation on behalf of all citizens who might be affected by personal information stolen from TJX stores. According to attorney Archie Lamb, whose firm is among those representing consumers and banks in their suits against TJX, "the costs to customers and banks will be enormous."

Even without lawsuit liabilities, Forrester Research estimates that the cost to TJX for the data breach could surpass $1 billion over five years, including costs for consultants, security upgrades, attorney fees, and additional marketing to reassure customers. TJX declined to comment on those numbers.

A report from Javelin Strategy & Research revealed that more than 75 percent of the consumers it surveyed would not continue to shop at stores that had been victimized by data theft. The same study showed that consumers trust credit card companies to protect their data far more than retailers. TJX was waiting to discover how much impact its security breach would have on the bottom line.

Sources: Robin Sidel, "Giant Retailer Reveals Customer Data Breach," *The Wall Street Journal,* January 18, 2007; Larry Greenemeier, "Data Theft, Pushback, and the TJX Effect," *InformationWeek,* August 13, 2007; "Secret Service Busts Four Fraudsters with Ties to T.J. Maxx Attack," *InformationWeek,* July 12, 2007, "Hack Attack Means Headaches for TJ Maxx," *Information Week,* February 3, 2007, and T.J. Maxx Probe Reveals Data Brach Worse Than Originally Thought," *InformationWeek,* February 21, 2007; Sharon Gaudin, "Mass. AG Heads Investigation into T.J. Maxx Security Breach, *InformationWeek,* February 9, 2007.

Case Study Questions

1. List and describe the security controls and weaknesses at TJX Companies.
2. What people, organization, and technology factors contributed to these weaknesses?
3. What was the business impact of TJX's data loss on TJX, consumers, and banks?
4. How effectively did TJX deal with these problems?
5. Who should be held liable for the losses caused by the use of fraudulent credit cards in this case? TJX? The banks issuing the credit cards? The consumers? Justify your answer.
6. What solutions would you suggest to prevent the problems?

Key System Applications for the Digital Age

PART III

Part III examines the core information system applications businesses are using today to improve operational excellence and decision making. These applications include enterprise systems; systems for supply chain management, customer relationship management, and knowledge management; e-commerce applications; decision-support systems; and executive support systems. This part answers questions such as these: How can enterprise applications improve business performance? How do firms use e-commerce to extend the reach of their businesses? How can systems improve decision making and help companies make better use of their knowledge assets?

Achieving Operational Excellence and Customer Intimacy: Enterprise Applications

8

STUDENT LEARNING OBJECTIVES

After completing this chapter, you will be able to answer the following questions:

1. How do enterprise systems help businesses achieve operational excellence?

2. How do supply chain management systems coordinate planning, production, and logistics with suppliers?

3. How do customer relationship management systems help firms achieve customer intimacy?

4. What are the challenges posed by enterprise applications?

5. How are enterprise applications used in platforms for new cross-functional services?

CHAPTER OUTLINE

TASTY BAKING COMPANY: AN ENTERPRISE SYSTEM TRANSFORMS AN OLD FAVORITE

Tasty Baking Company's name says it all. It is known for its Tastykake single-portion cupcakes, snack pies, cookies, and donuts, which are pre-wrapped fresh at its bakery and sold through approximately 15,500 convenience stores and supermarkets in the eastern United States. The Philadelphia-based company, which sold $28 in cakes its first day of business in 1914, rang up sales of $168 million in 2006.

Although Tasty Baking Company made customers smile, management and stockholders were frowning. Tasty is a fairly small enterprise in a maturing business, and saw its market share and sales dropping in the mid-1990s. In 2002, profitability levels were at an all-time low, with a -4.9 percent operating margin. To turn the company around, Tasty's new president and CEO Charles Pizzi introduced a new management team and strategic transformation plan.

The strategy required new manufacturing methods and new information systems. Tasty's existing systems were technically challenged, inflexible, and posed serious compliance and other business risks. Many key processes were traditional and heavily

manual, and the company did not have timely information for tracking manufacturing outputs and warehouse shipments. Tasty had to physically count all the items in its warehouses every day. Even so, inventory information was still inaccurate and out of date. Shipments were missed, and excess inventory had to be sold at a discount at bakery thrift stores. Tasty's market share and sales dropped while operating costs rose.

Much of Tasty's information about sales and products comes from its network of sales distributors. Tasty needed to create better connections with its sales operation to receive this information as soon as it was available.

Tasty's new management team decided to implement a new enterprise system using software from SAP designed specifically for the food and beverage industry. Consultants from SAP and Deloitte helped the company identify its business processes and figure out how to make them work with the SAP software. By limiting changes to the software and enforcing rigorous project management standards, the company was able to implement the new enterprise system on time and on budget in nine months. Tasty's SAP enterprise system uses a Microsoft SQL Server database and Windows operating system running on an Intel server.

Tasty was willing to make many changes in its business processes to take maximum advantage of the enterprise software's capabilities. It adopted Deloitte's template of best practices for the food and beverage industry. Tasty implemented the SAP modules for financials, order entry, manufacturing resource planning (MRP), and scheduling. The system integrates information that was previously maintained manually or in separate systems, and provides real-time information for inventory and warehouse management, financial activities, and centralized procurement. It provides more precise information about customer demand and inventory that helps managers make better decisions.

Since implementing SAP's enterprise system, Tasty's financial condition has become much healthier. The company has reduced inventory writedowns by 60 percent and price markdowns by 40 percent. Customer satisfaction has increased, as reflected in lower return rates and higher order fill rates. Tasty increased sales 11 percent without having to hire more staff.

Sources: "Tasty Baking Company,"and "Tasty Baking," www.mysap.com, accessed July 5, 2007 and "Tasty Baking Company 10-K Annual Report" filed March 14, 2007.

Tasty Banking Company's problems with its inventory and work processes illustrate the critical role of enterprise applications. The company's costs were too high because it did not have accurate and timely information to manage its inventory. Tasty also lost sales from missed shipments.

The chapter-opening diagram calls attention to important points raised by this case and this chapter. Tasty's fresh-baked products have a fairly short shelf life. Key business processes were manual, preventing the company from knowing exactly what items had shipped and what items were in inventory. Management couldn't access the data rapidly enough for daily decision making and planning.

Management could have chosen to add more employees or automate its existing business processes with newer technology. Instead, it decided to change many of its business processes to conform to industry-wide best practices and to implement an enterprise system. The enterprise system integrated financial, order entry, scheduling, and manufacturing information, and made it more widely available throughout the company. Data on manufacturing output and warehouse shipments are captured as soon as they are created. Instant availability of more timely and accurate information helps employees work more efficiently and helps managers make better decisions.

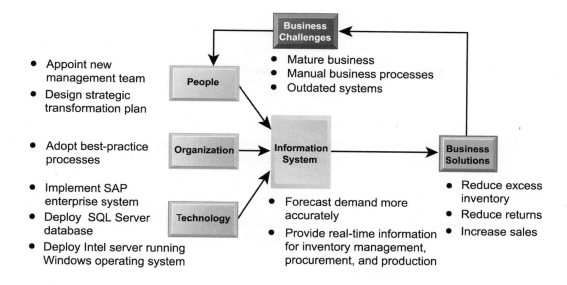

- Appoint new management team
- Design strategic transformation plan

- Adopt best-practice processes

- Implement SAP enterprise system
- Deploy SQL Server database
- Deploy Intel server running Windows operating system

People

Organization

Technology

Business Challenges

- Mature business
- Manual business processes
- Outdated systems

Information System

- Forecast demand more accurately
- Provide real-time information for inventory management, procurement, and production

Business Solutions

- Reduce excess inventory
- Reduce returns
- Increase sales

HEADS UP

This chapter focuses on how firms use enterprise-wide systems to achieve operational excellence, customer intimacy, and improved decision making. Enterprise systems and systems for supply chain management and customer relationship management help companies integrate information from many different parts of the business, forge closer ties with customers, and coordinate firm activities with those of suppliers and other business partners.

8.1 Enterprise Systems

Around the globe, companies are increasingly becoming more connected, both internally and with other companies. If you run a business, you will want to be able to react instantaneously when a customer places a large order or when a shipment from a supplier is delayed. You may also want to know the impact of these events on every part of the business and how the business is performing at any point in time, especially if you are running a large company. Enterprise systems provide the integration to make this possible. Let's look at how they work and what they can do for the firm.

WHAT ARE ENTERPRISE SYSTEMS?

Imagine that you had to run a business based on information from tens or even hundreds of different databases and systems, none of which could speak to one another? Imagine your company had 10 different major product lines, each produced in separate factories, and each with separate and incompatible sets of systems controlling production, warehousing, and distribution. At the very least, your decision making would often be based on manual hard copy reports, often out of date, and it would be difficult to really understand what is happening in the business as whole. You now have a good idea of why firms need a special enterprise system to integrate information.

Chapter 2 introduced enterprise systems, also known as enterprise resource planning (ERP) systems, which are based on a suite of integrated software modules and a common central database. The database collects data from many different divisions and departments in a firm, and from a large number of key business processes in manufacturing and production, finance and accounting, sales and marketing, and human resources, making the data available for applications that support nearly all of an organization's internal business activities. When new information is entered by one process, the information is made immediately available to other business processes (see Figure 8-1).

If a sales representative places an order for tire rims, for example, the system verifies the customer's credit limit, schedules the shipment, identifies the best shipping route, and reserves the necessary items from inventory. If inventory stock are insufficient to fill the order, the system schedules the manufacture of more rims, ordering the needed materials and components from suppliers. Sales and production forecasts are immediately updated. General ledger and corporate cash levels are automatically updated with the revenue and cost information from the order. Users can tap into the system and find out where that particular order was at any minute. Management can obtain information at any point in time about how the business was operating. The system can also generate enterprise-wide data for management analyses of product cost and profitability.

ENTERPRISE SOFTWARE

Enterprise software is built around thousands of predefined business processes that reflect best practices. Table 8.1 describes some of the major business processes supported by enterprise software.

Companies implementing this software would have to first select the functions of the system they wished to use and then map their business processes to the predefined business processes in the software. (One of our Learning Tracks shows how SAP enterprise software handles the procurement process for a new piece of equipment.) A firm would use configuration tables provided by the software to tailor a particular aspect of the system to the way it does business. For example, the firm could use these tables to select whether it wants to track revenue by product line, geographical unit, or distribution channel.

If the enterprise software does not support the way the organization does business, companies can rewrite some of the software to support the way their business processes work. However, enterprise software is unusually complex, and extensive customization may degrade system performance, compromising the information and process integration that are

Figure 8-1
How Enterprise Systems Work
Enterprise systems feature a set of integrated software modules and a central database that enables data to be shared by many different business processes and functional areas throughout the enterprise.

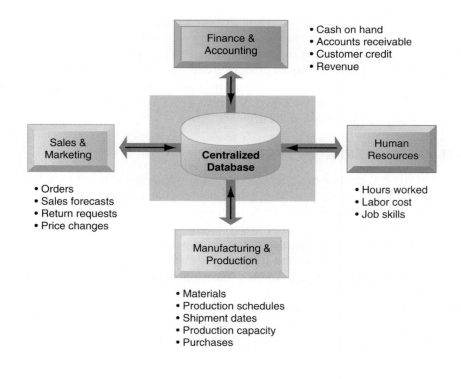

TABLE 8.1

Business Processes Supported by Enterprise Systems

Financial and accounting processes, including general ledger, accounts payable, accounts receivable, fixed assets, cash management and forecasting, product-cost accounting, cost center accounting, asset accounting, tax accounting, credit management, and financial reporting

Human resources processes, including personnel administration, time accounting, payroll, personnel planning and development, benefits accounting, applicant tracking, time management, compensation, workforce planning, performance management, and travel expense reporting

Manufacturing and production processes, including procurement, inventory management, purchasing, shipping, production planning, production scheduling, material requirements planning, quality control, distribution, transportation execution, and plant and equipment maintenance

Sales and marketing processes, including order processing, quotations, contracts, product configuration, pricing, billing, credit checking, incentive and commission management, and sales planning

the main benefits of the system. If companies want to reap the maximum benefits from enterprise software, they must change the way they work to conform to the business processes in the software.

Major enterprise software vendors include SAP, Oracle (with its acquisition PeopleSoft), and SSA Global. There are versions of enterprise software packages designed for small businesses and versions obtained through service providers over the Web. Although initially designed to automate the firm's internal "back-office" business processes, enterprise systems have become more externally oriented and capable of communicating with customers, suppliers, and other organizations.

BUSINESS VALUE OF ENTERPRISE SYSTEMS

Enterprise systems provide value both by increasing operational efficiency and by providing firmwide information to help managers make better decisions. Large companies with many operating units in different locations have used enterprise systems to enforce standard practices and data so that everyone does business the same way worldwide.

Coca-Cola, for instance, implemented a SAP enterprise system to standardize and coordinate important business processes in 200 countries. Lack of standard, companywide business processes prevented the company from leveraging its worldwide buying power to obtain lower prices for raw materials and from reacting rapidly to market changes.

Enterprise systems help firms respond rapidly to customer requests for information or products. Because the system integrates order, manufacturing, and delivery data, manufacturing is better informed about producing only what customers have ordered, procuring exactly the right amount of components or raw materials to fill actual orders, staging production, and minimizing the time that components or finished products are in inventory.

Enterprise software includes analytical tools for using data captured by the system to evaluate overall organizational performance. Enterprise system data have common standardized definitions and formats that are accepted by the entire organization. Performance figures mean the same thing across the company. Enterprise systems allow senior management to easily find out at any moment how a particular organizational unit is performing or to determine which products are most or least profitable.

8.2 Supply Chain Management Systems

If you manage a small firm that makes a few products or sells a few services, chances are you will have a small number of suppliers. You could coordinate your supplier orders and deliveries using a telephone and fax machine. But if you manage a firm that produces more complex products and services, then you will have hundreds of suppliers, and your suppliers will each have their own set of suppliers. Suddenly, you are in a situation where you will need to coordinate the activities of hundreds or even thousands of other firms in order to produce your products and services. Supply chain management systems, which we introduced in Chapter 2, are an answer to these problems of supply chain complexity and scale.

THE SUPPLY CHAIN

A firm's **supply chain** is a network of organizations and business processes for procuring raw materials, transforming these materials into intermediate and finished products, and distributing the finished products to customers. It links suppliers, manufacturing plants, distribution centers, retail outlets, and customers to supply goods and services from source through consumption. Materials, information, and payments flow through the supply chain in both directions.

Goods start out as raw materials and, as they move through the supply chain, are transformed into intermediate products (also referred to as components or parts), and finally, into finished products. The finished products are shipped to distribution centers and from there to retailers and customers. Returned items flow in the reverse direction from the buyer back to the seller.

Let's look at the supply chain for Nike sneakers as an example. Nike designs, markets, and sells sneakers, socks, athletic clothing, and accessories throughout the world. Its primary suppliers are contract manufacturers with factories in China, Thailand, Indonesia, Brazil, and other countries. These companies fashion Nike's finished products.

Nike's contract suppliers do not manufacture sneakers from scratch. They obtain components for the sneakers—the laces, eyelets, uppers, and soles—from other suppliers and then assemble them into finished sneakers. These suppliers in turn have their own suppliers. For example, the suppliers of soles have suppliers for synthetic rubber, suppliers for chemicals used to melt the rubber for molding, and suppliers for the molds into which to pour the rubber. Suppliers of laces have suppliers for their thread, for dyes, and for the plastic lace tips.

Figure 8-2 provides a simplified illustration of Nike's supply chain for sneakers; it shows the flow of information and materials among suppliers, Nike, and Nike's distributors, retailers, and customers. Nike's contract manufacturers are its primary suppliers. The suppliers of soles, eyelets, uppers, and laces are the secondary (Tier 2) suppliers. Suppliers to these suppliers are the tertiary (Tier 3) suppliers.

The *upstream* portion of the supply chain includes the company's suppliers, the suppliers' suppliers, and the processes for managing relationships with them. The *downstream* portion consists of the organizations and processes for distributing and delivering products to the final customers. Companies doing manufacturing, such as the Nike's contract suppliers of sneakers, also manage their own *internal supply chain* processes for transforming materials, components, and services furnished by their suppliers into finished products or intermediate products (components or parts) for their customers and for managing materials and inventory.

The supply chain illustrated in Figure 8-2 has been simplified. It only shows two contract manufacturers for sneakers and only the upstream supply chain for sneaker soles. Nike has hundreds of contract manufacturers turning out finished sneakers, socks, and athletic clothing, each with its own set of suppliers. The upstream portion of Nike's supply chain would actually comprise thousands of entities. Nike also has numerous distributors and many thousands of retail stores where its shoes are sold, so the downstream portion of its supply chain is also large and complex.

INFORMATION SYSTEMS AND SUPPLY CHAIN MANAGEMENT

Inefficiencies in the supply chain, such as parts shortages, underutilized plant capacity, excessive finished goods inventory, or high transportation costs, are caused by inaccurate or untimely information. For example, manufacturers may keep too many parts in inventory

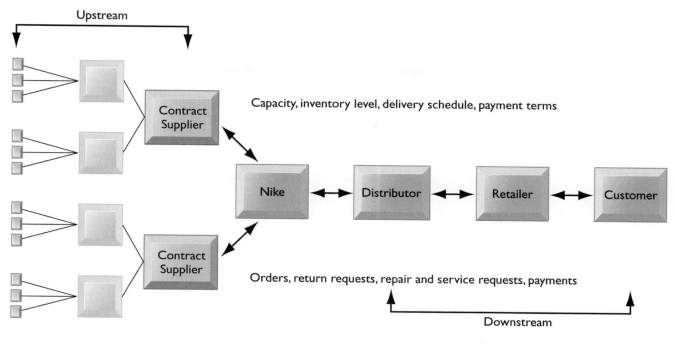

Tier 3   Tier 2   Tier I
Suppliers   Suppliers   Suppliers

Figure 8-2
Nike's Supply Chain
This figure illustrates the major entities in Nike's supply chain and the flow of information upstream and downstream to coordinate the activities involved in buying, making, and moving a product. Shown here is a simplified supply chain, with the upstream portion focusing only on the suppliers for sneakers and sneaker soles.

because they do not know exactly when they will receive their next shipments from their suppliers. Suppliers may order too few raw materials because they do not have precise information on demand. These supply chain inefficiencies waste as much as 25 percent of a company's operating costs.

If a manufacturer had perfect information about exactly how many units of product customers wanted, when they wanted them, and when they could be produced, it would be possible to implement a highly efficient **just-in-time** strategy. Components would arrive exactly at the moment they were needed, and finished goods would be shipped as they left the assembly line.

In a supply chain, however, uncertainties arise because many events cannot be foreseen—uncertain product demand, late shipments from suppliers, defective parts or raw materials, or production process breakdowns. To satisfy customers, manufacturers often deal with such uncertainties and unforeseen events by keeping more material or products in inventory than what they think they may actually need. The *safety stock* acts as a buffer for the lack of flexibility in the supply chain. Although excess inventory is expensive, low fill rates are also costly because business may be lost from canceled orders.

One recurring problem in supply chain management is the **bullwhip effect**, in which information about the demand for a product gets distorted as it passes from one entity to the next across the supply chain. A slight rise in demand for an item might cause different members in the supply chain—distributors, manufacturers, suppliers, secondary suppliers (suppliers' suppliers), and tertiary suppliers (suppliers' suppliers' suppliers)—to stockpile inventory so each has enough "just in case." These changes ripple throughout the supply chain, magnifying what started out as a small change from planned orders, creating excess inventory, production, warehousing, and shipping costs (see Figure 8-3).

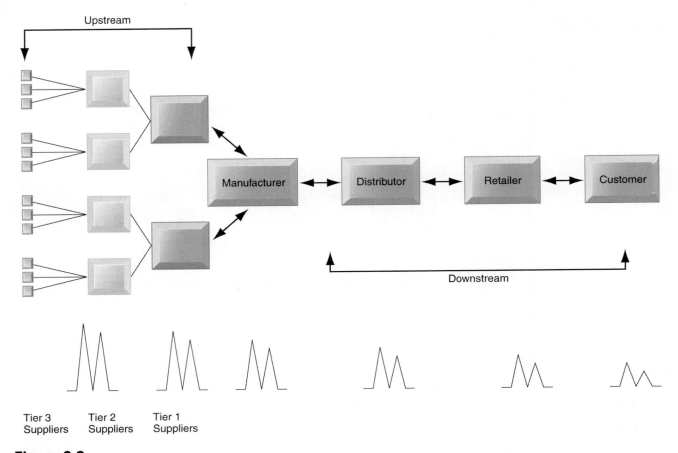

Figure 8-3
The Bullwhip Effect
Inaccurate information can cause minor fluctuations in demand for a product to be amplified as one moves further back in the supply chain. Minor fluctuations in retail sales for a product can create excess inventory for distributors, manufacturers, and suppliers.

For example, Procter & Gamble (P&G) found it had excessively high inventories of its Pampers disposable diapers at various points along its supply chain because of such distorted information. Although customer purchases in stores were fairly stable, orders from distributors would spike when P&G offered aggressive price promotions. Pampers and Pampers' components accumulated in warehouses along the supply chain to meet demand that did not actually exist. To eliminate this problem, P&G revised its marketing, sales, and supply chain processes and used more accurate demand forecasting.

The bullwhip is tamed by reducing uncertainties about demand and supply when all members of the supply chain have accurate and up-to-date information. If all supply chain members share dynamic information about inventory levels, schedules, forecasts, and shipments, they have more precise knowledge about how to adjust their sourcing, manufacturing, and distribution plans. Supply chain management systems provide the kind of information that helps members of the supply chain make better purchasing and scheduling decisions.

Supply Chain Management Software

Supply chain software is classified as either software to help businesses plan their supply chains (supply chain planning) or software to help them execute the supply chain steps (supply chain execution). **Supply chain planning systems** enable the firm to model its existing supply chain; generate demand forecasts for products, and develop optimal sourcing and manufacturing plans. Such systems help companies make better decisions such as determining how much of a specific product to manufacture in a given time period;

establishing inventory levels for raw materials, intermediate products, and finished goods; determining where to store finished goods; and identifying the transportation mode to use for product delivery.

For example, if a large customer places a larger order than usual or changes that order on short notice, it can have a widespread impact throughout the supply chain. Additional raw materials or a different mix of raw materials may need to be ordered from suppliers. Manufacturing may have to change job scheduling. A transportation carrier may have to reschedule deliveries. Supply chain planning software makes the necessary adjustments to production and distribution plans. Information about changes is shared among the relevant supply chain members so that their work can be coordinated. One of the most important—and complex—supply chain planning functions is **demand planning**, which determines how much product a business needs to make to satisfy all of its customers' demands.

Whirlpool Corporation, which produces washing machines, dryers, refrigerators, ovens and other home appliances, uses supply chain planning systems to make sure what it produces matches customer demand. The company uses supply chain planning software from i2 Technologies, which includes modules for Master Scheduling, Deployment Planning, and Inventory Planning. Whirlpool also installed i2's Web-based tool for Collaborative Planning, Forecasting, and Replenishment (CPFR) for sharing and combining its sales forecasts with those of its major sales partners. Improvements in supply chain planning helped Whirlpool increase availability of products in stock when customers needed them to 97 percent, while reducing the number of excess finished goods in inventory by 20 percent and forecasting errors by 50 percent (i2, 2007).

Supply chain execution systems manage the flow of products through distribution centers and warehouses to ensure that products are delivered to the right locations in the most efficient manner. They track the physical status of goods, the management of materials, warehouse and transportation operations, and financial information involving all parties. Haworth Incorporated's Transportation Management System and Warehouse Management System described in Chapter 2 are examples of such systems. Manugistics (acquired by JDA Software Group) and i2 Technologies are major supply chain management software vendors, and enterprise software vendors SAP and Oracle-PeopleSoft offer supply chain management modules.

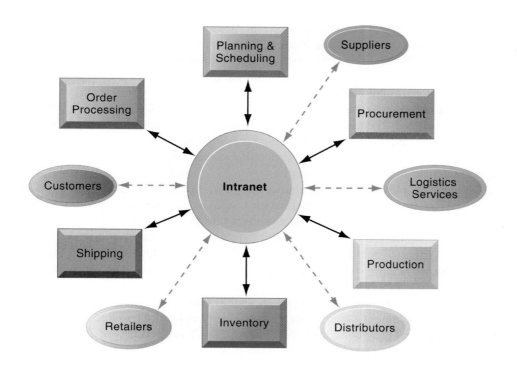

Figure 8-4
Intranets and Extranets for Supply Chain Management
Intranets integrate information from isolated business processes within the firm to help manage its internal supply chain. Access to these private intranets can also be extended to authorized suppliers, distributors, logistics services, and, sometimes, to retail customers to improve coordination of external supply chain processes.

GLOBAL SUPPLY CHAINS AND THE INTERNET

Before the Internet, supply chain coordination was hampered by the difficulties of making information flow smoothly among disparate internal supply chain systems for purchasing, materials management, manufacturing, and distribution. It was also difficult to share information with external supply chain partners because the systems of suppliers, distributors, or logistics providers were based on incompatible technology platforms and standards. Enterprise systems supply some integration of internal supply chain processes but they are not designed to deal with external supply chain processes.

Some supply chain integration is supplied inexpensively using Internet technology. Firms use intranets to improve coordination among their internal supply chain processes, and they use extranets to coordinate supply chain processes shared with their business partners (see Figure 8-4).

Using intranets and extranets, all members of the supply chain are instantly able to communicate with each other, using up-to-date information to adjust purchasing, logistics, manufacturing, packaging, and schedules. A manager will use a Web interface to tap into suppliers' systems to determine whether inventory and production capabilities match demand for the firm's products. Business partners will use Web-based supply chain management tools to collaborate online on forecasts. Sales representatives will access suppliers' production schedules and logistics information to monitor customers' order status.

Global Supply Chain Issues

More and more companies are entering international markets, outsourcing manufacturing operations and obtaining supplies from other countries as well as selling abroad. Their supply chains extend across multiple countries and regions. There are additional complexities and challenges to managing a global supply chain.

Global supply chains typically span greater geographic distances and time differences than domestic supply chains and have participants from a number of different countries. Although the purchase price of many goods might be lower abroad, there are often additional costs for transportation, inventory (the need for a larger buffer of safety stock), and local taxes or fees. Performance standards may vary from region to region or from nation to nation. Supply chain management may need to reflect foreign government regulations and cultural differences. All of these factors impact how a company takes orders, plans distribution, organizes warehousing, and manages inbound and outbound logistics throughout the global markets it services.

The Internet helps companies manage many aspects of their global supply chains, including sourcing, transportation, communications, and international finance. Today's apparel industry, for example, relies heavily on outsourcing to contract manufacturers in China and other low-wage countries. Apparel companies are starting to use the Web to manage their global supply chain and production issues.

Koret of California, a subsidiary of apparel maker Kellwood Co., uses e-SPS Web-based software to gain end-to-end visibility into its entire global supply chain. E-SPS features Web-based software for sourcing, work-in-progress tracking, production routing, product-development tracking, problem identification and collaboration, delivery-date projections, and production-related inquiries and reports.

As goods are being sourced, produced, and shipped, communication is required among retailers, manufacturers, contractors, agents, and logistics providers. Many, especially smaller companies, still share product information over the phone, via e-mail, or through faxes. These methods slow down the supply chain and also increase errors and uncertainty. With e-SPS, all supply chain members communicate through a Web-based system. If one of Koret's vendors makes a change in the status of a product, everyone in the supply chain sees the change.

In addition to contract manufacturing, globalization has encouraged outsourcing warehouse management, transportation management, and related operations to third-party logistics providers, such as UPS Supply Chain Services and American Port Services. These logistics services offer Web-based software to give their customers a better view of their global supply chains. American Port Services invested in software to synchronize processes with freight forwarders, logistics hubs, and warehouses around the world that it uses for managing its clients' shipments and inventory. Customers are able to check a secure Web site to monitor inventory and shipments, helping them run their global supply chains more efficiently.

Demand-Driven Supply Chains: From Push to Pull Manufacturing and Efficient Customer Response

In addition to reducing costs, supply chain management systems facilitate efficient customer response, enabling the workings of the business to be driven more by customer demand. (We introduced efficient customer response systems in Chapter 3.)

Earlier supply chain management systems were driven by a push-based model (also known as build-to-stock). In a **push-based model**, production master schedules are based on forecasts or best guesses of demand for products, and products are "pushed" to customers. With new flows of information made possible by Web-based tools, supply chain management more easily follows a **pull-based model**. In a pull-based model, also known as a demand-driven model or build-to-order, actual customer orders or purchases trigger events in the supply chain. Transactions to produce and deliver only what customers have ordered move up the supply chain from retailers to distributors to manufacturers and eventually to suppliers. Only products to fulfill these orders move back down the supply chain to the retailer. Manufacturers only use actual order-demand information to drive their production schedules and the procurement of components or raw materials, as illustrated in Figure 8-5. Wal-Mart's continuous replenishment system and Dell Computer's build-to-order system, both described in Chapter 3, are examples of the pull-based model.

The Internet and Internet technology make it possible to move from sequential supply chains, where information and materials flow sequentially from company to company, to concurrent supply chains, where information flows in many directions simultaneously among members of a supply chain network. Members of the network immediately adjust to changes in schedules or orders. Ultimately, the Internet could create a "digital logistics nervous system" throughout the supply chain (see Figure 8-6).

BUSINESS VALUE OF SUPPLY CHAIN MANAGEMENT SYSTEMS

You have just seen how supply chain management systems enable firms to streamline both their internal and external supply chain processes and provide management with more accurate information about what to produce, store, and move. By implementing a networked

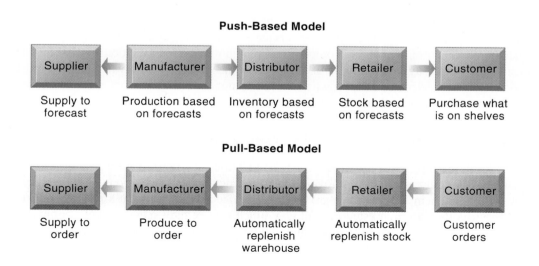

Push-Based Model

Supplier ← Manufacturer → Distributor → Retailer → Customer

Supply to forecast | Production based on forecasts | Inventory based on forecasts | Stock based on forecasts | Purchase what is on shelves

Pull-Based Model

Supplier ← Manufacturer ← Distributor ← Retailer ← Customer

Supply to order | Produce to order | Automatically replenish warehouse | Automatically replenish stock | Customer orders

Figure 8-5
Push- Versus Pull-Based Supply Chain Models
The difference between push- and pull-based models is summarized by the slogan "Make what we sell, not sell what we make."

Figure 8-6
The Future Internet-Driven Supply Chain
The future Internet-driven supply chain operates like a digital logistics nervous system.
It provides multidirectional communication among firms, networks of firms, and e-marketplaces so that entire networks of supply chain partners can immediately adjust inventories, orders, and capacities.

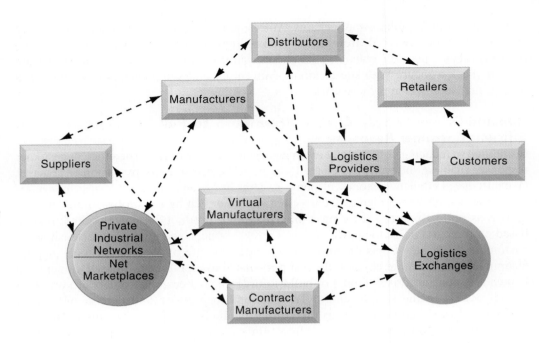

and integrated supply chain management system, companies match supply to demand, reduce inventory levels, improve delivery service, speed product time to market, and use assets more effectively.

Total supply chain costs represent the majority of operating expenses for many businesses and in some industries approach 75 percent of the total operating budget (Handfield and Nichols, 2002). Reducing supply chain costs may have a major impact on firm profitability.

In addition to reducing costs, supply chain management systems help increase sales. If a product is not available when a customer wants it, customers often try to purchase it from someone else. More precise control of the supply chain enhances the firm's ability to have the right product available for customer purchases at the right time, as illustrated by the previous discussion of Whirlpool.

8.3 Customer Relationship Management Systems

You have probably heard phrases such as "the customer is always right" or "the customer comes first." Today these words ring more true than ever. Because competitive advantage based on an innovative new product or service is often very short lived, companies are realizing that their only enduring competitive strength may be their relationships with their customers. Some say that the basis of competition has switched from who sells the most products and services to who "owns" the customer, and that customer relationships represent a firm's most valuable asset.

WHAT IS CUSTOMER RELATIONSHIP MANAGEMENT?

What kinds of information would you need to build and nurture strong, long-lasting relationships with customers? You would want to know exactly who your customers are, how to contact them, whether they are costly to service and sell to, what kinds of products and services they are interested in, and how much money they spend on your company. If you could, you would want to make sure you knew your each of your customers well, as if you were running a small-town store. And you would want to make your good customers feel special.

In a small business operating in a neighborhood, it is possible for business owners and managers to really know their customers on a personal, face-to-face basis. But in a large business operating on a metropolitan, regional, national, or even global basis, it is impossible to "know your customer" in this intimate way. In these kinds of businesses there are too many customers and too many different ways that customers interact with the firm (over the Web, the phone, fax, and face to face). It becomes especially difficult to integrate information from all theses sources and to deal with the large numbers of customers.

This is where customer relationship management systems help. Customer relationship management (CRM) systems, which we introduced in Chapter 2, capture and integrate customer data from all over the organization, consolidate the data, analyze the data, and then distribute the results to various systems and customer touch points across the enterprise. A **touch point** (also known as a contact point) is a method of interaction with the customer, such as telephone, e-mail, customer service desk, conventional mail, Web site, wireless device, or retail store.

Well-designed CRM systems provide a single enterprise view of customers that is useful for improving both sales and customer service. Such systems likewise provide customers with a single view of the company regardless of what touch point the customer uses (see Figure 8-7).

Good CRM systems provide data and analytical tools for answering questions such as these: "What is the value of a particular customer to the firm over his or her lifetime?" "Who are our most loyal customers?" (It can cost six times more to sell to a new customer than to an existing customer.) "Who are our most profitable customers?" and "What do these profitable customers want to buy?" Firms use the answers to these questions to acquire new customers, provide better service and support to existing customers, customize their offerings more precisely to customer preferences, and provide ongoing value to retain profitable customers.

CRM SOFTWARE

Commercial CRM software packages range from niche tools that perform limited functions, such as personalizing Web sites for specific customers, to large-scale enterprise applications that capture myriad interactions with customers, analyze them with sophisticated reporting tools, and link to other major enterprise applications, such as supply chain management and enterprise systems. The more comprehensive CRM packages contain modules for **partner relationship management (PRM)** and **employee relationship management (ERM)**.

**Figure 8-7
Customer Relationship Management (CRM Systems)**
CRM systems examine customers from a multifaceted perspective. These systems use a set of integrated applications to address all aspects of the customer relationship, including customer service, sales, and marketing.

PRM uses many of the same data, tools, and systems as customer relationship management to enhance collaboration between a company and its selling partners. If a company does not sell directly to customers but rather works through distributors or retailers, PRM helps these channels sell to customers directly. It provides a company and its selling partners with the ability to trade information and distribute leads and data about customers, integrating lead generation, pricing, promotions, order configurations, and availability. It also provides a firm with tools to assess its partners' performances so it can make sure its best partners receive the support they need to close more business.

ERM software deals with employee issues that are closely related to CRM, such as setting objectives, employee performance management, performance-based compensation, and employee training. Major CRM application software vendors include Oracle-owned Siebel Systems and PeopleSoft, SAP, and Salesforce.com.

Customer relationship management systems typically provide software and online tools for sales, customer service, and marketing. We briefly describe some of these capabilities.

Sales Force Automation (SFA)

Sales force automation modules in CRM systems help sales staff increase their productivity by focusing sales efforts on the most profitable customers, those who are good candidates for sales and services. CRM systems provide sales prospect and contact information, product information, product configuration capabilities, and sales quote generation capabilities. Such software can assemble information about a particular customer's past purchases to help the salesperson make personalized recommendations. CRM software enables sales, marketing, and delivery departments to easily share customer and prospect information. It increases each salesperson's efficiency in reducing the cost per sale as well as the cost of acquiring new customers and retaining old ones. CRM software also has capabilities for sales forecasting, territory management, and team selling.

Customer Service

Customer service modules in CRM systems provide information and tools to increase the efficiency of call centers, help desks, and customer support staff. They have capabilities for assigning and managing customer service requests.

One such capability is an appointment or advice telephone line: When a customer calls a standard phone number, the system routes the call to the correct service person, who inputs information about that customer into the system only once. Once the customer's data are in the system, any service representative can handle the customer relationship. Improved access to consistent and accurate customer information helps call centers handle more calls per day and decrease the duration of each call. Thus, call centers and customer service groups achieve greater productivity, reduced transaction time, and higher quality of service at lower cost. The customer is happier because he or she spends less time on the phone restating his or her problem to customer service representatives.

CRM systems may also include Web-based self-service capabilities: The company Web site can be set up to provide inquiring customers personalized support information as well as the option to contact customer service staff by phone for additional assistance.

Marketing

CRM systems support direct-marketing campaigns by providing capabilities for capturing prospect and customer data, for providing product and service information, for qualifying leads for targeted marketing, and for scheduling and tracking direct-marketing mailings or e-mail (see Figure 8-8). Marketing modules also include tools for analyzing marketing and customer data-identifying profitable and unprofitable customers, designing products and services to satisfy specific customer needs and interests, and identifying opportunities for cross-selling.

Cross-selling is the marketing of complementary products to customers. (For example, in financial services, a customer with a checking account might be sold a money market account or a home improvement loan.) CRM tools also help firms manage and execute marketing campaigns at all stages, from planning to determining the rate of success for each campaign.

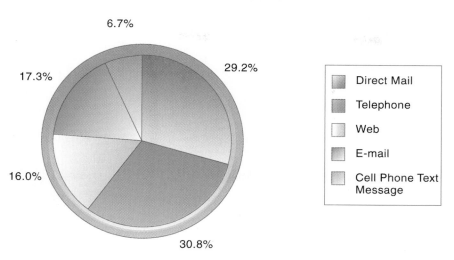

Responses by Channel for January 2008
Promotional Campaign

6.7%
17.3%
29.2%
16.0%
30.8%

Direct Mail
Telephone
Web
E-mail
Cell Phone Text Message

Figure 8-8
How CRM Systems Support Marketing
Customer relationship management software provides a single point for users to manage and evaluate marketing campaigns across multiple channels, including e-mail, direct mail, telephone, the Web, and wireless messages.

Figure 8-9 illustrates the most important capabilities for sales, service, and marketing processes that would be found in major CRM software products. Like enterprise software, this software is business-process driven, incorporating hundreds of business processes thought to represent best practices in each of these areas. To achieve maximum benefit, companies need to revise and model their business processes to conform to the best-practice business processes in the CRM software.

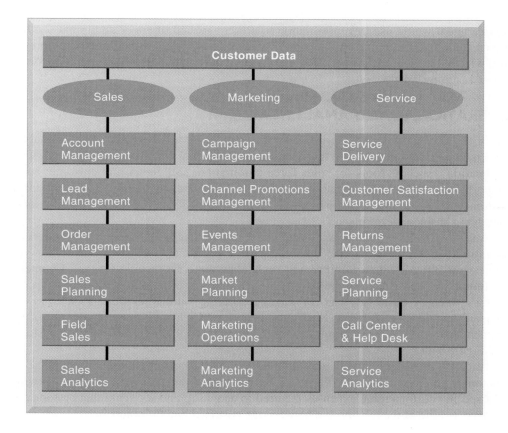

Figure 8-9
CRM Software Capabilities
The major CRM software products support business processes in sales, service, and marketing, integrating customer information from many different sources. Included are support for both the operational and analytical aspects of CRM.

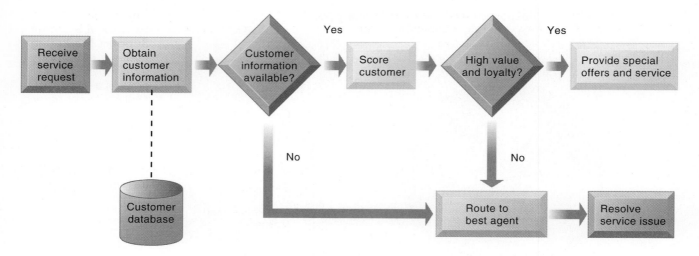

Figure 8-10
Customer Loyalty Management Process Map
This process map shows how a best practice for promoting customer loyalty through customer service would be modeled by customer relationship management software. The CRM software helps firms identify high-value customers for preferential treatment.

Figure 8-10 illustrates how a best practice for increasing customer loyalty through customer service might be modeled by CRM software. Directly servicing customers provides firms with opportunities to increase customer retention by singling out profitable long-term customers for preferential treatment. CRM software can assign each customer a score based on that person's value and loyalty to the company, and provide that information to help call centers route each customer's service request to agents who can best handle that customer's needs. The system would automatically provide the service agent with a detailed profile of that customer that includes his or her score for value and loyalty. The service agent would use this information to present special offers or additional service to the customer to encourage the customer to keep transacting business with the company. You will find more information on other best-practice business processes in CRM systems in our Learning Tracks.

OPERATIONAL AND ANALYTICAL CRM

All of the applications we have just described support either the operational or analytical aspects of customer relationship management. **Operational CRM** includes customer-facing applications, such as tools for sales force automation, call center and customer service support, and marketing automation. **Analytical CRM** includes applications that analyze customer data generated by operational CRM applications to provide information for improving business performance.

Analytical CRM applications are based on data warehouses that consolidate the data from operational CRM systems and customer touch points for use with online analytical processing (OLAP), data mining, and other data analysis techniques (see Chapter 5). Customer data collected by the organization might be combined with data from other sources, such as customer lists for direct-marketing campaigns purchased from other companies or demographic data. Such data are analyzed to identify buying patterns, to create segments for targeted marketing, and to pinpoint profitable and unprofitable customers (see Figure 8-11).

Another important output of analytical CRM is the customer's lifetime value to the firm. **Customer lifetime value (CLTV)** is based on the relationship between the revenue produced by a specific customer, the expenses incurred in acquiring and servicing that customer, and the expected life of the relationship between the customer and the company.

The Interactive Session on People describes how Alaska Airlines benefited from analytical CRM. To learn more about its customers and improve customer service, Alaska Airlines installed Oracle-Siebel Business Analytics software. As you read this case, try to identify the problem this company was facing; what alternative solutions were available to management; how well the chosen solution worked; and the people, organization, and technology issues that had to be addressed when developing the solution.

BUSINESS VALUE OF CUSTOMER RELATIONSHIP MANAGEMENT SYSTEMS

Companies with effective customer relationship management systems realize many benefits, including increased customer satisfaction, reduced direct-marketing costs, more effective marketing, and lower costs for customer acquisition and retention. Information from CRM systems increases sales revenue by identifying the most profitable customers and segments for focused marketing and cross-selling.

Customer churn is reduced as sales, service, and marketing better respond to customer needs. The **churn rate** measures the number of customers who stop using or purchasing products or services from a company. It is an important indicator of the growth or decline of a firm's customer base.

8.4 Enterprise Applications: New Opportunities and Challenges

Many firms have implemented enterprise systems and systems for supply chain management and customer relationship because they are such powerful instruments for achieving operational excellence and enhancing decision making. But precisely because they are so powerful in changing the way the organization works, they are challenging to implement. Let's briefly examine some of these challenges, as well as new ways of obtaining value from these systems.

ENTERPRISE APPLICATION CHALLENGES

Promises of dramatic reductions in inventory costs, order-to-delivery time, as well as more efficient customer response and higher product and customer profitability make enterprise

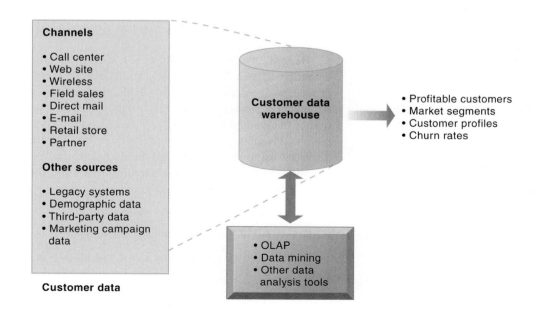

**Figure 8-11
Analytical CRM Data Warehouse**
Analytical CRM uses a customer data warehouse and tools to analyze customer data collected from the firm's customer touch points and from other sources.

INTERACTIVE SESSION: PEOPLE   Alaska Airlines Soars with Customer Relationship Management

The airline industry is very competitive and challenged by low profit margins and high fixed costs for wages, jet fuel, aircraft ownership and maintenance, and facilities. Customer loyalty achieved through strong customer service has been one of the best tools for airlines to fight these constrictions. Alaska Airlines continues to lead the way with award-winning customer service and dedication to technical innovation.

Formed in 1932, Alaska Airlines is a major passenger carrier in the Pacific Northwest, with an operating fleet of 114 jets. Over 17 million travelers flew on this airline in 2006. The company had been accumulating vast amounts of customer data for years, but could do very little with it.

Alaska Airlines' customer data existed in silos, stored in disparate systems across the company. The company was only able to use these data to track miles flown and price paid. To build a better and more relevant customer experience, the airline needed to integrate its customer data and find better ways to analyze them. Only then would the airline be able to gain a better understanding of customer trends and purchasing habits.

In its quest to provide better value for its customers than its competitors, Alaska Airlines invoked the same principles of continuous improvement that it applied to all of its business processes. These principles were based on the lean manufacturing system practiced to near perfection at Toyota (see the Chapter 2 Interactive Session on Organizations). The system led the airline to examine the processes of its customer service for holes rather than immediately searching for a CRM solution. The airline found that its executives were deprived of timely and accurate information that was crucial for strategic planning and meeting strategic objectives. With improved analytic capabilities, Alaska Airlines hoped to bring together its disparate data and use them to design marketing programs that would result in greater customer loyalty.

Alaska Airlines took a major step forward with its customer service in 2005 by selecting Oracle's Siebel Business Analytics software to complement its proprietary CRM system. The airline had evaluated solutions from four different vendors. Siebel was a good choice for a number of reasons. The system had the ability to access data from anywhere in the enterprise, including the Sabre distribution system the airline used to manage many of its reservations. The Siebel analytics software could also integrate the data from all these sources and provide actionable information rather than simply aggregate information. Up until this time, the airline had used an off-the-shelf SQL query and reporting tool that did not have such integration capabilities.

With Siebel Business Analytics, Alaska Airlines was able to create digital dashboards furnishing executives with customized views of information from disparate sources in a user-friendly manner. Among the other attractive elements of the Siebel system was the ease with which it could be implemented. Alaska Airlines looked for a solution that would not put a strain on its information systems department. Alaska Airlines deployed the system in about six weeks, and used Siebel's training, which proved to be very effective.

Also highly effective were Siebel's capabilities for measuring customer loyalty. Indicators for loyalty include how recently customers have flown, how frequently they fly, how much they have spent, the total mileage they have flown, and whether they are members of a frequent flier program. A customer's loyalty may depend on the flexibility of flight schedules, the ease of buying a ticket, check-in procedures, on-time rates, and seat selection. Siebel gave Alaska Airlines a clearer picture of all of these data points, highlighting the airline's strengths and weaknesses, and ultimately casting light on how well the company was serving its customers.

The new analytics helped Alaska Airlines improve another key component of customer service: providing customers with a highly relevant experience. By tracking customer interactions with the airline and combining that data with demographic data, the marketing department was in a better position to make targeted offers to customers. The Siebel system enabled Alaska Airlines to market more proactively while still respecting the privacy and time of customers. It also provided information for targeting special offers to specific customers to solicit business during "slow" travel periods.

Benefits from Siebel Business Analytics have extended to nearly all the operations and business processes at Alaska Airlines. CRM Director James Archuleta believes that it is really not the software solution or the data that have given Alaska Airlines a competitive advantage, but the people who are making the decisions using the software and the data. The employees are now better able to analyze customer behavior, identify trends, and design appropriate promotions.

Sources: "Alaska Airlines Soars in Meeting the Needs of More Than 17 Million Customers Annually," Oracle Customer Case Study, June 2006; Tony Kontzer, "Alaska Airlines Taps Siebel for Business Intelligence," *InformationWeek*, March 7, 2005; "Alaska Airlines Selects Siebel Business Analytics," *CRM Today*, March 8, 2005; and Alaska Air Group Inc. Report to the Securities and Exchange Commission on Form 10-K for the fiscal year ended December 31, 2006, accessed via www.alaskaair.com, July 9, 2007.

CASE STUDY QUESTIONS

1. What was the problem at Alaska Airlines in this story? How did the problem affect business performance?

2. What was the solution chosen by the airline? How well did this solution help the airline compete with its rivals?

3. What are the ways in which a typical customer interacts with an airline? List and briefly describe the customer data elements generated during these interactions (making a reservation, using frequent flyer miles, completing a flight.) How does information from CRM improve these interactions?

MIS IN ACTION

Go to www.alaskaair.com and answer the following questions:

1. What promotions is Alaska Airlines currently offering? (Promotions may be featured on the home page or found by using the Deals menu near the top of the page.)

2. What types of data do you think contributed to the airline's decision to offer these specific promotions?

3. Select a specific promotion or deal and make an educated guess as to why Alaska Airlines is featuring it. Who might be the target of this promotion? Do you think this is an effective marketing technique? Why or why not?

systems and systems for supply chain management and customer relationship management very alluring. But to obtain this value, you must clearly understand how your business has to change to use these systems effectively.

Enterprise applications involve complex pieces of software that are very expensive to purchase and implement. It might take a large company several years to complete a large-scale implementation of an enterprise system or a system for supply chain management or customer relationship management. The total implementation cost of a large system, including software, database tools, consulting fees, personnel costs, training, and perhaps hardware costs, might amount to four to five times the initial purchase price for the software.

Enterprise applications require not only deep-seated technological changes but also fundamental changes in the way the business operates. Companies must make sweeping changes to their business processes to work with the software. Employees must accept new job functions and responsibilities. They must learn how to perform a new set of work activities and understand how the information they enter into the system can affect other parts of the company. This requires new organizational learning.

Supply chain management systems require multiple organizations to share information and business processes. Each participant in the system may have to change some of its processes and the way it uses information to create a system that best serves the supply chain as a whole.

Some firms experienced enormous operating problems and losses when they first implemented enterprise applications because they did not understand how much organizational change was required. Kmart had trouble getting products to store shelves when it implemented supply chain management software from i2 Technologies in July 2000. The i2 software did not work well with Kmart's promotion-driven business model, which creates sharp spikes and drops in demand for products, and it was not designed to handle the massive number of products stocked in Kmart stores.

Hershey Foods' profitability dropped when it tried to implement SAP enterprise software, Manugistics SCM software, and Siebel Systems CRM software on a crash schedule in 1999 without thorough testing and employee training. Shipments ran two weeks late, and many customers did not receive enough candy to stock shelves during the busy

Halloween selling period. Hershey lost sales and customers during that period, although the new systems eventually improved operational efficiency.

The Interactive Session on Organizations describes another company's struggle to implement enterprise software. Invacare, a leading health care products manufacturer, had trouble making some of the modules of Oracle's E-Business Suite perform properly. Its experience illustrates some of the problems that occur when a company tries to make enterprise software work with its unique business processes.

Enterprise applications also introduce "switching costs." Once you adopt an enterprise application from a single vendor, such as SAP, Oracle, or others, it is very costly to switch vendors, and your firm becomes dependent on the vendor to upgrade its product and maintain your installation.

Enterprise applications are based on organization-wide definitions of data. You will need to understand exactly how your business uses its data and how the data would be organized in a customer relationship management, supply chain management, or enterprise system. CRM systems typically require some data cleansing work.

In a nutshell, it takes a lot of work to get enterprise applications to work properly. Everyone in the organization must be involved. Of course, for those companies that have successfully implemented CRM, SCM, and enterprise systems, the results have justified the effort.

EXTENDING ENTERPRISE SOFTWARE

Today many experienced business firms are looking for ways to wring more value from their enterprise applications. One way is to make them more flexible, Web-enabled, and capable of integration with other systems. The major enterprise software vendors have created what they call *enterprise solutions*, *enterprise suites*, or *e-business suites* to make their customer relationship management, supply chain management, and enterprise systems work closely together with each other, and link to systems of customers and suppliers. SAP's mySAP and Oracle's e-Business Suite are examples.

Service Platforms

Another way of leveraging investments in enterprise applications is to use them to create service platforms for new or improved business processes that integrate information from multiple functional areas. These enterprise-wide service platforms provide a greater degree of cross-functional integration than the traditional enterprise applications. A **service platform** integrates multiple applications from multiple business functions, business units, or business partners to deliver a seamless experience for the customer, employee, manager, or business partner.

For instance, the order-to-cash process involves receiving an order and seeing it all the way through obtaining payment for the order. This process begins with lead generation, marketing campaigns, and order entry, which are typically supported by CRM systems. Once the order is received, manufacturing is scheduled and parts availability is verified— processes that are usually supported by enterprise software. The order then is handled by processes for distribution planning, warehousing, order fulfillment, and shipping, which are usually supported by supply chain management systems. Finally, the order is billed to the customer, which is handled by either enterprise financial applications or accounts receivable. If the purchase at some point required customer service, customer relationship management systems would again be invoked.

A service such as order-to-cash requires data from enterprise applications and financial systems to be further integrated into an enterprise-wide composite process. To accomplish this, firms need software tools that use existing applications as building blocks for new cross-enterprise processes (see Figure 8-12). Enterprise application vendors provide middleware and tools that use XML and Web services for integrating enterprise applications with older legacy applications and systems from other vendors.

INTERACTIVE SESSION: ORGANIZATIONS

Invacare Struggles with Its Enterprise System Implementation

Invacare, headquartered in Elyria, Ohio, is the world's leading manufacturer and distributor of non-acute health care products, including wheel chairs, motorized scooters, home care beds, portable compressed oxygen systems, bath safety products, and skin and wound care products. It conducts business in over 80 countries, maintaining manufacturing plants in the United States and 11 other nations. Invacare sells its products primarily to over 25,000 home health care and medical equipment provider locations in the United States, Europe, Australia, New Zealand, and Canada, with the remainder of its sales primarily to government agencies and distributors. The company also distributes medical equipment and related supplies manufactured by other companies.

Invacare does not maintain much inventory. It manufactures most of its products to meet near-term demands, and it builds some of its products to order. It is constantly revising and expanding its numerous product lines.

In 2004, Invacare began working on replacing a collection of homemade legacy systems for purchase to payable processes with modules from Oracle's 11i E-Business Suite. Invacare had been using Oracle database software and had implemented the financial modules from Oracle E-Business Suite four years earlier. The company experienced no problems implementing and using the Oracle E-Business financial modules.

However, Invacare ran into problems when it went live with new order-to-cash modules, which let a company receive an order, allocate supplies to build it, and provide customer access to order status. Invacare's information systems specialists had tested the software under real-world business conditions and everyone felt the software was ready to be used in actual business operations.

When the new system went live in October 2005, the software would not perform properly. "Our systems were locking up," observed Greg Thompson, Invacare's Chief Financial Officer. Invacare call center representatives were unable to answer customer telephone calls in a timely manner. When they did talk with customers, they could not find complete information in the system about stock availability and shipment dates for products. The company was unable to ship products to customers within required lead times. Invacare's management never expected the implementation to be trouble-free, but it clearly did not foresee the magnitude of the problems it experienced with the new system.

As a result of the malfunctioning software, Invacare lost sales and had higher than usual levels of returned goods. It also incurred extra expenses for expediting product orders and for paying for employee overtime in its manufacturing, distribution, and customer-service departments. Two months of sales disruptions caused Invacare to cut its fourth-quarter 2005 revenue estimate to between $370 million and $380 million, lower than the previous year and well below the 2 percent sales increase the company had previously projected. Losses totaled $30 million for the quarter and extended into the first quarter of 2006.

The new system also changed some of the company's internal controls over financial reporting, and some of these controls did not function as intended. During the final quarter of 2005, Invacare had to perform a physical year-end inventory count for its North American operations, and take special steps to validate the figures used in financial statements.

According to Thompson, Invacare's problems were not caused by the Oracle software but by the way that Invacare configured the software and integrated its business processes with the new system. He and other Invacare management also believe that the company should have done more testing work.

Oracle worked closely with Invacare to resolve the problems, and Thompson was pleased by Oracle's response. "Oracle has been very helpful in working with our teams to resolve the issues we've identified," he said. Thompson anticipated all ordering and invoicing problems to be cleared up by early 2006.

Thompson also expressed hope that the new ERP system will provide enough value to offset the company's losses from the system. Invacare spent $20 million on its ERP implementation. The final phase of ERP implementation was scheduled for completion in late 2007 or early 2008, so it's still too early to tell whether Invacare's ERP system will justify its costs.

Sources: "Invacare Corporation 10-K Annual Report," filed March 3, 2007; Marc Songini, "Faulty ERP App Results in Shortfall for Medical Firm," *Computerworld*, January 2, 2006 and "Medical Products Maker Invacare Faces Rough ERP Ride," *Computerworld*, December 20, 2006.

CASE STUDY QUESTIONS

1. How did problems implementing the Oracle enterprise software affect Invacare's business performance?

2. What people, organization, and technology factors affected Invacare's ERP implementation?

3. If you were Invacare's management, what steps would you have taken to prevent these problems?

MIS IN ACTION

Visit the Oracle Web site and explore its section on Oracle E-Business Suite. Listen to one of Oracle's podcasts about this software. Then answer the following questions:

1. List and describe the capabilities of the order management modules.

2. How would the order management modules benefit a company such as Invacare? Describe how Invacare would use these capabilities.

Figure 8-12
Order-to-Cash Service
Order-to-cash is a composite process that integrates data from individual enterprise systems and legacy financial applications. The process must be modeled and translated into a software system using application integration tools.

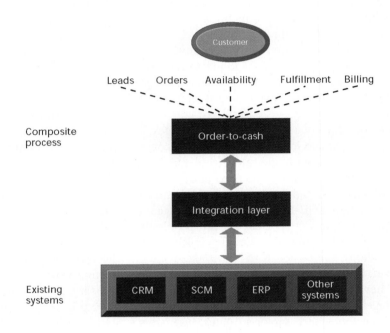

Increasingly, these new services will be delivered through portals. Today's portal products provide frameworks for building new composite services. Portal software can integrate information from enterprise applications and disparate in-house legacy systems, presenting it to users through a Web interface so that the information appears to be coming from a single source.

8.5 Hands-On MIS

The projects in this section give you hands-on experience evaluating supply chain management software for a real-world company, using database software to manage customer service requests, and evaluating supply chain management business services.

ACHIEVING OPERATIONAL EXCELLENCE: IDENTIFYING SUPPLY CHAIN MANAGEMENT SOLUTIONS

Software skills: Web browser and presentation software
Business skills: Locating and evaluating suppliers

In this project, you will use the Web to identify the best suppliers for one component of a dirt bike and appropriate supply chain management software for a small manufacturing company.

A growing number of Dirt Bikes's orders cannot be fulfilled on time because of delays in obtaining some important components and parts for its motorcycles, especially their fuel tanks. Complaints are mounting from distributors who fear losing sales if the dirt bikes they have ordered are delayed too long. Dirt Bikes's management has asked you to help it address some of its supply chain issues.

- Use the Internet to locate alternative suppliers for motorcycle fuel tanks. Identify two or three suppliers. Find out the amount of time and cost to ship a fuel tank (weighing about five pounds) by ground (surface delivery) from each supplier to Dirt Bikes in Carbondale, Colorado. Which supplier is most likely to take the shortest amount of time and cost the least to ship the fuel tanks?

- Dirt Bikes's management would like to know if there is any supply chain management software for a small business that would be appropriate for Dirt Bikes. Use the Internet to locate two supply chain management software providers for companies such as Dirt Bikes. Briefly describe the capabilities of the two software applications and indicate how they could help Dirt Bikes. Which supply chain management software product would be more appropriate for Dirt Bikes? Why?

- (Optional) Use electronic presentation software to summarize your findings for management.

IMPROVING DECISION MAKING: USING DATABASE SOFTWARE TO MANAGE CUSTOMER SERVICE REQUESTS

Software skills: Database design, querying, and reporting
Business skills: Customer service analysis

In this exercise, you will use database software to develop an application that tracks customer service requests and analyzes customer data to identify customers meriting priority treatment.

Prime Service is a large service company that provides maintenance and repair services for close to 1,200 commercial businesses in New York, New Jersey, and Connecticut. Its customers include businesses of all sizes. Customers with service needs call into its customer service department with requests for repairing heating ducts, broken windows, leaky roofs, broken water pipes, and other problems. The company assigns each request a number and writes down the service request number, identification number of the customer account, the date of the request, the type of equipment requiring repair, and a brief description of the problem. The service requests are handled on a first-come-first-served basis. After the service work has been completed, Prime calculates the cost of the work, enters the price on the service request form, and bills the client.

Management is not happy with this arrangement because the most important and profitable clients—those with accounts of more than $70,000—are treated no differently from its clients with small accounts. It would like to find a way to provide its best customers with better service. Management would also like to know which types of service problems occur the most frequently so that it can make sure it has adequate resources to address them.

Prime Service has a small database with client account information, which can be found on the Laudon Web site for Chapter 8. A sample is illustrated below. It includes fields for the account ID, company (account) name, street address, city, state, ZIP code, account size (in dollars), contact last name, contact first name, and contact telephone number. The contact is the name of the person in each company who is responsible for contacting Prime about maintenance and repair work. Use your database software to design a solution that would enable Prime's customer service representatives to identify the most important customers so that they could receive priority service. Your solution will require more than one table. Populate your database with at least 15 service requests. Create several reports that would be of inter-

	ACCT_ID	NAME	ADDR	CITY	STATE	ZIP	DOLLAR_SIZE	CONTACT_FIRS	CONTACT_LAS	PHONE
▶	1	Able Association	123 Axion Stree	Albertown	NY	11444-4444	$50,000	Alison	Ableson	(209) 111-1111
	2	Briggs Bakery	123 Boggs Stre	Brimstone	CT	11200-1234	$94,000	Barry	Berryman	(210) 111-1212
	3	Constant Carriers	31 Carmine Le	Carver	NJ	20111-1212	$200,000	Carl	Compress	(202) 123-1222
	4	Darning Drapers	1234 Dante Ave	Driblle	NY	12345-6849	$60,000	Delilah	Dilman	(209) 123-4321
	5	Eagle Engineers	Eagle Park	Edmonton	CT	11222-2313	$45,000	Eddie	Exeter	(210) 212-2233
*	(AutoNumber)						$0			

est to management, such as a list of the highest- and lowest-priority accounts or a report showing the most frequently occurring service problems. Create a report showing customer service representatives which service calls they should respond to first on a specific date.

ACHIEVING OPERATIONAL EXCELLENCE: EVALUATING SUPPLY CHAIN MANAGEMENT SERVICES

Software skills: Web browser and presentation software
Business skills: Evaluating supply chain management services

Trucking companies no longer merely carry goods from one place to another. Some also provide supply chain management services to their customers and help them manage their information. In this project, you will use the Web to research and evaluate two of these business services.

Investigate the Web sites of two companies, J.B. Hunt and Schneider Logistics, to see how these companies' services can be used for supply chain management. Then respond to the following questions:

- What supply chain processes can each of these companies support for their clients?
- How can customers use the Web sites of each company to help them with supply chain management?
- Compare the supply chain management services provided by these companies. Which company would you select to help your firm manage it supply chain? Why?

LEARNING TRACKS

The following Learning Tracks provide content relevant to topics covered in this chapter:

1. SAP Business Process Map
2. Business Processes in Supply Chain Management and Supply Chain Metrics
3. Best Practices Business Processes in CRM Software

Review Summary

1 **How do enterprise systems help businesses achieve operational excellence?**
Enterprise software is based on a suite of integrated software modules and a common central database. The database collects data from and feeds the data into numerous applications that can support nearly all of an organization's internal business activities. When new information is entered by one process, the information is made available immediately to other business processes.

Enterprise systems support organizational centralization by enforcing uniform data standards and business processes throughout the company and a single unified technology platform. The firmwide data generated by enterprise systems helps managers evaluate organizational performance.

2 How do supply chain management systems coordinate planning, production, and logistics with suppliers? Supply chain management systems automate the flow of information among members of the supply chain so they can use it to make better decisions about when and how much to purchase, produce, or ship. More accurate information from supply chain management systems reduces uncertainty and the impact of the bullwhip effect.

Supply chain management software includes software for supply chain planning and for supply chain execution. Internet technology facilitates the management of global supply chains by providing the connectivity for organizations in different countries to share supply chain information. Improved communication among supply chain members also facilitates efficient customer response and movement toward a demand-driven model.

3 How do customer relationship management systems help firms achieve customer intimacy? Customer relationship management (CRM) systems integrate and automate customer-facing processes in sales, marketing, and customer service, providing an enterprise-wide view of customers. Companies can use this customer knowledge when they interact with customers to provide them with better service or to sell new products and services. These systems also identify profitable or nonprofitable customers or opportunities to reduce the churn rate.

The major customer relationship management software packages provide capabilities for both operational CRM and analytical CRM. They often include modules for managing relationships with selling partners (partner relationship management) and for employee relationship management.

4 What are the challenges posed by enterprise applications? Enterprise applications are difficult to implement. They require extensive organizational change, large new software investments, and careful assessment of how these systems will enhance organizational performance. Enterprise applications cannot provide value if they are implemented atop flawed processes or if firms do not know how to use these systems to measure performance improvements. Employees require training to prepare for new procedures and roles. Attention to data management is essential.

5 How are enterprise applications used in platforms for new cross-functional services? Service platforms integrate data and processes from the various enterprise applications (customer relationship management, supply chain management, and enterprise systems), as well as from disparate legacy applications to create new composite business processes. Web services tie various systems together. The new services are delivered through enterprise portals, which can integrate disparate applications so that information appears to be coming from a single source.

Key Terms

Analytical CRM, 282
Bullwhip effect, 273
Churn rate, 283
Cross-selling, 280
Customer lifetime value (CLTV), 282
Demand planning, 275

Employee relationship management (ERM), 279
Just-in-time, 273
Operational CRM, 282
Partner relationship management (PRM), 279
Pull-based model, 277
Push-based model, 277

Service platform, 286
Supply chain, 272
Supply chain execution systems, 275
Supply chain planning systems, 274
Touch point, 279

Review Questions

1. How do enterprise systems help businesses achieve operational excellence?
- Define an enterprise system and explain how enterprise software works.
- Describe how enterprise systems provide value for a business.

2. How do supply chain management systems coordinate planning, production, and logistics with suppliers?
- Define a supply chain and identify each of its components.
- Explain how supply chain management systems help reduce the bullwhip effect and how they provide value for a business.
- Define and compare supply chain planning systems and supply chain execution systems.
- Describe the challenges of global supply chains and how Internet technology can help companies manage them better.
- Distinguish between a push-based and pull-based model of supply chain management and explain how contemporary supply chain management systems facilitate a pull-based model.

3. How do customer relationship management systems help firms achieve customer intimacy?
- Define customer relationship management and explain why customer relationships are so important today.
- Describe how partner relationship management (PRM) and employee relationship management (ERM) are related to customer relationship management (CRM).
- Describe the tools and capabilities of customer relationship management software for sales, marketing, and customer service.
- Distinguish between operational and analytical CRM.

4. What are the challenges posed by enterprise applications?
- List and describe the challenges posed by enterprise applications
- Explain how these challenges can be addressed.

5. How are enterprise applications used in platforms for new cross-functional services?
- Define a service platform and describe the tools for integrating data from enterprise applications.

Discussion Questions

1. Supply chain management is less about managing the physical movement of goods and more about managing information. Discuss the implications of this statement.

2. If a company wants to implement an enterprise application, it had better do its homework. Discuss the implications of this statement.

Video Case

You will find a video case illustrating some of the concepts in this chapter on the Laudon Web site along with questions to help you analyze the case.

Teamwork

Analyzing Enterprise Application Vendors

With a group of three or four students, use the Web to research and evaluate the products of two vendors of enterprise application software. You could compare, for example, the SAP and Oracle enterprise systems, the supply chain management systems from i2 and JDA Software's Manugistics, or the customer relationship management systems of Oracle's Siebel Systems and Salesforce.com. Use what you have learned from these companies' Web sites to compare the software packages you have selected in terms of business functions supported, technology platforms, cost, and ease of use. Which vendor would you select? Why? Would you select the same vendor for a small business as well as a large one? If possible, use electronic presentation software to present your findings to the class.

BUSINESS PROBLEM-SOLVING CASE

Sunsweet Growers Cultivates Its Supply Chain

Sunsweet Growers Inc. is an agricultural cooperative headquartered in Yuba City, California, and is the largest handler of dried tree fruits in the world. Sunsweet processes and markets 40,000 cases of dried fruit every day. In addition to dried cranberries, apricots, pineapples, and many other fruits, Sunsweet produces more than 50,000 tons of prunes annually for over one-third of the global market.

With 400 member-owners of orchards located primarily in the Sacramento and San Joaquin valleys of central California, Sunsweet has unique supply chain management issues. Most companies are constrained by either demand or supply, but not both. But in Sunsweet's case, both demand and supply are determined by factors that the company does not control. Sunsweet cannot control its supply, which is determined by the weather and growing season, or its demand, which is set by the market.

Like many manufacturers, Sunsweet sees spikes in demand for its products around holidays, such as Christmas and Easter. The growers harvest their fruit in August, September, and October, triggering a furious effort at the processing plant to dry, store, and package the fruit for delivery to retail stores. However, with the source limited to 400 growers in one geographic area, the supply of fruit varies significantly from year to year.

When demand peaked around the holidays, Sunsweet often found itself shelling out extra money to pay workers overtime in order to fulfill its orders. Scheduling and planning the production and distribution of dozens of varieties and sizes of fruits in packaging bearing 20 different languages was a complex operation.

Sunsweet needed to improve scheduling and line utilization while reducing inventory, transportation costs, and order lead time. To address these supply chain management issues, Sunsweet adopted a sales and operations planning (S&OP) program, which seeks to balance demand and supply on a regular and formal basis and keep them balanced as conditions change. S&OP helps businesses routinely handle unexpected events such as unanticipated demand, shortages in supply, and production disruptions.

Prior to implementing S&OP, Sunsweet managed its supply chain with a paper-based spreadsheet system. That system became increasingly inadequate as the business grew more complex due to outdated data, difficulty in supporting collaboration, and a lack of powerful tools for representing the business problem. Sunsweet's planners spent too much managing the spreadsheets, and performing tasks such as cost analysis often required up to three days of work. The company wanted to perform planning and analysis tasks in hours, not days, and the ability to model multiple versions of a production plan to schedule its plant production resources more efficiently. Sunsweet found the solution in the Zemeter S&OP supply chain management suite from Supply Chain Consultants.

With Zemeter replacing the old Excel-based system, Sunsweet revamped its forecast meetings. Previously, each group involved in the supply chain went to those monthly meetings with their own set of data and little understanding of any other department's data. One of the first, and most important, steps that Sunsweet took under its new S&OP project was to scrub all of its data and unify them in one database. Using one set of data was key to getting all supply chain participants to work most effectively with each other for the good of the whole cooperative.

Of course, getting line manufacturing supervisors, customer service representatives, schedulers, salespeople, engineers, and others on board with the new program required careful change management. Sunsweet's managers realized that it was important to show the value of S&OP early in the transformation. Such value would be demonstrated in the first phase of a five-phase implementation—demand visibility. By its very nature, improving demand visibility necessitated better communication and decision making at every level. It was also during this phase that all of Sunsweet's various groups first gained access to the same data and each other's goals.

Sunsweet needed just four weeks to implement the demand visibility phase. By its end, Sunsweet had also established parameters for training users, tested the scalability of the program, and initiated the program without disrupting the existing workflow.

The next phase of the S&OP project was demand planning. This phase provided Sunsweet's complete forecasting solution, which, in addition to providing a demand plan routinely, tracked and maintained improvements to the plan. Specific capabilities included creating and updating statistical forecasts, preparing plans for price changes and promotions, and analyzing demand data such as orders and shipments. Zemeter's Demand Planner module analyzes input from multiple sources and outputs the best plan from the proposals. Sunsweet gained an objective method of balancing sales forecasts and operational plans. Demand Planner also helped Sunsweet improve the accuracy of its operational budget.

The demand planning phase included implementation of an early-warning system that dispenses e-mail alerts to the proper employees under various circumstances. The alerts give departments a head start in reviewing metrics when events dictate that plans might need to be altered to keep operations in sync. For example, an increase in new customers or a change in the most popular items for a particular customer would be cause for a review. Continuous planning taking into account the latest available data became a key element of the company's business processes.

Inventory planning was the third phase of the S&OP project. The new inventory systems calculated current inventory and used data about inventory history to detect trends and predict problems before they caused significant losses.

In phase four, Sunsweet addressed supply planning. The cooperative added a Supply Planner module to raise the effectiveness of planning across its network of suppliers, with particular attention to maintaining a uniform labor force throughout the year. By taking into consideration the limits on production and supply in conjunction with a 15-month rolling forecast, Sunsweet evened out its production requirements instead of basing them on seasonal demands.

The fifth phase of the implementation was finite scheduling, which had to do with the daily operational activities at the cooperative's plant headquarters. Finite scheduling handles fruit-size issues, material availability, overtime and downtime, changeover times on the packing lines, and other shift and workday oriented issues.

Prior to implementing the S&OP program, Sunsweet left tasks such as sales forecasting, operational planning, inventory planning, and finite scheduling to monthly meetings using summarized sales information. These meetings resulted in a tendency to meet sales forecasts and customer requirements with little consideration for operational costs. With Zemeter in place, Sunsweet moved its planning processes to weekly meetings using the latest information. With everyone sharing the most up-to-date information about finite scheduling, daily production, and inventory levels, Sunsweet was better positioned to meet customer demands without throwing off operational costs and long-term production plans.

Sunsweet achieved its return on investment in its S&OP system in about half the time it anticipated—six and a half months—while the implementation was still ongoing. Sunsweet improved the accuracy of its forecasts by 15 to 20 percent while reducing the amount of time necessary to make forecasts. The early warning e-mail alert system moved up responses to problems such as supply shortages and order discrepancies by two to three weeks. Planning and cost analysis tasks that used to take days using spreadsheets are now completed in four to five hours. Information from the system enabled Sunsweet to reduce the number of production lines, production line changeovers, inventory, and transportation costs, and cut overtime from 30 percent down to 10 percent.

Another by-product of the program was a more efficient and collaborative environment. The integration of data across the company ushered in cross-functional metrics, such as measurements of how well current inventory supports forecasts.

Once the S&OP program was implemented, several obstacles remained. In some cases, the problem was modern supply chain software, which is very liberal in permitting custom configurations. As the circumstances surrounding an organization's business processes change, workers may find it difficult to make the necessary changes in the custom-configured software. Instead, with easy access to desktop productivity tools, they introduce ad-hoc solutions into the process, thereby weakening the mainstream system. Sunsweet mitigated this concern by incorporating the desktop into the integrated S&OP system. Employees were still able to work with data on their desktops, but the scrubbed and validated data on the system remained reliable.

In some supply chain planning implementations, only a few planners are responsible for the bulk of the application setup. When these planners move on to other tasks or other jobs, they take the knowledge of the initial setup methodology with them. Sunsweet avoided this complication by involving a wide swath of the organization in the planning phases. Furthermore, a large portion of the organization maintains access to the integrated data.

Another complexity of S&OP is that it addresses problems in the supply chain before they surface. This can create a false sense of security and lead to the conclusion that planning is no longer a critical issue. Rather than remaining dedicated to continuous planning, an organization may drop it as a high priority and begin to streamline the process. Sunsweet still confronts this issue regularly, looking for ways to stress that continuous refinement and improvement are paramount to a successful S&OP.

Successful S&OP programs include processes to sustain them. Among these are continuing education and training for departments whose decisions impact the supply chain; encouragement of management training;

ensuring transparency of decisions affecting the supply chain and supply chain data; development of a structure and budget that leave room for responding to crises; and recognition of achievements.

Today, Sunsweet is more successful at deploying its assets to satisfy demand projections. The cooperative has reduced inventory and transportations costs.

Sources: Harold Upton and Harpal Singh, "Balanced S&OP: Sunsweet Growers's Story," *Supply Chain Management Review*, March 1, 2007; Jane Lee, "Making Your Supply Chain a Competitive Advantage: Implementing S&OP," www.supplychainbrain.com, accessed June 6, 2007; Amy Roach Partridge, "Unwrapping Seasonality Challenges," www.inboundlogistics.com, November 2006; Chris Chiappinelli, "Sales and Operations Planning: The New Crystal Ball," www.managingautomation.com, January 22, 2007; "About Sunsweet," www.sunsweet.com, accessed June 6, 2007; and Jim Wasserman, "Growing Globally," *The Sacramento Bee*, December 4, 2005.

Case Study Questions

1. What are the constraints on Sunsweet Growers's supply chain?
2. What problems did Sunsweet Growers encounter as a result of these constraints? What was their business impact?
3. Describe sales and operations planning. What are its principles? What disciplines does it involve?
4. How did S&OP software help Sunsweet Growers better manage its supply chain?
5. What additional ways can you think of for Sunsweet Growers to ease its supply chain concerns?

E-commerce: Digital Markets, Digital Goods

CHAPTER 9

STUDENT LEARNING OBJECTIVES

After completing this chapter, you will be able to answer the following questions:

1. What are the unique features of e-commerce, digital markets, and digital goods?

2. How has Internet technology changed business models?

3. What are the various types of e-commerce, and how has e-commerce has changed consumer retailing and business-to-business transactions?

4. What is the role of m-commerce in business, and what are the most important m-commerce applications?

5. What are the principal payment systems for electronic commerce?

CHAPTER OUTLINE

PHOTOBUCKET: THE NEW FACE OF E-COMMERCE

Photobucket may very well be the most important site on the Web that few people understand. Its name is well-chosen. The purpose of the site is to create a "bucket" for storing your photos that allows you to show them anywhere else you want on the Internet.

While rival photo sites such as Kodak Gallery, Snapfish, or Shutterfly, are known for storing photos and providing services for making prints or picture books, Photobucket is best known for linking. Founded in 2003 by Alex Welch and Darren Crystal, Photobucket pioneered the concept of linking media from one Web site to multiple online sites. You store your photo or video there, and then link it to whatever other site you want—your MySpace page, an eBay auction page, or your personal blog. Photobucket makes it so easy to post photos to blogs or social networking sites that you can do it in one step.

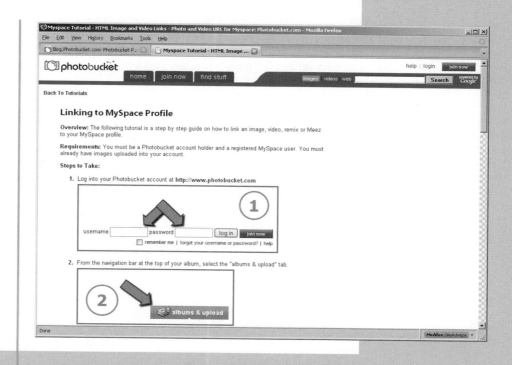

Photobucket lets users create a Remix—a presentation of photos or videos that have been mixed with music, graphics, special effects, and captions. These presentations take just seconds to make. Photobucket will also store avatars that people have created for use in Internet forums and let its users share their presentations via e-mail, instant messaging, and mobile devices.

What if you've outgrown MySpace and you want to switch to Facebook? No problem. You just link the photos you want to use that are stored in Photobucket to your new Web site. According to Photobucket CEO Alex Welch, "We're fad-proof...If one social networking site goes away and another comes up, the user just moves, but their content stays with Photobucket...We focus very much on not being a community. We let the communities build around us."

Photobucket is free for basic use and storage up to 1 gigabyte, but charges $25 per year for a premium subscription that includes extra storage space (up to 5 gigabytes) and the ability to store videos more than 5 minutes long. Photobucket also receives revenue from displaying advertisements to users when they manage their accounts. About 80 percent of Photobucket's revenue comes from these ads.

With these capabilities, Photobucket has become the largest and fastest-growing photo-sharing service on the Web. As of July 2007 it had 48 million users, compared to 14 million a year earlier, and 17 million unique visitors per month. Photobucket hosts over 3 billion images, and its visitors come to manage that photo and video stream. About 300,000 unique Web sites link back to Photobucket.

Photobucket's ability to attract and keep visitors makes the company a very hot target for advertisers and a very lucrative business. So lucrative, that it was acquired by Fox Interactive Media in July 2007.

Sources: David Kirkpatrick, "The Biggest Web Site You've Never Heard Of," *CNNMoney.com*, March 28, 2007; Brad Stone, "Fox Interactive Nears Deal to Buy Photobucket," *The New York Times*, May 8, 2007; and Walter Mossberg, "How the Big Photo-Sharing Sites Stack Up," *The Wall Street Journal*, August 1, 2007.

Photobucket very much epitomizes the "new" e-commerce. Selling physical goods on the Internet is still important, but much of the excitement and interest now centers around services—services for photo sharing, social networking, sharing music, sharing ideas, and software applications that you can put on your Web page or blog. Photobucket, MySpace, Facebook, Stylehive, Digg, and del.icio.us are examples. The ability to link with other users and with other Web sites has unleashed a huge wave of new businesses built around linking and sharing.

The chapter-opening diagram calls attention to important points raised by this case and this chapter. Photobucket was created to answer these questions: How do we make money on the Web today? How can we take advantage of more widespread broadband access to the Internet and to new Web 2.0 technologies? Photobucket's founders Alex Welch and Darren Crystal created a new service for people who want to share their photos and videos or store them in a single convenient location for use in other Web sites. Photobucket pioneered in linking media from one Web site to multiple online sites. The company's goal is to provide the easiest and most reliable Web site for sharing and linking all the media people use in their online lives. By making it so easy and inexpensive to store photos and link them to other Web sites, Photobucket has huge numbers of visitors and advertisers, and a continuing stream of revenue.

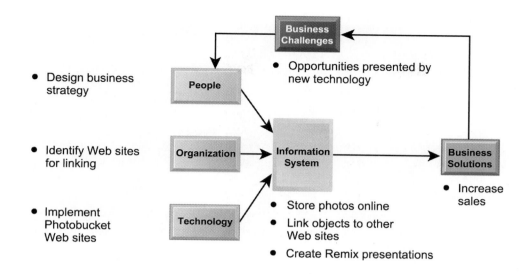

- Design business strategy
- Identify Web sites for linking
- Implement Photobucket Web sites

Business Challenges
- Opportunities presented by new technology

People

Organization

Technology

Information System
- Store photos online
- Link objects to other Web sites
- Create Remix presentations

Business Solutions
- Increase sales

HEADS UP

This chapter focuses on e-commerce and how businesses use e-commerce to achieve operational excellence and customer intimacy. E-commerce is also transforming business and industries. E-commerce advertising revenues are growing faster than other forms of advertising. Every large company, and most medium and small companies, have Web sites that speak directly to customers. If you work in business today, you need to know about e-commerce.

9.1 Electronic Commerce and the Internet

Have you ever purchased music over the Web? Have you ever used the Web to search for information about your sneakers before you bought them in a retail store? If so, you've participated in e-commerce. So have hundreds of millions of people around the globe. And although most purchases still take place through traditional channels, e-commerce continues to grow rapidly and to transform the way many companies do business.

E-COMMERCE TODAY

E-commerce refers to the use of the Internet and the Web to transact business. More formally, e-commerce is about digitally enabled commercial transactions between and among organizations and individuals. For the most part, this means transactions that occur over the Internet and the Web. Commercial transactions involve the exchange of value (e.g., money) across organizational or individual boundaries in return for products and services.

E-commerce began in 1995 when one of the first Internet portals, Netscape.com, accepted the first ads from major corporations and popularized the idea that the Web could be used as a new medium for advertising and sales. No one envisioned at the time what would turn out to be an exponential growth curve for e-commerce retail sales, which tripled and doubled in the early years. Only since 2006 has consumer e-commerce "slowed" to a 25-percent annual growth rate (Figure 9-1).

Figure 9-1
The Growth of E-commerce
Retail e-commerce revenues have grown exponentially since 1995 and have only recently "slowed" to a very rapid 25 percent annual increase, which is projected to remain at this growth rate through 2010.

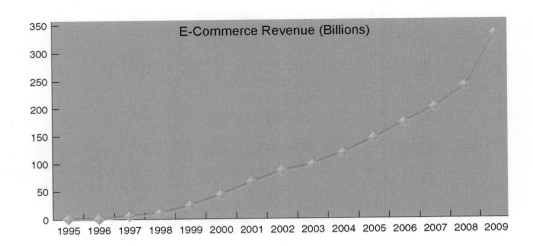

Mirroring the history of many technological innovations, such as the telephone, radio, and television, the very rapid growth in e-commerce in the early years created a market bubble in e-commerce stocks. Like all bubbles, the "dot-com" bubble burst in March 2001. A large number of e-commerce companies failed during this process. Yet for many others, such as Amazon, eBay, Expedia, and Google, the results have been more positive: soaring revenues, fine-tuned business models that produce profits, and rising stock prices. By 2006, e-commerce revenues returned to solid growth again.

- Online consumer sales increased by more than 25 percent in 2007 to an estimated $225 billion (including travel services), with 116 million people purchasing online and an additional 17 million shopping (gathering information) but not purchasing (eMarketer, 2007).
- The number of individuals online in the United States expanded to 170 million in 2007, up from 147 million in 2004. In the world, over one billion people are now connected to the Internet. Growth in the overall Internet population has spurred growth in e-commerce.
- On the average day, 92 million people go online, 76 million send e-mail, 11 million write on their blogs, 4 million share music on peer-to-peer networks, 26 million work on their social network profile, 26 million visit Wikipedia, and 3 million use the Internet to rate a person, product, or service (Pew Internet, 2007).
- B2B e-commerce—use of the Internet for business-to-business commerce—expanded 17 percent to more than $3.6 trillion and continues to strengthen.

The e-commerce revolution is still unfolding. Individuals and businesses will increasingly use the Internet to conduct commerce as more products and services come online and households switch to broadband telecommunications. More industries will be transformed by e-commerce, including travel reservations, music and entertainment, news, software, education, and finance. Table 9.1 highlights these new e-commerce developments.

WHY E-COMMERCE IS DIFFERENT

Why has e-commerce grown so rapidly? The answer lies in the unique nature of the Internet and the Web. Simply put, the Internet and e-commerce technologies are much more rich and powerful than previous technology revolutions. Table 9.2 on page 302 describes the unique features of the Internet and Web as a commercial medium. Let's explore each of these unique features in more detail.

Ubiquity

In traditional commerce, a marketplace is a physical place, such as a retail store, that you visit to transact business. E-commerce is ubiquitous, meaning that is it available just about everywhere, at all times. It makes it possible to shop from your desktop, at home, at work, or

TABLE 9.1

New Developments in E-commerce

BUSINESS TRANSFORMATION

- The first wave of e-commerce transformed the business world of books, music, and air travel. In the second wave, eight new industries are facing a similar transformation scenario: advertising, telephones, movies, television, jewelry, real estate, hotels, bill payments, and software.

- The breadth of e-commerce offerings grows, especially in the services economy of social networking, travel, information clearinghouses, entertainment, retail apparel, appliances, and home furnishings.

- The online demographics of shoppers broaden to match that of ordinary shoppers.

- Pure e-commerce business models will be refined further to achieve higher levels of profitability, whereas traditional retail brands, such as Sears, JCPenney, L.L.Bean, and Wal-Mart, will use e-commerce to retain their dominant retail positions.

- Small businesses and entrepreneurs continue to flood the e-commerce marketplace, often riding on the infrastructures created by industry giants, such as Amazon, eBay, and Overture.

TECHNOLOGY FOUNDATIONS

- Wireless Internet connections (Wi-Fi, WiMax, and 3G mobile phone) grow rapidly.

- New digital gadgets appear as powerful, handheld devices that support cellular telephone and music, with Wi-Fi connections. Podcasting takes off as a new medium for distribution of video, radio, and user-generated content.

- The Internet broadband foundation becomes stronger in households and businesses as transmission prices fall. More than 52 million households had broadband cable or DSL access to the Internet in 2007—about 43 percent of all households (eMarketer, 2007).

- RSS grows to become a major new form of user-controlled information distribution that rivals e-mail in some applications.

- New Internet-based models of computing, such as .NET and Web services, expand B2B opportunities.

NEW BUSINESS MODELS EMERGE

- More than half the Internet user population join an online social network, contribute to social bookmarking sites, create blogs, and share photos. Together these sites create a massive online audience that is attractive to marketers.

- The advertising business model is severely disrupted as Google and other technology players such as Microsoft and Yahoo! seek to dominate online advertising, and expand into offline ad brokerage for television and newspapers.

- Newspapers and other traditional media adopt online interactive models but are losing advertising revenues to the online players.

even from your car, using mobile commerce. The result is called a **marketspace**—a marketplace extended beyond traditional boundaries and removed from a temporal and geographic location.

From a consumer point of view, ubiquity reduces transaction costs—the costs of participating in a market. To transact business, it is no longer necessary that you spend time or money traveling to a market, and much less mental effort is required to make a purchase.

Global Reach

E-commerce technology permits commercial transactions to cross cultural and national boundaries far more conveniently and cost effectively than is true in traditional

E-commerce Technology Dimension	Business Significance
Ubiquity. Internet/Web technology is available everywhere: at work, at home, and elsewhere via mobile devices, anytime.	The marketplace is extended beyond traditional boundaries and is removed from a temporal and geographic location. "Marketspace" created; shopping can take place anywhere. Customer convenience is enhanced, and shopping costs are reduced.
Global Reach. The technology reaches across national boundaries, around the Earth.	Commerce is enabled across cultural and national boundaries seamlessly and without modification. The marketspace includes, potentially, billions of consumers and millions of businesses worldwide.
Universal Standards. There is one set of technology standards, namely Internet standards.	There is one set of technical standards across the globe so that disparate computer systems can easily communicate with each other.
Richness. Video, audio, and text messages are possible.	Video, audio, and text marketing messages are integrated into a single marketing message and consumer experience.
Interactivity. The technology works through interaction with the user.	Consumers are engaged in a dialog that dynamically adjusts the experience to the individual, and makes the consumer a co-participant in the process of delivering goods to the market.
Information Density. The technology reduces information costs and raises quality.	Information processing, storage, and communication costs drop dramatically, whereas currency, accuracy, and timeliness improve greatly. Information becomes plentiful, cheap, and more accurate.
Personalization/Customization. The technology allows personalized messages to be delivered to individuals as well as groups.	Personalization of marketing messages and customization of products and services are based on individual characteristics.
Social Technology. The technology promotes user content generation and social networking.	New Internet social and business models enable user content creation and distribution, and support social networks.

commerce. As a result, the potential market size for e-commerce merchants is roughly equal to the size of the world's online population (more than 1 billion, and growing rapidly).

In contrast, most traditional commerce is local or regional—it involves local merchants or national merchants with local outlets. Television and radio stations and newspapers, for instance, are primarily local and regional institutions with limited, but powerful, national networks that can attract a national audience but not easily cross national boundaries to a global audience.

Universal Standards

One strikingly unusual feature of e-commerce technologies is that the technical standards of the Internet and, therefore, the technical standards for conducting e-commerce are universal standards. They are shared by all nations around the world and enable any computer to link with any other computer regardless of the technology platform each is using. In contrast, most traditional commerce technologies differ from one nation to the next. For instance, television and radio standards differ around the world, as does cell telephone technology.

The universal technical standards of the Internet and e-commerce greatly lower **market entry costs**—the cost merchants must pay simply to bring their goods to market. At the same time, for consumers, universal standards reduce **search costs**—the effort required to find suitable products.

Richness

Information **richness** refers to the complexity and content of a message. Traditional markets, national sales forces, and small retail stores have great richness: they are able to provide personal, face-to-face service using aural and visual cues when making a sale. The richness of traditional markets makes them powerful selling or commercial environments. Prior to the development of the Web, there was a trade-off between richness and reach: the larger the audience reached, the less rich the message. The Web makes it possible to deliver rich messages with text, audio, and video simultaneously to large numbers of people.

Interactivity

Unlike any of the commercial technologies of the twentieth century, with the possible exception of the telephone, e-commerce technologies are interactive, meaning they allow for two-way communication between merchant and consumer. Traditional television, for instance, cannot ask viewers any questions or enter into conversations with them, and it cannot request that customer information be entered into a form. In contrast, all of these activities are possible on an e-commerce Web site. Interactivity allows an online merchant to engage a consumer in ways similar to a face-to-face experience but on a massive, global scale.

Information Density

The Internet and the Web vastly increase **information density**—the total amount and quality of information available to all market participants, consumers and merchants alike. E-commerce technologies reduce information collection, storage, processing, and communication costs while greatly increasing the currency, accuracy, and timeliness of information.

Information density in e-commerce markets make prices and costs more transparent. **Price transparency** refers to the ease with which consumers can find out the variety of prices in a market; **cost transparency** refers to the ability of consumers to discover the actual costs merchants pay for products.

There are advantages for merchants as well. Online merchants can discover much more about consumers than in the past. This allows merchants to segment the market into groups who are willing to pay different prices and permits the merchants to engage in **price discrimination**—selling the same goods, or nearly the same goods, to different targeted groups at different prices. For instance, an online merchant can discover a consumer's avid interest in expensive, exotic vacations and then pitch high-end vacation plans to that consumer at a premium price, knowing this person is willing to pay extra for such a vacation. At the same time, the online merchant can pitch the same vacation plan at a lower price to a more price-sensitive consumer. Information density also helps merchants differentiate their products in terms of cost, brand, and quality.

Personalization/Customization

E-commerce technologies permit **personalization**: Merchants can target their marketing messages to specific individuals by adjusting the message to a person's name, interests, and past purchases. The technology also permits **customization**—changing the delivered product or service based on a user's preferences or prior behavior. Given the interactive nature of e-commerce technology, much information about the consumer can be gathered in the marketplace at the moment of purchase. With the increase in information density, a great deal of information about the consumer's past purchases and behavior can be stored and used by online merchants.

The result is a level of personalization and customization unthinkable with traditional commerce technologies. For instance, you may be able to shape what you see on television by selecting a channel, but you cannot change the content of the channel you have chosen. In contrast, the *Wall Street Journal Online* allows you to select the type of news stories you want to see first and gives you the opportunity to be alerted when certain events happen.

Social Technology: User Content Generation and Social Networking

In contrast to previous technologies, the Internet and e-commerce technologies have evolved to be much more social by allowing users to create and share with a worldwide community content in the form of text, videos, music, or photos. Using these forms of communication, users are able to create new social networks and strengthen existing ones.

All previous mass media in modern history, including the printing press, use a broadcast model (one-to-many) where content is created in a central location by experts (professional writers, editors, directors, and producers), and audiences are concentrated in huge numbers to consume a standardized product. The new Internet and e-commerce empower users to create and distribute content on a large scale, and permit users to program their own content consumption. The Internet provides a many-to-many model of mass communications which is unique.

KEY CONCEPTS IN E-COMMERCE: DIGITAL MARKETS AND DIGITAL GOODS IN A GLOBAL MARKETPLACE

The location, timing, and revenue models of business are based in some part on the cost and distribution of information. The Internet has created a digital marketplace where millions of people all over the world are able to exchange massive amounts of information directly, instantly, and for free. As a result, the Internet has changed the way companies conduct business and increased their global reach.

The Internet shrinks information asymmetry. An **information asymmetry** exists when one party in a transaction has more information that is important for the transaction than the other party. That information helps determine their relative bargaining power. In digital markets, consumers and suppliers can "see" the prices being charged for goods, and in that sense digital markets are said to be more "transparent" than traditional markets.

For example, until auto retailing sites appeared on the Web, there was a pronounced information asymmetry between auto dealers and customers. Only the auto dealers knew the manufacturers' prices, and it was difficult for consumers to shop around for the best price. Auto dealers' profit margins depended on this asymmetry of information. Today's consumers have access to a legion of Web sites providing competitive pricing information, and three-fourths of U.S. auto buyers use the Internet to shop around for the best deal. Thus, the Web has reduced the information asymmetry surrounding an auto purchase. The Internet has also helped businesses seeking to purchase from other businesses reduce information asymmetries and locate better prices and terms.

Digital markets are very flexible and efficient because they operate with reduced search and transaction costs, lower **menu costs** (merchants' costs of changing prices), price discrimination, and the ability to change prices dynamically based on market conditions. In **dynamic pricing**, the price of a product varies depending on the demand characteristics of the customer or the supply situation of the seller.

These markets may either reduce or increase switching costs, depending on the nature of the product or service being sold, and they may cause some extra delay in gratification. Unlike a physical market, you can't immediately consume a product such as clothing purchased over the Web (although immediate consumption is possible with digital music downloads and other digital products.)

Digital markets provide many opportunities to sell directly to the consumer, bypassing intermediaries, such as distributors or retail outlets. Eliminating intermediaries in the distribution channel can significantly lower purchase transaction costs. To pay for all the steps in a traditional distribution channel, a product may have to be priced as high as 135 percent of its original cost to manufacture.

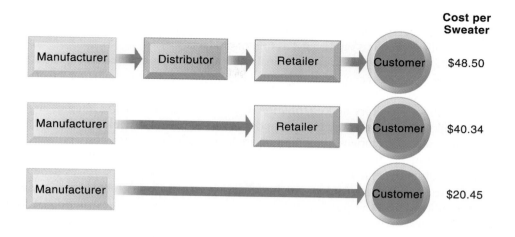

Figure 9-2
The Benefits of Disintermediation to the Consumer
The typical distribution channel has several intermediary layers, each of which adds to the final cost of a product, such as a sweater. Removing layers lowers the final cost to the consumer.

Figure 9-2 illustrates how much savings result from eliminating each of these layers in the distribution process. By selling directly to consumers or reducing the number of intermediaries, companies are able to raise profits while charging lower prices. The removal of organizations or business process layers responsible for intermediary steps in a value chain is called **disintermediation**.

Disintermediation is affecting the market for services. Airlines and hotels operating their own reservation sites online earn more per ticket because they have eliminated travel agents as intermediaries. Table 9.3 summarizes the differences between digital markets and traditional markets.

Digital Goods

The Internet digital marketplace has greatly expanded sales of digital goods. **Digital goods** are goods that can be delivered over a digital network. Music tracks, video, software, newspapers, magazines, and books can all be expressed, stored, delivered, and sold as

TABLE 9.3

Digital Markets Compared to Traditional Markets

	Digital Markets	Traditional Markets
Information asymmetry	Asymmetry reduced	Asymmetry high
Search costs	Low	High
Transaction costs	Low (sometimes virtually nothing)	High (time, travel)
Delayed gratification	High (or lower in the case of a digital good)	Lower: purchase now
Menu costs	Low	High
Dynamic Pricing	Low cost, instant	High cost, delayed
Price discrimination	Low cost, instant	High cost, delayed
Market segmentation	Low cost, moderate precision	High cost, less precision
Switching costs	Higher/lower (depending on product characteristics)	High
Network effects	Strong	Weaker
Disintermediation	More possible/likely	Less possible/unlikely

purely digital products. Currently, most of these products are sold as physical goods, for example, CDs, DVDs, and hard-copy books. But the Internet offers the possibility of delivering all these products on demand as digital products.

In general, for digital goods, the marginal cost of producing another unit is about zero (it costs nothing to make a copy of a music file). However, the cost of producing the original first unit is relatively high—in fact, it is nearly the total cost of the product because there are few other costs of inventory and distribution. Costs of delivery over the Internet are very low; marketing costs remain the same; and pricing can be highly variable. (On the Internet, the merchant can change prices as often as desired because of low menu costs.)

The impact of the Internet on the market for these kinds of digital goods is nothing short of revolutionary, and we see the results around us every day. Businesses dependent on the physical products for sales—such as bookstores, book publishers, music labels, and film studios—face the possibility of declining sales and even destruction of their businesses. Newspapers and magazines are losing readers to the Internet, and losing advertisers. Record label companies are losing sales to Internet piracy and record stores are going out of business. Video rental firms, such as Blockbuster, based on a physical DVD market and physical stores, have lost sales to NetFlix using an Internet model. Hollywood studios also face the prospect that Internet pirates will distribute their products as digital streams, bypassing Hollywood's monopoly on DVD rentals and sales, which now accounts for more than half of industry film revenues (see the Chapter 3 ending case). Table 9.4 describes digital goods and how they differ from traditional physical goods.

INTERNET BUSINESS MODELS

The bottom-line result of these changes in the economics of information is nearly a revolution in commerce, with many new business models appearing and many old business models no longer tenable. Table 9.5 describes some of the most important Internet business models that have emerged. All, in one way or another, use the Internet to add extra value to existing products and services or to provide the foundation for new products and services.

Communication and Social Networking

Some of these new business models take advantage of the Internet's rich communication capabilities. eBay is an online auction forum that uses e-mail and other interactive features of the Web. The system accepts bids entered on the Internet, evaluates the bids, and notifies the highest bidder. eBay collects a small commission on each listing and sale. eBay has become so popular that its site serves as a huge trading platform for other companies, hosting hundreds of thousands of "virtual storefronts." The Interactive Session on Organizations discusses eBay and its business model in greater detail.

TABLE 9.4

How the Internet Changes the Markets for Digital Goods

	Digital Goods	Traditional Goods
Marginal cost/unit	Zero	Greater than zero , high
Cost of production	High (most of the cost)	Variable
Copying cost	Approximately zero	Greater than zero, high
Distributed delivery cost	Low	High
Inventory cost	Low	High
Marketing cost	Variable	Variable
Pricing	More variable (bundling, random pricing games)	Fixed, based on unit costs

TABLE 9.5

Internet Business Models

Category	Description	Examples
Virtual storefront	Sells physical products directly to consumers or to individual businesses.	Amazon.com RedEnvelope.com
Information broker	Provides product, pricing, and availability information to individuals and businesses. Generates revenue from advertising or from directing buyers to sellers.	Edmunds.com Kbb.com Insweb.com Realtor.com
Transaction broker	Saves users money and time by processing online sales transactions and generating a fee each time a transaction occurs. Also provides information on rates and terms.	E*Trade.com Expedia.com
Online marketplace	Provides a digital environment where buyers and sellers can meet, search for products, display products, and establish prices for those products. Can provide online auctions or reverse auctions in which buyers submit bids to multiple sellers to purchase at a buyer-specified price as well as negotiated or fixed pricing. Can serve consumers or B2B e-commerce, generating revenue from transaction fees.	eBay.com Priceline.com ChemConnect.com
Content provider	Creates revenue by providing digital content, such as digital news, music, photos, or video, over the Web. The customer may pay to access the content, or revenue may be generated by selling advertising space.	WSJ.com GettyImages.com iTunes.com Games.com
Social network	Provides an online meeting place where people with similar interests can communicate and find useful information.	Linkedin.com MySpace.com iVillage.com
Portal	Provides initial point of entry to the Web along with specialized content and other services.	Yahoo.com MSN.com StarMedia.com
Service provider	Provides Web 2.0 applications such as photo sharing, video sharing, and user-generated content (in blogs and social networking sites) as services. Provides other services such as online data storage and backup.	Google Maps Photobucket.com YouTube.com Xdrive.com

Business-to-business auctions have also emerged. GoIndustry, for instance, features Web-based auction services for business-to-business sales of industrial equipment and machinery.

The Internet has created online communities where people with similar interests are able to communicate with each other from many different locations. A major source of revenue

INTERACTIVE SESSION: ORGANIZATIONS   Can eBay Continue Growing?

eBay advertises itself as the place to get "it," whatever it may be. "It" used to be goods and services purchased through its gigantic online auction and marketplace services. eBay derives the bulk of its revenue from fees and commissions associated with its trading services. Since the company was founded in 1995 by Pierre Omidyar and Jeff Skoll, the company has been profitable, and now boasts over 233 million registered users. In 2006, eBay users exchanged $50 billion worth of goods and were headed toward $60 billion in 2007.

A portion of eBay's revenue comes from direct advertising on the site, as well as end-to-end service providers whose services increase the ease and speed of eBay transactions. Deals with Yahoo! and Google will bring large streams of advertising revenue to eBay for the first time in 2007.

Not long ago, eBay's growth strategy focused on expansion in geography and scope and on continuing innovation to enhance the variety and appeal of products on its sites. More recently, after failing to take control of the Asian online auction market, the company's growth strategy has focused on diversification. eBay is now trying to develop and acquire new products and services that encompass all the activities people perform on the Internet. It is creating a diversified portfolio of companies with a hand in each of the Internet's big cash pots: shopping, communicating, search, and entertainment.

PayPal, whose service enables the exchange of money between individuals over the Internet, brings additional transaction-based fee revenue. eBay is banking on PayPal becoming the standard payment method for online transactions. The service already receives 40 percent of its $11.4 billion business from payment transactions that are not associated with eBay. PayPal has performed very well for eBay, even after Google Checkout emerged as a possible competitor.

In mid-2005, eBay agreed to buy Shopping.com, an online shopping comparison site, for $620 million. In September of that year, eBay acquired VoIP service provider Skype Technologies for $2.6 billion. Skype provides a service for free or low-cost voice calls over the Internet. eBay is betting heavily that Internet telephony will become an integral part of the e-commerce experience and accelerate trade on its Web site. The service could potentially generate $3.5 billion in revenue from markets that eBay traditionally had trouble penetrating, such as real estate, travel, new-car sales, and expensive collectibles. Those markets require more communication among buyers

and sellers than eBay currently offers, and Skype will provide voice communication services to help.

eBay also paid $310 million for the ticket reselling Web site StubHub, acquired a 25 percent stake in classified ad site Craigslist, and purchased Kurant, now ProStores, whose technology helps users set up online stores. With these moves, eBay extended its reach to new segments of e-commerce. The company is also working on new ways to bring its services to users, rather than expecting them to visit eBay.com. In the Web 2.0 era, users are spending their time on blogs, wikis, and mobile sites rather than on singularly purposed sites.

eBay recognized that today's Web surfers seek entertainment, socializing, and networking. Sites such as Facebook, MySpace, and YouTube have become the Web's gathering places. In response, eBay began developing tools and services that promote e-commerce anywhere on the Web. For example, the company is testing a tool that enables users to monitor their auctions without visiting eBay.com through the use of an embedded software widget called To Go. eBay is also having discussions with MySpace to allow eBay listings on MySpace pages. eBay wants to make it easier for all users to display eBay listings on their personal Web sites.

Some analysts report that while many of eBay's individual acquisitions appear successful, their overall cost is not justified because they haven't created the synergy that was intended. Analysts and shareholders don't necessarily agree that diversification is the correct strategy for growth. They are especially concerned that this expansion has come at the expense of eBay's core business, auctions.

Shopping was responsible for almost 70 percent of the company's revenue in 2006, but sales growth has dropped from 40 percent annually to 23 percent. New users are no longer joining the site at the same rate they used to join. The overall volume of items listed is also down nearly 4 percent. Sales have suffered as a result of sellers filling their eBay stores with slow-selling and undesirable merchandise, or pricing their quality merchandise at unattractive prices. Fraud, identity theft, and abuse are still big problems for the company, but eBay is paying more attention to them.

In light of these problems, eBay is trying to improve its site's user experience to keep its loyal customer base happy. It is reducing the clutter of its Web page design, especially the home page, which has been described as one of the most confusing and cluttered in the industry. The overhaul is also enhancing the feedback criteria that buyers use to rate sellers and make sellers' shipping costs more transparent. eBay is looking to improve product search results and give buyers more guidance in finding the products they are looking for without having to scour through hundreds of listings.

One area in which eBay seems to be ahead of the curve is in its Web services architecture. eBay has opened up its application programming interfaces (APIs), free of charge, to a growing community of independent developers. This network of developers builds applications that connect to eBay's core computing platform and help the site grow in new ways. For example, one such program sends auction status information to buyers on their mobile phones.

Keeping the community happy is of utmost importance to the future of eBay. A loyal user base

may be the company's most valuable asset, and one which competitors will be challenged to replicate. But even if eBay deals successfully with these issues, how much more can it grow? As Global Crown Capital analyst Martin Pyykkonen put it, "They're not really screwing up, and it's not that Meg Whitman needs to go or they've gone in the wrong direction. It's just that there are some finite limits to growth, and they're reaching that."

Sources: Catherine Holahan, "Going, Going…Everywhere," *Business Week*, June 18, 2007, "eBay's Changing Identity," *Business Week*, April 23, 2007, and "eBay Holds Its Turf Against Google," January 25, 2007; Edward Cone, "Inside eBay's Innovation Machine," *CIO Insight*, December 6, 2006; Brad Stone, "Stirring Up the Cubicles at eBay," *The New York Times*, February 21, 2007; Rob Hof, "Is eBay on the Mend," *Business Week*, April 18, 2007; The Associated Press, "eBay Rethinks Its Ways as It Enters Middleage," accessed via Cnn.com, June 18, 2007; and Bob Tedeschi, "eBay Moves to Recharge Its Auctions," *The New York Times*, June 18, 2007.

CASE STUDY QUESTIONS

1. What is eBay's business model and business strategy? How successful has it been? What are the problems that eBay is currently facing?

2. How is eBay trying to solve these problems? Are these good solutions? Are there any other solutions that eBay should consider?

3. What people, organization, and technology factors play a role in eBay's response to its problems?

4. Will eBay be successful in the long run? Why or why not?

MIS IN ACTION

Go to the home page of eBay at www.eBay.com and answer the following questions:

1. How would you describe eBay's home page? Does it appear cluttered? Does the site seem like it would be easy to use? What suggestions would you make for improving the appearance or organization of the site from a user's perspective?

2. Search eBay's auction listings for a high definition, LCD flat panel TV. How would you describe the results you get? Are they helpful? How would you feel about buying this product from an eBay auction?

3. What evidence do you see on eBay.com that the company is moving toward being a diversified portfolio of Internet businesses rather than just an online auction site? Have you seen evidence of this elsewhere on the Internet?

for these communities involves providing ways for corporate clients to target customers, including the placement of banner ads and pop-up ads on their Web sites. A **banner ad** is a graphic display on a Web page used for advertising. The banner is linked to the advertiser's Web site so that a person clicking the banner is transported to a Web page with more information about the advertiser. **Pop-up ads** work in the opposite manner. They automatically open up when a user accesses a specific Web site, and the user must click the ad to make it disappear.

Social networking sites are a type of online community that has become extremely popular. Social networking is the practice of expanding the number of one's business or social contacts by making connections through individuals. MySpace, Facebook, and

Friendster appeal to people who are primarily interested in extending their friendships, while LinkedIn focuses on job networking.

Members of social networking sites spend hours surfing pages, checking out other members, and exchanging messages, revealing a great deal of information about themselves. Businesses harvest this information to create carefully targeted promotions that far surpass the typical text and display ads found on the Web. They also use the sites to interact with potential customers. The most popular of these sites attract so many visitors and are so "sticky" that they have become very powerful marketing tools. The Interactive Session on People discusses MySpace as a business model.

Social networking is so appealing that it has inspired a new type of e-commerce experience called **social shopping**. Social shopping sites such as Kaboodle, ThisNext, and StyleHive provide online meeting places for swapping shopping tips and for displaying favorite purchases.

Digital Content, Entertainment, and Services

The ability to deliver digital goods and digital content over the Web has created new alternatives to traditional print and broadcast media. There are Web sites for digital versions of print publications, such as the *New York Times* or the *Wall Street Journal*, and for new online journals such as Salon.com.

Some of the most popular Web sites deliver entertainment in digital form. Online games attract huge numbers of players. For example, Blizzard Entertainment's online role-playing game World of Warcraft has 8 million subscribers.

You can listen to some of your favorite radio channels, such as Classic Rock or the BBC, on the Web as well as many independent channels. Because the radio signal is relayed over the Internet, it is possible to access stations from anywhere in the world. Services such as Yahoo!'s LAUNCHcast and RealNetworks Rhapsody even put together individualized radio channels for listeners.

Broadband connections now make it possible for Web sites to display full-length films and television shows. Apple, Amazon, Movielink, and CinemaNow have downloading services for full-length movies. MLB.com, the Web site for Major League Baseball, delivers live streaming video of MLB baseball games to paid subscribers. Some online television and video services, such as iVillage Live, provide instant messaging capabilities allowing viewers to discuss the show as it is being broadcast.

Many of you use the Web to preview and download music. Although some of this Internet music is free of charge, Apple's iTunes and other sites are generating revenue by charging for each song or album downloaded from their Web sites. The phenomenal popularity of Apple's iTunes music service and Apple's iPod portable music player have inspired a new form of digital content delivery called *podcasting*. **Podcasting** is a method of publishing audio broadcasts via the Internet, allowing subscribing users to download audio files onto their personal computers or portable music players. Video clips designed to be downloaded and viewed on a portable device are called *vcasts*.

Podcasts also have internal uses for businesses who want to distribute information in audio form to their employees. Internet security firm SonicWALL uses podcasts to demonstrate its expertise to customers and to provide new product information to its resellers.

Portals have emerged as an Internet business model to help individuals and organizations locate information more efficiently. In Chapter 2, we defined a portal as a Web interface for presenting integrated, personalized information from a variety of sources. As an e-commerce business model, a *portal* is a "supersite" that provides a comprehensive entry point for a huge array of resources and services on the Internet.

Yahoo! is an example. It provides capabilities for locating information on the Internet along with news, sports, weather, telephone directories, maps, games, shopping, e-mail, chat, discussion boards, and links to other sites. Specialized portals help users with specific interests. For example, StarMedia is a portal customized for Hispanic Internet users.

Yahoo! and other portals and Web content sites often combine content and applications from many different sources and service providers. Other Internet business models use

INTERACTIVE SESSION: PEOPLE   The Allure of MySpace

MySpace.com is nothing short of a phenomenon. It is the most popular social networking site on the Web and competes with Yahoo as the most highly visited Web site in the United States. Its ascent has been exceptionally swift, since it has only been in business since January 2004.

MySpace offers a rich array of features, including message boards, e-mail, instant messaging, video clips, classified ads, online games, blogs, job searches, music, and, of course, the ability to network with other people online and perhaps meet them in person. It provides tools for users to customize personal Web pages using their own video, graphics, and music. Although MySpace touts itself as a private community for people to talk about the things they love in a personal way, it's also big business. News Corp paid $580 million to acquire MySpace in late 2005.

Advertisers are enthralled with the opportunity to create personal relationships with millions of young people. "What we really struck upon is the power of friendship," said Michael Barrett, chief revenue officer for News Corp.'s Fox Interactive Media. And MySpace's circle of friends is huge. About 105 million people visit the site each month. with users spending an average of 30 minutes on each visit to the site. In early August 2007, MySpace was hosting about 180 million personal profiles.

Companies are allowed to pay MySpace to set up profiles of their products as if they were members of the community. MySpace users can become "friends" of Toyota Motor's Yaris car, Burger King, or films, such as *Punk's Not Dead*. Profile sponsors are able to see exactly who is interested in their product and gather rich data on age, marital status, location, language, gender, occupation, and personal interests.

Procter & Gamble used MySpace to launch its Secret Sparkle deodorant for 16- to 24-year-old women by linking the product to the Web pages of musicians that used MySpace and appealed to the same demographic group. When users listened to new songs by The Donnas and Bonnie McKey, they were exposed to ads for Secret Sparkle and offered a chance to participate in a Secret Sparkle sweepstakes.

On August 8, 2006, Google agreed to pay Fox Interactive Media $900 million to have MySpace use its search engine so that it could place text ads alongside search results generated by MySpace users. Besides the Google deal, MySpace will be able to generate revenue from display advertising, video advertising, and ads on key MySpace destinations such as the music page, the main comedy page, or the home page. MySpace also has its own technology for tailoring online ads to the personal information maintained by its active users on their profile pages. The company is expected to generate nearly $500 million in advertising revenue in 2007.

Sounds like good business—except that MySpace is also very controversial. Many teenage subscribers post suggestive photos of themselves and lie about their age. About one-fourth of all MySpace users are registered as minors under 18 years of age, but that number could be much larger. Connecticut Attorney General Richard Blumenthal called MySpace a "virtual playground" for predators. Media outlets reported almost 100 criminal incidents across the United States involving adults who used MySpace to prey or attempt to prey on children in 2006.

Blumenthal and attorneys general from seven other states demanded that MySpace identify registered sex offenders who use the site and remove their profiles. MySpace agreed to turn over registered sex offenders' names, addresses, and online profiles and to delete profiles of convicted sex offenders identified by matching its profile data against databases of registered sex offenders.

MySpace has some restrictions on how adults contact its younger users. It prohibits children under 13 from setting up accounts and displays only partial profiles of registered 14- or 15-year-olds unless the person viewing the profile is already on the teen's list of friends. (Partial profiles display gender, age, and city, while full profiles describe hobbies, schools, and other personal details.) Friends' lists are no longer available to MySpace users over 18 unless they already know the youth's full name or e-mail address. However, users under 18 can still make contact, and MySpace has no mechanism for verifying that users submit their true age when registering. So adults can sign up as minors and join a 14-year-old's list of friends.

To further appease critics, MySpace is planning to offer free parental notification software that allows parents to find out the name, age, and location their children are using to represent themselves on MySpace. The software doesn't enable parents to see their child's e-mail or profile page. MySpace is also fine-tuning its ad-targeting to avoid displaying gambling and other adult-themed sites on minors' profile pages.

Sources: K.C. Jones, "On the Defensive, MySpace Emphasizes Its Progress," *Information Week*, July 30, 2007; Julia Angwin, "MySpace Moves to Give Parents More Information," *The Wall Street Journal*, January 17, 2007; Brad Stone, "MySpace to Share Data with States on Offenders," *The New York Times*, May 22, 2007; Elizabeth Holmes, "On MySpace, Millions of Users Make 'Friends' with Ads," *The Wall Street Journal*, August 7, 2006; "MySpace Plans New Age Restrictions," Associated Press, June 21, 2006; Anick Jesdanun, "Online Age Verification May Prove Complex," Associated Press, July 17, 2006.

CASE STUDY QUESTIONS

1. How do businesses benefit from MySpace? How do MySpace members benefit?

2. Does MySpace create an ethical dilemma? Why or why not?

3. Do parent and schools' objections to MySpace have any merit? Should a site such as MySpace be allowed to operate? Why or why not?

4. Is there anything that MySpace management can do to make the site less controversial?

MIS IN ACTION

Explore MySpace.com, examining the features and tools that are not restricted to registered members. View the profile created for a product such as the Toyota Yaris, Burger King, or a movie of your choice and related profiles about individuals who are "friends" of that product. Then answer the following questions.

1. What information can you find out about the product from its MySpace profile?

2. What features of the profile would attract teenage and college buyers? How does this profile differ from display advertising on the Web?

3. Explore some of the profiles of "friends" of this product. What kind of information is available about them?

4. Is using MySpace a good way to promote this product? Why or why not?

Toyota set up a MySpace profile for the Yaris to attract the attention of young buyers and gather marketing data.

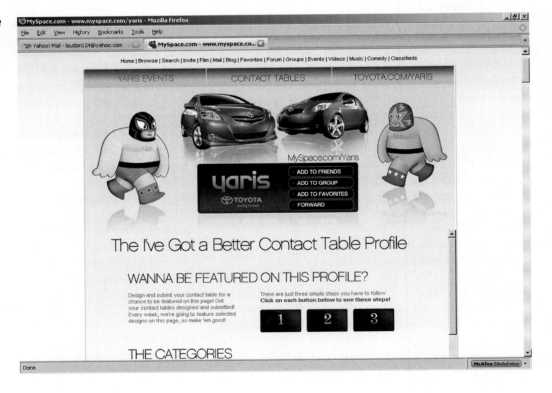

syndication as well providing additional value. For example, E*Trade, the discount Web trading site, purchases most of its content from outsider sources such as Reuters (news) and BigCharts.com (charts). Online **syndicators**, who aggregate content or applications from multiple sources, package them for distribution, and resell them to third-party Web sites, have emerged as another variant of the online content provider business model. The Web makes it much easier for companies to aggregate, repackage, and distribute information and information-based services.

The chapter-opening case study describes Photobucket, a photo-sharing service that works with other Web 2.0 applications and services. Other online service providers offer services such as remote storage of data (Xdrive.com). Online service providers generate revenue from subscription fees or from advertising.

Most of the business models described in Table 9.5 are called **pure-play** business models because they are based purely on the Internet. These firms did not have an existing bricks-and-mortar business when they designed their Internet business. However, many existing retail firms, such as L.L.Bean, Office Depot, R.E.I., and the *Wall Street Journal*, have developed Web sites as extensions of their traditional bricks-and-mortar businesses. Such businesses represent a hybrid **clicks-and-mortar** business model.

9.2 Electronic Commerce

Although most commercial transactions still take place through traditional retail channels, rising numbers of consumers and businesses are using the Internet for electronic commerce. Today, e-commerce revenue represents about 5 percent of all retail sales in the United States, and there is tremendous upside potential for growth.

TYPES OF ELECTRONIC COMMERCE

There are many ways to classify electronic commerce transactions. One is by looking at the nature of the participants in the electronic commerce transaction. The three major electronic commerce categories are business-to-consumer (B2C) e-commerce, business-to-business (B2B) e-commerce, and consumer-to-consumer (C2C) e-commerce.

- **Business-to-consumer (B2C) electronic commerce** involves retailing products and services to individual shoppers. Barnesandnoble.com, which sells books, software, and music to individual consumers, is an example of B2C e-commerce.
- **Business-to-business (B2B) electronic commerce** involves sales of goods and services among businesses. ChemConnect's Web site for buying and selling natural gas liquids, refined and intermediate fuels, chemicals, and plastics is an example of B2B e-commerce.
- **Consumer-to-consumer (C2C) electronic commerce** involves consumers selling directly to consumers. For example, eBay, the giant Web auction site, enables people to sell their goods to other consumers by auctioning the merchandise off to the highest bidder.

Another way of classifying electronic commerce transactions is in terms of the participants' physical connection to the Web. Until recently, almost all e-commerce transactions took place over wired networks. Now mobile phones and other wireless handheld digital appliances are Internet-enabled to send text messages and e-mail, access Web sites, and make purchases. Companies are offering new types of Web-based products and services that can be accessed by these wireless devices. The use of handheld wireless devices for purchasing goods and services from any location has been termed **mobile commerce** or **m-commerce**. Both business-to-business and business-to-consumer e-commerce transactions can take place using m-commerce technology, which we discuss in detail in Section 9.3.

ACHIEVING CUSTOMER INTIMACY: INTERACTIVE MARKETING, PERSONALIZATION, AND SELF-SERVICE

The unique dimensions of e-commerce technologies that we have just described offer many new possibilities for marketing and selling. The Internet provides companies with additional channels of communication and interaction for closer yet more cost-effective relationships with customers in sales, marketing, and customer support.

Interactive Marketing and Personalization

The Internet and e-commerce have helped some merchants achieve the holy grail of marketing: making products for millions of consumers that are personal, an impossible task in traditional markets. Web sites such as those for Lands' End (shirts and pants), Nike (athletic shoes), and VistaPrint (business cards, note cards, and labels) feature online tools that allow consumers to purchase products tailored to their individual specifications.

Web sites have become a bountiful source of detailed information about customer behavior, preferences, needs, and buying patterns that companies can use to tailor promotions, products, services, and pricing. Some customer information may be obtained by asking visitors to "register" online and provide information about themselves, but many companies also collect customer information using software tools that track the activities of Web site visitors.

Clickstream tracking tools collect data on customer activities at Web sites and store them in a log. The tools record the site that users visited prior to coming to a particular Web site and where these users go when they leave that site. They also record the specific pages visited on the particular site, the time spent on each page of the site, the types of pages visited, and what the visitors purchased (see Figure 9-3). Firms analyze this information about customer interests and behavior to develop precise profiles of existing and potential customers.

Such information enables firms to create unique personalized Web pages that display content or ads for products or services of special interest to each user, improving the customer's experience and creating additional value (see Figure 9-4). By using personalization technology to modify the Web pages presented to each customer, marketers achieve the benefits of using individual salespeople at dramatically lower costs.

Figure 9-3
Web Site Visitor Tracking

E-commerce Web sites have tools to track a shopper's every step through an online store. Close examination of customer behavior at a Web site selling women's clothing shows what the store might learn at each step and what actions it could take to increase sales.

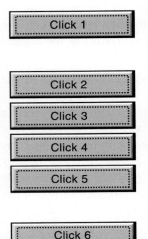

The shopper clicks on the home page. The store can tell that the shopper arrived from the Yahoo! portal at 2:30 PM (which might help determine staffing for customer service centers) and how long she lingered on the home page (which might indicate trouble navigating the site).

The shopper clicks on blouses, clicks to select a woman's white blouse, then clicks to view the same item in pink. The shopper clicks to select this item in a size 10 in pink and clicks to place it in her shopping cart. This information can help the store determine which sizes and colors are most popular.

From the shopping cart page, the shopper clicks to close the browser to leave the Web site without purchasing the blouse. This action could indicate the shopper changed her mind or that she had a problem with the Web site's checkout and payment process. Such behavior might signal that the Web site was not well designed.

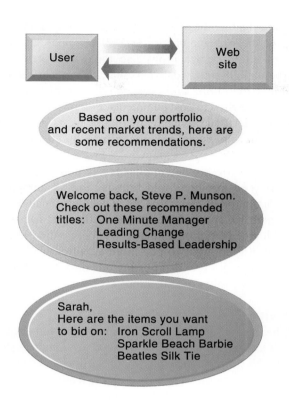

Figure 9-4
Web Site Personalization
Firms can create unique personalized Web pages that display content or ads for products or services of special interest to individual users, improving the customer experience, and creating additional value.

One technique for Web personalization is **collaborative filtering**, which compares information gathered about a specific user's behavior at a Web site to data about other customers with similar interests to predict what the user would like to see next. The software then makes recommendations to users based on their assumed interests. For example, Amazon and Barnesandnoble.com use collaborative filtering software to prepare personalized book recommendations: "Customers who bought this book also bought...." These recommendations are made just at the point of purchase, an ideal time to prompt a consumer into purchasing a related product.

Blogs and Wikis

Blogs, which we introduced in Chapter 6, have emerged as another promising Web-based tool for marketing. A blog, the popular term for a Weblog, is a personal Web page that typically contains a series of chronological entries (newest to oldest) by its author, and links to related Web pages.

The blog may include a *blogroll* (a collection of links to other blogs) and TrackBacks (a list of entries in other blogs that refer to a post on the first blog). Most blogs allow readers to post comments on the blog entries as well. The act of creating a blog is often referred to as "blogging." Blogs are either hosted by a third-party site such as Blogger.com, LiveJournal.com, Typepad.com, and Xanga.com, or prospective bloggers can download software such as Movable Type and bBlog to create a blog that is housed by the user's ISP. Blogger and Twitter have added features to allow users to post short notes and photos to their blogs from cell phones.

Blog pages are usually variations on templates provided by the blogging service or software. Therefore, millions of people without HTML skills of any kind can post their own Web pages and share content with others. The totality of blog-related Web sites is often referred to as the **blogosphere**.

The content of blogs range from individual musings to corporate communications. Blogs have a significant impact on political affairs, and have gained increasing notice for their role in breaking and shaping the news. Blogs have become hugely popular. There are at least 70 million blogs on the Web and nearly 100,000 new ones added daily.

Companies that maintain public blogs use them as a new channel for reaching customers. These corporate blogs provide a personal and conversational way for businesses to present information to the public and prospective customers about new products and services. Readers are often invited to post comments. For example, Stonyfield Farm Inc., the world's third-largest organic food company, maintains blogs on childrearing and organic dairy farms to create a more personal relationship with consumers than the traditional selling relationship.

Marketers are analyzing blogs as well as chat groups and message boards to see what is being said online about new products, old brands, and ad campaigns. Blog-watching services that monitor popular blogs claim that "blog watching" can be cheaper and faster for analyzing consumer interests and sentiment than traditional focus groups and surveys. For example, Polaroid learned from blogs that consumers online frequently discuss photo longevity and archiving, prompting it to pay more attention to long-lasting photos in its product development. Companies are also posting ads on some of the most popular blogs published by individuals or by other organizations.

Customer Self-Service

Many companies use their Web sites and e-mail to answer customer questions or to provide customers with product information, reducing the need for human customer-support expert. For instance, American, Northwest, and other major airlines have created Web sites where customers can review flight departure and arrival times, seating charts, and airport logistics; check frequent-flyer miles; and purchase tickets online. Chapter 1 describes how customers of UPS use its Web site to track shipments, calculate shipping costs, determine time in transit, and arrange for a package pickup. FedEx and other package delivery firms provide similar Web-based services. Automated self-service or other Web-based responses to customer questions cost only a fraction of what a live customer service representative on the telephone would cost.

Stonyfield Farms' Baby Babble blog provides a channel for the company to talk to customers with young children directly and hear back from them.

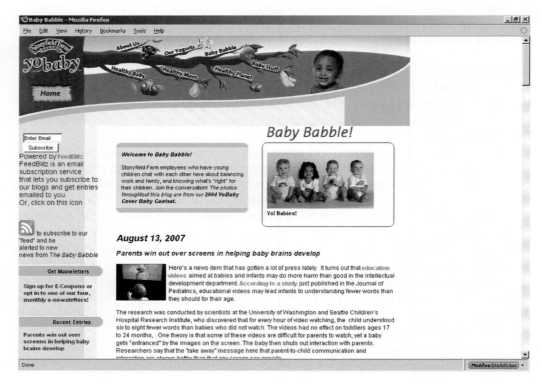

New software products are even integrating the Web with customer call centers, where customer service problems have been traditionally handled over the telephone. A **call center** is an organizational department responsible for handling customer service issues by telephone and other channels. For example, visitors to the Lands' End Web site can request a phone call from customer service by entering his or her telephone number. A call-center system directs a customer service representative to place a voice telephone call to the user's phone.

BUSINESS-TO-BUSINESS ELECTRONIC COMMERCE: NEW EFFICIENCIES AND RELATIONSHIPS

About 80 percent of B2B e-commerce is still based on proprietary systems for electronic data interchange (EDI). **Electronic data interchange** (**EDI**) enables the computer-to-computer exchange between two organizations of standard transactions such as invoices, bills of lading, shipment schedules, or purchase orders. Transactions are automatically transmitted from one information system to another through a network, eliminating the printing and handling of paper at one end and the inputting of data at the other. Each major industry in the United States and much of the rest of the world has EDI standards that define the structure and information fields of electronic documents for that industry.

EDI originally automated the exchange of documents such as purchase orders, invoices, and shipping notices. Although some companies still use EDI for document automation, firms engaged in just-in-time inventory replenishment and continuous production use EDI as a system for continuous replenishment. Suppliers have online access to selected parts of the purchasing firm's production and delivery schedules and automatically ship materials and goods to meet prespecified targets without intervention by firm purchasing agents (see Figure 9-5).

Although many organizations still use private networks for EDI, they are increasingly Web-enabled because Internet technology provides a much more flexible and low-cost platform for linking to other firms. Businesses are able to extend digital technology to a wider range of activities and broaden their circle of trading partners.

Take procurement, for example. **Procurement** involves not only purchasing goods and materials but also sourcing, negotiating with suppliers, paying for goods, and making delivery arrangements. Businesses can now use the Internet to locate the most low-cost supplier, search online catalogs of supplier products, negotiate with suppliers, place orders, make payments, and arrange transportation. They are not limited to partners linked by traditional EDI networks.

The Internet and Web technology enable businesses to create new electronic storefronts for selling to other businesses with multimedia graphic displays and interactive features similar to those for B2C commerce. Alternatively, businesses can use Internet technology to create extranets or electronic marketplaces for linking to other businesses for purchase and sale transactions.

Figure 9-5
Electronic Data Interchange (EDI)
Companies use EDI to automate transactions for B2B e-commerce and continuous inventory replenishment. Suppliers can automatically send data about shipments to purchasing firms. The purchasing firms can use EDI to provide production and inventory requirements and payment data to suppliers.

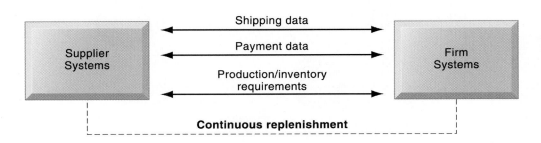

Private industrial networks typically consist of a large firm using an extranet to link to its suppliers and other key business partners (see Figure 9-6). The network is owned by the buyer, and it permits the firm and designated suppliers, distributors, and other business partners to share product design and development, marketing, production scheduling, inventory management, and unstructured communication, including graphics and e-mail. Another term for a private industrial network is a **private exchange**.

An example is VW Group Supply, which links the Volkswagen Group and its suppliers. VW Group Supply handles 90 percent of all global purchasing for Volkswagen, including all automotive and parts components.

Net marketplaces, which are sometimes called *e-hubs*, provide a single, digital marketplace based on Internet technology for many different buyers and sellers (see Figure 9-7). They are industry owned or operate as independent intermediaries between buyers and sellers. Net marketplaces generate revenue from purchase and sale transactions and other services provided to clients. Participants in Net marketplaces can establish prices through online negotiations, auctions, or requests for quotations, or they can use fixed prices.

There are many different types of Net marketplaces and ways of classifying them. Some Net marketplaces sell direct goods and some sell indirect goods. *Direct goods* are goods used in a production process, such as sheet steel for auto body production. *Indirect goods* are all other goods not directly involved in the production process, such as office supplies or products for maintenance and repair. Some Net marketplaces support contractual purchasing based on long-term relationships with designated suppliers, and others support short-term spot purchasing, where goods are purchased based on immediate needs, often from many different suppliers.

Some Net marketplaces serve vertical markets for specific industries, such as automobiles, telecommunications, or machine tools, whereas others serve horizontal markets for goods and services that can be found in many different industries, such as office equipment or transportation.

Exostar is an example of an industry-owned net marketplace, focusing on long-term contract purchasing relationships and on providing common networks and computing platforms for reducing supply chain inefficiencies. This aerospace and defense industry-sponsored Net marketplace was founded jointly by BAE Systems, Boeing, Lockheed Martin, Raytheon, and Rolls-Royce PLC to connect these companies to their suppliers and

Figure 9-6
A Private Industrial Network
A private industrial network, also known as a private exchange, links a firm to its suppliers, distributors, and other key business partners for efficient supply chain management and other collaborative commerce activities.

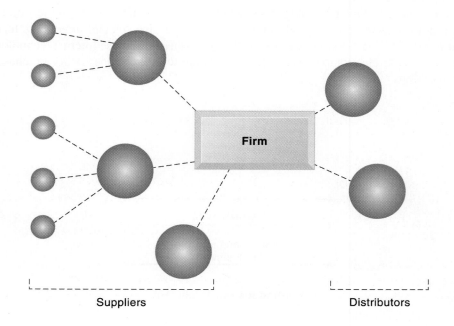

Suppliers   Distributors

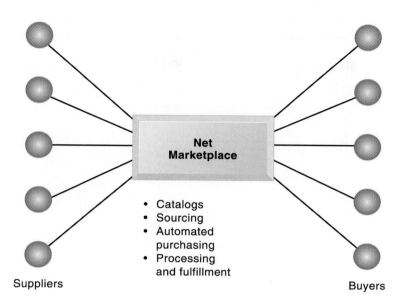

Figure 9-7
A Net Marketplace
Net marketplaces are online marketplaces where multiple buyers can purchase from multiple sellers.

Net Marketplace

- Catalogs
- Sourcing
- Automated purchasing
- Processing and fulfillment

Suppliers

Buyers

facilitate collaboration. More than 16,000 trading partners in the commercial, military, and government sectors use Exostar's sourcing, e-procurement, and collaboration tools for both direct and indirect goods.

Exchanges are independently owned third-party Net marketplaces that connect thousands of suppliers and buyers for spot purchasing. Many exchanges provide vertical markets for a single industry, such as food, electronics, or industrial equipment, and they primarily deal with direct inputs. For example, FoodTrader.com automates spot purchases among buyers and sellers from more than 180 countries in the food and agriculture industry.

Exchanges proliferated during the early years of e-commerce, but many have failed. Suppliers were reluctant to participate because the exchanges encouraged competitive bidding that drove prices down and did not offer any long-term relationships with buyers or services to make lowering prices worthwhile. Many essential direct purchases are not conducted on a spot basis because they require contracts and consideration of issues such as delivery timing, customization, and quality of products.

9.3 M-commerce

Wireless mobile devices are starting to be used for purchasing goods and services as well as for transmitting messages. Although m-commerce represents a small fraction of total e-commerce transactions, revenue has been steadily growing (see Figure 9-8). In 2007, there were an estimated 2.2 billion wireless and mobile devices worldwide.

M-COMMERCE SERVICES AND APPLICATIONS

M-commerce applications have taken off for services that are time-critical, that appeal to people on the move, or that accomplish a task more efficiently than other methods. They are especially popular in Europe, Japan, South Korea, and other countries where fees for conventional Internet usage are very expensive. Here are some examples.

Location-Based Services

Services such as Mobio and Where enable users to locate nearby restaurants and gasoline stations, find local entertainment and movie times, and call a cab, providing maps showing

Figure 9-8
Global
M-commerce
Revenue,
2000–2009
*M-commerce sales
represent a small
fraction of total
e-commerce sales,
but that percentage is
steadily growing.
(Totals for 2007–2008
are estimated.)*

Sources: Jupiter Research,
e-Marketer, 2006, and
authors.

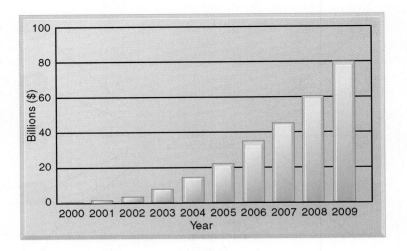

how to reach their locations. New York-based MeetMoi provides a dating service that helps users identify people who are nearby and looking for dates. Smarter Agent enables users of cell phones with the global positioning system (GPS) to find nearby vacant apartments.

Banking and Financial Services

Banks are rolling out services that let customers manage their bank accounts from their cell phones or other mobile devices. Citibank and Bank of America customers can use their cell phones to check account balances, transfer funds, and pay bills.

Wireless Advertising

Cell phone service providers have information valuable to advertisers about where subscribers live, their location the moment they view ads, their age, and the games, music, and other services they use on their phones. Advertisers must find a way to deal with privacy issues and consumer reactions to ads on their phones. But when done right, mobile campaigns yield high response rates and increased consumer engagement. With over 2 billion cell phone users worldwide, the market for mobile advertising is expected to reach $11.3 billion by 2011 (Sylvers, 2007).

Yahoo! displays ads on its mobile home page for companies such as Pepsi, Procter & Gamble, Hilton, Nissan, and Intel. News Corp. has a mobile campaign to encourage people to vote for winners of its *American Idol* television show. Google is displaying ads linked to cell phone searches by users of the mobile version of its search engine. Ads are starting to be embedded in downloadable applications such as games and videos.

Games and Entertainment

Cell phones are quickly turning into portable entertainment platforms. Mobile phone services offer downloadable digital games, music, and **ringtones** (digitized snippets of music that play on mobile phones when a user receives or places a call). Some handset models combine the features of a cell phone and a portable music player.

Users of broadband services from the major wireless vendors can download on-demand video clips, news clips, and weather reports. MobiTV, offered by Sprint and AT&T Wireless, features live TV programs, including MSNBC and Fox Sports. Film companies are starting to produce short films explicitly designed to play on mobile phones. The News Corporation, which owns the Fox Network, coined the trademark "mobisodes" for short cell phone videos.

User-generated content is also appearing in mobile form. See Me TV, a service from European cell phone providers, allows users to shoot video on their mobile phones and post it to a gallery for viewing on other mobile phones. A selection of YouTube videos are available to Verizon Wireless customers who subscribe to its VCast media service. MySpace arranged with Vodafone Group PLC and AT&T to allow European and American users to post comments, photos, and eventually videos to the MySpace Web site from their mobile phones.

ACCESSING INFORMATION FROM THE WIRELESS WEB

Although cell phones, PDAs, and other handheld mobile devices are able to access the Web at anytime and from any place, the amount of information that they can actually handle at one time is very limited. Until 3G broadband service comes into widespread use, these devices will not be able to transmit or receive large amounts data. The information must fit onto small display screens.

Major search providers Google, Yahoo!, and Microsoft have introduced search services for mobile phones that provide useful information with minimal typing. Their **wireless portals** (also known as *mobile portals*) feature content and services optimized for mobile devices to steer users to the information they are most likely to need. Google's mobile service remembers recent place names in searches, so that when users initiate a search for "movies," it returns a list of movies playing locally and makes it easy to find show times and purchase tickets. Microsoft's TellMe service allows users to speak into their phones to search movie listings, stock quotes, news, and other information and then see the results on their phone screens.

9.4 Electronic Commerce Payment Systems

Special electronic payment systems have been developed to pay for goods electronically on the Internet. Electronic payment systems for the Internet include systems for digital credit card payments, digital wallets, accumulated balance digital payment systems, online stored value payment systems, digital checking, and electronic billing presentment and payment systems.

TYPES OF ELECTRONIC PAYMENT SYSTEMS

Nearly all online payments in the United States (90 percent) use credit cards, or rely on the credit card system. Businesses can also contract with services that extend the functionality of existing credit card payment systems. **Digital wallets** make paying for purchases over the Web more efficient by eliminating the need for shoppers to enter their address and credit card information repeatedly each time they buy something. The digital wallet securely stores credit card and owner identification information and enters the shopper's name, credit card number, and shipping information automatically when invoked to complete a purchase. Google Checkout is an example.

Micropayment systems have been developed for purchases of less than $10, such as downloads of individual articles or music clips, which would be too small for conventional credit card payments. **Accumulated balance digital payment systems** enable users to make micropayments and purchases on the Web, accumulating a debit balance that they must pay periodically on their credit card or telephone bills. Examples are Valista's PaymentsPlus used by AOL, Vodafone, and NTT DoCoMo, and Clickshare, which is widely used by the online newspaper and publishing industry.

Online **stored value payment systems** enable consumers to make instant online payments to merchants and other individuals based on value stored in an online digital account. Some online stored value payment systems, such as Valista, are merchant platforms. Others are focused on peer-to-peer payments, such as PayPal. PayPal is owned by eBay and makes it possible for people to send money to vendors or individuals who are not set up to accept credit card payments.

Digital checking systems such as PayByCheck extend the functionality of existing checking accounts so they can be used for online shopping payments. Digital checks are processed much faster than traditional paper-based checking.

Electronic billing presentment and payment systems are used for paying routine monthly bills. They enable users to view their bills electronically and pay them through electronic fund transfers from bank or credit card accounts. These services notify purchasers about bills that are due, present the bills, and process the payments. Some of these services, such as CheckFree, consolidate subscribers' bills from various sources so that they can all be paid at one time. Table 9.6 summarizes the features of some of these e-commerce payment systems.

DIGITAL PAYMENT SYSTEMS FOR M-COMMERCE

Use of mobile handsets as payment devices is already well established in Europe, Japan, and South Korea. Three kinds of mobile payments systems are used in Japan, and these provide a glimpse of the future of mobile payment in the United States. Japanese cell phones support stored value systems charged by credit cards or bank accounts, mobile debit cards (tied to personal bank accounts), and mobile credit cards. Japanese cell phones act like mobile wallets, containing a variety of payment mechanisms. Consumers can pay merchants by simply waving the cell phone at a merchant payment device that can accept payments. Japan's largest phone company, NTT DoCoMo, introduced wireless RFID cell phones and a related payment system (FeliCa) in 2004. Currently, 10 million wallet phones are in use in Japan.

In the United States, the cell phone has not yet evolved into a fully capable mobile commerce and payment system. The cell phone in the United States is not connected to a wide network of financial institutions, but instead resides behind the walled garden of the telephone providers. In Europe and Asia, cell phone users can pay for a very wide variety of real goods and services, and there, phones are integrated with a large array of financial institutions.

TABLE 9.6

Examples of Electronic Payment Systems for E-commerce

Payment System	Description	Commercial Example
Credit card payment systems	Protect information transmitted among users, merchant sites, and processing banks	Visa, MasterCard, American Express
Digital wallet	Software that stores credit card and other information to facilitate form completion and payment for goods on the Web	Google Checkout
Accumulated balance digital payment systems	Accumulates micropayment purchases as a debit balance that must be paid periodically on credit card or telephone bills	Valista PaymentsPlus, Clickshare
Stored value payment systems	Enables consumers to make instant payments to merchants or individuals based on value stored in a digital account	PayPal, Valista
Digital checking	Electronic check with a secure digital signature	PayByCheck
Electronic billing presentment and payment systems	Supports electronic payment for online and physical store purchases of goods or services after the purchase has taken place	CheckFree, Yahoo Bill Pay

9.5 Hands-On MIS

The projects in this section give you hands-on experience developing an e-commerce strategy for a real-world company, using spreadsheet software to analyze the profitability of an e-commerce company, and using Web tools to research and evaluate e-commerce hosting services.

ACHIEVING OPERATIONAL EXCELLENCE: DEVELOPING AN E-COMMERCE STRATEGY

Software skills: Web browser software, Web page development software
Business skills: Strategic analysis

This project provides an opportunity for you to develop an e-commerce strategy for a real-world business and to use a Web page development tool to create part of the company's Web site.

Dirt Bikes's management believes that the company could benefit from e-commerce. The company has sold motorcycles and parts primarily through authorized dealers. Dirt Bikes advertises in various magazines catering to dirt bike enthusiasts and maintains booths at important off-road motorcycle racing events. You have been asked to explore how Dirt Bikes could benefit from e-commerce and a Dirt Bikes Web site. Prepare a report for management that answers the following questions:

- How could Dirt Bikes benefit from e-commerce? Should it sell motorcycles or parts over the Web? Should it use its Web site primarily to advertise its products and services? Should it use the Web for customer service?
- How would a Web site provide value to Dirt Bikes? Use the Web to research the cost of an e-commerce site for a small- to medium-sized company. How much revenue or cost savings would the Web site have to produce to make it a worthwhile investment for Dirt Bikes?
- Prepare specifications describing the functions that should be performed by Dirt Bikes's Web site. Include links to other Web sites or other systems in your specifications.
- (Optional) Design the home page for Dirt Bikes's Web site and an important secondary page linked to the home page using the Web page creation capabilities of word processing software or a Web page development tool of your choice.

IMPROVING DECISION MAKING: USING SPREADSHEET SOFTWARE TO ANALYZE A DOT-COM BUSINESS

Software skills: Spreadsheet downloading, formatting, and formulas
Business skills: Financial statement analysis

Publicly traded companies, including those specializing in e-commerce, are required to file financial data with the Securities and Exchange Commission. By analyzing this information, you can determine the profitability of an e-commerce company and the viability of its business model.

Pick one e-commerce company on the Internet: for example, Ashford.com, Buy.com, Yahoo.com, or Priceline.com. Study the Web pages that describe the company and explain its purpose and structure. Use the Web to find articles that comment on the company. Then visit the Securities and Exchange Commission's Web site at www.sec.gov and select Filings and Forms to access the company's 10-K (annual report) form showing income statements and balance sheets. Select only the sections of the 10-K form containing the desired portions of financial statements that you need to examine, and download them into your spreadsheet. Create simplified spreadsheets of the company's balance sheets and income statements for the past three years.

- Is the company a dot-com success, borderline business, or failure? What information dictates the basis of your decision? Why? When answering these questions, pay special attention to the company's three-year trends in revenues, costs of sales, gross margins, operating expenses, and net margins.

• Prepare an electronic presentation (with a minimum of five slides), including appropriate spreadsheets or charts, and present your work to your professor and classmates.

ACHIEVING OPERATIONAL EXCELLENCE: EVALUATING E-COMMERCE HOSTING SERVICES

Software skills: Web browser software
Business skills: Evaluating e-commerce hosting services

You would like to set up a Web site to sell towels, linens, pottery, and tableware from Portugal and are examining services for hosting small-business Internet storefronts. Your Web site should be able to take secure credit card payments and to calculate shipping costs and taxes. Initially, you would like to display photos and descriptions of 40 different products. Visit Yahoo! Small Business and Freemerchant.com and compare the range of e-commerce hosting services they offer to small business, their capabilities, and costs. Also examine the tools they provide for creating an e-commerce site. Compare both of these services and decide which of the two you would use if you were actually establishing a Web store. Write a brief report indicating your choice and explaining the strengths and weaknesses of both.

LEARNING TRACKS

The following Learning Tracks provide content relevant to topics covered in this chapter:

1. E-commerce Challenges: The Story of Online Groceries
2. Build an E-commerce Business Plan

Review Summary

1 What are the unique features of e-commerce, digital markets, and digital goods? E-commerce involves digitally enabled commercial transactions between and among organizations and individuals. Unique features of e-commerce technology include ubiquity, global reach, universal technology standards, richness, interactivity, information density, capabilities for personalization and customization, and social technology.

Digital markets are said to be more "transparent" than traditional markets, with reduced information asymmetry, search costs, transaction costs, and menu costs, along with the ability to change prices dynamically based on market conditions. Digital goods, such as music, video, software, and books, can be delivered over a digital network. Once a digital product has been produced, the cost of delivering that product digitally is extremely low.

2 How has Internet technology changed business models? The Internet can help companies add extra value to existing products and services or create new products and services. Many different business models for electronic commerce on the Internet have emerged, including virtual storefronts, information brokers, transaction brokers, online marketplaces, content providers, social networks, service providers, and portals. Business models that take advantage of the Internet's capabilities for communication, community-building, and digital goods distribution have become especially prominent.

3 **What are the various types of e-commerce, and how has e-commerce changed consumer retailing and business-to-business transactions?** The three major types of electronic commerce are business-to-consumer (B2C), business-to-business (B2B), and consumer-to-consumer (C2C). Mobile commerce, or m-commerce, is the purchase of goods and services using handheld wireless devices.

The Internet creates new channels for marketing, sales, and customer support and to eliminate intermediaries in buy-and-sell transactions. Interactive capabilities on the Web can be used to build closer relationships with customers in marketing and customer support. Web personalization technologies deliver Web pages with content geared to the specific interests of each user. Web sites and e-mail reduce transaction costs for placing orders and customer service.

B2B e-commerce generates efficiencies by enabling companies to locate suppliers, solicit bids, place orders, and track shipments in transit electronically. Net marketplaces provide a single, digital marketplace for many buyers and sellers. Private industrial networks link a firm with its suppliers and other strategic business partners to develop highly efficient and responsive supply chains.

4 **What is the role of m-commerce in business, and what are the most important m-commerce applications?** M-commerce is especially well-suited for location-based applications, such as finding local hotels and restaurants, monitoring local traffic and weather, and providing personalized location-based marketing. Mobile phones and handhelds are being used for mobile bill payment; banking; securities trading; transportation schedule updates; and downloads of digital content, such as music, games, and video clips. M-commerce requires wireless portals and special digital payment systems that can handle micropayments.

5 **What are the principal payment systems for electronic commerce?** The principal e-commerce payment systems are digital credit card payment systems, digital wallets, accumulated balance digital payment systems, stored value payment systems, digital checking, and electronic billing presentment and payment systems.

Key Terms

Accumulated balance digital
    payment systems, 321
Banner ad, 309
Blogosphere, 315
Business-to-business (B2B)
    electronic commerce, 313
Business-to-consumer (B2C)
    electronic commerce, 313
Call center, 317
Clicks-and-mortar, 313
Clickstream tracking, 314
Collaborative filtering, 315
Consumer-to-consumer
    (C2C) electronic
    commerce, 313
Cost transparency, 303
Customization, 303
Digital checking, 321
Digital goods, 305

Digital wallets, 321
Disintermediation, 305
Dynamic pricing, 304
Electronic billing
    presentment and payment
    systems, 322
Electronic data interchange
    (EDI), 317
Exchanges, 319
Information asymmetry, 304
Information density, 303
Market entry costs, 303
Marketspace, 301
Menu costs, 304
Micropayment, 321
Mobile commerce
    (m-commerce), 313
Net marketplaces, 318
Personalization, 303

Podcasting, 310
Pop-up ads, 309
Price discrimination, 303
Price transparency, 303
Private exchange, 318
Private industrial
    networks, 318
Procurement, 317
Pure-play, 313
Richness, 303
Ringtones, 320
Search costs, 303
Social networking, 309
Social shopping, 310
Stored value payment
    systems, 321
Syndicators, 313
Wireless portals, 321

Review Questions

1. What are the unique features of e-commerce, digital markets, and digital goods?
- Name and describe four business trends and three technology trends shaping e-commerce today.
- List and describe the eight unique features of e-commerce.
- Define *digital market* and *digital goods* and describe their distinguishing features.

2. How has Internet technology changed business models?
- Explain how the Internet is changing the economics of information and business models.
- Name and describe six Internet business models for electronic commerce. Distinguish between a pure-play Internet business model and a clicks-and-mortar business model.

3. What are the various types of e-commerce, and how has e-commerce changed consumer retailing and business-to-business transactions?
- Name and describe the various categories of electronic commerce.
- Explain how the Internet facilitates sales and marketing for individual customers, and describe the role played by Web personalization.
- Explain how the Internet can enhance customer service.
- Explain how Internet technology supports business-to-business electronic commerce.
- Define and describe Net marketplaces, and explain how they differ from private industrial networks (private exchanges).

4. What is the role of m-commerce in business, and what are the most important m-commerce applications?
- List and describe important types of m-commerce services and applications.
- Explain how wireless portals help users access information on the wireless Web.
- Describe some of the barriers to m-commerce.

5. What are the principal payment systems for electronic commerce?
- Name and describe the principal electronic payment systems used on the Internet.
- Describe the types of payment systems used in m-commerce.

Discussion Questions

1. How does the Internet change consumer and supplier relationships?

2. The Internet may not make corporations obsolete, but the corporations will have to change their business models. Do you agree? Why or why not?

Video Case

You will find a video case illustrating some of the concepts in this chapter on the Laudon Web site along with questions to help you analyze the case.

Teamwork

Performing a Competitive Analysis of E-commerce Sites

Form a group with three or four of your classmates. Select two businesses that are competitors in the same industry and that use their Web sites for electronic commerce. Visit these Web sites. You might compare, for example, the Web sites for iTunes and Napster, Amazon and Barnesandnoble.com, or E*Trade and Scottrade. Prepare an evaluation of each business's Web site in terms of its functions, user friendliness, and ability to support the company's business strategy. Which Web site does a better job? Why? Can you make some recommendations to improve these Web sites?

BUSINESS PROBLEM-SOLVING CASE

Can J&R Electronics Grow with E-commerce?

J&R Electronics is a mom-and-pop shop for the modern age. Joe and Rachelle Friedman started the business as an audio equipment store in 1971. They funded the original business, a 500-square-foot storefront near New York's City Hall, with money they received for their wedding. Over 35 years, the Friedmans expanded the business, adding records, office equipment, cameras, computers, movies, and games. Today, J&R Electronics encompasses a lucrative catalog business and 10 specialty electronics stores covering 300,000 square feet of retail space on that same city block in Manhattan. Among the stores are the famed J&R Music World and J&R Computer World.

The J&R empire sells nearly every type of electronic device imaginable. However, the Friedmans have resisted the advice of suppliers, such as record companies, who have told them the only way to survive and compete with big box stores was to become a chain. Rachelle Friedman explained that "by staying on the block...we maintain control, which the chain stores lose."

How does J&R continue to survive with only one location in an industry dominated by Wal-Mart, Best Buy, and Circuit City? Quite appropriately, the Friedmans have their son to thank for that.

Jason Friedman is the vice president of e-commerce for J&R electronics. In 1998, Jason, who started out as the company's database manager, lobbied his parents to invest in the Web as an outlet for the company. J&R went online using e-commerce software developed by InterWorld Corp., a highly regarded product of the first dot-com boom. InterWorld's Commerce Exchange served J&R well enough to satisfy the notion that e-commerce would play a major role in the company's future.

In 2000, J&R was ready to upgrade to a new version of the InterWorld software, which was touted as being much more robust than the previous versions that J&R had installed. Within a year, the upgrade process at J&R was thrown off track as the dot-com bust brought about the demise of InterWorld. Jason Friedman was forced to continue development of J&R's online presence without support from the software vendor. He and his staff managed to piece together a customized e-commerce application that could handle the 400,000 products that J&R sold. However, the solution did not support some of the features that online retail competitors offered, such as the ability to collect and display customer reviews and provide information on inventory statistics, and shipping time.

By that time, with 30 percent of J&R's $400 million in revenue being generated by JR.com, Friedman was looking to inject new life into the Web site. With a staff of 50 IT workers backing him up, he explored ways to ensure that the JR.com would remain as popular a destination online as the bricks-and-mortar store was in the real world. For the new site, he chose an e-commerce platform from Blue Martini and a CRM package made by Loyalty Lab. In addition, Friedman planned to bring JR.com in line with Web 2.0 concepts by populating the site with videos and introducing customer reviews. Those features were valuable tools that customers could use to educate themselves about products and comparison-shop before they committed to buying.

In May 2006, J&R unveiled an online loyalty program to encourage shoppers to visit JR.com directly rather than connect from a link on another site, such as a price comparison search engine. The strategy intends to raise the number of unique visitors to the site and, as Jason Friedman put it, relieve J&R from "fighting over pennies with our competitors." For participating in the program, customers receive gift cards equaling 2 percent of their purchases. If successful, the loyalty program will keep past customers from giving their business to other stores, as well as entice new customers to join the J&R community. Catalog shoppers are also eligible for loyalty rewards.

Mark H. Goldstein, CEO of Loyalty Lab, noted that J&R already had a loyal customer base as a result of its top-notch customer service and focus on building relationships. All that the company lacked was a program that recognized customer loyalty. Loyalty Lab's CRM package helped fill that void by hosting the modules that enabled J&R customers to register for accounts, manage their accounts, and redeem the incentives they have earned. J&R's marketers can control the services from Loyalty Lab with simple graphical online tools using any standard Web browser. Goldstein points to additional benefits for J&R from the program in form of saving what he calls "the Google tax." This is the 20 to 30 percent charge that J&R pays to search sites when visitors are directed to J&R from another site, a fee that J&R avoids when shoppers visit JR.com directly.

J&R selected Blue Martini as its new e-commerce platform because Blue Martini functions well with J&R's ERP software from a technical perspective. The two systems are able to exchange data easily. Blue Martini provides a better opportunity to share the strengths of J&R's bricks-and-mortar channels online. By doing so, the company hopes to achieve a greater competitive advantage over its chain store rivals. Blue Martini has to showcase online the standout features of a visit to a J&R Electronics store. Only then can customers throughout the country respond to the business with the same sense of loyalty as those who physically visit the stores in lower Manhattan.

J&R has plenty of advantages, or differentiators, to showcase. Its prices are very competitive, yet it maintains a vast inventory that rarely leaves customers disappointed. J&R also has a reputation for being at the leading edge of new technology. The company has a penchant for being the first retailer to sell new products or the latest versions of already popular products. Furthermore, J&R is known to have a good sense for technology trends, such as the transition from VHS to DVD and the rising popularity of Apple products. J&R often caters to those trends before other stores are prepared to do so. Aside from good prices, perhaps the element of J&R that appeals to customers most is its sales staff. Customers who enter J&R stores know that the workers they encounter will be well informed and adept at explaining the features and specifications of even the newest and most high-tech products.

With Blue Martini, J&R will try to emulate the expertise of its sales staff online. The platform provides a Guided Selling application, which collects input from the shopper and produces a narrowed-down view of the product catalog that is tailored for the requirements and preferences of a particular customer. Customers are able to view products by brand, price, popularity, size, and availability of special offers. By providing interactive recommendations, J&R can put more information about products in the hands of the customers, which makes them more comfortable in their purchases.

Comprehensive product descriptions, product reviews from customers and other sources, and comparison grids will also make it easier for shoppers to understand and select products. Going a step further, Blue Martini enables J&R to deepen its Web content with videos, including hundreds of clips that feature staff members giving tutorials on specific products. The videos bring a personalization to the online shopping experience that normally would be available only in a bricks-and-mortar store. J&R even films the videos in its actual stores.

The new e-commerce platform will also enhance the capabilities of software that J&R was already using. For example, under the old system, J&R had to run its Endeca Web site search software separately from the InterWorld site. The Endeca software helps customers find, analyze, and determine relevancy in search results, but these features could not be fully utilized in that environment. On the new site, J&R can integrate Endeca with its PowerReviews customer reviews to help customers refine and sort products. Endeca also features merchandising functionality that J&R will now be able to deploy for tracking the activities of customers across the JR.com site.

The new JR.com launched in March 2007 with a host of new customer conveniences. If a customer selects a product that is out of stock, the site is prepared with a list of similar products. The site also has real-time integration with store inventory, so onsite purchases are reflected in the availability of products online. J&R has also made the checkout process more efficient so shoppers arrive at final price more quickly. The shipping section has been restructured to improve the accuracy of delivery dates and shipping fees.

Jason Friedman recognizes that, despite the increased functionality provided by Blue Martini, his company is still limited by having physical stores located solely in New York City. He notes that where chain stores can offer customers the option of ordering merchandise online and picking it up that day in person at the nearest store, J&R can only make that option available to customers in the New York City area. However, he feels that emphasizing e-commerce carries great potential for the business and represents the company's future.

Maris Daugherty, a senior consultant with J.C. Williams Group, a global retail consultancy, believes that J&R should not expect too much too soon. She says that there is space in the retail market for a niche entity like J&R, but success will likely come from a long-term focus rather than a short-term revolution.

Sources: Laton McCartney, "Mid-Market Case: J&R Electronics Pumps Up the Volume," *Baseline Magazine*, March 13, 2007; "J&R Electronics Taps Loyalty Lab's On-Demand Suite for First Shopper Loyalty Program," *Rtmilestones.com*, accessed May 1, 2007; "J&R Electronics Migrating to Blue Martini E-Commerce Platform," *Internetretailer.com*, November 8, 2006; "Encyclopedia of Company Histories—J&R Electronics, Inc.," Answers.com, accessed April 25, 2007; and Heather Retzlaff, "J&R Tests Online Loyalty Program," *MultichannelMerchant.com*, August 1, 2006.

Case Study Questions

1. Analyze J&R Electronics using the competitive forces and value chain models. What is its business model and business strategy? How does it provide value?

2. What is the role of the Internet in J&R's business strategy? Is it providing a solution to J&R's problems? Why or why not?

3. Can J&R keep up with the competition since it is more or less a local brand competing with nation-wide chains? How would you measure its success in keeping up with the competition?

4. Visit J&R's online store at JR.com. What features described in this case are you able to find on the site? How effective is the implementation of these features? Do they seem to be achieving the goals that J&R set for them?

5. Compare JR.com to the Web sites of Circuit City or Best Buy. Evaluate them in terms of product selection and availability, tools for providing product information and customer service, and ease of use. Which site would you use to purchase a computer or MP3 player? Why?

6. What do you think of the notion that J&R's new Web site and emphasis on e-commerce are not likely to result in a short-term windfall but should be part of a long-term growth strategy? How does this concept fit in with the company's strategy?

Improving Decision Making and Managing Knowledge

CHAPTER 10

STUDENT LEARNING OBJECTIVES

After completing this chapter, you will be able to answer the following questions:

1. What are the different types of decisions, and how does the decision-making process work?

2. How do information systems help people working individually and in groups make decisions more effectively?

3. What are the business benefits of using intelligent techniques in decision making and knowledge management?

4. What types of systems are used for enterprise-wide knowledge management, and how do they provide value for businesses?

5. What are the major types of knowledge work systems, and how do they provide value for firms?

Chapter Outline

EASTERN MOUNTAIN SPORTS FORGES A TRAIL TO BETTER DECISIONS

Founded in 1967 by two rock climbers, Eastern Mountain Sports (EMS) has grown into one of the leading outdoor specialty retailers in the United States, with more than 80 retail stores in 16 states, a seasonal catalogue, and a growing online presence. EMS designs and offers a wide variety of gear and clothing for outdoor enthusiasts.

Until recently, however, the company's information systems for management reporting were dated and clumsy. It was very difficult for senior management to have a picture of customer purchasing patterns and company operations because data were stored in disparate sources: legacy merchandising systems, financial systems, and point-of-sale devices. Employees crafted most of the reports by hand, wasting valuable people resources on producing information rather than analyzing it.

After evaluating several leading business intelligence products, EMS selected WebFOCUS and iWay middleware from Information Builders. EMS believed WebFOCUS was better than other tools in combining data from various sources and

presenting the results in a user-friendly view. It is Web-based and easy to implement, taking EMS only 90 days to be up and running.

iWay extracts point-of-sale data from EMS's legacy enterprise system running on an IBM AS/400 midrange computer and loads them into a data mart running Microsoft's SQL Server database management system. WebFOCUS then creates a series of executive dashboards accessible through Web browsers, which provide a common view of the data to more than 200 users at headquarters and retail stores.

The dashboards provide a high-level view of key performance indicators such as sales, inventory, and margin levels, but enable users to drill down for more detail on specific transactions. Merchandising managers monitor inventory levels and the rate that items turn over. E-commerce managers monitor hour-by-hour Web sales, visitors, and conversion rates. A color-coded system of red, yellow, and green alerts indicates metrics that are over, under, or at plan.

EMS is adding wikis and blogs to enable managers and employees to share tips and initiate dialogues about key pieces of data. For example, in identifying top-selling items and stores, EMS sales managers noticed that inner soles were moving very briskly in specialty stores. These stores had perfected a multi-step sales technique that included the recommendation of socks designed for specific uses, such as running or hiking, along with an inner sole that could be custom-fit to each customer. Wikis and blogs made it easier for managers to discuss this tactic and share it with the rest of the retail network.

Longer term, EMS is planning for more detailed interactions with its suppliers. By sharing inventory and sales data with suppliers EMS will be able to quickly re-stock inventory to meet customer demand, while suppliers will know when to ramp up production.

Sources: Jeffrey Neville, "X-treme Web 2.0," *Optimize Magazine*, January 2007 and "Web 2.0's Wild Blue Yonder," *Information Week*, January 1/8, 2007; "Eastern Mountain Sports Forges a Trail to Merchandising Visibility," www.informationbuilders.com, accessed August 6, 2007.

Eastern Mountain Sports' executive dashboards are a powerful illustration of how information systems improve decision making. Management was unable to make good decisions about how and where to stock stores because the required data were scattered in many different systems and were difficult to access. Management reporting was excessively manual. Bad decisions about how to stock stores and warehouses increased operating costs and prevented EMS stores from responding quickly to customer needs.

EMS management could have continued to use its outdated management reporting system or implemented a large-scale enterprise-wide database and software, which would have been extremely expensive and time-consuming to complete. Instead, it opted for a business intelligence solution that could extract, consolidate, and analyze sales and merchandising data from its various legacy systems. It chose a platform from WebFOCUS because the tools were user-friendly and capable of pulling together data from many different sources.

The chosen solution populates a data mart with data from point-of-sale and legacy systems, and then pulls information from the data mart into a central series of executive dashboards visible to authorized users throughout the organization. Decision-makers can quickly access a unified high-level view of key performance indicators such as sales, inventory, and margin levels or drill down to obtain more detail about specific transactions. Increased availability of this information has helped EMS managers make better decisions about increasing sales, allocating resources, and propagating best practices.

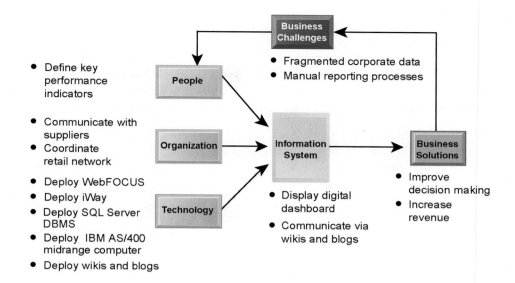

- Define key performance indicators

- Communicate with suppliers
- Coordinate retail network

- Deploy WebFOCUS
- Deploy iWay
- Deploy SQL Server DBMS
- Deploy IBM AS/400 midrange computer
- Deploy wikis and blogs

Business Challenges

- Fragmented corporate data
- Manual reporting processes

People

Organization

Technology

Information System

- Display digital dashboard
- Communicate via wikis and blogs

Business Solutions

- Improve decision making
- Increase revenue

HEADS UP

This chapter focuses on how business firms use information systems to improve decision making. Until the past decade, most businesses and their managers and employees operated in an information and knowledge fog, making decisions based on best guesses about the past and present, and making expensive errors in the process. Today, firms use a wide variety of information systems to directly improve decision making throughout the firm from the executive suite to the call center customer service representative, from the financial advisor's desk to the factory floor. Even customers are provided with systems to help them make better decisions. It would not be an overstatement to say that a primary contribution of information systems to business firms has been to improve decision making at all levels.

10.1 Decision Making and Information Systems

One of the main contributions of information systems has been to improve decision making, both for individuals and groups. Decision making in businesses used to be limited to management. Today, lower-level employees are responsible for some of these decisions, as information systems make information available to lower levels of the business. But what do we mean by better decision making? How does decision making take place in businesses and other organizations? Let's take a closer look.

BUSINESS VALUE OF IMPROVED DECISION MAKING

What does it mean to the business to be able to make a better decision? What is the monetary value to the business of better, improved decision making? Table 10.1 attempts to measure the monetary value of improved decision making for a small U.S. manufacturing firm with $280 million in annual revenue and 140 employees. The firm has identified a number of key decisions where new system investments might improve the quality of decision making. The table provides selected estimates of annual value (in the form of cost savings or increased revenue) from improved decision making in selected areas of the business.

TABLE 10.1

Business Value of Enhanced Decision Making

Example Decision	Decision Maker	Number of Annual Decisions	Estimated Value to Firm of a Single Improved Decision	Annual Vaue
Allocate support to most valuable customers	Accounts manager	12	$100,000	$1,200,000
Predict call center daily demand	Call Center management	4	150,000	600,000
Decide parts inventory levels daily	Inventory manager	365	5,000	1,825,000
Identify competitive bids from major suppliers	Senior management	1	2,000,000	2,000,000
Schedule production to fill orders	Manufacturing manager	150	10,000	1,500,000
Allocate labor to complete a job	Production floor manager	100	4,000	400,000

We can see from Table 10.1 that decisions are made at all levels of the firm, and that some of these decisions are common, routine, and numerous. Although the value of improving any single decision may be small, improving hundreds of thousands of "small" decisions adds up to a large annual value for the business.

TYPES OF DECISIONS

Chapter 2 showed that there are different levels in an organization. Each of these levels has different information requirements for decision support and responsibility for different types of decisions (see Figure 10-1). Decisions are classified as structured, semistructured, and unstructured.

Figure 10-1
Information Requirements of Key Decision-Making Groups in a Firm
Senior managers, middle managers, operational managers, and employees have different types of decisions and information requirements.

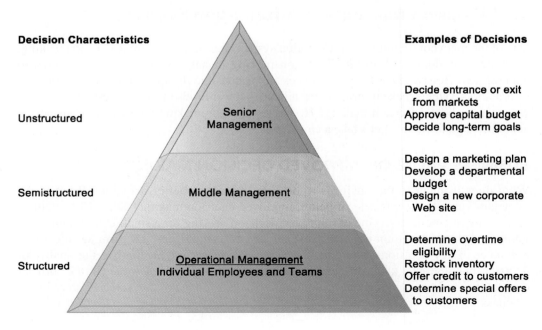

Decision Characteristics		Examples of Decisions
Unstructured	Senior Management	Decide entrance or exit from markets Approve capital budget Decide long-term goals
Semistructured	Middle Management	Design a marketing plan Develop a departmental budget Design a new corporate Web site
Structured	Operational Management Individual Employees and Teams	Determine overtime eligibility Restock inventory Offer credit to customers Determine special offers to customers

Unstructured decisions are those in which the decision maker must provide judgment, evaluation, and insight to solve the problem. Each of these decisions is novel, important, and nonroutine, and there is no well-understood or agreed-on procedure for making them.

Structured decisions, by contrast, are repetitive and routine, and they involve a definite procedure for handling them so that they do not have to be treated each time as if they were new. Many decisions have elements of both types of decisions and are **semistructured**, where only part of the problem has a clear-cut answer provided by an accepted procedure. In general, structured decisions are more prevalent at lower organizational levels, whereas unstructured problems are more common at higher levels of the firm.

Senior executives face many unstructured decision situations, such as establishing the firm's five- or ten-year goals or deciding new markets to enter. Answering the question "Should we enter a new market?" would require access to news, government reports, and industry views, as well as high-level summaries of firm performance. However, the answer would also require senior managers to use their own best judgment and poll other managers for their opinions.

Middle management faces more structured decision scenarios, but their decisions may include unstructured components. A typical middle-level management decision might be "Why is the reported order fulfillment showing a decline over the past six months at a distribution center in Minneapolis?" This middle manager could obtain a report from the firm's enterprise system or distribution management system on order activity and operational efficiency at the Minneapolis distribution center. This is the structured part of the decision. But before arriving at an answer, this middle manager will have to interview employees and gather more unstructured information from external sources about local economic conditions or sales trends.

Operational management and rank-and-file employees tend to make more structured decisions. For example, a supervisor on an assembly line has to decide whether an hourly paid worker is entitled to overtime pay. If the employee worked more than eight hours on a particular day, the supervisor would routinely grant overtime pay for any time beyond eight hours that was clocked on that day.

A sales account representative often has to make decisions about extending credit to customers by consulting the firm's customer database that contains credit information. If the customer met the firm's prespecified criteria for granting credit, the account representative would grant that customer credit to make a purchase. In both instances, the decisions are highly structured and are routinely made thousands of times each day in most large firms. The answer has been preprogrammed into the firm's payroll and accounts receivable systems.

THE DECISION-MAKING PROCESS

Making a decision is a multistep process. Simon (1960) described four different stages in decision making: intelligence, design, choice, and implementation (see Figure 10-2). These stages correspond to the four steps in problem-solving used throughout this book.

Intelligence consists of discovering, identifying, and understanding the problems occurring in the organization—why is there a problem, where, and what effects it is having on the firm.

Design involves identifying and exploring various solutions to the problem.

Choice consists of choosing among solution alternatives.

Implementation involves making the chosen alternative work and continuing to monitor how well the solution is working.

What happens if the solution you have chosen does not work? Figure 10-2 shows that you can return to an earlier stage in the decision-making process and repeat it, if necessary. For instance, in the face of declining sales, a sales management team may decide to pay the sales force a higher commission for making more sales to spur on the sales effort. If this

Figure 10-2
Stages in Decision Making
The decision-making process can be broken down into four stages.

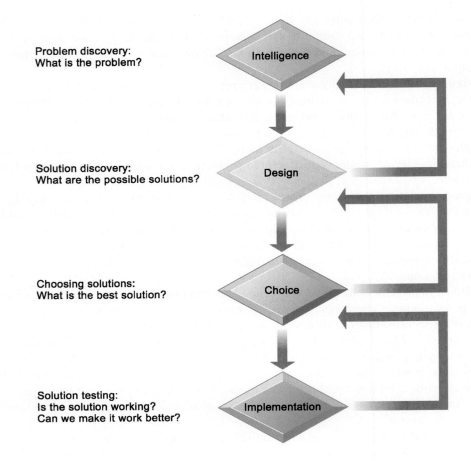

Problem discovery:
What is the problem? — Intelligence

Solution discovery:
What are the possible solutions? — Design

Choosing solutions:
What is the best solution? — Choice

Solution testing:
Is the solution working?
Can we make it work better? — Implementation

does not produce sales increases, managers would need to investigate whether the problem stems from poor product design, inadequate customer support, or a host of other causes that call for a different solution.

QUALITY OF DECISIONS AND DECISION MAKING

How can you tell if a decision has become "better" or the decision-making process "improved?" Accuracy is one important dimension of quality: In general, we think decisions are "better" if they accurately reflect the real-world data. Speed is another dimension: We tend to think that the decision-making process should be efficient, even speedy. For instance, when you apply for car insurance, you want the decision making by the insurance firm to be fast and accurate. But there are many other dimensions of quality in decisions and the decision-making process to consider. Which is important for you will depend on the business firm where you work, the various parties involved in the decision, and your own personal values. Table 10.2 describes some quality dimensions for decision making. When we describe how systems "improve decisions and the decision-making process" in this chapter, we are referencing the dimensions in this table.

SYSTEMS AND TECHNOLOGIES FOR SUPPORTING DECISIONS

There are four kinds of systems for supporting the different levels and types of decisions we have just described. We introduced these systems in Chapter 2. *Management information systems (MIS)* deliver routine reports and summaries of transaction-level data to middle- and operational-level managers to provide answers to structured and

Quality Dimension	Description
Accuracy	Decision reflects reality
Comprehensiveness	Decision reflects a full consideration of the facts and circumstances
Fairness	Decision faithfully reflects the concerns and interests of affected parties
Speed (efficiency)	Decision making is efficient with respect to time and other resources, including the time and resources of affected parties, such as customers
Coherence	Decision reflects a rational process that can be explained to others and made understandable
Due process	Decision is the result of a known process and can be appealed to a higher authority

TABLE 10.2

Qualities of Decisions and the Decision-Making Process

semistructured decision problems. *Decision support systems (DSS)* provide analytical models or tools for analyzing large quantities of data and supportive interactive queries for middle managers who face semistructured decision situations. *Executive support systems (ESS)* are systems that provide senior management, making primarily unstructured decisions, with external information (news, stock analyses, and industry trends) and high-level summaries of firm performance. *Group decision-support systems (GDSS)* are specialized systems that provide a group electronic environment in which managers and teams can collectively make decisions and design solutions for unstructured and semistructured problems.

Decision making is also enhanced by intelligent techniques and knowledge management systems. **Intelligent techniques** consist of expert systems, case-based reasoning, genetic algorithms, neural networks, fuzzy logic, and intelligent agents. These technologies aid decision makers by capturing individual and collective knowledge, discovering patterns and behaviors in very large quantities of data, and generating solutions to problems that are too large and complex for human beings to solve on their own.

Knowledge management systems, which we introduced in Chapter 2, and knowledge work systems provide tools for knowledge discovery, communication, and collaboration that make knowledge more easily available to decision makers and integrate it into the business processes of the firm.

10.2 Systems for Decision Support

Exactly how do these different types of systems for supporting decisions affect a business? What can today's decision-support systems do for a business? Let's look more closely at how each major type of decision-support system works and provides value.

MANAGEMENT INFORMATION SYSTEMS (MIS)

Management information systems (MIS), which we introduced in Chapter 2, help managers monitor and control the business by providing information on the firm's performance. They typically produce fixed, regularly scheduled reports based on data extracted and summarized from the firm's underlying transaction processing systems (TPS). The formats for these reports are often specified in advance. A typical MIS report might show a summary of monthly or annual sales for each of the major sales territories of a company. Sometimes,

TABLE 10.3

Examples of MIS Applications

Company	MIS Application
California Pizza Kitchen	Inventory Express application "remembers" each restaurant's ordering patterns and compares the amount of ingredients used per menu item to predefined portion measurements established by management. The system identifies restaurants with out-of-line portions and notifies their managers so that corrective actions can be taken.
PharMark	Extranet MIS identifies patients with drug-use patterns that place them at risk for adverse outcomes.
Black & Veatch	Intranet MIS tracks construction costs for various projects across the United States.
Taco Bell	Total Automation of Company Operations (TACO) system provides information on food, labor, and period-to-date costs for each restaurant.

MIS reports are exception reports, highlighting only exceptional conditions, such as when the sales quotas for a specific territory fall below an anticipated level or employees have exceeded their spending limits in a dental care plan.

Traditional MIS produce primarily hard-copy reports. Today, many of these reports are available online through an intranet, and more MIS reports can be generated on demand. Table 10.3 provides some examples of MIS applications.

DECISION-SUPPORT SYSTEMS (DSS)

Whereas MIS primarily address structured problems, DSS support semistructured and unstructured problem analysis. The earliest DSS were heavily model driven, using some type of model to perform "what-if" and other kinds of analyses. In a "what if" analysis, a model is developed, various input factors are changed, and the output changes are measured (see the following section). DSS analysis capabilities were based on a strong theory or model combined with a good user interface that made the system easy to use.

The Interactive Session on People describes a model-driven DSS. In this particular case, the system did not perform as well as expected because of the assumptions driving the model and user efforts to circumvent the system. As you read this case, try to identify the problem these companies were facing, what alternative solutions were available to management, and how well the chosen solution worked.

Some contemporary DSS are data driven, using online analytical processing (OLAP) and data mining to analyze large pools of data in major corporate systems. The business intelligence applications described in Chapter 5 are examples of these data-driven DSS. They support decision making by enabling users to extract useful information that was previously buried in large quantities of data.

For example, Compass Bank, a leading financial holding company with 376 banking centers and more than $28 billion in assets, uses a data-driven DSS to help it minimize default risk in its credit card business. The system analyzes the relationship between a customer's checking and savings account activity and that person's credit card default risk. The system is able to pull together and analyze 13 months of detailed data from multiple databases to flag customer accounts in danger of defaulting.

INTERACTIVE SESSION: PEOPLE   Too Many Bumped Fliers: Why?

In a seemingly simpler and less hectic time, over-booked flights presented an opportunity. Frequent travelers regularly and eagerly chose to give up their seats and delay their departures by a few hours in exchange for rewards such as a voucher for a free ticket.

Today, fewer people are volunteering to give up their seats for a flight because there are fewer and fewer seats to be bumped to. Airlines are struggling to stay in business and look to save costs wherever possible. They are scheduling fewer flights and those flights are more crowded. Instead of delaying his or her trip by a few hours, a passenger that accepts a voucher for being bumped may have to wait several days before a seat becomes available on another flight. And passengers are being bumped from flights involuntarily more often.

Airlines routinely overbook flights to compensate for the millions of no-shows that cut into expected revenue. The purpose of overbooking is not to leave passengers without a seat but to come as close as possible to filling every seat on every flight. The revenue lost from an empty seat is much greater than the costs of compensating a bumped passenger. Airlines are much closer today to filling every seat on flights than at any point in their history. The problem is, the most popular routes often sell out, so bumped passengers may be stranded for days.

The airlines do not approach overbooking haphazardly. They employ young, sharp minds with backgrounds in math and economics as analysts. The analysts use computer modeling to predict how many passengers will fail to show up for a flight. They recommend overbooking based on the numbers generated by the software.

The software used by US Airways, for example, analyzes the historical record of no-shows on flights and looks at the rate at every fare level available. The lowest-priced fares are generally nonrefundable, and passengers at those fare levels tend to carry their reservations through. Business travelers with the high-priced fares no-show more often. The software examines the fares people are booking on each upcoming flight and takes other data into account, such as the rate of no-shows on flights originating from certain geographic regions. Analysts then predict the number of no-shows on a particular flight, based on which fares passengers have booked, and overbook the flight accordingly.

Of course, the analysts do not always guess correctly. And their efforts can be hampered by a number of factors. Ticket agents report that faulty computer algorithms result in miscalculations. Changes in weather can introduce unanticipated weight restrictions. Sometimes a smaller plane is substituted for the scheduled plane. All of these circumstances result in fewer seats being available for the same number of passengers, which might have been set too high already.

Regardless of how much support the analysts have from airline management, gate attendants complain because they are the ones who receive the brunt of overbooked passengers' wrath. Attendants have been known to call in sick to avoid dealing with the havoc caused by overbooked flights.

Some gate attendants have gone as far as creating phony reservations, sometimes in the names of airline executives or cartoon characters, such as Mickey Mouse, in an effort to stop analysts from overbooking. This tactic may save the attendants some grief in the short term, but their actions often come back to haunt them. The modeling software counts the phony reservations as no-shows, which leads the analysts to overbook the flight even more the next time. Thomas Trenga, vice president for revenue management at US Airways, refers to this game of chicken as "the death spiral." US Airways discourages the practice of entering phony reservations.

With fewer passengers volunteering to accept vouchers, tensions can escalate. The number of passengers bumped involuntarily in 2006 rose 23 percent from the previous year and has continued to rise. The encouraging statistic is that only 676,408 of the 555 million people who flew in 2006 were bumped, voluntarily or involuntarily.

W. Douglas Parker, CEO of US Airways, says that airlines have to overbook their flights as long as they allow passengers to no-show without penalty. US Airways has a no-show rate of between 7 and 8 percent. The airline's revenue in 2006 was $11.56 billion. US Airways claims that overbooking contributed to at least $1 billion of that revenue. With a profit of only $304 million, that extra revenue becomes critical to the survival of the business. Some airlines, such as JetBlue, have avoided the overbooking controversy by offering only nonrefundable tickets. No-shows cannot reclaim the price of their tickets. Business travelers often buy the most expensive seats, but also want the flexibility of refundable tickets, so JetBlue is considering a change in its policy.

The airlines are supposed to hold their analysts accountable for their work, but they are rarely subject to critical review. Some analysts make an effort to accommodate the wishes of the airport workers by finding a compromise in the overbooking rate. Unfortunately, analysts often leave their jobs for new challenges once they become proficient at overbooking.

Sources: Jeff Bailey, "Bumped Fliers and Plan B," *The New York Times*, May 30, 2007; Alice LaPlante, "Travel Problems? Blame Technology," *InformationWeek.com*, June 11, 2007; Noelle Phillips, "More Fliers, Fewer Flights Mean More Bumping," *TheState.com*, May 31, 2007; and "When Airlines Do the Bump, You Can Push Back," ocregister.com, June 10, 2007.

CASE STUDY QUESTIONS

1. Is the decision support system being used by airlines to overbook flights working well? Answer from the perspective of the airlines and from the perspective of customers.

2. What is the impact on the airlines if they are bumping too many passengers?

3. What are the inputs, processes, and outputs of this DSS?

4. What people, organization, and technology factors are responsible for excessive bumping problems?

5. How much of this is a "people" problem? Explain your answer.

MIS IN ACTION

Visit the Web sites for US Airways, JetBlue, and Continental. Search the sites to answer the following questions:

1. What is the policy of each of these airlines for dealing with involuntary refunds (overbookings)? (Hint: these matters are often covered in the Contract of Carriage.)

2. In your opinion, which airline has the best policy? What makes this policy better than the others?

3. How are each of these policies intended to benefit customers? How do they benefit the airlines?

Components of DSS

Figure 10-3 illustrates the components of a DSS. They include a database of data used for query and analysis; a software system with models, data mining, and other analytical tools; and a user interface.

The **DSS database** is a collection of current or historical data from a number of applications or groups. It may be a small database residing on a PC that contains a subset of corporate data that has been downloaded and possibly combined with external data. Alternatively, the DSS database may be a massive data warehouse that is continuously updated by major corporate TPS (including enterprise systems and data generated by Web site transactions). The data in DSS databases are generally extracts or copies of production databases so that using the DSS does not interfere with critical operational systems.

The **DSS software system** contains the software tools that are used for data analysis. It may contain various OLAP tools, data mining tools, or a collection of mathematical and analytical models that easily can be made accessible to the DSS user. A **model** is an abstract representation that illustrates the components or relationships of a phenomenon. A model can be a physical model (such as a model airplane), a mathematical model (such as an equation), or a verbal model (such as a description of a procedure for writing an order).

Statistical modeling helps establish relationships, such as relating product sales to differences in age, income, or other factors between communities. Optimization models determine optimal resource allocation to maximize or minimize specified variables, such as cost or time. A classic use of optimization models is to determine the proper mix of products within a given market to maximize profits. P&G uses optimization models to determine how to maximize its return on investment from the organization of its supply chain.

Forecasting models often are used to forecast sales. The user of this type of model might supply a range of historical data to project future conditions and the sales that might result

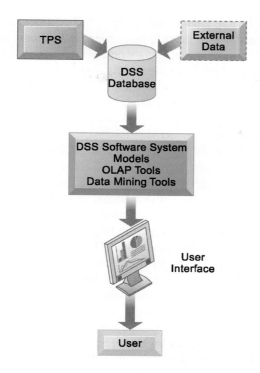

Figure 10-3
Overview of a Decision-Support System
The main components of the DSS are the DSS database, the DSS software system, and the user interface. The DSS database may be a small database residing on a PC or a large data warehouse.

from those conditions. The decision maker could vary those future conditions (entering, for example, a rise in raw materials costs or the entry of a new, low-priced competitor in the market) to determine how new conditions might affect sales.

Sensitivity analysis models ask "what-if" questions repeatedly to determine the impact on outcomes of changes in one or more factors. *What-if analysis*—working forward from known or assumed conditions—allows the user to vary certain values to test results to better predict outcomes if changes occur in those values. What happens if we raise product price by 5 percent or increase the advertising budget by $100,000? What happens if we keep the price and advertising budgets the same? Spreadsheet software, such as Microsoft Excel, is often used for this purpose (see Figure 10-4). Backward sensitivity analysis software helps decision makers with goal seeking: If I want to sell one million product units next year, how much must I reduce the price of the product?

The DSS user interface permits easy interaction between users of the system and the DSS software tools. Many DSS today have Web interfaces to take advantage of graphic displays, interactivity, and ease of use.

Figure 10-4
Sensitivity Analysis
This table displays the results of a sensitivity analysis of the effect of changing the sales price of a necktie and the cost per unit on the product's break-even point. It answers the question, "What happens to the break-even point if the sales price and the cost to make each unit increase or decrease?"

Total fixed costs	19000					
Variable cost per unit	3					
Average sales price	17					
Contribution margin	14					
Break-even point	1357					
			Variable Cost per Unit			
Sales	1357	2	3	4	5	6
Price	14	1583	1727	1900	2111	2375
	15	1462	1583	1727	1900	2111
	16	1357	1462	1583	1727	1900
	17	1267	1357	1462	1583	1727
	18	1188	1267	1357	1462	1583

Using Spreadsheet Pivot Tables to Support Decision Making

Managers also use spreadsheets to identify and understand patterns in business information. For instance, let's a take a look at one day's worth of transactions at an online firm Online Management Training Inc. (OMT Inc.) that sells online management training videos and books to corporations and individuals who want to improve their management techniques. On a single day the firm experienced 517 order transactions. Figure 10-5 shows the first 25 records of transactions produced at the firm's Web site on that day. The names of customers and other identifiers have been removed from this list.

You can think of this list as a database composed of transaction records (the rows). The fields (column headings) for each customer record are: customer ID, region of purchase, payment method, source of contact (e-mail versus Web banner ad), amount of purchase, the product purchased (either online training or a book), and time of day (in 24 hour time).

There is a great deal of valuable information in this transaction list that could help managers answer important questions and make important decisions:

- Where do most of our customers come from? The answer might tell managers where to spend more marketing resources or to initiate new marketing efforts.
- Are there regional differences in the sources of our customers? Perhaps in some regions, e-mail is the most effective marketing tool, whereas in other regions, Web banner ads are more effective. The answer to this more complicated question could help managers develop a regional marketing strategy.
- Where are the average purchases higher? The answer might tell managers where to focus marketing and sales resources or to pitch different messages to different regions.
- What form of payment is the most common? The answer could be used to emphasize in advertising the most preferred means of payment.
- Are there any times of day when purchases are most common? Do people buy products while at work (likely during the day) or at home (likely in the evening)?
- Are there regional differences in the average purchase? If one region is much more lucrative, managers could focus their marketing and advertising resources on that region.

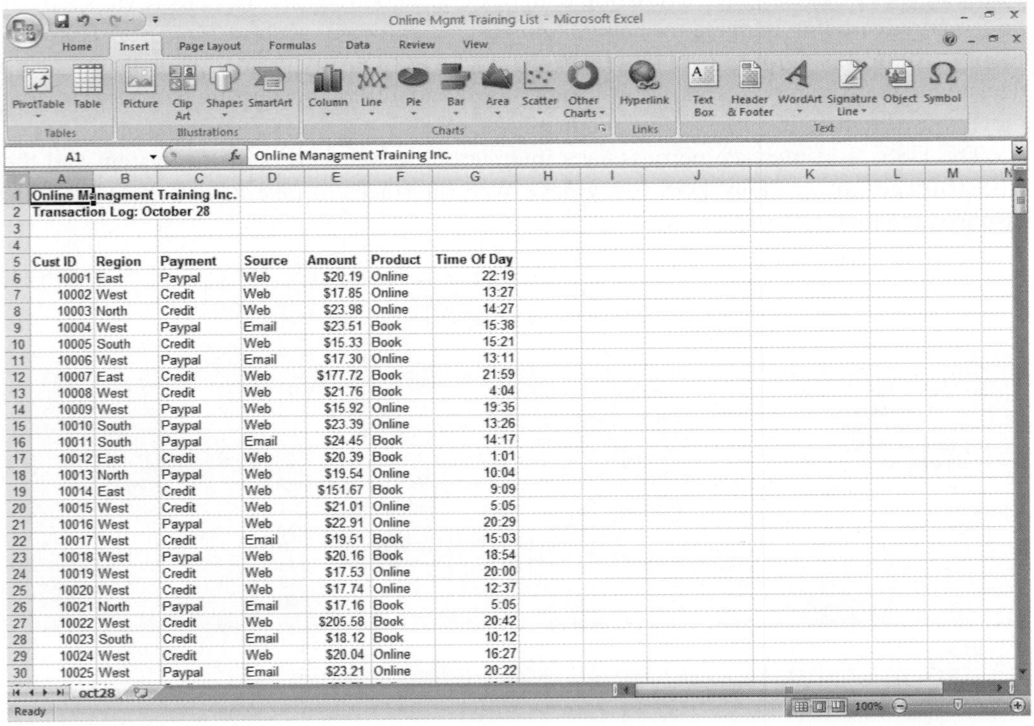
Online Managment Training Inc.
Transaction Log: October 28

Cust ID	Region	Payment	Source	Amount	Product	Time Of Day
10001	East	Paypal	Web	$20.19	Online	22:19
10002	West	Credit	Web	$17.85	Online	13:27
10003	North	Credit	Web	$23.98	Online	14:27
10004	West	Paypal	Email	$23.51	Book	15:38
10005	South	Credit	Web	$15.33	Book	15:21
10006	West	Paypal	Email	$17.30	Online	13:11
10007	East	Credit	Web	$177.72	Book	21:59
10008	West	Credit	Web	$21.76	Book	4:04
10009	West	Paypal	Web	$15.92	Online	19:35
10010	South	Paypal	Web	$23.39	Online	13:26
10011	South	Paypal	Email	$24.45	Book	14:17
10012	East	Credit	Web	$20.39	Book	1:01
10013	North	Paypal	Web	$19.54	Online	10:04
10014	East	Credit	Web	$151.67	Book	9:09
10015	West	Credit	Web	$21.01	Online	5:05
10016	West	Paypal	Web	$22.91	Online	20:29
10017	West	Credit	Email	$19.51	Book	15:03
10018	West	Paypal	Web	$20.16	Book	18:54
10019	West	Credit	Web	$17.53	Online	20:00
10020	West	Credit	Web	$17.74	Online	12:37
10021	North	Paypal	Email	$17.16	Book	5:05
10022	West	Credit	Web	$205.58	Book	20:42
10023	South	Credit	Email	$18.12	Book	10:12
10024	West	Credit	Web	$20.04	Online	16:27
10025	West	Paypal	Email	$23.21	Online	20:22

Figure 10-5
Sample List of Transactions for Online Management Training Inc.
This list shows a portion of the order transactions for Online Management Training Inc. on October 28, 2007.

Notice that these questions often involve multiple dimensions: region and average purchase; time of day and average purchase; payment type and average purchase; and region, source of customer, and purchase. Also, some of the dimensions are categorical, such as payment type, region, and source. If the list were small, you could simply inspect the list and find patterns in the data. But this is impossible when you have a list of over 500 transactions.

Fortunately, the spreadsheet pivot table provides a powerful tool for answering such questions using large data sets. A **pivot table** is a table that displays two or more dimensions of data in a convenient format. Microsoft Excel's PivotTable capability makes it easy to analyze lists and databases by automatically extracting, organizing, and summarizing the data.

For instance, let's take the first question, "Where do our customers come from?" We will start with region and ask the question "How many customers come from each region?" To find the answer using Excel 2007, you would create a pivot table by selecting the range of data, fields you want to analyze, and a location for the PivotTable report, as illustrated in Figure 10-6. The pivot table shows most customers come from the Western region.

Does the source of the customer make a difference in addition to region? We have two sources of customers: e-mail campaigns and online banner advertising. In a few seconds, you can find the answer shown in Figure 10-7. The pivot table shows that Web banner advertising produces most of the customers, and this is true of all the regions.

You can use pivot tables to answer all the questions we have posed about the Online Management Training data. The complete Excel file for these examples is available on our companion Web site. The Hands-On MIS section of this chapter asks you to find answers to a number of other questions regarding this data file.

Data Visualization and Geographic Information Systems

Data from information systems can be made easier for users to digest and act on by using graphics, charts, tables, maps, digital images, three-dimensional presentations, animations, and other data visualization technologies. By presenting data in graphical form, **data visualization** tools help users see patterns and relationships in large amounts of data that would be difficult to discern if the data were presented as traditional lists of text.

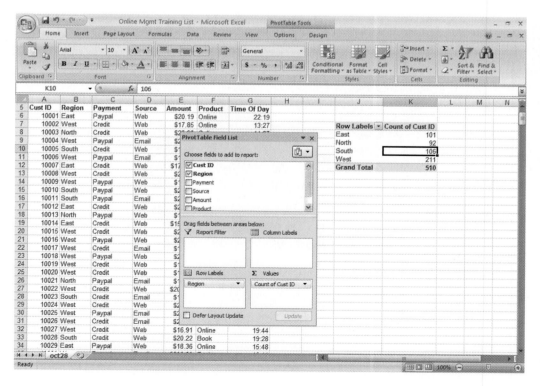

Figure 10-6
A Pivot Table That Determines the Regional Distribution of Customers
This pivot table was created using Excel 2007 to quickly produce a table showing the relationship between region and number of customers.

Figure 10-7
A Pivot Table that Examines Customer Regional Distribution and Advertising Source
In this pivot table, we can examine where customers come from in terms of region and advertising source. It appears nearly 30 percent of the customers respond to e-mail campaigns, and there are some regional variations.

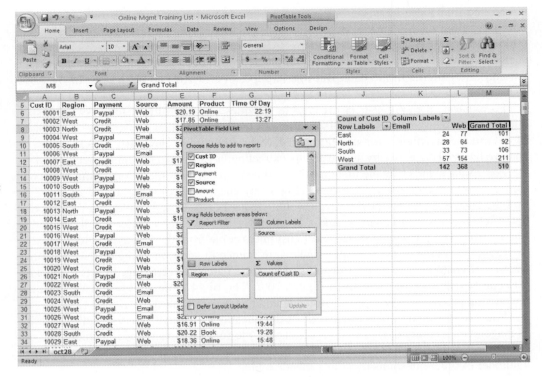

Geographic information systems (GIS) are a special category of DSS that use data visualization technology to analyze and display data for planning and decision making in the form of digitized maps. The software assembles, stores, manipulates, and displays geographically referenced information, tying data to points, lines, and areas on a map. GIS have modeling capabilities, enabling managers to change data and automatically revise business scenarios.

South Carolina used a GIS-based program called HAZUS to estimate and map the regional damage and losses resulting from an earthquake of a given location and intensity. HAZUS estimates the degree and geographic extent of earthquake damage across the state based on inputs of building use, type, and construction materials. The GIS helps the state plan for natural hazards mitigation and response.

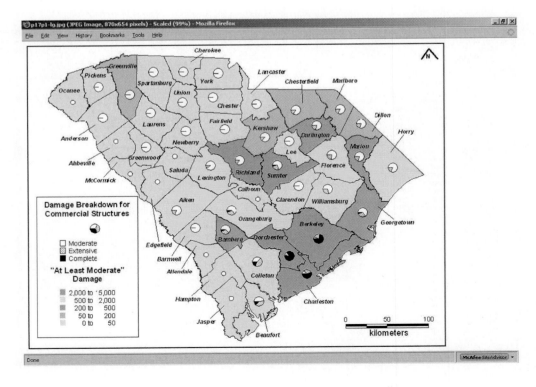

GIS support decisions that require knowledge about the geographic distribution of people or other resources. For example, GIS might be used to help state and local governments calculate emergency response times to natural disasters, to help retail chains identify profitable new store locations, or to help banks identify the best locations for installing new branches or automatic teller machine (ATM) terminals.

Web-Based Customer Decision-Support Systems

DSS based on the Web and the Internet support decision making by providing online access to various databases and information pools along with software for data analysis. **Customer decision-support systems (CDSS)** support the decision-making process of an existing or potential customer.

People interested in purchasing a product or service can use Internet search engines, intelligent agents, online catalogs, Web directories, newsgroup discussions, e-mail, and other tools to help them locate the information they need to help with their decision. Companies have developed specific customer Web sites where all the information, models, or other analytical tools for evaluating alternatives are concentrated in one location. Web-based DSS have become especially popular in the financial services area because so many people are trying to manage their own assets and retirement savings. For example, the T. Rowe Price Web site offers a series of online tools and planning guides for college planning, retirement planning, investment planning, tax planning, and estate planning.

EXECUTIVE SUPPORT SYSTEMS

If you were a senior executive and you wanted a picture of the overall performance of your firm, where would you find that information? You would turn to an executive support system. Executive support systems (ESS), which we introduced in Chapter 2, help solve unstructured and semistructured problems by focusing on the information needs of senior management. Contemporary ESS bring together data from many different internal and external sources, including data from the Web, often through a portal. These systems provide easy-to-use analytical tools and online displays to help users select, access, and tailor the data as needed.

You can think of ESS as generalized computing, communications, and graphic systems that, similar to a zoom lens, can focus quickly on detailed problems or retract back for a broad view of the company. ESS have a capability to **drill down**, moving from a piece of summary data to lower and lower levels of detail. Some display a high-level view of firm performance in the form of a digital dashboard. A **digital dashboard**, or "executive dashboard," displays on a single screen all of the critical measurements for piloting a company, similar to the cockpit of an airplane or an automobile dashboard. The dashboard presents key performance indicators as graphs and charts, providing a one-page overview of all the critical measurements necessary to make key executive decisions. The EMS dashboards described in the chapter-opening case are an example.

ESS help senior executives monitor organizational performance, track activities of competitors, identify changing market conditions, spot problems, identify opportunities, and forecast trends. Employees lower down in the corporate hierarchy also use these systems to monitor and measure business performance in their areas of responsibility.

GROUP DECISION-SUPPORT SYSTEMS

The systems we have just described focus primarily on helping you make a decision acting alone. But what if you are part of a team and need to make a decision as a group? You would use a special category of systems called group decision-support systems (GDSS) for this purpose.

A **group decision-support system (GDSS)** is an interactive computer-based system for facilitating the solution of unstructured problems by a set of decision makers working together as a group in the same location or in different locations. Groupware and

Web-based tools for videoconferencing and electronic meetings described earlier in this text support some group decision processes, but their focus is primarily on communication. GDSS, however, provide tools and technologies geared explicitly toward group decision making.

GDSS-guided meetings take place in conference rooms with special hardware and software tools to facilitate group decision making. The hardware includes computer and networking equipment, overhead projectors, and display screens. Special electronic meeting software collects, documents, ranks, edits, and stores the ideas offered in a decision-making meeting. The more elaborate GDSS use a professional facilitator and support staff. The facilitator selects the software tools and helps organize and run the meeting.

A sophisticated GDSS provides each attendee with a dedicated desktop computer under that person's individual control. No one will be able to see what individuals do on their computers until those participants are ready to share information. Their input is transmitted over a network to a central server that stores information generated by the meeting and makes it available to all on the meeting network. Data can also be projected on a large screen in the meeting room.

GDSS make it possible to increase meeting size while at the same time increasing productivity because individuals contribute simultaneously rather than one at a time. A GDSS promotes a collaborative atmosphere by guaranteeing contributors' anonymity so that attendees can focus on evaluating the ideas themselves without fear of personally being criticized or of having their ideas rejected based on the contributor. GDSS software tools follow structured methods for organizing and evaluating ideas and for preserving the results of meetings, enabling nonattendees to locate needed information after the meeting. GDSS effectiveness depends on the nature of the problem and the group and on how well a meeting is planned and conducted.

10.3 Intelligent Systems for Decision Support

A number of intelligent techniques for enhancing decision making are based on **artificial intelligence (AI)** technology, which consists of computer-based systems (both hardware and software) that attempt to emulate human behavior and thought patterns. These techniques include expert systems, case-based reasoning, fuzzy logic, neural networks, genetic algorithms, and intelligent agents.

EXPERT SYSTEMS

What if employees in your firm had to make decisions that required some special knowledge, such as how to formulate a fast-drying sealing compound or how to diagnose and repair a malfunctioning diesel engine, but all the people with that expertise had left the firm? Expert systems are one type of decision-making aid that could help you out. An **expert system** captures human expertise in a limited domain of knowledge as a set of rules in a software system that can be used by others in the organization. These systems typically perform a limited number of tasks that can be performed by professionals in a few minutes or hours, such as diagnosing a malfunctioning machine or determining whether to grant credit for a loan. They are useful in decision-making situations where expertise is expensive or in short supply.

How Expert Systems Work

Human knowledge must be modeled or represented in a form that a computer can process. Expert systems model human knowledge as a set of rules that collectively are called the **knowledge base**. Expert systems can have from 200 to as many as 10,000 of these rules, depending on the complexity of the decision-making problem. These rules are much more interconnected and nested than in a traditional software program (see Figure 10-8).

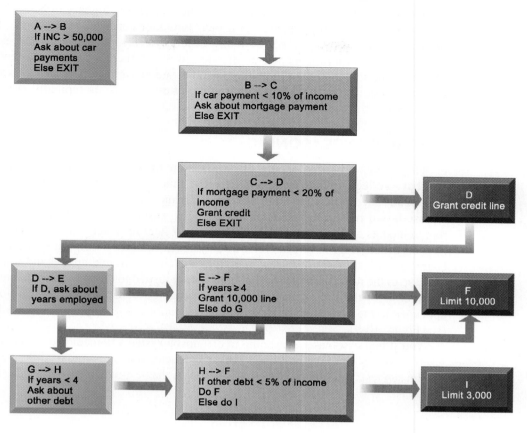

Figure 10-8
Rules in an Expert System

An expert system contains a set of rules to be followed when used. The rules are interconnected; the number of outcomes is known in advance and is limited; there are multiple paths to the same outcome; and the system can consider multiple rules at a single time. The rules illustrated are for a simple credit-granting expert system.

The strategy used to search through the collection of rules and formulate conclusions is called the **inference engine**. The inference engine works by searching through the rules and "firing" those rules that are triggered by facts gathered and entered by the user.

Expert systems provide businesses with an array of benefits, including improved decisions, reduced errors, reduced costs, reduced training time, and improved quality and service. For example, Con-Way Transportation built an expert system called Line-haul to automate and optimize planning of overnight shipment routes for its nationwide freight-trucking business. The expert system captures the business rules that dispatchers follow when assigning drivers, trucks, and trailers to transport 50,000 shipments of heavy freight each night across 25 U.S. states and Canada and when plotting their routes. Line-haul runs on a Sun platform and uses data on daily customer shipment requests, available drivers, trucks, trailer space, and weight stored in an Oracle database. The expert system uses thousands of rules and 100,000 lines of program code written in C++ to crunch the numbers and create optimum routing plans for 95 percent of daily freight shipments. Con-Way dispatchers tweak the routing plan provided by the expert system and relay final routing specifications to field personnel responsible for packing the trailers for their nighttime runs. Con-Way recouped its $3 million investment in the system within two years by reducing the number of drivers, packing more freight per trailer, and reducing damage from rehandling. The system also reduces dispatchers' arduous nightly tasks (Pastore, 2003).

Although expert systems lack the robust and general intelligence of human beings, they can provide benefits to organizations if their limitations are well understood. Only certain classes of problems can be solved using expert systems. Virtually all successful expert systems deal with problems of classification in which there are relatively few alternative outcomes and in which these possible outcomes are all known in advance. Expert systems are much less useful for dealing with unstructured problems typically encountered by managers.

CASE-BASED REASONING

Expert systems primarily capture the knowledge of individual experts, but organizations also have collective knowledge and expertise that they have built up over the years. This organizational knowledge can be captured and stored using case-based reasoning. In **case-based reasoning (CBR)**, knowledge and past experiences of human specialists are represented as cases and stored in a database for later retrieval when the user encounters a new case with similar parameters. The system searches for stored cases with problem characteristics similar to the new one, finds the closest fit, and applies the solutions of the old case to the new case. Successful solutions are tagged to the new case and both are stored together with the other cases in the knowledge base. Unsuccessful solutions also are appended to the case database along with explanations as to why the solutions did not work (see Figure 10-9).

You'll find case-based reasoning in diagnostic systems in medicine or customer support where users can retrieve past cases whose characteristics are similar to the new case. The system suggests a solution or diagnosis based on the best-matching retrieved case.

Figure 10-9
How Case-Based Reasoning Works
Case-based reasoning represents knowledge as a database of past cases and their solutions. The system uses a six-step process to generate solutions to new problems encountered by the user.

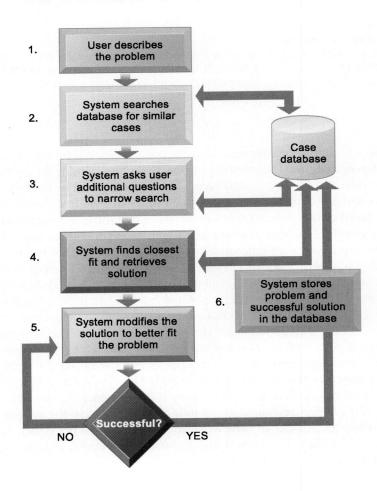

FUZZY LOGIC SYSTEMS

Most people do not think in terms of traditional IF-THEN rules or precise numbers. Humans tend to categorize things imprecisely, using rules for making decisions that may have many shades of meaning. For example, a man or a woman may be *strong* or *intelligent*. A company may be *large, medium,* or *small* in size. Temperature may be *hot, cold, cool,* or *warm*. These categories represent a range of values.

Fuzzy logic is a rule-based technology that represents such imprecision by creating rules that use approximate or subjective values. It describes a particular phenomenon or process linguistically and then represents that description in a small number of flexible rules.

Let's look at the way fuzzy logic would represent various temperatures in a computer application to control room temperature automatically. The terms (known as *membership functions*) are imprecisely defined so that, for example, in Figure 10-10, cool is between 45 degrees and 70 degrees, although the temperature is most clearly cool between about 60 degrees and 67 degrees. Note that *cool* is overlapped by *cold* or *norm*. To control the room environment using this logic, the programmer would develop similarly imprecise definitions for humidity and other factors, such as outdoor wind and temperature. The rules might include one that says, "If the temperature is *cool* or *cold* and the humidity is low while the outdoor wind is high and the outdoor temperature is low, raise the heat and humidity in the room." The computer would combine the membership function readings in a weighted manner and, using all the rules, raise and lower the temperature and humidity.

Fuzzy logic provides solutions to problems requiring expertise that is difficult to represent in the form of crisp IF-THEN rules. In Japan, Sendai's subway system uses fuzzy logic controls to accelerate so smoothly that standing passengers need not hold on. Fuzzy logic allows incremental changes in inputs to produce smooth changes in outputs instead of discontinuous ones, making it useful for consumer electronics and engineering applications.

NEURAL NETWORKS

Neural networks are used for solving complex, poorly understood problems for which large amounts of data have been collected. They find patterns and relationships in massive amounts of data that would be too complicated and difficult for a human being

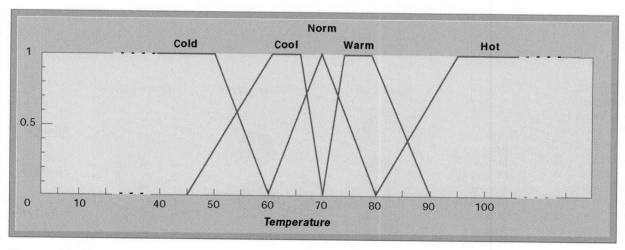

Figure 10-10
Fuzzy Logic for Temperature Control
The membership functions for the input called temperature are in the logic of the thermostat to control the room temperature. Membership functions help translate linguistic expressions, such as warm, into numbers that the computer can manipulate

to analyze. Neural networks discover this knowledge by using hardware and software that parallel the processing patterns of the biological or human brain. Neural networks "learn" patterns from large quantities of data by sifting through data, searching for relationships, building models, and correcting over and over again the model's own mistakes.

A neural network has a large number of sensing and processing nodes that continuously interact with each other. Figure 10-11 represents one type of neural network comprising an input layer, an output layer, and a hidden processing layer. Humans "train" the network by feeding it a set of training data for which the inputs produce a known set of outputs or conclusions. This helps the computer learn the correct solution by example. As the computer is fed more data, each case is compared with the known outcome. If it differs, a correction is calculated and applied to the nodes in the hidden processing layer. These steps are repeated until a condition, such as corrections being less than a certain amount, is reached. The neural network in Figure 10-11 has learned how to identify a fraudulent credit card purchase. Also, self-organizing neural networks can be trained by exposing them to large amounts of data and allowing them to discover the patterns and relationships in the data.

Whereas expert systems seek to emulate or model a human expert's way of solving problems, neural network builders claim that they do not program solutions and do not aim to solve specific problems. Instead, neural network designers seek to put intelligence into the hardware in the form of a generalized capability to learn. In contrast, the expert system is highly specific to a given problem and cannot be retrained easily.

Neural network applications in medicine, science, and business address problems in pattern classification, prediction, financial analysis, and control and optimization. In medicine, neural network applications are used for screening patients for coronary artery disease, for diagnosing patients with epilepsy and Alzheimer's disease, and for performing pattern recognition of pathology images. The financial industry uses neural networks to discern patterns in vast pools of data that might help investment firms predict the performance of equities, corporate bond ratings, or corporate bankruptcies. Visa International uses a neural network to help detect credit card fraud by monitoring all Visa transactions for sudden changes in the buying patterns of cardholders.

There are many puzzling aspects of neural networks. Unlike expert systems, which typically provide explanations for their solutions, neural networks cannot always explain why they arrived at a particular solution. They may not perform well if their training covers too little or too much data. In most current applications, neural networks are best used as aids to human decision makers instead of substitutes for them.

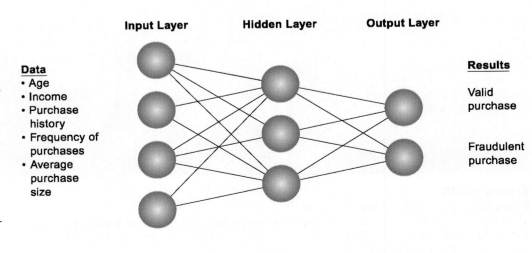

Figure 10-11
How a Neural Network Works

A neural network uses rules it "learns" from patterns in data to construct a hidden layer of logic. The hidden layer then processes inputs, classifying them based on the experience of the model. In this example, the neural network has been trained to distinguish between valid and fraudulent credit card purchases.

Input Layer   **Hidden Layer**   **Output Layer**

Data
• Age
• Income
• Purchase history
• Frequency of purchases
• Average purchase size

Results

Valid purchase

Fraudulent purchase

GENETIC ALGORITHMS

Genetic algorithms are useful for finding the optimal solution for a specific problem by examining a very large number of alternative solutions for that problem. They are based on techniques inspired by evolutionary biology, such as inheritance, mutation, selection, and crossover (recombination).

A genetic algorithm works by representing a solution as a string of 0s and 1s. The genetic algorithm searches a population of randomly generated strings of binary digits to identify the right string representing the best possible solution for the problem. As solutions alter and combine, the worst ones are discarded and the better ones survive to go on to produce even better solutions.

In Figure 10-12, each string corresponds to one of the variables in the problem. One applies a test for fitness, ranking the strings in the population according to their level of desirability as possible solutions. After the initial population is evaluated for fitness, the algorithm then produces the next generation of strings, consisting of strings that survived the fitness test plus offspring strings produced from mating pairs of strings, and tests their fitness. The process continues until a solution is reached.

Genetic algorithms are used to solve complex problems that are very dynamic and complex, involving hundreds or thousands of variables or formulas. The problem must be one where the range of possible solutions can be represented genetically and criteria can be established for evaluating fitness. Genetic algorithms expedite the solution because they can evaluate many solution alternatives quickly to find the best one. For example, General Electric engineers used genetic algorithms to help optimize the design for jet turbine aircraft engines, where each design change required changes in up to 100 variables. The supply-chain management software from i2 Technologies uses genetic algorithms to optimize production-scheduling models, incorporating hundreds of thousands of details about customer orders, material and resource availability, manufacturing and distribution capability, and delivery dates.

INTELLIGENT AGENTS

Intelligent agent technology helps businesses and decision makers navigate through large amounts of data to locate and act on information that is considered important.

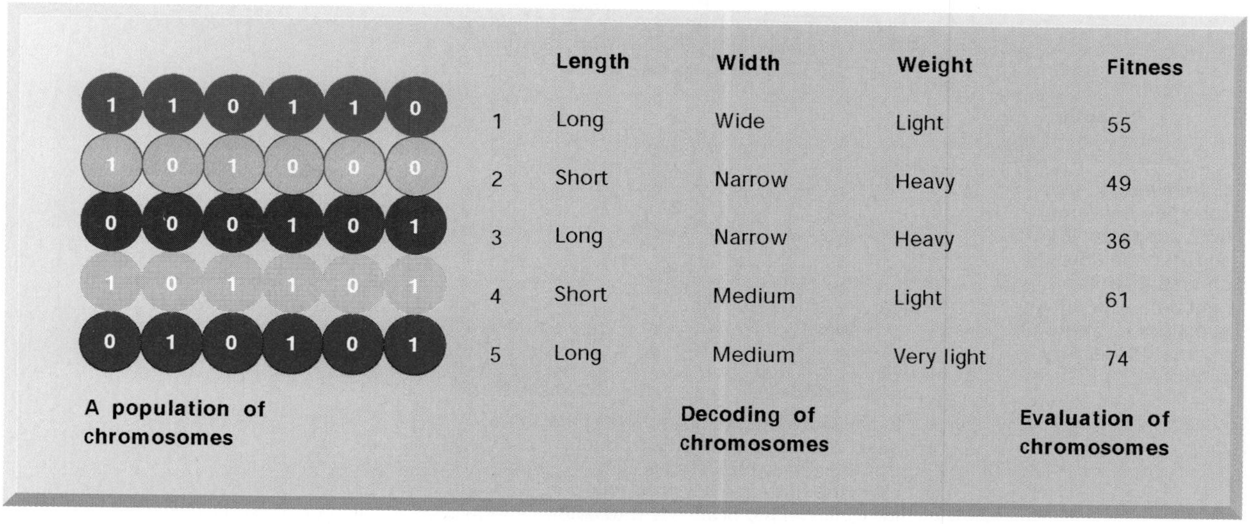

		Length	Width	Weight	Fitness
	1	Long	Wide	Light	55
	2	Short	Narrow	Heavy	49
	3	Long	Narrow	Heavy	36
	4	Short	Medium	Light	61
	5	Long	Medium	Very light	74
A population of chromosomes			Decoding of chromosomes		Evaluation of chromosomes

Figure 10-12
The Components of a Genetic Algorithm
This example illustrates an initial population of "chromosomes," each representing a different solution. The genetic algorithm uses an iterative process to refine the initial solutions so that the better ones, those with the higher fitness, are more likely to emerge as the best solution.

Intelligent agents are software programs that work in the background without direct human intervention to carry out specific, repetitive, and predictable tasks for an individual user, business process, or software application. The agent uses a limited built-in or learned knowledge base to accomplish tasks or make decisions on the user's behalf, such as deleting junk e-mail, scheduling appointments, or finding the cheapest airfare to California.

There are many intelligent agent applications today in operating systems, application software, e-mail systems, mobile computing software, and network tools. Of special interest to business are intelligent agents that search for information on the Internet. Chapter 6 describes how shopping bots help consumers find products they want and assists them in comparing prices and other features.

Procter & Gamble (P&G) used intelligent agent technology to make its supply chain more efficient (see Figure 10-13). It modeled a complex supply chain as a group of semiautonomous "agents" representing individual supply-chain components, such as trucks, production facilities, distributors, and retail stores. The behavior of each agent is programmed to follow rules that mimic actual behavior, such as "order an item when it is out of stock." Simulations using the agents enable the company to perform what-if analyses on inventory levels, in-store stockouts, and transportation costs.

Using intelligent agent models, P&G discovered that trucks should often be dispatched before being fully loaded. Although transportation costs would be higher using partially loaded trucks, the simulation showed that retail store stockouts would occur less often, thus reducing the amount of lost sales, which would more than make up for the higher distribution costs. Agent-based modeling has saved P&G $300 million annually on an investment of less than 1 percent of that amount (Anthes, 2003).

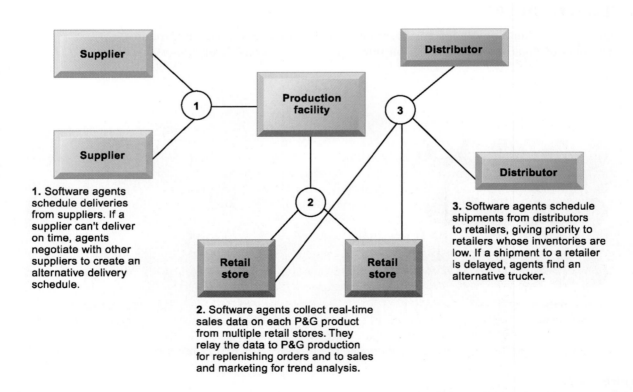

Figure 10-13
Intelligent Agents in P&G's Supply-Chain Network
Intelligent agents are helping Procter & Gamble shorten the replenishment cycles for products, such as a box of Tide.

10.4 Systems for Managing Knowledge

Systems for knowledge management improve the quality and utilization of knowledge used in the decision-making process. **Knowledge management** refers to the set of business processes developed in an organization to create, store, transfer, and apply knowledge. Knowledge management increases the ability of the organization to learn from its environment and to incorporate knowledge into its business processes and decision making.

Knowledge that is not shared and applied to the problems facing firms and managers does not add any value to the business. Knowing how to do things effectively and efficiently in ways that other organizations cannot duplicate is a major source of profit and competitive advantage. Why? Because the knowledge you generate about your own production processes, and about your customers, usually stays within your firm and cannot be sold or purchased on the open market. In this sense, self-generated business knowledge is a strategic resource and can provide strategic advantage. Businesses will operate less effectively and efficiently if this unique knowledge is not available for decision making and ongoing operations. There are two major types of knowledge management systems: enterprise-wide knowledge management systems and knowledge work systems.

ENTERPRISE-WIDE KNOWLEDGE MANAGEMENT SYSTEMS

Firms must deal with at least three kinds of knowledge. Some knowledge exists within the firm in the form of structured text documents (reports and presentations). Decision makers also need knowledge that is semistructured, such as e-mail, voice mail, chat room exchanges, videos, digital pictures, brochures, or bulletin board postings. In still other cases, there is no formal or digital information of any kind, and the knowledge resides in the heads of employees. Much of this knowledge is **tacit knowledge** and is rarely written down.

Enterprise-wide knowledge management systems deal with all three types of knowledge. Enterprise-wide knowledge management systems are general-purpose, firmwide systems that collect, store, distribute, and apply digital content and knowledge. These systems include capabilities for searching for information, storing both structured and unstructured data, and locating employee expertise within the firm. They also include supporting technologies such as portals, search engines, collaboration tools (e-mail, instant messaging, wikis, blogs, social bookmarking, and groupware) and learning management systems.

Enterprise Content Management Systems

Businesses today need to organize and manage both structured and semistructured knowledge assets. **Structured knowledge** is explicit knowledge that exists in formal documents, as well as in formal rules that organizations derive by observing experts and their decision-making behaviors. But, according to experts, at least 80 percent of an organization's business content is semistructured or unstructured—information in folders, messages, memos, proposals, e-mails, graphics, electronic slide presentations, and even videos created in different formats and stored in many locations.

Enterprise content management systems help organizations manage both types of information. They have capabilities for knowledge capture, storage, retrieval, distribution, and preservation to help firms improve their business processes and decisions. Such systems include corporate repositories of documents, reports, presentations, and best practices, as well as capabilities for collecting and organizing semistructured knowledge such as e-mail (see Figure 10-14). Major enterprise content management systems also enable users to access external sources of information, such as news feeds and research, and to communicate via e-mail, chat/instant messaging, discussion groups, and videoconferencing.

A key problem in managing knowledge is the creation of an appropriate classification scheme to organize information into meaningful categories. Once the categories for classifying knowledge have been created, each knowledge object needs to be "tagged," or classified, so that it can be easily retrieved. Enterprise content management systems have

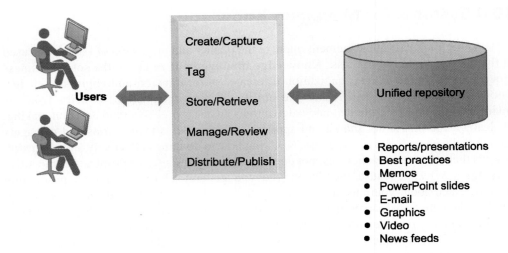

Figure 10-14
An Enterprise Content Management System
An enterprise content management system has capabilities for classifying, organizing, and managing structured and semistructured knowledge and making it available throughout the enterprise.

capabilities for tagging, interfacing with corporate databases where the documents are stored, and creating an enterprise portal environment for employees to use when searching for corporate knowledge.

BAE Systems, the largest aerospace and defense company in Europe, used Autonomy enterprise content management software to aggregate structured and unstructured content from many different sources, including reports, e-mail, resumes, profiles, intranet content, and 10,000 news feeds per day. The system automatically categorizes and tags the content and alerts its 130,000 employees to documents in the system that relate to their jobs. It has reduced the amount of time spent retrieving information by over 90 percent (Lamont, 2006).

Firms in publishing, advertising, broadcasting, and entertainment have special needs for storing and managing unstructured digital data such as photographs, graphic images, video, and audio content. **Digital asset management systems** help them classify, store, and distribute these digital objects.

Knowledge Network Systems

Knowledge network systems, also known as *expertise location and management systems*, address the problem that arises when the appropriate knowledge is not in the form of a digital document but instead resides in the memory of expert individuals in the firm. Knowledge network systems provide an online directory of corporate experts in well-defined knowledge domains and use communication technologies to make it easy for employees to find the appropriate expert in a company. Some knowledge network systems go further by systematizing the solutions developed by experts and then storing the solutions in a knowledge database as a best-practices or frequently asked questions (FAQs) repository (see Figure 10-15). AskMe, Tacit ActiveNet, and Xpert SHARE provide tools for internal corporate use. Tacit offers another service called Illumio, which allows users to solicit expertise from friends, colleagues, and business experts over the open Internet.

Collaboration Tools and Learning Management Systems

Companies are starting to use consumer Web technologies such as blogs, wikis, and social bookmarking for internal use to foster collaboration and information exchange between individuals and teams. Blogs and wikis help capture, consolidate, and centralize this knowledge for the firm.

Wikis, which we introduced in Chapter 6, are inexpensive and easy to implement. Wikis provide a central repository for all types of corporate data that can be displayed in a Web browser, including electronic pages of documents, spreadsheets, and electronic slides, and can embed e-mail and instant messages. Although users are able to modify wiki content

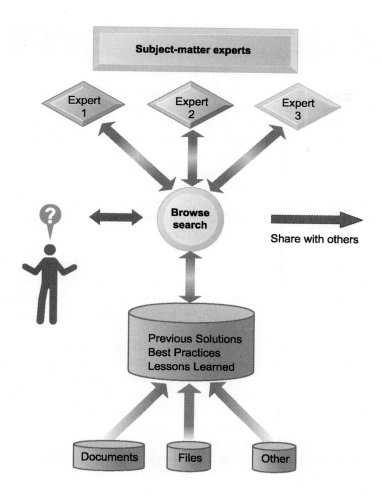

Figure 10-15
An Enterprise Knowledge Network System
A knowledge network maintains a database of firm experts, as well as accepted solutions to known problems, and then facilitates the communication between employees looking for knowledge and experts who have that knowledge. Solutions created in this communication are then added to a database of solutions in the form of frequently asked questions (FAQs), best practices, or other documents.

contributed by others, wikis have capabilities for tracking these changes and tools for reverting to earlier versions. A wiki is most appropriate for information that is revised frequently but must remain available perpetually as it changes.

The Interactive Session on Organizations describes some of these corporate uses of Web 2.0 tools. As you read this case, try to identify the problem these companies were facing, what alternative solutions were available to management, and how well the chosen solution worked.

Social bookmarking makes it easier to search for and share information by allowing users to save their bookmarks to Web pages on a public Web site and tag these bookmarks with keywords. These tags can be used to organize and search for the documents. Lists of tags can be shared with other people to help them find information of interest. The user-created taxonomies created for shared bookmarks are called "folksonomies." Del.icio.us and Digg are two popular social bookmarking sites.

Suppose, for example, that you are on a corporate team researching wind power. If you did a Web search and found relevant Web pages on wind power, you would click on a bookmarking button on a social bookmarking site and create a tag identifying each Web document you found to link it to wind power. By clicking on the "tags" button at the social networking site, you would be able to see a list of all the tags you created and select the documents you need.

Companies need ways to keep track of and manage employee learning and to integrate it more fully into their knowledge management and other corporate systems. A **learning management system (LMS)** provides tools for the management, delivery, tracking, and assessment of various types of employee learning and training.

INTERACTIVE SESSION: ORGANIZATIONS   Managing with Web 2.0

Who's blogging? It is not just twenty-somethings who want to chronicle their experiences, vent about consumer products, or put out a political message. Today's blogger might very well be an employee at IBM, Intel, Procter & Gamble, or any number of companies that have embraced Web 2.0 tools. Blogs, wikis, and social networking are emerging as powerful tools to boost communication and productivity in the corporate workforce. McKinsey & Co. reported that approximately one-third of the top executives it polled have Web 2.0 tools in use or plan to deploy them.

Web 2.0 tools have made inroads into the business world because the software that supports them is generally inexpensive and user-friendly. A manager who wants to communicate with his or her team via a blog or have the progress of a project documented on a wiki can institute the technology without help from the IT department and without superiors worrying about high costs.

At Sun Microsystems, management compelled its engineers to create wiki pages that described their projects. Once the engineers were comfortable with the technology, it was easier for them to transition to using wikis for the company's formal software documentation. The use of wikis also spread to meeting notes, project plans, and software reports, resulting in a total four-fold increase in the amount of documented information at Sun.

At IBM, over 26,000 employees have created blogs on the company's network to post about technology and the work they are doing. Project team members use wikis to store information and share memos. IBM's Wiki Central manages over 20,000 company wikis with over 125,000 participants. The company created a wiki to help 50 of its experts on law, economics, government, and technology to collaborate on an intellectual property manifesto that serves as the foundation of its new patent policy.

Web 2.0 tools are particularly valuable at IBM, where 42 percent of the workforce operates remotely, either from home or from client offices. Brian Goodman, who is the Connecticut-based manager of a software development team with members in New York and Massachusetts, says that the wikis give him "a single view of the projects and their status without pinging each" worker every day with an instant message.

The use of social networking in business is so far limited mostly to recruiting and making sales contacts. Recruiters at Microsoft and Starbucks have used LinkedIn to search for potential job candidates. At IBM, however, employees engage in social networking internally through its corporate directory, BluePages, which is edited by employees and serves as a sort of internal corporate MySpace. The directory contains basic information on 400,000 employees and is accessed six million times daily. Employees have control of most of the content on their individual entries, and can post their own photos and resumes to their corporate "profiles."

Two of the biggest challenges for companies using Web 2.0 technologies are convincing workers to embrace these tools and regulating their use. IBM reminds employees to remember the rules of privacy, respect, and confidentiality in its corporate code of conduct and does not allow any anonymous online communication.

Some companies, such as Nokia and Frankfurt-based investment bank Dresdner Kleinwort, started wiki or blog implementations with a small group of employees. Once other managers and employees saw the business benefits, ease of use, and versatility of the tools, their departments were quick to adopt the technology.

A few pioneers in the London office IT department of Dresdner Kleinwort sent the Socialtext wiki software program to several IT groups to see how it might be used to facilitate some of their tasks. The program spread so rapidly that Dresdner launched a corporate wiki for collaborating on materials related to meetings, supporting brainstorming sessions, and developing presentations. Some employees were initially uncertain about how to use the wiki. They were ordered to use the wiki instead of sending e-mail. By 2006, the wiki had nearly 8,000 users.

Alex Thill, who leads a team of 52 that designs and maintains Web sites for many Dresdner divisions, reports that using the wiki along with blogs and instant messaging has cut down his group's e-mail use by at least 75 percent. He and his team also save time because the key metrics on the 80 Web sites they monitor are on a single wiki page. Each user only needs about 30 seconds to enter his or her data and make it available to the whole team. In the past, Till had to sift and sort these data from 80 sources, a process that might take weeks.

Sources: Michael Totty, "Social Studies," *The Wall Street Journal*, June 18, 2007; William M. Bulkeley, "Playing Well with Others," *The Wall Street Journal*, June 18, 2007; Vauhini Vara, "Wikis at Work," *The Wall Street Journal*, June 18, 2007; Dan Carlin, "Corporate Wikis Go Viral," *BusinessWeek*, March 12, 2007; and Rachael King, "No Rest for the Wiki," *BusinessWeek*, March 12, 2007.

CASE STUDY QUESTIONS

1. How do Web 2.0 tools help companies manage knowledge, coordinate work, and enhance decision making?

2. What business problems do blogs, wikis, and other social networking tools help solve?

3. Describe how a company such as Wal-Mart or Procter & Gamble would benefit from using Web 2.0 tools internally.

4. What challenges do companies face in spreading the use of Web 2.0? What issues should managers be concerned with?

MIS IN ACTION

Go to Sun Microsystems' Blogs home page at http://blogs.sun.com and click the Blog Directory tab. Select a blog from the directory and then answer the following questions:

1. What is the name of the blog you selected?

2. Who is the intended audience of this blog?

3. What subjects does the blog address?

4. Visit several more blogs in Sun's directory. If you were a Sun employee, do you think you would find these blogs helpful? Why or why not? Do you think there is value in blog entries that discuss the author's personal life instead of work-related matters?

For example, the Whirlpool Corporation uses CERTPOINT's learning management system to manage the registration, scheduling, reporting, and content for its training programs for 3,500 salespeople. The system helps Whirlpool tailor course content to the right audience, track the people who took courses and their scores, and compile metrics on employee performance (Summerfield, 2007).

KNOWLEDGE WORK SYSTEMS

The enterprise-wide knowledge systems we have just described provide a wide range of capabilities used by many, if not all, the workers and groups in an organization. Firms also have specialized systems for knowledge workers to help them create new knowledge for improving the firm's business processes and decision making. **Knowledge work systems (KWS)** are specialized systems for engineers, scientists, and other knowledge workers that are designed to promote the creation of knowledge and to ensure that new knowledge and technical expertise are properly integrated into the business.

Requirements of Knowledge Work Systems

Knowledge work systems give knowledge workers the specialized tools they need, such as powerful graphics, analytical tools, and communications and document management. These systems require great computing power to handle the sophisticated graphics or complex calculations necessary for such knowledge workers as scientific researchers, product designers, and financial analysts. Because knowledge workers are so focused on knowledge in the external world, these systems also must give the worker quick and easy access to external databases. They typically feature user-friendly interfaces that enable users to perform needed tasks without having to spend a lot of time learning how to use the computer. Figure 10-16 summarizes the requirements of knowledge work systems.

Knowledge workstations often are designed and optimized for the specific tasks to be performed. Design engineers need graphics with enough power to handle three-dimensional, computer-aided design (CAD) systems. However, financial analysts are more interested in access to a myriad of external databases and technology for efficiently storing and accessing massive amounts of financial data.

Figure 10-16
Requirements of Knowledge Work Systems
Knowledge work systems require strong links to external knowledge bases in addition to specialized hardware and software.

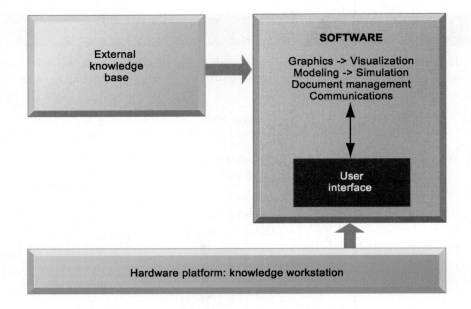

Examples of Knowledge Work Systems

Major knowledge work applications include computer-aided design (CAD) systems (which we introduced in Chapter 3), virtual reality systems for simulation and modeling, and financial workstations.

Contemporary CAD systems are capable of generating realistic-looking three-dimensional graphic designs that can be rotated and viewed from all sides. Architects from Skidmore, Owings, & Merrill LLP used a three-dimensional CAD program called Revit to work out the creative and technical details of the design for the Freedom Tower at the site of the former World Trade Center. The software enabled the architects to strip away the outer layer to manipulate the shape of the floors. Changes appeared immediately in the entire model, and the software automatically recalculated the technical details in the blueprints.

Virtual reality systems use interactive graphics software to create computer-generated simulations that are so close to reality that users almost believe they are participating in a real-world situation. In many virtual reality systems, the user dons special clothing, headgear, and equipment, depending on the application. The clothing contains sensors that record the user's movements and immediately transmit that information back to the computer. For instance, to walk through a virtual reality simulation of a house, you would need garb that monitors the movement of your feet, hands, and head. You also would need goggles containing video screens and sometimes audio attachments and feeling gloves so that you are immersed in the computer feedback.

Virtual reality is just starting to provide benefits in educational, scientific, and business work. For example, neuroradiologists at New York's Beth Israel Medical Center use the Siemens Medical Systems 3D Virtuoso System to peek at the interplay of tiny blood vessels or take a fly-through of the aorta. Surgeons at New York University School of Medicine use three-dimensional modeling to target brain tumors more precisely, thereby reducing bleeding and trauma during surgery.

Virtual reality applications developed for the Web use a standard called **Virtual Reality Modeling Language** (**VRML**). VRML is a set of specifications for interactive, three-dimensional modeling on the World Wide Web that organize multiple media types, including animation, images, and audio to put users in a simulated real-world environment. VRML is platform independent, operates over a desktop computer, and requires little bandwidth.

DuPont, the Wilmington, Delaware, chemical company, created a VRML application called HyperPlant, which enables users to access three-dimensional data over the Internet using Web browser software. Engineers can go through three-dimensional models as if they were physically walking through a plant, viewing objects at eye level. This level of detail reduces the number of mistakes they make during construction of oil rigs, oil plants, and other structures.

The financial industry is using specialized **investment workstations** to leverage the knowledge and time of its brokers, traders, and portfolio managers. Firms such as Merrill Lynch and UBS Financial Services have installed investment workstations that integrate a wide range of data from both internal and external sources, including contact management data, real-time and historical market data, and research reports. Previously, financial professionals had to spend considerable time accessing data from separate systems and piecing together the information they needed. By providing one-stop information faster and with fewer errors, the workstations streamline the entire investment process from stock selection to updating client records.

10.5 Hands-On MIS

The projects in this section give you hands-on experience using spreadsheet software to analyze the impact of changes in prices of component parts on production costs for a real-world company, using a spreadsheet pivot table to analyze sales data, and using intelligent agents to research products for sale on the Web.

IMPROVING DECISION MAKING: ANALYZING THE IMPACT OF COMPONENT PRICE CHANGES

Software skills: Spreadsheet formulas, two-variable data table
Business skills: Manufacturing bill of materials sensitivity analysis

A bill of materials is used in manufacturing and production to show all of the parts and materials required to manufacture a specific item or for the subassembly of a finished product, such as a motorcycle. The information in the bill of materials is useful for determining product costs, coordinating orders, and managing inventory. It can also show how product costs will be affected by price changes in components or raw materials. This project provides you with an opportunity to use spreadsheet software to perform a sensitivity analysis showing the impact of various prices for component parts on the total costs of a dirt bike. The bill of materials for this project has been simplified for instructional purposes.

Dirt Bikes's management has asked you to explore the impact of changes in some of its parts components on production costs. Review the following bill of materials information for the brake system for Dirt Bikes's Moto 300 model.

The completed bill of materials contains the description of the component, the identification number of each component, the supplier (source) of the component, the unit cost of each component, the quantity of each component needed to make each finished brake system, the extended cost of each component, and the total materials cost. The extended cost is calculated by multiplying the quantity of each component needed to produce the finished brake system by the unit cost. The prices of components are constantly changing, and you will need to develop a spreadsheet application that can show management the impact of such price changes on the cost to produce each brake system and on total production costs for the Moto 300 model.

- Complete the bill of materials by calculating the extended cost of each component and the total materials cost for each brake system.
- Develop a sensitivity analysis to show the impact on total brake system materials costs if the front brake calipers unit cost ranges from $103 to $107 and if the brake pipe unit cost ranges from $27 to $30.

Bill of Materials: Moto 300 Brake System

Component	Component No.	Source	Unit Cost	Quantity	Extended Cost
Brake cable	M0593	Nissin	$27.81	1	
Brake pedal	M0546	Harrison Billet	$6.03	2	
Brake pad	M3203	Russell	$27.05	2	
Front brake pump	M0959	Brembo	$66.05	1	
Rear brake pump	M4739	Brembo	$54.00	1	
Front brake caliper	M5930	Nissin	$105.20	1	
Rear brake caliper	M7942	Nissin	$106.78	1	
Front brake disc	M3920	Russell	$143.80	1	
Rear brake disc	M0588	Russell	$56.42	1	
Brake pipe	M0943	Harrison Billet	$28.52	1	
Brake lever cover	M1059	Brembo	$2.62	1	

- The brake system represents 30 percent of the total materials cost for one Moto 300 motorcycle. Use sensitivity analysis again to show the impact of the changes in front brake caliper unit costs and brake pipe unit costs described previously on total materials costs for this motorcycle model.

IMPROVING DECISION MAKING: USING PIVOT TABLES TO ANALYZE SALES DATA

Software skills: Pivot tables
Business skills: Analyzing sales data

This project gives you an opportunity to learn how to use Excel's PivotTable functionality to analyze a database or data list.

Use the data file for Online Management Training Inc. described earlier in the chapter. This is a list of the sales transactions at OMT for one day. You can find this spreadsheet file at the Laudon Web site for this chapter.

Use Excel's PivotTable to help you answer the following questions:

- Where are the average purchases higher? The answer might tell managers where to focus marketing and sales resources, or pitch different messages to different regions.
- What form of payment is the most common? The answer could be used to emphasize in advertising the most preferred means of payment.
- Are there any times of day when purchases are most common? Do people buy are products while at work (likely during the day) or at home (likely in the evening)?
- What's the relationship between region, type of product purchased, and average sales price?

We provide instructions on how to use Excel PivotTables in our Learning Tracks.

IMPROVING DECISION MAKING: USING INTELLIGENT AGENTS FOR COMPARISON SHOPPING

Software skills: Web browser and shopping bot software
Business skills: Product evaluation and selection

This project will give you experience using shopping bots to search online for products, find product information, and find the best prices and vendors.

You have decided to purchase a new digital camera. Select a digital camera you might want to purchase, such as the Canon PowerShot SD 1000 or the Fuji FinePix A900. To purchase the camera as inexpensively as possible, try several of the shopping bot sites, which do the price comparisons for you. Visit MySimon (www.mysimon.com), BizRate.com (www.bizrate.com), and Google Product Search. Compare these shopping sites in terms of their ease of use, number of offerings, speed in obtaining information, thoroughness of information offered about the product and seller, and price selection. Which site or sites would you use and why? Which camera would you select and why? How helpful were these sites for making your decision?

LEARNING TRACKS

The following Learning Tracks provide content relevant to topics covered in this chapter:

1. Building and Using Pivot Tables
2. How an Expert System Inference Engine Works
3. Challenges of Implementing and Using Knowledge Management Systems

---

Review Summary

1 **What are the different types of decisions, and how does the decision-making process work?** Decisions may be structured, semistructured, or unstructured, with structured decisions clustering at the operational level of the organization and unstructured decisions at the strategic level. Decision making can be performed by individuals or groups and includes employees as well as operational, middle, and senior managers. There are four stages in decision making: intelligence, design, choice, and implementation.

2 **How do information systems help people working individually and in groups make decisions more effectively?** Systems specifically designed to help managers and employees make better decisions include management information systems (MIS), decision-support systems (DSS), group decision-support systems (GDSS), and executive support systems (ESS).

MIS provide information on firm performance to help managers monitor and control the business, often in the form of fixed regularly scheduled reports based on data summarized from the firm's transaction processing systems. MIS support structured decisions and some semistructured decisions.

Decision-support systems combine data, sophisticated analytical models and tools, and user-friendly software into a single powerful system that can support semistructured or unstructured decision making. Geographic information systems (GIS) uses data visualization technology to analyze and display data for planning and decision making with digitized maps.

Group decision-support systems (GDSS) help people meeting together in a group arrive at decisions more efficiently. GDSS feature special conference room facilities where participants contribute their ideas using networked computers and software tools for organizing ideas, gathering information, ranking and setting priorities, and documenting meeting sessions.

Executive support systems (ESS) help senior managers with unstructured problems by combining data from internal and external sources for high-level overviews or drilling down to detailed transaction data.

3 **What are the business benefits of using intelligent techniques in decision making and knowledge management?** Expert systems capture tacit knowledge from a limited domain of human expertise and express that knowledge in the form of rules. The strategy used to search through the knowledge base is called the *inference engine*. Case-based reasoning represents organizational knowledge as a database of cases that can be continually expanded and refined.

Fuzzy logic is a software technology for expressing knowledge in the form of rules that use approximate or subjective values. Neural networks consist of hardware and software that attempt to mimic the thought processes of the human brain. Neural networks are notable for their ability to learn without programming and to recognize patterns in massive amounts of data.

Genetic algorithms develop solutions to particular problems using genetically based processes, such as fitness, crossover, and mutation. Intelligent agents are software programs with built-in or learned knowledge bases that carry out specific, repetitive, and predictable tasks for an individual user, business process, or software application.

4 **What types of systems are used for enterprise-wide knowledge management, and how do they provide value for businesses?** Enterprise content management systems feature databases and tools for organizing and storing structured documents and semistructured knowledge, such as e-mail or rich media. Knowledge network systems provide directories and tools for locating firm employees with special expertise who are important sources of tacit knowledge. Often these systems include group collaboration tools, portals to simplify information access, search tools, and tools for classifying information based on a taxonomy that is appropriate for the organization. Learning management systems provide tools for the management, delivery, tracking, and assessment of various types of employee learning and training.

5 **What are the major types of knowledge work systems, and how do they provide value for firms?** Knowledge work systems (KWS) support the creation of new knowledge and its integration into the organization. KWS require easy access to an external knowledge base; powerful computer hardware that can support software with intensive graphics, analysis, document management, and communications capabilities; and a user-friendly interface.

Key Terms

Artificial intelligence (AI), 346	Choice, 335	Design, 335
Case-based reasoning (CBR), 348	Customer decision-support systems (CDSS), 345	Digital asset management systems, 354
	Data visualization, 343	Digital dashboard, 345

Review Questions

1. What are the different types of decisions, and how does the decision-making process work?
- List and describe the different decision-making levels and decision-making groups in organizations and their decision-making requirements.
- Distinguish between an unstructured, semistructured, and structured decision.
- List and describe the stages in decision making.

2. How do information systems help people working individually and in groups make decisions more effectively?
- Distinguish between a decision-support system (DSS) and a management information system (MIS).
- List and describe the three basic components of a DSS.
- Define a geographic information system (GIS), and explain how it supports decision making.
- Define a customer decision-support system (CDSS), and explain how the Internet is used for this purpose.
- Define an executive support system (ESS), and explain how its capabilities enhance managerial decision making and provide value for a business.
- Define a group decision-support system (GDSS), explaining how it works and the problems it solves.

3. What are the business benefits of using intelligent techniques in decision making and knowledge management?
- Define an expert system, describe how it works, and explain its value to business.
- Define case-based reasoning, and explain how it differs from an expert system.
- Define a neural network, and describe how it works and how it benefits businesses.
- Define and describe fuzzy logic, genetic algorithms, and intelligent agents. Explain how each works and the kinds of problems for which each is suited.

4. What types of systems are used for enterprise-wide knowledge management, and how do they provide value for businesses?
- Define knowledge management, and explain its value to businesses.
- Define and describe the various types of enterprise-wide knowledge systems, and explain how they provide value for businesses.
- Describe how the various types of collaboration tools and learning management systems facilitate knowledge management.

5. What are the major types of knowledge work systems, and how do they provide value for firms?

- Define knowledge work systems, and describe the generic requirements of knowledge work systems.
- Describe how the following systems support knowledge work: computer-aided design (CAD), virtual reality, and investment workstations.

Discussion Questions

1. If businesses used DSS, GDSS, and ESS more widely, would they make better decisions? Do you agree? Why or why not?

2. Describe various ways that knowledge management systems could help firms with sales and marketing or with manufacturing and production.

Video Case

You will find a video case illustrating some of the concepts in this chapter on the Laudon Web site along with questions to help you analyze the case.

Teamwork

Designing a University GDSS

With three or four of your classmates, identify several groups in your university that could benefit from a GDSS. Design a GDSS for one of those groups, describing its hardware, software and people elements. If possible, use electronic presentation software to present your findings to the class.

BUSINESS PROBLEM-SOLVING CASE

HSBC's Mortgage Lending Decisions: What Went Wrong?

One of the biggest news stories of late summer and fall of 2007 was about the U.S. subprime mortgage loan crisis and its effect on worldwide financial markets. A major player in this crisis was HSBC Holdings PLC, the third largest bank in the world based on market value. With headquarters in London, HSBC operates in 76 countries and territories. In 2006, it had become one of the largest lenders of subprime mortgages in the United States.

Subprime mortgages are targeted toward low-end borrowers who represent a risk of default, but, at times, a good business opportunity to the lender. Subprime customers often have blemished credit histories, low incomes, or other traits that suggest a greater likelihood of defaulting on a loan. Generally speaking, lenders try to avoid making such loans. However, during a housing boom, competition for customers motivates lenders to relax their lending standards. During such a time, subprime mortgages, including those that do not require a down payment and have very low introductory rates, become far more prevalent, as they did between 2001 and 2006 in the United States.

By 2007, 12 percent of the total $8.4 trillion U.S. mortgage market consisted of subprime mortgages, up from just 7.5 percent near the end of 2001. In early February 2007, HSBC revealed that this risky lending technique had become a major problem.

As the U.S. real estate market slowed in 2006, the growth rate of home values also slowed. With the coinciding rise in interest rates, many borrowers with adjustable-rate mortgages were unable to make their mortgage payments and defaulted on their loans. HSBC anticipated seeing the number of delinquent and defaulted accounts grow, but not to the level it actually discovered.

Mortgage lenders in the United States participate in a complicated business that involves more than a simple lender-borrower relationship. A bank or mortgage broker that originates a mortgage may not keep it. Mortgage wholesalers often buy loans and then turn right around and resell them to large financial institutions. The default risk passes along to whomever winds up with the account last. HSBC participated in several zones of the mortgage market. One unit of HSBC Mortgage Services originated mortgages, often of the subprime variety. HSBC flipped some of these loans to other companies, but kept others as investments. The ones HSBC kept provided revenue from the interest they generated, assuming the borrowers kept current with their payments. If the borrowers fell behind or defaulted, HSBC suffered the losses.

In its quest for higher revenue, HSBC began buying up subprime loans from other sources. In 2005 and 2006, with the housing boom in its final stages, HSBC bought billions of dollars of subprime loans from as many as 250 wholesale mortgage companies, which had acquired the loans from independent brokers and banks. HSBC found the high interest rates of these loans to be very alluring. Many of these loans were second-lien, or piggyback loans, which allow home owners who are unable to come up with a downpayment for a house to qualify for a mortgage by borrowing the downpayment amount, so they actually borrow the entire purchase price of a home.

HSBC stated it had a process for forecasting how many of the loans it purchased from wholesalers were likely to default. First, the bank would tell the wholesaler what types of loans it was interested in, based on the income and credit scores of the borrowers. Once the wholesaler offered a pool of mortgages, HSBC analysts evaluated the lot to determine whether it met HSBC standards.

Perhaps due to the intense competition for mortgages, HSBC accepted pools that included stated-income loans. These are loans for which the borrower simply states his or her income with providing any documentation to verify it. According to Martin Eakes, CEO of the Center for Responsible Lending, 90 percent of stated-income loan applicants declare their incomes to be higher than they are in IRS records. Sixty percent of these people inflate their incomes by 50 percent or more. Many also exaggerate their employment positions to coincide with the inflated income. As a result, they receive approval for loans that are much larger than they can actually afford.

Between September 2005 and March 2006, HSBC bought nearly $4 billion in second-lien loans. The surge increased the bank's second-lien to a total of $10.24 billion. Earlier in 2005, Bobby Mehta, the top HSBC executive in the United States, described the development of the bank's mortgage portfolio as disciplined. He reported to investors, "We've done them conservatively based on analytics and based on our ability to earn a good return for the risks that we undertake."

In early February 2007, HSBC shook up Wall Street when it announced a much higher percentage of its subprime loans defaulted than it had anticipated. It would have to make provisions for $10.6 billion in bad debt stemming from loan delinquencies in 2006. In the third quarter of 2006, the percentage of all HSBC Mortgage Services loans that were overdue by 60 days or more jumped from 2.95 to 3.74. The bank announced that a similar increase was expected for the fourth quarter. In short, the subprime mortgage market was in distress, and profits from the high-risk loans were disappearing.

HSBC had begun lending to American consumers in 2003, when it purchased Household International Inc., a major subprime lender based in Prospect Heights, Illinois. Household's CEO William Aldinger touted his company's ability to assess credit risk using modeling techniques designed by 150 Ph.Ds. The system, called the Worldwide Household International Revolving Lending System, or Whirl, helped Household underwrite credit card debt and support collection services in the United States, Mexico, the United Kingdom, and the Middle East.

Lenders such as HSBC who are analyzing applicants for credit cards, car loans, and fixed-rate mortgages use a credit rating from Fair Isaac Corp. of Minneapolis called a FICO score. However, FICO scores had not yet been proven reliable tools for predicting the performance, during a weakening housing market, of second-lien loans or of adjustable-rate mortgages taken out by subprime borrowers. Data on subprime borrowers who made small or no down payments were scarce, and the FICO scores did not adequately distinguish between loans where borrowers had put their own money down and loans with no downpayment. Nor did the models take into account what would happen if housing prices fell to the point where the amount owed on some mortgages exceeded the value of the homes they covered.

Nevertheless, HSBC used FICO scores to screen subprime applicants for both second-lien loans and adjustable-rate mortgages.

In response to its subprime loan crisis, HSBC made changes in both personnel and policy. The company ceased originating and purchasing stated-income loans and boosted the required FICO score for some loans. Tom Detelich, who had led the transition from Household to HSBC's consumer lending business, was appointed head of HSBC Mortgage Services.

HSBC doubled the number of customer representatives who call on borrowers who have missed payments and discuss payment plans that are more manageable. Those operations now run seven days a week. HSBC is also utilizing information technology to pinpoint ahead of time which customers are most in danger of failing to meet their monthly payments once their adjustable-rate mortgages (ARMs) jump from their initial teaser interest rates to higher rates. In some cases, the adjustment can increase a monthly payment by $500. With so many mortgages originated in 2005 and 2006, HSBC could be facing another onslaught of delinquencies and defaults over the next two years. The Center for Responsible Lending predicted that 20 percent of subprime mortgages sold during those two years would result in foreclosure.

HSBC adopted business analytics software from Experian-Scorex to help support the decision making of its credit application processing staff. The software provides users with the ability to consistently deploy scoring models and portfolio segmentation. It also includes tools for managing customer relationships and improving risk management decisions. By using these tools, HSBC should be able to create strategies for individual applicants, assess the value of each applicant, and then customize a loan offer that suits the customer's needs as well as the bank's business.

Sources: Carrick Mollenkamp, "In Home-Lending Push, Banks Misjudged Risk," *The Wall Street Journal*, February 8, 2007; Joe Niedzielski, "A Sinking Sensation for Subprime Loans," *BusinessWeek*, February 14, 2007; Carrick Mollenkamp, "HSBC Taps 2 to Help Fix U.S. Mortgage Unit Woes," *The Wall Street Journal*, February 9, 2007; Edward Chancellor and Mike Verdin, "Subprime Lenders' Miscue," *The Wall Street Journal*, February 9, 2007; "Rising Subprime Defaults Hit Local HSBC Unit," Reuters, accessed via www.chicagobusiness.com, February 8, 2007; and "HSBC Implements Experian-Scorex Decision Support Software," www.finextra.com, February 23, 2007.

Case Study Questions

1. What problem did HSBC face in this case? What people, technology, and organization factors were responsible for the problem? Did HSBC management correctly identify the problem?

2. HSBC had sophisticated information systems and analytical tools for predicting the risk presented by subprime mortgage applicants. Why did HSBC still run into trouble? If HSBC had a solution to the problem all along, why was the right solution not used?

3. What solutions is HSBC relying on to deal with its problem going forward? Will these solutions be sufficient to turn the subprime mortgage business around? Are there additional factors for which HSBC has not accounted? What are they?

4. What are the possible consequences of HSBC changing its approach to subprime lending? How might these changes affect the business? How might they affect the customer? How might they affect the U.S. economy?

5. HSBC made a decision to pursue subprime mortgages as a segment of its business. Explain how this was a structured, unstructured, or semistructured decision. Then, present your opinion about where in the decision-making process HSBC went wrong. Finally, apply the decision quality concepts of accuracy and comprehensiveness to this case.

Building and Managing Systems

PART IV

Part IV shows how to use the knowledge acquired in earlier chapters to analyze and design information system solutions to business problems. This part answers questions such as these: How can I develop a solution to an information system problem that provides genuine business benefits? How can the firm adjust to the changes introduced by the new system solution? What alternative approaches are available for building system solutions? What broader ethical and social issues should be addressed when building and using information systems?

Building Information Systems and Managing Projects

11

STUDENT LEARNING OBJECTIVES

After completing this chapter, you will be able to answer the following questions:

1. What are the core problem-solving steps for developing new information systems?

2. What are the alternative methods for building information systems?

3. What are the principal methodologies for modeling and designing systems?

4. How should information systems projects be selected and evaluated?

5. How should information systems projects be managed?

CHAPTER OUTLINE

A NEW ORDERING SYSTEM FOR GIRL SCOUT COOKIES

Peanut Butter Petites, Caramel DeLites, Thin Mints—Girl Scout Cookies have been American favorites since the organization's first cookie drive in 1917. The Girl Scouts have been so successful selling cookies that cookie sales are a major source of funding for this organization. The Girl Scouts sell so many cookies that collecting, counting, and organizing the annual avalanche of orders has become a tremendous challenge.

The Girl Scouts' traditional cookie-ordering process depends on mountains of paperwork. During the peak sales period in January, each Girl Scout marked her sales on an individual order card and turned the card in to the troop leader when she was finished. The troop leader would transfer the information onto a five-part form and give this form to a community volunteer who tabulated the orders. From there, the orders data passed to a regional council headquarters, where they would be batched into final orders for the manufacturer, ABC Cookies. In addition to ordering, Girl Scout volunteers and troop members had to coordinate cookie deliveries, from the manufacturer to regional warehouses, to local drop-off sites, to each scout, and to the customers themselves.

The Patriots' Trail Girl Scout Council, representing 65 communities and 18,000 Girl Scouts in the greater Boston area, sold more than 1.6 million boxes of eight different cookie varieties in 2004 alone. According to its associate executive director Deborah Deacetis, the paperwork had become "overwhelming." "It changed hands too many times. There was a lot of opportunity for error, because of all the added columns, multiple prices per box, and calculations that had to be made by different people, all on deadline."

The Patriots' Trail Council first looked into building a computerized system using Microsoft Access database management and application development tools. But this alternative would have cost $25,000 to develop and would have taken at least three to four months to get the system up and running. It was too time consuming, complex, and expensive for the Girl Scouts. In addition to Microsoft Access software, the Girl Scouts would have to purchase a server to run the system, plus pay for networking and Web site maintenance services so the system could be made available on the Web.

After consulting with management consultants Dovetail Associates, the council selected Intuit's QuickBase for Corporate Workgroups. QuickBase is a hosted Web-based software service for small businesses and corporate workgroups. It is especially well suited for building simple database applications very quickly and does not require a great deal of training to use. QuickBase is customizable and designed to collect, organize, and share data among teams in many different locations.

A Dovetail consultant created a working QuickBase prototype with some basic functions for the Girl Scouts within a few hours. It only took two months to build, test, and implement the entire system using this software. The cost for developing the entire system was a fraction of the Microsoft Access solution. The Girl Scouts do not have to pay for any hardware, software, or networking services because QuickBase runs everything for them on its servers. QuickBase costs $500 per month for organizations with 100 users and $1,500 per month for organizations with up to 500 users. It is very easy to use.

The QuickBase solution eliminates paperwork and calculation errors by providing a clear central source of data for the entire council and easy online entry of cookie orders over the Web. Troop leaders collect the Girl Scouts' order cards and enter them directly into the QuickBase system using their home computers linked to the Web. With a few mouse clicks, the council office consolidates the unit totals and transmits the orders electronically to ABC Cookies.

In the past the council relied on volunteers to handle their paperwork, dropping it off at the council office or mailing it in. "Now we have a way to actually watch the orders coming in," Deacetis notes. As local orders come in, local section leaders can track the data in real time.

The Patriots' Trail Girl Scout Council also uses the QuickBase system to manage the Cookie Cupboard warehouse, where volunteers pick up their cookie orders. Volunteers use the system to make reservations so that the warehouse can prepare the orders in advance, saving time and inventory management costs. The trucking companies that deliver cookie shipments now receive their instructions electronically through QuickBase so that they can create efficient delivery schedules.

Since its implementation, the QuickBase system has cut paperwork by more than 90 percent, reduced errors to 1 percent, and reduced the time spent by volunteers by 50 percent. The old system used to take two months to tally the orders and determine which Scouts should be rewarded for selling the most cookies. Now that time has been cut to 48 hours.

Sources: Intuit Inc., "QuickBase Customers: Patriots' Trail Girl Scouts," www.quickbase.com, accessed August 1, 2007 and "Girl Scouts Unite Behind Order Tracking," *Customer Relationship Management*, May 2005.

The experience of the Patriots' Trail Girl Scout Council illustrates some of the steps required to design and build new information systems. It also illustrates some of the benefits of a new system solution. The Girl Scouts had an outdated manual paper-based system for processing cookie orders that was excessively time consuming and error ridden. The Girl Scouts tried several alternative solutions before opting for a new ordering system based on the QuickBase software service. In this chapter, we will examine the Girl Scouts' search for a system solution as we describe each step of building a new information system using the problem-solving process.

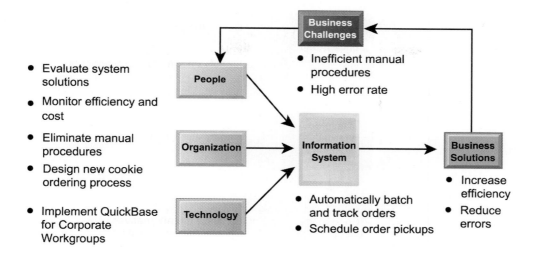

- Evaluate system solutions
- Monitor efficiency and cost
- Eliminate manual procedures
- Design new cookie ordering process
- Implement QuickBase for Corporate Workgroups

Business Challenges
- Inefficient manual procedures
- High error rate

People

Organization

Technology

Information System
- Automatically batch and track orders
- Schedule order pickups

Business Solutions
- Increase efficiency
- Reduce errors

HEADS UP

During your career, you will undoubtedly be asked to work on the development of a new system to solve an important challenge for your business. In the process of building new systems, you will face many choices about hardware and software, and you will have to think about how to redesign business processes and jobs in order to maximize the value derived from the new system. You will also have to manage the system-building project and any changes related to new technology and ways of working. But the most important decisions you will face involve understanding just exactly what it is you want the new system to do and what value it will bring to your firm. This chapter provides you with a methodology to guide you through the problem-solving process of building new information systems and information systems project management.

11.1 Problem Solving and Systems Development

We have already described the problem-solving process and how it helps us analyze and understand the role of information systems in business. This problem-solving process is especially valuable when we need to build new systems. A new information system is built as a solution to a problem or set of problems the organization perceives it is facing. The problem may be one in which managers and employees believe that the business is not performing as well as expected, or it may come from the realization that the organization should take advantage of new opportunities to perform more effectively.

Let's apply this problem-solving process to system building. Figure 11-1 illustrates the four steps we would need to take: (1) define and understand the problem, (2) develop alternative solutions, (3) choose the best solution, and (4) implement the solution.

Before a problem can be solved, it first must be properly defined. Members of the organization must agree that a problem actually exists and that it is serious. The problem must be investigated so that it can be better understood. Next comes a period of devising alternative solutions, then one of evaluating each alternative and selecting the best solution. The final stage is one of implementing the solution, in which a detailed design for the solution is specified, translated into a physical system, tested, introduced to the organization, and further refined as it is used over time.

Figure 11-1
**Developing an
Information System
Solution**
*Developing an informa-
tion system solution is
based on the problem-
solving process.*

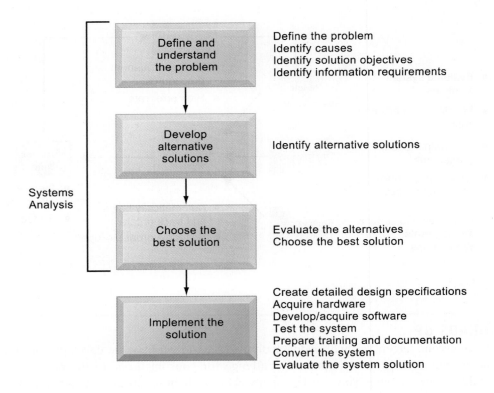

In the information systems world, we have a special name for these activities. Figure 11-1 shows that the first three problem-solving steps, where we identify the problem, gather information, devise alternative solutions, and make a decision about the best solution, are called **systems analysis**.

DEFINING AND UNDERSTANDING THE PROBLEM

Defining the problem may take some work because various members of the company may have different ideas about the nature of the problem and its severity. What caused the problem? Why is it still around? Why wasn't it solved long ago? Systems analysts typically gather facts about existing systems and problems by examining documents, work papers, procedures, and system operations and by interviewing key users of the system.

Information systems problems in the business world typically result from a combination of people, organization, and technology factors. When identifying a key issue or problem, ask what kind of problem it is: Is it a people problem, an organizational problem, a technology problem, or a combination of these? What people, organizational, and technological factors contributed to the problem?

Once the problem has been defined and analyzed, it is possible to make some decisions about what should and can be done. What are the objectives of a solution to the problem? Is the firm's objective to reduce costs, increase sales, or improve relationships with customers, suppliers, or employees? Do managers have sufficient information for decision-making? What information is required to achieve these objectives?

At the most basic level, the **information requirements** of a new system identify who needs what information, where, when, and how. Requirements analysis carefully defines the objectives of the new or modified system and develops a detailed description of the functions that the new system must perform. A system designed around the wrong set of requirements will either have to be discarded because of poor performance or will need to undergo major modifications. Section 11.2 describes alternative approaches to eliciting requirements that help minimize this problem.

Let's return to our opening case about the Girl Scouts. The problem here is that the Girl Scout ordering process is heavily manual and cannot support the large number of volunteers and cookie orders that must be coordinated. As a result, cookie ordering is extremely inefficient with high error rates and volunteers spending excessive time organizing orders and deliveries.

Organizationally, the Girl Scouts are a voluntary organization distributed across a large area, with cookie sales as the primary source of revenue. The Scouts rely on volunteers with little or no business or computer experience for sales and management of orders and deliveries. They have almost no financial resources and volunteers are strapped for time. The Girl Scout cookie-ordering process requires many steps and coordination of multiple groups and organizations—individual Girl Scouts, volunteers, the council office, the cookie manufacturing factory, trucking companies, and the Cookie Cupboard warehouse.

The objectives of a solution for the Girl Scouts would be to reduce the amount of time, effort, and errors in the cookie-ordering process. Information requirements for the solution include the ability to rapidly total and organize order transactions for transmittal to ABC Cookies; the ability to track orders by type of cookie, troop, and individual Girl Scout; the ability to schedule deliveries to the Cookie Cupboard; and the ability to schedule order pickups from the Cookie Cupboard.

DEVELOPING ALTERNATIVE SOLUTIONS

What alternative solutions are possible for achieving these objectives and meeting these information requirements? The systems analysis lays out the most likely paths to follow given the nature of the problem. Some possible solutions do not require an information system solution but instead call for an adjustment in management, additional training, or refinement of existing organizational procedures. Some, however, do require modifications to the firm's existing information systems or an entirely new information system.

EVALUATING AND CHOOSING SOLUTIONS

The systems analysis includes a **feasibility study** to determine whether each proposed solution is feasible, or achievable, from a financial, technical, and organizational standpoint. The feasibility study establishes whether each alternative solution is a good investment, whether the technology needed for the system is available and can be handled by the firm's information systems staff, and whether the organization is capable of accommodating the changes introduced by the system.

A written systems proposal report describes the costs and benefits, and advantages and disadvantages of each alternative solution. Which solution is best in a financial sense? Which works best for the organization? The systems analysis will detail the costs and benefits of each alternative and the changes that the organization will have to make to use the solution effectively. We provide a detailed discussion of how to determine the business value of systems and manage change in the following section. On the basis of this report, management will select what it believes is the best solution for the company.

The Patriots' Trail Girl Scouts had three alternative solutions. One was to streamline existing processes, continuing to rely on manual procedures. However, given the large number of Girl Scouts and cookie orders, as well as relationships with manufacturers and shippers, redesigning and streamlining a manual ordering and delivery process would not have provided many benefits. The Girl Scouts needed an automated solution that accurately tracked thousands of order and delivery transactions, reduced paperwork, and created a central real-time source of sales data that could be accessed by council headquarters and individual volunteers.

A second alternative was to custom-build a cookie ordering system using Microsoft Access. This alternative was considered too time consuming, expensive, and technically challenging for the Girl Scouts. It required $25,000 in initial programming costs, plus the purchase of hardware and networking equipment to run the system and link it to the Internet, as well as trained staff to run and maintain the system.

The third alternative was to rapidly create a system using an application service provider. QuickBase provides templates and tools for creating simple database systems in very short periods, provides the hardware for running the application and Web site, and can be accessed by many different users over the Web. This solution does not require the Girl Scouts to purchase any hardware, software, or networking technology or to maintain any information system staff to support the system. This last alternative was the most feasible for the Girl Scouts.

IMPLEMENTING THE SOLUTION

The first step in implementing a system solution is to create detailed design specifications. **Systems design** shows how the chosen solution should be realized. The system design is the model or blueprint for an information system solution and consists of all the specifications that will deliver the functions identified during systems analysis. These specifications should address all of the technical, organizational, and people components of the system solution. Table 11.1 lists the types of specifications that would be produced during system design.

A Dovetail Associates consultant elicited information requirements and created a design for the new Girl Scout cookie system. Table 11.2 shows some of the design specifications for the new system.

Completing Implementation

In the final steps of implementing a system solution, the following activities would be performed:

- *Hardware selection and acquisition.* System builders select appropriate hardware for the application. They would either purchase the necessary computers and networking hardware or lease them from a technology provider.

TABLE 11.1

System Design Specifications

Output	Medium and Content
	Timing
Input	Flow
	Data entry
User interface	Feedback and error handling
Database	Logical data model
	Volume and speed requirements
	File and record specifications
Processing	Program logic and computations
Manual procedures	What activities, who, when, how, and where
Security and controls	Access controls
	Input, processing, and output controls
Conversion	Testing method
	Conversion strategy
Training and documentation	Training modules and platforms
	Systems, user, and operations documentation
Organizational changes	Process design
	Organizational structure changes

Output	Online reports
	Hard copy reports
	Online queries
	Order transactions for ABC Cookies
	Delivery tickets for the trucking firm
Input	Order data entry form
	Troop data entry form
	Girl Scout data entry form
	Shipping/delivery data entry form
User interface	Graphical Web interface
Database	Database with cookie order file, delivery file, troop contact file
Processing	Calculate order totals by type of cookie and number of boxes
	Track orders by troop and individual Girl Scout
	Schedule pickups at the Cookie Cupboard
	Update Girl Scout and troop data for address and member changes
Manual procedures	Girl Scouts take orders with paper forms
	Troop leaders collect order cards from Scouts and enter the order data online
Security and controls	Online passwords
	Control totals
Conversion	Input Girl Scout and troop data
	Transfer factory and delivery data
	Test system
Training and documentation	System guide for users
	Online practice demonstration
	Online training sessions
	Training for ABC Cookies and trucking companies to accept data and instructions automatically from the Girl Scout system
Organizational changes	Job design: Volunteers no longer have to tabulate orders
	Process design: Take orders on manual cards but enter them online into the system
	Schedule order pickups from the Cookie Cupboard online

TABLE 11.2

Design Specifications for the Girl Scout Cookie System

- *Software development and programming.* Software is custom programmed in-house or purchased from an external source, such as an outsourcing vendor, an application software package vendor, or an application service provider.

The Girl Scouts did not have to purchase additional hardware or software. QuickBase offers templates for generating simple database applications. Dovetail consultants used the QuickBase tools to rapidly create the software for the system. The system runs on QuickBase servers.

- *Testing.* The system is thoroughly tested to ensure it produces the right results. The **testing** process requires detailed testing of individual computer programs, called **unit testing**, as well as **system testing**, which tests the performance of the information system as a whole. **Acceptance testing** provides the final certification that the system is ready to be used in a production setting. Information systems tests are evaluated by users and reviewed by management. When all parties are satisfied that the new system meets their standards, the system is formally accepted for installation.

The systems development team works with users to devise a systematic test plan. The **test plan** includes all of the preparations for the series of tests we have just described. Figure 11-2 shows a sample from a test plan that might have been used for the Girl Scout cookie system. The condition being tested is online access of an existing record for a specific Girl Scout troop.

- *Training and documentation.* End users and information system specialists require training so that they will be able to use the new system. Detailed **documentation** showing how the system works from both a technical and end-user standpoint must be prepared.

The Girl Scout cookie system provides an online practice area for users to practice entering data into the system by following step-by-step instructions. Also available on the Web is a step-by-step instruction guide for the system that can be downloaded and printed as a hard copy manual.

- ***Conversion*** is the process of changing from the old system to the new system. There are three main conversion strategies: the parallel strategy, the direct cutover strategy, and the phased approach strategy.

In a **parallel strategy**, both the old system and its potential replacement are run together for a time until everyone is assured that the new one functions correctly. The old system remains available as a backup in case of problems. The **direct cutover strategy** replaces the old system entirely with the new system on an appointed day, carrying the risk that there is no system to fall back on if problems arise. A **phased approach** introduces the system in stages (such as first introducing the modules for ordering Girl Scout cookies and then introducing the modules for transmitting orders and instructions to the cookie factory and shipper).

Figure 11-2
A Sample Test Plan for the Girl Scout Cookie System
When developing a test plan, it is imperative to include the various conditions to be tested, the requirements for each condition tested, and the expected results. Test plans require input from both end users and information systems specialists.

Test Case Number: GS02-010

Prepared by: A. Nelson	Date: February 15, 2008

Objective: This subtest checks for accessing an existing troop record

Specific Environment: QuickBase for WorkGroups

Procedure Description:
Click on My Troop Summary link.
Enter Troop Number

Expected Result:
When user clicks on My Troop Summary, the Troop Summary screen appears.
When user enters the correct Troop Number, the Troop record appears.
When user enters the wrong Troop Number, the error message "Wrong Troop Number" appears.

Test Results:
All OK.

- *Production and maintenance*. After the new system is installed and conversion is complete, the system is said to be in **production**. During this stage, users and technical specialists review the solution to determine how well it has met its original objectives and to decide whether any revisions or modifications are in order. Changes in hardware, software, documentation, or procedures to a production system to correct errors, meet new requirements, or improve processing efficiency are termed **maintenance.**

The Girl Scouts continued to improve and refine their QuickBase cookie system. In 2005, the system was made more efficient for users with slow Internet connections. Other recent enhancements include capabilities for paying for orders more rapidly, entering troop information and initial orders without waiting for a specified starting date, and receiving online confirmation for reservations to pick up orders from the Cookie Cupboard.

Managing the Change

Developing a new information systems solution is not merely a matter of installing hardware and software. The business must also deal with the organizational changes that the new solution will bring about—new information, new business processes, and perhaps new reporting relationships and decision-making power. A very well-designed solution may not work unless it is introduced to the organization very carefully. The process of planning change in an organization so that it is implemented in an orderly and effective manner is so critical to the success or failure of information system solutions that we devote the next section to a detailed discussion of this topic.

To manage the transition from the old manual cookie-ordering processes to the new system, the Girl Scouts would have to inform troop leaders and volunteers about changes in cookie-ordering procedures, provide training, and provide resources for answering any questions that arose as parents and volunteers started using the system. They would need to work with ABC Cookies and their shippers on new procedures for transmitting and delivering orders.

11.2 Alternative Systems-Building Approaches

There are alternative methods for building systems using the basic problem-solving model we have just described. These alternative methods include the traditional systems lifecycle, prototyping, end-user development, application software packages, and outsourcing.

TRADITIONAL SYSTEMS DEVELOPMENT LIFECYCLE

The **systems development lifecycle (SDLC)** is the oldest method for building information systems. The lifecycle methodology is a phased approach to building a system, dividing systems development into a series of formal stages, as illustrated in Figure 11-3. Although systems builders can go back and forth among stages in the lifecycle, the systems lifecycle is predominantly a "waterfall" approach in which tasks in one stage are completed before work for the next stage begins.

This approach maintains a very formal division of labor between end users and information systems specialists. Technical specialists, such as system analysts and programmers, are responsible for much of the systems analysis, design, and implementation work; end users are limited to providing information requirements and reviewing the technical staff's work. The lifecycle also emphasizes formal specifications and paperwork, so many documents are generated during the course of a systems project.

The systems lifecycle is still used for building large complex systems that require rigorous and formal requirements analysis, predefined specifications, and tight controls over the systems-building process. However, this approach is also time consuming and expensive to use. Tasks in one stage are supposed to be completed before work for the next stage begins. Activities can be repeated, but volumes of new documents must be generated and steps retraced if requirements and specifications need to be revised. This encourages

Figure 11-3
The Traditional Systems Development Lifecycle
The systems development lifecycle partitions systems development into formal stages, with each stage requiring completion before the next stage can begin.

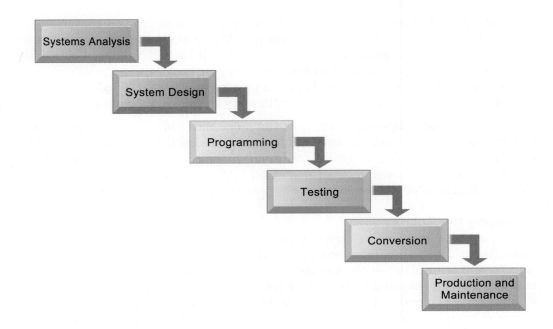

freezing of specifications relatively early in the development process. The lifecycle approach is also not suitable for many small desktop systems, which tend to be less structured and more individualized.

PROTOTYPING

Prototyping consists of building an experimental system rapidly and inexpensively for end users to evaluate. The prototype is a working version of an information system or part of the system, but it is intended as only a preliminary model. Users interact with the prototype to get a better idea of their information requirements, refining the prototype multiple times. The chapter-opening case describes how Dovetail Associates used QuickBase to create a prototype that helped the Patriots' Trail Girl Scout Council refine their specifications for their cookie ordering system. When the design is finalized, the prototype will be converted to a polished production system. Figure 11-4 shows a four-step model of the prototyping process.

Step 1: *Identify the user's basic requirements.* The system designer (usually an information systems specialist) works with the user only long enough to capture the user's basic information needs.

Step 2: *Develop an initial prototype.* The system designer creates a working prototype quickly, using tools for rapidly generating software.

Step 3: *Use the prototype.* The user is encouraged to work with the system to determine how well the prototype meets his or her needs and to make suggestions for improving the prototype.

Step 4: *Revise and enhance the prototype.* The system builder notes all changes the user requests and refines the prototype accordingly. After the prototype has been revised, the cycle returns to step 3. Steps 3 and 4 are repeated until the user is satisfied.

Prototyping is especially useful in designing an information system's user interface. Because prototyping encourages intense end-user involvement throughout the systems-development process, it is more likely to produce systems that fulfill user requirements.

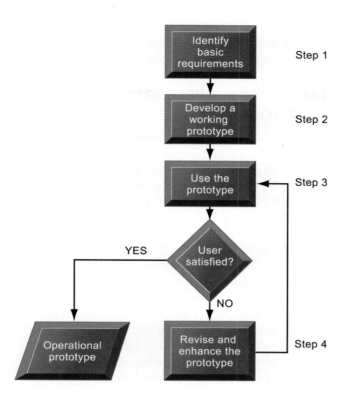

Figure 11-4
The Prototyping Process
The process of developing a prototype consists of four steps. Because a prototype can be developed quickly and inexpensively, systems builders can go through several iterations, repeating steps 3 and 4, to refine and enhance the prototype before arriving at the final operational one.

However, rapid prototyping may gloss over essential steps in systems development, such as thorough testing and documentation. If the completed prototype works reasonably well, management may not see the need to build a polished production system. Some hastily constructed systems do not easily accommodate large quantities of data or a large number of users in a production environment.

END-USER DEVELOPMENT

End-user development allows end users, with little or no formal assistance from technical specialists, to create simple information systems, reducing the time and steps required to produce a finished application. Using fourth-generation languages, graphics languages, and PC software tools, end users can access data, create reports, and develop entire information systems on their own, with little or no help from professional systems analysts or programmers.

For example Elie Tahari Ltd., a leading designer of women's fashions, uses InformationBuilders Inc.'s WebFOCUS software to enable authorized users to obtain self-service reports on orders, inventory, sales, and finance. Sales executives use the system to view their accounts, to determine what merchandise is selling, and to see what customers have ordered. Users can also create ad-hoc reports by themselves to obtain specific pieces of information or more detailed data (Information Builders, 2007).

On the whole, end-user-developed systems are completed more rapidly than those developed with conventional programming tools. Allowing users to specify their own business needs improves requirements gathering and often leads to a higher level of user involvement and satisfaction with the system. However, fourth-generation tools still cannot replace conventional tools for some business applications because they cannot easily handle the processing of large numbers of transactions or applications with extensive procedural logic and updating requirements.

End-user development also poses organizational risks because systems are created rapidly, without a formal development methodology, testing, and documentation. To help organizations maximize the benefits of end-user applications development, management should require cost justification of end-user information system projects and establish hardware, software, and quality standards for user-developed applications.

PURCHASING SOLUTIONS: APPLICATION SOFTWARE PACKAGES AND OUTSOURCING

Chapter 4 points out that the software for most systems today is not developed in-house but is purchased from external sources. Firms may choose to purchase a software package from a commercial vendor, rent the software from a service provider, or outsource the development work to another firm. Selection of the software or software service is often is based on a **Request for Proposal (RFP)**, which is a detailed list of questions submitted to external vendors to see how well they meet the requirements for the proposed system.

Application Software Packages

Most new information systems today are built using an application software package or preprogrammed software components. Many applications are common to all business organizations—for example, payroll, accounts receivable, general ledger, or inventory control. For such universal functions with standard processes that do not change a great deal over time, a generalized system will fulfill the requirements of many organizations.

If a software package can fulfill most of an organization's requirements, the company does not have to write its own software. The company saves time and money by using the prewritten, predesigned, pretested software programs from the package.

Many packages include capabilities for customization to meet unique requirements not addressed by the package software. **Customization** features allow a software package to be modified to meet an organization's unique requirements without destroying the integrity of the packaged software. However, if extensive customization is required, additional programming and customization work may become so expensive and time consuming that it negates many of the advantages of software packages. If the package cannot be customized, the organization will have to adapt to the package and change its procedures.

Outsourcing

If a firm does not want to use its internal resources to build or operate information systems, it can outsource the work to an external organization that specializes in providing these services. Software service providers, which we describe in Chapter 4, are one form of outsourcing. An example would be the Girl Scouts leasing the software and hardware from QuickBase to run their cookie-ordering system. Subscribing companies use the software and computer hardware of the service provider as the technical platform for their systems. In another form of outsourcing, a company would hire an external vendor to design and create the software for its system, but that company would operate the system on its own computers.

The outsourcing vendor might be domestic or in another country. Domestic outsourcing is driven primarily by the fact that outsourcing firms possess skills, resources, and assets which their clients do not have. Installing a new supply chain management system in a very large company might require hiring an additional 30–50 people with specific expertise in supply chain management software licensed, say, from Manugistics or another vendor. Rather than hire permanent new employees, most of whom would need extensive training in the software package, and then release them after the new system is built, it makes more sense, and is often less expensive, to outsource this work for a 12 month period.

In the case of offshore outsourcing, the decision tends to be much more cost-driven. A skilled programmer in India or Russia earns about U.S. $10,000 per year, compared to $70,000 per year for a comparable programmer in the United States. The Internet and low-cost communications technology have drastically reduced the expense and difficulty of coordinating the work of global teams in faraway locations. In addition to cost savings, many offshore outsourcing firms offer world-class technology assets and skills.

For example, Pinnacle West Capital Corporation, which sells and delivers electricity and energy-related services to one million customers in the western United States, turned to outsourcing to reduce operational costs. It contracted with the Indian software and service provider Wipro Ltd. to handle its application development. Wipro develops Pinnacle West's applications, services system enhancements, and provides 24-hour system support. Outsourcing to Wipro helped Pinnacle West accomplish 12 months of development work in 7 months while reducing computer processing and application development costs (Wipro, 2007).

There is a very strong chance that at some point in your career, you'll be working with offshore outsourcers or global teams. Your firm is most likely to benefit from outsourcing if it takes the time to evaluate all the risks and to make sure outsourcing is appropriate for its particular needs. Any company that outsources its applications must thoroughly understand the project, including its requirements, method of implementation, source of expected benefits, cost components, and metrics for measuring performance.

Many firms underestimate costs for identifying and evaluating vendors of information technology services, for transitioning to a new vendor, for improving internal software development methods to match those of outsourcing vendors, and for monitoring vendors to make sure they are fulfilling their contractual obligations. Outsourcing offshore incurs additional costs for coping with cultural differences that drain productivity and dealing with human resources issues, such as terminating or relocating domestic employees. These hidden costs undercut some of the anticipated benefits from outsourcing. Firms should be especially cautious when using an outsourcer to develop or to operate applications that give it some type of competitive advantage.

Figure 11-5 shows best- and worst-case scenarios for the total cost of an offshore outsourcing project. It shows how much hidden costs affect the total project cost. The best case reflects the lowest estimates for additional costs, and the worst case reflects the highest estimates for these costs. As you can see, hidden costs increase the total cost of an offshore outsourcing project by an extra 15 to 57 percent. Even with these extra costs, many firms will benefit from offshore outsourcing if they manage the work well.

TOTAL COST OF OFFSHORE OUTSOURCING					
Cost of outsourcing contract				**$10,000,000**	
Hidden Costs	Best Case	Additional Cost ($)	Worst Case	Additional Cost ($)	
1. Vendor selection	0.2%	20,000	2%	200,000	
2. Transition costs	2%	200,000	3%	300,000	
3. Layoffs & retention	3%	300,000	5%	500,000	
4. Lost productivity/cultural issues	3%	300,000	27%	2,700,000	
5. Improving development processes	1%	100,000	10%	1,000,000	
6. Managing the contract	6%	600,000	10%	1,000,000	
Total additional costs		**1,520,000**		**5,700,000**	
	Outstanding Contract ($)	Additional Cost ($)	Total Cost ($)	Additional Cost	
Total cost of outsourcing (TCO) best case	10,000,000	1,520,000	11,520,000	15.2%	
Total cost of outsourcing (TCO) worst case	10,000,000	5,700,000	15,700,000	57.0%	

Figure 11-5
Total Cost of Offshore Outsourcing
If a firm spends $10 million on offshore outsourcing contracts, that company will actually spend 15.2 percent in extra costs even under the best-case scenario. In the worst-case scenario, where there is a dramatic drop in productivity along with exceptionally high transition and layoff costs, a firm can expect to pay up to 57 percent in extra costs on top of the $10 million outlay for an offshore contract.

RAPID APPLICATION DEVELOPMENT FOR E-BUSINESS

Technologies and business conditions are changing so rapidly that agility and scalability have become critical elements of system solutions. Companies are adopting shorter, more informal development processes for many of their e-commerce and e-business applications, processes that provide fast solutions that do not disrupt their core transaction processing systems and organizational databases. In addition to using software packages, application service providers, and other outsourcing services, they are relying more heavily on fast-cycle techniques, such as joint application design (JAD), prototypes, and reusable standardized software components that can be assembled into a complete set of services for e-commerce and e-business.

The term **rapid application development (RAD)** refers to the process of creating workable systems in a very short period of time. RAD includes the use of visual programming and other tools for building graphical user interfaces, iterative prototyping of key system elements, the automation of program code generation, and close teamwork among end users and information systems specialists. Simple systems often can be assembled from prebuilt components (see Section 11.3). The process does not have to be sequential, and key parts of development can occur simultaneously.

Sometimes a technique called **joint application design (JAD)** will be used to accelerate the generation of information requirements and to develop the initial systems design. JAD brings end users and information systems specialists together in an interactive session to discuss the system's design. Properly prepared and facilitated, JAD sessions can significantly speed up the design phase and involve users at an intense level.

11.3 Modeling and Designing Systems

We have just described alternative methods for building systems. There are also alternative methodologies for modeling and designing systems. The two most prominent are structured methodologies and object-oriented development.

STRUCTURED METHODOLOGIES

Structured methodologies have been used to document, analyze, and design information systems since the 1970s. **Structured** refers to the fact that the techniques are step by step, with each step building on the previous one. Structured methodologies are top-down, progressing from the highest, most abstract level to the lowest level of detail—from the general to the specific.

Structured development methods are process-oriented, focusing primarily on modeling the processes, or actions, that capture, store, manipulate, and distribute data as the data flow through a system. These methods separate data from processes. A separate programming procedure must be written every time someone wants to take an action on a particular piece of data. The procedures act on data that the program passes to them.

The primary tool for representing a system's component processes and the flow of data between them is the **data flow diagram (DFD)**. The data flow diagram offers a logical graphic model of information flow, partitioning a system into modules that show manageable levels of detail. It rigorously specifies the processes or transformations that occur within each module and the interfaces that exist between them.

Figure 11-6 shows a simple data flow diagram for a mail-in university course registration system. The rounded boxes represent processes, which portray the transformation of data. The square box represents an external entity, which is an originator or receiver of information located outside the boundaries of the system being modeled. The open rectangles represent data stores, which are either manual or automated inventories of data. The arrows represent data flows, which show the movement between processes, external entities, and data stores. They always contain packets of data with the name or content of each data flow listed beside the arrow.

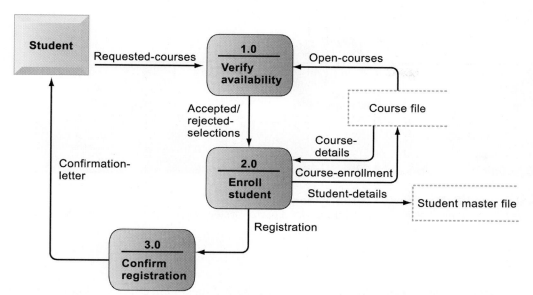

Figure 11-6
Data Flow Diagram for Mail-in University Registration System
The system has three processes: Verify availability (1.0), Enroll student (2.0), and Confirm registration (3.0). The name and content of each of the data flows appear adjacent to each arrow. There is one external entity in this system: the student. There are two data stores: the student master file and the course file.

This data flow diagram shows that students submit registration forms with their names, identification numbers, and the numbers of the courses they wish to take. In process 1.0 the system verifies that each course selected is still open by referencing the university's course file. The file distinguishes courses that are open from those that have been canceled or filled. Process 1.0 then determines which of the student's selections can be accepted or rejected. Process 2.0 enrolls the student in the courses for which he or she has been accepted. It updates the university's course file with the student's name and identification number and recalculates the class size. If maximum enrollment has been reached, the course number is flagged as closed. Process 2.0 also updates the university's student master file with information about new students or changes in address. Process 3.0 then sends each student applicant a confirmation-of-registration letter listing the courses for which he or she is registered and noting the course selections that could not be fulfilled.

Through leveled data flow diagrams, a complex process can be broken down into successive levels of detail. An entire system can be divided into subsystems with a high-level data flow diagram. Each subsystem, in turn, can be divided into additional subsystems with lower-level data flow diagrams, and the lower-level subsystems can be broken down again until the lowest level of detail has been reached. **Process specifications** describe the transformation occurring within the lowest level of the data flow diagrams, showing the logic for each process.

In structured methodology, software design is modeled using hierarchical structure charts. The **structure chart** is a top-down chart, showing each level of design, its relationship to other levels, and its place in the overall design structure. The design first considers the main function of a program or system, then breaks this function into subfunctions, and decomposes each subfunction until the lowest level of detail has been reached. Figure 11-7 shows a high-level structure chart for a payroll system. If a design has too many levels to fit onto one structure chart, it can be broken down further on more detailed structure charts. A structure chart may document one program, one system (a set of programs), or part of one program.

OBJECT-ORIENTED DEVELOPMENT

Structured methods treat data and processes as logically separate entities, whereas in the real world such separation seems unnatural. Different modeling conventions are used for analysis (the data flow diagram) and for design (the structure chart).

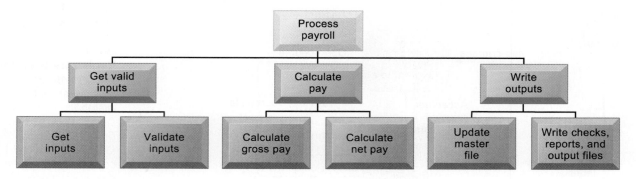

Figure 11-7 High-Level Structure Chart for a Payroll System
This structure chart shows the highest or most abstract level of design for a payroll system, providing an overview of the entire system.

Object-oriented development addresses these issues. Object-oriented development uses the object, which we introduced in Chapter 4, as the basic unit of systems analysis and design. An object combines data and the specific processes that operate on those data. Data encapsulated in an object can be accessed and modified only by the operations, or methods, associated with that object. Instead of passing data to procedures, programs send a message for an object to perform an operation that is already embedded in it. The system is modeled as a collection of objects and the relationships among them. Because processing logic resides within objects rather that in separate software programs, objects must collaborate with each other to make the system work.

Object-oriented modeling is based on the concepts of *class* and *inheritance*. Objects belonging to a certain class, or general categories of similar objects, have the features of that class. Classes of objects in turn inherit all the structure and behaviors of a more general class and then add variables and behaviors unique to each object. New classes of objects are created by choosing an existing class and specifying how the new class differs from the existing class, instead of starting from scratch each time.

We can see how class and inheritance work in Figure 11-8, which illustrates the relationships among classes concerning employees and how they are paid. Employee is the common ancestor, or superclass, for the other three classes. Salaried, Hourly, and Temporary are subclasses of Employee. The class name is in the top compartment, the attributes for each class are in the middle portion of each box, and the list of operations is in the bottom portion of each box. The features that are shared by all employees (ID, name, address, date hired, position, and pay) are stored in the Employee superclass, whereas each subclass stores features that are specific to that particular type of employee. Specific to Hourly employees, for example, are their hourly rates and overtime rates. A solid line from the subclass to the superclass is a generalization path showing that the subclasses Salaried, Hourly, and Temporary have common features that can be generalized into the superclass Employee.

Object-oriented development is more iterative and incremental than traditional structured development. During systems analysis, systems builders document the functional requirements of the system, specifying its most important properties and what the proposed system must do. Interactions between the system and its users are analyzed to identify objects, which include both data and processes. The object-oriented design phase describes how the objects will behave and how they will interact with one other. Similar objects are grouped together to form a class, and classes are grouped into hierarchies in which a subclass inherits the attributes and methods from its superclass.

The information system is implemented by translating the design into program code, reusing classes that are already available in a library of reusable software objects and adding new ones created during the object-oriented design phase. Implementation may also involve

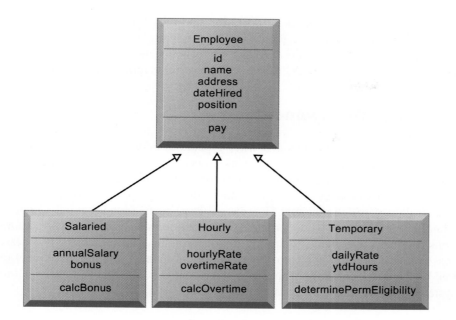

Figure 11-8
Class and Inheritance
This figure illustrates how classes inherit the common features of their superclass.

the creation of an object-oriented database. The resulting system must be thoroughly tested and evaluated.

Because objects are reusable, object-oriented development could potentially reduce the time and cost of writing software if organizations reuse software objects that have already been created as building blocks for other applications. New systems can be created by using some existing objects, changing others, and adding a few new objects.

Component-Based Development and Web Services

To further expedite software creation, groups of objects have been assembled into software components for common functions, such as a graphical user interface or online ordering capability, and these components can be combined to create large-scale business applications. This approach to software development is called **component-based development**. Businesses are using component-based development to create their e-commerce applications by combining commercially available components for shopping carts, user authentication, search engines, and catalogs with pieces of software for their own unique business requirements.

Chapter 4 introduced Web services as loosely coupled, reusable software components based on extensible markup language (XML) and other open protocols and standards that enable one application to communicate with another with no custom programming required. In addition to supporting internal and external integration of systems, Web services provide nonproprietary tools for building new information system applications or enhancing existing systems. For example, eDiets.com, an online provider of diet information and packaged meals to dieters, used an address-verification Web service from StrikeIron.com to quickly build its system for shipping meals to the right address (Babcock, 2006).

COMPUTER-AIDED SOFTWARE ENGINEERING (CASE)

Computer-aided software engineering (CASE)—sometimes called computer-aided systems engineering—provides software tools to automate the methodologies we have just described to reduce the amount of repetitive work in systems development. CASE tools provide automated graphics facilities for producing charts and diagrams, screen and report generators, data dictionaries, extensive reporting facilities, analysis and checking tools, code generators, and documentation generators. CASE tools also contain features for validating design diagrams and specifications.

CASE tools facilitate clear documentation and coordination of team development efforts. Team members can share their work by accessing each other's files to review or modify what has been done. Modest productivity benefits are achieved if the tools are used properly. Many CASE tools are PC based, with powerful graphical capabilities.

11.4 Project Management

Your company might have developed what appears to be an excellent system solution. Yet when the system is in use, it does not work properly or it doesn't deliver the benefits that were promised. If this occurs, your firm is not alone. There is a very high failure rate among information systems projects because they have not been properly managed. The Standish Group consultancy, which monitors IT project success rates, found that only 29 percent of all technology investments were completed on time, on budget, and with all features and functions originally specified (Levinson, 2006). Firms may have incorrectly assessed the business value of the new system or were unable to manage the organizational change required by the new technology. That's why it's essential to know how to manage information systems projects and the reasons why they succeed or fail.

PROJECT MANAGEMENT OBJECTIVES

A **project** is a planned series of related activities for achieving a specific business objective. Information systems projects include the development of new information systems, enhancing existing systems, or projects for replacing or upgrading the firm's information technology (IT) infrastructure.

Project management refers to the application of knowledge, skills, tools, and techniques to achieve specific targets within specified budget and time constraints. Project management activities include planning the work, assessing risk, estimating resources required to accomplish the work, organizing the work, acquiring human and material resources, assigning tasks, directing activities, controlling project execution, reporting progress, and analyzing the results. As in other areas of business, project management for information systems must deal with five major variables: scope, time, cost, quality, and risk.

Scope defines what work is or is not included in a project. For example, the scope of a project for a new order processing system might include new modules for inputting orders and transmitting them to production and accounting but not any changes to related accounts receivable, manufacturing, distribution, or inventory control systems. Project management defines all the work required to complete a project successfully, and should ensure that the scope of a project not expand beyond what was originally intended.

Time is the amount of time required to complete the project. Project management typically establishes the amount of time required to complete major components of a project. Each of these components is further broken down into activities and tasks. Project management tries to determine the time required to complete each task and establish a schedule for completing the work.

Cost is based on the time to complete a project multiplied by the daily cost of human resources required to complete the project. Information systems project costs also include the cost of hardware, software, and work space. Project management develops a budget for the project and monitors ongoing project expenses.

Quality is an indicator of how well the end result of a project satisfies the objectives specified by management. The quality of information systems projects usually boils down to improved organizational performance and decision making. Quality also considers the accuracy and timeliness of information produced by the new system and ease of use.

Risk refers to potential problems that would threaten the success of a project. These potential problems might prevent a project from achieving its objectives by increasing time and cost, lowering the quality of project outputs, or preventing the project from being completed altogether. We discuss the most important risk factors for information systems projects later in this section.

SELECTING PROJECTS: MAKING THE BUSINESS CASE FOR A NEW SYSTEM

Companies typically are presented with many different projects for solving problems and improving performance. There are far more ideas for systems projects than there are resources. You will need to select the projects that promise the greatest benefit to the business.

Determining Project Costs and Benefits

As we pointed out earlier, the systems analysis includes an assessment of the economic feasibility of each alternative solution—whether each solution represents a good investment for the company. In order to identify the information systems projects that will deliver the most business value, you'll need to identify their costs and benefits and how they relate to the firm's information systems plan.

Table 11.3 lists some of the more common costs and benefits of systems. **Tangible benefits** can be quantified and assigned a monetary value. **Intangible benefits**, such as more efficient customer service or enhanced decision making, cannot be immediately quantified. Yet systems that produce mainly intangible benefits may still be good investments if they produce quantifiable gains in the long run.

To determine the benefits of a particular solution, you'll need to calculate all of its costs and all of its benefits. Obviously, a solution where costs exceed benefits should be rejected. But even if the benefits outweigh the costs, some additional financial analysis is required to determine whether the investment represents a good return on the firm's invested capital. Capital budgeting methods, such as net present value, internal rate of return (IRR), or accounting rate of return on investment (ROI), would typically be employed to evaluate the proposed information system solution as an investment. You can find out more about how these capital budgeting methods are used to justify information system investments in our Learning Tracks.

TABLE 11.3

Costs and Benefits of Information Systems

IMPLEMENTATION COSTS
Hardware
Telecommunications
Software
Personnel costs

OPERATIONAL COSTS
Computer processing time
Maintenance
Operating staff
User time
Ongoing training costs
Facility costs

TANGIBLE BENEFITS
Increased productivity
Lower operational costs
Reduced workforce
Lower computer expenses
Lower outside vendor costs
Lower clerical and professional costs
Reduced rate of growth in expenses
Reduced facility costs
Increased sales

INTANGIBLE BENEFITS
Improved asset utilization
Improved resource control
Improved organizational planning
Increased organizational flexibility
More timely information
More information
Increased organizational learning
Legal requirements attained
Enhanced employee goodwill
Increased job satisfaction
Improved decision making
Improved operations
Higher client satisfaction
Better corporate image

Some of the tangible benefits obtained by the Girl Scouts were increased productivity and lower operational costs resulting from automating the ordering process and from reducing errors. Intangible benefits include enhanced volunteer job satisfaction and improved operations.

The Information Systems Plan

An **information systems plan** shows how specific information systems fit into a company's overall business plan and business strategy. Table 11.4 lists the major components of such a plan. The plan contains a statement of corporate goals and specifies how information technology will help the business attain these goals. The report shows how general goals will be achieved by specific systems projects. It identifies specific target dates and milestones that can be used later to evaluate the plan's progress in terms of how many objectives were actually attained in the time frame specified in the plan. The plan indicates the key management decisions concerning hardware acquisition; telecommunications; centralization/decentralization of authority, data, and hardware; and required organizational change.

The plan should describe organizational changes, including management and employee training requirements; changes in business processes; and changes in authority, structure, or management practice. When you are making the business case for a new information system project, you show how the proposed system fits into that plan.

Portfolio Analysis

Once you have determined the overall direction of systems development, **portfolio analysis** will help you evaluate alternative system projects. Portfolio analysis inventories all of the firm's information systems projects and assets, including infrastructure, outsourcing contracts, and licenses. This portfolio of information systems investments can be described as having a certain profile of risk and benefit to the firm (see Figure 11-9), similar to a financial portfolio. Each information systems project carries its own set of risks and benefits. Firms try to improve the return on their information system portfolios by balancing the risk and return from their systems investments.

Obviously, you begin first by focusing on systems of high benefit and low risk. These promise early returns and low risks. Second, high-benefit, high-risk systems should be examined; low-benefit, high-risk systems should be totally avoided; and low-benefit, low-risk systems should be reexamined for the possibility of rebuilding and replacing them with more desirable systems having higher benefits. By using portfolio analysis, management can determine the optimal mix of investment risk and reward for their firms, balancing riskier, high-reward projects with safer, lower-reward ones.

The U.S. Army's Office of the CIO/G6, which oversees an annual IT budget of more than $7 billion and manages over 1500 systems and programs, uses portfolio analysis to

Figure 11-9
A System Portfolio
Companies should examine their portfolio of projects in terms of potential benefits and likely risks. Certain kinds of projects should be avoided altogether and others developed rapidly. There is no ideal mix. Companies in different industries have different information systems needs.

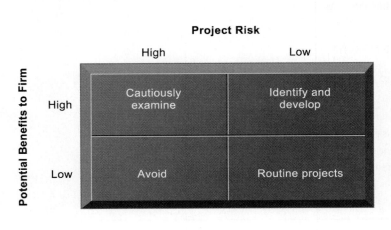

TABLE 11.4

Information Systems
Plan

1. **Purpose of the Plan**
    Overview of plan contents
    Current business organization and future organization
    Key business processes
    Management strategy

2. **Strategic Business Plan Rationale**
    Current situation
    Current business organization
    Changing environments
    Major goals of the business plan
    Firm's strategic plan

3. **Current Systems**
    Major systems supporting business functions and processes
    Current infrastructure capabilities
        Hardware
        Software
        Database
        Telecommunications and the Internet
    Difficulties meeting business requirements
    Anticipated future demands

4. **New Developments**
    New system projects
        Project descriptions
        Business rationale
        Applications' role in strategy
    New infrastructure capabilities required
        Hardware
        Software
        Database
        Telecommunications and the Internet

5. **Management Strategy**
    Acquisition plans
    Milestones and timing
    Organizational realignment
    Internal reorganization
    Management controls
    Major training initiatives
    Personnel strategy

6. **Implementation of the Plan**
    Anticipated difficulties in implementation
    Progress reports

7. **Budget Requirements**
    Requirements
    Potential savings
    Financing
    Acquisition cycle

inventory, evaluate, and rank its IT investments. Portfolio analysis helped the Office identify redundant systems and ensure that its IT investments provide needed capabilities. ("Winning the IT Portfolio Battle," 2007).

Another method for evaluating alternative system solutions is a **scoring model**. Scoring models give alternative systems a single score based on the extent to which they meet selected objectives. Table 11.5 shows part of a simple scoring model that could have been used by the Girl Scouts in evaluating their alternative systems. The first column lists the criteria that decision makers use to evaluate the systems. Table 11.5 shows that the Girl Scouts attach the most importance to capabilities for sales order processing, ease of use, ability to support users in many different locations, and low cost. The second column in Table 11.5 lists the weights that decision makers attached to the decision criteria. Columns 3 and 5 show the percentage of requirements for each function that each alternative system meets. Each alternative's score is calculated by multiplying the percentage of requirements met for each function by the weight attached to that function. The QuickBase solution has the highest total score.

MANAGING PROJECT RISK AND SYSTEM-RELATED CHANGE

Some systems development projects are more likely to run into problems or to suffer delays because they carry a much higher level of risk than others. The level of project risk is influenced by project size, project structure, and the level of technical expertise of the information systems staff and project team. The larger the project—as indicated by the

TABLE 11.5

Example of a Scoring Model for the Girl Scouts Cookie System

Criteria	Weight	Microsoft Access System (%)	Microsoft Access System Score	QuickBase System (%)	QuickBase System Score
1.0 Order processing					
1.1 Online order entry	5	67	335	83	415
1.2 Order tracking by troop	5	81	405	87	435
1.3 Order tracking by individual Girl Scout	5	72	360	80	400
1.4 Reserving warehouse pickups	3	66	198	79	237
Total order processing			1,298		1,487
2.0 Ease of use					
2.1 Web access from multiple locations	5	55	275	92	460
2.2 Short training time	4	79	316	85	340
2.3 User-friendly screens and data entry forms	4	65	260	87	348
Total ease of use			851		1,148
3.0 Costs					
3.1 Software costs	3	51	153	65	195
3.2 Hardware (server) costs	4	57	228	90	360
3.3 Maintenance and support costs	4	42	168	89	356
Total costs			549		911
Grand Total			2,698		3,546

dollars spent, project team size, and how many parts of the organization will be affected by the new system—the greater the risk. Very large scale systems projects have a failure rate that is 50 to 75 percent higher than that for other projects because such projects are complex and difficult to control. Risks are also higher for systems where information requirements are not clear and straightforward or the project team must master new technology.

Implementation and Change Management

Dealing with these project risks requires an understanding of the implementation process and change management. A broader definition of **implementation** refers to all the organizational activities working toward the adoption and management of an innovation, such as a new information system. Successful implementation requires a high level of user involvement in a project and management support.

If users are heavily involved in the development of a system, they have more opportunities to mold the system according to their priorities and business requirements, and more opportunities to control the outcome. They also are more likely to react positively to the completed system because they have been active participants in the change process. Incorporating user knowledge and expertise leads to better solutions.

The relationship between end users and information systems specialists has traditionally been a problem area for information systems implementation efforts because of differing backgrounds, interests, and priorities. These differences create a **user-designer communications gap**. Information systems specialists often have a highly technical orientation to problem solving, focusing on technical solutions in which hardware and software efficiency is optimized at the expense of ease of use or organizational effectiveness. End users prefer systems that are oriented toward solving business problems or facilitating organizational tasks. Often the orientations of both groups are so at odds that they appear to speak in different tongues.

These differences are illustrated in Table 11.6, which depicts the typical concerns of end users and technical specialists (information systems designers) regarding the development of a new information system. Communication problems between end users and designers are a major reason why user requirements are not properly incorporated into information systems and why users are driven out of the implementation process.

If an information systems project has the backing and commitment of management at various levels, it is more likely to receive higher priority from both users and the technical information systems staff. Management backing also ensures that a systems project receives sufficient funding and resources to be successful. Furthermore, to be enforced effectively, all the changes in work habits and procedures and any organizational realignments associated with a new system depend on management backing.

The Interactive Session on People demonstrates the importance of user involvement in designing and developing a successful solution. Dorfman Pacific, a manufacturer of

User Concerns	Designer Concerns
Will the system deliver the information I need for my work?	How much disk storage space will the master file consume?
How quickly can I access the data?	How many lines of program code will it take to perform this function?
How easily can I retrieve the data?	How can we cut down on CPU time when we run the system?
How much clerical support will I need to enter data into the system?	What is the most efficient way of storing the data?
How will the operation of the system fit into my daily business schedule?	What database management system should we use?

TABLE 11.6

The User-Designer Communications Gap

headwear and handbags, could not effectively expand its business because it was hampered by an outdated warehouse system and heavily manual processes. It decided to implement a new wireless warehouse that changed the way it worked. As you read this case, try to identify the problem this organization was facing, what alternative solutions were available to management, and how well the chosen solution worked.

Controlling Risk Factors

There are strategies you can follow to deal with project risk and increase the chances of a successful system solution. If the new system involves challenging and complex technology, you can recruit project leaders with strong technical and administrative experience. Outsourcing or using external consultants are options if your firm does not have staff with the required technical skills or expertise.

Large projects benefit from appropriate use of **formal planning and tools** for documenting and monitoring project plans. The two most commonly used methods for documenting project plans are Gantt charts and PERT charts. A Gantt chart lists project activities and their corresponding start and completion dates. The **Gantt chart** visually represents the timing and duration of different tasks in a development project as well as their human resource requirements (see Figure 11-10). It shows each task as a horizontal bar whose length is proportional to the time required to complete it.

Although Gantt charts show when project activities begin and end, they don't depict task dependencies, how one task is affected if another is behind schedule, or how tasks should be ordered. That is where **PERT charts** are useful. PERT stands for Program Evaluation and Review Technique, a methodology developed by the U.S. Navy during the 1950's to manage the Polaris submarine missile program. A PERT chart graphically depicts project tasks and their interrelationships. The PERT chart lists the specific activities that make up a project and the activities that must be completed before a specific activity can start, as illustrated in Figure 11-11 on page 394.

The PERT chart portrays a project as a network diagram consisting of numbered nodes (either circles or rectangles) representing project tasks. Each node is numbered and shows the task, its duration, the starting date, and the completion date. The direction of the arrows on the lines indicates the sequence of tasks and shows which activities must be completed before the commencement of another activity. In Figure 11-11, the tasks in nodes 2, 3, and 4 are not dependent on each other and can be undertaken simultaneously, but each is dependent on completion of the first task.

Project Management Software Commercial software tools are available to automate the creation of Gantt and PERT charts and to facilitate the project management process. Project management software typically features capabilities for defining and ordering tasks, assigning resources to tasks, establishing starting and ending dates for tasks, tracking progress, and facilitating modifications to tasks and resources. The most widely used project management tool today is Microsoft Project.

Overcoming User Resistance

You can overcome user resistance by promoting user participation (to elicit commitment as well as to improve design), by making user education and training easily available, and by providing better incentives for users who cooperate. End users can become active members of the project team, take on leadership roles, and take charge of system installation and training.

You should pay special attention to areas where users interface with the system, with sensitivity to ergonomics issues. **Ergonomics** refers to the interaction of people and machines in the work environment. It considers the design of jobs, health issues, and the end-user interface of information systems. For instance, if a system has a series of complicated online data entry screens that are extremely difficult or time-consuming to work with, users will reject the system if it increases their work load or level of job stress.

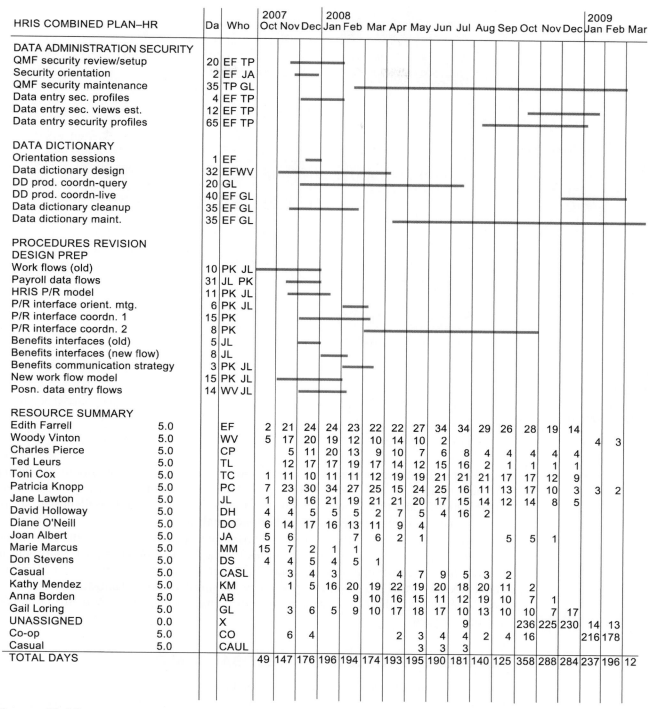

The HRIS Combined Plan–HR Gantt chart contains the following information:

HRIS COMBINED PLAN–HR	Da	Who
DATA ADMINISTRATION SECURITY		
QMF security review/setup	20	EF TP
Security orientation	2	EF JA
QMF security maintenance	35	TP GL
Data entry sec. profiles	4	EF TP
Data entry sec. views est.	12	EF TP
Data entry security profiles	65	EF TP
DATA DICTIONARY		
Orientation sessions	1	EF
Data dictionary design	32	EFWV
DD prod. coordn-query	20	GL
DD prod. coordn-live	40	EF GL
Data dictionary cleanup	35	EF GL
Data dictionary maint.	35	EF GL
PROCEDURES REVISION DESIGN PREP		
Work flows (old)	10	PK JL
Payroll data flows	31	JL PK
HRIS P/R model	11	PK JL
P/R interface orient. mtg.	6	PK JL
P/R interface coordn. 1	15	PK
P/R interface coordn. 2	8	PK
Benefits interfaces (old)	5	JL
Benefits interfaces (new flow)	8	JL
Benefits communication strategy	3	PK JL
New work flow model	15	PK JL
Posn. data entry flows	14	WV JL

RESOURCE SUMMARY (monthly person-days, Oct 2007 – Mar 2009)

	2007			2008												2009		
Name (rate) / Who	Oct	Nov	Dec	Jan	Feb	Mar	Apr	May	Jun	Jul	Aug	Sep	Oct	Nov	Dec	Jan	Feb	Mar
Edith Farrell 5.0 — EF	2	21	24	24	23	22	22	27	34	34	29	26	28	19	14			
Woody Vinton 5.0 — WV	5	17	20	19	12	10	14	10	2							4	3	
Charles Pierce 5.0 — CP			5	11	20	13	9	10	7	6	8	4	4	4	4			
Ted Leurs 5.0 — TL		12	17	17	19	17	14	12	15	16	2	1	1	1	1			
Toni Cox 5.0 — TC	1	11	10	11	11	12	19	19	21	21	21	17	17	12	9			
Patricia Knopp 5.0 — PC	7	23	30	34	27	25	15	24	25	16	11	13	17	10	3	3	2	
Jane Lawton 5.0 — JL	1	9	16	21	19	21	21	20	17	15	14	12	14	8	5			
David Holloway 5.0 — DH	4	4	5	5	5	2	7	5	4	16	2							
Diane O'Neill 5.0 — DO	6	14	17	16	13	11	9	4										
Joan Albert 5.0 — JA	5	6			7	6	2	1				5	5	1				
Marie Marcus 5.0 — MM	15	7	2	1	1													
Don Stevens 5.0 — DS	4	4	5	4	5	1												
Casual 5.0 — CASL		3	4	3			4	7	9	5	3	2						
Kathy Mendez 5.0 — KM			1	5	16	20	19	22	19	20	18	20	11	2				
Anna Borden 5.0 — AB						9	10	16	15	11	12	19	10	7	1			
Gail Loring 5.0 — GL			3	6	5	9	10	17	18	17	10	13	10	10	7	17		
UNASSIGNED 0.0 — X												9	236	225	230	14	13	
Co-op 5.0 — CO		6	4					2	3	4	4	2	4	16		216	178	
Casual 5.0 — CAUL									3	3	3							
TOTAL DAYS	49	147	176	196	194	174	193	195	190	181	140	125	358	288	284	237	196	12

Figure 11-10

A Gantt chart

The Gantt chart in this figure shows the task, person-days, and initials of each responsible person, as well as the start and finish dates for each task. The resource summary provides a good manager with the total person-days for each month and for each person working on the project to manage the project successfully. The project described here is a data administration project.

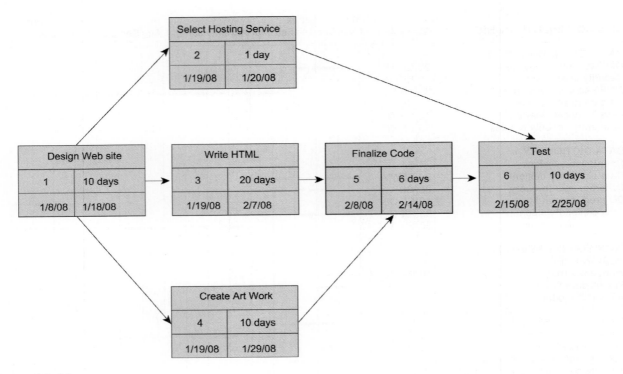

Figure 11-11
A PERT chart
This is a simplified PERT chart for creating a small Web site. It shows the ordering of project tasks and the relationship of a task with preceding and succeeding tasks.

Users will be more cooperative if organizational problems are solved prior to introducing the new system. In addition to procedural changes, transformations in job functions, organizational structure, power relationships, and behavior should be identified during systems analysis using an **organizational impact analysis**.

You will see some of these project management issues at work in the Interactive Session on Organizations, which describes the experience of Maine's Department of Human Services in implementing a new information system for processing Medicaid claims. As you read this case, try to identify the problem this organization was facing, what alternative solutions were available to management, and how well the chosen solution worked.

MANAGING PROJECTS ON A GLOBAL SCALE

As globalization proceeds, companies will be building many more new systems that are global in scale, spanning many different units in many different countries. The project management challenges for global systems are similar to those for domestic systems, but they are complicated by the international environment. User information requirements, business processes, and work cultures differ from country to country. It is difficult to convince local managers anywhere in the world to change their business processes and ways of working to align with units in other countries, especially if this might interfere with their local performance.

Involving people in change, assuring them that change is in the best interests of the company and their local units, is a key tactic for convincing users to adopt global systems and standards. Information systems projects should involve users in the design without giving up control over the project to parochial interests.

INTERACTIVE SESSION: PEOPLE   Dorfman Pacific Rolls Out a New Wireless Warehouse

You may not have heard of Dorfman Pacific, but you've probably seen its hats on celebrities featured in People and *InStyle* magazines. Dorfman Pacific, based in Stockton, California, has been manufacturing and distributing headwear and handbags for over 85 years. The company's philosophy has been to keep up with fashion trends while offering quality products with strong customer service, on-time deliveries, and competitive prices.

Traditionally, Dorfman served the mom-and-pop sector of the retail market. The company's warehouse processes reflected this. Warehouse activities relied on paper-based processes and tacit knowledge of the facility and Dorfman Pacific's customers.

In the 1980s and 1990s, Dorfman Pacific started adding big-box stores like Wal-Mart and JC Penney to its roster of customers. Such stores quickly came to represent half of Dorfman's business. More significantly, the large retailers had a much greater appetite for thousands of different items and box types.

Serving retailers like Wal-Mart with a paper-based order-picking process in a 100,000-square-foot warehouse was stressful and an ineffective means of doing business. During seasonal peaks in demand, Dorfman had to hire extra workers and pay hefty overtime wages to satisfy the demand. The extra wages amounted to $250,000 every year. The company's IT systems were spread out over various functional areas and did little to support a transparent inventory.

Dorfman eventually increased its warehouse space to 275,000 square feet, but the space alone was not enough to overcome flawed business processes. Top management at Dorfman realized that major changes were necessary if the company was going to expand its operations successfully. In 2001, CEO Douglass Highsmith committed to a complete overhaul of the technology in the warehouse. He wanted to eliminate the paper systems and replace them with wireless technology.

The traditional order-fulfillment process at Dorfman began with a warehouse worker, called a picker, receiving a paper pick ticket from a supervisor. The picker then drove a forklift to the area of the warehouse where he or she expected to find the bin that stored the product on the ticket. The worker manually picked boxes off of the shelf and then brought them to a packing area to be boxed, labeled, and loaded onto a truck. The warehouse was really set up only for picking, which left the remaining order-fulfillment processes as afterthoughts.

Confusing the process were bins that were labeled manually, making them difficult to read, and boxes that sometimes held more than one product. Additionally, each picker had his or her own preferred path to performing picking duties. The inefficiencies of these practices were magnified by special orders. The company's ERP system offered little help because it did not integrate well with other systems. Mark Dulle, Dorfman's IT Services Director, recognized that picking by order wasn't going to work in an era of expansion.

Dorfman approached the change as a business project rather than an IT project. A cross-functional team consisting of an outside consultant as project manager and managers from distribution, purchasing, customer service, and sales worked on the transformation. The IT department took responsibility for choosing hardware, installing the hardware and software for the wireless warehouse, and appointing an administrator for the new warehouse management system.

Highsmith's goals were to reduce labor costs and create the most efficient way for a streamlined warehouse staff to pick products with the smallest error rate. A successful implementation required a number of steps. First, the project team sought to learn everything it could about how Dorfman's 25,000 products were received, replenished, picked, packed, and shipped. This study included measuring the dimension and weight of each product, as well as the size of every bin and storage shelf, and determining whether products were stored in the correct places.

Next, Dorfman brought in Texas Bar Code Systems to test the feasibility of a wireless system in the warehouse. The project would have been fruitless if wireless signals did not function properly amidst the warehouse's concrete walls, steel doors, and metal storage shelves. The testing also helped to determine where the best wireless access points were located. Dorfman's warehouse required an unusually high number of access points, fifteen, because the floor space expansions over the years created an irregular layout, which was dense with inventory.

Dulle led the effort to revamp Dorfman's IT infrastructure, including replacing all of the old networking cables and switches with the most advanced networking technology available. He also reconfigured the ERP system and installed a new warehouse management system from HighJump Software complete with wireless capabilities and the ability to sort through warehouse and shipping data. To this system, which was based on a wireless LAN, Dulle added bar-coding equipment from Zebra Technologies, integration software, durable mobile computers, and additional computers mounted on forklifts.

With these components in place, paper was no longer necessary. The new ERP system and the warehouse management system used software to manage the picking, packing, and shipping processes. Pickers carrying mobile devices receive data telling them where to go, what to pick, and where to bring the merchandise using the most efficient route.

Dorfman employees had to change the way they worked. The new warehouse management system required a different warehouse floor configuration as well as new ways to pick, pack and ship products. Dorfman took the job of selling the new systems to its workers very seriously, convincing them that the

wireless warehouse would improve their lives and their job performance.

Once the new warehouse system was deployed, pickers armed with wireless scanning devices could be assured that the bar-code-labeled bins to which they were directed contained only one product type each. Tracking inventory became seamless. According to Dulle, Dorfman can now handle twice the number of orders during peak seasons and labor costs are down almost 30 percent. Eliminating the need for temporary workers and overtime has saved the company $250,000 and counting.

Sources: Thomas Wailgum, "How to Take Your Warehouse Wireless," and "Wireless—Five Steps to a Successful Wireless Rollout," *CIO Magazine*, February 1, 2007; Jim Fulcher, "Rise of User-Friendly Devices Propels Strategic Use of Wireless Technology," *Manufacturing Business Technology*, February 18, 2007; Lisa M. Kempfer, "Hats Off to Wireless," *Material Handling Management*, January 2007; and "Hats-Off: Dorfman Pacific Implements Symbol Enterprise Mobility Solution for Paperless Warehouse Operations," www.symbol.com, September 13, 2006.

CASE STUDY QUESTIONS

1. Compare Dorfman Pacific's old and new order-picking processes. Diagram the processes.

2. What role did end users play in developing Dorfman's wireless warehouse system? What would have happened to the project if users hadn't been so involved? Explain your answer.

3. What types of system-building methods and tools did Dorfman use for building its wireless warehouse system?

4. How did the new system change the way Dorfman ran its business?

5. What problems did the new system solve? Was it successful?

MIS IN ACTION

Use your Web-searching capabilities to answer the following questions.

1. What are some of the components of a wireless warehouse system?

2. What companies manufacture these components?

3. What other businesses or organizations have implemented wireless wirehouses?

4. If you were implementing a wireless warehouse, what potential problems would worry you most?

One tactic is to permit each country unit in a global corporation to develop one transnational application first in its home territory, and then throughout the world. In this manner, each major country systems group is given a piece of the action in developing a transnational system, and local units feel a sense of ownership in the transnational effort. On the downside, this assumes the ability to develop high-quality systems is widely distributed, and that, a German team, for example, can successfully implement systems in France and Italy. This will not always be the case.

A second tactic is to develop new transnational centers of excellence, or a single center of excellence. These centers draw heavily from local national units, are based on multinational teams, and must report to worldwide management. Centers of excellence

INTERACTIVE SESSION: ORGANIZATIONS   What Went Wrong with Maine's New Medicaid System?

The state of Maine provides medical coverage for over 260,000 of its residents through its Medicaid program, called MaineCare. Healthcare providers submit claims to MaineCare in order to be paid for the services they provide to Medicaid patients. As the 1990s drew to a close, Maine, like many other states, began planning for a complete overhaul of its Medicaid claims processing systems to comply with the Health Insurance Portability and Accountability Act of 1996 (HIPAA). HIPAA was enacted to standardize the management of patient health and records, and, most notably the protection of patient privacy. HIPAA provided a deadline of October 1, 2002 to meet its patient privacy and security standards.

The Medicaid program, as outlined by the federal government, was becoming increasingly complex as new services were added, each with codes and subcodes assigned to them. The state also wanted to offer providers access to patient eligibility and claim status data online in the hopes of reducing the volume of calls to the state Bureau of Medical Services, which ran Medicaid under the Department of Human Services (DHS).

At the time, Maine was processing over 100,000 Medicaid claims per week on a Honeywell mainframe that dated back to the 1970s. The system was not capable of supporting HIPAA requirements or the online access that the state wished to implement. The state's IT department decided that a completely new system would be more cost-effective and easier to maintain than an upgrade of the old system. DHS believed a new custom-built system would be more flexible because they could make it rule-based in order to accommodate frequent changes in Medicaid rules.

For such a large and significant project, the DHS enlisted a private contractor to work with its IT staff. CNSI, which had never before designed a Medicaid claims system, received the contract for its $15 million proposal. The deal called for CNSI to deploy the new processing system by the HIPAA compliance deadline, which was 12 months away. The system debuted on January 21, 2005, almost 27 months later, failing on many levels.

Shortly after its rollout, the new system was rejecting claims much more frequently than the old system had. Most of the rejected claims were being held up as suspended, a designation usually applied to claim forms that contained errors. The suspended file grew quickly, causing millions of dollars in claims to be held back.

Within two months, 300,000 claims were frozen. The number would eventually reach nearly 650,000.

The Bureau of Medical Services could keep up neither with the number of phone calls nor the processing of the suspended claims. The 65 members of the DHS/CNSI team worked feverishly to fix glitches in the error-prone claims software, but their efforts were accompanied by a lack of regard for critical management guidelines. Meanwhile, some providers who weren't getting paid were forced to turn away Medicaid patients or even shut down their operations. Others sought bank loans to keep their practices fluid. Maine began issuing interim payments to providers that were based on their average claims, the only backup plan the state had in place.

Providers were having difficulty filling out the lengthy new claim forms correctly. The incorrect forms were among those claims that were flagged for the suspended file. CNSI recommended that all providers re-enroll so that their information would be complete according to the new system's requirements. The department chose, instead, to transfer existing information from the old system, which was considered incomplete by the new system. Only 13 people were on staff to handle customer service calls from 7,000 providers. The disaster cost the state an additional $30 million. More than a year after rolling out the new system, Maine was the only state that still had not satisfied the HIPAA requirements.

The project team had difficulty obtaining input from the Medicaid experts on staff at the Bureau of Medical Services, forcing the project team to make judgments about Medicaid rules and requirements without them. The team then had to reprogram parts of the system once the Medicaid experts became available. Although the federal body that runs Medicaid extended the HIPAA deadline to October 1, 2003, the DHS team still had an uphill fight. Sensing that they would never catch up, the team began to take shortcuts.

When the DHS launched the new claims processing system in January 2005, it made a clean break from the legacy system. There was no backup or parallel system to support the deployment because the legacy system was incompatible with the new code numbers and electronic claim forms, and a parallel system was not feasible economically or technically. The malfunctioning new system was the only one available for claims processing work. The Bureau of Medical Services could not remedy the botched claims as fast they were coming in, creating a crisis in Maine's healthcare system.

Later in 2005, Maine hired XWave, a project management consultant specializing in integration for over $860,000 to right the ship. The state added an Oracle database specialist, who filled the role of operations manager and worked to improve communications and prioritize troubleshooting.

Dr. Laureen Biczak was appointed the organization's Medicaid expert. Beginning in January 2006, questions from providers were filtered to Medicaid specialists working under Biczak if they were business-process issues, or to the IT department if they were hardware or software issues. With this filtering system in effect, Maine was able to reduce the claim suspension rate to about 15%.

By the fall of 2006 the project cost between $30 million and $40 million over the initial bid of $15 million. In the spring of 2007, Maine decided to cut its losses. The state reached an agreement to have CNSI continue maintaining the system and add functionality until a new vendor was chosen by June 2008.

CNSI lost around $10 million on the project. Its president, B. Chatterjee, believed that CNSI and the state bore responsibility for half of the problems, and providers who made mistakes on their claim forms could be blamed for the other half. He also insisted that Maine is better positioned to go forward than other states that updated their existing systems rather than building state-of-the-art new systems. CNSI received additional state Medicaid contracts in the wake of its work with Maine.

Sources: Adam Wilson, "Glitches Delay State Project," *The Olympian*, July 13, 2007; Patty Enrado, "Maine Medicaid Cuts Losses on $50M of IT," www.healthcareitnews.com, April 1, 2007 and "CMS Investigating New Maine Medicaid System," www.healthcareitnews.com, October 1, 2006; "Maine Struggles with Medicaid Billing System," www.fiercehealthit.com, November 26, 2006; and Allan Holmes, "Maine's Medicaid Mistakes," *CIO Magazine*, April 15, 2006.

CASE STUDY QUESTIONS

1. How important are information systems for Maine's Department of Human Services? Analyze the impact of its faulty Medicaid claims processing system.

2. Evaluate the risks of the Medicaid claims processing system project and key risk factors.

3. Classify and describe the problems the Maine Department of Human Services faced in implementing its new Medicaid claims processing system. What people, organization, and technology factors caused these problems?

4. Describe the steps you would have taken to control the risk in the Maine Medicaid project. If you were in charge of managing this project, what else would you have done differently to increase chances for success?

MIS IN ACTION

Visit the Office of MaineCare Services on the Web at www.maine.gov/bms/ and then answer the following questions:

1. What services are available through MaineCare online?

2. What information is available regarding MaineCare and its compliance with HIPAA standards?

3. What information is available for providers who have had or are still having problems using MaineCare's claims processing system?

4. How easy is it to obtain this information?

perform the business and systems analysis and accomplish all design and testing. Implementation, however, and pilot testing are rolled out to other parts of the globe. Recruiting a wide range of local groups to transnational centers of excellence helps send the message that all significant groups are involved in the design and will have an influence.

11.5 Hands-On MIS

The projects in this section give you hands-on experience designing and building an employee training and skills tracking system for a real world company, designing and building a customer system for auto sales, and analyzing Web site information requirements.

ACHIEVING OPERATIONAL EXCELLENCE: DESIGNING AN EMPLOYEE TRAINING AND SKILLS TRACKING SYSTEM AND DATABASE

Software skills: Database design, querying, and reporting
Business skills: Employee training and skills tracking

This project requires you to perform a systems analysis and then design a system solution using database software.

Dirt Bikes promotes itself as a "learning company." It pays for employees to take training courses or college courses to help them advance in their careers. As employees move on, their job positions become vacant and Dirt Bikes must quickly fill them to maintain its pace of production. Dirt Bikes's human resources staff would like to find a way to quickly identify qualified employees who have the training to fill vacant positions. Once the company knows who these employees are, it has a better chance of filling open positions internally rather than paying to recruit outsiders. Dirt Bikes would like to track each employee's years of education and the title and date completed of training classes that each employee has attended.

Dirt Bikes currently cannot identify such employees. Its existing employee database is limited to basic human resources data, such as employee name, identification number, birth date, address, telephone number, marital status, job position, and salary. A portion of this database is illustrated here. You can find some sample records from this database on the Laudon Web site. Dirt Bikes's human resources staff keeps skills and training data in paper folders.

tblEmployee : Table

Emp_SS#	Last_Name	First_Name	Street	City	State	Zip	Telephone	Birth_Date	Marital
012-34-5678	Munoz	Luis	11 Ram Ridge	Carbondale	CO	81623	970-945-4338	8/29/1971	M
123-45-6789	Lattimore	Joseph	302 Garden St.	Carbondale	CO	81623	970-945-7002	7/3/1972	S
234-56-7890	Artis	Patricia	45 William St.	Basalt	CO	81621	970-945-0087	4/11/1973	S
345-67-8901	Renaldo	Carlos	793 Ridge Rd.	Basalt	CO	81621	970-945-1883	5/8/1969	M
456-78-9012	Norwick	Robert	10 Webb St.	Carbondale	CO	81623	970-945-5654	9/1/1970	M
567-89-0123	O'Donnell	James	56 Mountainview	Carbondale	CO	81623	970-945-3021	2/9/1969	M
678-90-1234	Morrissey	Richard	93 Pond Drive	Basalt	CO	81621	970-945-2838	1/30/1960	D
789-01-2345	Kamp	Timothy	39 Brook Dr.	Basalt	CO	81621	970-945-5944	6/27/1964	M
890-12-3456	Franz	George	8 Powder Tr.	Carbondale	CO	81623	970-945-9304	9/21/1964	S
901-23-4567	Collins	Dawn	9 Young Ave.	Glenwood Sprin	CO	81602	970-945-2648	11/3/1974	S
987-65-4321	Stokes	Brian	5 Saddle Tr.	Carbondale	CO	81623	970-945-8943	5/14/1963	D

Record: 1 of 11

Prepare a systems analysis report describing Dirt Bikes's problem and a system solution that can be implemented using PC database software. Then use the database software to develop a simple system solution. Your report should include the following:

- Description of the problem and its organizational and business impact.
- Proposed solution and solution objectives.
- Information requirements to be addressed by the solution.
- People, organization, and technology issues to be addressed by the solution, including changes in business processes.

On the basis of the requirements you have identified, design the solution using database software and populate it with at least 10 records per table. Consider whether you can use or modify the existing employee database in your design. Print out the design for each table in your new application. Use the system you have created to create queries and reports that would be of most interest to management, such as which employees have college education or which employees have training in project management or advanced computer-aided design [CAD] tools.

If possible, use electronic presentation software to summarize your findings for management.

IMPROVING DECISION MAKING: USING DATABASE SOFTWARE TO DESIGN A CUSTOMER SYSTEM FOR AUTO SALES

Software skills: Database design, querying, reporting, and forms
Business skills: Sales lead and customer analysis

This project requires you to perform a systems analysis and then design a system solution using database software.

Ace Auto Dealers specializes in selling new vehicles from Subaru. The company advertises in local newspapers and also is listed as an authorized dealer on the Subaru Web site and other major Web sites for auto buyers. The company benefits from a good local word-of-mouth reputation and name recognition and is a leading source of information for Subaru vehicles in the Portland, Oregon, area.

When a prospective customer enters the showroom, he or she is greeted by an Ace sales representative. The sales representative manually fills out a form with information such as the prospective customer's name, address, telephone number, date of visit, and model and make of the vehicle in which the customer is interested. The representative also asks where the prospect heard about Ace—whether it was from a newspaper ad, the Web, or word of mouth—and this information is noted on the form also. If the customer decides to purchase an auto, the dealer fills out a bill of sale form.

Ace does not believe it has enough information about its customers. It cannot easily determine which prospects have made auto purchases, nor can it identify which customer touch points have produced the greatest number of sales leads or actual sales so it can focus advertising and marketing more on the channels that generate the most revenue. Are purchasers discovering Ace from newspaper ads, from word of mouth, or from the Web?

Prepare a systems analysis report detailing Ace's problem and a system solution that can be implemented using PC database management software. Then use database software to develop a simple system solution. Your systems analysis report should include the following:

- Description of the problem and its organizational and business impact.
- Proposed solution, solution objectives, and solution feasibility.
- Costs and benefits of the solution you have selected. The company has a PC with Internet access and the full suite of Microsoft Office desktop productivity tools.
- Information requirements to be addressed by the solution.
- People, organization, and technology issues to be addressed by the solution, including changes in business processes.

On the basis of the requirements you have identified, design the database and populate it with at least 10 records per table. Consider whether you can use or modify the existing customer database in your design. Print out the database design. Then use the system you have created to generate queries and reports that would be of most interest to management. Create several prototype data input forms for the system and review them with your instructor. Then revise the prototypes.

ACHIEVING OPERATIONAL EXCELLENCE: ANALYZING WEB SITE DESIGN AND INFORMATION REQUIREMENTS

Software skills: Web browser software
Business skills: Information requirements analysis, Web site design

Visit the Web site of your choice and explore it thoroughly. Prepare a report analyzing the various functions provided by that Web site and its information requirements. Your report should answer these questions: What functions does the Web site perform? What data does it use? What are its inputs, outputs, and processing? What are some of its other design specifications? Does the Web site link to any internal systems or systems of other organizations? What value does this Web site provide the firm?

Review Summary

1 **What are the core problem-solving steps for developing new information systems?** The core problem-solving steps for developing new information systems are: (1) define and understand the problem, (2) develop alternative solutions, (3) evaluate and choose the solution, and (4) implement the solution. The third step includes an assessment of the technical, financial, and organizational feasibility of each alternative. The fourth step entails finalizing design specifications, acquiring hardware and software, testing, providing training and documentation, conversion, and evaluating the system solution once it is in production.

2 **What are the alternative methods for building information systems?** The systems lifecycle requires that information systems be developed in formal stages. The stages must proceed sequentially and have defined outputs; each requires formal approval before the next stage can commence. The system lifecycle is rigid and costly but nevertheless useful for large projects.

Prototyping consists of building an experimental system rapidly and inexpensively for end users to interact with and evaluate. The prototype is refined and enhanced until users are satisfied that it includes all of their requirements and can be used as a template to create the final system. End-user-developed systems can be created rapidly and informally using fourth-generation software tools. End-user development can improve requirements determination and reduce application backlog.

Application software packages eliminate the need for writing software programs when developing an information system. Application software packages are helpful if a firm does not have the internal information systems staff or financial resources to custom develop a system.

Outsourcing consists of using an external vendor to build (or operate) a firm's information systems. If it is properly managed, outsourcing can save application development costs or enable firms to develop applications without an internal information systems staff.

Rapid application design, joint application design (JAD), and reusable software components (including Web services) can be used to speed up the systems development process.

3 **What are the principal methodologies for modeling and designing systems?** The two principal methodologies for modeling and designing information systems are structured methodologies and object-oriented development. Structured methodologies focus on modeling processes and data separately. The data flow diagram is the principal tool for structured analysis and the structure chart is the principal tool for representing structured software design. Object-oriented development models a system as a collection of objects that combine processes and data.

4 **How should information systems projects be selected and evaluated?** To determine whether an information system project is a good investment, one must calculate its costs and benefits. Tangible benefits are quantifiable, and intangible benefits cannot be immediately quantified but may provide quantifiable benefits in the future. Benefits that exceed costs should then be analyzed using capital budgeting methods to make sure they represent a good return on the firm's invested capital.

Organizations should develop information systems plans that describe how information technology supports the company's overall business plan and strategy. Portfolio analysis and scoring models can be used to evaluate alternative information systems projects.

5 **How should information systems projects be managed?** Information systems projects and the entire implementation process should be managed as planned organizational change using an organizational impact analysis. Management support and control of the implementation process are essential, as are mechanisms for dealing with the level of risk in each new systems project. Project risks are influenced by project size, project structure, and the level of technical expertise of the information systems staff and project team. Formal planning and control tools (including Gantt and PERT charts) track the resource allocations and specific project activities. Users can be encouraged to take active roles in systems development and become involved in installation and training. Global information systems projects should involve local units in the creation of the design without giving up control of the project to parochial interests.

Key Terms

Acceptance testing, 376
Component-based
    development, 385
Computer-aided software
    engineering (CASE), 385
Conversion, 376
Customization, 380
Data flow diagram
    (DFD), 382
Direct cutover, 376
Documentation, 376
End-user development, 379
Ergonomics, 392
Feasibility study, 373
Formal planning and
    tools, 392
Gantt chart, 392
Implementation, 391
Information
    requirements, 372

Information systems
    plan, 388
Intangible benefits, 387
Joint application design
    (JAD), 382
Maintenance, 377
Object-oriented
    development, 384
Organizational impact
    analysis, 394
Parallel strategy, 376
PERT charts, 392
Phased approach, 376
Portfolio analysis, 388
Process specifications, 383
Production, 377
Project, 386
Project management, 386
Prototyping, 378

Rapid application
    development (RAD), 382
Request for Proposal
    (RFP), 380
Scope, 386
Scoring model, 390
Structure chart, 383
Structured, 382
System testing, 376
Systems analysis, 372
Systems design, 374
Systems development
    lifecycle (SDLC), 377
Tangible benefits, 387
Test plan, 376
Testing, 376
Unit testing, 376
User-designer communica-
    tions gap, 391

Review Questions

1. What are the core problem-solving steps for developing new information systems?
- List and describe the problem-solving steps for building a new system.
- Define information requirements and explain why they are important for developing a system solution.
- List the various types of design specifications required for a new information system.
- Explain why the testing stage of systems development is so important. Name and describe the three stages of testing for an information system.
- Describe the roles of documentation, conversion, production, and maintenance in systems development.

2. What are the alternative methods for building information systems?
- Define the traditional systems lifecycle and describe its advantages and disadvantages for systems building.
- Define information system prototyping and describe its benefits and limitations. List and describe the steps in the prototyping process.
- Define end-user development and explain its advantages and disadvantages.
- Describe the advantages and disadvantages of developing information systems based on application software packages.
- Define outsourcing. Describe the circumstances in which it should be used for building information systems. List and describe the hidden costs of offshore software outsourcing.
- Explain how businesses can rapidly develop e-business applications.

3. What are the principal methodologies for modeling and designing systems?
- Compare object-oriented and traditional structured approaches for modeling and designing systems.

4. How should information systems projects be selected and evaluated?
- Explain the difference between tangible and intangible benefits.
- List six tangible benefits and six intangible benefits.
- List and describe the major components of an information systems plan.
- Describe how portfolio analysis and scoring models can be used to establish the worth of systems.

5. How should information systems projects be managed?
- Explain the importance of implementation for managing the organizational change surrounding a new information system.
- Define the user-designer communications gap and explain the kinds of implementation problems it creates.
- List and describe the factors that influence project risk and describe strategies for minimizing project risks.
- Describe tactics for managing global projects.

Discussion Questions

1. Discuss the role of business end users and information system professionals in developing a system solution. How do both roles differ when the solution is developed using prototyping or end-user development?

2. It has been said that systems fail when systems builders ignore "people" problems. Why might this be so?

Video Case

You will find a video case illustrating some of the concepts in this chapter on the Laudon Web site along with questions to help you analyze the case.

Teamwork

Analyzing Web Site Requirements

With three or four of your classmates, visit the Web site of iTunes, MP3.com, the Internet Movie Database, or a company described in this text that uses the Web. Review the Web site for the company you select. Use what you have learned from the Web site and this chapter to prepare a report describing the functions of that Web site and some of its design specifications. If possible, use electronic presentation software to present your findings to the class.

BUSINESS PROBLEM-SOLVING CASE

Citizens National Bank Searches for a System Solution

Citizens National Bank of Texas is a private, full-service bank with headquarters in Waxahachie, Texas, and 200 employees that has operated independently since 1868. Citizens National serves businesses and consumers in Ellis County and other nearby counties, primarily in communities with populations of 25,000 or less. The bank counts total assets of $400 million and is growing annually at a rate of 12 percent. Since 1999, the number of branches has increased from four to fifteen, with locations in ten cities. Citizens National would like to increase its market share to at least 50 percent in eight counties south of the Dallas-Fort Worth area

A major part of Citizen National's strategy for continuing growth was to implement customer relationship management (CRM) software. The CRM strategy targeted the bank's two main contact points with customers: the bank's call center and its sales force. The call center receives around 4,000 calls per day, which are handled by between 10 and 20 customer service representatives. The sales force consists of 16 representatives, who are known by the title of relationship bankers. It is the relationship bankers that drive business for Citizens National. Their contacts with customers generate loan sales and deposits that make money for the bank.

In 2001 CEO Mark Singleton oversaw the adoption of a CRM package from Siebel Systems (Siebel is now owned by Oracle). The main goal for the implementation was to increase sales by raising the number of contacts relationship bankers were making and improving the tracking of these activities so that the bank could learn more from them. The CRM package promised additional benefits. The bank would be able to approve credit and loan applications more quickly. It would also finally have a method for storing the interactions between relationship bankers and customers electronically.

Electronic records were key for two reasons. Under the old paper system, a salesperson that left Citizens National could take records of customer interaction with him or her, leaving the bank with no information to maintain the relationship. The paper system also created too much information for Singleton and his branch managers to process effectively.

For Singleton, the decision to move to a CRM system was not a slam dunk. While he recognized the great value that automated systems provided to businesses, he placed even greater value on the person-to-person interactions between his relationship bankers and their customers. He feared that an overreaching CRM system might interfere with those interactions and diminish the relationship bankers' rapport with customers. The track record for the old fashioned way was impressive. For retail customers, the bank's cross-sale ratio was between 2 and 2.5, meaning that the average customer used at least two of the bank's products. The top commercial and personal customers were using between 6 and 7 products.

With this strength in mind, Singleton insisted that any CRM implementation at Citizens National be able to fortify the relationship bankers' knowledge of their customers and potential customers, including their previous interactions with the bank. The Siebel package, which had a price tag of $150,000, was supposed to fulfill this goal. The bank contracted with a local consulting firm, The Small Business Solution, to help install the package. The union of old-fashioned business sensibility with powerful enterprise software was a mismatch almost immediately. The approach of Citizens National toward nearly all business functions, from tracking customer leads to generating reports about them, was very basic. The Siebel software was simply too rich in features. The bank spent an inordinate amount of time switching off features that hindered productivity.

For example, Siebel had a complex module for handling customer support cases. It included capabilities for detailed managing of complaints from initial call through subsequent calls to options for resolving the issue. Customer complaints at Citizens National rarely went that far. A representative at the call center handled them immediately. In cases where a second interaction was necessary, the representative simply sent an e-mail to the employee responsible for carrying out the action.

Jim Davis, an expert on CRM from Deloitte Consulting, characterized the situation at Citizens National by saying, "The problem with Siebel is that it has everything." At Citizens National, the sheer size of the package was not the only issue. Employees found the software to be too complicated. They were surprised to learn, for example, that the system did not automatically generate potential business opportunities for customers on their records. They had to assign the potential transaction to the customer. Furthermore, bankers were not able to view multiple relationships between a customer and the bank on the same screen. The extra navigation was confusing and inefficient. Not surprisingly, the relationship bankers resisted the new system. It didn't make sense for them to change their tried-and-true methods simply because new software required change.

According to Davis, the disconnect between the relationship bankers and the new system was at the crux of the implementation's failure. The relationship bankers were the key employees; the system was intended to be of value to them, and, in turn, provide value to the bank. However, they found no incentive in the Siebel environment because their compensation was based on sales, and sales had become harder to make.

Citizens National also experienced compatibility issues between the database formats in Siebel and those used by the bank's core banking application, developed by Kirchman. The Kirchman software combined customer first and last names into one field, whereas Siebel had separate fields for first and last names. As a result, the two systems had difficulty exchanging information properly. The bank was forced to spend a significant amount of time fixing such compatibility issues, which negatively impacted its ability to serve customers.

Citizens National spent three years trying to make its Siebel CRM implementation work. In 2004, having derived no quantifiable benefit from the effort, the bank finally decided to cut its losses. In addition to the initial $150,000 purchase, it had spent $350,000 on solving integration issues. Singleton referred to the process as "a $500,000 education."

David Furney, president and CEO of The Small Business Solution, began searching for another CRM solution for Citizens National. Furney happened upon a hosted online database system from Intuit called QuickBase, which was used by small businesses and consumers, including the Patriots' Trail Girl Scout Council discussed in the chapter-opening case. Intuit was best known for its financial management applications such as Quicken and QuickBooks. The company did not have a defined reputation in the CRM market.

QuickBase included modules for databases, spreadsheets, and sales management, all of which could be easily manipulated for the bank's business functions. QuickBase was designed for organizing, tracking, and sharing information among team members in the workplace while encouraging progress by notifying workers via automated e-mails of updated files, new task assignments, and approaching deadlines. Intuit offered in the product ready-made applications for general purposes, such as project management, sales management, and marketing management, as well as more specific purposes, such as healthcare, IT, legal, and real estate.

Furney referred to QuickBase as "the ultimate in rapid application development" and "a kind of do-it-yourself application." Citizens National people, including Singleton, would be able to customize the package themselves rather than having to solicit help from the manufacturer or an IT specialist. To make changes in the Siebel system, the bank had to request help from Siebel. Because QuickBase was not programmed as a specific business application, businesses could modify its database structure to meet specific business functions. The Citizens National staff were able to make changes to QuickBase themselves, so the cost of ownership and maintenance fees were much lower.

QuickBase offered Citizens National flexibility that it did not have previously. Because the system was Web-based, the relationship bankers were able to use it anywhere that they had access to a browser. In addition to the cost of ownership savings, Citizens National saved a small fortune with QuickBase, which started with a one-time fee of $249 for the first 10 users and increased by $3 per month for each additional user (the cost is now $249 per month plus $15 per month for every five additional users).

Singleton still had to deal with the fact that some of relationship bankers would have preferred to push technology aside altogether. To give the system its best chance of success, Singleton permitted these bankers to dictate their activity to administrative assistants. The assistants then entered the information into QuickBase for the bankers. Davis observed that this may not have been the best practice, but it was fairly common and, more importantly, very worthwhile if the bankers were devoting their time to making money for the bank rather than wasting it wrestling with technology. Citizens National made the transition easier additionally by implementing QuickBase using a phased rollout, starting with the call center.

Also central to the success of QuickBase at Citizens National was Furney's ability to integrate the system with the Kirchman core banking application. Furney configured QuickBase to upload new account information to the core system every night via an XML interface. Relationship bankers and management received daily updated access to all interactions and transactions, enabling them to track business in a way that was never possible previously. For the first time, Citizens National was able to completely track sales opportunities and, as Singleton said, "where we lost business, so we know where we need to make those extra 10 or 15 sales calls."

Sources: Doug Bartholomew, "A Banker's $500,000 Lesson in CRM," *Baseline Magazine*, February 26, 2007; Mark Singleton, as told to Colin Beasty, "Secret of My Success: Getting More for the Money," www.destinationcrm.com, March 1, 2006; "QuickBase: A Better Way to Work," www.quickbase.com, accessed March 30, 2007; "QuickBase: How It Works," www.quickbase.com, accessed March 30, 2007; and "Siebel Customer Relationship Management Applications," www.oracle.com, March 30, 2007.

Case Study Questions

1. What was the initial problem that Mark Singleton was trying to solve at Citizens National? How well did he apply the four steps of problem solving?
2. What was the business case for implementing a new system? What were some of the tangible benefits? What were some of the intangible benefits?
3. Why didn't the implementation of the Siebel CRM solution work out for Citizens National? What were the biggest factors? How would you classify these factors in terms of organization, technology, and people issues?
4. Was QuickBase a better solution for Citizens National? If so, why? What factors suggest that the bank ended up with the right approach and the right choice of product?
5. Based on this case study, what kind of organization do you think would benefit from using the Siebel CRM package? Give an example of such an organization and justify your choice. You may use the Web to research your answer, including Oracle's Web site.
6. Could Citizens National have made a better choice of software for its CRM system the first time around? Explain your answer.

Ethical and Social Issues in Information Systems

CHAPTER 12

After completing this chapter, you will be able to answer the following questions:

1. What ethical, social, and political issues are raised by information systems?

2. What specific principles for conduct can be used to guide ethical decisions?

3. Why do contemporary information systems technology and the Internet pose challenges to the protection of individual privacy and intellectual property?

4. How have information systems affected everyday life?

CHAPTER OUTLINE

IS YOUR STUDENT LOAN DATA ON LOAN?

Have you ever applied for a student loan to finance your college education? If so, you had to provide information about your date of birth, your address, your Social Security number, your financial status, your college, the amount of your loan, and perhaps your e-mail address. You probably assumed that this sensitive information was kept highly confidential. If you had a direct loan from the U.S. Department of Education, you were wrong.

The U.S. Department of Education maintains data about Title IV loans and grant amounts, outstanding balances, loan statuses, and disbursements in its National Student Loan Data System (NSLDS). It set up NSLDS in 1993 to help universities and lenders share information on student loans. The system includes information from schools and agencies that guarantee loans, as well as from the Direct Loan, Pell Grant, and other Education Department programs. NSLDS is managed by the U.S. Education Department's Office of Federal Student Aid.

About 29,000 university financial aid administrators and 7,500 loan company employees have access to the NSLDS database, which has data on 60 million student

borrowers. Access is granted solely to determine the eligibility of an applicant for federal student aid or to facilitate the collection of federal student loans and grant overpayments. The information may not be used for any other purpose.

However, employees of some of the loan companies with access to the database were mining the system to market products and services to borrowers and their families. The Education Department first noticed the problem in mid-2003 when loan consolidation became more popular. As loan companies began looking for more low-risk borrowers to target for their consolidation plans, they started using the database to identify prospective customers. The student loan database is set up so that users can only view one student record at a time, and the Education Department can monitor each time a record is viewed. When IT staff members observed an unusual amount of activity accessing student records, they sent out warning letters in April 2005 to database users that inappropriate use of the system could have their access revoked. The letters said the agency was "specifically troubled" that lenders were giving unauthorized users, such as marketing firms, debt collection agencies, and brokerage firms, access to the database.

After the warnings, inappropriate use of the student loan system seemed to decline, but resurged in early 2007. Student loan companies were trying to access the system several thousand times per minute. At the same time, students with direct loans were being inundated with mass mailings for loan consolidations. In April 2007 the Education Department temporarily suspended loan companies' access to the system. (Loan borrowers and university officials continued to have access.) While access to the database was suspended, the Office of Inspector General reviewed how the database has been used or misused and whether certain companies should have their access cut off permanently.

Since 2003, the Office of Federal Student Aid has invested more than $650,000 to improve system security and protect student information. It has revoked more than 52,000 user IDs, 261 of which belonged to lenders, loan holders, guaranty agencies, loan servicers, and schools believed to have engaged in suspicious activity.

Sources: Larry Greenemeier, "Data on Loan," *Information Week*, April 23, 2007 and Amit R. Paley, "Lenders Misusing Student Database," *The Washington Post*, April 15, 2007.

Misuse of the National Student Loan Data System described in the chapter-opening case shows that technology can be a double-edged sword. It can be the source of many benefits (including expediting low-cost loans to students) and it can also create new opportunities for breaking the law or taking benefits away from others.

The chapter-opening diagram calls attention to important points raised by this case and this chapter. The U.S. Department of Education was looking for a way to make it easier for lenders to evaluate candidates for student loans and collect these loans and for students to keep track of their loans. The National Student Loan Data System, featuring a comprehensive database of student loan data, provided a solution, but it also made it possible for information about students and their loans to be used for the wrong purpose.

This solution created what we call an "ethical dilemma," pitting the legitimate need to know about student borrowers against the possibility that such information could be used to threaten individual privacy. Another ethical dilemma might occur if you were implementing a new information system that reduced labor costs and eliminated employees' jobs. You need to be aware of the negative impacts of information systems and you need to balance the negative consequences with the positive ones.

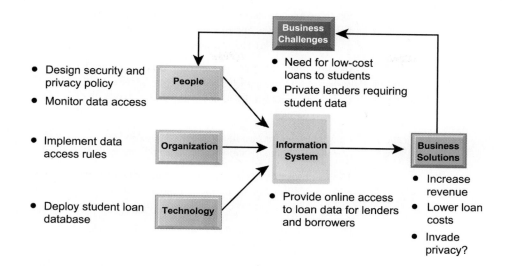

- Design security and privacy policy
- Monitor data access

- Implement data access rules

- Deploy student loan database

People

Organization

Technology

Business Challenges

- Need for low-cost loans to students
- Private lenders requiring student data

Information System

- Provide online access to loan data for lenders and borrowers

Business Solutions

- Increase revenue
- Lower loan costs
- Invade privacy?

HEADS UP

Information systems raise new and often-perplexing ethical problems. This is more true today than ever because of the challenges posed by the Internet and electronic commerce to the protection of privacy and intellectual property. Other ethical issues raised by widespread use of information system include establishing accountability for the consequences of information systems, setting standards to safeguard system quality that protect the safety of individuals and society, and preserving values and institutions considered essential to the quality of life in an information society. Whether you run your own business or work in a large company, you'll be confronting these issues, and you'll need to know how to deal with them.

12.1 Understanding Ethical and Social Issues Related to Systems

In the past five years we have witnessed, arguably, one of the most ethically challenging periods for U.S. and global business. Table 12.1 provides a small sample of recent cases demonstrating failed ethical judgment by senior and middle managers. These lapses in management ethical and business judgment occurred across a broad spectrum of industries.

In today's new legal environment, managers who violate the law and are convicted will most likely spend time in prison. U.S. Federal Sentencing Guidelines adopted in 1987 mandate that federal judges impose stiff sentences on business executives based on the monetary value of the crime, the presence of a conspiracy to prevent discovery of the crime, the use of structured financial transactions to hide the crime, and failure to cooperate with prosecutors (U.S. Sentencing Commission 2004).

Although in the past business firms would often pay for the legal defense of their employees enmeshed in civil charges and criminal investigations, now firms are encouraged to cooperate with prosecutors to reduce charges against the entire firm for obstructing investigations. These developments mean that, more than ever, as a manager or an employee, you will have to decide for yourself what constitutes proper legal and ethical conduct.

TABLE 12.1

Recent Examples of Failed Ethical Judgment by Managers

Enron	Top three executives convicted for misstating earnings using illegal accounting schemes and making false representations to shareholders. Bankruptcy declared in 2001.
WorldCom	Second-largest U.S. telecommunications firm. Chief executive convicted for improperly inflating revenue by billions using illegal accounting methods. Bankruptcy declared in July 2002 with $41 billion in debts.
Brocade Communications	CEO convicted for backdating stock options and concealing millions of dollars of compensation expenses from shareholders.
Parmalat	10 executives in Italy's eighth-largest industrial group convicted for misstating more than $5 billion in revenues, earnings, and assets over several years.
Bristol-Myers Squibb	Pharmaceutical firm agreed to pay a fine of $150 million for misstating its revenues by $1.5 billion, and inflating its stock value.

Although these major instances of failed ethical and legal judgment were not masterminded by information systems departments, information systems were instrumental in many of these frauds. In many cases, the perpetrators of these crimes artfully used financial reporting information systems to bury their decisions from public scrutiny in the vain hope they would never be caught. We deal with the issue of control in information systems in Chapter 7. In this chapter we talk about the ethical dimensions of these and other actions based on the use of information systems.

Ethics refers to the principles of right and wrong that individuals, acting as free moral agents, use to make choices to guide their behaviors. Information systems raise new ethical questions for both individuals and societies because they create opportunities for intense social change, and thus threaten existing distributions of power, money, rights, and obligations. Like other technologies, such as steam engines, electricity, the telephone, and the radio, information technology can be used to achieve social progress, but it can also be used to commit crimes and threaten cherished social values. The development of information technology will produce benefits for many and costs for others.

Ethical issues in information systems have been given new urgency by the rise of the Internet and electronic commerce. Internet and digital firm technologies make it easier than ever to assemble, integrate, and distribute information, unleashing new concerns about the appropriate use of customer information, the protection of personal privacy, and the protection of intellectual property.

Other pressing ethical issues raised by information systems include establishing accountability for the consequences of information systems, setting standards to safeguard system quality that protect the safety of the individual and society, and preserving values and institutions considered essential to the quality of life in an information society. When using information systems, it is essential to ask, "What is the ethical and socially responsible course of action?"

A MODEL FOR THINKING ABOUT ETHICAL, SOCIAL, AND POLITICAL ISSUES

Ethical, social, and political issues are closely linked. The ethical dilemma you may face as a manager of information systems typically is reflected in social and political debate. One way to think about these relationships is given in Figure 12-1. Imagine society as a more or less calm pond on a summer day, a delicate ecosystem in partial equilibrium with individuals and with social and political institutions. Individuals know how to act in this

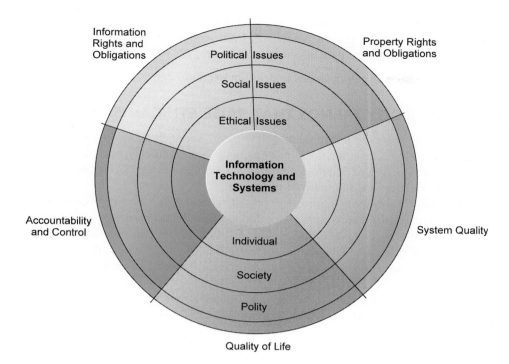

Figure 12-1
The Relationship Between Ethical, Social, and Political Issues in an Information Society
The introduction of new information technology has a ripple effect, raising new ethical, social, and political issues that must be dealt with on the individual, social, and political levels. These issues have five moral dimensions: information rights and obligations, property rights and obligations, system quality, quality of life, and accountability and control.

pond because social institutions (family, education, organizations) have developed well-honed rules of behavior, and these are supported by laws developed in the political sector that prescribe behavior and promise sanctions for violations. Now toss a rock into the center of the pond. But imagine instead of a rock that the disturbing force is a powerful shock of new information technology and systems hitting a society more or less at rest. What happens? Ripples, of course.

Suddenly individual actors are confronted with new situations often not covered by the old rules. Social institutions cannot respond overnight to these ripples—it may take years to develop etiquette, expectations, social responsibility, politically correct attitudes, or approved rules. Political institutions also require time before developing new laws and often require the demonstration of real harm before they act. In the meantime, you may have to act. You may be forced to act in a legal gray area.

We can use this model to illustrate the dynamics that connect ethical, social, and political issues. This model is also useful for identifying the main moral dimensions of the information society, which cut across various levels of action—individual, social, and political.

FIVE MORAL DIMENSIONS OF THE INFORMATION AGE

The major ethical, social, and political issues raised by information systems include the following moral dimensions:

Information rights and obligations. What **information rights** do individuals and organizations possess with respect to themselves? What can they protect? What obligations do individuals and organizations have concerning this information?

Property rights and obligations. How will traditional intellectual property rights be protected in a digital society in which tracing and accounting for ownership are difficult and ignoring such property rights is so easy?

Accountability and control. Who can and will be held accountable and liable for the harm done to individual and collective information and property rights?

System quality. What standards of data and system quality should we demand to protect individual rights and the safety of society?

Quality of life. What values should be preserved in an information- and knowledge-based society? Which institutions should we protect from violation? Which cultural values and practices are supported by the new information technology?

We explore these moral dimensions in detail in Section 12.3.

KEY TECHNOLOGY TRENDS THAT RAISE ETHICAL ISSUES

Ethical issues long preceded information technology. Nevertheless, information technology has heightened ethical concerns, taxed existing social arrangements, and made some laws obsolete or severely crippled. There are four key technological trends responsible for these ethical stresses and they are summarized in Table 12.2.

The doubling of computing power every 18 months has made it possible for most organizations to use information systems for their core production processes. As a result, our dependence on systems and our vulnerability to system errors and poor data quality have increased. Social rules and laws have not yet adjusted to this dependence. Standards for ensuring the accuracy and reliability of information systems (see Chapter 7) are not universally accepted or enforced.

Advances in data storage techniques and rapidly declining storage costs have been responsible for the multiplying databases on individuals—employees, customers, and potential customers—maintained by private and public organizations. These advances in data storage have made the routine violation of individual privacy both cheap and effective. Already massive data storage systems are cheap enough for regional and even local retailing firms to use in identifying customers.

Advances in data analysis techniques for large pools of data are another technological trend that heightens ethical concerns because companies and government agencies are able to find out much detailed personal information about individuals. With contemporary data management tools (see Chapter 5), companies can assemble and combine the myriad pieces of information about you stored on computers much more easily than in the past.

Think of all the ways you generate computer information about yourself—credit card purchases; telephone calls; magazine subscriptions; video rentals; mail-order purchases; banking records; local, state, and federal government records (including court and police records); and visits to Web sites. Put together and mined properly, this information could reveal not only your credit information but also your driving habits, your tastes, your associations, and your political interests.

Companies with products to sell purchase relevant information from these sources to help them more finely target their marketing campaigns. Chapters 3 and 5 describe how companies can analyze large pools of data from multiple sources to rapidly identify buying

---

TABLE 12.2

Technology Trends That Raise Ethical Issues

Trend	Impact
Computing power doubles every 18 months	More organizations depend on computer systems for critical operations
Data storage costs rapidly declining	Organizations can easily maintain detailed databases on individuals
Data analysis advances	Companies can analyze vast quantities of data gathered on individuals to develop detailed profiles of individual behavior
Networking advances and the Internet	Copying data from one location to another and accessing personal data from remote locations are much easier

Credit card purchases can make personal information available to market researchers, telemarketers, and direct-mail companies. Advances in information technology facilitate the invasion of privacy.

patterns of customers and suggest individual responses. The use of computers to combine data from multiple sources and create electronic dossiers of detailed information on individuals is called **profiling**.

For example, hundreds of Web sites allow DoubleClick (www.doubleclick.net), an Internet advertising broker, to track the activities of their visitors in exchange for revenue from advertisements based on visitor information DoubleClick gathers. DoubleClick uses this information to create a profile of each online visitor, adding more detail to the profile as the visitor accesses an associated DoubleClick site. Over time, DoubleClick can create a detailed dossier of a person's spending and computing habits on the Web that can be sold to companies to help them target their Web ads more precisely.

ChoicePoint, described in the Interactive Session on Organizations, gathers data from police, criminal, and motor vehicle records; credit and employment histories; current and previous addresses; professional licenses; and insurance claims to assemble and maintain electronic dossiers on almost every adult in the United Sates. The company sells this personal information to businesses and government agencies. Demand for personal data is so enormous that data broker businesses such as ChoicePoint are booming.

A new data analysis technology called **nonobvious relationship awareness** (**NORA**) has given both the government and the private sector even more powerful profiling capabilities. NORA can take information about people from many disparate sources, such as employment applications, telephone records, customer listings, and "wanted" lists, and correlate relationships to find obscure hidden connections that might help identify criminals or terrorists (see Figure 12-2 on page 417).

NORA technology scans data and extracts information as the data are being generated so that it could, for example, instantly discover a man at an airline ticket counter who shares a phone number with a known terrorist before that person boards an airplane. The technology is considered a valuable tool for homeland security but does have privacy implications because it can provide such a detailed picture of the activities and associations of a single individual.

Finally, advances in networking, including the Internet, promise to reduce greatly the costs of moving and accessing large quantities of data and open the possibility of mining large pools of data remotely using small desktop machines, permitting an invasion of

INTERACTIVE SESSION: ORGANIZATIONS   Data for Sale

Want a list of 3877 charity donors in Detroit? You can buy it from USAData for $465.24. Through USAData's Web site, which is linked to large databases maintained by Acxiom and Dun & Bradstreet, anyone with a credit card can buy marketing lists of consumers broken down by location, demographics, and interests. The College Board sells data on graduating high school seniors to 1700 colleges and universities for 28 cents per student. These businesses are entirely legal. Also selling data are businesses that obtain credit card and cell phone records illegally and sell them to private investigators and law enforcement. The buying and selling of personal data has become a multibillion dollar business that's growing by leaps and bounds.

Unlike banks or companies selling credit reports, these private data brokers are largely unregulated There has been little or no federal or state oversight of how they collect, maintain, and sell their data. But they have been allowed to flourish because there is such a huge market for personal information and they provide useful services for insurance companies, banks, employers, and federal, state, and local government agencies.

For example, the Internal Revenue Service and departments of Homeland Security, Justice, and State paid data brokers $30 million in 2005 for data used in law enforcement and counterterrorism. The Internal Revenue Service signed a five-year $200 milllion deal to access ChoicePoint's databases to locate assets of delinquent taxpayers. After the September 11, 2001 terrorist attacks, ChoicePoint helped the U.S. government screen candidates for the new federally controlled airport security workforce.

ChoicePoint is one of the largest data brokers, with more than 5,000 employees serving businesses of all sizes as well as federal, state, and local governments. In 2004, ChoicePoint performed more than seven million background checks. It processes thousands of credit card transactions every second.

ChoicePoint builds its vast repository of personal data through an extensive network of contractors who gather bits of information from public filings, financial-services firms, phone directories, and loan application forms. The contractors use police departments, school districts, departments of motor vehicles, and local courts to fill their caches. All of the information is public and legal.

ChoicePoint possesses 19 billion records containing personal information on the vast majority of American adult consumers. According to Daniel J. Solove, associate professor of law at George Washington University, the company has collected information on nearly every adult American and "these are dossiers that J. Edgar Hoover would be envious of."

The downside to the massive databases maintained by ChoicePoint and other data brokers is the threat they pose to personal privacy and social well being. The quality of the data they maintain can be unreliable, causing people to lose their jobs and their savings. In one case, Boston Market fired an employee after receiving a background check from ChoicePoint that showed felony convictions. However, the report had been wrong. In another, a retired GE assembly-line worker was charged a higher insurance premium because another person's driving record, with multiple accidents, had been added to his ChoicePoint file.

ChoicePoint came under fire in early 2005 for selling information on 145,000 customers to criminals posing as legitimate businesses. The criminals then used the identities of some of the individuals on whom ChoicePoint maintained data to open fraudulent credit card accounts. Since then, ChoicePoint curtailed the sale of products that contain sensitive data, such as social security and driver's license identification numbers and limited access by small businesses, including private investigators, collection agencies, and non-bank financial institutions. ChoicePoint also revised its security policy and procedures, implementing more rigorous processes to verify customer authenticity.

Marc Rotenberg of the Electronic Privacy Information Center in Washington, D.C., believes that the ChoicePoint case is a clear demonstration that self-regulation does not work in the information business and that more comprehensive laws are needed. California, 22 other states, and New York City have passed laws requiring companies to inform customers when their personal data files have been compromised. More than a dozen data security bills were introduced in Congress in 2006 and some type of federal data security and privacy legislation will result. Privacy advocates are hoping for a broad federal law with a uniform set of standards for privacy protection practices.

Sources: Lemecha, Darryl. "Best Practices: ChoicePoint: Back from the Breach?," *Optimize Magazine*, May, 2007; Rick Whiting, "Who's Buying and Selling Your Data? Everybody," *Information Week*, July 10, 2006; and Christopher Wolf, "Dazed and Confused: Data Law Disarray," *Business Week*, June 8, 2006.

CASE STUDY QUESTIONS

1. Do data brokers pose an ethical dilemma? Explain your answer.

2. What are the problems caused by the proliferation of data brokers? What people, organization, and technology factors are responsible for these problems?

3. How effective are existing solutions to these problems?

4. Should the U.S. federal government regulate private data brokers? Why or why not? What are the advantages and disadvantages?

MIS IN ACTION

Explore the Web site of USAData (usadata.com). Click on Consumer Lists/Leads to start the process of ordering a consumer mailing list online but do not use your credit card to pay for the list. Answer the following questions:

1. What kind of data does this company provide? How does it obtain the data?

2. Who uses the data sold by USAData? Are there any restrictions on who can use the data?

3. What kind of information can you obtain by ordering a mailing list online? How detailed is this information? How easy is it to purchase this information? Can someone use this online capability to find out how much money you make?

4. Does this capability raise any privacy issues? Explain your answer.

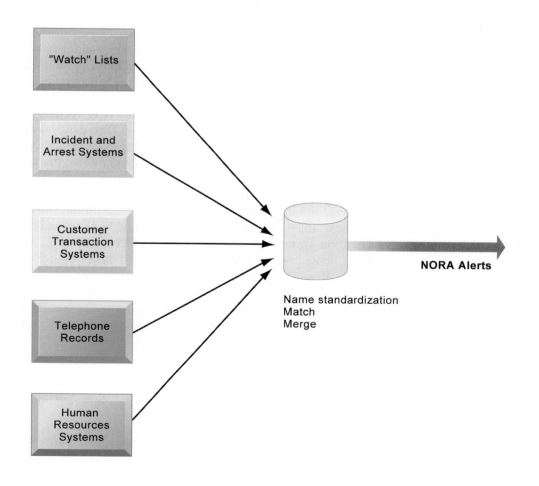

Figure 12-2
Nonobvious Relationship Awareness (NORA)
NORA technology can take information about people from disparate sources and find obscure, nonobvious relationships. It might discover, for example, that an applicant for a job at a casino shares a telephone number with a known criminal and issue an alert to the hiring manager.

privacy on a scale and with a precision heretofore unimaginable. If computing and network-ing technologies continue to advance at the same pace as in the past, by 2023 large organizations will be able to devote the equivalent of a contemporary desktop personal computer to monitoring each of the 350 million individuals who will then be living in the United States (Farmer and Mann, 2003).

The development of global digital communication networks widely available to individ-uals and businesses poses many ethical and social concerns. Who will account for the flow of information over these networks? Will you be able to trace information collected about you? What will these networks do to the traditional relationships between family, work, and leisure? How will traditional job designs be altered when millions of "employees" become subcontractors using mobile offices for which they themselves must pay? In the next section we consider some ethical principles and analytical techniques for dealing with these kinds of ethical and social concerns.

12.2 Ethics in an Information Society

Ethics is a concern of humans who have freedom of choice. Ethics is about individual choice: When faced with alternative courses of action, what is the correct moral choice? What are the main features of ethical choice?

BASIC CONCEPTS: RESPONSIBILITY, ACCOUNTABILITY, AND LIABILITY

Ethical choices are decisions made by individuals who are responsible for the consequences of their actions. **Responsibility** is a key element of ethical action. Responsibility means that you accept the potential costs, duties, and obligations for the decisions you make. **Accountability** is a feature of systems and social institutions: It means that mechanisms are in place to determine who took responsible action, who is responsible. Systems and institutions in which it is impossible to find out who took what action are inherently incapable of ethical analysis or ethical action. Liability extends the concept of responsibility further to the area of laws. **Liability** is a feature of political systems in which a body of laws is in place that permits individuals to recover the damages done to them by other actors, systems, or organizations. **Due process** is a related feature of law-governed societies and is a process in which laws are known and understood and there is an ability to appeal to higher authorities to ensure that the laws are applied correctly.

These basic concepts form the underpinning of an ethical analysis of information systems and those who manage them. First, information technologies are filtered through social institutions, organizations, and individuals. Systems do not have impacts by themselves. Whatever information system impacts exist are products of institutional, organizational, and individual actions and behaviors. Second, responsibility for the consequences of technology falls clearly on the institutions, organizations, and individual managers who choose to use the technology. Using information technology in a socially responsible manner means that you can and will be held accountable for the consequences of your actions. Third, in an ethical, political society, individuals and others can recover damages done to them through a set of laws characterized by due process.

ETHICAL ANALYSIS

When confronted with a situation that seems to present ethical issues, how should you analyze it? The following five-step process should help.

1. *Identify and describe clearly the facts.* Find out who did what to whom, and where, when, and how. In many instances, you will be surprised at the errors in the initially reported facts, and often you will find that simply getting the facts straight helps define

the solution. It also helps to get the opposing parties involved in an ethical dilemma to agree on the facts.

2. *Define the conflict or dilemma and identify the higher-order values involved.* Ethical, social, and political issues always reference higher values. The parties to a dispute all claim to be pursuing higher values (e.g., freedom, privacy, protection of property, and the free enterprise system). Typically, an ethical issue involves a dilemma: two diametrically opposed courses of action that support worthwhile values. For example, the chapter-ending case study illustrates two competing values: the need to facilitate communication and access to information on the Internet and the need to protect children.

3. *Identify the stakeholders.* Every ethical, social, and political issue has stakeholders: players in the game who have an interest in the outcome, who have invested in the situation, and usually who have vocal opinions. Find out the identity of these groups and what they want. This will be useful later when designing a solution.

4. *Identify the options that you can reasonably take.* You may find that none of the options satisfy all the interests involved, but that some options do a better job than others. Sometimes arriving at a good or ethical solution may not always be a balancing of consequences to stakeholders.

5. *Identify the potential consequences of your options.* Some options may be ethically correct but disastrous from other points of view. Other options may work in one instance but not in other similar instances. Always ask yourself, "What if I choose this option consistently over time?"

CANDIDATE ETHICAL PRINCIPLES

Once your analysis is complete, what ethical principles or rules should you use to make a decision? What higher-order values should inform your judgment? Although you are the only one who can decide which among many ethical principles you will follow, and how you will prioritize them, it is helpful to consider some ethical principles with deep roots in many cultures that have survived throughout recorded history.

1. Do unto others as you would have them do unto you (the Golden Rule). Putting yourself into the place of others, and thinking of yourself as the object of the decision, can help you think about fairness in decision making.

2. If an action is not right for everyone to take, it is not right for anyone (**Immanuel Kant's Categorical Imperative**). Ask yourself, "If everyone did this, could the organization, or society, survive?"

3. If an action cannot be taken repeatedly, it is not right to take at all (**Descartes' rule of change**). This is the slippery-slope rule: An action may bring about a small change now that is acceptable, but if it is repeated, it would bring unacceptable changes in the long run. In the vernacular, it might be stated as "once started down a slippery path, you may not be able to stop."

4. Take the action that achieves the higher or greater value (the **Utilitarian Principle**). This rule assumes you can prioritize values in a rank order and understand the consequences of various courses of action.

5. Take the action that produces the least harm or the least potential cost (**Risk Aversion Principle**). Some actions have extremely high failure costs of very low probability (e.g., building a nuclear generating facility in an urban area) or extremely high failure costs of moderate probability (speeding and automobile accidents). Avoid these high-failure-cost actions, paying greater attention obviously to high-failure-cost potential of moderate to high probability.

6. Assume that virtually all tangible and intangible objects are owned by someone else unless there is a specific declaration otherwise. (This is the **ethical "no free lunch" rule**.) If something someone else has created is useful to you, it has value, and you should assume the creator wants compensation for this work.

Although these ethical rules cannot be guides to action, actions that do not easily pass these rules deserve some very close attention and a great deal of caution. The appearance of unethical behavior may do as much harm to you and your company as actual unethical behavior.

PROFESSIONAL CODES OF CONDUCT

When groups of people claim to be professionals, they take on special rights and obligations because of their special claims to knowledge, wisdom, and respect. Professional codes of conduct are promulgated by associations of professionals, such as the American Medical Association (AMA), the American Bar Association (ABA), the Association of Information Technology Professionals (AITP), and the Association for Computing Machinery (ACM). These professional groups take responsibility for the partial regulation of their professions by determining entrance qualifications and competence. Codes of ethics are promises by professions to regulate themselves in the general interest of society. For example, avoiding harm to others, honoring property rights (including intellectual property), and respecting privacy are among the General Moral Imperatives of the ACM's Code of Ethics and Professional Conduct.

SOME REAL-WORLD ETHICAL DILEMMAS

Information systems have created new ethical dilemmas in which one set of interests is pitted against another. For example, many of the large telephone companies in the United States are using information technology to reduce the sizes of their workforces. Voice recognition software reduces the need for human operators by enabling computers to recognize a customer's responses to a series of computerized questions. Many companies monitor what their employees are doing on the Internet to prevent them from wasting company resources on non-business activities (see the Chapter 6 Interactive Session on People).

In each instance, you can find competing values at work, with groups lined up on either side of a debate. A company may argue, for example, that it has a right to use information systems to increase productivity and reduce the size of its workforce to lower costs and stay in business. Employees displaced by information systems may argue that employers have some responsibility for their welfare. Business owners might feel obligated to monitor employee e-mail and Internet use to minimize drains on productivity. Employees might believe they should be able to use the Internet for short personal tasks in place of the telephone. A close analysis of the facts can sometimes produce compromised solutions that give each side "half a loaf." Try to apply some of the principles of ethical analysis described to each of these cases. What is the right thing to do?

12.3 The Moral Dimensions of Information Systems

In this section, we take a closer look at the five moral dimensions of information systems first described in Figure 12-1. In each dimension we identify the ethical, social, and political levels of analysis and use real-world examples to illustrate the values involved, the stakeholders, and the options chosen.

INFORMATION RIGHTS: PRIVACY AND FREEDOM IN THE INTERNET AGE

Privacy is the claim of individuals to be left alone, free from surveillance or interference from other individuals or organizations, including the state. Claims to privacy are also involved at the workplace: Millions of employees are subject to electronic and other forms of high-tech surveillance (Ball, 2001). Information technology and systems threaten individual claims to privacy by making the invasion of privacy cheap, profitable, and effective.

The claim to privacy is protected in the U.S., Canadian, and German constitutions in a variety of different ways and in other countries through various statutes. In the United States, the claim to privacy is protected primarily by the First Amendment guarantees of freedom of speech and association, the Fourth Amendment protections against unreasonable search and seizure of one's personal documents or home, and the guarantee of due process.

Table 12.3 describes the major U.S. federal statutes that set forth the conditions for handling information about individuals in such areas as credit reporting, education, financial records, newspaper records, and electronic communications. The Privacy Act of 1974 has been the most important of these laws, regulating the federal government's collection, use, and disclosure of information. At present, most U.S. federal privacy laws apply only to the federal government and regulate very few areas of the private sector.

Most American and European privacy law is based on a regime called Fair Information Practices first set forth in a report written in 1973 by a federal government advisory committee (U.S. Department of Health, Education, and Welfare, 1973). **Fair Information Practices (FIP)** is a set of principles governing the collection and use of information about individuals. FIP principles are based on the notion of a mutuality of interest between the record holder and the individual. The individual has an interest in engaging in a transaction, and the record keeper—usually a business or government agency—requires information about the individual to support the transaction. Once information is gathered, the individual maintains an interest in the record, and the record may not be used to support other activities without the individual's consent. In 1998, the Federal Trade Commission (FTC) restated and extended the original FIP to provide guidelines for protecting online privacy. Table 12.4 describes the FTC's Fair Information Practice principles.

The FTC's FIP are being used as guidelines to drive changes in privacy legislation. In July 1998, the U.S. Congress passed the Children's Online Privacy Protection Act (COPPA), requiring Web sites to obtain parental permission before collecting information on children under the age of 13. (This law is in danger of being overturned.) The FTC has recommended additional legislation to protect online consumer privacy in advertising networks that collect records of consumer Web activity to develop detailed

TABLE 12.3

Federal Privacy Laws in the United States

General Federal Privacy Laws	Privacy Laws Affecting Private Institutions
Freedom of Information Act of 1966 as Amended (5 USC 552)	Fair Credit Reporting Act of 1970
Privacy Act of 1974 as Amended (5 USC 552a)	Family Educational Rights and Privacy Act of 1974
Electronic Communications Privacy Act of 1986	Right to Financial Privacy Act of 1978
Computer Matching and Privacy Protection Act of 1988	Privacy Protection Act of 1980
Computer Security Act of 1987	Cable Communications Policy Act of 1984
Federal Managers Financial Integrity Act of 1982	Electronic Communications Privacy Act of 1986
Driver's Privacy Protection Act of 1994	Video Privacy Protection Act of 1988
E-Government Act of 2002	The Health Insurance Portability and Accountability Act of 1996 (HIPAA)
	Children's Online Privacy Protection Act of 1998 (COPPA)
	Financial Modernization Act (Gramm–Leach-Bliley Act) of 1999

TABLE 12.4

Federal Trade Commission Fair Information Practice Principles

1. Notice/awareness (core principle). Web sites must disclose their information practices before collecting data. Includes identification of collector; uses of data; other recipients of data; nature of collection (active/inactive); voluntary or required status; consequences of refusal; and steps taken to protect confidentiality, integrity, and quality of the data.

2. Choice/consent (core principle). There must be a choice regime in place allowing consumers to choose how their information will be used for secondary purposes other than supporting the transaction, including internal use and transfer to third parties.

3. Access/participation. Consumers should be able to review and contest the accuracy and completeness of data collected about them in a timely, inexpensive process.

4. Security. Data collectors must take responsible steps to assure that consumer information is accurate and secure from unauthorized use.

5. Enforcement. There must be in place a mechanism to enforce FIP principles. This can involve self-regulation, legislation giving consumers legal remedies for violations, or federal statutes and regulations.

profiles, which are then used by other companies to target online ads. Other proposed Internet privacy legislation focuses on protecting the online use of personal identification numbers, such as social security numbers; protecting personal information collected on the Internet that deals with individuals not covered by the Children's Online Privacy Protection Act of 1998; and limiting the use of data mining for homeland security.

Privacy protections have also been added to recent laws deregulating financial services and safeguarding the maintenance and transmission of health information about individuals. The Gramm-Leach-Bliley Act of 1999, which repeals earlier restrictions on affiliations among banks, securities firms, and insurance companies, includes some privacy protection for consumers of financial services. All financial institutions are required to disclose their policies and practices for protecting the privacy of nonpublic personal information and to allow customers to opt out of information-sharing arrangements with nonaffiliated third parties.

The Health Insurance Portability and Accountability Act of 1996 (HIPAA), which took effect on April 14, 2003, includes privacy protection for medical records. The law gives patients access to their personal medical records maintained by healthcare providers, hospitals, and health insurers and the right to authorize how protected information about themselves can be used or disclosed. Doctors, hospitals, and other healthcare providers must limit the disclosure of personal information about patients to the minimum amount necessary to achieve a given purpose.

The European Directive on Data Protection

In Europe, privacy protection is much more stringent than in the United States. Unlike the United States, European countries do not allow businesses to use personally identifiable information without consumers' prior consent. On October 25, 1998, the European Commission's Directive on Data Protection went into effect, broadening privacy protection in the European Union (EU) nations. The directive requires companies to inform people when they collect information about them and disclose how it will be stored and used. Customers must provide their informed consent before any company can legally use data about them, and they have the right to access that information, correct it, and request that no further data be collected. **Informed consent** can be defined as consent given with knowledge of all the facts needed to make a rational decision. EU member nations must translate these principles into their own laws and cannot transfer personal data to countries, such as the United States, that do not have similar privacy protection regulations.

Working with the European Commission, the U.S. Department of Commerce developed a safe harbor framework for U.S. firms. A **safe harbor** is a private, self-regulating policy and enforcement mechanism that meets the objectives of government regulators and legislation but does not involve government regulation or enforcement. U.S. businesses would be allowed to use personal data from EU countries if they develop privacy protection policies that meet EU standards. Enforcement would occur in the United States using self-policing, regulation, and government enforcement of fair trade statutes.

Internet Challenges to Privacy

Internet technology has posed new challenges for the protection of individual privacy. Information sent over this vast network of networks may pass through many different computer systems before it reaches its final destination. Each of these systems is capable of monitoring, capturing, and storing communications that pass through it.

It is possible to record many online activities, including which online newsgroups or files a person has accessed, which Web sites and Web pages he or she has visited, and what items that person has inspected or purchased over the Web. Much of this monitoring and tracking of Web site visitors occurs in the background without the visitor's knowledge. Tools to monitor visits to the World Wide Web have become popular because they help organizations determine who is visiting their Web sites and how to better target their offerings. (Some firms also monitor the Internet usage of their employees to see how they are using company network resources.) Web retailers now have access to software that lets them "watch" the online shopping behavior of individuals and groups while they are visiting a Web site and making purchases. The commercial demand for this personal information is virtually insatiable.

Web sites can learn the identities of their visitors if the visitors voluntarily register at the site to purchase a product or service or to obtain a free service, such as information. Web sites can also capture information about visitors without their knowledge using cookie technology.

Cookies are tiny files deposited on a computer hard drive when a user visits certain Web sites. Cookies identify the visitor's Web browser software and track visits to the Web site. When the visitor returns to a site that has stored a cookie, the Web site software will search the visitor's computer, find the cookie, and know what that person has done in the past. It may also update the cookie, depending on the activity during the visit. In this way, the site can customize its contents for each visitor's interests. For example, if you purchase a book on the Amazon.com Web site and return later from the same browser, the site will welcome you by name and recommend other books of interest based on your past purchases. DoubleClick, described earlier in this chapter, uses cookies to build its dossiers with details of online purchases and to examine the behavior of Web site visitors. Figure 12-3 on page 424 illustrates how cookies work.

Web sites using cookie technology cannot directly obtain visitors' names and addresses. However, if a person has registered at a site, that information can be combined with cookie data to identify the visitor. Web site owners can also combine the data they have gathered from cookies and other Web site monitoring tools with personal data from other sources, such as offline data collected from surveys or paper catalog purchases, to develop very detailed profiles of their visitors.

There are now even more subtle and surreptitious tools for surveillance of Internet users. Marketers use Web bugs as another tool to monitor online behavior. **Web bugs** are tiny graphic files embedded in e-mail messages and Web pages that are designed to monitor who is reading the e-mail message or Web page and transmit that information to another computer. Other **spyware** can secretly install itself on an Internet user's computer by piggybacking on larger applications. Once installed, the spyware calls out to Web sites to send banner ads and other unsolicited material to the user, and it can also report the user's movements on the Internet to other computers. More information is available about Web bugs, spyware, and other intrusive software in Chapter 7.

Figure 12-3
How Cookies Identify Web Visitors
Cookies are written by a Web site on a visitor's hard drive. When the visitor returns to that Web site, the Web server requests the ID number from the cookie and uses it to access the data stored by that server on that visitor. The Web site can then use these data to display personalized information.

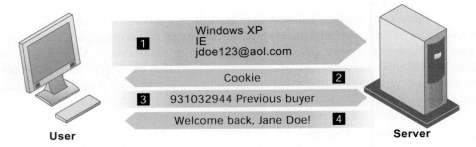

User   Server

1. The Web server reads the user's Web browser and determines the operating system, browser name, version number, Internet address, and other information.
2. The server transmits a tiny text file with user identification information called a cookie, which the user's browser receives and stores on the user's computer hard drive.
3. When the user returns to the Web site, the server requests the contents of any cookie it deposited previously in the user's computer.
4. The Web server reads the cookie, identifies the visitor, and calls up data on the user.a

Google has been using tools to scan the contents of messages received by users of its free Web-based e-mail service called Gmail. Ads that users see when they read their e-mail are related to the subjects of these messages. Privacy advocates find the practice offensive.

The United States has allowed businesses to gather transaction information generated in the marketplace and then use that information for other marketing purposes without obtaining the informed consent of the individual whose information is being used. U.S. e-commerce sites are largely content to publish statements on their Web sites informing visitors about how their information will be used. Some have added opt-out selection boxes to these information policy statements. An **opt-out** model of informed consent permits the collection of personal information until the consumer specifically requests that the data not be collected. Privacy advocates would like to see wider use of an **opt-in** model of informed consent in which a business is prohibited from collecting any personal information unless the consumer specifically takes action to approve information collection and use.

The online industry has preferred self-regulation to privacy legislation for protecting consumers. In 1998, the online industry formed the Online Privacy Alliance to encourage self-regulation to develop a set of privacy guidelines for its members. The group promotes the use of online seals, such as that of TRUSTe, certifying Web sites adhering to certain privacy principles. Members of the advertising network industry, including DoubleClick, have created an additional industry association called the Network Advertising Initiative (NAI) to develop its own privacy policies to help consumers opt out of advertising network programs and provide consumers redress from abuses.

In general, however, most Internet businesses do little to protect the privacy of their customers, and consumers do not do as much as they should to protect themselves. Many companies with Web sites do not have privacy policies. Of the companies that do post privacy polices on their Web sites, about half do not monitor their sites to ensure they adhere to these policies. The vast majority of online customers claim they are concerned about online privacy, but less than half read the privacy statements on Web sites (Laudon and Traver, 2007).

Technical Solutions

In addition to legislation, new technologies are available to protect user privacy during interactions with Web sites. Many of these tools are used for encrypting e-mail, for making e-mail or surfing activities appear anonymous, for preventing client computers from accepting cookies, or for detecting and eliminating spyware.

There are now tools to help users determine the kind of personal data that can be extracted by Web sites. The Platform for Privacy Preferences, known as P3P, enables automatic communication of privacy policies between an e-commerce site and its visitors.

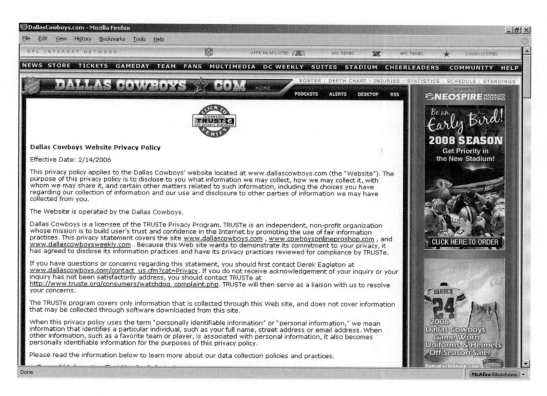

Web sites are posting their privacy policies for visitors to review. The TRUSTe seal designates Web sites that have agreed to adhere to TRUSTe's established privacy principles of disclosure, choice, access, and security.

P3P provides a standard for communicating a Web site's privacy policy to Internet users and for comparing that policy to the user's preferences or to other standards, such as the FTC's new FIP guidelines or the European Directive on Data Protection. Users can use P3P to select the level of privacy they wish to maintain when interacting with the Web site.

The P3P standard allows Web sites to publish privacy policies in a form that computers can understand. Once it is codified according to P3P rules, the privacy policy becomes part of the software for individual Web pages (see Figure 12-4). Users of Microsoft Internet Explorer Web browsing software can access and read the P3P site's privacy policy and a list of all cookies coming from the site. Internet Explorer enables users to adjust their computers to screen out all cookies or let in selected cookies based on specific levels of privacy. For example, the "medium" level accepts cookies from first-party host sites that have opt-in or opt-out policies but rejects third-party cookies that use personally identifiable information without an opt-in policy.

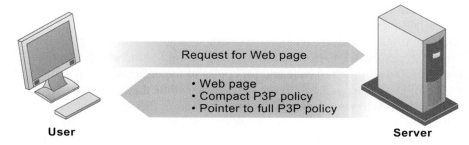

User   **Server**

1. The user with P3P Web browsing software requests a Web page.
2. The Web server returns the Web page along with a compact version of the Web site's policy and a pointer to the full P3P policy. If the Web site is not P3P compliant, no P3P data are returned.
3. The user's Web browsing software compares the response from the Web site with the user's privacy preferences. If the Web site does not have a P3P policy or the policy does not match the privacy levels established by the user, it warns the user or rejects the cookies from the Web site. Otherwise, the Web page loads normally.

Figure 12-4
The P3P Standard
P3P enables Web sites to translate their privacy policies into a standard format that can be read by the user's Web browser software. The user's Web browser software evaluates the Web site's privacy policy to determine whether it is compatible with the user's privacy preferences.

However, P3P only works with Web sites of members of the World Wide Web Consortium who have translated their Web site privacy policies into P3P format. The technology will display cookies from Web sites that are not part of the consortium, but users will not be able to obtain sender information or privacy statements. Many users may also need to be educated about interpreting company privacy statements and P3P levels of privacy.

PROPERTY RIGHTS: INTELLECTUAL PROPERTY

Contemporary information systems have severely challenged existing law and social practices that protect private intellectual property. **Intellectual property** is considered to be intangible property created by individuals or corporations. Information technology has made it difficult to protect intellectual property because computerized information can be so easily copied or distributed on networks. Intellectual property is subject to a variety of protections under three different legal traditions: trade secrets, copyright, and patent law.

Trade Secrets

Any intellectual work product—a formula, device, pattern, or compilation of data—used for a business purpose can be classified as a **trade secret**, provided it is not based on information in the public domain. Protections for trade secrets vary from state to state. In general, trade secret laws grant a monopoly on the ideas behind a work product, but it can be a very tenuous monopoly.

Software that contains novel or unique elements, procedures, or compilations can be included as a trade secret. Trade secret law protects the actual ideas in a work product, not only their manifestation. To make this claim, the creator or owner must take care to bind employees and customers with nondisclosure agreements and to prevent the secret from falling into the public domain.

The limitation of trade secret protection is that, although virtually all software programs of any complexity contain unique elements of some sort, it is difficult to prevent the ideas in the work from falling into the public domain when the software is widely distributed.

Copyright

Copyright is a statutory grant that protects creators of intellectual property from having their work copied by others for any purpose during the life of the author plus an additional 70 years after the author's death. For corporate-owned works, copyright protection lasts for 95 years after their initial creation. Congress has extended copyright protection to books, periodicals, lectures, dramas, musical compositions, maps, drawings, artwork of any kind, and motion pictures. The intent behind copyright laws has been to encourage creativity and authorship by ensuring that creative people receive the financial and other benefits of their work. Most industrial nations have their own copyright laws, and there are several international conventions and bilateral agreements through which nations coordinate and enforce their laws.

In the mid-1960s, the Copyright Office began registering software programs, and in 1980 Congress passed the Computer Software Copyright Act, which clearly provides protection for software program code and for copies of the original sold in commerce, and sets forth the rights of the purchaser to use the software while the creator retains legal title.

Copyright protects against copying of entire programs or their parts. Damages and relief are readily obtained for infringement. The drawback to copyright protection is that the underlying ideas behind a work are not protected, only their manifestation in a work. A competitor can use your software, understand how it works, and build new software that follows the same concepts without infringing on a copyright.

"Look and feel" copyright infringement lawsuits are precisely about the distinction between an idea and its expression. For instance, in the early 1990s Apple Computer sued Microsoft Corporation and Hewlett-Packard for infringement of the expression of Apple's Macintosh interface, claiming that the defendants copied the expression of overlapping windows. The defendants countered that the idea of overlapping windows can be expressed only in a single way and, therefore, was not protectable under the merger doctrine of copyright law. When ideas and their expression merge, the expression cannot be copyrighted.

In general, courts appear to be following the reasoning of a 1989 case—*Brown Bag Software vs. Symantec Corp.*—in which the court dissected the elements of software alleged to be infringing. The court found that similar concept, function, general functional features (e.g., drop-down menus), and colors are not protectable by copyright law (*Brown Bag* vs. *Symantec Corp.*, 1992).

Patents

A **patent** grants the owner an exclusive monopoly on the ideas behind an invention for 20 years. The congressional intent behind patent law was to ensure that inventors of new machines, devices, or methods receive the full financial and other rewards of their labor and yet still make widespread use of the invention possible by providing detailed diagrams for those wishing to use the idea under license from the patent's owner. The granting of a patent is determined by the Patent Office and relies on court rulings.

The key concepts in patent law are originality, novelty, and invention. The Patent Office did not accept applications for software patents routinely until a 1981 Supreme Court decision that held that computer programs could be a part of a patentable process. Since that time, hundreds of patents have been granted and thousands await consideration.

The strength of patent protection is that it grants a monopoly on the underlying concepts and ideas of software. The difficulty is passing stringent criteria of nonobviousness (e.g., the work must reflect some special understanding and contribution), originality, and novelty, as well as years of waiting to receive protection.

Challenges to Intellectual Property Rights

Contemporary information technologies, especially software, pose severe challenges to existing intellectual property regimes and, therefore, create significant ethical, social, and political issues. Digital media differ from books, periodicals, and other media in terms of ease of replication; ease of transmission; ease of alteration; difficulty in classifying a software work as a program, book, or even music; compactness—making theft easy; and difficulties in establishing uniqueness.

The proliferation of electronic networks, including the Internet, has made it even more difficult to protect intellectual property. Before widespread use of networks, copies of software, books, magazine articles, or films had to be stored on physical media, such as paper, computer disks, or videotape, creating some hurdles to distribution. Using networks, information can be more widely reproduced and distributed. The Fourth Annual Global Software Piracy Study conducted by the International Data Corporation and the Business Software Alliance found that 35 percent of the software installed in 2006 on PCs worldwide was obtained illegally, representing nearly $40 billion in global losses from software piracy (Business Software Alliance, 2007).

The Internet was designed to transmit information freely around the world, including copyrighted information. With the World Wide Web in particular, you can easily copy and distribute virtually anything to thousands and even millions of people around the world, even if they are using different types of computer systems. Information can be illicitly copied from one place and distributed through other systems and networks even though these parties do not willingly participate in the infringement.

Individuals have been illegally copying and distributing digitized MP3 music files on the Internet for a number of years. File sharing services such as Napster, and later Grokster, Kazaa, and Morpheus sprung up to help users locate and swap digital music files, including those protected by copyright. Illegal file-sharing became so widespread that it threatened the viability of the music recording industry. The recording industry won some legal battles for shutting these services down, but has not been able to halt illegal file sharing entirely. As more and more homes adopt high-speed Internet access, illegal file sharing of videos will pose similar threats to the motion picture industry (see the case study concluding Chapter 3).

Mechanisms are being developed to sell and distribute books, articles, and other intellectual property legally on the Internet, and the **Digital Millennium Copyright Act (DMCA)** of 1998 is providing some copyright protection. The DMCA implemented a World Intellectual Property Organization Treaty that makes it illegal to circumvent technology-based protections of copyrighted materials. Internet service providers (ISPs) are required to take down sites of copyright infringers that they are hosting once they are notified of the problem.

Microsoft and 1,400 other software and information content firms are represented by the Software and Information Industry Association (SIIA), which lobbies for new laws and enforcement of existing laws to protect intellectual property around the world. (SIIA was formed on January 1, 1999, from the merger of the Software Publishers Association [SPA] and the Information Industry Association [IIA].) The SIIA runs an antipiracy hotline for individuals to report piracy activities and educational programs to help organizations combat software piracy and has published guidelines for employee use of software.

ACCOUNTABILITY, LIABILITY, AND CONTROL

Along with privacy and property laws, new information technologies are challenging existing liability law and social practices for holding individuals and institutions accountable. If a person is injured by a machine controlled, in part, by software, who should be held accountable and, therefore, held liable? Should a public bulletin board or an electronic service, such as America Online, permit the transmission of pornographic or offensive material (as broadcasters), or should they be held harmless against any liability for what users transmit (as is true of common carriers, such as the telephone system)? What about the Internet? If you outsource your information processing, can you hold the external vendor liable for injuries done to your customers? Some real-world examples may shed light on these questions.

Computer-Related Liability Problems

During the weekend of March 15, 2002, tens of thousands of Bank of America customers in California, Arizona, and Nevada were unable to use their paychecks and social security payments that had just been deposited electronically. Checks bounced. Withdrawals were blocked because of insufficient funds. Because of an operating error at the bank's computer center in Nevada, a batch of direct deposit transactions was not processed. The bank lost track of money that should have been credited to customers' accounts, and it took days to rectify the problem (Carr and Gallagher, 2002). Who is liable for any economic harm caused to individuals or businesses that could not access their full account balances in this period?

This case reveals the difficulties faced by information systems executives who ultimately are responsible for any harm done by systems developed by their staffs. In general, insofar as computer software is part of a machine, and the machine injures someone physically or economically, the producer of the software and the operator can be held liable for damages. Insofar as the software acts like a book, storing and displaying information, courts have been reluctant to hold authors, publishers, and booksellers liable for contents (the exception being instances of fraud or defamation), and hence courts have been wary of holding software authors liable for booklike software.

In general, it is very difficult (if not impossible) to hold software producers liable for their software products when those products are considered like books are, regardless of the physical or economic harm that results. Historically, print publishers, books, and periodicals have not been held liable because of fears that liability claims would interfere with First Amendment rights guaranteeing freedom of expression.

What about software as service? ATM machines are a service provided to bank customers. Should this service fail, customers will be inconvenienced and perhaps harmed economically if they cannot access their funds in a timely manner. Should liability protections be extended to software publishers and operators of defective financial, accounting, simulation, or marketing systems?

Software is very different from books. Software users may develop expectations of infallibility about software; software is less easily inspected than a book, and it is more difficult to compare with other software products for quality; software claims actually to perform a task rather than describe a task, as a book does; and people come to depend on services essentially based on software. Given the centrality of software to everyday life, the chances are excellent that liability law will extend its reach to include software even when the software merely provides an information service.

Telephone systems have not been held liable for the messages transmitted because they are regulated common carriers. In return for their right to provide telephone service, they must provide access to all, at reasonable rates, and achieve acceptable reliability. But broadcasters and cable television systems are subject to a wide variety of federal and local constraints on content and facilities. Organizations can be held liable for offensive content on their Web sites; and online services, such as America Online, might be held liable for postings by their users. Although U.S. courts have increasingly exonerated Web sites and ISPs for posting material by third parties, the threat of legal action still has a chilling effect on small companies or individuals who cannot afford to take their cases to trial.

SYSTEM QUALITY: DATA QUALITY AND SYSTEM ERRORS

The debate over liability and accountability for unintentional consequences of system use raises a related but independent moral dimension: What is an acceptable, technologically feasible level of system quality? At what point should system managers say, "Stop testing, we've done all we can to perfect this software. Ship it!" Individuals and organizations may be held responsible for avoidable and foreseeable consequences, which they have a duty to perceive and correct. And the gray area is that some system errors are foreseeable and correctable only at very great expense, an expense so great that pursuing this level of perfection is not feasible economically—no one could afford the product.

For example, although software companies try to debug their products before releasing them to the marketplace, they knowingly ship buggy products because the time and cost of fixing all minor errors would prevent these products from ever being released. What if the product was not offered on the marketplace, would social welfare as a whole not advance and perhaps even decline? Carrying this further, just what is the responsibility of a producer of computer services—should it withdraw the product that can never be perfect, warn the user, or forget about the risk (let the buyer beware)?

Three principal sources of poor system performance are (1) software bugs and errors, (2) hardware or facility failures caused by natural or other causes, and (3) poor input data quality. Chapter 7 discusses why zero defects in software code of any complexity cannot be achieved and why the seriousness of remaining bugs cannot be estimated. Hence, there is a technological barrier to perfect software, and users must be aware of the potential for catastrophic failure. The software industry has not yet arrived at testing standards for producing software of acceptable but not perfect performance.

Although software bugs and facility catastrophes are likely to be widely reported in the press, by far the most common source of business system failure is data quality. Few companies routinely measure the quality of their data, but individual organizations report data error rates ranging from 0.5 to 30 percent.

QUALITY OF LIFE: EQUITY, ACCESS, AND BOUNDARIES

The negative social costs of introducing information technologies and systems are beginning to mount along with the power of the technology. Many of these negative social consequences are not violations of individual rights or property crimes. Nevertheless, these negative consequences can be extremely harmful to individuals, societies, and political institutions. Computers and information technologies potentially can destroy valuable elements of our culture and society even while they bring us benefits. If there is a balance of good and bad consequences of using information systems, who do we hold responsible for the bad consequences? Next, we briefly examine some of the negative social consequences of systems, considering individual, social, and political responses.

Balancing Power: Center Versus Periphery

An early fear of the computer age was that huge, centralized mainframe computers would centralize power at corporate headquarters and in the nation's capital, resulting in a Big Brother society, as was suggested in George Orwell's novel *1984*. The shift toward highly decentralized computing, coupled with an ideology of empowerment of thousands of workers, and the decentralization of decision making to lower organizational levels have reduced the fears of power centralization in institutions. Yet much of the empowerment described in popular business magazines is trivial. Lower-level employees may be empowered to make minor decisions, but the key policy decisions may be as centralized as in the past.

Rapidity of Change: Reduced Response Time to Competition

Information systems have helped to create much more efficient national and international markets. The now-more-efficient global marketplace has reduced the normal social buffers that permitted businesses many years to adjust to competition. Time-based competition has an ugly side: The business you work for may not have enough time to respond to global competitors and may be wiped out in a year, along with your job. We stand the risk of developing a "just-in-time society" with "just-in-time jobs" and "just-in-time" workplaces, families, and vacations.

Maintaining Boundaries: Family, Work, and Leisure

Parts of this book were produced on trains and planes, as well as on family vacations and during what otherwise might have been "family" time. The danger to ubiquitous computing, telecommuting, nomad computing, and the "do anything anywhere" computing environment is that it might actually come true. If so, the traditional boundaries that separate work from family and just plain leisure will be weakened.

Although authors have traditionally worked just about anywhere (typewriters have been portable for nearly a century), the advent of information systems, coupled with the growth of knowledge-work occupations, means that more and more people will be working when traditionally they would have been playing or communicating with family and friends. The work umbrella now extends far beyond the eight-hour day.

Even leisure time spent on the computer threatens these close social relationships. Extensive Internet use, even for entertainment or recreational purposes, takes people away from their family and friends. The chapter-ending case study explores this topic.

Weakening these institutions poses clear-cut risks. Family and friends historically have provided powerful support mechanisms for individuals, and they act as balance points in a society by preserving private life, providing a place for people to collect their thoughts, allowing people to think in ways contrary to their employer, and dream.

Dependence and Vulnerability

Today, our businesses, governments, schools, and private associations, such as churches, are incredibly dependent on information systems and are, therefore, highly vulnerable if these systems fail. With systems now as ubiquitous as the telephone system, it is startling to remember that there are no regulatory or standard-setting forces in place that are similar to telephone, electrical, radio, television, or other public-utility technologies. The absence of standards and the criticality of some system applications will probably call forth demands for national standards and perhaps regulatory oversight.

Computer Crime and Abuse

New technologies, including computers, create new opportunities for committing crime by creating new valuable items to steal, new ways to steal them, and new ways to harm others. *Computer crime* is the commission of illegal acts through the use of a computer or against a computer system. Computers or computer systems can be the object of the crime (destroying a company's computer center or a company's computer files), as well as the instrument of a crime (stealing computer lists by illegally gaining access to a computer

Although some people enjoy the convenience of working at home, the do anything anywhere computing environment can blur the traditional boundaries between work and family time.

system using a home computer). Simply accessing a computer system without authorization or with intent to do harm, even by accident, is now a federal crime.

Computer abuse is the commission of acts involving a computer that may not be illegal but that are considered unethical. The popularity of the Internet and e-mail has turned one form of computer abuse—spamming—into a serious problem for both individuals and businesses. **Spam** is junk e-mail sent by an organization or individual to a mass audience of Internet users who have expressed no interest in the product or service being marketed. Spammers tend to market pornography, fraudulent deals and services, outright scams, and other products not widely approved in most civilized societies. Some countries have passed laws to outlaw spamming or to restrict its use. In the United States, it is still legal if it does not involve fraud and the sender and subject of the e-mail are properly identified.

Spamming has mushroomed because it only costs a few cents to send thousands of messages advertising wares to Internet users. Spam now accounts for more than 70 percent of Internet e-mail traffic worldwide. Spam costs for businesses are very high (an estimated $50 billion per year) because of the computing and network resources consumed by billions of unwanted e-mail messages and the time required to deal with them.

Internet service providers and individuals can combat spam by using spam filtering software to block suspicious e-mail before it enters a recipient's e-mail inbox. However, spam filters may block legitimate messages. Spammers know how to skirt around filters by continually changing their e-mail accounts, by incorporating spam messages in images, by embedding spam in e-mail attachments and electronic greeting cards, and by using other people's computers that have been hijacked by botnets (see Chapter 7). Many spam messages are sent from one country while another country hosts the spam Web site.

Spamming is more tightly regulated in Europe than in the United States. On May 30, 2002, the European Parliament passed a ban on unsolicited commercial messaging. Electronic marketing can be targeted only to people who have given prior consent.

The U.S. CAN-SPAM Act of 2003, which went into effect on January 1, 2004, does not outlaw spamming but does ban deceptive e-mail practices by requiring commercial e-mail messages to display accurate subject lines, identify the true senders, and offer recipients an easy way to remove their names from e-mail lists. It also prohibits the use of fake return addresses. A few people have been prosecuted under the law, but spamming increased since it went into effect.

Employment: Trickle-Down Technology and Reengineering Job Loss

Reengineering work is typically hailed in the information systems community as a major benefit of new information technology. It is much less frequently noted that redesigning business processes could potentially cause millions of middle-level managers and clerical workers to lose their jobs. One economist has raised the possibility that we will create a society run by a small "high tech elite of corporate professionals . . . in a nation of the permanently unemployed" (Rifkin, 1993).

Other economists are much more sanguine about the potential job losses. They believe relieving bright, educated workers from reengineered jobs will result in these workers moving to better jobs in fast-growth industries. Missing from this equation are unskilled, blue-collar workers and older, less well-educated middle managers. It is not clear that these groups can be retrained easily for high-quality (high-paying) jobs. Careful planning and sensitivity to employee needs can help companies redesign work to minimize job losses.

The Interactive Session on People explores another consequence of reengineered jobs. In this case, Wal-Mart's changes in job scheduling for more efficient use of its employees did not cause employees to lose their jobs directly. But it did impact their personal lives and forced them to accept more irregular part-time work. As you read this case, try to identify the problem this company is facing; what alternative solutions are available to management; and whether the chosen solution was the best way to address this problem.

Equity and Access: Increasing Racial and Social Class Cleavages

Does everyone have an equal opportunity to participate in the digital age? Will the social, economic, and cultural gaps that exist in the United States and other societies be reduced by information systems technology? Or will the cleavages be increased, permitting the better off to become even more better off relative to others?

These questions have not yet been fully answered because the impact of systems technology on various groups in society has not been thoroughly studied. What is known is that information, knowledge, computers, and access to these resources through educational institutions and public libraries are inequitably distributed along ethnic and social class lines, as are many other information resources. Several studies have found that certain ethnic and income groups in the United States are less likely to have computers or online Internet access even though computer ownership and Internet access have soared in the past five years. Although the gap is narrowing, higher-income families in each ethnic group are still more likely to have home computers and Internet access than lower-income families in the same group.

A similar **digital divide** exists in U.S. schools, with schools in high-poverty areas less likely to have computers, high-quality educational technology programs, or Internet access availability for their students. Left uncorrected, the digital divide could lead to a society of information haves, computer literate and skilled, versus a large group of information have-nots, computer illiterate and unskilled. Public interest groups want to narrow this digital divide by making digital information services—including the Internet—available to virtually everyone, just as basic telephone service is now.

Health Risks: RSI, CVS, and Technostress

The most important occupational disease today is **repetitive stress injury** (**RSI**). RSI occurs when muscle groups are forced through repetitive actions often with high-impact loads (such as tennis) or tens of thousands of repetitions under low-impact loads (such as working at a computer keyboard).

The single largest source of RSI is computer keyboards. The most common kind of computer-related RSI is **carpal tunnel syndrome** (**CTS**), in which pressure on the median nerve through the wrist's bony structure, called a carpal tunnel, produces pain. The pressure is caused by constant repetition of keystrokes: In a single shift, a word processor may perform 23,000 keystrokes. Symptoms of carpal tunnel syndrome include numbness, shooting pain, inability to grasp objects, and tingling. Millions of workers have been diagnosed with carpal tunnel syndrome.

INTERACTIVE SESSION: PEOPLE   Flexible Scheduling at Wal-Mart: Good or Bad for Employees?

With nearly 1.3 million workers domestically, Wal-Mart is the largest private employer in the United States. Wal-Mart is also the nation's number one retailer in terms of sales, registering nearly $345 billion in sales revenue for the fiscal year ending January 31, 2006. Wal-Mart achieved its lofty status through a combination of low prices and low operational costs, enabled by a superb continuous inventory replenishment system. .

Now Wal-Mart is trying to lower costs further by changing its methods for scheduling the work shifts of its employees. In early 2007 Wal-Mart revealed that it was adopting a computerized scheduling system, a move that has been roundly criticized by worker's rights advocates for the impact it may have on employees' lives.

Traditionally, scheduling employee shifts at big box stores such as Wal-Mart was the domain of store managers who arranged schedules manually. They based their decisions in part on current store promotions as well as on weekly sales data from the previous year. Typically, the process required a full day of effort for a store manager. Multiply that labor intensity by the number of stores in a chain and you have an expensive task with results that are marginally beneficial to the company.

By using a computerized scheduling system, such as the system from Kronos that Wal-Mart adopted, a retail enterprise can produce work schedules for every store in its chain in a matter of hours. Meanwhile, store managers can devote their time to running their individual stores more effectively.

The Kronos scheduling system tracks individual store sales, transactions, units sold, and customer traffic. The system logs these metrics over 15-minute increments for seven weeks at a time, and then measures them against the same data from the previous year. It can also integrate data such as the number of in-store customers at certain hours or the average time required to sell a television set or unload a truck and predict the number of workers needed at any given hour.

A typical result of this type of scheduling might call for a sparse staff early in the day, a significant increase for the midday rush, scaling back toward the end of the day, and then fortifying the staff once again for an evening crowd. However, for a chain like Wal-Mart, which operates thousands of 24-hour stores and has also run into trouble previously for its labor practices, the transition to a computerized scheduling system has resulted in controversy.

For Wal-Mart, using Kronos translates to improved productivity and customer satisfaction. For Wal-Mart employees, known to the company as associates, the change may decrease the stability of their jobs and, possibly, create financial hardship. The scheduling generated by Kronos can be unpredictable, requiring associates to be more flexible with their work hours. Stores may ask them to be on call in case of a rush, or to go home during a slow spell. Irregular hours, and inconsistent paychecks, make it more difficult for employees to organize their lives, from scheduling babysitters to paying bills. Alerts from the system may also enable store managers to avoid paying overtime or full-time wages by cutting back the hours of associates who are approaching the thresholds that cause extra benefits to kick in. Associates are almost always people who need all the work they can get.

According to Paul Blank of the Web site WakeUpWalMart.com, which is supported by the United Food and Commercial Workers union, "What the computer is trying to optimize is the most number of part-time and least number of full-time workers at lower labor costs, with no regard for the effect that it has on workers' lives." Sarah Clark, speaking on behalf of Wal-Mart, insists that system's goal is simply to improve customer service by shortening checkout lines and better meeting the needs of shoppers.

To assist in the deployment of its computerized scheduling system in all of its stores, Wal-Mart requests that its associates submit "personal availability" forms. Language on the form instructs associates that "Limiting your personal availability may restrict the number of hours you are scheduled." Anecdotal evidence suggests that some workers have indeed seen their hours cut and their shifts bounced around. Experienced associates with high pay rates have expressed concern that the system enables managers to pressure them into quitting. If they are unwilling to work nights and weekends, managers have a justification for replacing them with new workers who will make much less per hour. Sarah Clark denies that the system is used in this manner.

Critics of the system can cite the Clayton Antitrust Act of 1914, which states, "The labor of a human being is not a commodity or article of commerce." No legal battles over computerized scheduling appear imminent, so interpreting whether Wal-Mart's strategy equals treating its labor force as a commodity will have to wait.

In the meantime, Wal-Mart is once again at the forefront of technology trends in its industry. Kronos also has agreements for scheduling systems with Ikea, Radio Shack, Fossil, and New Look.

Sources: Kris Maher, "Wal-Mart Seeks New Flexibility in Worker Shifts," *The Wall Street Journal*, January 3, 2007; Bob Evans, "Wal-Mart's Latest 'Orwellian' Technology Move: Get Over It," *InformationWeek*, April 6, 2007 and "More Opinions on Wal-Mart's Flexible Scheduling," *InformationWeek*, April 17, 2007; www.walmartstores.com; and www.kronos.com, accessed May 24, 2007.

CASE STUDY QUESTIONS

1. What is the ethical dilemma facing Wal-Mart in this case? Do Wal-Mart's associates also face an ethical dilemma? If so, what is it?

2. What ethical principles apply to this case? How do they apply?

3. What are the potential effects of computerized scheduling on employee morale? What are the consequences of these effects for Wal-Mart?

MIS IN ACTION

Visit the Web site at www.WakeUpWalMart.com and then answer the following questions.

1. How well does the Web site serve their cause? Does the site help their cause or hurt it?

2. What are this group's major points of contention about Wal-Mart?

3. What other approach could the organization take to bring about change?

Using Wal-Mart's Web site and Google for research, answer the following questions:

4. How does Wal-Mart address the issues raised by organizations such as WakeUpWalMart.com?

5. Are the company's methods effective?

6. If you were a public relations expert advising Wal-Mart, what suggestions would you make for handling criticism?

Repetitive stress injury (RSI) is the leading occupational disease today. The single largest cause of RSI is computer keyboard work.

RSI is avoidable. Designing workstations for a neutral wrist position (using a wrist rest to support the wrist), proper monitor stands, and footrests all contribute to proper posture and reduced RSI. New, ergonomically correct keyboards are also an option. These measures should be supported by frequent rest breaks and rotation of employees to different jobs.

RSI is not the only occupational illness computers cause. Back and neck pain, leg stress, and foot pain also result from poor ergonomic designs of workstations. **Computer vision syndrome (CVS)** refers to any eyestrain condition related to computer display screen use. Its symptoms, which are usually temporary, include headaches, blurred vision, and dry and irritated eyes.

The newest computer-related malady is **technostress**, which is stress induced by computer use. Its symptoms include aggravation, hostility toward humans, impatience, and fatigue. According to experts, humans working continuously with computers come to expect other humans and human institutions to behave like computers, providing instant responses, attentiveness, and an absence of emotion. Technostress is thought to be related to high levels of job turnover in the computer industry, high levels of early retirement from computer-intense occupations, and elevated levels of drug and alcohol abuse.

The incidence of technostress is not known but is thought to be in the millions and growing rapidly in the United States. Computer-related jobs now top the list of stressful occupations based on health statistics in several industrialized countries.

To date, the role of radiation from computer display screens in occupational disease has not been proved. Video display terminals (VDTs) emit nonionizing electric and magnetic fields at low frequencies. These rays enter the body and have unknown effects on enzymes, molecules, chromosomes, and cell membranes. Long-term studies are investigating low-level electromagnetic fields and birth defects, stress, low birth weight, and other diseases. All manufacturers have reduced display screen emissions since the early 1980s, and European countries, such as Sweden, have adopted stiff radiation emission standards.

The computer has become a part of our lives—personally as well as socially, culturally, and politically. It is unlikely that the issues and our choices will become easier as information technology continues to transform our world. The growth of the Internet and the information economy suggests that all the ethical and social issues we have described will be heightened further as we move into the first digital century.

12.4 Hands-On MIS

The projects in this section give you hands-on experience in developing a privacy policy for a real-world company, using Web page development tools to design and create a simple Web site, and using Internet newsgroups for market research.

ACHIEVING OPERATIONAL EXCELLENCE: DEVELOPING A WEB SITE PRIVACY POLICY

Software skills: Web browser software and presentation software
Business skills: Corporate privacy policy formulation

Dirt Bikes's management wants to make sure it has policies and procedures in place to protect the privacy of visitors to its Web site. You have been asked to develop Dirt Bikes's Web site privacy policy. The TRUSTe Web site at www.truste.org has Model Privacy Disclosures in its Privacy Resources that you can download and review to help you draft Dirt Bikes's privacy policy. You can also examine specific companies' privacy policies by searching for Web site privacy policies on Yahoo!, Google, or another search engine. Prepare a report for management that addresses the following issues:

- How much data should Dirt Bikes collect on visitors to its Web site? What information could it discover by tracking visitors' activities at its Web site? What value would this information provide the company? What are the privacy problems raised by collecting such data?

- Should Dirt Bike use cookies? What are the advantages of using cookies for both Dirt Bikes and its Web site visitors? What privacy issues do they create for Dirt Bikes?
- Should Dirt Bikes join an organization such as TRUSTe to certify that it has adopted approved privacy practices? Why or why not?
- Should Dirt Bikes design its site so that it conforms to P3P standards? Why or why not?
- Should Dirt Bikes adopt an opt-in or opt-out model of informed consent?
- Include in your report a short (two to three pages) privacy statement for the Dirt Bikes Web site. You can use the categories of the TRUSTe Model Privacy Disclosures as a guideline if you wish.
- (Optional) Use electronic presentation software to summarize your recommendations for management.

ACHIEVING OPERATIONAL EXCELLENCE: CREATING A SIMPLE WEB SITE USING WEB PAGE DEVELOPMENT TOOLS

Software skills: Web page creation
Business skills: Web page design

In this project, you'll learn how to build a simple Web site of your own design for a business using the Web page creation function of Microsoft Word, Microsoft FrontPage, or a Web page development tool of your choice.

Build a simple Web site for a business. The Web site should include a homepage with a description of your business and at least one picture or graphic. From the homepage, you must be able to link to a second Web page and, from there, link to a third Web page. Make the homepage long enough so that when you arrive at the bottom of the page, you can no longer see the top. At the bottom of your Web page include a link back to the top. Also include a link to one of the secondary Web pages. On the secondary page, include a link to the top of that page and a link back to the top of the homepage. Also include a link to the third page, which should contain a link to its own top and a link back to the top of the homepage. Finally, on one of the secondary pages, include another picture or graphic, and on the other page include an object that you create using Microsoft Excel or other spreadsheet software. The Laudon Web site includes instructions for completing this project and a Learning Track on Web page creation using Microsoft FrontPage. If you have tested every function and all work to your satisfaction, save the pages you have created for submission to your instructor.

IMPROVING DECISION MAKING: USING INTERNET NEWSGROUPS FOR ONLINE MARKET RESEARCH

Software Skills: Web browser software and Internet newsgroups
Business Skills: Using Internet newsgroups to identify potential customers

This project will help develop your Internet skills in using newsgroups for marketing. It will also ask you to think about the ethical implications of using information in online discussion groups for business purposes.

You are producing hiking boots that you are selling through a few stores at this time. You think your boots are more comfortable than those of your competition. You believe you can undersell many of your competitors if you can significantly increase your production and sales. You would like to use Internet discussion groups interested in hiking, climbing, and camping both to sell your boots and to make them well known. Visit groups.google.com, which stores discussion postings from many thousands of newsgroups. Through this site you can locate all relevant newsgroups and search them by keyword, author's name, forum, date, and subject. Choose a message and examine it carefully, noting all the information you can obtain, including information about the author.

- How could you use these newsgroups to market your boots?
- What ethical principles might you be violating if you use these messages to sell your boots? Do you think there are ethical problems in using newsgroups this way? Explain your answer.

- Next use Google or Yahoo.com to search for the hiking boots industry and locate sites that will help you develop other new ideas for contacting potential customers.
- Given what you have learned in this and previous chapters, prepare a plan to use newsgroups and other alternative methods to begin attracting visitors to your site.

LEARNING TRACKS

The following Learning Tracks provide content relevant to the topics covered in this chapter:

1. Developing a Corporate Code of Ethics for Information Systems
2. Creating a Web Page

Review Summary

1 **What ethical, social, and political issues are raised by information systems?** Information technology is introducing changes for which laws and rules of acceptable conduct have not yet been developed. Increasing computing power, storage, and networking capabilities—including the Internet—expand the reach of individual and organizational actions and magnify their impacts. The ease and anonymity with which information is now communicated, copied, and manipulated in online environments pose new challenges to the protection of privacy and intellectual property. The main ethical, social, and political issues raised by information systems center around information rights and obligations, property rights and obligations, accountability and control, system quality, and quality of life.

2 **What specific principles for conduct can be used to guide ethical decisions?** Six ethical principles for judging conduct include the Golden Rule, Immanuel Kant's Categorical Imperative, Descartes' rule of change, the Utilitarian Principle, the Risk Aversion Principle, and the ethical "no free lunch" rule. These principles should be used in conjunction with an ethical analysis.

3 **Why do contemporary information systems technology and the Internet pose challenges to the protection of individual privacy and intellectual property?** Contemporary data storage and data analysis technology enables companies to easily gather personal data about individuals from many different sources and analyze these data to create detailed electronic profiles about individuals and their behaviors. Data flowing over the Internet can be monitored at many points. Cookies and other Web monitoring tools closely track the activities of Web site visitors. Not all Web sites have strong privacy protection policies, and they do not always allow for informed consent regarding the use of personal information. Traditional copyright laws are insufficient to protect against software piracy because digital material can be copied so easily and transmitted to many different locations simultaneously over the Internet.

4 **How have information systems affected everyday life?** Although computer systems have been sources of efficiency and wealth, they have some negative impacts. Computer errors can cause serious harm to individuals and organizations. Poor data quality is also responsible for disruptions and losses for businesses. Jobs can be lost when computers replace workers or tasks become unnecessary in reengineered business processes. The ability to own and use a computer may be exacerbating socioeconomic disparities among different racial groups and social classes. Widespread use of computers increases opportunities for computer crime and computer abuse. Computers can also create health problems, such as repetitive stress injury, computer vision syndrome, and technostress.

Key Terms

Accountability, 410, 412, 413, 420, 422, 428, 436, 440

Carpal tunnel syndrome (CTS), 432

Computer vision syndrome (CVS), 435

Cookies, 423– 426, 434

Copyright, 426–428

Descartes' rule of change, 419, 437

Digital divide, 432

Digital Millennium Copyright Act (DMCA), 428

Due process, 418, 421

Ethical "no free lunch" rule, 410–414, 418, 420, 422, 431, 435–436

Ethics, 412, 418, 420, 437

Fair Information Practices (FIP), 421

Immanuel Kant's Categorical Imperative, 419, 437

Information rights, 413, 420, 437

Informed consent, 422, 424, 436–437

Intellectual property, 411–413, 420, 423, 426–428, 437

Liability, 418, 428–429, 441

Nonobvious relationship awareness (NORA), 415, 417

Opt-in, 424–425, 436

Opt-out, 424–425, 436

P3P, 424–426, 436

Patent, 426–427

Privacy, 410, 412, 414—415, 418, 420–426, 428, 435–436

Profiling, 415

Repetitive stress injury (RSI), 432, 434

Responsibility, 413, 418, 420, 429

Risk Aversion Principle, 419, 437

Safe harbor, 423

Spam, 431

Spyware, 423–424

Technostress, 432, 435, 438

Trade secret, 426

Utilitarian Principle, 419, 437

Web bugs, 423

Review Questions

1. What ethical, social, and political issues are raised by information systems?
- Explain how ethical, social, and political issues are connected and give some examples.
- List and describe the key technological trends that heighten ethical concerns.
- Differentiate between responsibility, accountability, and liability.

2. What specific principles for conduct can be used to guide ethical decisions?
- List and describe the five steps in an ethical analysis.
- Identify and describe six ethical principles.

3. Why do contemporary information systems technology and the Internet pose challenges to the protection of individual privacy and intellectual property?
- Define privacy and fair information practices.
- Explain how the Internet challenges the protection of individual privacy and intellectual property.
- Explain how informed consent, legislation, industry self-regulation, and technology tools help protect the individual privacy of Internet users.
- List and define three different regimes that protect intellectual property rights.

4. How have information systems affected everyday life?
- Explain why it is so difficult to hold software services liable for failure or injury.
- List and describe the principal causes of system quality problems.
- Name and describe four quality of life impacts of computers and information systems.
- Define and describe technostress and repetitive stress injury (RSI) and explain their relationship to information technology.

Discussion Questions

1. Should producers of software-based services, such as ATMs, be held liable for economic injuries suffered when their systems fail?

2. Should companies be responsible for unemployment caused by their information systems? Why or why not?

Video Case

You will find a video case illustrating some of the concepts in this chapter on the Laudon Web site along with questions to help you analyze the case.

Teamwork

Developing a Corporate Ethics Code

With three or four of your classmates, develop a corporate ethics code on privacy that addresses both employee privacy and the privacy of customers and users of the corporate Web site. Be sure to consider e-mail privacy and employer monitoring of worksites, as well as corporate use of information about employees concerning their off-the-job behavior (e.g., lifestyle, marital arrangements, and so forth). If possible, use electronic presentation software to present your ethics code to the class.

BUSINESS PROBLEM-SOLVING CASE

The Internet: Friend or Foe to Children?

The Internet has so much to offer people of all ages, including children. School-age children typically use the Internet for school assignments, downloading music, playing games, and connecting with others.

A report issued by the National Telecommunications and Information Administration (NTIA) on "How Access Benefits Children: Connecting Our Kids to the World of Information" outlines five major avenues that the Internet opens for children. It gives them opportunities to explore artistic expression, such as composing music and art electronically and sharing it with teachers and peers.

The Internet enables children to make connections across social and geographic boundaries. In one instance, young students formed e-pal relationships with nursing home residents and learned what it was like to grow up in rural Nebraska in the first part of the twentieth century.

Being connected online also opens doors for kids to contribute to their communities. In Holland, Texas, a group of schoolchildren embarked on a successful e-mail campaign to convince the state highway department to install a traffic signal on a busy street they had to cross on their way to school.

In the state of Massachusetts, several school districts have demonstrated how the Internet can help students be better prepared to enter the workforce. They accomplished this by teaching skills such as resume writing, Web page designing, and data graphing, as well as by establishing ties between the schools and local businesses that might one day employ the students.

But there's a dark side to all that Internet use. It can also socially isolate children and expose them to unhealthy activities and experiences. According to child and adolescent psychiatrist Dr. David Bassler, certain children become too isolated as a result of heavy Internet use. When children spend too much time online, they don't do their homework or can't focus on their work in school because their online activities have drained their energy. They miss out on sports and other activities and they don't spend enough time with their real-world peers and family members.

Dr. Robert Kraut, a Carnegie-Mellon University professor who has studied online behavior for more than a decade, found that the more people use the Internet, the less they socialize and the less they communicate with family members. Many hours spent online in casual conversation with other strangers don't translate into meaningful relationships.

E-mail and instant messaging can help youngsters stay in touch with friends and family but they have also become instruments for "cyberbullying." Kids will use these tools to send insulting remarks to each other or to broadcast personal details meant for a few close friends. Kylie Kenney was an eighth-grader when some students in her school created a Web site named "Kill Kylie Incorporated" specifically to disparage her. The insulting remarks on the site were available for the entire school to read. The humiliation caused by this act of cyberbullying caused Kylie to change schools, and she was still suffering from the emotional wounds two years later.

The anonymity and reach of the Internet empowers bullies by giving them a large audience and the opportunity to hide their real identity. School administrators have come under increasing pressure to deal with cyberbullying incidents. While school officials are quick to denounce such behavior, they have been hesitant to lend their authority to activities that originate outside of school.

However, in recent months, school districts have been working with state legislatures to enact policies that address cyberbullying. Many of these policies authorize school administrators to intervene when the fallout from cyberbullying conducted on students' home computers disrupts the school environment. Such policies must be crafted and instituted without infringing on students' First Amendment rights to free speech.

Ten million young people use the Internet each day and one in five have been solicited or approached by a child predator, according to the FBI. Federal arrests for online exploitation of children doubled from 863 to 1649 between 2003 and 2005. Fifty percent of child victims of online sex abuse are in the seventh through ninth grades.

Online predators monitor screen names and scrutinize personal information on social networking sites such as MySpace, Friendster, and Facebook to find youngsters with self-esteem problems. They'll ask youngsters questions such as "Do you like this band? Can I help you with your homework?" Then they'll try to arrange a physical meeting with these juveniles. MySpace recently counted 29,000 registered sex offenders with profiles on its site and deleted those profiles. Social networking and virtual world sites aimed specifically at children set up safeguards to ensure that conduct between participants is appropriate. But many parents still fear that the virtual characters their children are socializing with online are actually controlled by predators instead of other children.

Parents have a number of tools at their disposal for protecting their children from online threats. Concerned parents can obtain these tools by purchasing software or by activating them through an ISP or operating system that provides them. Among the parental controls available are different types of filters that limit access to Web sites. A blacklist filter denies access to Web sites based on categories, such as sexual content, violence, or hate speech. A white list filter restricts Web surfing to a pre-approved list of Web sites.

For parents who want to maintain tighter control over the activity on their home computers, monitoring software is available. In addition to blocking Web sites, monitoring software can log site visits, usage time, and the content of instant messages. Some parents view this technique of protection as spying and say that it undermines trust in the household. It may also hinder the ability of children to develop their own common sense.

While filtering tools can certainly bring a degree of peace of mind, they are not a guaranteed solution. Many children these days are computer savvy and will simply find ways to work around parental controls. Some organizations that are opposed to any form of censorship even give instructions on how to defeat blocking software on their Web sites. No matter what technology is available, making the Internet a safe place for children should still involve education, communication, and parental supervision.

Virtual worlds targeted at young people and online stores that offer instant gratification present financial challenges for parents as well. Gone are the days when kids could only purchase toys, games, and music to the extent of the cash in their pockets. These days parents may find their credit card bills inflated by song downloads, eBay purchases, and game subscriptions and purchases of virtual cash to pay for an advanced user experience on sites like Stardoll.com and Zwinktopia.

The online marketplace gives children exposure and access to materials that are not suitable for consumers under the age of 18. Movie studios generally do not advertise R-rated movies during television shows that are popular with young audiences, but they do advertise on Web sites that cater to that demographic. Underage Web surfers are also able to purchase tickets to R-rated movies as well as unrated and R-rated DVDs with a significant rate of success. The prevalence of violent entertainment, whether in movies or video games, poses a particular problem for concerned parents.

Obesity, now an epidemic in the United States, is especially prevalent among youngsters who sit at their computers for hours at a time munching on snack food. And there are plenty of Web sites encouraging them to do just that.

Food companies aggressively use Internet games and other perks such as screen-saver downloads to entice children into buying their brands. Their Web sites offer children's' games linked to snacks, such as Chips Ahoy Soccer Shootout, Pop-Tart Slalom, and Lucky Charms Wild Chocolate Mine. Some Web sites enable kids to take care of virtual pets by feeding them foods that are not the basis of a healthy diet. Children may then associate these foods with fun, putting parents who are trying to promote healthy eating at a disadvantage.

A Kaiser Family Foundation study found that between June and November 2005 more than 12.2 million children had visited 77 food company Web sites it examined. According to the study's lead researcher Vicky Rideout, Internet advertising "still doesn't have the reach TV advertising has. But who it does reach, it reaches more deeply."

The Center for Digital Democracy and American University released a report in May 2007 that also painted a bleak picture for parents trying to curb the influence of online marketing on their children. According to Kathryn Montgomery, a communications professor at American, parents are hard-pressed to fight the appeal of high-sugar and high-fat foods to children and teenagers.

Some brand names that sell these foods request to be added as friends on the profiles of young people who use social networking sites. The companies then encourage the young people to endorse the brands to real-life friends in exchange for giveaways. Montgomery concludes that this type of brand association is much more powerful than a television commercial. Burger King even created a page on MySpace for its mascot, "The King," and had over 150,000 users submit friend requests.

Some companies have altered their approach to youth-targeting advertising in response to criticism. Kraft no longer markets to children under six, and limits advertisements targeted at 6-to-11-year-olds to "better-for-you" products. General Mills uses avatars on its kid-centric virtual town site, Millsberry.com, to encourage healthy eating habits. Avatars obtain their food from a grocery store in the town. They score more health points, and perform better in online games, when they eat healthier foods such as fruits, vegetables, and whole grains.

Sources: Catherine Holahan, "Is Online Marketing Making Kids Obese?" *BusinessWeek*, May 17, 2007; Anne Marie Chaker, "Schools Act to Short-Circuit Spread of 'Cyberbullying,'" *The Wall Street Journal*, January 24, 2007; Alina Tugend, "Tools to Keep the Web Safe for Children," *The New York Times*, April 14, 2007; Jessica E. Vascellaro, "Virtual Worlds Now Cater to Kids, But Are They Safe?" *The Wall Street Journal*, April 30, 2007; Michael Cieply, "Report Says the Young Buy Violent Games and Movies," *The New York Times*, April 13, 2007; Brad Stone, "Young Turn to Web Sites Without Rules," *The New York Times*, January 2, 2007; United States Department of Commerce, "How Access Benefits Children: Connecting Our Kids to the World of Information," www.ntia.doc.gov, accessed August 14, 2007; Johanna Ambrosio, "Connected to Nowhere," *Information Week*, May 1, 2006; and Curtis L. Taylor, "Kids Swallowing Online Food Company Lures," *Newsday*, July 20, 2006.

Case Study Questions

1. Does use of the Internet by children and teenagers pose an ethical dilemma? Why or why not?

2. Should parents restrict use of the Internet by children or teenagers? Why or why not?

3. What are the consequences of allowing children unfettered access to the Internet? What are the consequences of restricting access?

4. Who should deal with cyberbullying? The schools? Parents? Explain your answer.

5. Apply the concepts of responsibility, accountability, and liability to the following scenario: Two junior high school students get into an argument while exchanging instant messages from their respective home computers. The next day, one student assaults the other on school property. Who bears responsibility for the assault? Accountability? Liability?

Glossary

3G networks High-speed cellular networks based on packet-switched technology, enabling users to transmit video, graphics, and other rich media, in addition to voice.

acceptable use policy (AUP) Defines acceptable uses of the firm's information resources and computing equipment, including desktop and laptop computers, wireless devices, telephones, and the Internet, and specifies consequences for noncompliance.

acceptance testing Provides the final certification that the system is ready to be used in a production setting.

access control Policies and procedures a company uses to prevent improper access to systems by unauthorized insiders and outsiders.

accountability The mechanisms for assessing responsibility for decisions made and actions taken.

accumulated balance digital payment systems Systems enabling users to make micropayments and purchases on the Web, accumulating a debit balance on their credit card or telephone bills.

Ajax Technology for creating interactive Web applications capable of updating the user interface without reloading the entire browser page.

analytical CRM Customer relationship management applications dealing with the analysis of customer data to provide information for improving business performance.

antivirus software Software designed to detect, and often eliminate, computer viruses from an information system.

applet Miniature program designed to reside on centralized network servers.

application proxy filtering Firewall screening technology that uses a proxy server to inspect and transmit data packets flowing into and out of the organization so that all the organization's internal applications communicate with the outside using a proxy application.

application server Software that handles all application operations between browser-based computers and a company's back-end business applications or databases.

application software Programs written for a specific application to perform functions specified by end users.

artificial intelligence (AI) The effort to develop computer-based systems that can behave like humans, with the ability to learn languages, accomplish physical tasks, use a perceptual apparatus, and emulate human expertise and decision making.

attributes Pieces of information describing a particular entity.

audio input Voice input devices such as microphones that convert spoken words into digital form for processing by the computer.

audio output Voice output devices that convert digital output data back into intelligible speech.

authentication The ability of each party in a transaction to ascertain the identity of the other party.

authorization management systems Systems for allowing each user access only to those portions of a system or the Web that person is permitted to enter, based on information established by a set of access rules.

authorization policies Determine differing levels of access to information assets for different levels of users in an organization.

autonomic computing Effort to develop systems that can manage themselves without user intervention.

backbone Part of a network handling the major traffic and providing the primary path for traffic flowing to or from other networks.

bandwidth The capacity of a communications channel as measured by the difference between the highest and lowest frequencies that can be transmitted by that channel.

banner ad A graphic display on a Web page used for advertising. The banner is linked to the advertiser's Web site so that a person clicking on it will be transported to the advertiser's Web site.

batch processing A method of collecting and processing data in which transactions are accumulated and stored until a specified time when it is convenient or necessary to process them as a group.

benchmarking Setting strict standards for products, services, or activities and measuring organizational performance against those standards.

best practices The most successful solutions or problem-solving methods that have been developed by a specific organization or industry.

biometric authentication Technology for authenticating system users that compares a person's unique characteristics such as fingerprints, face, or retinal image, against a stored set profile of these characteristics.

bit A binary digit representing the smallest unit of data in a computer system. It can only have one of two states, representing 0 or 1.

blog Popular term for Weblog, designating an informal yet structured Web site where individuals can publish stories, opinions, and links to other Web sites of interest.

blogosphere The totality of blog-related Web sites.

Bluetooth Standard for wireless personal area networks that can transmit up to 722 Kbps within a 10-meter area.

botnet A group of computers that have been infected with bot malware without users' knowledge, enabling a hacker to use the amassed resources of the computers to launch distributed denial-of-service attacks, phishing campaigns or spam.

broadband High-speed transmission technology. Also designates a single communications medium that can transmit multiple channels of data simultaneously.

bullwhip effect Distortion of information about the demand for a product as it passes from one entity to the next across the supply chain.

bundling Cross-selling in which a combination of products is sold as a bundle at a price lower than the total cost of the individual products.

bus networks Network topology linking a number of computers by a single circuit with all messages broadcast to the entire network.

business A formal organization whose aim is to produce products or provide services for a profit

business continuity planning Planning that focuses on how the company can restore business operations after a disaster strikes.

business intelligence (BI) Applications and technologies to help users make better business decisions.

business model An abstraction of what an enterprise is and how the enterprise delivers a product or service, showing how the enterprise creates wealth.

business process reengineering (BPR) The radical redesign of business processes, combining steps to cut waste and eliminating repetitive, paper-intensive tasks in order to improve cost, quality, and service, and to maximize the benefits of information technology.

business processes The unique ways in which organizations coordinate and organize work activities, information, and knowledge to produce a product or service.

business strategy Set of activities and decisions that determine the products and services the firm produces, the industries in which the firm competes, firm competitors, suppliers, and customers, and the firm's long-term goals.

business-to-business (B2B) electronic commerce Electronic sales of goods and services among businesses.

business-to-consumer (B2C) electronic commerce Electronic retailing of products and services directly to individual consumers.

C A powerful programming language with tight control and efficiency of execution; is portable across different microprocessors and is used primarily with PCs.

cable Internet connections Use digital cable coaxial lines to deliver high-speed Internet access to homes and businesses.

call center An organizational department responsible for handling customer service issues by telephone and other channels.

campus area network (CAN) An interconnected set of local area networks in a limited geographical area such as a college or corporate campus.

capacity planning The process of predicting when a computer hardware system becomes saturated to ensure that adequate computing resources are available for work of different priorities and that the firm has enough computing power for its current and future needs.

carpal tunnel syndrome (CTS) Type of RSI in which pressure on the median nerve through the wrist's bony carpal tunnel structure produces pain.

case-based reasoning (CBR) Artificial intelligence technology that represents knowledge as a database of cases and solutions.

cathode ray tube (CRT) Electronic gun that shoots a beam of electrons illuminating pixels on a display screen.

CD-ROM (compact disk read-only memory) Read-only optical disk storage used for imaging, reference, and database applications with massive amounts of unchanging data and for multimedia.

CD-RW (CD-ReWritable) Optical disk storage that can be rewritten many times by users.

cellular telephones (cell phones) A device that transmits voice or data, using radio waves to communicate with radio antennas placed within adjacent geographic areas called cells.

central processing unit (CPU) Area of the computer system that manipulates symbols, numbers, and letters, and controls the other parts of the computer system.

centralized processing Processing that is accomplished by one large central computer.

change agent In the context of implementation, the individual acting as the catalyst during the change process to ensure successful organizational adaptation to a new system or innovation.

change management Giving proper consideration to the impact of organizational change associated with a new system or alteration of an existing system.

chat Live, interactive conversations over a public network.

chief knowledge officer (CKO) Responsible for the firm's knowledge management program.

chief information officer (CIO) Senior manager in charge of the information systems function in the firm.

chief privacy officer (CPO) Responsible for ensuring the company complies with existing data privacy laws.

chief security officer (CSO) Heads a formal security function for the organization and is responsible for enforcing the firm's security policy.

choice Simon's third stage of decision making, when the individual selects among the various solution alternatives.

churn rate Measurement of the number of customers who stop using or purchasing products or services from a company. Used as an indicator of the growth or decline of a firm's customer base.

clicks-and-mortar Business model where the Web site is an extension of a traditional bricks-and-mortar business.

clickstream tracking Tracking data about customer activities at Web sites and storing them in a log.

client The user point-of-entry for the required function in client/server computing. Normally a desktop computer, workstation, or laptop computer.

client/server computing A model for computing that splits processing between clients and servers on a network, assigning functions to the machine most able to perform the function.

cloud computing Web-based applications that are stored on remote servers and accessed via the "cloud" of the Internet using a standard Web browser.

coaxial cable A transmission medium consisting of thickly insulated copper wire; can transmit large volumes of data quickly.

COBOL (Common Business Oriented Language) Major programming language for business applications because it can process large data files with alphanumeric characters.

collaborative filtering Tracking users' movements on a Web site, comparing the information gleaned about a user's behavior against data about other customers with similar interests to predict what the user would like to see next.

co-location Web hosting approach in which the firm actually purchases and owns the server computer housing its Web site but locates the server in the physical facility of the hosting service.

competitive forces model Model used to describe the interaction of external influences, specifically threats and opportunities, that affect an organization's strategy and ability to compete.

component-based development Building large software systems by combining pre-existing software components.

computer Physical device that takes data as an input, transforms the data by executing stored instructions, and outputs information to a number of devices.

computer abuse The commission of acts involving a computer that may not be illegal but are considered unethical.

computer crime The commission of illegal acts through the use of a computer or against a computer system.

computer forensics The scientific collection, examination, authentication, preservation, and analysis of data held on or retrieved from computer storage media in such a way that the information can be used as evidence in a court of law.

computer hardware Physical equipment used for input, processing, and output activities in an information system.

computer literacy Knowledge about information technology, focusing on understanding of how computer-based technologies work.

computer software Detailed, preprogrammed instructions that control and coordinate the work of computer hardware components in an information system.

computer virus Rogue software program that attaches itself to other software programs or data files in order to be executed, often causing hardware and software malfunctions.

computer vision syndrome (CVS) Eyestrain condition related to computer display screen use; symptoms include headaches, blurred vision, and dry and irritated eyes.

computer-aided design (CAD) system Information system that automates the creation and revision of designs using sophisticated graphics software.

computer-aided software engineering (CASE) Automation of step-by-step methodologies for software and systems development to reduce the amounts of repetitive work the developer needs to do.

consumer-to-consumer (C2C) electronic commerce electronic commerce Consumers selling goods and services electronically to other consumers.

controls All of the methods, policies, and procedures that ensure protection of the organization's assets, accuracy and reliability of its records, and operational adherence to management standards.

conversion The process of changing from the old system to the new system.

cookies Tiny file deposited on a computer hard drive when an individual visits certain Web sites. Used to identify the visitor and track visits to the Web site.

copyright A statutory grant that protects creators of intellectual property against copying by others for any purpose during the life of the author plus an additional 70 years after the author's death.

core competency Activity at which a firm excels as a world-class leader.

cost-benefit ratio A method for calculating the returns from a capital expenditure by dividing total benefits by total costs.

cost transparency The ability of consumers to discover the actual costs merchants pay for products.

cracker A hacker with criminal intent.

critical thinking Sustained suspension of judgment with an awareness of multiple perspectives and alternatives.

cross-selling Marketing complementary products to customers.

culture Fundamental set of assumptions, values, and ways of doing things that has been accepted by most members of an organization.

customer decision-support systems (CDSS) Systems to support the decision-making process of an existing or potential customer.

customer lifetime value (CLTV) Difference between revenues produced by a specific customer and the expenses for acquiring and servicing that customer minus the cost of promotional marketing over the lifetime of the customer relationship, expressed in today's dollars.

customer relationship management (CRM) systems Information systems that track all the ways in which a company interacts with its customers and analyze these interactions to optimize revenue, profitability, customer satisfaction, and customer retention.

customization The modification of a software package to meet an organization's unique requirements without destroying the package software's integrity.

cybervandalism Intentional disruption, defacement, or even destruction of a Web site or corporate information system.

cycle time The total elapsed time from the beginning of a process to its end.

data Streams of raw facts representing events occurring in organizations or the physical environment before they have been organized and arranged into a form that people can understand and use.

data administration A special organizational function for managing the organization's data resources, concerned with information policy, data planning, maintenance of data dictionaries, and data quality standards.

data cleansing Activities for detecting and correcting data in a database or file that are incorrect, incomplete, improperly formatted, or redundant. Also known as data scrubbing.

data definition Specifies the structure of the content of a database.

data dictionary An automated or manual tool for storing and organizing information about the data maintained in a database.

data flow diagram (DFD) Primary tool for structured analysis that graphically illustrates a system's component process and the flow of data between them.

data management software Software used for creating and manipulating lists, creating files and databases to store data, and combining information for reports.

data management technology The software that governs the organization of data on physical storage media.

data manipulation language A language associated with a database management system that end users and programmers use to manipulate data in the database.

data mart A small data warehouse containing only a portion of the organization's data for a specified function or population of users.

data mining Analysis of large pools of data to find patterns and rules that can be used to guide decision making and predict future behavior.

data quality audit A survey and/or sample of files to determine accuracy and completeness of data in an information system.

data visualization Technology for helping users see patterns and relationships in large amounts of data by presenting the data in graphical form.

data warehouse A database, with reporting and query tools, that stores current and historical data extracted from various operational systems and consolidated for management reporting and analysis.

data workers People such as secretaries or bookkeepers who process the organization's paperwork.

database A group of related files.

database administration Refers to the more technical and operational aspects of managing data, including physical database design and maintenance.

database management system (DBMS) Special software to create and maintain a database and enable individual business applications to extract the data they need without having to create separate files or data definitions in their computer programs.

database server A computer in a client/server environment that is responsible for running a DBMS to process SQL statements and perform database management tasks.

decision-support systems (DSS) Information systems at the organization's management level that combine data and sophisticated analytical models or data analysis tools to support semistructured and unstructured decision making.

deep packet inspection (DPI) Technology for managing network traffic by examining data packets, sorting out low-priority data from higher priority business-critical data, and sending packets in order of priority.

demand planning Determining how much product a business needs to make to satisfy all its customers' demands.

denial of service (DoS) attack Flooding a network server or Web server with false communications or requests for services in order to crash the network.

Descartes' rule of change A principle that states that if an action cannot be taken repeatedly, then it is not right to be taken at any time.

design Simon's second stage of decision making, when the individual conceives of possible alternative solutions to a problem.

digital asset management systems Classify, store, and distribute digital objects such as photographs, graphic images, video, and audio content.

digital certificates Attachments to an electronic message to verify the identity of the sender and to provide the receiver with the means to encode a reply.

digital checking Systems that extend the functionality of existing checking accounts so they can be used for online shopping payments.

digital dashboard Displays all of a firm's key performance indicators as graphs and charts on a single screen to provide one-page overview of all the critical measurements necessary to make key executive decisions

digital divide Large disparities in access to computers and the Internet among different social groups and different locations.

digital goods Goods that can be delivered over a digital network.

digital market A marketplace that is created by computer and communication technologies that link many buyers and sellers.

Digital Millennium Copyright Act (DMCA) Adjusts copyright laws to the Internet Age by making it illegal to make, distribute, or use devices that circumvent technology-based protections of copy-righted materials.

digital signature A digital code that can be attached to an electronically transmitted message to uniquely identify its contents and the sender.

digital subscriber line (DSL) A group of technologies providing high-capacity transmission over existing copper telephone lines.

digital video disk (DVD) High-capacity optical storage medium that can store full-length videos and large amounts of data.

digital wallet Software that stores credit card, electronic cash, owner identification, and address information and provides this data automatically during electronic commerce purchase transactions.

direct cutover A risky conversion approach where the new system completely replaces the old one on an appointed day.

disaster recovery planning Planning for the restoration of computing and communications services after they have been disrupted.

disintermediation The removal of organizations or business process layers responsible for certain intermediary steps in a value chain.

disruptive technologies Technologies with disruptive impact on industries and businesses, rendering existing products, services and business models obsolete.

distributed denial-of-service (DDoS) attack Uses numerous computers to inundate and overwhelm a network from numerous launch points.

distributed processing The distribution of computer processing work among multiple computers linked by a communications network.

documentation Descriptions of how an information system works from either a technical or end-user standpoint.

domain name English-like name that corresponds to the unique 32-bit numeric Internet Protocol (IP) address for each computer connected to the Internet.

Domain Name System (DNS) A hierarchical system of servers maintaining a database enabling the conversion of domain names to their numeric IP addresses.

domestic exporter Form of business organization characterized by heavy centralization of corporate activities in the home county of origin.

downtime Period of time in which an information system is not operational.

drill down The ability to move from summary data to lower and lower levels of detail.

DSS database A collection of current or historical data from a number of applications or groups. Can be a small PC database or a massive data warehouse.

DSS software system Collection of software tools that are used for data analysis, such as OLAP tools, datamining tools, or a collection of mathematical and analytical models.

due process A process in which laws are well-known and understood and there is an ability to appeal to higher authorities to ensure that laws are applied correctly.

dynamic pricing Pricing of items based on real-time interactions between buyers and sellers that determine what a item is worth at any particular moment.

e-government Use of the Internet and related technologies to digitally enable government and public sector agencies' relationships with citizens, businesses, and other arms of government.

edge computing Method for distributing the computing load (or work) across many layers of Internet computers in order to minimize response time.

efficient customer response system System that directly links consumer behavior back to distribution, production, and supply chains.

electronic billing presentment and payment systems Systems used for paying routine monthly bills that allow users to view their bills electronically and pay them through electronic funds transfers from banks or credit card accounts.

electronic business (e-business) The use of the Internet and digital technology to execute all the business processes in the enterprise. Includes e-commerce as well as processes for the internal management of the firm and for coordination with suppliers and other business partners.

electronic commerce (e-commerce) The process of buying and selling goods and services electronically involving transactions using the Internet, networks, and other digital technologies.

electronic data interchange (EDI) The direct computer-to-computer exchange between two organizations of standard business transactions, such as orders, shipment instructions, or payments.

electronic mail (e-mail) The computer-to-computer exchange of messages.

electronic records management (ERM) Policies, procedures, and tools for managing the retention, destruction, and storage of electronic records.

employee relationship management (ERM) Software dealing with employee issues that are closely related to CRM, such as setting objectives, employee performance management, performance-based compensation, and employee training.

encryption The coding and scrambling of messages to prevent their being read or accessed without authorization.

end users Representatives of departments outside the information systems group for whom applications are developed.

end-user development The development of information systems by end users with little or no formal assistance from technical specialists.

end-user interface The part of an information system through which the end user interacts with the system, such as on-line screens and commands.

enterprise applications Systems that can coordinate activities, decisions, and knowledge across many different functions, levels, and business units in a firm. Include enterprise systems, supply chain management systems, customer relationship management systems, and knowledge management systems.

enterprise content management systems Help organizations manage structured and semistructured knowledge, providing corporate repositories of documents, reports, presentations, and best practices and capabilities for collecting and organizing e-mail and graphic objects.

enterprise software Set of integrated modules for applications such as sales and distribution, financial accounting, investment management, materials management, production planning, plant maintenance, and human resources that allow data to be used by multiple functions and business processes.

enterprise systems Integrated enterprise-wide information systems that coordinate key internal processes of the firm. Also known as enterprise resource planning (ERP).

enterprise-wide knowledge management systems General-purpose, firmwide systems that collect, store, distribute, and apply digital content and knowledge.

entity A person, place, thing, or event about which information must be kept.

entity-relationship diagram A methodology for documenting databases illustrating the relationship between various entities in the database.

ergonomics The interaction of people and machines in the work environment, including the design of jobs, health issues, and the end-user interface of information systems.

Ethernet The dominant LAN standard at the physical network level, specifying the physical medium to carry signals between computers; access control rules; and a standardized set of bits to carry data over the system.

ethical "no free lunch" rule Assumption that all tangible and intangible objects are owned by someone else, unless there is a specific declaration otherwise, and that the creator wants compensation for this work.

ethics Principles of right and wrong that can be used by individuals acting as free moral agents to make choices to guide their behavior.

evil twins Wireless networks that pretend to be legitimate Wi-Fi networks to entice participants to log on and reveal passwords or credit card numbers.

exchanges Third-party Net marketplaces that are primarily transaction oriented and that connects many buyers and suppliers for spot purchasing.

executive support systems (ESS) Information systems at the organization's strategic level designed to address unstructured decision making through advanced graphics and communications.

expert systems Knowledge-intensive computer programs that capture the expertise of a human in limited domains of knowledge.

Extensible Markup Language (XML) A more powerful and flexible markup language than hypertext markup language (HTML) for Web pages.

extranets Private intranets that are accessible to authorized outsiders.

Fair Information Practices (FIP) A set of principles originally set forth in 1973 that governs the collection and use of information about individuals and forms the basis of most U.S. and European privacy laws.

fault-tolerant computer systems Systems that contain extra hardware, software, and power supply components that can back a system up and keep it running to prevent system failure.

feasibility study As part of the systems analysis process, the way to determine whether the solution is achievable, given the organization's resources and constraints.

feedback Output that is returned to the appropriate members of the organization to help them evaluate or correct input.

fiber-optic cable A fast, light, and durable transmission medium consisting of thin strands of clear glass fiber bound into cables. Data are transmitted as light pulses.

field A grouping of characters into a word, a group of words, or a complete number, such as a person's name or age.

file transfer protocol (FTP) Tool for retrieving and transferring files from a remote computer.

finance and accounting information systems Systems keep track of the firm's financial assets and fund flows.

firewalls Hardware and software placed between an organization's internal network and an external network to prevent outsiders from invading private networks.

FLOPS Stands for floating point operations per second and is a measure of computer processing speed.

foreign key Field in a database table that enables users to find related information in another database table.

formal planning and control tools Improve project management by listing the specific activities that make up a project, their duration, and the sequence and timing of tasks.

fourth-generation languages Programming languages that can be employed directly by end users or less-skilled programmers to develop computer applications more rapidly than conventional programming languages.

franchiser Form of business organization in which a product is created, designed, financed, and initially produced in the home country, but for product-specific reasons relies heavily on foreign personnel for further production, marketing, and human resources.

fuzzy logic Rule-based AI that tolerates imprecision by using nonspecific terms called membership functions to solve problems.

Gantt chart Visually represents the timing, duration, and human resource requirements of project tasks, with each task represented as a horizontal bar whose length is proportional to the time required to complete it.

genetic algorithms Problem-solving methods that promote the evolution of solutions to specified problems using the model of living organisms adapting to their environment.

geographic information systems (GIS) Systems with software that can analyze and display data using digitized maps to enhance planning and decision-making.

gigabyte Approximately one billion bytes.

Gramm-Leach-Bliley Act Requires financial institutions to ensure the security and confidentiality of customer data.

graphical user interface (GUI) The part of an operating system users interact with that uses graphic icons and the computer mouse to issue commands and make selections.

grid computing Applying the resources of many computers in a network to a single problem.

group decision-support system (GDSS) An interactive computer-based system to facilitate the solution to unstructured problems by a set of decision makers working together as a group.

groupware Software that provides functions and services that support the collaborative activities of work groups.

hacker A person who gains unauthorized access to a computer network for profit, criminal mischief, or personal pleasure.

hertz Measure of frequency of electrical impulses per second, with 1 Hertz equivalent to 1 cycle per second.

high-availability computing Tools and technologies ,including backup hardware resources, to enable a system to recover quickly from a crash.

HIPAA Law outlining medical security and privacy rules and procedures for simplifying the administration of healthcare billing and automating the transfer of healthcare data between healthcare providers, payers, and plans.

home page A World Wide Web text and graphical screen display that welcomes the user and explains the organization that has established the page.

hotspots Specific geographic locations in which an access point provides public Wi-Fi network service.

hubs Very simple devices that connect network components, sending a packet of data to all other connected devices.

human resources information systems Systems that maintain employee records, track employee skills, job performance and training, and support planning for employee compensation and career development.

hypertext markup language (HTML) Page description language for creating Web pages and other hypermedia documents.

hypertext transport protocol (HTTP) The communications standard used to transfer pages on the Web. Defines how messages are formatted and transmitted.

identity theft Theft of key pieces of personal information, such as credit card or Social Security numbers, in order to obtain merchandise and services in the name of the victim or to obtain false credentials.

Immanuel Kant's Categorical Imperative A principle that states that if an action is not right for everyone to take it is not right for anyone.

implementation Simon's final stage of decision-making, when the individual puts the decision into effect and reports on the progress of the solution.

inference engine The strategy used to search through the rule base in an expert system; can be forward or backward chaining.

information Data that have been shaped into a form that is meaningful and useful to human beings.

information appliance Device that has been customized to perform a few specialized computing tasks well with minimal user effort.

information asymmetry Situation where the relative bargaining power of two parties in a transaction is determined by one party in the transaction possessing more information essential to the transaction than the other party.

information density The total amount and quality of information available to all market participants, consumers, and merchants

information policy Formal rules governing the maintenance, distribution, and use of information in an organization.

information requirements A detailed statement of the information needs that a new system must satisfy; identifies who needs what information, and when, where, and how the information is needed.

information rights The rights that individuals and organizations have with respect to information that pertains to themselves.

information system Interrelated components working together to collect, process, store, and disseminate information to support decision making, coordination, control, analysis, and visualization in an organization.

information systems department The formal organizational unit that is responsible for the information systems function in the organization.

information systems literacy Broad-based understanding of information systems that includes behavioral knowledge about organizations and individuals using information systems as well as technical knowledge about computers.

information systems managers Leaders of the various specialists in the information systems department.

information systems plan A road map indicating the direction of systems development the rationale, the current situation, the management strategy, the implementation plan, and the budget.

information technology (IT) All the hardware and software technologies that a firm needs to use in order to achieve its business objectives.

information technology (IT) infrastructure Computer hardware, software, data, storage technology, and networks providing a portfolio of shared IT resources for the organization.

informed consent Consent given with knowledge of all the facts needed to make a rational decision.

input The capture or collection of raw data from within the organization or from its external environment for processing in an information system.

input devices Device which gathers data and converts them into electronic form for use by the computer.

instant messaging Chat service that allows participants to create their own private chat channels so that a person can be alerted whenever someone on his or her private list is on-line to initiate a chat session with that particular individual.

intangible benefits Benefits that are not easily quantified; they include more efficient customer service or enhanced decision making.

intellectual property Intangible property created by individuals or corporations that is subject to protections under trade secret, copyright, and patent law.

intelligence The first of Simon's four stages of decision making, when the individual collects information to identify problems occurring in the organization.

intelligent agents Software programs that use a built-in or learned knowledge base to carry out specific, repetitive, and predictable tasks for an individual user, business process, or software application.

intelligent techniques Technologies that aid decision makers by capturing individual and collective knowledge, discovering patterns and behaviors in very large quantities of data, and generating solutions to problems that are too large and complex for human beings to solve on their own.

Internet global network of networks using univeral standards to connect millions of different networks.

Internet Protocol (IP) address Four-part numeric address indicating a unique computer location on the Internet.

Internet service provider (ISP) A commercial organization with a permanent connection to the Internet that sells temporary connections to subscribers.

Internet telephony Technologies that use the Internet Protocol's packet-switched connections for voice service.

Internet2 Research network with new protocols and transmission speeds that provides an infrastructure for supporting high-bandwidth Internet applications.

internetworking The linking of separate networks, each of which retains its own identity, into an interconnected network.

interorganizational system Information systems that automate the flow of information across organizational boundaries and link a company to its customers, distributors, or suppliers.

intranets Internal networks based on Internet and World Wide Web technology and standards.

intrusion detection systems Tools to monitor the most vulnerable points in a network to detect and deter unauthorized intruders.

investment workstations Powerful desktop computers for financial specialists, which are optimized to access and manipulate massive amounts of financial data.

Java An operating system-independent, processor-independent, object-oriented programming language that has become a leading interactive programming environment for the Web.

Joint application design (JAD) Process to accelerate the generation of information requirements by having end users and information systems specialists work together in intensive interactive design sessions.

just-in-time Scheduling system for minimizing inventory by having components arrive exactly at the moment they are needed and finished goods shipped as soon as they leave the assembly line.

key field A field in a record that uniquely identifies instances of that record so that it can be retrieved, updated, or sorted.

key loggers Spyware that records every keystroke made on a computer.

knowledge base Model of human knowledge that is used by expert systems.

knowledge management The set of processes developed in an organization to create, gather, store, maintain, and disseminate the firm's knowledge.

knowledge management systems (KMS) Systems that support the creation, capture, storage, and dissemination of firm expertise and knowledge.

knowledge network systems Online directory for locating corporate experts in well-defined knowledge domains.

knowledge work systems Information systems that aid knowledge workers in the creation and integration of new knowledge in the organization.

knowledge workers People such as engineers or architects who design products or services and create knowledge for the organization.

learning management system (LMS) Tools for the management, delivery, tracking, and assessment of various types of employee learning.

legacy systems System that have been in existence for a long time and that continue to be used to avoid the high cost of replacing or redesigning them.

liability The existence of laws that permit individuals to recover the damages done to them by other actors, systems, or organizations.

Linux Reliable and compactly designed operating system that is an open-source offshoot of UNIX and that can run on many different hardware platforms and is available free or at very low cost.

local area network (LAN) A telecommunications network that requires its own dedicated channels and that encompasses a limited distance, usually one building or several buildings in close proximity.

magnetic disk A secondary storage medium in which data are stored by means of magnetized spots on a hard or floppy disk.

magnetic tape Inexpensive, older secondary-storage medium in which large volumes of information are stored sequentially by means of magnetized and nonmagnetized spots on tape.

mainframe Largest category of computer, used for major business processing.

maintenance Changes in hardware, software, documentation, or procedures to a production system to correct errors, meet new requirements, or improve processing efficiency.

malware Malicious software programs such as computer viruses, worms, and Trojan horses.

managed security service providers (MSSPs) Companies that provide security management services for subscribing clients.

management information systems (MIS) The study of information systems focusing on their use in business and management..

manufacturing and production information systems Systems that deal with the planning, development, and production of products and services and with controlling the flow of production.

market entry costs The cost merchants must pay simply to bring their goods to market.

marketspace A marketplace extended beyond traditional boundaries and removed from a temporal and geographic location.

mashups Composite software applications that depend on high-speed networks, universal communication standards, and open source code and are intended to be greater than the sum of their parts.

mass customization The capacity to offer individually tailored products or services on a large scale.

menu prices Merchants' costs of changing prices.

metropolitan area network (MAN) Network that spans a metropolitan area, usually a city and its major suburbs. Its geographic scope falls between a WAN and a LAN.

microbrowser Web browser software with a small file size that can work with low-memory constraints, tiny screens of handheld wireless devices, and low bandwidth of wireless networks.

micropayment Payment for a very small sum of money, often less
than $10.

microprocessor Very large scale integrated circuit technology that integrates the computer's memory, logic, and control on a single chip.

microwave A high-volume, long-distance, point-to-point transmission in which high-frequency radio signals are transmitted through the atmosphere from one terrestrial transmission station to another.

middle management People in the middle of the organizational hierarchy who are responsible for carrying out the plans and goals of senior management.

middleware Software that connects two disparate applications, allowing them to communicate with each other and to exchange data.

midrange computers Middle-size computers that are capable of supporting the computing needs of smaller organizations or of managing networks of other computers.

minicomputers Middle-range computers used in systems for universities, factories, or research laboratories.

MIS audit Identifies all the controls that govern individual information systems and assesses their effectiveness.

mobile commerce (m-commerce) The use of wireless devices, such as cell phones or handheld digital information appliances, to conduct both business-to-consumer and business-to-business e-commerce transactions over the Internet.

model An abstract representation that illustrates the components or relationships of a phenomenon.

modem A device for translating a computer's digital signals into analog form for transmission over ordinary telephone lines, or for translating analog signals back into digital form for reception by a computer.

mouse Handheld input device with point-and-click capabilities that is usually connected to the computer by a cable.

multicore processor Integrated circuit to which two or more processors have been attached for enhanced performance, reduced power consumption and more efficient simultaneous processing of multiple tasks.

multinational Form of business organization that concentrates financial management and control out of a central home base while decentralizing

MP3 (MPEG3) Standard for compressing audio files for transfer over the Internet.

nanotechnology Technology that builds structures and processes based on the manipulation of individual atoms and molecules.

natural languages Nonprocedural languages that enable users to communicate with the computer using conversational commands resembling human speech.

net marketplaces Digital marketplaces based on Internet technology linking many buyers to many sellers.

network The linking of two or more computers to share data or resources, such as a printer.

network address translation (NAT) Conceals the IP addresses of the organization's internal host computer(s) to prevent sniffer programs outside the firewall from ascertaining them and using that information to penetrate internal systems.

network economics Model of strategic systems at the industry level based on the concept of a network where adding another participant entails zero marginal costs but can create much larger marginal gains.

network interface card (NIC) Expansion card inserted into a computer to enable it to connect to a network.

network operating system (NOS) Special software that routes and manages communications on the network and coordinates network resources.

networking and telecommunications technology Physical devices and software that link various pieces of hardware and transfer data from one physical location to another.

neural networks Hardware or software that attempts to emulate the processing patterns of the biological brain.

nonobvious relationship awareness (NORA) Technology that can find obscure hidden connections between people or other entities by analyzing information from many different sources to correlate relationships.

normalization The process of creating small stable data structures from complex groups of data when designing a relational database.

n-tier client/server architecture Client/server arrangement which balances the work of the entire network over multiple levels of servers.

object Software building block that combines data and the procedures acting on the data.

object-oriented DBMS An approach to data management that stores both data and the procedures acting on the data as objects that can be automatically retrieved and shared; the objects can contain multimedia.

object-oriented development Approach to systems development that uses the object as the basic unit of systems analysis and design. The system is modeled as a collection o objects and the relationship between them.

object-relational DBMS A database management system that combines the capabilities of a relational DBMS for storing traditional information and the capabilities of an object-oriented DBMS for storing graphics and multimedia.

Office 2007 Microsoft desktop software suite with capabilities for supporting collaborative work on the Web or incorporating information from the Web into documents.

offshore software outsourcing Outsourcing systems development work or maintenance of existing systems to external vendors in another country.

on-demand computing Firms off-loading peak demand for computing power to remote, large-scale data processing centers, investing just enough to handle average processing loads and paying for only as much additional computing power as they need. Also called utility computing.

online analytical processing (OLAP) Capability for manipulating and analyzing large volumes of data from multiple perspectives.

online processing A method of collecting and processing data in which transactions are entered directly into the computer system and processed immediately.

online transaction processing Transaction processing mode in which transactions entered on-line are immediately processed by the computer.

open source software Software that provides free access to its program code, allowing users to modify the program code to make improvements or fix errors.

operating system The system software that manages and controls the activities of the computer.

operational CRM Customer-facing applications, such as sales force automation, call center and customer service support, and marketing automation.

operational management People who monitor the day-to-day activities of the organization.

opt-in Model of informed consent permitting prohibiting an organization from collecting any personal information unless the individual specifically takes action to approve information collection and use.

opt-out Model of informed consent permitting the collection of personal information until the consumer specifically requests that the data not be collected.

organizational impact analysis Study of the way a proposed system will affect organizational structure, attitudes, decision making, and operations.

output The distribution of processed information to the people who will use it or to the activities for which it will be used.

output devices Device that displays data after they have been processed.

outsourcing The practice of contracting computer center operations, telecommunications networks, or applications development to external vendors.

P3P Industry standard designed to give users more control over personal information gathered on Web sites they visit. Stands for Platform for Privacy Preferences Project.

packet filtering Examines selected fields in the headers of data packets flowing back and forth between the trusted network and the Internet

packet switching Technology that breaks messages into small, fixed bundles of data and routes them in the most economical way through any available communications channel.

parallel processing Type of processing in which more than one instruction can be processed at a time by breaking down a problem into smaller parts and processing them simultaneously with multiple processors.

parallel strategy A safe and conservative conversion approach where both the old system and its potential replacement are run together for a time until everyone is assured that the new one functions correctly.

partner relationship management (PRM) Automation of the firm's relationships with its selling partners using customer data and analytical tools to improve coordination and customer sales.

patches Small pieces of software that repair flaws in programs without disturbing the proper operation of the software.

patent A legal document that grants the owner an exclusive monopoly on the ideas behind an invention for 17 years; designed to ensure that inventors of new machines or methods are rewarded for their labor while making widespread use of their inventions.

peer-to-peer Network architecture that gives equal power to all computers on the network; used primarily in small networks.

people perspective Consideration of the firm's management, as well as employees as individuals and their interrelationships in workgroups.

personal computer (PC) Small desktop or portable computer.

Personal digital assistants (PDA) Small, pen-based, handheld computers with built-in wireless telecommunications capable of entirely digital communications transmission.

personal-area networks (PANs) Computer networks used for communication among digital devices (including telephones and PDAs) that are close to one person.

personalization Ability of merchants to target their marketing messages to specific individuals by adjusting the message to a person's name, interests, and past purchases.

PERT chart Graphically depicts project tasks and their interrelationships, showing the specific activities that must be completed before others can start.

pharming Phishing technique that redirects users to a bogus Web page, even when the individual types the correct Web page address into his or her browser.

phased approach Introduces the new system in stages either by functions or by organizational units.

phishing A form of spoofing involving setting up fake Web sites or sending e-mail messages that look like those of legitimate businesses to ask users for confidential personal data.

pilot study A strategy to introduce the new system to a limited area of the organization until it is proven to be fully functional; only then can the conversion to the new system across the entire organization take place.

pivot table Spreadsheet tool for reorganizing and summarizing two or more dimensions of data in a tabular format.

podcasting Method of publishing audio broadcasts via the Internet, allowing subscribing users to download audio files onto their personal computers or portable music players.

pop-up ads Ads that open automatically and do not disappear until the user clicks on them.

portal Web interface for presenting integrated personalized content from a variety of sources. Also refers to a Web site service that provides an initial point of entry to the Web.

portfolio analysis An analysis of the portfolio of potential applications within a firm to determine the risks and benefits, and to select among alternatives for information systems.

predictive analysis Use of datamining techniques, historical data, and assumptions about future conditions to predict outcomes of events.

presentation graphics Software to create professional-quality graphics presentations that can incorporate charts, sound, animation, photos, and video clips.

price discrimination Selling the same goods, or nearly the same goods, to different targeted groups at different prices.

price transparency the ease with which consumers can find out the variety of prices in a market.

primary activities Activities most directly related to the production and distribution of a firm's products or services.

primary key Unique identifier for all the information in any row of a database table.

privacy The claim of individuals to be left alone, free from surveillance or interference from other individuals, organizations, or the state.

private exchange Another term for a private industrial network.

private industrial networks Web-enabled networks linking systems of multiple firms in an industry for the coordination of trans-organizational business processes.

process specifications Describe the logic of the processes occurring within the lowest levels of a data flow diagram.

processing The conversion, manipulation, and analysis of raw input into a form that is more meaningful to humans.

procurement Sourcing goods and materials, negotiating with suppliers, paying for goods, and making delivery arrangements.

product differentiation Competitive strategy for creating brand loyalty by developing new and unique products and services that are not easily duplicated by competitors.

production The stage after the new system is installed and the conversion is complete; during this time the system is reviewed by users and technical specialists to determine how well it has met its original goals.

production or service workers People who actually produce the products or services of the organization.

profiling The use of computers to combine data from multiple sources and create electronic dossiers of detailed information on individuals.

program Series of instructions for the computer.

programmers Highly trained technical specialists who write computer software instructions.

programming The process of translating the system specifications prepared during the design stage into program code.

project A planned series of related activities for achieving a specific business objective.

project management Application of knowledge, skills, tools and techniques to achieve specific targets within specified budget and time constraints.

protocol A set of rules and procedures that govern transmission between the components in a network.

prototyping The process of building an experimental system quickly and inexpensively for demonstration and evaluation so that users can better determine information requirements.

public key encryption Uses two keys one shared (or public) and one private.

public key infrastructure (PKI) System for creating public and private keys using a certificate authority (CA) and digital certificates for authentication.

pull-based model Supply chain driven by actual customer orders or purchases so that members of the supply chain produce and deliver only what customers have ordered.

pure-play Business models based purely on the Internet.

push-based model Supply chain driven by production master schedules based on forecasts or best guesses of demand for products, and products are "pushed" to customers.

quality Product or service's conformance to specifications and standards.

query languages Software tools that provide immediate online answers to requests for information that are not predefined.

radio frequency identification (RFID) Technology using tiny tags with embedded microchips containing data about an item and its location to transmit short-distance radio signals to special RFID readers that then pass the data on to a computer for processing.

Rapid application development (RAD) Process for developing systems in a very short time period by using prototyping, fourth-generation tools, and close teamwork among users and systems specialists.

rationalization of procedures The streamlining of standard operating procedures, eliminating obvious bottlenecks, so that automation makes operating procedures more efficient.

reach Measurement of how many people a business can connect with and how many products it can offer those people.

records Groups of related fields.

recovery-oriented computing Computer systems designed to recover rapidly when mishaps occur.

referential integrity Rules to ensure that relationships between coupled database tables remain consistent.

relational database A type of logical database model that treats data as if they were stored in two-dimensional tables. It can relate data stored in one table to data in another as long as the two tables share a common data element.

repetitive stress injury (RSI) Occupational disease that occurs when muscle groups are forced through repetitive actions with high-impact loads or thousands of repetitions with low-impact loads.

Request for Proposal (RFP) A detailed list of questions submitted to vendors of software or other services to determine how well the vendor's product can meet the organization's specific requirements.

responsibility Accepting the potential costs, duties, and obligations for the decisions one makes.

richness Measurement of the depth and detail of information that a business can supply to the customer as well as information the business collects about the customer.

ring networks A network topology in which all computers are linked by a closed loop in a manner that passes data in one direction from one computer to another.

ringtones Digitized snippets of music that play on mobile phones when a user receives or places a call.

risk assessment Determining the potential frequency of the occurrence of a problem and the potential damage if the problem were to occur. Used to determine the cost/benefit of a control.

Risk Aversion Principle Principle that one should take the action that produces the least harm or incurs the least cost.

router Specialized communications processor that forwards packets of data from one network to another network.

RSS Technology using aggregator software to pull content from Web sites and feed it automatically to subscribers' computers.

SaaS (Software as a Service) Services for delivering and providing access to software remotely as a Web-based service.

safe harbor Private self-regulating policy and enforcement mechanism that meets the objectives of government regulations but does not involve government regulation or enforcement.

sales and marketing information systems Systems that help the firm identify customers for the firm's products or services, develop products and services to meet their needs, promote these products and services, sell the products and services, and provide ongoing customer support.

Sarbanes-Oxley Act Law passed in 2002 that imposes responsibility on companies and their management to protect investors by safeguarding the accuracy and integrity of financial information that is used internally and released externally.

satellites The transmission of data using orbiting satellites that serve as relay stations for transmitting microwave signals over very long distances.

scalability The ability of a computer, product, or system to expand to serve a larger number of users without breaking down.

scope Defines what work is or is not included in a project.

scoring model A quick method for deciding among alternative systems based on a system of ratings for selected objectives.

search costs The time and money spent locating a suitable product and determining the best price for that product.

search engine marketing Use of search engines to deliver sponsored links, for which advertisers have paid, in search engine results.

search engines Tools for locating specific sites or information on the Internet.

secondary storage Relatively long term, nonvolatile storage of data outside the CPU and primary storage.

Secure Hypertext Transfer Protocol (S-HTTP) Protocol used for encrypting data flowing over the Internet; limited to individual messages.

Secure Sockets Layer (SSL) Enables client and server computers to manage encryption and decryption activities as they communicate with each other during a secure Web session.

security Policies, procedures, and technical measures used to prevent unauthorized access, alteration, theft, or physical damage to information systems.

security policy Statements ranking information risks, identifying acceptable security goals, and identifying the mechanisms for achieving these goals.

Semantic web Collaborative effort led by the World Wide Web Consortium to make Web searching more efficient by reducing the amount of human involvement in searching for and processing web information.

semistructured decisions Decisions in which only part of the problem has a clear-cut answer provided by an accepted procedure.

semistructured knowledge Information in the form of less structured objects, such as e-mail, chat room exchanges, videos, graphics, brochures, or bulletin boards.

senior management People occupying the topmost hierarchy in an organization who are responsible for making long-range decisions.

sensitivity analysis Models that ask "what-if" questions repeatedly to determine the impact of changes in one or more factors on the outcomes.

sensors Devices that collect data directly from the environment for input into a computer system.

server Computer specifically optimized to provide software and other resources to other computers over a network.

service level agreement (SLA) Formal contract between customers and their service providers that defines the specific responsibilities of the service provider and the level of service expected by the customer.

service-oriented architecture (SOA) Software architecture of a firm built on a collection of software programs that communicate with each other to perform assigned tasks to create a working software application.

service platform Integration of multiple applications from multiple business functions or business units to deliver a seamless experience for the customer, employee, manager, or business partner.

shopping bots Software with varying levels of built-in intelligence to help electronic commerce shoppers locate and evaluate products or service they might wish to purchase.

six sigma A specific measure of quality, representing 3.4 defects per million opportunities; used to designate a set of methodologies and techniques for improving quality and reducing costs.

smart card A credit-card-size plastic card that stores digital information and that can be used for electronic payments in place of cash.

smartphones Wireless phones with voice, messaging, scheduling, e-mail, and Internet capabilities.

sniffer A type of eavesdropping program that monitors information traveling over a network.

social bookmarking Capability for users to save their bookmarks to Web pages on a public Web site and tag these bookmarks with keywords to organize documents and share information with others.

social engineering Tricking people into revealing their passwords by pretending to be legitimate users or members of a company in need of information.

social networking Online community for expanding users' business or social contacts by making connections through their mutual business or personal connections.

social shopping Use of Web sites featuring user-created Web pages to share knowledge about items of interest to other shoppers.

software package A prewritten, precoded, commercially available set of programs that eliminates the need to write software programs for certain functions.

spam Unsolicited commercial e-mail.

spamming A form of abuse in which thousands and even hundreds of thousands of unsolicited e-mail and electronic messages are sent out, creating a nuisance for both businesses and individual users.

spoofing Misrepresenting one's identity on the Internet or redirecting a Web link to an address different from the intended one, with the site masquerading as the intended destination.

spreadsheet Software displaying data in a grid of columns and rows, with the capability of easily recalculating numerical data.

spyware Technology that aids in gathering information about a person or organization without their knowledge.

star network A network topology in which all computers and other devices are connected to a central host computer. All communications between network devices must pass through the host computer.

stateful inspection Provides additional security by determining whether packets are part of an ongoing dialogue between a sender and a receiver.

Storage area networks (SAN) High-speed networks dedicated to storage that connects different kinds of storage devices, such as tape libraries and disk arrays so they can be shared by multiple servers.

stored value payment systems Systems enabling consumers to make instant on-line payments to merchants and other individuals based on value stored in a digital account.

strategic information system Computer system at any level of the organization that changes goals, operations, products, services, or environmental relationships to help the organization gain a competitive advantage.

strategic transitions A movement from one level of sociotechnical system to another. Often required when adopting strategic systems that demand changes in the social and technical elements of an organization.

structure chart System documentation showing each level of design, the relationship among the levels, and the overall place in the design structure; can document one program, one system, or part of one program.

structured Refers to the fact that techniques are carefully drawn up, step by step, with each step building on a previous one.

structured decisions Decisions that are repetitive, routine, and have a definite procedure for handling them.

structured knowledge Knowledge in the form of structured documents and reports.

structured knowledge systems Systems for organizing structured knowledge in a repository where it can be accessed throughout the organization. Also known as content management systems.

Structured Query Language (SQL) The standard data manipulation language for relational database management systems.

supercomputer Highly sophisticated and powerful computer that can perform very complex computations extremely rapidly.

supply chain Network of organizations and business processes for procuring materials, transforming raw materials into intermediate and finished products, and distributing the finished products to customers.

supply chain execution systems Systems to manage the flow of products through distribution centers and warehouses to ensure that products are delivered to the right locations in the most efficient manner.

supply chain management (SCM) systems Information systems that automate the flow of information between a firm and its suppliers in order to optimize the planning, sourcing, manufacturing, and delivery of products and services.

supply chain planning systems Systems that enable a firm to generate demand forecasts for a product and to develop sourcing and manufacturing plans for that product.

support activities Activities that make the delivery of a firm's primary activities possible. Consist of the organization's infrastructure, human resources, technology, and procurement.

switch Device to connect network components that has more intelligence than a hub and can filter and forward data to a specified destination.

switching costs The expense a customer or company incurs in lost time and expenditure of resources when changing from one supplier or system to a competing supplier or system.

syndicators Business aggregating content or applications from multiple sources, packaging them for distribution, and reselling them to third-party Web sites.

system software Generalized programs that manage the computer's resources, such as the central processor, communications links, and peripheral devices.

system testing Tests the functioning of the information system as a whole in order to determine if discrete modules will function together as planned.

systems analysis The analysis of a problem that the organization will try to solve with an information system.

systems analysts Specialists who translate business problems and requirements into information requirements and systems, acting as liaison between the information systems department and the rest of the organization.

systems design Details how a system will meet the information requirements as determined by the systems analysis.

systems development The activities that go into producing an information systems solution to an organizational problem or opportunity.

systems development life cycle (SDLC) A traditional methodology for developing an information system that partitions the systems development process into formal stages that must be completed sequentially with a very formal division of labor between end users and information systems specialists.

systems integration Ensuring that a new infrastructure works with a firm's older, so-called legacy systems and that the new elements of the infrastructure work with one another.

T lines High-speed data lines leased from communications providers, such as T-1 lines (with a transmission capacity of 1.544 Mbps).

tacit knowledge Expertise and experience of organizational members that has not been formally documented.

tangible benefits Benefits that can be quantified and assigned a monetary value; they include lower operational costs and increased cash flows.

taxonomy Method of classifying things according to a predetermined system.

technostress Stress induced by computer use; symptoms include aggravation, hostility toward humans, impatience, and enervation.

terabyte Approximately one trillion bytes.

test plan Prepared by the development team in conjunction with the users; it includes all of the preparations for the series of tests to be performed on the system.

testing The exhaustive and thorough process that determines whether the system produces the desired results under known conditions.

token Physical device, similar to an identification card, that is designed to prove the identity of a single user.

topology The way in which the components of a network are connected.

Total cost of ownership (TCO) Designates the total cost of owning technology resources, including initial purchase costs, the cost of hardware and software upgrades, maintenance, technical support, and training.

Total quality management (TQM) A concept that makes quality control a responsibility to be shared by all people in an organization.

touch point Method of firm interaction with a customer, such as telephone, e-mail, customer service desk, conventional mail, or point-of-purchase.

touch screen Device that allows users to enter limited amounts of data by touching the surface of a sensitized video display monitor with a finger or a pointer.

trade secret Any intellectual work or product used for a business purpose that can be classified as belonging to that business, provided it is not based on information in the public domain.

transaction costs The costs of participating in a market.

transaction processing systems (TPS) Computerized systems that perform and record the daily routine transactions necessary to conduct the business; they serve the organization's operational level.

Transmission Control Protocol/Internet Protocol (TCP/IP) Dominant model for achieving connectivity among different networks. Provides a universally agree-on method for breaking up digital messages into packets, routing them to the proper addresses, and then reassembling them into coherent messages.

transnational Truly global form of business organization where value-added activities are managed from a global perspective without reference to national borders, optimizing sources of supply and demand and local competitive advantage.

Trojan horse A software program that appears legitimate but contains a second hidden function that may cause damage.

tuples Rows or records in a relational database.

twisted wire A transmission medium consisting of pairs of twisted copper wires; used to transmit analog phone conversations but can be used for data transmission.

Uniform Resource Locator (URL) The address of a specific resource on the Internet.

unit testing The process of testing each program separately in the system. Sometimes called program testing.

UNIX Operating system for all types of computers, which is machine independent and supports multiuser processing, multitasking, and networking. Used in high-end workstations and servers.

unstructured decisions Nonroutine decisions in which the decision maker must provide judgment, evaluation, and insights into the problem definition; there is no agreed-upon procedure for making such decisions.

up-selling Marketing higher-value products or services to new or existing customers.

user interface The part of the information system through which the end user interacts with the system; type of hardware and the series of on-screen commands and responses required for a user to work with the system.

user-designer communications gap The difference in backgrounds, interests, and priorities that impede communication and problem solving among end users and information systems specialists.

Utilitarian Principle Principle that assumes one can put values in rank order and understand the consequences of various courses of action.

utility computing Model of computing in which companies pay only for the information technology resources they actually use during a specified time period. Also called on-demand computing or usage-based pricing.

value chain model Model that highlights the primary or support activities that add a margin of value to a firm's products or services where information systems can best be applied to achieve a competitive advantage.

value web Customer-driven network of independent firms who use information technology to coordinate their value chains to collectively produce a product or service for a market.

virtual company Uses networks to link people, assets, and ideas, enabling it to ally with other companies to create and distribute products and services without being limited by traditional organizational boundaries or physical locations.

Virtual private network (VPN) A secure connection between two points across the Internet to transmit corporate data. Provides a low-cost alternative to a private network.

Virtual Reality Modeling Language (VRML) A set of specifications for interactive three-dimensional modeling on the World Wide Web.

virtual reality systems Interactive graphics software and hardware that create computer-generated simulations that provide sensations that emulate real-world activities.

virtualization Presenting a set of computing resources so that they can all be accessed in ways that are not restricted by physical configuration or geographic location.

visual programming language Allows users to manipulate graphic or iconic elements to create programs.

Voice over IP (VoIP) Facilities for managing the delivery of voice information using the Internet Protocol (IP).

voice portals Capability for accepting voice commands for accessing Web content, e-mail, and other electronic applications from a cell phone or standard telephone and for translating responses to user requests for information back into speech for the customer.

war driving An eavesdropping technique in which eavesdroppers drive by buildings or park outside and try to intercept wireless network traffic.

Web 2.0 Second-generation, interactive Internet-based services that enable people to collaborate, share information, and create new services online, including mashups, blogs, RSS, and wikis.

Web browsers Easy-to-use software tool for accessing the World Wide Web and the Internet.

Web bugs Tiny graphic files embedded in e-mail messages and Web pages that are designed to monitor online Internet user behavior.

Web hosting service Company with large Web server computers to maintain the Web sites of fee-paying subscribers.

Web server Software that manages requests for Web pages on the computer where they are stored and that delivers the page to the user's computer.

Web services Set of universal standards using Internet technology for integrating different applications from different sources without time-consuming custom coding. Used for linking systems of different organizations or for linking disparate systems within the same organization.

Web site All of the World Wide Web pages maintained by an organization or an individual.

Webmaster The person in charge of an organization's Web site.

Wide area networks (WANs) Telecommunications networks that span a large geographical distance. May consist of a variety of cable, satellite, and microwave technologies.

widget Small software program that can be added to a Web page or placed on the desktop to provide additional functionality.

Wi-Fi Standards for Wireless Fidelity and refers to the 802.11 family of wireless networking standards.

wiki Collaborative Web site where visitors can add, delete, or modify content on the site, including the work of previous authors.

WiMax Popular term for IEEE Standard 802.16 for wireless networking over a range of up to 31 miles with a data transfer rate of up to 75 Mbps. Stands for Worldwide Interoperability for Microwave Access.

Windows Server 2003 Most recent Windows operating system for servers.

Windows Vista Microsoft Windows operating system featuring improved security; diagnostics; parental controls; usability; desktop searching, synchronization with mobile devices, cameras, and Internet services; and better support for video and TV.

Windows XP Powerful Windows operating system that provides reliability, robustness, and ease of use for both corporate and home PC users.

wireless portals Portals with content and services optimized for mobile devices to steer users to the information they are most likely to need.

wireless sensor networks (WSNs) Networks of interconnected wireless devices with built-in processing, storage, and radio frequency sensors and antennas that are embedded into the physical environment to provide measurements of many points over large spaces.

Word processing software Software for electronically creating, editing, formatting, and printing documents.

workflow management The process of streamlining business procedures so that documents can be moved easily and efficiently from one location to another.

workstation Desktop computer with powerful graphics and mathematical capabilities and the ability to perform several complicated tasks at once.

World Wide Web A system with universally accepted standards for storing, retrieving, formatting, and displaying information in a networked environment.

worms Independent software programs that propagate themselves to disrupt the operation of computer networks or destroy data and other programs.

References

CHAPTER 1

Benbasat, Izak, and **Robert W. Zmud**. "The Identity Crisis within the IS Discipline: Defining and Communicating the Discipline's Core Properties." *MIS Quarterly* 27, no. 2 (June 2003).

Belson, Ken. "Technology Lets High-End Hotels Anticipate Guests' Whims." *The New York Times* (November 16, 2005).

Brynjolfsson, Erik. "VII Pillars of IT Productivity." *Optimize* (May 2005).

Bureau of Economic Analysis. *National Income and Product Accounts*, 2007. Table 5.3.5. Private Fixed Investment by Type (A) (Q).

Carr, Nicholas. "IT Doesn't Matter." *Harvard Business Review* (May 2003).

Deloitte Research. "The Power of Synchronization." Deloitte Research (2005).

Dutta, Amitava, and **Rahul Roy**. "Offshore Outsourcing: A Dynamic Causal Model of Counteracting Forces." *Journal of Management Information Systems* 22, no. 2 (Fall 2005).

Friedman, Thomas. *The World is Flat*. New York: Farrar, Straus, and Giroux (2006).

Garretson, Rob. "IT Still Matters." *CIO Insight* 81 (May 2007).

Greenspan Alan. "The Revolution in Information Technology." Boston College Conference on the New Economy (March 6, 2000).

Gurbaxani, Vijay, and **Phillippe Jorion**. "The Value of Information Systems Outsourcing Arrangements: An Event Study Analysis." Center for Research on IT and Organizations, University of California, Irvine, Draft (April 2005).

Information Technology Association of America. "The Comprehensive Impact of Offshore Software and IT Services Outsourcing on the U.S. Economy and the IT Industry." *Global Insight* (October, 2005).

Ives, Blake, Joseph S. Valacich, Richard T. Watson, and **Robert W. Zmud**. "What Every Business Student Needs to Know about Information Systems." *CAIS* 9, Article 30 (December 2002).

Lohr, Steve. "At I.B.M., a Smarter Way to Outsource." *The New York Times* (July 5, 2007).

Pew Internet and American Life Project. Daily Internet Activities, Table, 2007. www.pewinternet.org, accessed 8/20/07.

Ross, Jeanne W., and **Peter Weill**. "Six IT Decisions Your IT People Shouldn't Make." *Harvard Business Review* (November 2002).

Tam, Pui-Wing, and **Jackie Range**. "Second Thoughts: Some in Silicon Valley Begin to Sour on India." *The Wall Street Journal* (July 3, 2007).

Triplett, Jack E., and **Barry P. Bosworth**. "Productivity in Services Industries: Trends and Measurement Issues. The Brookings Institution, Washington DC (2003).

Tuomi, Ilkka. "Data Is More Than Knowledge. *Journal of Management Information Systems* 16, no. 3 (Winter 1999-2000).

U.S. Bureau of Labor Statistics. "Tomorrow's Jobs." http://bls.gov/oco/oco2003.htm,

U.S. Census Bureau. *Statistical Abstract of the United States* 2007 .

CHAPTER 2

Anthony, R. N. *Planning and Control Systems: A Framework for Analysis*. Cambridge, MA: Harvard University Press (1965).

eMarketer. "Wireless Subscribers: North America." (March, 2007).

Gruman, Galen. "Strategic HR Integration." *CIO Magazine* (August 15, 2005).

Gupta, Amar. "Expanding the 24-Hour Workplace." *The New York Times* (September 15, 2007).

Hof, Robert D. "The End of Work as You Know It." *Business Week* (August 20, 2007).

Huber, George P. "Organizational Information Systems: Determinants of Their Performance and Behavior." *Management Science* 28, no. 2 (1984).

Johnston, Russell, and **Michael J. Vitale**. "Creating Competitive Advantage with Interorganizational Information Systems." *MIS Quarterly* 12, no. 2 (June 1988).

Johnson, Bradfor, James Manyika, and **Lareina Yee**. "The Next Revolution in Interactions," *McKinsey Quarterly* No. 4 (2005).

Kalakota, Ravi, and **Marcia Robinson**. *e-Business2.0: Roadmap for Success*. Reading, MA: Addison-Wesley (2001).

Lamonica, Martin. "IBM Warms to Social Networking." *ZDNet News* (October 3, 2006).

Malone, Thomas M., Kevin Crowston, Jintae Lee, and **Brian Pentland**. "Tools for Inventing Organizations: Toward a Handbook of Organizational Processes." *Management Science* 45, no. 3 (March 1999).

Mamberto, Carola."Instant Messaging Invades the Office," The Wall Street Journal (July 24, 2007).

Nolan, Richard, and **F. Warren McFarland**. "Information Technology and the Board of Directors." *Harvard Business Review* (October 1, 2005).

Oracle Corporation. "Alcoa Implements Oracle Solution 20% below Projected Cost, Eliminates 43 Legacy Systems." www.oracle.com, accessed August 21, 2005.

Picarelle, Lisa. Planes, Trains, and Automobiles." *Customer Relationship Management* (February 2004).

Radicatti Group. "Taming the Growth of E-Mail: An ROI Analysis." (July, 2007).

SAP. "Alcan Packaging Implements mySAP SCM to Increase Shareholder Value." www.mysap.com, accessed August 20, 2005.

Siebel Systesms. "Saab Cars USA Increases Lead Follow-Up from 38 Percent to 50 Percent with Siebel Automotive." www.siebel.com, accessed October 15, 2005.

Sprague, Ralph H., Jr., and **Eric D. Carlson**. *Building Effective Decision Support Systems*. Englewood Cliffs, NJ: Prentice Hall (1982)

Sullivan, Laurie. "ERPzilla." *Information Week* (July 11, 2005).

Tapscott, Don and **Anthony D. Williams**. "The Global Plant Floor." *Business Week* (March 20, 2007).

Vara, Vauhini. "Wikis at Work." *The Wall Street Journal* (June 18, 2007).

Weill, Peter, and **Jeanne Ross**. "A Matrixed Approach to Designing IT Governance." *MIT Sloan Management Review* 46, no. 2 (Winter 2005).

CHAPTER 3

Basu, Amit and **Steve Muylle**. "How to Plan E-Business Initiatives in Established Companies." *MIT Sloan Management Review* 49, no. 1 (Fall 2007).

Bhatt, Ganesh D., and **Varun Grover**. "Types of Information Technology Capabilities and Their Role in Competitive Advantage." *Journal of Management Information Systems* 22, no.2 (Fall 2005).

Champy, James A. *X-Engineering the Corporation: Reinventing Your Business in the Digital Age*. New York: Warner Books (2002).

Chen, Pei-Yu (Sharon), and **Lorin M. Hitt**. "Measuring Switching Costs and the Determinants of Customer Retention in Internet-Enabled Businesses: A Study of the Online Brokerage Industry." *Information Systems Research* 13, no.3 (September 2002).

Christensen, Clayton. "The Past and Future of Competitive Advantage." *Sloan Management Review* 42, no. 2 (Winter 2001).

Cohen, Beth, Peter Sorrentino, and Walt DuLaney. "Customization Goes into Overdrive." *Optimize* (March 2005).

Copeland, Michael V. "The Mighty Micro-Multinational." *Business 2.0* (July 28, 2006).

Davenport, Thomas H. and Jeanne G. Harris. *Competing on Analytics: The New Science of Winning* Boston: Harvard Business School Press (2007).

———. "Rethinking the Mobile Workforce." *Optimize* (August 2005).

Dean, Jason and Pui-Wing Tam. "The Laptop Trail." *The Wall Street Journal* (June 9, 2005).

Deans, Candace P., and Michael J. Kane. *International Dimensions of Information Systems and Technology.* Boston: PWS-Kent (1992).

Eisenhardt, Kathleen M. "Has Strategy Changed?" *Sloan Management Review* 43, no.2 (Winter 2002).

El Sawy, Omar A. *Redesigning Enterprise Processes for E-Business.* New York: McGraw-Hill (2001).

Ferguson, Glover, Sanjay Mathur, and Baiju Shah. "Evolving from Information to Insight." *MIT Sloan Management Review* 46, no. 2 (Winter 2005).

Fine, Charles H., Roger Vardan, Robert Pethick, and Jamal E-Hout. "Rapid-Response Capability in Value-Chain Design." *Sloan Management Review* 43, no.2 (Winter 2002).

Garretson, Rob. "IS IT Still Strategic?" *CIO Insight* (May 7, 2007).

Hagel, John, III, and John Seeley Brown. "The Shifting Industrial Landscape." *Optimize* (April 2005).

Hammer, Michael. "Process Management and the Future of Six Sigma." *Sloan Management Review* 43, no.2 (Winter 2002).

Hammer, Michael, and James Champy. *Reengineering the Corporation.* New York: HarperCollins (1993).

Holweg, Matthias, and Frits K. Pil. "Successful Build-to-Order Strategies Start with the Customer." *Sloan Management Review* 43, no. 1 (Fall 2001).

Iansiti, Marco, and Roy Levien. "Strategy as Ecology." *Harvard Business Review* (March 2004).

IBM. "Clarion Malaysia Reduces Design Time by 50 Percent with CATIA V5." www.306-ibm.com/software/success, accessed August 31, 2005.

Kauffman, Robert J., and Yu-Ming Wang. "The Network Externalities Hypothesis and Competitive Network Growth." *Journal of Organizational Computing and Electronic Commerce* 12, no. 1 (2002).

King, William R., and Vikram Sethi. "An Empirical Analysis of the Organization of Transnational Information Systems." *Journal of Management Information Systems* 15, no. 4 (Spring 1999).

Koulopoulos, Thomas, and James Champy. "Building Digital Value Chains." *Optimize* (September 2005).

Krishnan, M.S. "Moving Beyond Alignment: IT Grabs the Baton."*Optimize Magazine* (April 2007).

Luftman, Jerry. *Competing in the Information Age: Align in the Sand.* Oxford University Press (2003).

Piccoli, Gabriele, and Blake Ives. "Review: IT-Dependent Strategic Initiatives and Sustained Competitive Advantage: A Review and Synthesis of the Literature." *MIS Quarterly* 29, no. 4 (December 2005).

Porter, Michael E., and Scott Stern. "Location Matters." *Sloan Management Review* 42, no. 4 (Summer 2001).

Porter, Michael. *Competitive Advantage.* New York: Free Press (1985).

———. *Competitive Strategy.* New York: Free Press (1980).

———. "Strategy and the Internet." *Harvard Business Review* (March 2001).

Prahalad, C. K., and Venkatram Ramaswamy. "The New Frontier of Experience Innovation." *MIS Sloan Management Review* 44, no. 4 (Summer 2003).

Ray, Gautam, Waleed A. Muhanna, and Jay B. Barney. "Information Technology and the Performance of the Customer Service Process: A Resource-Based Analysis." *MIS Quarterly* 29, no. 4 (December 2005).

Roche, Edward M. *Managing Information Technology in Multinational Corporations.* New York: Macmillan (1992).

Rowsell-Jones, Andrew, and Mark McDonald. "Giving Global Strategies Local Flavor." *Optimize* (April 2005).

Shapiro, Carl, and Hal R. Varian. Information Rules. Boston: Harvard Business School Press (1999).

Shpilberg, David, Steve Berez, Rudy Puryear, and Sachin Shah. "Avoiding the Alignment Trap in Information Technology." *MIT Sloan Management Review* 49, no. 1 (Fall 2007).

Varian, Hal R. "Technology Levels the Business Playing Field." *The New York Times* (August 25, 2005).

CHAPTER 4

Ante, Spencer E., Heather Green and Catherine Holahan. "The Next Small Thing." *Business Week* (July 23,2007).

Babcock, Charles. "Software Ecosystems." *Information Week* (May 28, 2007).

——— "The Relentless Pace of Linux." Information Week (October 22, 2007).

Carr, Nicholas G. "The End of Corporate Computing." *MIT Sloan Management Review* 46, no.3 (Spring 2005).

Champy, James. "Re-examining the Infrastructure." *Optimize* 23 (September 2003).

Chou, Timothy. "The Reinvention of Software." *Optimize Magazine* (June 2007).

Crosman, Penny. "Wall Street-Style Power." *Information Week* (April 16, 2007).

David, Julie Smith, David Schuff, and Robert St. Louis. "Managing Your IT Total Cost of Ownership." *Communications of the ACM* 45, no. 1 (January 2002).

Dubey, Abhijit and Dilip Wagle. "Delivering Software as a Service." *McKinsey Quarterly* (June 2007).

Eisenberg, Anne. "Do the Mash (Even If You Don't Know All the Steps)." *The New York Times* (September 2, 2007).

Fox, Armando, and David Patterson. "Self-Repairing Computers." *Scientific American* (May 2003.).

Ganek, A. G., and T. A. Corbi. "The Dawning of the Autonomic Computing Era." *IBM Systems Journal* 42, no 1, (2003).

Hagel, John, III, and John Seeley Brown. "Your Next IT Strategy." *Harvard Business Review* (October 2001).

Laudon, Kenneth C. "Data Quality and Due Process in Large Interorganizational Record Systems." *Communications of the ACM* 29 (January 1986a).

Lawton, Christopher. "Linux Shoots for Big League of Servers." The *Wall Street Journal* (June 19, 2007).

Lawton, Christopher and Don Clark. "'Virtualization' is Pumping Up Servers." *The Wall Street Journal* (March 6, 2007).

Loo, Alfred W. "The Future of Peer-to-Peer Computing." *Communications of the ACM* 46, no. 9 (September 2003).

Markoff, John. "Competing as Software Goes to Web." *The New York Times* (June 5, 2007).

——— "Software Via the Internet: Microsoft in 'Cloud' Computing." *The New York Times* (September 3, 2007).

McAfee, Andrew. "Will Web Services Really Transform Collaboration?" *MIT Sloan Management Review* 46, no. 2 (Winter 2005).

McDougall, Paul. "Dow Hires IBM to Take VoIP Project Over from EDS." *Information Week* (August 3, 2004).

National Science Foundation. "Revolutionizing Science and Engineering through Cyberinfrastructure: Report of the National Science Foundation Blue-Ribbon Advisory Panel on Cyberinfrastructure." Washington DC (January 2003).

Patel, Samir, and Suneel Saigal. "When Computers Learn to Talk: A Web Services Primer." *McKinsey Quarterly* no. 1 (2002).

Schuff, David, and Robert St. Louis. "Centralization vs. Decentralization of Application Software." *Communications of the ACM* 44, no. 6 (June 2001).

Tallon, Paul P. and Richard Scannell. "Information Life Cycle Management." *Communications of the ACM* 50, no. 11 (November 2007).

Tatemura, Junichi, et al. "Acceleration of Web Service Workflow Execution through Edge Computing." NEC Laboratories America, Inc. (2003).

Weier, Mary Hayes. "Mashups Start to Make More Sense for Business." *Information Week* (February 19, 2007).

Weill, Peter, and Marianne Broadbent. *Leveraging the New Infrastructure.* Cambridge, MA: Harvard Business School Press (1998).

Weill, Peter, Mani Subramani, and Marianne Broadbent. "Building IT Infrastructure for Strategic Agility." *Sloan Management Review* 44, no. 1 (Fall 2002).

Zaino, Jennifer. "Client-Side Evolution." *Optimize Magazine* 81 (May 2007).

CHAPTER 5

Cappiello, Cinzia, Chiara Francalanci, and Barbara Pernici. "Time-Related Factors of Data Quality in Multichannel Information Systems." *Journal of Management Information Systems* 20, no. 3 (Winter 2004).

Chen, Andrew N. K., Paulo B. Goes, and James R. Marsden. "A Query-Driven Approach to the Design and Management of Flexible Database Systems." *Journal of Management Information Systems* 19, no. 3 (Winter 2002-2003).

Cooper, Brian L., Hugh J. Watson, Barbara H. Wixom, and Dale L. Goodhue. "Data Warehousing Supports Corporate Strategy at First American Corporation." *MIS Quarterly* (December 2000).

DeFelice, Alexander. "What's in a Name?" *Customer Relationship Management* (July 2005).

Eckerson, Wayne W. "Data Quality and the Bottom Line." The Data Warehousing Institute (2002).

Foshay, Neil, Avinandan Mukherjee and Andrew Taylor. "Does Data Warehouse End-User Metadata Add Value? *Communications of the ACM* 50, no. 11 (November 2007).

Goodhue, Dale L., Laurie J. Kirsch, Judith A. Quillard, and Michael D. Wybo. "Strategic Data Planning: Lessons from the Field." *MIS Quarterly* 16, no. 1 (March 1992).

Goodhue, Dale L., Michael D. Wybo, and Laurie J. Kirsch. "The Impact of Data Integration on the Costs and Benefits of Information Systems." *MIS Quarterly* 16, no. 3 (September 1992).

Kim, Yong Jin, Rajiv Kishore, and G. Lawrence Sanders. "From DQ to EQ: Understanding Data Quality in the Context of E-Business Systems. "*Communications of the ACM* 48, no. 10 (October 2005).

Klau, Rick. "Data Quality and CRM." Line56.com, accessed March 4, 2003.

Lee, Yang W., and Diane M. Strong. "Knowing-Why about Data Processes and Data Quality." *Journal of Management Information Systems* 20, no. 3 (Winter 2004).

Loveman, Gary. "Diamonds in the Datamine." *Harvard Business Review* (May 2003).

Hoffer, Jeffrey A., Mary Prescott, and Fred McFadden. *Modern Database Management*, 8th ed. Upper Saddle River, NJ: Prentice Hall (2007).

Morrison, Mike, Joline Morrison, and Anthony Keys. "Integrating Web Sites and Databases." *Communications of the ACM* 45, no.9 (September 2002).

Pierce, Elizabeth M. "Assessing Data Quality with Control Matrices." *Communications of the ACM* 47, no. 2 (February 2004).

Redman, Thomas. "The Impact of Poor Data Quality on the Typical Enterprise." *Communications of the ACM* 41, no. 2 (February 1998).

Stanley, Tim. "High-Stakes Analytics." *Optimize Magazine* (February 2006).

Strong, Diane M., Yang W. Lee, and Richard Y. Wang. "Data Quality in Context." *Communications of the ACM* 40, no. 5 (May 1997).

Totty, Michael. "Making Sense of It All." *The Wall Street Journal* (September 24, 2007).

Wang, Richard Y., Yang W. Lee, Leo L. Pipino, and Diane M. Strong. "Manage Your Information as a Product." *Sloan Management Review* 39, no. 4 (Summer 1998).

CHAPTER 6

Ben Ameur, Walid, and Herve Kerivin. "New Economical Virtual Private Networks." *Communications of the ACM* 46, no 6 (June 2003).

Borland, John. "A Smarter Web." *Technology Review* (March/April 2007).

Chopra, Sunil and Manmohan S. Sodhi. "In Search of RFID's Sweet Spot." *The Wall Street Journal* (March 3, 2007).

Dekleva, Sasha, J.P. Shim, Upkar Varshney, and Geoffrey Knoerzer. "Evolution and Emerging Issues in Mobile Wireless Networks." *Communications of the ACM* 50, No. 6 (June 2007).

Fish, Lynn A. and Wayne C. Forrest. "A Worldwide Look at RFID." *Supply Chain Management Review* (April 1, 2007).

Frauenfelder, Mark. "Sir Tim Berners-Lee." *Technology Review* (October 2004).

Greenemeier, Larry. "RFID Tags Are on the Menu." *Information Week* (February 5, 2007).

Hof, Rob."You Tube Launches Video Ads." *Business Week* (August 21, 2007).

Hoover, J. Nicholas. "Enterprise 2.0." *Information Week* (February 26, 2007).

———"Video on Demand: A Business Priority," *Information Week* (April 2, 2007).

Housel, Tom, and Eric Skopec. *Global Telecommunication Revolution: The Business Perspective.* New York: McGraw-Hill (2001).

Jesdanun, Anick. "Researchers Explore Scrapping Internet."Associated Press (April 13, 2007).

Mamberto, Carola. "Instant Messaging Invades the Office." *The Wall Street Journal* (July 24, 2007).

National Research Council. *The Internet's Coming of Age.* Washington, DC: National Academy Press (2000).

Niemeyer, Alex, Minsok H. Pak, and Sanjay E. Ramaswamy. "Smart Tags for Your Supply Chain." *McKinsey Quarterly* no. 4 (2003).

Pottie, G. J., and W.J Kaiser. "Wireless Integrated Network Sensors." *Communications of the ACM* 43, no. 5 (May 2000).

Talbot, David. "The Internet Is Broken." *Technology Review* (December 2005/January 2006).

Varshney, Upkar, Andy Snow, Matt McGivern, and Christi Howard. "Voice Over IP." *Communications of the ACM* 45, no. 1 (January 2002).

Vascellaro, Jessica E. "What's a Cellphone For?" *The Wall Street Journal* (March 26, 2007).

Vascellaro, Jessica E. and Amol Sharma. "Cellphones Get Wi-Fi, Adding Network Options." *The Wall Street Journal* (June 27, 2007).

Xiao, Bo and Izak Benbasat. "E-Commerce Product Recommendation Agents: Use, Characteristics, and Impact." *MIS Quarterly 31*, no. 1 (March 2007).

CHAPTER 7

Agence France Presse." China Hacked into Pentagon Computer Network." *Yahoo! News* (September 4. 2007).

Anti-Phishing Working Group. "Phishing Activity Trends Report for the Month of May, 2007." (May 2007).www.antiphishing.org, accessed July 24, 2007.

Austin, Robert D., and Christopher A. R. Darby. "The Myth of Secure Computing." *Harvard Business Review* (June 2003).

Australian IT News. "US China Main Sources of Malware." *News Limited* (January 23, 2007).

Baker, Wade H., Loren Paul Rees, and Peter S. Tippett: "Necessary Measures: Metric-Driven Information Security Risk Assessment and Decision Making." *Communications of the ACM* 50, no. 10 (October 2007).

Banham, Russ. "Personal Data for Sale: Calculating the Cost of Security Breaches." *The Wall Street Journal* (June 5, 2007).

Bartholomew, Doug. "IT Controls Yield Greater Productivity-and Revenue," *CIO Insight* (March 22, 2007).

Brandel, Mary."Keeping Secrets in a WikiBlogTubeSpace World." *Computerworld* (March19, 2007).

Brenner, Susan W. "U.S. Cygbercrime Law: Defining Offenses." *Information Systems Frontiers* 6, no. 2 (June 2004).

Byers, Simon, and **Dave Kormann**. "802.11b Access Point Mapping." *Communications of the ACM* 46, no. 5 (May 2003).

Cam Winget, Nancy, Russ Housley, David Wagner, and **Jesse Walker**. "Security Flaws in 802.11b Data Link Protocols." *Communications of the ACM* 46, no. 5 (May 2003).

Cavusoglu, Huseyin, Birendra Mishra, and **Srinivasan Raghunathan**. "A Model for Evaluating IT Security Investments." *Communications of the ACM* 47, no. 7 (July 2004).

D'arcy, John and **Anat Hovav**. "Deterring Internal Information Systems Use." *Communications of the ACM* 50, no. 10 (October 2007).

Delaney, Kevin J. "'Evil Twins' and 'Pharming'." *The Wall Street Journal* (May 17, 2005).

Duvall, Mel. "Virtual Project Yields Real-World Benefits." *Baseline* (August 2007).

Gaudin, Sharon. "Prosecutors: Medco 'Bomber' Would have Wreaked Havoc." *Information Week* (January 1/8, 2007).

———— "Storm Turns into a Hurricane: Is a Botnet Attack Brewing?" *Information Week* (August 6, 2007).

Gaur, Nalneesh and **Bob Kiep**. "Managing Mobile Menaces." *Optimize Magazine* (May 2007).

Giordano, Scott M. "Electronic Evidence and the Law." *Information Systems Frontiers* 6, no. 2 (June 2004).

Housley, Russ, and **William Arbaugh**. "Security Problems in 802.11b Networks." *Communications of the ACM* 46, no. 5 (May 2003).

Ives, Blake, Kenneth R. Walsh, and **Helmut Schneider**. "The Domino Effect of Password Reuse." *Communications of the ACM* 47, no.4 (April 2004).

Jagatic Tom, Nathaniel Johnson, Markus Jakobsson, and **Filippo Menczer**. "Social Phishing." *Communications of the ACM* 50, no. 10 (October 2007).

Keizer, Gregg. "Hacker Scheme Steals Sponsored Google Links" *CSO* (April 26, 2007).

Koch, Christopher. "Don't Maroon Security." *CIO Magazine* (May 15, 2005).

Leyden, John. "The Strange Decline in Computer Worms." *The Register*, www.channelregister.co.uk/2005/03/17/f-secure_websec/, accessed March 17, 2005.

Martin, Richard. "RIM Service Outage Leads to 'BlankBerrys' and Questions." *Information Week* (April 23, 2007).

McDougall, Paul. "High Cost of Data Loss." *Information Week* (March 20,2006).

Mercuri, Rebeca T. "Analyzing Security Costs." *Communications of the ACM* 46, no. 6 (June 2003).

Mercuri, Rebecca T. "The HIPAA-potamus in Health Care Data Security." *Communications of the ACM* 47, no. 7 (July 2004).

Mitchell, Dan. "It's Here: It's There; It's Spyware." *The New York Times* (May 20, 2006).

Newman, Robert. *Enterprise Security*. Upper Saddle River, NJ: Prentice Hall (2003).

OpenDNS. "Phishtank Annual Report," OpenDNS Corporation, October 9, 2007.

Panko, Raymond R. *Corporate Computer and Network Security*. Upper Saddle River, NJ: Pearson Prentice Hall (2004).

Richmond, Riva. "A New Battleground for Computer Security." *The Wall Street Journal* (March 6, 2007).

Rivlin, Gary. "Purloined Lives." *The New York Times* (March 17, 2005).

Roberts, Paul. "Fake Microsoft Security Trojan on the Loose, Antivirus Firm Says," ID News Service (April 8, 2005).

Robertson, Jordan. "Hackers: Social Networking Sites Flawed." Associated Press (August 3, 2007).

Roche, Edward M., and **George Van Nostrand**. *Information Systems, Computer Crime and Criminal Justice*. New York: Barraclough Ltd. (2004).

Schmidt, Howard. "Cyber Anxiety." *Optimize Magazine* (May 2007).

Schwerha, Joseph J., IV. "Cybercrime: Legal Standards Governing the Collection of Digital Evidence." *Information Systems Frontiers* 6, no. 2 (June 2004).

Secure Computing. "White Paper: In Today's Web 2.0 Environment, Proactive Security is Paramount. Are You Protected?" (2007).

Shukla, Sudhindra, and **Fiona Fui-Hoon Nah**. "Web Browsing and Spyware Intrusion." *Communications of the ACM* 48, no. 8 (August 2005).

Software World. "U.S. Consumers Losing Billions in Cyber Attacks." (September 1, 2006).

Stempel, Jonathan. "U.S. Identity Theft Losses Fall: Study." Reuters (February 1, 2007).

Straub, Detmar W., and **Richard J. Welke**. "Coping with Systems Risk: Security Planning Models for Management Decision Making." *MIS Quarterly* 22, no. 4 (December 1998).

Symantec, "Symantec Internet Security Report," Volume XI, Symantec Corporation, (March, 2007).

Thompson, Roger. "Why Spyware Poses Multiple Threats to Security." *Communications of the ACM* 48, no. 8 (August 2005).

Thomson, Iain. "Akamai Investigates Denial of Service Attack." vunet.com, accessed June 17, 2004.

Vara, Vauhini. "Lurking in the Shadows." *The Wall Street Journal*, Technology Report (July 18, 2005).

Vaas,Lisa. "The Final 'Final'Nail in WEP's Coffin?" *EWeek* (April 5, 2007).

Volonino, Linda., Reynaldo Anzaldua, and **Jana Godwin**: *Computer Forensics: Principles and Practices*. Upper Saddle River, NJ: Prentice Hall (2007).

Volonino, Linda, and **Stephen R. Robinson**. *Principles and Practices of Information Security*. Upper Saddle River, NJ: Prentice Hall (2004).

Warkentin, Merrill, Xin Luo, and **Gary F. Templeton**. "A Framework for Spyware Assessement." *Communications of the ACM* 48, no. 8 (August 2005).

Westerman, George. *IT Risk: Turning Business Threats into Competitive Advantage*. Harvard Business School Publishing (2007) www.itl.nist.gov/div897/docs/samate.html, accessed August 1, 2005.

Watson, Brian P. "Botnets: How they Attack and How They Can Be Defeated." *Baseline Magazine* (June 2007).

White, Bobby. "A Question of Priorities." *The Wall Street Journal* (July 30, 2007).

CHAPTER 8

Anderson, James C., and **James A. Narus**. "Selectively Pursuing More of Your Customer's Business." *MIT Sloan Management Review* 44, no. 3 (Spring 2003).

D'Avanzo, Robert, Hans von Lewinski, and **Luk N. Van Wassenhove**. "The Link between Supply Chain and Financial Performance." *Supply Chain Management Review* (November 1, 2003).

Davenport, Thomas H. *Mission Critical: Realizing the Promise of Enterprise Systems*. Boston: Harvard Business School Press (2000).

————. "Putting the Enterprise into Enterprise Systems." *Harvard Business Review* (July-August 1998).

Day, George S. "Creating a Superior Customer-Relating Capability." *MIT Sloan Management Review* 44, no. 3 (Spring 2003).

Ferrer, Jaume, Johan Karlberg, and **Jamie Hintlian**."Integration: The Key to Global Success." *Supply Chain Management Review* (March 1, 2007).

Fleisch, Elgar, Hubert Oesterle, and **Stephen Powell**. "Rapid Implementation of Enterprise Resource Planning Systems." *Journal of Organizational Computing and Electronic Commerce* 14, no. 2 (2004).

Garber, Randy and **Suman Sarkar**. "Want a More Flexible Supply Chain?" *Supply Chain Management Review* (January 1, 2007).

Goodhue, Dale L., Barbara H. Wixom, and **Hugh J. Watson**. "Realizing Business Benefits through CRM: Hitting the Right Target in the Right Way." *MIS Quarterly Executive* 1, no. 2 (June 2002).

Gosain, Sanjay, Arvind Malhotra, and **Omar A. ElSawy**. "Coordinating for Flexibility in E-Business Supply Chains." *Journal of Management Information Systems* 21, no. 3 (Winter 2004–2005).

Handfield, Robert B. and **Ernest L. Nichols**. *Supply Chain Redesign: Transforming Supply Chains into Integrated Value Systems*. Financial Times Press (2002).

Hitt, Lorin, D. J. Wu, and **Xiaoge Zhou**. "Investment in Enterprise Resource Planning: Business Impact and Productivity Measures." *Journal of Management Information Systems* 19, no. 1 (Summer 2002).

Jaiswal. M. P. "Implementing ERP Systems." *Dataquest* (June 30, 2003).

Kalakota, Ravi, and **Marcia Robinson**. *E-Business 2.0*. Boston: Addison-Wesley (2001).

———. *Services Blueprint: Roadmap for Execution*. Boston: Addison-Wesley (2003).

Kanakamedala, Kishore, Glenn Ramsdell, and **Vats Srivatsan**. "Getting Supply Chain Software Right." *McKinsey Quarterly* no. 1 (2003).

Kopczak, Laura Rock, and **M. Eric Johnson**. "The Supply-Chain Management Effect." *MIT Sloan Management Review* 44, no. 3 (Spring 2003).

Lee, Hau. "The Triple-A Supply Chain." *Harvard Business Review* (October 2004).

Lee, Hau, L., V. Padmanabhan, and **Seugin Whang**. "The Bullwhip Effect in Supply Chains." *Sloan Management Review* (Spring 1997).

Liang, Huigang, Nilesh Sharaf, Quing Hu, and **Yajiong Xue**. "Assimilation of Enterprise Systems: The Effect of Institutional Pressures and the Mediating Role of Top Management." *MIS Quarterly* 31, no. 1 (March 2007).

Malhotra, Arvind, Sanjay Gosain, and **Omar A. El Sawy**. "Absorptive Capacity Configurations in Supply Chains: Gearing for Partner-Enabled Market Knowledge Creation." *MIS Quarterly* 29, no. 1 (March 2005).

Maylett, Tracy and **Kate Vitasek**. "For Closer Collaboration, Try Education." *Supply Chain Management Review* (January 1, 2007).

Rai, Arun, Ravi Patnayakuni, and **Nainika Seth**. "Firm Performance Impacts of Digitally Enabled Supply Chain Integration Capabilities." *MIS Quarterly* 30 No. 2 (June 2006).

Ranganathan, C. and **Carol V. Brown**. "ERP Iinvestments and the Market Value of Firms: Toward an Understanding of Influential ERP Project Variables." *Information Systems Research* 17, No. 2 (June 2006).

Rayport, Jeffrey F. "Who Knows the Customer Best?" *Optimize* (March 2005).

Robey, Daniel, Jeanne W. Ross, and **Marie-Claude Boudreau**. "Learning to Implement Enterprise Systems: An Exploratory Study of the Dialectics of Change." *Journal of Management Information Systems* 19, no. 1 (Summer 2002).

Scott, Judy E., and **Iris Vessey**. "Managing Risks in Enterprise Systems Implementations." *Communications of the ACM* 45, no. 4 (April 2002).

Whiting, Rick. "You Look Marvelous!" *Information Week* (July 24, 2006).

CHAPTER 9

Abboud, Leila. "Cellphones' Coming Attraction: You!" *The Wall Street Journal* (March 8, 2007).

Adomavicius, Gediminas and **Alexander Tuzhilin**. "Personalization Technologies: A Process-Oriented Perspective." *Communications of the ACM* 48, no. 10 (October 2005).

Bakos, Yannis. "The Emerging Role of Electronic Marketplaces and the Internet." *Communications of the ACM* 41, no. 8 (August 1998).

Bhargava, Hemant K. and Vidyanand Chourhary. "Economics of an Information Intermediary with Aggregation Benefits." *Information Systems Research* 15, no. 1 (March 2004).

Brynjolfsson, Erik, Yu Hu, and **Michael D. Smith**. "Consumer Surpus in the Digital Economy: Estimating the Value of Increased Product Variety at Online Booksellers." *Management Science* 49, no. 11 (November 2003).

Christiaanse, Ellen. "Performance Benefits Through Integration Hubs." *Communications of the ACM* 48, No.5 (April 2005).

Cotteleer, Mark J., Christopher A. Cotteleer, and **Andrew Prochmow**. "Cutting Checks: Challenges and Choices in B2B E-Payments." *Communications of the ACM* 50, No. 6 (June 2007).

Dewan, Rajiv M., Marshall L. Freimer, and **Jie Zhang**. "Management and Valuation of Advertisement-Supported Web Sites." *Journal of Management Information Systems* 19, no. 3 (Winter 2002-2003).

eMarketer. "Mobile Spending: *US Non-Voice Services.*" September 2007).

——— "US Retail E-commerce: Entering the Multi-Channel Era" (May 2007).

Evans, Philip and **Thomas S. Wurster**. *Blown to Bits: How the New Economics of Information Transforms Strategy*. Boston, MA: Harvard Business School Press (2000).

Helft, Miguel. "Big Money in Little Screens." *The New York Times* (April 20, 2007).

Iansiti, Marco, F. Warren McFarlan and **George Wessterman**. "Leveraging the Incumbent's Advantage." *MIS Sloan Management Review* 44, no. 4 (Summer 2003).

Kaplan, Steven and **Mohanbir Sawhney**. "E-Hubs: the New B2B Marketplaces." *Harvard Business Review* (May-June 2000).

Kauffman, Robert J. and **Bin Wang**. "New Buyers' Arrival Under Dynamic Pricing Market Microstructure: The Case of Group-Buying Discounts on the Internet, *Journal of Management Information Systems* 18, no. 2 (Fall 2001).

Kim, Jane J. "Mobile Banking Shifts into High Gear." *The Wall Street Journal* (February 21, 2007).

King, Rachael. "Tapping Wikis for Web Community-Building." *BusinessWeek* (March 12, 2007).

Laseter, Timothy M., Elliott Rabinovich, Kenneth K. Boyer, and **M. Johnny Rungtusanatham**. "Critical Issues in Internet Retailing." *MIT Sloan Management Review* 48, no. 3 (Spring 2007).

Laudon, Kenneth C. and **Carol Guercio Traver**. *E-Commerce: Business, Technology, Society*. Upper Saddle River, NJ: Prentice Hall (2008).

Lee, Hau L. and **Seungin Whang**. "Winning the Last Mile of E-Commerce." *Sloan Management Review* 42, no. 4 (Summer 2001).

Magretta, Joan. "Why Business Models Matter." *Harvard Business Review* (May 2002).

Mc Knight, D. Harrison, Vivek Choudhury, and **Charlea Kacmar**. "Developing and Validating Trust Measures for e-Commerce: An Integrative Typology." *Information Systems Research* 13, no.3 (September 2002).

Patrick, Aaron O. "Tapping into Customers' Online Chatter." *The Wall Street Journal* (May 18, 2007).

Pavlou, Paul A., Huigang Liang, and **Yajiong Xue**. "Understanding and Mitigating Uncertainty in Online Exchange Relationships: A Principal-Agent Perspective." *MIS Quarterly* 31, no. 1 (March 2007).

Pew Internet and **American Life**. "Trends." (2007).

Pinker, Edieal, Abraham Seidmann, and **Riginald C. Foster**." Strategies for Transitioning 'Old Economy' Firms to E-Business." *Communications of the ACM* 45, no. 5 (May 2002).

Prahalad, C.K. and **Venkatram Ramaswamy**. "Coopting Consumer Competence." *Harvard Business Review* (January-February 2000).

Rayport, Jeffrey F. "Demand-Side Innovation: Where IT Meets Marketing." *Optimize Magazine* (February 2007).

Sawhney, Mohanbir, Emanuela Prandelli, and **Gianmario Verona**. "The Power of Innomediation." *MIT Sloan Management Review* (Winter 2003).

Schiesel, Seth. "In a Virtual Universe, the Politics Turn Real." *The New York Times* (June 7, 2007).

Schultze, Ulrike and **Wanda J. Orlikowski.** "A Practice Perspective on Technology-Mediated Network Relations: The Use of Internet-Based Self-Serve Technologies." *Information Systems Research* 15, no. 1 (March 2004).

Seybold, Patricia. "Customer-Controlled Innovation." *Optimize Magazine* (February 2007).

Sharma, Amol. "Comjpanies VIe for Ad Dollars on Mobile Web." *The Wall Street Journal* (January 17, 2007).

———— "What's New In Wireless." *The Wall Street Journal* (March 26, 2007).

Smith, Michael D., Joseph Bailey and **Erik Brynjolfsson.** "Understanding Digital Markets: Review and Assessment" in Erik Brynjolfsson and Brian Kahin, ed. *Understanding the Digital Economy.* Cambridge, MA: MIT Press (1999).

Story, Louise. "Yes, the Screen is Tiny, but the Plans Are Big." *The New York Times* (June 17, 2007).

Sylvers, Eric. "The Ad-Free Cellphone May Soon Be Extinct." *The New York Times* (February 14, 2007).

Tedeschi, Bob. "Like Shopping? Social Networking? Try Social Shopping." *The New York Times* (September 11, 2006).

Urbaczewski, Andrew, Leonard M. Jessup, and **Bradley Wheeler.** "Electronic Commerce Research: A Taxonomy and Synthesis." Journal of Organizational Computing and Electronic Commerce 12, no. 2 (2002).

Vascellaro, Jessica E. and **Kevin J. Delaney.** "Search Engines Seek to Get Inside Your Head." *The Wall Street Journal* (April 25, 2007).

Wagner, Christian and **Ann Majchrzak.** "Enabling Customer-Centricity Using Wikis and the Wiki Way." *Journal of Management Information Systems* 23, No. 3 (Winter 2006-7).

Yen, Benjamin P.-C. and **Elsie O.S. Ng.** "The Impact of Electronic Commerce on Procurement." *Journal of Organizational Computing and Electronic Commerce* 13, no. 3 & 4 (2003).

Yoo, Byungjoon, Vidyanand Choudhary, and **Tridas Mukhopadhyay.** ""A Model of Neutral B2B Intermediaries." *Journal of Management Information Systems* 19, no. 3 (Winter 2002–2003).

CHAPTER 10

Alavi, Maryam, and **Dorothy Leidner.** "Knowledge Management and Knowledge Management Systems: Conceptual Foundations and Research Issues." *MIS Quarterly 25,* no. 1 (March 2001).

———— Timothy R. Kayworth, and Dorothy E. Leidner. "An Empirical Investigation of the Influence of Organizational Culture on Knowledge Management Practices." *Journal of Management Information Systems* 22, No.3 (Winter 2006).

Anson, Rob, and **Bjorn Erik Munkvold.** "Beyond Face-to-Face: A Field Study of Electronic Meetings in Different Time and Place Modes." *Journal of Organizational Computing and Electronic Commerce* 14, no. 2 (2004).

Bargeron, David, Jonathan Grudin, Anoop Gupta, Elizabeth Sanocki, Francis Li, and **Scott Le Tiernan.** "Asynchronous Collaboration around Multimedia Applied to On-Demand Education." *Journal of Management Information Systems* 18, no. 4 (Spring 2002).

Becerra-Fernandez, Irma, Avelino Gonzalez, and **Rajiv Sabherwal.** *Knowledge Management.* Upper Saddle River, NJ: Prentice Hall (2004).

Birkinshaw, Julian, and **Tony Sheehan.** "Managing the Knowledge Life Cycle." *MIT Sloan Management Review* 44, no. 1 (Fall 2002).

Bodendorf, Freimut, and **Roland Zimmermann.** "Proactive Supply Chain Event Management with Agent Technology." *International Journal of Electronic Commerce* 9, no. 4 (Summer 2005).

Booth, Corey, and **Shashi Buluswar.** "The Return of Artificial Intelligence." *McKinsey Quarterly* no. 2 (2002).

Burtka, Michael. "Generic Algorithms." *The Stern Information Systems Review* 1, no. 1 (Spring 1993).

Carlin, Dan. "Corporate Wikis Go Viral." *Business Week* (March 12, 2007);

Cavalieri, Sergio, Vittorio Cesarotti, and **Vito Introna.** "A Multiagent Model for Coordinated Distribution Chain Planning." *Journal of Organizational Computing and Electronic Commerce* 13, nos. 3 & 4 (2003).

Clark, Thomas D., Mary C. Jones, and **Curtis P. Armstrong.** "The Dynamic Structure of Management Support Systems: Theory Development, Research Focus, and Direction. *MIS Quarterly* 31, no. 3 (September 2007).

Davenport. Thomas H., and **Jeanne G. Harris.** "Automated Decision Making Comes of Age." *MIT Sloan Management Review* 46 no. 4 (Summer 2005).

Davenport, Thomas H., and **Lawrence Prusak.** *Working Knowledge: How Organizations Manage What They Know.* Boston: Harvard Business School Press (1997).

Davenport, Thomas H., David W. DeLong, and **Michael C. Beers.** "Successful Knowledge Management Projects." *Sloan Management Review* 39, no. 2 (Winter 1998).

Davenport, Thomas H., Robert J. Thomas, and **Susan Cantrell.** "The Mysterious Art and Science of Knowledge-Worker Performance." *MIT Sloan Management Review* 44, no. 1 (Fall 2002).

Dennis, Alan R., and **Bryan A. Reinicke.** "Beta versus VHS and the Acceptance of Electronic Brainstorming Technology." *MIS Quarterly* 28, no. 1 (March 2004).

Dennis, Alan R., Jay E. Aronson, William G. Henriger, and **Edward D. Walker III.** "Structuring Time and Task in Electronic Brainstorming." *MIS Quarterly* 23, no. 1 (March 1999).

Dennis, Alan R., Jay F. Nunamaker, Jr., and **Douglas R. Vogel.** "A Comparison of Laboratory and Field Research in the Study of Electronic Meeting Systems." *Journal of Management Information Systems* 7, no. 3 (Winter 1990-1991).

DeSanctis, Geraldine, and **R. Brent Gallup**e. "A Foundation for the Study of Group Decision Support Systems." *Management Science* 33, no. 5 (May 1987).

Dhar, Vasant, and **Roger Stein.** *Intelligent Decision Support Methods: The Science of Knowledge Work.* Upper Saddle River, NJ: Prentice Hall (1997).

Du, Timon C., Eldon Y. Li, and **An-pin Chang.** "Mobile Agents in Distributed Network Management." *Communications of the ACM* 46, no.7 (July 2003).

Earl, Michael. "Knowledge Management Strategies: Toward a Taxonomy." *Journal of Management Information Systems* 18, no. 1 (Summer 2001).

Easley, Robert F., Sarv Devaraj, and **J. Michael Crant.** "Relating Collaborative Technology Use to Teamwork Quality and Performance: An Empirical Analysis." *Journal of Management Information Systems* 19, no. 4 (Spring 2003).

El Sawy, Omar. "Personal Information Systems for Strategic Scanning in Turbulent Environments." *MIS Quarterly* 9, no. 1 (March 1985).

Fjermestad, Jerry, and **Starr Roxanne Hiltz.** "An Assessment of Group Support Systems Experimental Research: Methodology, and Results." *Journal of Management Information Systems* 15, no. 3 (Winter, 1998-1999).

Frangos, Alex. "New Dimensions in Design." *The Wall Street Journal* (July 7, 2004).

Gallupe, R. Brent, Geraldine DeSanctis, and **Gary W. Dickson.** "Computer-Based Support for Group Problem-Finding: An Experimental Investigation." *MIS Quarterly* 12, no. 2 (June 1988).

Gelernter, David. "Aritificial Intelligence Is Lost in the Woods." *Technology Review* (July/August 2007).

Gorry, G. Anthony, and **Michael S. Scott Morton.** "A Framework for Management Information Systems." *Sloan Management Review* 13, no. 1 (Fall 1971).

Grover, Varun, and **Thomas H. Davenport.** "General Perspectives on Knowledge Management: Fostering a Research Agenda." *Journal of Management Information Systems* 18, no. 1 (Summer 2001).

Holland, John H. "Genetic Algorithms." Scientific American (July 1992).

Hoover, J. Nicholas. "Enterprise 2.0." *Information Week* (February 26, 2007).

Housel, Tom, and **Arthur A. Bell**. *Measuring and Managing Knowledge*. New York: McGraw-Hill (2001).

Jarvenpaa, Sirkka L., and **D. Sandy Staples**. "Exploring Perceptions of Organizational Ownership of Information and Expertise." *Journal of Management Information Systems* 18, no. 1 (Summer 2001).

King, Rachael. "No Rest for the Wiki." *Business Week* (March 12, 2007).

King, William R., **Peter V. Marks, Jr.**, and **Scott McCoy**. "The Most Important Issues in Knowledge Management." *Communications of the ACM* 45, no.9 (September 2002).

Kuo, R. J., **K. Chang**, and **S. Y.Chien**. "Integration and Self-Organizing Feature Maps and Genetic-Algorithm-Based Clustering Method for Market Segmentation." *Journal of Organizational Computing and Electronic Commerce* 14, no. 1 (2004).

Lamont, Judith. "Finding Experts-Explicit and Implicit." *KM World* (June 2006).

Leidner, Dorothy E., and **Joyce Elam**. "Executive Information Systems: Their Impact on Executive Decision Making." *Journal of Management Information Systems* (Winter 1993–1994).

Leidner, Dorothy E., and **Joyce Elam**. "The Impact of Executive Information Systems on Organizational Design, Intelligence, and Decision Making." *Organization Science* 6, no. 6 (November–December 1995).

Lilien, Gary L., **Arvind Rangaswamy**, **Gerrit H. Van Bruggen**, and **Katrin Starke**. "DSS Effectiveness in Marketing Resource Allocation Decisions: Reality vs. Perception." *Information Systems Research* 15, no. 3 (September 2004).

Maglio, Paul P., and **Christopher S. Campbell**. "Attentive Agents." *Communications of the ACM* 46, no. 3 (March 2003).

O'Keefe, Robert M., and **Tim McEachern**. "Web-based Customer Decision Support Systems." *Communications of the ACM* 41, no. 3 (March 1998).

Pastore, Richard. "Cruise Control." *CIO Magazine* (February 1, 2003).

Pinsonneault, Alain, **Henri Barki**, **R. Brent Gallupe**, and **Norberto Hoppen**. "Electronic Brainstorming: The Illusion of Productivity." *Information Systems Research* 10, no. 2 (July 1999).

Sadeh, Norman, **David W. Hildum**, and **Dag Kjenstad**. "Agent-Based E-Supply Chain Decision Support." *Journal of Organizational Computing and Electronic Commerce* 13, nos. 3 & 4 (2003)

Samuelson, Douglas A. and **Charles M. Macal**. "Agent-Based Simulation." *OR/MS Today* (August 2006).

Schultze, Ulrike, and **Dorothy Leidner**. "Studying Knowledge Management in Information Systems Research: Discourses and Theoretical Assumptions." *MIS Quarterly* 26, no. 3 (September 2002).

Schwabe, Gerhard. "Providing for Organizational Memory in Computer-Supported Meetings." *Journal of Organizational Computing and Electronic Commerce* 9, nos. 2 & 3 (1999).

Siebel Systems. "Compass Bank Reduces Loan Write-Offs by 7 Percent Using Siebel Business Analytics." www.siebel.com/business-intelligence/success-stories.shtm, accessed August 14, 2005.

Simon, H. A. *The New Science of Management Decision*. New York: Harper & Row (1960).

Singer, Emily. "Silicon Brains." *Technology Review* (May/June 2007).

Singh, Rahul, **A. F.Salam**, and **Lakshmi Iyer**. "Agents in E-Supply Chains." *Communications of the ACM* 48, no.6 (June 2005).

Suh, Kil-Soo, and **Young Eun Lee**. "The Effects of Virtual Reality on Consumer Learning: An Empirical Investigation." *MIS Quarterly* 29, no.4 (December 2005).

Summerfield, Brian. "Whirpool Corp." Learning Grows with the Business." *Chief Learning Officer* (August 2007).

Tanriverdi, Huseyin. "Information Technology Relatedness, Knowledge Management Capability, and Performance of Multibusiness Firms." *MIS Quarterly* 29, no. 2 (June 2005).

Totty, Michael. "Making Sense of It All." *The Wall Street Journal* (September 24, 2007).

Totty, Michael. "Rethinking the Inbox." *The Wall Street Journal* (March 26, 2007).

Turban, Efraim, and **Jay E. Aronson**. *Business Intelligence and Decision Support Systems*, 8th ed. Upper Saddle River, NJ: Prentice Hall (2007).

Walczak, Steven. "Gaining Competitive Advantage for Trading in Emerging Capital Markets with Neural Networks. " *Journal of Management Information Systems* 16, no. 2 (Fall 1999).

Wang, Huaiqing, **John Mylopoulos**, and **Stephen Liao**. "Intelligent Agents and Financial Risk Monitoring Systems." *Communications of the ACM* 45, no. 3 (March 2002).

Zack, Michael H. "Rethinking the Knowledge-Based Organization." *MIT Sloan Management Review* 44, no. 4 (Summer 2003).

Zadeh, Lotfi A. "Fuzzy Logic, Neural Networks, and Soft Computing." *Communications of the ACM* 37, no. 3 (March 1994).

CHAPTER 11

Agarwal, Ritu, and **Viswanath Venkatesnh**. "Assessing a Firm's Web Presence: A Heuristic Evaluation Procedure for the Measurement of Usability." *Information Systems Research* 13, no. 3 (September 2002).

Andres, Howard P., and **Robert W. Zmud**. "A Contingency Approach to Software Project Coordination." *Journal of Management Information Systems* 18, no. 3 (Winter 2001-2002).

Armstrong, Deborah J. and **Bill C. Hardgrove**. "Understanding Mindshift Learning: The Transition to Object-Oriented Development." *MIS Quarterly* 31, no. 3 (September 2007).

Aron, Ravi, **Eric K.Clemons**, and **Sashi Reddi**. "Just Right Outsourcing: Understanding and Managing Risk." *Journal of Management Information Systems* 22, no. 1 (Summer 2005).

Avison, David E., and **Guy Fitzgerald**. "Where Now for Development Methodologies?" *Communications of the ACM* 41, no. 1 (January 2003).

Babcock, Charles. "Web Services by the Dozen." *Information Week* (March 13, 2006).

Baily, Martin N., and **Diana Farrell**. "Exploding the Myths of Offshoring." *McKinsey Quarterly* (July 2004).

Barki, Henri, **Suzanne Rivard**, and **Jean Talbot**. "An Integrative Contingency Model of Software Project Risk Management." *Journal of Management Information Systems* 17, no. 4 (Spring 2001).

Biehl, Markus. "Success Factors For Implementing Global Information Systems." *Communications of the ACM* 50, No. 1 (January 2007).

Brown, Susan A., **Norman L. Chervany**, and **Bryan A. Reinicke**. "What Matters When Introducing New Technology." *Communications of the ACM* 50, No. 9 (September 2007).

Davern, Michael J., and **Robert J. Kauffman**. "Discovering Potential and Realizing Value from Information Technology Investments." *Journal of Management Information Systems* 16, no. 4 (Spring 2000).

Delone, William H., and **Ephraim R. McLean**. "The Delone and McLean Model of Information Systems Success: A Ten-Year Update. *Journal of Management Information Systems* 19, no. 4 (Spring 2003).

Feeny, David, **Mary Lacity**, and **Leslie P. Willcocks**. "Taking the Measure of Outsourcing Providers." *MIT Sloan Management Review* 46, no. 3 (Spring 2005).

Gallivan, Michael J., **Valerie K. Spitler**, and **Marios Koufaris**. "Does Information Technology Training Really Matter?" *Journal of Management Information Systems* 22, no. 1 (Summer 2005).

George, Joey, **Dinesh Batra**, **Joseph S. Valacich**, and **Jeffrey A. Hoffer**. *Object Oriented System Analysis and Design*, 2nd ed. Upper Saddle River, NJ: Prentice Hall (2007).

Hickey, Ann M., and **Alan M. Davis**. "A Unified Model of Requirements Elicitation." *Journal of Management Information Systems* 20, no. 4 (Spring 2004).

Hitt, Lorin, **D. J. Wu**, and **Xiaoge Zhou**. "Investment in Enterprise Resource Planning: Business Impact and Productivity Measures." *Journal of Management Information Systems* 19, no. 1 (Summer 2002).

Hoffer, Jeffrey, Joey George, and Joseph Valacich. *Modern Systems Analysis and Design*, 5th ed. Upper Saddle River, NJ: Prentice Hall (2008).

Housel, Thomas J., Omar El Sawy, JianfangJ. Zhong, and Waymond Rodgers. "Measuring the Return on e-Business Initiatives at the Process Level: The Knowledge Value-Added Approach." ICIS (2001).

Information Builders."Elie Tahari Ltd. Unveils New End-User Reporting Framework." www.informationbuilders.com, accessed October 21, 2007.

Irwin, Gretchen. "The Role of Similarity in the Reuse of Object-Oriented Analysis Models." *Journal of Management Information Systems* 19, no. 2 (Fall 2002).

Ivari, Juhani, Rudy Hirscheim, and Heinz K. Klein. "A Dynamic Framework for Classifying Information Systems Development Methodologies and Approaches." *Journal of Management Information Systems* 17, no. 3 (Winter 2000–2001).

Jasperson, Jon (Sean), Pamela E. Carter, and Robert W. Zmud. "A Comprehensive Conceptualization of Post-Adoptive Behaviors Associated with Information Technology Enabled Work Systems." *MIS Quarterly* 29, no. 3 (September 2005).

Jeffrey, Mark, and Ingmar Leliveld. "Best Practices in IT Portfolio Management." *MIT Sloan Management Review* 45, no. 3 (Spring 2004).

Kalin, Sari. "Making IT Portfolio Management a Reality." *CIO Magazine* (June 1, 2006).

Keen, Peter W. "Information Systems and Organizational Change." *Communications of the ACM* 24 (January 1981).

Keil, Mark, Joan Mann, and Arun Rai. "Why Software Projects Escalate: An Empirical Analysis and Test of Four Theoretical Models." *MIS Quarterly* 24, no. 4 (December 2000).

Kendall, Kenneth E., and Julie E. Kendall. *Systems Analysis and Design*, 8th ed. Upper Saddle River, NJ: Prentice Hall (2008).

Kettinger, William J., and Choong C. Lee. "Understanding the IS-User Divide in IT Innovation." *Communications of the ACM* 45, no.2 (February 2002).

Kirsch, Laurie J. "Deploying Common Systems Globally: The Dynamic of Control." *Information Systems Research* 15, no. 4 (December 2004).

Koh, Christine, Song Ang, and Detmar W. Straub. "IT Outsourcing Success: A Psychological Contract Perspective." *Information Systems Research* 15 no. 4 (December 2004).

Kolb, D. A., and A. L. Frohman. "An Organization Development Approach to Consulting." *Sloan Management Review* 12 (Fall 1970).

Krishna, S., Sundeep Sahay, and Geoff Walsham. "Managing Cross-Cultural Issues in Global Software Outsourcing." *Communications of the ACM* 47, no. 4 (April 2004).

Lapointe, Liette, and Suzanne Rivard. "A Multilevel Model of Resistance to Information Technology Implementation." *MIS Quarterly* 29, no. 3 (September2005).

Lee, Jae Nam, Shaila M. Miranda, and Yong-Mi Kim. "IT Outsourcing Strategies: Universalistic, Contingency, and Configurational Explanations of Success." *Information Systems Research* 15, no. 2 (June 2004).

Levina, Natalia, and Jeanne W. Ross. "From the Vendor's Perspective: Exploring the Value Proposition in Information Technology Outsourcing." *MIS Quarterly* 27, no. 3 (September 2003).

Limayem, Moez, Mohamed Khalifa, and Wynne W. Chin. "Case Tools Usage and Impact on System Development Performance." *Journal of Organizational Computing and Electronic Commerce* 14, no. 3 (2004).

Luftman, Jerry, and Hunter Muller. "Total Value of Ownership: A New Model." *Optimize* (July 2005).

Majchrzak, Ann, Cynthia M. Beath, and Ricardo A. Lim. "Managing Client Dialogues during Information Systems Design to Facilitate Client Learning." *MIS Quarterly* 29, no. 4 (December 2005).

Markus, M. Lynne, and Robert I. Benjamin. "The Magic Bullet Theory of IT-Enabled Transformation." *Sloan Management Review* (Winter 1997).

Martin, James. *Application Development without Programmers*. Englewood Cliffs, NJ: Prentice Hall (1982).

Martin, James, and Carma McClure. *Structured Techniques: The Basis of CASE*. Englewood Cliffs, NJ: Prentice Hall (1988).

McFarlan, F. Warren. "Portfolio Approach to Information Systems." *Harvard Business Review* (September-October 1981).

Mumford, Enid, and Mary Weir. *Computer Systems in Work Design*: The ETHICS Method. New York: John Wiley (1979).

Nadkarni, Sucheta and Reetika Gupta. "A Task-Based Model of Perceived Website Complexity." *MIS Quarterly* 31, no. 3 (September 2007).

Nidumolu, Sarma R., and Mani Subramani. "The Matrix of Control: Combining Process and Structure Approaches to Managing Software Development." *Journal of Management Information Systems* 20, no. 4 (Winter 2004).

Overby, Stephanie. "The Hidden Costs of Offshore Outsourcing," *CIO Magazine* (September 1, 2003).

Palmer, Jonathan W. "Web Site Usability, Design and Performance Metrics." *Information Systems Research* 13, no.3 (September 2002).

Prahalad, C. K., and M. S. Krishnan. "Synchronizing Strategy and Information Technology." *Sloan Management Review* 43, no. 4 (Summer 2002).

Rai, Arun, Sandra S. Lang, and Robert B. Welker. "Assessing the Validity of IS Success Models: An Empirical Test and Theoretical Analysis." *Information Systems Research* 13, no. 1 (March 2002).

Ravichandran, T., and Marcus A. Rothenberger. "Software Reuse Strategies and Component Markets." *Communications of the ACM* 46, no. 8 (August 2003).

Robey, Daniel, Jeanne W. Ross, and Marie-Claude Boudreau. "Learning to Implement Enterprise Systems: An Exploratory Study of the Dialectics of Change." *Journal of Management Information Systems* 19, no. 1 (Summer 2002).

Ryan, Sherry D., David A. Harrison, and Lawrence L Schkade. "Information Technology Investment Decisions: When Do Cost and Benefits in the Social Subsystem Matter?" *Journal of Management Information Systems* 19, no. 2 (Fall 2002).

Sakthivel, S. "Managing Risk in Offshore Systems Development." *Communications of the ACM* 50, No. 4 (April 2007).

Sauer, Chris, Andrew Gemino, and Blaize Horner Reich. "The Impact of Size and Volatility on IT Project Performance. "*Communications of the ACM* 50, no. 11 (November 2007).

Sharma, Rajeev and Philip Yetton. "The Contingent Effects of Training, Technical Complexity, and Task Interdependence on Successful Information Systems Implementation." *MIS Quarterly* 31, no. 2 (June 2007).

Silva, Leiser and Rudy Hirschheim. "Fighting Against Windmills: Strategic Information Systems and Organizational Deep Structures." *MIS Quarterly* 31, no. 2 (June 2007).

Sircar, Sumit, Sridhar P. Nerur, and Radhakanta Mahapatra. "Revolution or Evolution? A Comparison of Object-Oriented and Structured Systems Development Methods." *MIS Quarterly* 25, no. 4 (December 2001).

Smith, H. Jeff, Mark Keil, and Gordon Depledge. "Keeping Mum as the Project Goes Under." *Journal of Management Information Systems* 18, no. 2 (Fall 2001).

Schwalbe, Kathy. *Information Technology Project Management, 5/e*. Course Technology (2007).

Simonsen, Jasper. "Involving Top Management in IT Projects." *Communications of the ACM 50,* No. 8 (August 2007).

Swanson, E. Burton, and Enrique Dans. "System Life Expectancy and the Maintenance Effort: Exploring Their Equilibration." *MIS Quarterly* 24, no. 2 (June 2000).

Thatcher, Matt E., and Jim R. Oliver. "The Impact of Technology Investments on a Firm's Production Efficiency, Product Quality, and Productivity." *Journal of Management Information Systems* 18, no. 2 (Fall 2001).

Turetken, Ozgur, David Schuff, Ramesh Sharda, and **Terence T. Ow**. "Supporting Systems Analysis and Design through Fisheye Views." *Communications of the ACM* 47, no. 9 (September 2004).

Venkatesh, Viswanath, Michael G. Morris, Gordon B Davis, and **Fred D. Davis**. "User Acceptance of Information Technology: Toward a Unified View." *MIS Quarterly* 27, no. 3 (September 2003).

Wang, Eric T.G., Gary Klein, and **James J. Jiang**. "ERP Misfit: Country of Origin and Organizational Factors." *Journal of Management Information Systems* 23, No. 1 (Summer 2006).

Weinberg Allen and Weinberg Allen and William Forrest."Infrastructure's Outer Limits." *Optimize Magazine* (April 2006)

Wipro Technologies. "Case Studies: Pinacle West."www.wipro.com, accessed October 21, 2007.

Wulf, Volker, and **Matthias Jarke**. "The Economics of End-User Development." *Communications of the ACM* 47, no. 9 (September 2004).

Xia, Weidong, and **Gwanhoo Lee**. "Complexity of Information Systems Development Projects." *Journal of Management Information Systems* 22, no. 1 (Summer 2005).

"Winning the IT Portfolio Battle," Projects@Work (September 6, 2007).

Zhu, Kevin, Kenneth L. Kraemer, Sean Xu, and **Jason Dedrick**. "Information Technology Payoff in E-Business Environments: An International Perspective on Value Creation of E-business in the Financial Services Industry." *Journal of Management Information Systems* 21, no. 1 (Summer 2004).

CHAPTER 12

American Management Association and The ePolicy Institute. "2005 Electronic Monitoring & Surveillance Survey" (May 18, 2005).

Anton, Annie I., Elisa Bertino, Ninghui Li, and **Ting Yu**. "A Roadmap for Comprehensive Online Privacy Policy Management." *Communications of the ACM* 50, No. 7 (July 2007).

Association of Computing Machinery. "ACM's Code of Ethics and Professional Conduct." *Communications of the ACM* 36, no. 12 (December 1993).

Ball, Kirstie S. "Situating Workplace Surveillance: Ethics and Computer-based Performance Monitoring." *Ethics and Information Technology* 3, no. 3 (2001).

Bank, David. "Companies Seek to Hold Software Makers Liable for Flaws." *The Wall Street Journal* (February 24, 2005).

Bellman, Steven, Eric J. Johnson, and **Gerald L. Lohse**. "To Opt-in or Opt-out? It Depends on the Question. Communications of the ACM 44, no. 2 (February 2001).

Bennett, Colin J. "Cookies, Web Bugs, Webcams, and Cue Cats: Patterns of Surveillance on the World Wide Web." *Ethics and Information Technology* 3, no. 3 (2001).

Bowen, Jonathan. "The Ethics of Safety-Critical Systems." *Communications of the ACM* 43, no. 3 (April 2000).

Brown Bag Software vs. Symantec Corp. 960 F2D 1465 (Ninth Circuit, 1992).

Carr, David F., and **Sean Gallagher**. "BofA's Direct-Deposit Debacle." *Baseline* (May 15, 2002).

Collins, W. Robert, Keith W. Miller, Bethany J. Spielman, and **Phillip Wherry**. "How Good Is Good Enough? An Ethical Analysis of Software Construction and Use." *Communications of the ACM* 37, no. 1 (January 1994).

Congressional Research Service. "Internet Privacy: Overview and Pending Legislation"(May 16, 2005).

Earp. Julia B., and **David Baumer**. "Innovative Web Use to Learn about Consumer Behavior and Online Privacy." *Communications of the ACM* 46, no. 4 (April 2003).

eMarketer. "US Online Sales Lost Due to Privacy/Security Concerns, 2000–2006" (November 23, 2005).

Farmer, Dan, and **Charles C. Mann**. "Surveillance Nation." Part I *Technology Review* (April 2003) and Part II *Technology Review* (May 2003).

Fox, Susannah. "Digital Divisions." Pew Internet and American Life Project (October 5, 2005).

Goodman, Joshua, Gordon V. Cormack, and **David Herckerman**. "Spam and the Ongoing Battle for the Inbox." *Communications of the ACM* 50, No. 2 (February 2007)

Grimes, Galen A. "Compliance with the CAN-SPAM Act of 2003," *Communications of the ACM* 50, No. 2 (February 2007)..

Hui, Kai-Lung, Hock Hai Teo, and **Sang-Yong Tom Lee**. "The Value of Privacy Assurance: An Exploratory Field Experiment." *MIS Quarterly* 31, no. 1 (March 2007).

Jackson, Linda A., Alexander von Eye, Gretchen Barbatsis, Frank Biocca, Hiram E. Fitzgerald, and **Yong Zhao**. "The Impact of Internet Use on the Other Side of the Digital Divide." *Communications of the ACM* 47, no. 7 (July 2004).

Jackson, Thomas W., Ray Dawson, and **Darren Wilson**. "Understanding Email Interaction Increases Organizational Productivity." *Communications of the ACM* 46, no. 8 (August 2003).

Kobsa, Alfred. "Privacy-Enhancing Personalization." *Communications of the ACM* 50, No.8 (August 2007).

Laudon, Kenneth C. *Dossier Society: Value Choices in the Design of National Information Systems.* New York: Columbia University Press (1986b).

———. "Ethical Concepts and Information Technology." *Communications of the ACM* 38, no. 12 (December 1995).

Laudon, Kenneth C., and **Carol Guercio Traver**. *E-Commerce: Business, Technology, Society.* Upper Saddle River, NJ: Prentice Hall (2008).

Lee, Jintae. "An End-User Perspective on File-Sharing Systems." *Communications of the ACM* 46, no. 2 (February 2003).

Maltz, Elliott, and **Vincent Chiappetta**. "Maximizing Value in the Digital World." *Sloan Management Review* 43, no. 3 (Spring 2002).

Mann, Catherine L. "What Global Sourcing Means for U.S. I.T. Workers and for the U.S. Economy." *Communications of the ACM* 47, no. 7 (July 2004).

Payton, Fay Cobb. "Rethinking the Digital Divide." *Communications of the ACM* 46, no. 6 (June 2003).

Petrecca, Laura. "Memo to Managers: Don't Expect High Workplace Productivity on Monday," *USA Today* (November 27, 2005).

Pew Internet and American Life Project. "Demographics of Internet Users." http://www.pewinternet.org/trends/User_Demo_12.05.05.htm, accessed December 9, 2005.

Pollach, Irene. "What's Wrong with Online Privacy Policies? *Communications of the ACM* 50, No. 9 (September 2007).

Rifkin, Jeremy. "Watch Out for Trickle-Down Technology." *The New York Times* (March 16, 1993).

Rigdon, Joan E. "Frequent Glitches in New Software Bug Users." *The Wall Street Journal* (January 18, 1995).

Sewell, Graham, and **James R. Barker**. "Neither Good, nor Bad, but Dangerous: Surveillance as an Ethical Paradox." *Ethics and Information Technology* 3, no. 3 (2001).

Sipior, Janice C. "Unintended Invitation: Organizational Wi-Fi Use by External Roaming Users." *Communications of the ACM* 50, No. 8 (August 2007).

Smith, H. Jeff. "The Shareholders vs. Stakeholders Debate." *MIT Sloan Management Review* 44, no. 4 (Summer 2003).

Smith, Marcia S. "Spyware: Background and Policy Issues for Congress." Congressional Research Service (May 18, 2005).

U.S. Department of Health, Education, and Welfare. *Records, Computers, and the Rights of Citizens.* Cambridge: MIT Press (1973).

Van Kirk, Andrew. "Platform for Privacy Preferences (P3P): Privacy without Teeth," Working Paper, Duke University (March 10, 2005).

Wellman, Barry. "Designing the Internet for a Networked Society." *Communications of the ACM* 45, no. 5 (May 2002).

Zeller, Tom. "Critics Press Companies on Internet Rights Issues." *The New York Times* (November 8, 2005).

———. "Study Says Software Makers Supply Tools to Censor Web." *The New York Times* (October 12, 2005).

Index

International Organizations Index

Subject Index